W9-BTD-254

CHINESE POLITICS IN THE XI JINPING ERA

CHINESE POLITICS IN THE XI JINPING ERA

Reassessing Collective Leadership

CHENG LI

BROOKINGS INSTITUTION PRESS
Washington, D.C.

Copyright © 2016
THE BROOKINGS INSTITUTION
1775 Massachusetts Avenue, N.W., Washington, D.C. 20036
www.brookings.edu

The Brookings Institution is a private nonprofit organization devoted to research, education, and publication on important issues of domestic and foreign policy. Its principal purpose is to bring the highest quality independent research and analysis to bear on current and emerging policy problems. Interpretations or conclusions in Brookings publications should be understood to be solely those of the authors.

Library of Congress Cataloging-in-Publication data

Names: Li, Cheng, 1956– author.
Title: Chinese politics in the Xi Jinping era : reassessing collective
    leadership / Cheng Li.
Description: Washington, D.C. : Brookings Institution Press, 2016. |
    Includes index.
Identifiers: LCCN 2016017497 | ISBN 9780815726920 (paperback : alk. paper) |
    ISBN 9780815726937 (epub) | ISBN 9780815726944 (pdf)
Subjects: LCSH: China—Politics and government—2002– | Political
    Leadership—China. | Xi, Jinping. | BISAC: POLITICAL SCIENCE /
    Political Ideologies / Communism & Socialism. | POLITICAL
    SCIENCE / International Relations / General.
Classification: LCC DS779.46 .L5227 2016 | DDC 951.06/12—dc23
LC record available at https://lccn.loc.gov/2016017497

9 8 7 6 5 4 3 2 1

Typeset in Minion

Composition by Westchester Publishing Services

DEDICATED TO
LYNN T. WHITE III
A GREAT TEACHER, MENTOR, AND FRIEND
SINCE MY GRADUATE STUDENT YEARS
AT PRINCETON

CONTENTS

LIST OF FIGURES AND TABLES

TABLES

ACKNOWLEDGMENTS

Preparations for this book began in the autumn of 2013, approximately one year after the Chinese Communist Party's seminal 18th Congress. By then, it was already clear that major shifts were under way in China's political framework, though the extent and direction of those changes remained unclear. I owe my own understanding of and analysis on these changes—where they derive from and what they might spell for the future—to a long list of individuals without whose creative thinking and insights this book project would never have been possible.

The intellectual inspiration and mentorship that guided this study, however, date back to the late 1980s and early 1990s, when I had the privilege of studying under leading scholars in the China-watching community. Although these academic gurus are no longer with us, their work continues to serve as an important foundation for today's scholarship. By standing on their shoulders, we can see just a little farther and a little more clearly than we would otherwise be able to. For their direct mentorship, I am grateful to Professor A. Doak Barnett; Arthur W. Hummel Jr., and James R. Lilley, both former ambassadors to China; Professor Lucian W. Pye; Professor Michel Oksenberg; and especially Professor Robert A. Scalapino, who advised my master's thesis at the University of California, Berkeley. I owe equally profound thanks to Professors Ho Ping-ti, Ray Huang, and Tang Tsou for their groundbreaking works on Chinese elite studies, though I regret that I never worked with them directly.

In parsing the dimensions of contemporary Chinese politics, I benefited from frequent thought-provoking discussions with foremost leaders and thinkers in the United States. For generously sharing their time, observations, and insights with me, I extend my heartfelt thanks to Henry Kissinger, Henry Paulson Jr., William Cohen, Stephen Hadley, Ambassador Carla Hills, Ambassador Robert B. Zoellick, Ambassador Jon Huntsman, Ambassador James Sasser, Ambassador Gary F. Locke, Barbara H. Franklin, Senator Mark Kirk, and Congressman Rick Larsen.

This book's structure took shape under the feedback and guidance of Michael O'Hanlon, my colleague at the Brookings Institution, where he is the director of research for the Foreign Policy program and the co-director of the Center for 21st Century Security and Intelligence. Michael inspected the manuscript with his characteristic thoroughness, clarity, and precision. His detailed comments and suggestions guided major improvements at both the micro and macro levels. Bruce Jones, vice president and director of the Foreign Policy program, also provided many astute recommendations, which strengthened the core arguments of the book. I owe similarly profound thanks to two anonymous reviewers whose constructive criticisms resulted in a more detailed, nuanced, and balanced analysis, not to mention an argument better grounded in both empirical evidence and comparative perspectives.

I am humbled every day by the incredible knowledge and balanced analysis of my colleagues at Brookings. For sharing with me their wisdom, I am grateful to senior fellows Jeffrey Bader, Kenneth Lieberthal, Jonathan Pollack, David Dollar, Richard Bush, Qi Ye, and Katherine H.S. Moon, as well as nonresident fellows Thomas Christensen, Charles W. Freeman III, Evan Osnos, Pavneet Singh, Rachel Stern, and Daniel B. Wright. Outside of Brookings, I have been influenced and inspired over the years by the original work of seasoned China analysts who operate across a range of institutions, including Joseph Fewsmith, Paul Gewirtz, Avery Goldstein, David Mike Lampton, Susan V. Lawrence, Woo Lee, Deborah Lehr, Yawei Liu, Richard McGregor, Alice Miller, Andrew J. Nathan, Minxin Pei, Joshua Cooper Ramo, Anthony Saich, David Shambaugh, Victor C. Shih, Susan L. Shirk, Ezra F. Vogel, Dali Yang, Rachel Zhang and Zheng Yongnian.

No words can fully convey my gratitude to John L. Thornton, co-chair of the Brookings Board of Trustees, professor and director of the Global Leadership Program at Tsinghua University, and executive chairman of Barrick Gold Corporation. That John can dedicate himself fully to three demanding roles—and achieve uncompromised success in each—speaks to his boundless energy and the value he brings to any endeavor he touches. His intellectual contributions to and financial support of the China Center at Brookings— named after him—adhere to no earthly limits. John's charitable spirit extends to his faith in the abilities of those around him, and I am humbled to have his continued trust and confidence. Furthermore, as one of only a few Americans to have enjoyed prolonged, intimate exposure to China's leaders throughout much of its rise on the world stage, John's insights into Chinese leadership politics have been invaluable in shaping my own views and understanding.

I extend my utmost thanks to others whose generosity sustains important scholarly inquiries into China, U.S.-China relations, and Chinese politics: the Chubb Charitable Foundation, including my dear friend Evan Greenberg, chairman and chief executive officer of Chubb Limited; and Lee Folger, chairman of Folger Nolan Fleming Douglas Incorporated. Their support was instrumental in moving this project forward. I am also grateful for the support and encouragement of members of the Brookings China Council: Michael Ahearn, Anla Cheng, Deng Feng, Ding Jian, Jiang Weiming, Shen Nanpeng, Vaughan Smith, Michael Sweeney, Tang Xiaodan, Jerry Yang, Yang Yuanqing, and Zhang Chi. These individuals and institutions have given admirably and selflessly to sponsor impartial, objective research, no matter the findings.

Managing one of the country's oldest think tanks amid a period of profound economic and political change—both domestically and internationally— is no simple task, but the highly capable Brookings leadership has navigated these uncharted waters with ease and vision. For helping preserve a space for independent research in support of the public interest, and for providing a stable home in which the John L. Thornton China Center can continue to pursue its mission, I offer tremendous thanks to Strobe Talbott, president of Brookings; Martin Indyk, executive vice president of Brookings; and Ted Piccone, who was acting vice president and director of the Foreign Policy program at Brookings during the initial stages of this book and is now senior fellow in the Foreign Policy program's Latin America Initiative. I am enormously grateful to Bruce Jones, mentioned above, for his initiative and great input— along with Martin Indyk—of the Order from Chaos project at Brookings, with its emphasis on leadership issues across numerous countries.

The John L. Thornton China Center strives and thrives only through the tireless efforts of those who manage daily operations and contribute substantial research and editorial support. Immense thanks are due, first and foremost, to Ryan McElveen, assistant director of the China Center. With respect to this project, Ryan not only provided a thorough first round of edits that shaped the course of all future drafts, but also supplied indispensable managerial support throughout this lengthy process. Lucy Xu—my multitalented, polyglot research assistant—displayed inimitable patience and resolve in poring over the manuscript three times. Her edits were consistently thoughtful and perceptive, and she exercised a keen and rigorous ability to identify and correct errors, greatly enhancing the academic quality of this work. Zach Balin, a research assistant and the publications coordinator in the China Center, similarly contributed through his persistently excellent edits, ideas, and recommendations. That he joined this project in the late stages and yet helped immensely to improve the analysis and presentation of the book is a testament to his robust editorial skills. I extend my sincere thanks, as well, to longtime friends Sally Carman and Andrew Marble for their editorial help, and to a group of extremely talented young research assistants and interns that I have been fortunate to work with over the past three years: Eve Cary, Claire Jin, Jordan Lee, Aubrey Kenton Thibaut, Benjamin Tsui, James Tyson, Will Zeng, Jing Jing Zhang, Yuxin Zhang, and Tony Zhao. And a special thanks goes to Vincent Wang for his skillful management of complex logistics, including his effortless coordination across wide time zones.

Thank you to the excellent team of the Brookings Institution Press and Westchester Publishing Services, who diligently shepherded this project through the final stretches. The following individuals contributed meticulous eyes, thoughtful suggestions, and an unwavering commitment to quality in all aspects of their work: Valentina Kalk, director of the Brookings Institution Press; Bill Finan, editorial director and content strategist at the Brookings Institution Press; and Janet Walker, managing editor at the Brookings Institution Press. Likewise, from Westchester Publishing Services, I thank Angela Piliouras, production editor; Robert Griffin, copy editor; and Jamie Keenan, cover designer. Of course, the arguments in this book, including any and all remaining errors, are solely my own.

Immeasurable thanks are owed to my spouse, Yinsheng Li, whose contributions included countless hours of research and proofreading, and whose support extended far beyond those tasks. I could not ask for a better companion with whom to pursue a deeper understanding of our native land.

Last but never least, this book is dedicated to Lynn White, professor emeritus at Princeton University, whom I am privileged to call both a mentor and a friend. Lynn and I have co-authored numerous articles over the past two decades, and both within and outside of those projects I have learned a tremendous amount from him. He is, at his core, a teacher—always willing to pass along the lessons he has acquired over a long and successful career and eager to help those around him thrive. Lynn has been a role model for me and many others, building bridges between academia and non-academia and vigorously promoting mutual understanding on both ends of the vast Pacific Ocean.

Cheng Li
June 2016

PROLOGUE
Leadership

A Central Issue in Chinese Politics

Leaders don't create followers; they create more leaders.
—TOM PETERS

Every solution is an admission ticket to another problem.
—HENRY KISSINGER

China often confounds outside observers with the opacity of its decision-making processes and the seemingly contradictory trends in its political evolution. The selection process for members of the Politburo Standing Committee (PSC) of the Chinese Communist Party (CCP)—arguably the most important decision to be made, from the perspective of the Chinese authorities—is characteristically inscrutable. China analysts use the term "black box manipulation" (暗箱操作, *anxiang caozuo*) to describe the extraordinarily complex and multifaceted process of deal cutting and trade-offs (usually among a handful of heavyweight politicians), which ultimately determines the composition of this supreme leadership body. Very little information is available in the public domain about how personnel decisions are made at this topmost level. Both the mysterious selection process and the enormous power of the PSC reflect the importance of what the Chinese call "collective leadership" (集体领导, *jiti lingdao*).

Yet the Chinese public is increasingly aware of the battles among ambitious politicians for PSC membership, as well as of broader political tensions, ideological disputes, and policy differences within the leadership. Before the last political succession at the 18th National Party Congress in the fall of 2012, the country witnessed unprecedented political lobbying, most evident in the aggressive, self-promotional campaign of former Chongqing party secretary Bo Xilai. First in Chongqing, China's most populous municipality, and then on the national stage, Bo vigorously promoted the so-called Chongqing model of socioeconomic development, which emphasizes an authoritarian anticorruption campaign, rural land reform, an urban socialist welfare economy, and ultranationalism.[1]

Bo also aggressively implemented two idiosyncratic initiatives known collectively as "singing red songs and striking at the black triads" (唱红打黑, *changhong dahei*). Under the first initiative, Bo, well known as a princeling who was born into a communist veteran leader's family, encouraged officials and ordinary Chongqing residents to sing revolutionary "red songs" to lift their political spirits. This was a way for Bo to show that his communist princeling pedigree made him an ideal leader of the red regime established by his father's generation. Through the second initiative, Bo ordered Chongqing's law enforcement personnel to arrest a large number of people he labeled "gangsters of the underground mafia," citing a need to maintain social stability.[2] Despite these ambitious programs, Bo's political fortunes turned quickly in February 2012, when former Chongqing police chief Wang Lijun defected in dramatic fashion and fled to the U.S. consulate in Chengdu. Wang allegedly implicated Bo's wife, Gu Kailai, in the murder of a family friend, British businessman Neil Heywood. Consequently, Bo's campaign came to an end, as did his political career.[3]

The Bo Xilai episode epitomizes the challenge of selecting national leaders in the absence of venerated figures such as Mao Zedong and Deng Xiaoping. The CCP must find a new mechanism to choose its top officials. As is widely recognized both in China and abroad, Bo launched his initiatives in an attempt to secure a seat on the PSC or even in the top leadership. This was precisely because he sensed—perhaps earlier than other leaders—that the old method of elite selection had become increasingly inadequate and that the CCP required new sources of legitimacy. But in trying something new and bold, Bo provoked a great deal of anxiety in certain political circles. He was viewed with apprehension, partly because of his ideologically provocative approach and partly because of his notorious egoism.[4] The party perhaps needed someone to change the game of elite selection in order to keep abreast of the times, but Bo was the wrong person to take up the gauntlet.

The first step in Bo's downfall occurred when, in a notable departure from standard practice, several prominent leaders openly criticized his campaign. Indeed, former premier Wen Jiabao implied that Bo and his "leftist" (or Maoist) followers, who opposed further economic and political reforms, were "remnants of the Cultural Revolution" (文革余孽, *wenge yunie*).[5] Wang Yang—then Guangdong party secretary and, as another political rising star, Bo's main political rival at the time—began to promote his own Guangdong model, a more market-driven plan for China's economic growth, which advocated economic innovation and political reform.[6] Wen and Wang's actions further illustrate how political competition in China both shapes and reflects broader ideological and policy disputes. Interestingly, the events leading up to the 2012 Party Congress illustrated the new trend of political rivals seeking support from the public and various interest groups

Following the purge of Bo, China's politicians largely stopped reaching out to the public to bolster their candidacies for top leadership positions. Although the Chinese system of governance appears increasingly ill suited to meet the growing pluralism of political life, which has resulted from remarkable socioeconomic changes over the past three decades, top leaders are noticeably hesitant to risk opening the Pandora's box of change—a dilemma that could lead to a split in the party leadership. But the search for a more competitive, institutionalized, and transparent political system in this rapidly changing country will not end as a result of these recent upheavals. Given China's ongoing socioeconomic transformation, unprecedented telecommunications revolution, and upcoming generational change in the political elite, this search inevitably will begin anew.

Bo Xilai's rise and fall have laid bare the fundamental flaws of the political system of the People's Republic of China. But this episode has also demonstrated the resilience of the CCP leadership in confronting challenges to its legitimacy. In other words, the Bo scandal itself has revealed the simultaneous inertia and dynamism of the inner workings of China's political establishment.

In equally dramatic fashion, within the first three years of his tenure as top party leader, Xi Jinping has surprised many in China and around the world with his bold and vigorous anticorruption campaign. Approximately 160 senior officials, including civilian leaders at the vice-minister and vice-governor levels or above and military officers with the rank of major general or higher, have been arrested on corruption charges. They include some of the most formidable power brokers in Chinese politics: former PSC member Zhou Yongkang, who was in charge of China's security apparatus for a decade; former director of the General Office of the CCP Central Committee Ling Jihua, who was the most important confidant to former secretary general Hu Jintao and the person in charge of daily affairs for the top leadership operation; and former vice-chairs of the Central Military Commission Xu Caihou and Guo Boxiong, the two highest-ranking military officers from the previous administration.

Xi's quick and impressive consolidation of individual power has been a fascinating and significant political development.[7] In addition to holding the top posts in the party, government, and military, Xi chairs the newly established National Security Committee, the Central Leading Group for

Comprehensively Deepening Reforms, and several central leading groups in important functional areas, including foreign affairs, finance and the economy, cybersecurity and information technology, and military reform. Some analysts in both China and abroad believe that Xi's political dominance undermines the supreme role of the PSC and even reverses the trend of collective leadership, which has been a defining characteristic of Chinese elite politics for the past two decades.

Was Xi lucky enough to arrive at just the moment in history when his consolidation of power—to upset the inertia and possibly even prevent a split of the CCP leadership—was appealing to the Chinese public and most other Chinese leaders, especially those in the current PSC? Or did he achieve control more through "hook and crook," Machiavellian dealings, and the assembly of strong loyalist networks, thus returning the CCP to an era of strongman politics? Or is it that Xi's bold political moves are endorsed by the political establishment, but only as urgent, ad hoc measures to safeguard CCP rule? Is Xi interested in—or capable of—replacing the collective leadership?

While Xi Jinping's reliance on a mass campaign to deal with official corruption and his inclination to establish a personality cult bring to mind Bo's initiatives, Xi and Bo differ profoundly in meaningful ways. Xi's call for legal and judicial development and his ambitious market reform agenda contrast noticeably from Bo's well-known defiance of both legal professionals and private entrepreneurs.[8] The ways in which Xi and Bo treat their colleagues and subordinates—the strong personal ties and loyalty of the former and the authoritarian personality of the latter, especially evident in Bo's handling of Wang Lijun—reflect important differences in personal character and leadership style between these two individuals who otherwise have similar princeling backgrounds.

Interestingly, and perhaps ironically, the primary objective of Xi's consolidation of power is to appoint his protégés to key leadership posts so that they are well positioned for membership in the Politburo and, most important, in the PSC that will be formed at the 19th Party Congress in the fall of 2017. The battle for the next round of leadership selection is apparently well under way. The focus of competition will likely continue to be the composition of the new PSC.

The dramatic and complicated developments of the past few years call for a more systematic and empirical analysis of the structure and dynamics of the party and its leadership. Wang Qishan, the party's "anticorruption tsar" and Xi's strongest political ally, recently told an American delegation of Democrats and Republicans in Beijing that the "CCP leadership is the defining characteristic of Chinese politics, and foreign countries simply cannot deal with China without an understanding of the party."[9] Although

China analysts may not take Wang's remarks at face value, they must rethink how Chinese politics is analyzed—how they can reconcile the tensions between the trend of collective leadership, which emphasizes deal making based on accepted rules and norms, and the new party boss's aggressive consolidation of power. This is an urgent task for Sinologists, as the Middle Kingdom now has more influence on the global economy and regional security than at any other point in modern history.

Ultimately, all of these astonishing—and seemingly unplanned—episodes in Chinese politics over recent years raise new questions about the legitimacy of the process through which the CCP selects its leaders and sets its structure of governance. As illustrated by Henry Kissinger's words in the above epigraph, for the Chinese nation, every solution to a critical problem—of governance or otherwise—only leads to a new challenge.[10]

CHAPTER 1

Governance

Collective Leadership Revisited

Things don't have to be or look identical in order to be balanced or equal.
—MAYA LIN 林瓔

This book examines how the structure and dynamics of the leadership of the Chinese Communist Party (CCP) have evolved in response to the challenges the party has confronted since the late 1990s. This study pays special attention to the issue of leadership selection and composition, which is a perpetual concern in Chinese politics. Using both quantitative and qualitative analyses, this volume assesses the changing nature of elite recruitment, the generational attributes of the leadership, the checks and balances between competing political coalitions or factions, the behavioral patterns and institutional constraints of heavyweight politicians in the collective leadership, and the interplay between elite politics and broad changes in Chinese society. This study also links new trends in elite politics to emerging currents within the Chinese intellectual discourse on the tension between strongman politics and collective leadership and its implications for political reforms. A systematic analysis of these developments—and some seeming contradictions—will help shed valuable light on how the world's most populous country will be governed in the remaining years of the Xi Jinping era and beyond.

This study argues that the survival of the CCP regime in the wake of major political crises such as the Bo Xilai episode and rampant official corruption is not due to "authoritarian resilience"—the capacity of the Chinese communist system to resist political and institutional changes—as some foreign China analysts have theorized. Rather, China's leadership has survived and thrived over the past three decades because it has continually sought new mechanisms, institutional regulations, policy measures, and political norms to resolve its inherent deficiencies and inadequacies. Whether foreign analysts like them or not, some of these institutional developments are actually much more extensive and even more "democratic" (at least at the intraparty level) than the outside world has generally recognized or appreciated. By keeping abreast of changes—especially those resulting from the development of new, dynamic forces in Chinese society—and adapting accordingly, the CCP has maintained its grip on one-party rule.

XI'S CONSOLIDATION OF POWER: REVERSING THE TREND OF COLLECTIVE LEADERSHIP?

Over the past two decades, China has undergone a major transition in leadership structure and governance. The shift has often been characterized as a move from an era shaped by the arbitrary authority of an all-powerful strongman—first Mao, and then Deng—to a new era of collective leadership. This change means that the composition of the Politburo Standing Committee (PSC) is more important than ever before. Of particular significance are the idiosyncrasies of the body's members, its group dynamics, and the balance of power between its factions. Over the past two periods of leadership, the party's chief, beginning with Jiang Zemin of the third generation, and then Hu Jintao of the fourth generation, was merely seen as the "first among equals" in the collective leadership of the PSC.[1] In contrast to the eras of Mao and Deng, China's political structure, the rules and norms that govern its elite politics, and associated decisionmaking processes appear to have changed dramatically.

Five Main Areas of Change under Xi's New Leadership

With the arrival of Xi Jinping in 2012 to 2013, the existing trend toward collective leadership has become less apparent, or possibly even reversed. Some observers argue that Xi's leadership represents the "end of collective leadership" and the "reemergence of strongman politics."[2] In the first three years of his tenure as top leader, Xi Jinping surprised many China analysts with his bold and effective political moves and policy undertakings. To date, the initiatives that have stood out in Xi's administration fall on five main fronts.

First, Xi quickly and skillfully concluded the Bo Xilai trial, which both the Chinese and international media called China's "trial of the century."[3] The Bo Xilai case represented the greatest challenge to the party's legitimacy since the 1989 Tiananmen Square incident and was widely perceived to be a "no-win" situation for the CCP leadership. The scandal exposed the decadent lifestyles of some high-ranking party leaders, including involvement with sex, drugs, money laundering, and even murder. Xi and his colleagues handled the case wisely. Prosecutors focused on Bo's official corruption, not on his other unlawful or immoral behavior, thus avoiding a broader exposure of the Chinese political system's flaws. They used social media to disseminate details of the courtroom proceedings, thereby undermining potential criticism of lack of openness. Bo's verdict of life imprisonment seemed appropriate—neither too severe nor too lenient.

Second, with the support of his principal political ally in the PSC, "anticorruption tsar" Wang Qishan, Xi launched a remarkably tough national antigraft campaign. In 2013, for example, the Wang-led Central Commission for Discipline Inspection along with the Ministry of Supervision handled 172,000 corruption cases and investigated 182,000 officials—the highest annual number of cases in thirty years.[4] By May 2016, the Xi leadership had purged a total of about 160 leaders at the vice-ministerial and provincial levels (副省部级, *fushengbuji*) on corruption charges, including twenty members of the 18th Central Committee of the CCP and one member of the Central Commission for Discipline Inspection.[5] The twenty recently purged members of the 18th Central Committee are Ling Jihua (full member and former director of the United Front Work Department), Zhou Benshun (full member and former party secretary of Hebei), Yang Dongliang (full member and former director of the State Administration of Work Safety), Su Shulin (full member and former governor of Fujian), Li Dongsheng (full member and former executive vice-minister of Public Security), Jiang Jiemin (full member and former minister of the State-owned Assets Supervision and Administration Commission), Yang Jinshan (full member and former vice-commander of the Chengdu Military Region), Wang Min (full member and former party secretary of Liaoning), Li Chuncheng (alternate member and former deputy party secretary of Sichuan), Wang Yongchun (alternate member and former vice president of the China National Petroleum Corporation), Wan Qingliang (alternate member and former party secretary of Guangzhou), Chen Chuanping (alternate member and former party secretary of Taiyuan), Pan Yiyang (alternate member and former executive vice-governor of Neimenggu), Zhu Mingguo (alternate member and former chair of the Guangdong People's Political Consultative Conference), Fan Changmi (alternate member and former deputy political commissar of the Lanzhou Military Region), Wang Min (alternate member and former party secretary of Jinan), Yang Weize (alternate member and former party secretary of Nanjing), Qiu He (alternate member and former deputy party secretary of Yunnan), Yu Yuanhui (alternate member and former party secretary of Nanning City), and Lu Xiwen (alternate member and former deputy party secretary of Beijing). Seven of these former officials (Su Shulin, Chen Chuanping, Wang Yongchun, Wan Qingliang, Pan Yiyang, Yang Weize, and

Yu Yuanhui) were born in the 1960s and thus had been considered up-and-coming leaders of the future generation.

In an even bolder move, Xi sent four heavyweight leaders to jail: former PSC member Zhou Yongkang, who for ten years controlled China's security and law enforcement apparatus; former vice-chairs of the Central Military Commission (CMC), Xu Caihou and Guo Boxiong, the highest-ranking generals, who for a decade were in charge of military personnel affairs; and Ling Jihua, who was in charge of the General Office of the Central Committee under Hu Jintao and oversaw all of the activities and document flows of the top leadership. These moves to clean up corruption within the party greatly bolstered public confidence and support for Xi, contributing to his image as a strong leader.

Third, Xi has shown dexterity on the foreign policy front. Although the outside world views China as increasingly assertive and even belligerent, the Chinese public generally interprets foreign policy issues from its own more patriotic perspective.[6] As is evident in China's official broadcasts and social media, the public tends to believe that China has been on the defensive in disputes in the East and South China Seas and that maritime tensions are largely due to a U.S.-led effort to contain China. To many Chinese, China's foreign policy under Xi has been a great success. Xi's "proactive" foreign policy approach (奋发有为, fenfa youwei) represents a remarkable departure from that of his predecessor, Hu Jintao, who was often seen as following a policy of "inaction" (无为, wuwei).[7] For example, Xi has significantly improved China's relationship with South Korea, even at the risk of antagonizing North Korea's Kim Jong-un. Xi also presided over a defining event in Sino-Russian relations: the signing of a thirty-year gas deal with Russian president Vladimir Putin in 2014. Some Chinese scholars have argued that China now seems to have more leverage in the U.S.-China-Russia triad, which contrasts with the Cold War era, when the United States carried more clout.[8] At the Conference on Interaction and Confidence-Building Measures in Asia, held in Shanghai in May 2014, Xi again asserted China's right to influence regional matters. He claimed that "ultimately Asian affairs should be decided by Asians, and Asian security should be protected by Asian nations."[9] On the world stage, China has many economic cards to play with nations of the European Union, and China's influence in Africa and South America has grown unprecedentedly strong.

Fourth, in late 2015 and early 2016, while China's economic slowdown and the resulting socioeconomic tensions within the country were dominating public concerns in China and abroad, Xi Jinping achieved a milestone victory in restructuring the People's Liberation Army (PLA). With this unprecedentedly large-scale and multifaceted transformation, known simply as the "military reform" (军改, jungai), Xi has profoundly revamped the PLA administrative lineup, restructured its regional organization, and reshuffled officers across departments, regions, and services. These far-reaching changes are also paving the way for the rapid promotion of "young guards," many of whom are seen either as Xi's long-time protégés or his new loyalists.[10] Xi's "ability to impose his will on the PLA," as the *Wall Street Journal* has observed, is in stunning contrast to his predecessors.[11] His "sweeping change" to the PLA reflects "a skill that his predecessor Hu Jintao lacked utterly and that Jiang Zemin wielded inconsistently," notes a seasoned overseas scholar of the Chinese military.[12]

Although it will take a total of five years to complete the military reform as scheduled for 2020, some major structural changes occurred immediately after Xi Jinping's important speech on the detailed plans about the transformation of the PLA under his administration in November 2015. It has been widely recognized for decades that the Chinese military is markedly unprepared for modern warfare, as the PLA structure has not been conducive to commanding joint force operations. Xi's grand military reform at least partially aims to address this deficiency. Several aspects of military reform are intended to alter the long-standing "dominance of the army" (大陆军, *dalujun*) in the Chinese military. These include downgrading of the four general departments (which have been dominated by officers from the army), establishing the Army Headquarters (which aims to make the army equal to, instead of superior to, other services such as the navy and air force), founding the Strategic Support Force, and emphasizing joint operations within the new structure of theater-based commands. These measures all contribute to a strategic shift away from a Soviet-style, army-centric system and toward what analysts call "a Western-style joint command."[13]

Finally, and perhaps most important, Xi is determined to reform and revitalize China's economy. He has championed his vision of a "Chinese dream," defined as the rejuvenation of the Chinese nation and the opportunity for all Chinese to attain a middle-class lifestyle. As evident from the Third Plenum of the 18th Central Committee, held in November 2013, the overall objectives of Xi's economic policy are to make the private sector the "decisive driver" of the Chinese economy, to satisfy the desires of the Chinese middle class, and to allow more members of the lower class to attain middle-class status.[14] Xi aims to present China and the world with a blueprint for this new phase of China's economic reform. With a road map for financial liberalization, service-sector development, and a new stage of environmentally friendly urbanization, Xi has set a bold agenda for economic change that aims to be as consequential as Deng Xiaoping's landmark decision to pursue economic reform and opening in 1978.[15]

These five far-reaching measures have greatly bolstered public confidence in the new party boss in Zhongnanhai (the headquarters of the CCP and the Chinese government). These are clear manifestations of Xi's very impressive rise over the past three years. Specifically, they demonstrate how Xi Jinping was able to identify potential threats to the party's legitimacy and supremacy—Bo Xilai's dramatic scandal, public dissatisfaction with both rampant official corruption and an ineffective leadership structure for making policy, Chinese nationalist sentiment in a rapidly changing international environment, the exigency of military reform, and the growing demands and desires of an emerging middle class—and then turn them to his advantage as a way to consolidate power.

No less significant has been the consolidation of Xi Jinping's power through the many top leadership positions that he has assumed. Previously, Presidents Jiang and Hu both first became general secretary of the party and then, after waiting months or years, took over the country's top military post. In contrast to his predecessors, Xi immediately took control of both pillars of party strength. Xi also chairs the newly established National Security Committee (NSC) and the Central Leading Group for Comprehensively Deepening Reforms (CLGCDF), two crucial decisionmaking bodies. In addition, he holds the top position in several central leading groups in important functional areas such as foreign affairs, finance and the economy, cybersecurity and information technology, and military reform.[16] Altogether, Xi now holds a total of twelve top posts in the country's most powerful leadership bodies (see table 1-1).

Given Xi's seeming monopoly of power in the Chinese political system, Chinese and foreign analysts have begun to refer to the current top leadership as the "Xi administration," rather than the "Xi-Li administration" (which refers also to Premier Li Keqiang). This contrasts with the naming convention for previous administrations, namely, the "Jiang Zemin-Zhu Rongji administration" and the "Hu Jintao-Wen Jiabao administration."[17] Observers argue that Premier Li has been marginalized, as Xi has taken over all of the top posts in economic affairs, which traditionally fall within the purview of the premier.[18] Zhang Lifan, a well-known Chinese historian and outspoken public intellectual, has argued that Xi hopes to be "as strong as [Vladimir] Putin when dealing with domestic and foreign affairs."[19] As Zhang noted during Xi's 2013 visit to Moscow, Xi's and Putin's personalities are very similar.

Reviewing the Trend of Collective Leadership and Interpreting Xi's Recent Initiatives

The developments that have followed Xi's ascent to the top leadership at the 18th National Party Congress raise a critical question: Will Xi's ongoing concentration of power reverse the trend of collective leadership, which has been a defining characteristic of post-Deng Chinese politics?

SKEPTICISM ABOUT XI'S DOMINANCE

It is one thing to recognize Xi Jinping's remarkable achievements in consolidating power over the first three years of his tenure as top CCP leader, but quite another to conclude that he has become a paramount and charismatic leader in the manner of Mao or Deng. Some scholars of Chinese politics have remained skeptical of the claim that Xi has attained supreme stature.[36] They believe it is far too early to forecast Xi's political trajectory and personal ambitions. Because the bold anticorruption campaign and comprehensive market reform will undermine various vested interest groups, including party officials and state-owned enterprise (SOE) executives, Xi needs to maximize his power and authority to achieve these objectives. Without this power, as Singapore-based political scientist Zheng Yongnian argues, Xi simply cannot do anything.[37]

From a different perspective, Xi's concentration of power may betray "an acute sense of insecurity."[38] In the words of British political scientist Steve Tsang, Xi may feel that "he needs to exert a high level of control over the party in order to make the reforms that China needs."[39] Xi's like-minded colleagues in the top leadership, of course, strongly support his endeavor to save the CCP. But their support for Xi's amassment of individual power could be temporary rather than permanent. Also, at a time of rapid change, with the two-decade-long practice of collective decisionmaking facing a serious test, there is understandably a certain amount of disagreement about what in fact is taking place in the leadership. Critics have highlighted four major factors that may undermine Xi's capacity to end collective leadership and become a Mao- or Denglike figure in Chinese politics.

Absence of Legendary Revolution or War Experience

The power and charisma of Mao and Deng grew out of their extraordinary leadership through revolution and war, as well as their decades of political networking.[40] Mao's authority stemmed largely from his leadership during the Long March and his enormous contribution to the founding of the PRC in 1949. Mao's followers—the Long Marchers and other revolutionary veterans—occupied an overwhelming majority of leadership positions during the first two decades of the PRC. Mao himself wielded enormous— almost unchallengeable—personal power after the Communist victory and was viewed as a godlike figure, especially during the Cultural Revolution. He routinely made major policy decisions alone, including the establishment of the "interior third front" (三线建设, *sanxian jianshe*), which was the large-scale construction of the defense industry and the development of electric and transportation infrastructure in China's interior that began in

1964, and the invitation that led to President Nixon's historic visit to China in 1972.[41] The most convincing evidence of Mao's individual power is, of course, his launch of the devastating Great Leap Forward and the Cultural Revolution.[42]

Furthermore, Mao treated succession as if it were his own private matter; discussion of the transition of power after Mao was taboo, and he literally did away with two expected successors when they displeased him: Liu Shaoqi in 1966 and Lin Biao in 1971. The omnipresent slogan "Long Live Chairman Mao!" reinforced the illusion of Mao's "immortality." The chairman literally held power until he exhaled his dying breath in September 1976. The result was a cataclysmic succession struggle that led, ironically, to Deng Xiaoping's rise to power and the reversal of most of the policies that characterized Mao's China.

Like Mao, Deng had a legendary revolutionary career, during which he cultivated a robust political network. He also drastically and imaginatively changed the country's course of development in the post-Mao reform era. When Deng returned to power in 1978 (the third rehabilitation in his incredible political career), he promoted some of his "revolutionary comrades in arms" from the Anti-Japanese War and the Chinese Civil War to key military posts in the PLA. In 1988, of the seventeen full generals who held the highest military ranks after the Cultural Revolution, ten came from the Second Field Army, to which Deng had personal ties. Some, including Defense Minister Qin Jiwei and Director of the General Political Department of the PLA Yang Baibing, came from the 129th Division—Deng's own unit.[43]

The loyalty of these military leaders to Deng was among the most crucial factors that enabled him to remain in power after the 1989 Tiananmen crisis. The same loyalists also made the military the "protector and escort" of Deng's economic reform and opening-up policy.[44] As a result of Deng's legendary political career and formidable mentor-protégé ties, a set of reform initiatives—establishing special economic zones and initiating programs that allowed Chinese students to study in the West—were implemented with little resistance.[45]

Also, like Mao, Deng's selection of his successor was pretty much his decision alone. In fact, he twice removed leaders he had tagged to succeed him—Hu Yaobang in 1986 and Zhao Ziyang in 1989—because he saw them as being too soft on democracy protesters. But unlike Mao, Deng did not pursue large-scale political purges, nor did he cause drastic disruptions to society. During the Deng era, political succession and generational change in the Chinese leadership became a matter of public concern. Whereas Mao was seen as a godlike figure, Deng was just a political strongman (政治强人, *zhengzhi qiangren*). For many years in the 1990s, people in China and Sinologists abroad speculated about geriatric Deng's imminent death, often causing stock markets in Hong Kong and China to fluctuate wildly. In actuality, Deng effectively handed over the reins of power to Jiang before he died in 1997.

Those who doubt Xi's preeminence claim that holding twelve leadership posts is not necessarily a sign of strength. They argue that for all of his influence, Deng Xiaoping did not hold any leadership positions between 1989 and 1997, except for the post of honorary chair of the China Bridge Association, and yet no one would doubt that Deng was the real boss of Zhongnanhai in most of his final years. He Pin argues that even though Xi may be able to acquire monopolized powerful positions (集权, *jiquan*), he will not be able to exert actual authority and power (威权, *weiquan*).[46] In He's view, establishing a personality cult to bolster Xi's image would be counterproductive and detrimental, not only for present-day China but also for Xi himself.[47]

Because of his generational attributes, Xi cannot boast political associations based on his revolutionary or war experiences, nor does he command a large team of devoted and well-positioned protégés in the current leadership. Even though Xi has recently promoted many "young guards" to the military leadership, their loyalty to Xi is something new—not based on decades-long bonds forged as army comrades, as was the case for Mao and Deng with their loyalists. Also, Xi's new loyalists must share power with other military leaders whose careers were not advanced through mentor-protégé ties. As Perry Link has observed, both Mao and Deng "were shrewd and powerful men who could dictate ideas and then either force or manipulate others into obedience. Top leaders after Deng have not been able to rule in this way; they have needed to balance power interests and continually watch rivals over their shoulders."[48]

There has been widespread concern in China and abroad that Xi's ambitious economic reform agenda announced at the Third Plenum in the fall of 2013 cannot be effectively implemented due to bureaucratic resistance, "suggesting that Xi is not quite as all-powerful as it may seem."[49] Along the same lines, critics believe that Xi's bold anticorruption campaign may create many enemies, provoking a backlash against him within Chinese officialdom.

Xi's Relatively Short Tenure as Heir Apparent

Unlike his two predecessors, Jiang Zemin and Hu Jintao, who served for many years in the top decisionmaking circle as presumed future leaders before assuming power, Xi has found the path to succession rather short. He served only one term in the PSC and two years as vice-chair of the CMC before becoming party boss in the fall of 2012. By contrast, when Jiang was appointed to top posts in the party, state, and military soon after the 1989 Tiananmen crisis, he had spent many years working in the shadow of the paramount leader Deng Xiaoping. While Deng "ruled behind a screen" (垂帘听政, *chuilian tingzheng*), Jiang reinforced his power gradually by promoting many of his close friends to the national leadership—most noticeably his former junior colleagues at the First Ministry of Machine Building, Li Lanqing, Jia Qinglin, and Zeng Peiyan, and his protégés in Shanghai, Zeng Qinghong, Wu Bangguo, and Huang Ju. All but one of these men later became members of the PSC.[50]

Similarly, as heir apparent, Hu Jintao served two terms on the PSC and five years as vice-chair of the CMC. He had already formed a strong mentor-protégé network of former colleagues through the Chinese Communist Youth League (CCYL), which he led in the early 1980s. Many of these so-called CCYL factional leaders (团派, *tuanpai*) were well positioned in the national leadership when Hu succeeded Jiang as top leader in 2002.[51] Notable examples include Song Defu (Fujian party secretary), Wang Lequan (Xinjiang party secretary and Politburo member), Li Keqiang (Henan party secretary), Li Yuanchao (Jiangsu party secretary), Wang Yang (executive deputy secretary-general of the State Council), Liu Yandong (director of the CCP United Front Work Department), Du Qinglin (minister of Agriculture), Meng Xuenong (Beijing mayor), and Huang Huahua (Guangdong governor). These long-time protégés constituted Hu's power base when he served as the CCP general secretary, and some of them currently serve on the PSC, Politburo, and Secretariat.

For Xi Jinping, the experiences of his predecessors have likely motivated him to move quickly to form his own strong team with which he can more effectively lead, both now and in the future. Xi, of course, is not without political allies in the top leadership, but political allies are not the same as personal protégés. Xi was not responsible for the ascent of his powerful political allies to the PSC, which contrasts with Jiang and Hu's involvement in the rise of their own personal protégés. In a sense, Xi's basis of power and authority is not as infallible as it seems. This also raises an important question as to what that basis is. Indeed, an important distinction exists between Xi's individual power and the group power generated by the dominance of his political allies in the top leadership.

Distinction between Xi's Individual Power and the Dominance of His Allies on the PSC

The first three years of the Xi administration brought remarkable changes in politics and policy as Xi took control of the leadership agenda. But these achievements arguably had more to do with the factional makeup of the PSC than with Xi's authority and command. In the post-Deng era, two major political coalitions associated with former general secretaries Jiang Zemin and Hu Jintao (who both still wield considerable influence) have been competing for power, influence, and control over policy initiatives. The first coalition, which was born from the Jiang era and is currently led by President Xi Jinping, can be named the Jiang-Xi camp (江习阵营, *jiangxi zhenying*). Its core membership was once the Shanghai Gang (上海帮, *shanghaibang*)—leaders who worked under Jiang when he was a top municipal leader in the city and later moved to Beijing to serve in the national leadership. Increasingly, the Jiang-Xi camp consists of "princelings" (太子党, *taizidang*)—leaders born to the families of revolutionaries or other high-ranking officials. Both Jiang and Xi are princelings themselves, though other princelings in Beijing have long harbored suspicions about the "authenticity" of Jiang's pedigree.[52]

The second coalition, known as the Hu-Li camp (胡李阵营, *huli zhenying*), was previously led by Hu Jintao and is now headed by Premier Li Keqiang. Its core faction is *tuanpai* officials, leaders who advanced their political career primarily through the leadership of the CCYL when they were young, as both Hu and Li did. They usually have humble family backgrounds and often have leadership experience in less developed inland regions. This bifurcation has created within China's one-party polity something approximating a system of checks and balances, as the two coalitions attempt to direct the policymaking process. This informal experiment in Chinese elite politics, which this author calls the "one party, two coalitions" mechanism (一党两派, *yidang liangpai*), has been one of the most important political developments in post-Deng China.

At the 18th National Party Congress, the Jiang-Xi camp won an overwhelming majority of the seats on the PSC. It secured six of the seven spots, while the Hu-Li camp is now only represented by Li Keqiang.[53] This six-to-one ratio in favor of the Jiang-Xi camp is a crucially important political factor in present-day Chinese leadership, yielding Xi, the protégé of Jiang, tremendous support and power. It explains why he can so quickly and boldly carry out his new initiatives—the successful closure of the Bo Xilai trial, the strong anticorruption drive, a more proactive foreign policy, military reform, and an ambitious market reform agenda. This is also the reason the PSC has been able to grant Xi twelve top leadership posts.

Yet, it should also be noted that the five members of the PSC who are Xi's political allies are expected to retire, as a result of age limits, at the 19th National Party Congress planned for 2017. They include Wang Qishan, a skilled political tactician and Xi's longtime friend, who has played an instrumental role in the anticorruption campaign and financial reforms, and Yu Zhengsheng, another seasoned politician who has ties with Xi's family reaching back almost seven decades.[54] Even before the 18th National Party Congress in November 2012, some analysts were predicting that following the Hu-Wen administration, these three heavyweight politicians would form the "iron triangle" (铁三角, *tiesanjiao*) in the top leadership.[55] It is likely that the Jiang-Xi camp will no longer enjoy as overwhelming a majority after the next round of leadership turnover.

The Enduring Power of the Opposition Camp

The dominance of Jiang's men in the current PSC does not necessarily mean that "the winner takes all" in Chinese elite politics. Leaders of the Hu-Li camp are still well represented in other important leadership bodies. Although the Jiang-Xi camp dominates the PSC, the other eighteen Politburo seats are divided equally between the Jiang-Xi and Hu-Li camps (see table 1-2). On the seven-member Secretariat, five members advanced their careers largely through the ranks of the CCYL; three of these—Director of the CCP Organization Department Liu Qibao, Vice-Chair of the Chinese People's Political Consultative Conference (CPPCC) Du Qinglin, and State Councilor Yang Jing—are Hu's *tuanpai* protégés.[56] Of the ten members on the executive committee of the State Council, four officials—Li Keqiang, Liu Yandong, Wang Yang, and Yang Jing—are prominent *tuanpai* leaders.

It is also notable that in each of the nine most important leadership organs of the PRC—namely, the PSC, the PRC presidency (president and vice-president), the State Council, the CMC, the CCP Secretariat, the NPC, the CPPCC, the Supreme People's Court, and the Supreme People's Procuratorate—the top-ranked leader (第一把手, *diyibashou*) and the second-ranked leader (第二把手, *di'erbashou*) are split between the two competing coalitions (see table 1-3). This suggests that China's current collective leadership maintains a factional balance of power.

Another factor contributing to factional balance is the ascent of numerous *tuanpai* leaders to the 376-member Central Committee. Many of them serve as provincial party secretaries, governors, and ministers of the State Council or their deputies, or in other important leadership posts. More specifically, *tuanpai* leaders, whose time working with the CCYL coincided with Hu Jintao or Li Keqiang's leadership of the league, now occupy ninety-nine seats on the 18th Central Committee, constituting 26.3 percent of this crucial decisionmaking body.[57]

As the "one party, two coalitions" dynamic appears to be a new experiment in Chinese elite politics, it is possible that the CCP will also experiment with a new mechanism of "factional rotation" (派系轮换, *paixi lunhuan*). This may partially explain why the Hu-Li camp quietly acquiesced to its significant minority in the 18th PSC. Based on political norms and age requirements in elite Chinese politics, leading candidates for the 2017 PSC will likely include several leaders from the Hu-Li camp, such as Vice-Premier Wang Yang, Guangdong Party Secretary Hu Chunhua, and Director of the

TABLE 1-2. Factional Identity of Members of the Politburo, 2016

Name	Age (2016)	Confirmed and designated leadership post	Jiang-Xi camp	Hu-Li camp
Xi Jinping*	63	Party Secretary-General, Chair of CMC, PRC President	X	
Li Keqiang*	61	Premier of the State Council		X
Zhang Dejiang*	70	Chair of the National People's Congress	X	
Yu Zhengsheng*	71	Chair of the CPPCC	X	
Liu Yunshan*	69	Executive Secretary of the Secretariat	X	
Wang Qishan*	68	Secretary of the CCDI	X	
Zhang Gaoli*	70	Executive Vice-Premier of the State Council	X	
Ma Kai	70	Vice-Premier of the State Council	X	
Wang Huning	61	Director of the CCP Central Policy Research Office	X	
Liu Yandong (f)	71	Vice-Premier of the State Council		X
Liu Qibao	63	Director of the CCP Propaganda Department		X
Xu Qiliang	66	Vice-Chair of the CMC	X	
Sun Chunlan (f)	66	Director of the CCP United Front Work Department		X
Sun Zhengcai	53	Chongqing Party Secretary	X	
Li Jianguo	70	Vice-Chair of NPC		X
Li Yuanchao	66	Vice-President of the PRC		X
Wang Yang	61	Vice-Premier of the State Council		X
Zhang Chunxian	63	Xinjiang Party Secretary	X	
Fan Changlong	69	Vice-Chair of the CMC		X
Meng Jianzhu	69	Secretary of the Commission of Political Science and Law	X	
Zhao Leji	59	Director of the CCP Organization Department	X	
Hu Chunhua	53	Guangdong Party Secretary		X
Li Zhanshu	66	Director of the CCP General Office	X	
Guo Jinlong	69	Beijing Party Secretary		X
Han Zheng	62	Shanghai Party Secretary	X	

Notes and Source: * Refers to Politburo Standing Committee members. Jiang-Xi camp = Jiang Zemin and Xi Jinping camp; Hu-Li camp = Hu Jintao and Li Keqiang camp; CMC = Central Military Commission; CPPCC = Chinese People's Political Consultative Conference; CCDI = Central Commission for Discipline Inspection; (f) = female; CCP = Chinese Communist Party; NPC = National People's Congress; PRC = People's Republic of China. Cheng Li, "Opportunity Lost? Inside China's Leadership Transition," *Foreign Policy* Online, November 16, 2012 (http://www.foreignpolicy.com/articles/2012/11/16/opportunity_lost).

TABLE 1-3. Factional Affiliation of Top Two Leaders in the Most Important People's Republic of China Leadership Organs, 2016

Leadership organ	Top-ranked leader		Second-ranked leader	
	Name	Faction	Name	Faction
Politburo Standing Committee (PSC, two highest-ranking members)	Xi Jinping	Jiang-Xi camp (princeling)	Li Keqiang	Hu-Li camp (*tuanpai*)
PRC Presidency (President & Vice-President)	Xi Jinping	Jiang-Xi camp (princeling)	Li Yuanchao	Hu-Li camp (*tuanpai*)
State Council (Premier & Executive Vice-Premier)	Li Keqiang	Hu-Li camp (*tuanpai*)	Zhang Gaoli	Jiang-Xi camp
Central Military Commission (Chair & Executive Vice-Chair)	Xi Jinping	Jiang-Xi camp (princeling)	Fan Changlong	Hu-Li camp
CCP Secretariat (two highest-ranking members)	Liu Yunshan	Jiang-Xi camp	Liu Qibao	Hu-Li camp (*tuanpai*)
National People's Congress (Chair & Executive Vice-Chair)	Zhang Dejiang	Jiang-Xi camp (princeling)	Li Jianguo	Hu-Li camp
CPPCC (Chair & Executive Vice-Chair)	Yu Zhengsheng	Jiang-Xi camp (princeling)	Du Qinglin	Hu-Li camp (*tuanpai*)
Supreme People's Court (President & Executive Vice-President)	Zhou Qiang	Hu-Li camp (*tuanpai*)	Shen Deyong	Jiang-Xi camp
Supreme People's Procuratorate (President & Executive Vice-President)	Cao Jianming	Jiang-Xi camp (Shanghai gang)	Hu Zejun	Hu-Li camp (*tuanpai*)

Note and Source: CCP = Chinese Communist Party; CMC = Central Military Commission; CPPCC = Chinese People's Political Consultative Conference; NPC = National People's Congress; PRC = People's Republic of China. Cheng Li, "A Biographical and Factional Analysis of the Post-2012 Politburo," *China Leadership Monitor*, no. 41 (June 6, 2013), 11.

CCP Propaganda Department Liu Qibao. All of these leaders currently serve on the Politburo, and all are known as *tuanpai* leaders who worked very closely with Hu Jintao in the leadership of the CCYL in the 1980s. Hu Chunhua, one of the two so-called sixth-generation leaders in the current Politburo, is viewed by some analysts as the heir apparent to Xi, in line to succeed him at the 20th Party Congress in 2022.[58]

It is interesting to note that Xi's ongoing anticorruption campaign is not directly motivated by factional politics, although the political capital and public confidence acquired through the campaign's achievements will potentially allow Xi to appoint more of his protégés to the top leadership in the next round of political succession. Five out of the six largest corruption cases that have been investigated over the past three years have involved Jiang's protégés, namely, former Politburo member Bo Xilai, former minister of Railways Liu Zhijun, former PSC member Zhou Yongkang, and former vice-chairs of the CMC, Xu Caihou and Guo Boxiong.

Different reasons led to these five leaders being charged, but in each case, the crimes were outrageous in scope. In some cases, such as the Bo Xilai-Wang Lijun episode, the fallen official was unlucky enough to have his crimes publicly exposed. The publicity was likely a result of Xi's need to prove his ability to curtail rampant official corruption, to improve the tarnished image of the CCP, and, most important, to quell public resentment over the convergence of political power and economic wealth that emerged from a government primarily run by princelings and Jiang's protégés.[59] In fact, the anticorruption tsar, Wang Qishan, is also a princeling and Jiang's protégé. In demonstrating that princelings can crack down on other princelings or their political allies, Xi and Wang have effectively headed off criticism that the new leadership's anticorruption campaign is merely motivated by factional politics.

Only after the trial of Bo Xilai and arrests of the other four aforementioned leaders did Xi and Wang begin to purge some of the heavyweight leaders in the Hu-Li camp, most noticeably the prominent *tuanpai* leader Ling Jihua. Ling was Hu Jintao's confidant, formerly serving as the director of the Central United Front Work Department and director of the Central General Office. In the lead-up to the 18th National Party Congress, Ling was a top contender for PSC membership. But he faced a political Waterloo during the last leadership succession due to fallout from a scandal involving his son, who was killed when he crashed a Ferrari driving at high speeds in Beijing. Ling's alleged cover-up, as well as suspicion of a cross-factional conspiracy between him and Zhou Yongkang, brought his political ambitions to ruin.[60] Ling's brother, Ling Zhengce, the former director of the Development and Reform Commission in Shanxi Province, was arrested earlier in 2014 on corruption charges. That it took two years to remove Ling Jihua may reflect caution on the part of Xi Jinping and Wang Qishan in handling cases that involve Hu's *tuanpai* protégés.

It remains to be seen whether they will pursue other cases against prominent *tuanpai* leaders. One does not need to be a seasoned China watcher to realize that further purges of heavyweight *tuanpai* leaders will be widely perceived as faction driven and could carry grave consequences. But even if the leadership structure or factional lineup changes in accordance with Xi's political desire, the broad political circumstances in this rapidly changing country are unlikely to make a return of strongman politics feasible.

BROAD CHALLENGES CONFRONTING THE XI LEADERSHIP

The tension between Xi's concentration of individual power and China's past practice of collective leadership has become especially significant at a time when the country is confronting many daunting challenges. Over the past several decades, China has been beset by growing wealth disparities, repeated industrial and environmental disasters, resource scarcity, public health and food safety crises, frequent instances of social unrest, and a manual labor shortage in some coastal cities, coinciding with high unemployment rates among college graduates. China's economy faces serious and interrelated problems, including mounting local debt, the proliferation of shadow banking, overcapacity in certain industrial sectors, and a growing property bubble. The old development model, which relied on export-driven and cheap labor-oriented growth, has come to an end. Chinese labor costs have risen rapidly, and the country can no longer tolerate the previous growth model's severe damage to the environment, including the pollution of air, water, and soil. But the new consumption-driven, innovation-led, and service sector–centric model has yet to fully take flight.

Of course, Xi and his generation of leaders did not create these problems; they have largely inherited them from their predecessors. In fact, Xi's bold economic reform agenda has sought to address many of these issues. Some argue that factional deadlock in collective leadership led to the Hu-Wen administration's ineffectiveness during the so-called lost decade, when seemingly little could be done to counter rampant official corruption and the monopolization of SOEs. This rationale has apparently bolstered the case for Xi's more forceful personal leadership.[61] If a more balanced factional composition in the PSC leads to infighting, political fragmentation, and policy deadlock, why should China not organize leadership so that power is concentrated in the hands of Xi and his team? If collective leadership assigns each PSC member one functional area and thus leads to political fragmentation and poor coordination, why should more power not be given to the general secretary? If local governments have been the main source of resistance to reform initiatives, why should Zhongnanhai not establish the Leading Group for Comprehensively Deepening Reforms at various levels of government to facilitate policy implementation? This line of thinking seems to explain the basis for the six-to-one split of the current PSC and Xi's twelve top leadership posts.

But in consolidating power, Xi also runs a major political risk: If he cannot deliver what he has promised as part of his economic reform agenda, he will not have anyone else with whom to share the blame. The recent stock market crisis in China and the very strong government interference in order to "save the market" reflect Xi's political vulnerability and his sense of urgency. Xi's popularity among the general public, including the majority of the middle class, is always subject to change if China's economic conditions deteriorate.

Furthermore, Xi's inclination for monopolizing power has alienated a large swath of China's public intellectuals, especially liberal intellectuals. They were particularly dismayed in the early months of Xi's tenure by orders instructing them not to speak about seven sensitive issues: universal values, freedom of the press, civil society, civil rights, past mistakes by the CCP, crony capitalism, and judicial independence.[62] In public discourse, some of these topics remain very sensitive or even taboo. Media censorship has tightened under Xi's leadership, as has the state monitoring and management of research institutes, universities, and NGOs.

It should be noted that Xi's politically conservative and economically liberal approach to governing mirrors the method preferred by his predecessors, who always seemed to take one step forward economically while taking a step backward politically. During his famous "Southern Tour" (南巡, *nanxun*) in 1992, Deng called for greater market reform and economic privatization, while continuing to crack down on political dissent. Jiang broadened the CCP's power base by recruiting entrepreneurs and other new socioeconomic players, a formulation known as the "Three Represents" (三个代表, *sange daibiao*), while launching a harsh political campaign against the Falun Gong, an emerging religious group. Hu's populist appeal for a "harmonious society" sought to reduce economic disparities and social tensions, all while tightening police control of society, especially in regions with a high proportion of ethnic minorities.

And yet, Xi seems to face deeper and rougher political waters than any Chinese leader since Mao, with the very survival of the party-state resting in his hands. With the revolution in telecommunications and social media, the way China's authorities manage domestic political issues—from human rights and religious freedom to ethnic tensions and media censorship—has increasingly caught the eye of the Chinese public and the international community. Xi's decision to prioritize economic reforms may be strategically sound, but he may not be able to postpone much-needed political reform for too long. Xi must make bold, timely moves to implement political reforms—including increasing political openness and expanding the role of civil society—and address issues that are currently preventing China from blossoming into a true innovation-driven economy.

Likewise, Xi's ambitious anticorruption campaign has not come without serious political risks. Though popular among the Chinese public, this ad hoc initiative may ultimately alienate the officialdom—the very group on which the system relies for steady governance. Ultimately, Xi's limited crackdown on official corruption should not serve as a replacement for reinforcing the rule of law, adopting institutional mechanisms like official income disclosure and conflict of interest regulations, and, most important, taking concrete steps to establish an independent judicial system in China. Otherwise, it will only be a matter of time before a new wave of official corruption leaves the public cynical about Xi's true intentions and the effectiveness of his signature campaign.

From an even broader standpoint, China's history under Mao and Deng was one of arbitrary decisionmaking by one individual leader. This method is arguably unsuitable for governing a pluralistic society amid increasingly active interest group politics. Despite its deficiencies, collective leadership generally entails a more dynamic and pluralistic decisionmaking process through which political leaders can represent various socioeconomic and geographic constituencies. Bringing together leaders from contending political camps with different expertise, credentials, and experiences contributes to the development of more-effective governmental institutions. Common interests in domestic social stability and a shared aspiration to further China's rise on the world stage may make collective leadership both feasible and sustainable. In this sense, Xi can modify and improve the system of collective leadership, which is still largely experimental. But it would be pretentious and detrimental to attempt to replace most of the rules and norms that have governed elite politics over the past two decades. One simply cannot turn the clock back to the old days of the Mao era, when China was far less pluralistic and far more isolated from the outside world.

INADEQUACIES OF SCHOLARLY DEBATES

For the international community, a well-informed, accurate, and sophisticated understanding of China's leadership structure and politics is essential in today's world. One of the most unfortunate gaps in the growing literature on contemporary China is the relative lack of insightful and informed research on leadership politics. Many authors have held forth at length about China's foreign policy, strategic behavior, military capabilities, social tensions, economic prospects, and demographic challenges, but few have addressed the topic that underpins all of these areas, namely, the changes and developments in politics and decisionmaking at the leadership level.[63]

With China emerging as a global economic powerhouse, PRC government policies—relating to the domestic economy, trade, taxation, industry, the environment, and energy—will continue to have a major impact on the global economy. The Chinese political structure and leadership, including the decisionmaking process and personal characteristics of leaders, will be among the most important factors that shape these policies. Unity or division within the leadership will undoubtedly affect China's overall political stability. Growing tensions in the East China Sea and South China Sea and the widespread view among the Chinese public that the United States wants to contain China have further clouded Chinese leadership politics. At the same time, China's foreign policy is increasingly influenced by domestic considerations, including elite competition, the economy, energy security, nationalism, and maintaining political support from the military. These domestic and international factors mean that the study of Chinese leadership politics is more important than ever before. For U.S. policymakers, misjudging Xi's power or drawing unbalanced assessments of the status and trends of collective leadership risks rendering policies toward China ineffective.

Though the overseas media has reported extensively on China's elite politics—including the importance of the PSC, the characteristics of top leaders, and Xi's efforts to consolidate his power—numerous facets of Chinese collective leadership have escaped rigorous scholarly scrutiny.[64] Unfortunately, many analysts have gravitated to either of two extremes. Some researchers remain burdened by stale perceptions and vulnerable to rumors. They are obsessed with investigating information obtained from unverified "secret documents" in China and often rely on outmoded analytical frameworks with ideologically loaded terminology to analyze the PRC's increasingly complicated governing structure. Many overseas analyses of Chinese politics are based on rumors, myths, and speculation rather than verifiable and empirical facts.

Meanwhile, other scholars and observers are so impressed by the capacity and achievements of Chinese leaders that they have abandoned their critical lens, sometimes overlooking fundamental deficiencies in China's political system and serious shortcomings in individual leaders.[65] The most notable recent example is a book written by Robert Lawrence Kuhn, a businessman who has become a biographer of PRC senior leaders. After extensive interviews with many rising stars of the fifth generation of PRC leaders, Kuhn offers substantial if not absolute praise of their talent, wisdom, and vision.[66] To be fair, Kuhn's interviews with Chinese senior leaders are informative and insightful, providing an important perspective. But he and other like-minded overseas analysts have often overlooked the long-standing problems of the authoritarian system when it comes to selecting national leaders. Until a more legitimate mechanism for selecting leaders is implemented, these problems will likely continue to undermine the unity of the leadership and the party's governance capacity.

In academic studies of Chinese politics, two contending views have prevailed over the past decade. One is the analytical paradigm of authoritarian resilience. Western scholarship on the durability of the party-state regime began to emerge in the mid-1990s and has become the mainstream position over the last decade.[67] After the CCP survived the political turmoil of the 1989 Tiananmen incident, which caused a serious legitimacy crisis, some China analysts began to appreciate the endurance and adaptability of the Chinese leadership in handling daunting challenges both at home and abroad. These analysts view the CCP as adaptable enough to respond quickly to changes in its environment and to become more competent over time. "The result," some scholars observe, "has been to create a power system characterized by 'authoritarian resilience.'"[68]

By definition, the CCP's resilient authoritarianism refers to a one-party political system that is able to "enhance the capacity of the state to govern effectively" through institutional adaptations and policy adjustments.[69] A key component of the authoritarian resilience thesis is the argument or perception that the CCP's system can successfully resist or suppress demands for democracy in the country and around the world.[70] Not surprisingly, party leaders and conservative public intellectuals seek to reinforce the belief that "democracy is not appropriate for China," but that a resilient authoritarian system is.[71]

In his analysis of why the CCP has been able to retain power since the 1989 Tiananmen incident, Andrew Nathan outlines four important institutional developments in the Chinese political system:

1. the increasingly norm-bound nature of its succession politics;
2. the increase in meritocratic, as opposed to factional, considerations in the promotion of political elites;
3. the differentiation and functional specialization of institutions within the regime; and
4. the establishment of institutions for political participation that strengthen the CCP's legitimacy among the public at large.[72]

Establishing these institutional mechanisms has certainly been a part of the CCP leadership's agenda. Indeed, over the past decade some of these processes have influenced the political behavior of leaders and changed the game of China's elite politics. But one can also argue that, for now, they all have serious limitations. None has been effective enough to make the overall

Chinese political system more resilient.[73] The "norm-bound nature of its succession politics" has been overshadowed by widespread "black box manipulation," which is anything but meritocratic. Nepotism in various forms— blood ties, school ties, regional identities, and mentor-protégé ties—continues to play a crucial role in elite selection. Similarly, the CCP has explicitly stated that it is not interested in pursuing a Western-style tripartite division of government. Instead, the Chinese leadership has proposed an institutional separation of the party into three divisions, namely, decisionmaking, policy implementation, and supervision. Given that CCP power remains unchecked, however, the party leadership's promotion of "functional specialization of institutions within the regime" has been mostly empty rhetoric. And CCP paranoia about group protests, petitions, and the rise of social media forums is a serious obstacle in the way of institutionalized public participation.

In general, the authoritarian resilience thesis tends to underestimate the vulnerability of the authoritarian political system. It largely overlooks the fact that new socioeconomic forces in the country pose serious challenges to the CCP's monopoly on power and will make it more difficult for prominent leaders such as Bo Xilai and Zhou Yongkang to benefit from misuse of personal influence. As described earlier, competing factions within the party leadership may fail to broker the necessary deals to preserve party unity. The authoritarian resilience paradigm also neglects to adequately consider strong demands for democracy by liberal-minded intellectuals and a burgeoning Chinese middle class. New experiments in the management or reform of party institutions should lead to deeper changes if the system is genuinely resilient. A truly durable political system remains open to new ideas and new experiments. It would therefore be able to evolve institutionally and politically and avoid becoming dogmatic and stagnant.

Opposite to the "authoritarian resilience" camp, another group of scholars holds the belief that the CCP—but not the country—is in danger of collapse. In his remarks at the China Reform Forum in December 2011, scholar Zhang Lifan argued that "China is not in danger, but the CCP is."[74] In his view, many CCP officials are aware of the party's tenuous legitimacy. They ultimately do not care whether or not the CCP survives and are instead concerned only with the well-being of their own families. Rampant official corruption, the tendency of leaders to transfer their personal assets abroad for safekeeping, and the phenomenon of officials sending their family members to study or live in the West all reflect party elites' lack of confidence in the country's sociopolitical stability.[75] Observers often note that the Chinese government budget for national defense in 2012 was 670.3 billion yuan, whereas the budget for police and other domestic security expenditures amounted to 701.8 billion yuan.[76]

Critics also point out the unprecedentedly large presence of princelings in the top leadership, the role of mentor-protégé ties in elite promotion (for example, the prevalence of *tuanpai* and *mishu* in the leadership), and the fact that those who do not have strong family backgrounds or political connections have routinely used bribes to "purchase office" (买官, *maiguan*). Minxin Pei, a prominent U.S.-based scholar of China's elite politics, has identified the trend of China's leaders using "fake or dubiously acquired academic credentials to burnish their resumes." All of the above have tarnished the CCP elite's claims of legitimacy and meritocracy.[77]

Scholars who predict the CCP's collapse are often cynical about Xi's intentions and capacity to pursue serious political and legal reforms, which they believe are essential to the party's survival. In the lead-up to the 18th National Party Congress, Zhang Lifang stated bluntly, "If the next generation of leaders do not pursue political reforms in their first term, there is no point in doing so in their second term." In his words, "China should witness either reforms in the first five years, or the end of the CCP in ten years."[78] David Shambaugh's famous article "The Coming Chinese Crackup" argues along the same line of thinking while highlighting the imminent nature of this doomsday scenario for the CCP and, in particular, for Xi.[79]

Just as proponents of the authoritarian resilience thesis have not adequately considered societal factors, scholars associated with the collapse paradigm tend to underestimate the strong incentive for CCP leaders to ensure the party's survival and the wealth of political resources that those leaders have to change the odds against them. In a sense, critics see China's problems as dynamic, but they do not give the country's leadership the same credit. The assumption that the CCP leadership is static and stubborn proves problematic, as it disregards the recent political measures and policy changes enacted by Xi and his new leadership team in the wake of scandals relating to Bo Xilai and others.

China's political future, especially the survival or transformation of its one-party system, is a complex issue that demands more intellectually rigorous analysis and debate. The resilience and collapse paradigms are based on some valid empirical evidence and analytical insight, but both are too deterministic in forecasting China's political trajectory. Neither has seriously scrutinized the remarkable changes in the formation of the CCP elite or the Chinese conception of collective leadership and its intriguing role in the transformation of Chinese society.

Some PRC scholars have recently argued that collective leadership is a uniquely Chinese form of governance. In his new book *The System of Collective Leadership in China*, Hu Angang, an influential scholar and director of the Institute for Contemporary China Studies at Tsinghua University, goes a step further and glorified China for developing, in his view, a political system of collective leadership that is more democratic, more responsive, and superior to the presidential system (总统制, *zongtongzhi*) in the United States.[80] In criticizing the U.S. system, he cites several negative features, including the influence of money in presidential politics, the empty promises of presidential candidates, lack of long-term strategic planning, widespread bureaucratic inefficiency, monopolized executive power, and dysfunction due to partisan bickering.

According to Hu Angang, the most important feature of the Chinese political system at present is that it is "collective"—Hu coined the term *collective presidency* to refer to the Chinese collective leadership—and therefore differs from the U.S. presidential system, which emphasizes the "individual."[81] The Chinese system values "collective wisdom" rather than "individual wisdom" and relies on "collective decisionmaking" instead of the "individual decisionmaking" favored by the U.S. presidential system.[82] The diverse backgrounds and expertise of the PSC members are invaluable assets in the decisionmaking process, helping the body avoid reaching arbitrary, ill-considered conclusions more reliably than an individual leader. In Hu's view, PSC members who also lead other institutions not only represent diverse interests but also more effectively coordinate and implement policies.[83] Hu also elaborates on what he calls the five mechanisms of Chinese collective leadership: division and coordination of responsibility, generational succession, group learning, separate investigations and visits, and collective decisionmaking.[84]

Hu proposes thirteen ways in which the Chinese collective leadership can improve—including by adopting regulations on procedures and voting for major decisions, ensuring against the resurgence of the personality cult, soliciting external consultant work, and strengthening political accountability—but he hardly discusses any fundamental flaws of China's political system. Most notably, Hu does not address China's political and institutional vulnerabilities. Not surprisingly, Hu Angang's thesis has received far more criticism than praise in Chinese semiofficial news circuits and social media channels, as well as in Chinese academic circles. Critics especially find fault in Hu's simplistic assessment of both American and Chinese political systems and his contradictions about the "monopolized power" and "powerlessness" of the U.S. president.[85]

Nevertheless, Hu Angang has made both the Chinese public and the intellectual community pay greater attention to the origin, operation, and implications of collective leadership, especially the pivotal role of the PSC. Western scholars of Chinese politics have not yet engaged in the serious research that this subject demands. Analysis of Xi Jinping's ascent and recent consolidation of power and its impact on collective leadership has relevance beyond China's future trajectory. It can also contribute to a broader understanding of the political transition processes in authoritarian regimes in general. An empirically grounded, comprehensive study of China's search for collective leadership can enrich the wider academic literature on comparative political systems.

THE OVERARCHING ARGUMENT AND KEY THEMES OF THIS BOOK

The overarching argument of this book is that despite the persistence of one-party rule in the PRC, the ruling party has continued to evolve and reform itself over the past three decades. China's governance structure and political dynamics in general have progressed significantly, becoming far more institutionalized than many of the system's harshest critics in the West acknowledge. One must recognize that China's experiment with orderly, institutionalized transfer of power is relatively new. Yet, in what is no insignificant feat, the country has twice completed a generally peaceful, systematic transition of leadership: first in 2002 and again in 2012. A more comprehensive analysis of the inner workings of China's collective leadership—its structure, composition, internal dynamics, limitations, and the role of the top leader—yields vital insights regarding the party's stability and future prospects.

The CCP is apparently unwilling to relinquish its monopoly on political power and experiment with a Western-style system based on a separation of powers between the executive, legislative, and judicial branches of government. This does not mean, however, that the CCP is a politically stagnant institution completely resistant to institutional change, nor does it mean that there is a total absence of checks and balances in the Chinese political system. Furthermore, leadership under the one-party system does not necessarily consist of a monolithic group of elites that share similar personal and professional backgrounds, political experiences, policy preferences, and worldviews.

Certain institutional rules and norms—including the retirement age requirement, term limits, regional representation, and multicandidate elections for the Central Committee—have proven enduring and effective. While these institutional mechanisms cannot fully eliminate the nepotism inherent in elite promotion, they have nevertheless imparted a new sense of consistency and fairness, and even changed competitive political behavior among the elite.

The elite transformation in China during the past three decades is not simply generational; it is also occupational. In fact, the background of the CCP leadership has shifted twice over the past three decades. The first transition was from a revolutionary party consisting primarily of peasants, soldiers, and urban workers to a ruling party dominated by technocrats (that is, officials who were trained as engineers and natural scientists before they advanced politically in the mid-1980s and 1990s). The second shift occurred at the beginning of the twenty-first century, when a different set of leaders, this time with formal training in law, economics, and other social sciences, rose to power at both the national and provincial levels. Perhaps even more important than the fluidity of elite turnover and the growing diversity in educational and occupational experiences among political leaders is the trend, within the upper echelons of the CCP, toward competition between the two informal coalitions described earlier in the chapter.

This study pays special attention to what the Chinese term *inner-party democracy,* a conceptualization of the new period of collective leadership that emphasizes deal making and compromise between competing factions or coalitions, in addition to the observance of commonly accepted guidelines affecting various forms of representation—be they regional, institutional, or professional. A far cry from liberal democracy, this experiment expands political choice for members of the party establishment in a fairly limited way. However, the gradual evolution of this emergent inner-party competition and cooperation may pave the way for a more significant transformation within the Chinese political system.

To a certain extent, Xi's remarkable rise and quick consolidation of power also reflect important changes in Chinese leadership politics, particularly new adjustments in its institutional governance framework over the past three decades. These largely unanticipated developments call for analysts both in China and abroad to reassess collective leadership. This study rejects as being too extreme two widely held perceptions of Xi Jinping: one maintains that Xi has already become a Mao-like dictator; the other argues that Xi's grip on power is tenuous at best, claiming that he has made too many enemies and cannot get anything done due to strong bureaucratic and local resistance.

The truth—a more realistic assessment—lies somewhere in between: Xi has indeed emerged as a powerful leader, but not powerful enough to neglect the norms and regulations of collective leadership. Chinese politics can hardly return to the days of Maoists' zero-sum game. Deng and other Chinese leaders who followed Mao were determined to prevent any future leader from running away with the system, as Mao had, and to make it similarly difficult to abandon or depart from the strategy of reform and opening.[86] In addition, Chinese society today differs fundamentally from that of the Mao era.

What do the above findings and arguments mean for foreign leaders, especially for U.S. policymakers? A balanced and accurate understanding of Chinese leadership politics, especially the sources of and constraints on Xi's power, is essential as foreign countries develop their strategies toward China under Xi's leadership.[87] Foreign analysts must be careful not to overstate any one dimension of Xi's leadership while ignoring others. Furthermore, it would be a huge mistake to conclude that any of Xi's policy decisions— either domestic or foreign—are predetermined or made in isolation. It would be even more dangerous for U.S. decisionmakers to assume that a major confrontation or war with China is inevitable. It is still too early to make a definitive judgment about Xi's intentions, political savvy, and historical legacy. Ultimately, of course, China will decide its own path, and Xi will pursue his priorities to the best of his ability. But policymakers in Washington have a strong influence over China's trajectory and a huge incentive to encourage the Chinese political system to develop stronger checks and balances and to ensure that U.S.-China relations remain stable. A more complete understanding of Xi's motivations and the dynamics of the environment in which he operates will help serve this mutually beneficial goal.

SOURCES AND METHODOLOGY OF THE STUDY

Generally speaking, the field of Chinese political studies has benefited tremendously from several new developments that facilitate research. These include the Internet revolution, the availability of new and open sources in China, and the growing accessibility of Chinese public intellectuals and policymakers for meetings and interviews. The rapid growth of the Internet has allowed quicker and more-comprehensive access to official and unofficial Chinese sources of hard data and qualitative information.

Despite lack of transparency and the mysterious nature of Chinese elite politics, publicized biographical information on Chinese leaders has become increasingly detailed and standardized. In recent years, Chinese authorities have made deliberate efforts to release more-comprehensive biographical data about officials at various levels of leadership, including information that was once considered highly sensitive, such as accounts of the mentor-protégé ties of party leaders. Meanwhile, Chinese books published in Hong Kong, Taiwan, and overseas provide additional—though often unverified— information about Chinese leaders' backgrounds, family ties, and political networks.[88] Some specialized online websites run by the CCP are devoted to biographies of leaders in the party, the government, certain major state-owned enterprises, and the military.[89]

Since former PRC president Yang Shangkun published his diary in 2001, China has witnessed a wave of memoirs, diaries, and autobiographies of senior leaders in the country, especially of those who have retired.[90] Jiang Zemin, Li Peng, Zhu Rongji, Wen Jiabao, Li Ruihuan, Qiao Shi, Wu Guanzheng, Li Lanqing, and other former PSC members have all published their memoirs and diaries.[91] In addition to the writings of retired leaders, top political figures also released biographies while they were in power. For example, works about Hu Jintao and Wen Jiabao, written by two senior Chinese journalists and published in Hong Kong and Taiwan, were available in bookstores across the mainland while Hu and Wen still served in top leadership positions.[92] Furthermore, popular Chinese newspapers and magazines such as *Southern Weekly, Southern People Weekly, China Newsweek,* and *Phoenix Weekly* frequently publish long profiles and interviews with rising stars in the provincial and ministerial leadership.[93] In 2013, for example, both *Southern People Weekly* and *Phoenix Weekly* carried long feature stories about Wang Qishan, including his background, characteristics, circles of associates, and his four-decade-long friendship with Xi Jinping.[94]

Xi himself had published extensively before becoming a national leader. The collection of essays he wrote as party secretary of Zhejiang, entitled *New Thoughts in Zhejiang,* was published before he moved to Beijing in 2007.[95] From 1998 to 2002, while Xi attended a part-time doctoral program at Tsinghua University, he wrote, edited, or coedited five books on rural reform and agricultural development as well as science and technology policy.[96] Most significant, information about Xi Jinping's associates and protégés is publicly available and quite reliable, as Xi himself has recently spoken with the media both in China and abroad about the relationships he has developed throughout his career.[97]

Altogether, these biographical materials complement one another, presenting comprehensive and detailed information about top leaders' family backgrounds, paths to office, political networking, and attitudinal and behavioral attributes. Such a wealth of information about the Chinese leadership was unimaginable just a few years ago. However, this bounty presents a new challenge for scholars of China's elite politics, as accessibility to more data does not necessarily translate into better scholarship or more-insightful analysis. Scholars must now more carefully distinguish between important and trivial information, between insider accounts and deliberate misinformation from stakeholders, and between facts and rumors. It is a great challenge to use all of the relevant pieces, while taking advantage of multiple sources and means of analysis, to construct a holistic framework that brings new clarity to China's leadership politics. In a way, this study also pursues the middle-ground approach between voluminous Chinese-language commentary on elite politics—much of it focused on personal power struggles and relationships—and Western political science literature, with its ever-increasing emphasis on quantitative and data-driven assessment, rational choice modeling, interest group interactions, and policy analysis.

This study incorporates four methodological approaches: (1) a structural assessment of the regime's new distribution of power and the evolving tensions between various functional leadership bodies, with a special focus on recent institutional changes under the Xi administration, including highly fluid ad hoc leading groups and intriguing ties between the civilian and military leadership; (2) a large-scale quantitative analysis of biographical data of the 376 full and alternate members of the 18th Central Committee of the Chinese Communist Party; (3) a comprehensive presentation of the author's analytical model, "one party, two coalitions"; and (4) a qualitative examination (based on both a literature review and interviews with Chinese leaders and their advisers) of recent ideological and policy discourse in the country.[98]

ORGANIZATION OF THIS VOLUME

Each of the following chapters adopts one of the above methodologies or a combination of approaches. Altogether, these chapters consider a wide range of information to analyze important attributes of and key dynamics within the Chinese political system. These thematically focused discussions should be useful not only to a broad set of China specialists but also to non-China specialists who are eager to understand what is happening in the Middle Kingdom. Below are brief previews of each chapter, highlighting the organizational components and logical framework of this volume as a whole.

Chapter 2 offers a concise overview of the structure of China's party-state, with an emphasis on the supreme power of the PSC. The chapter examines the respective roles of various leadership institutions in the party and the government. It also assesses interactions between those institutions, as well as the functions of ad hoc coordinating bodies such as functional central leading groups and aims to present a clear framework of the inner workings of the Chinese political system and its decisionmaking mechanisms.

Chapter 3 provides detailed empirical data that illustrate the transformation in the generational and professional attributes of Chinese elites over the past three decades. The main body of the chapter is a comprehensive biographical analysis of the 376 full and alternate members of the 18th Central Committee of the CCP, the leadership body that includes almost all of the most powerful leaders in the country. Data examined include the leaders' personal and professional backgrounds, demographic distribution, career paths, and political affiliations.

Crucial to any analysis of China's political trajectory is an understanding of the kind of leadership that is governing the country. This is even more important now, given the emergence of a new group of political elites with distinct educational and professional credentials who will run the country for the next decade and beyond. Throughout PRC history, changes in the composition of the political elite have often reflected—and sometimes heralded—broader social, economic, political, and ideological changes.

Chapter 4 examines educational backgrounds of the 18th Central Committee of the CCP. Based on both qualitative and quantitative analyses, the chapter highlights the change and new attributes of the educational credentials—including the trend of advanced degrees and foreign study and work experiences—of the Chinese elite over the past three decades. The emphasis, or overemphasis, on advanced educational attainment among political elites has also led to many leaders receiving education, especially in postgraduate programs, on a part-time basis, often from the Central Party School (CPS). This phenomenon has drawn much public criticism, undermining the credibility and legitimacy of the CCP elites.

Chapter 5 traces the remarkable rise and decline of technocrats (engineers-turned-political leaders) and also reveals the growing occupational diversity and rapid rise of two new elite groups: first, entrepreneurs (from both the private sector and SOEs), and second, lawyers and legal professionals in the Chinese leadership. This study divides these leaders with legal professional backgrounds into three subgroups: (1) leaders who hold a law degree in name only, as they primarily studied Marxism or politics instead of receiving legal training, (2) leaders who are legally trained but have never practiced law, and (3) leaders who are legal professionals in terms of both educational credentials and professional practice in the field of law. An important theoretical proposition in Western social science literature on political elites is that the occupational identities of political leaders usually have some bearing on other characteristics of a country's political system. The ongoing elite transformation embodied in the growing power and influence of entrepreneur and lawyers—just like the previous elite transformation, known as "technocratic turnover"—will likely shape the leadership's socio-economic and political policies. It may also change the way the world's most populous country is governed.

Mentor-protégé ties play an important role in elite formation in virtually all political systems. But arguably no country gives greater advantage, in terms of bestowing promotions to those who have previously served as personal assistants (秘书, *mishu*) to senior leaders, than China. Chapter 6 focuses on the spread of the *mishu* phenomenon in the CCP leadership. After examining the historical, administrative, and political factors that led to the *mishu* phenomenon, the chapter reveals how this development has contributed to rampant official corruption in the country. The chapter concludes with a discussion of the diversity of Xi's *mishu* cluster, which broadens his power base and affords him more options when assembling an effective leadership team and also setting a diverse policy agenda.

Chapter 7 explores the factional composition of the CCP leadership, examines how the factions were formed, and explains why dynamic factionalism is intrinsic to a system of collective leadership. Based on a meticulous tracing of mentor-protégé ties and various forms of political networking, this chapter argues that two informal coalitions within the CCP leadership are actively competing for power, influence, and control over policy initiatives in post-Deng China. The chapter aims to deepen the understanding of China's new factional dynamics, especially the main characteristics of its "one party, two coalitions" mechanism.

The dominance of his political allies in the PSC has enabled Xi Jinping to pursue an ambitious anticorruption and market reform agenda during his first term. The effectiveness of Xi's policies and the political legacy of his leadership, however, will depend significantly on the political positioning of his protégés during his second term. Chapter 8 examines the basis of Xi's power, including the "Shaanxi Gang" (陕西帮, shaanxibang), friends whom Xi met during his formative years, and local leaders who worked with Xi before he moved to Beijing, as well as his mishu cluster. These groups make up Xi's inner circle of allies, serving as his hands, ears, mouth, and brain. An analysis of Xi's most trusted associates will identify some of the stars poised to rise in the next round of leadership turnover.

Chapter 9, the concluding chapter, aims to forecast two trends in China's continuing transformation. One is the CCP leadership and the other is state-society relations. A forecast about the upcoming leadership turnover at the 2017 Party Congress can shed valuable light on the prospects for the survival and revival of collective leadership in the Xi era. With the arrival of many novel sociopolitical players and the public's increasing engagement with policy issues in China, the interaction between elite politics and socioeconomic forces is more dynamic than ever before. This chapter places the Chinese political experiments and intellectual debates in the broader context of the country's long and painful journey toward rule of law and democratization. This discussion reaffirms the main thesis of the volume: Xi's legacy will largely depend on whether he encourages or obstructs this trend of political institutionalization in the governance of an increasingly pluralistic country.

As a whole, this volume highlights several important paradoxical developments in Chinese politics and society: a rigid political system confronting a rapid circulation of political elites; Xi's quick accession to and hold on power in the name of effective implementation of domestic and foreign policies, despite the persistence of strong institutional norms and constraints stemming from collective leadership; the influence of mentor-protégé ties on elite selection in the face of increasing public demand for political representation and transparency; and the stagnation of political reform and tight ideological control in the midst of an increasingly dynamic society and blossoming intellectual firmament. The complex interplay between these seemingly contradictory developments in Chinese politics constitutes one of the most important political dramas of our time.

CHAPTER 2

Structure

China's Party-State System

Chinese politics is nothing more than personnel and structure.
—QIAN MU 钱穆

The defining feature of the Chinese communist system is its party-state structure. The Chinese Communist Party (CCP) has ruled the country since the founding of the People's Republic of China (PRC) in 1949, and it is currently the world's largest ruling political party.[1] With the exception of a few tumultuous years during the early phases of the Cultural Revolution, the CCP has always been the ultimate source of political power in China—only the Korean Workers' Party of North Korea has held on to power longer. Indeed, for the past sixty-seven years, the only serious episodes of political contention in China have been power struggles within the CCP leadership.

The CCP has made it clear that it is not willing to cede its monopoly on political power to experiment with multiparty democracy, and party leaders do not seem interested in moving toward a Western-style system based on a separation of powers between the executive, legislative, and judicial branches of government. This does not mean, however, that the CCP is a stagnant institution that has completely resisted political and institutional change. Nor does it mean that the Chinese political system is bereft of checks and balances, as evidenced by interest group politics within the party leadership itself. Though other important institutions and leadership bodies are indeed under the firm control of the CCP, they still assert their bureaucratic interests and influence in decisionmaking. To understand the complex relationship between the CCP and the PRC government, it is essential to grasp the basic structure of these key organizations.

41

A comprehensive analysis of China's political structure can illustrate the roles and responsibilities of various leadership bodies in the party and the state and diagram the ways in which they interact. Deeper knowledge of these mechanisms cannot only shed valuable light on both the sources of continuity in China's long-standing party-state system and some of the more recent and profound changes in the PRC's political landscape, but also yield important predictors of future Chinese political institutionalization.

THE ORGANIZATIONAL STRUCTURE OF THE CHINESE COMMUNIST PARTY

The world's largest ruling party, the CCP, has a hierarchical organizational structure and currently boasts 4.4 million grassroots organizations or branches. As shown in figure 2-1, CCP membership has increased from about 5 million in 1949, when the party first came to power, to 87.8 million as of the end of 2014.[2] Note that more than half of this growth has occurred since the end of the Mao era in 1976. In 2011, 3.1 million new members were admitted to the CCP out of 21.6 million applicants.[3] However, the party's total membership still constitutes only about 7.5 percent of the total eligible population (those over eighteen years old).

With such a bloated bureaucratic structure, party officials at various levels of leadership must concentrate on office work, personnel management, ideological affairs, disciplinary issues, and other administrative matters. According to Yang Jisheng, a well-known scholar of the Chinese leadership and a former senior reporter for *Xinhua News*, the total number of CCP and government officials and staff increased from roughly 2 million in 1966 to 10.6 million in 2000, leading to pervasive overstaffing (see figure 2-2). According to the data released by then vice-minister of Civil Affairs Hou Jianliang in 2005, China had a total of 6.37 million civil servants (公务员, *gongwuyuan*) employed at various levels of government.[4] Among them, 475,000 worked in the central government and its local offices; 535,500 in the provincial governments; 1,446,000 at the prefecture and municipal level of government; 2,852,000 at the county level; and 1,061,000 at the township level.[5]

Because China operates under a party-state structure, it is no accident that since the establishment of the PRC, the top leaders of the CCP have concurrently held the most important positions in the government. Top party officials serve as president of the PRC, premier of the State Council (the cabinet), chair of the National People's Congress (NPC, the legislature), and chair of the Central Military Commission (CMC). CCP leaders at various levels—provincial, municipal, county, and township—often also serve as officials in local government organizations. The head of the party

FIGURE 2-1. Chinese Communist Party Membership, 1949–2014

Millions of members

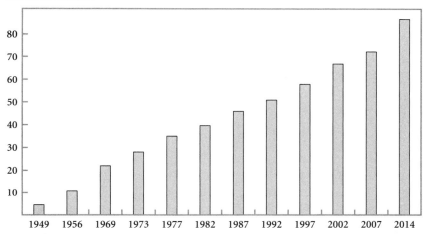

Note and Source: Figures represent total party membership at the founding of the People's Republic of China and at each subsequent National Party Congress until 2007. See Cheng Li, "China's Communist Party-State: The Structure and Dynamics of Power," in *Politics in China,* 2d ed., ed. William A. Joseph (Oxford University Press, 2014). For the data for 2014, see *Shijie ribao* [World Journal], July 1, 2015, A5.

organization—the party secretary—is the de facto "boss" in local political and policy matters at any level of administration. In the case of Shanghai, which has both a party secretary and a mayor, the party secretary has greater authority even though the mayor is also a high-ranking party member.

The institutions of party and state are intimately intertwined, which is why the PRC, like the former Soviet Union, is referred to as a communist party-state. Marxist doctrine defines the communist party as the "vanguard" of the proletariat or working class. The preamble to the Constitution of the PRC makes several mentions of the leadership of the CCP, and Article 1 describes the PRC as "a socialist state under the people's democratic dictatorship led by the working class and based on the alliance of workers and peasants." However, the document is rather vague about who wields supreme political power in China.[6] In practice, the CCP is unequivocally in charge at all levels, and the state merely executes party directives.

Although high-ranking Chinese leaders have sporadically called for a greater separation between the party and the state, over the last two decades the overwhelming trend has been to consolidate and revitalize the party rather than to reduce its leadership role. The watchword of the Chinese leadership has been to "enhance the governing capacity of the ruling party."[7]

FIGURE 2-2. Officials and Staff in the Chinese Communist Party and Government, 1966–2000

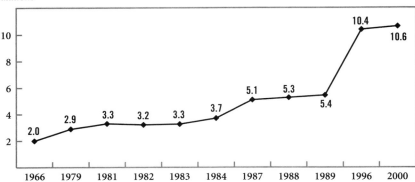

Source: Yang Jisheng, *Zhongguo dangdai shehui gejieceng fenxi* [Analysis of social strata of contemporary China] (Lanzhou: Gansu renmin chubanshe, 2006), 284.

To achieve that aim, the CCP has frequently arranged for party officials, especially rising stars at various levels of the leadership, to simultaneously hold important positions within both the party and the government.

Two important observations can be made regarding the current party-state structure in China. First, the party has the power to make all of the state's most important personnel and policy decisions. Second, although the party is the lead decisionmaker, many important policy discussions, as well as most policy implementation, take place in or through government institutions, not CCP organizations.

Figure 2-3 provides an overview of all the levels of CCP organization and membership, using numbers taken primarily from the 18th National Party Congress. Party organizations exist at all administrative levels, from the center in Beijing down to the 4.4 million primary or "grassroots" units (基层组织, *jiceng zuzhi*), which, according to the CCP Constitution, "are formed in enterprises, rural areas, government organs, schools, research institutes, communities, social organizations, companies of the PLA and other basic units, where there are at least three full party members."[8] According to official data released in late June 2014, the CCP had a total of 3,219 party committees at three important local levels: 31 at the provincial level, 395 at the municipal and prefecture level, and 2,793 at the county level.[9] The party's reach extends throughout the country, but power is highly concentrated at the center. The twenty-five-member Politburo (or Political Bureau), especially the seven members who concurrently serve on its Standing Committee, has the most clout by far.

FIGURE 2-3. Organization of the Chinese Communist Party, 2016[a]

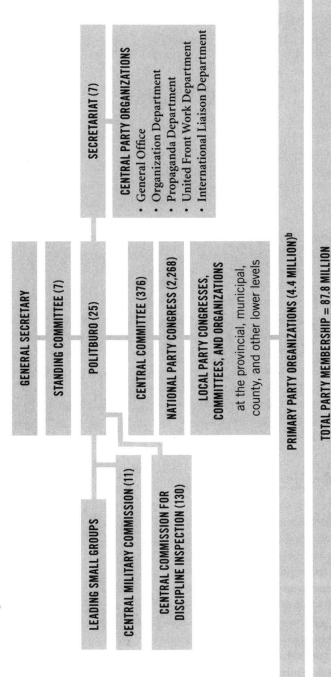

GENERAL SECRETARY

STANDING COMMITTEE (7)

POLITBURO (25)

LEADING SMALL GROUPS

CENTRAL MILITARY COMMISSION (11)

CENTRAL COMMISSION FOR DISCIPLINE INSPECTION (130)

CENTRAL COMMITTEE (376)

NATIONAL PARTY CONGRESS (2,268)

LOCAL PARTY CONGRESSES, COMMITTEES, AND ORGANIZATIONS

at the provincial, municipal, county, and other lower levels

SECRETARIAT (7)

CENTRAL PARTY ORGANIZATIONS
- General Office
- Organization Department
- Propaganda Department
- United Front Work Department
- International Liaison Department

PRIMARY PARTY ORGANIZATIONS (4.4 MILLION)[b]

TOTAL PARTY MEMBERSHIP = 87.8 MILLION

Source: Cheng Li, "China's Communist Party-State: The Structure and Dynamics of Power," in *Politics in China*, 2d ed., ed. William A. Joseph (Oxford University Press, 2014). The number of the primary party organizations and total party members reflect late 2014 figures; see *Shijie ribao* [World Journal], July 1, 2015, A5.

a. Numbers in parentheses represent membership as of July 1, 2013.

b. Formed in enterprises, rural areas, government organs, schools, research institutes, communities, social organizations, companies of the People's Liberation Army, and other basic units where there are at least three full party members.

The National Party Congress: The Most Important Convention in China

The National Congress of the CCP (or National Party Congress), which meets every five years for about two weeks in the fall, is the most important political convention in the country. All delegates must be CCP members. Two types of delegates, regular and invited, attended the most recent party congress in November 2012. The 2,268 regular delegates were elected, or more precisely, chosen, by their respective constituencies to serve in thirty-eight delegations. About 70 percent of these delegates were party leaders at various levels and the others were representatives of grassroots units.[10]

Delegations included China's thirty-one provincial-level administrations: twenty-two provinces, five administrative regions, and four large cities directly under central administration. The other seven delegations represented (1) ethnic Taiwanese who are citizens of the PRC and members of the CCP, (2) the central departments of the party, (3) ministries and commissions of the central government, (4) major state-owned enterprises (SOEs), (5) the country's largest banks and financial institutions, (6) the PLA, and (7) the People's Armed Police.[11]

Fifty-seven specially invited delegates—mostly retired party elders—also attended. This group was eligible to vote with other members and can be considered China's equivalent of the "superdelegates" to the Democratic Party Convention in the United States. There were also 314 nonvoting observers and 147 noncommunists who were invited to attend the opening and closing sessions of the 18th National Party Congress.[12] Similar to the Democratic or Republican Party Conventions in the United States every four years, China's National Party Congress takes place once every five years.

The Central Committee: The First Rung on the Ladder of Top Leadership

The chief responsibility of National Party Congress delegates is to elect members of the Central Committee (376 members, including 205 full members and 171 alternate members) and the Central Commission for Discipline Inspection (130 members). The Central Committee consists primarily of the country's most powerful national and provincial-level leaders, including top officials in the party, government, military, and SOEs. The Chinese leadership uses multicandidate elections for the Central Committee and often eliminates those who finish in the bottom 10 percent.

By CCP norms, the elected full members are listed in order based on the number of strokes in the Chinese characters of their names. The elected alternate members are listed in sequence according to the number of the votes they have received in the election. If there is a vacancy in the full membership resulting from a death or a purge, the alternate member atop the list will automatically assume full membership. Chapter 3 provides a detailed analysis of the regional and institutional constituencies, career paths, political affiliations, and generational and occupational pedigrees of members of the 18th Central Committee.

The Central Committee convenes at least once per year for meetings called plenums or plenary sessions (全会, *quanhui*). All full and alternate members attend these sessions. Top officials in the central organs of the CCP, government ministries, provincial administrations, and the military who are not members of the Central Committee are usually also invited to attend the plenary sessions as nonvoting participants. Plenary sessions provide an opportunity to announce new policy initiatives and major personnel appointments. For example, at the Third Plenum of the 11th Central Committee, held in December 1978, Deng Xiaoping introduced his reform and opening-up proposals. That specific plenary session is often viewed as a critical juncture in the CCP's shift away from the ideology and politics of the Cultural Revolution, toward a new emphasis on economic reform.

According to tradition, in its first plenary session, each Central Committee selects the members of the party's most powerful organizations: the Politburo (twenty-five members), the Politburo Standing Committee (PSC, seven members), and the CMC (eleven members). A Central Committee also elects the general secretary, which is the top position in the CCP. In practice, however, the process is top-down rather than bottom-up: the party's leading organizations closely guide the selection of the Central Committee members, to whom they then present a slate of candidates for the incoming Politburo and PSC for "approval."

The Central Commission for Discipline Inspection: An Anticorruption Body

The CCDI, while less important than the Central Committee, plays a crucial role in monitoring and investigating party officials for abuse of power, corruption, and other wrongdoings—and disciplining them, if necessary. The commission primarily handles cases involving party leadership and administers a range of punishments, the most serious being the purge and expulsion of senior-level officials from the party. When the CCDI determines that a crime might have been committed, the matter is handed over to the state judicial system.

Lower-level party organizations, including provincial, municipal, and county-level bodies, also have discipline inspection commissions that report directly to the anticorruption commission one level above them. The chiefs of the local discipline inspection commissions are usually not selected from the localities that they serve, but are transferred in from elsewhere to reduce the possibility of favoritism. Under Xi's unprecedented campaign against corruption in the leadership, the CCDI—especially its secretary, Wang Qishan—has become enormously powerful. The current CCDI is the "most powerful discipline inspection commission in CCP history," and the secretary of the provincial discipline inspection commission ranks below only the provincial party secretary and two deputy secretaries in status.[13]

The current CCDI has eight deputy secretaries, including executive deputy secretary of the CCDI Zhao Hongzhu, who also serves on the Secretariat, one leader from the Ministry of Supervision of the State Council (Minister Huang Shuxian), and one from the PLA (General Du Jincai, secretary of the PLA Commission of Discipline Inspection). Members of the CCDI do not usually serve on the Central Committee. Currently, however, there are four leaders of the 130-member CCDI who also serve on the 18th Central Committee: the three officials mentioned above and Wang Qishan.

Under the leadership of Wang Qishan, the CCDI has tried to achieve a more independent position within the CCP establishment in order to provide more effective oversight. In line with this objective, the CCDI has concentrated on three major areas. First, given that the heads of various leadership bodies, known as "the number one leader" tend to abuse power, the CCDI pays particular attention to party chiefs. According to some official Chinese sources, more than one-third of the corrupt officials above the county level punished and purged within the past few years were "the number one leaders."[14] Another recent study showed that out of the senior executives of major Chinese SOEs arrested in 2013, two-thirds were "number one leaders."[15] These party chiefs have often used their enormous power of elite promotion to control various branches of the leadership, making localities or institutions into personal "independent kingdoms." This was most evident in the case of Chongqing under Bo Xilai. The CCDI now calls for closer supervision of the power and jurisdiction of top officials in various levels of administration, reinforcing the division of responsibility within the collective leadership.[16]

Second, the CCDI has mandated more stringent institutionalized supervision, transparency, and financial auditing. It has enhanced the power of its inspection tour teams (巡视组, *xunshizu*), which audit and investigate provincial and ministerial leadership. In addition, the CCDI has also stationed fifty-three discipline inspection teams (纪检组, *jijianzu*) in forty-eight leadership bodies among the various ministries and agencies of the State Council, the Supreme People's Court, the Supreme People's Procuratorate, and major SOEs such as the State Grid Corporation of China.[17]

Finally, the CCDI has encouraged the public's supervision of officials, especially through mass media. The CCDI has its shared offices and operations (合署办公, *heshu bangong*) with the Ministry of Supervision of the State Council. Both institutions have established a joint website that allows the public to file a report of official wrongdoing (举报, *jubao*). The site links to similar websites run by provincial and ministerial-level institutions; and in the past few years, several senior leaders have been caught primarily as the result of a *jubao* .[18] Liu Tienan, former vice-minister of the National Development and Reform Commission (NDRC) and former director of the National Energy Administration, for example, was convicted following a *jubao* by Luo Changping, a well-known reporter from *Caijing* magazine.[19]

The Politburo and the Politburo Standing Committee: Where the Supreme Power Lies

According to the CCP Constitution, the Central Committee elects members of the Politburo, members of the PSC, and the General Secretary; and members of the Politburo must be chosen from the Central Committee, members of the PSC from the Politburo, and the CCP General Secretary from the PSC. As discussed in chapter 1, to call the process of choosing the Politburo and the PSC by the Central Committee an election would be misguided. The CCP has never used multicandidate elections for the Politburo or the PSC. In fact, these top bodies are selected by the outgoing PSC, under the supervision of retired or retiring senior leaders. For example, Deng Xiaoping personally chose Jiang Zemin to take over the position of CCP general secretary in 1989, and Jiang is widely believed to have played a major role in shaping the subsequent PSCs.

Over the past two decades, the outgoing PSC has usually held a closed-door meeting during the summer of the year that the National Party Congress convenes. The exclusive conference takes place at Beidaihe, a resort near Beijing, and has the purpose of deciding the preliminary slate of leaders to be elected to the next Politburo and PSC. Before and after this meeting, the outgoing PSC is likely to consult retired top leaders, including retired PSC members. The PSC will then meet again in the fall, several weeks prior to when the National Party Congress convenes, to finalize a list of candidates. In addition, the outgoing PSC may conduct a straw poll among the outgoing Central Committee members, as well as other newly appointed top ministerial and provincial leaders who are not Central Committee members, to nominate candidates for the new Politburo to the next Party Congress. This has been the practice at recent National Party Congresses—one example is the straw poll held in June 2007, prior to the 17th National Party Congress.[20]

The outgoing PSC's selection of the next iteration of leadership is an extraordinarily complex and multifaceted deal-making process. Analysts are often not privy to the detailed story of how each member is chosen (i.e., the factional bargaining that may take place or the types of information about candidates that influence the decisions). However, analysts can identify potential candidates for the new PSC based on the current members of the Politburo and the Central Committee, and whether they meet the age qualification for another five-year term.

The number of members in all of these leadership bodies—the Central Committee, the Politburo, and the PSC—is subject to change, as the CCP Constitution does not specify any fixed quantity. For the past two decades, the five previous Central Committees have averaged about 350 members. The three latest Politburos have consistently had twenty-five members. Among the members of the current Politburo, eight represent party organizations, nine come from government organizations, two from the military, and six from province-level administrative units (representing Beijing, Shanghai, Tianjin, Chongqing, Guangdong, and Xinjiang).

Previously, the number of seats in the PSC fluctuated. The PSC formed at the 13th National Party Congress in 1987 had only five members, and the PSCs formed at both the 14th National Party Congress in 1992 and 15th in 1997 had seven. At the two party congresses in the 2000s, both PSCs had nine members. The current PSC formed at the 18th National Party Congress in 2012 consists of seven members. These changes in the number of PSC seats largely reflect the difficulty competing factions have in making deals with each other. Top leaders had to change the number of seats to satisfy the concerns and political interests of some heavyweight politicians and power networks.

As always, all PSC members also hold top posts in other leadership bodies. Over the past twenty years, the general secretary has always concurrently served as president of the PRC. With the exception of General Secretary Hu Jintao, who waited two years to succeed his predecessor, Jiang Zemin, as chair of the powerful CMC, all general secretaries have assumed leadership of the military following the First Plenum of the National Party Congress.

PSC members are selected to concurrently serve as leaders of the CMC and other institutions, a phenomenon that reflects the great importance of these bodies. Table 2-1 shows that traditionally, in addition to the president of the PRC, the premier of the State Council, the chair of the NPC, the chair of the Chinese People's Political Consultative Conference (CPPCC), the executive vice-premier of the State Council, and the executive secretary of the Secretariat are all also members of the PSC. In the last four iterations of the PSC, the secretary of the CCDI, also known as the anticorruption tsar, has also been guaranteed a seat.[21] The chair of the Central Spiritual Civilization Steering Committee (CSCSC), who heads the propaganda coordinating body, has also served on the PSC since 2002.

Prior to 1997, the post of vice-president of the PRC was largely ceremonial. Soong Ching-ling (Sun Yat-sen's widow), Ulanhu (an ethnic minority leader),

TABLE 2-1. Concurrent Leadership Positions Held by
Politburo Standing Committee Members, 1992–2012

	Politburo Standing Committee				
Concurrent Leadership Position	14th 1992–97 N = 7	15th 1997–02 N = 7	16th 2002–07 N = 9	17th 2007–12 N = 9	18th 2012– present N = 7
General Secretary of the CCP	X	X	X	X	X
President of the People's Republic of China	X	X	X	X	X
Chair of the Central Military Commission	X	X	X	X	X
Premier of the State Council	X	X	X	X	X
Chair of the National People's Congress	X	X	X	X	X
Chair of the CPPCC	X	X	X	X	X
Executive Vice-Premier of the State Council	X	X	X	X	X
Executive Secretary of the Secretariat	X	X	X	X	X
Secretary of the CCDI		X	X	X	X
Chair of the CSCSC			X	X	X
Vice-President		X	X	X	
Chair of the Politics and Law Committee of the CCP			X	X	
Vice-Chair of the Central Military Commission	X*	X	X	X	

Note: N = total number, * = military officer. CCDI = Central Commission for Discipline Inspection, CCP = Chinese Communist Party, CPPCC = Chinese People's Political Consultative Conference, CSCSC = Central Spiritual Civilization Steering Committee.

Wang Zhen (a retired PLA general), and Rong Yiren (a rich private entrepreneur) have all held the position. When Hu Jintao was appointed vice-president in 1997, this was a turning point. The appointment indicated that Hu would succeed Jiang Zemin as general secretary and president. The same applied to Xi Jinping when he became vice-president in 2007. Other vice-presidents include Zeng Qinghong, who served on the 16th PSC, and current vice-president Li Yuanchao. Zeng was a heavyweight politician who often played the role of dealmaker in Chinese elite politics; however, he was not seen as a possible successor to the presidency, but rather as an influential figure who could balance power in the top leadership. Currently, Li Yuanchao is only a member of the Politburo. Although an influential political figure, Li lost the battle for a PSC seat at the 18th National Party Congress. While Li may still have a slight chance of becoming a PSC member at the next party congress in 2017, he is not considered a likely successor to Xi because of his age and other factors.[22]

For a decade (2002–12), the secretary of the Politics and Law Committee (PLC) of the CCP, first Luo Gan and then Zhou Yongkang, served on the PSC. The PLC oversees all legal enforcement, and its primary responsibility is to coordinate various state agencies to maintain the sociopolitical stability of the country.[23] The committee consists of the minister of Public Security, minister of State Security, minister of Justice, president of the Supreme People's Court, procurator general of the Supreme People's Procuratorate, commander of the People's Armed Police, and others. The presence of the secretary of the PLC on the PSC reflected the enormous power of the police and law enforcement apparatus in the country. As secretary of the PLC, Zhou Yongkang intended to use this position of power to create his own "independent kingdom" and often refused the directives of the Hu-Wen leadership.[24] According to one study, the PLC, under the direction of Secretary Qiao Shi, ordered the People's Armed Police to engage in a social stability task only once in a seven-year period (1985–92). In contrast, Zhou ordered the police to conduct fifteen such exercises in just his first year as secretary of the PLC.[25]

Some Chinese intellectuals who believe that the PRC should move toward a true rule of law system have spoken out against the unchecked power of the PLC. One such intellectual is Peking University law professor He Weifang, who has been a consistent critic of party interference in legal affairs. In 2006 he bluntly criticized Zhou Yongkang, then minister of Public Security and deputy secretary of the PLC (and also a member of the Politburo), for his heavy-handed "oversight" of the Supreme People's Court. According to Professor He, Zhou's actions exemplified China's lack of a genuinely independent judicial system. "There is no other country in the world," Professor He said, "in which the chief justice reports to the chief of police."[26] In his view, the fact that the president of the Supreme People's Court is now supposed to report to the secretary of the PLC or to the police chief (minister of Public Security), rather than to the NPC as specified by China's Constitution, severely undermines the country's legal development. He pointedly asks, "How can a judiciary like this exercise effective supervision and constraint over police power?"[27]

He Weifang and many like-minded Chinese legal scholars criticize the CCP's interference in the country's legal system, especially via the all-powerful PLC. They believe that many recent well-known cases of injustice were largely due to the "invisible hand" of the PLC, and they have called for a fundamental change in the role and presence of the PLC, including abolition of the PLC at all subnational levels.[28] The fact that the secretary of the

PLC now no longer serves on the current PSC can be seen as a positive development in reducing the power and influence of the police and law enforcement in the supreme decisionmaking body.

Table 2-1 shows that over the past two decades, only one military leader has served on the PSC: vice-chair of the CMC Liu Huaqing, who ascended to the Standing Committee following the 14th National Party Congress and stayed from 1992 to 1997. Since the 15th National Party Congress in 1997, the PLA has had two representatives sitting on the Politburo, but none has served on the PSC. This has helped reinforce the civilian leadership's control over the military.

There is no term limit for membership in the Central Committee, the Politburo, or the PSC. However, according to *The Interim Regulations of the Tenure of Party and Government Officials*, issued by the Central General Office of the CCP in 2006, a leader in the party or government cannot work in the same position for more than two terms and cannot work in the same level of the leadership for more than fifteen years.[29] This means that if a PSC member switches to another leadership post after two terms of membership on the PSC (e.g., from the post of premier to the chair of the NPC or to the general secretary), that leader can still stay on the PSC for a third five-year term (but no longer than that).

PSC members usually have broad administrative experience and established leadership credentials in their assigned area of responsibility. For example, with the exception of China's first premier, Zhou Enlai, all of the PRC's six other premiers (Hua Guofeng, Zhao Ziyang, Li Peng, Zhu Rongji, Wen Jiaobao, and Li Keqiang) had previously served as vice-premier of the State Council before becoming premier. Most of them could also boast broad leadership experience in other departments, especially in economic affairs.

In accordance with *The Interim Regulations of the Tenure of Party and Government Officials*, any party and government leader at various levels elected for a five-year term can be reelected for one additional term.[30] It is expected that the party and government leader will serve two full terms and that a leadership transition will take place every decade. For example, Xi Jinping took over as general secretary in 2012 from Hu Jintao, who was first elected in 2002 and then reelected in 2007. Barring unforeseen events, Xi will be reelected at the 19th National Party Congress in 2017 and will serve until 2022. Recent practice has been that the heir apparent is anointed at the halfway point of the current general secretary's term and elevated to a number of preparatory positions, including a seat on the PSC, vice-president of the PRC, and vice-chair of the CMC. Thus, by the fall of 2017, when the 19th National Party Congress meets, it should be clear who is likely to ascend to China's top post for the 2022–32 period. However, Xi's amassing of personal power in the past three years causes some analysts to believe that this important political norm may change, as Xi may want to stay in power beyond his second term. Many analysts in both China and abroad have also expressed growing doubt that the political structure and leadership succession will remain unchanged in the coming decades.

The Secretariat and Five Central Party Organs: Key Chinese Communist Party Apparatchiks

The Secretariat, which has seven members, is a crucial leadership body that manages the party's routine business and administrative matters. Generally speaking, Secretariat members meet almost daily and are responsible for coordinating the country's major events and meetings. In comparison, the Politburo and the PSC, two more powerful organizations, meet only once a month and once a week, respectively. Like the members of the PSC, all members of the Secretariat live in Beijing. Some Politburo members reside in other cities, where they serve concurrently as provincial or municipal party chiefs. Of the seven members of the current Secretariat, three also serve as members of the Politburo (Li Zhanshu, director of the Central General Office; Zhao Leji, director of the Central Organization Department; and Liu Qibao, director of the Central Propaganda Department), with one member (Liu Yunshan, executive secretary) serving on the PSC.

The Secretariat supervises the work of the CCP's administrative coordinating body, the Central General Office of the CCP, as well as the party's four most important central departments: the Central Organization Department, the Central Propaganda (or Publicity) Department, the Central United Front Work Department, and the Central International Liaison Department. Presently, the directors of the Central General Office, the Central Organization Department, and the Central Propaganda Department also concurrently serve on both the Secretariat and the Politburo.

The Central General Office is an enormously important organ of the Chinese leadership, akin to the Executive Office of the President in the United States, for the crucial role it plays within power circles. Although the office is supposed to manage only secretarial and logistical affairs for the top party leadership, it in fact controls the flow of information, monitors daily events, drafts important documents, coordinates major meetings, handles the security of top leaders, and is directly involved in the decisionmaking process. All ten previous directors in the history of the Central General Office, with the exception of Ling Jihua, served on the Politburo either concurrently or later in their careers. Seven of them served on the PSC, including such heavyweight politicians as former CCP vice-chair Wang Dongxing, former PRC president Yang Shangkun, former vice-president Zeng Qinghong, and former premier Wen Jiabao. The directors of the Central General Office are usually the confidants of top leaders: examples include Wang Dongxing (confidant of Mao), Wang Zhaoguo (Deng), Zeng Qinghong (Jiang), and Ling Jihua (Hu).

The current director, Li Zhanshu, is a confidant of Xi Jinping. Their friendship began about three decades ago when Xi served as deputy party secretary and then party secretary of Zhengding County in Hebei from 1982 to 1985. Li Zhanshu served as party secretary of Wuji County in the same province during roughly the same period.[31] Both counties belong to Shijiazhuang prefecture and are close geographically, so Xi and Li developed a good working relationship during that time. Li is also widely seen as a member of the "Shaanxi Gang," Xi's most important power base, which will be elaborated on in chapter 8. Li will be a top contender for the next PSC.

The Central Organization Department (COD) determines the personnel appointments of several thousand high-ranking leadership (or cadre) positions in the party, government, and military, as well as in large business firms and banks, key universities, and other important institutions. These positions are part of the *nomenklatura*, the "list of official posts" (干部职务名称表, *ganbu zhiwu mingchengbiao*) system that was adopted from the Soviet Communist Party. Control of the cadre appointment process is one of the CCP's most important sources of power.

Since the founding of the PRC, the COD has been granted the power and authority to nominate and appoint cadres to the country's long list of important leadership posts. The CCP's organizational apparatchiks consist of a large number of staff members. In 1985, for example, there were 96,615 officials altogether working on the party's organization affairs, including 509 in the COD, 2,741 in the provincial level of administrations (94 per province on average), 17,087 in the municipal and prefecture level of administrations (47 per city or prefecture), 37,928 in the county level (17 per county), and 38,350 in townships.[32]

In the reform era, the total number of posts on the list controlled by the COD has been reduced from about 13,000 prior to 1984 to about 4,200 in recent years.[33] This decentralization of power means that the COD now handles a single tier of personnel appointments, as opposed to the previous two-tier hierarchy. The department now manages only the official posts at the ministerial and provincial levels of the leadership or above, while lists of official posts at the department- and bureau-level (厅局级, *tingjuji*) and prefectural level (地级, *diji*) are managed by ministerial personnel departments and provincial party organization departments, respectively.[34] Appointments to these lower levels of leadership posts now require only that a list of names be put on record (备案, *bei'an*) with the COD. Nevertheless, the department still exerts tremendous power in selecting the 4,200 most powerful cadres for virtually all of the important leadership bodies in the PRC.

The primary task of the CCP's organizational apparatchiks is to identify and select reserve cadres (后备干部 *houbei ganbu*).[35] Also in the mid-1980s, the COD had a total of 1,054 reserve cadres for the provincial and ministerial levels of leadership; the provincial organization departments and ministerial personnel departments had a total of 18,000 reserve cadres for the prefecture- and bureau-level leadership. Municipal and prefectural organization departments had a total of 96,000 reserve cadre for the county- and division-level leadership.[36] The document "Plan on the establishment of the reserve system for provincial and ministerial cadres," which was issued by the COD in 1983, specified that the COD select about 200 reserve cadres for provincial party secretary, governor, and minister positions and about 800 reserve cadres for deputy provincial party secretaries, provincial party standing committee members, executive vice-governors, vice-governors, and vice-ministers.[37] This matrix of reserve cadres leaves about 1,000 reserve cadres for the provincial and ministerial level of leadership, 6,000 for the municipal and departmental level, and 40,000 for the county and division level (县处级, *xianchuji*).[38] The reserve cadres are required to be forty-five to fifty years old at the provincial and ministerial level, forty to forty-five at the municipal and departmental level, and thirty-five to forty at the county and division level.[39]

In his insightful analysis of the COD, Richard McGregor of the *Financial Times* creates a hypothetical parallel body in Washington to illustrate the astonishing scope of the COD's personnel control in China:

> The imaginary department would oversee the appointment of U.S. state governors and their deputies; the mayors of big cities; heads of federal regulatory agencies; the chief executives of General Electric, Exxon Mobil, Wal-Mart and 50-odd of the remaining largest companies; justices on the Supreme Court; the editors of *The New York Times, The Wall Street Journal* and *The Washington Post*, the bosses of the television networks and cable stations, the presidents of Yale and Harvard and other big universities, and the heads of think-tanks such as the Brookings Institution and the Heritage Foundation.[40]

The Central Propaganda Department, the most important organ in China's propaganda system, is primarily responsible for controlling the media and spreading the party's message. This is evidenced by the fact that the newly appointed PRC minister of Culture, Luo Shugang, the newly appointed president of the Xinhua News Agency, Cai Mingzhao, the newly appointed director of the State Council Information Office, Jiang Jianguo, the director of the Cyberspace Affairs Administration, Lu Wei, and the director of the State Administration of Press, Publication, Radio, Film and Television, Cai Fuchao, all concurrently serve as deputy directors of the department. While the Central Propaganda Department has a well-deserved reputation for conservatism due to its rigid ideological orientation and strong control over media and freedom of expression, not all senior officials of the department are hard-line conservatives or communist ideologues. Liberal leaders in the CCP, such as Xi Zhongxun (1953–54), Hu Yaobang (1978–80), and Zhu Houze (1985–87), all served as director of the Central Propaganda Department.

The Central United Front Work Department deals with noncommunist organizations, including the eight "democratic parties" (which will be discussed later in this chapter), ethnic and religious policy, business and commerce organizations, overseas Chinese affairs, and issues concerning Taiwan, Tibet, Hong Kong, and Macao. The notion of the united front (统一战线, *tongyi zhanxian*) originated in the Anti-Japanese War period, during which the CCP called for the creation of a broader front that would bring together all of the Chinese forces and groups to unite against the Japanese invaders. In many aspects, the Central United Front Work Department's purview is similar to that of the CPPCC, which will also be discussed later in this chapter.

At its founding in the early 1950s, the mission of the Central International Liaison Department (CILD) was to establish party-to-party relations between the CCP and foreign communist parties. In the past three decades, however, the CILD has profoundly broadened its functional responsibility by establishing formal contact with over 400 political parties of various political stripes in 140 countries. In some ways, the division of labor between the CILD and the Ministry of Foreign Affairs has become blurred. On the personnel front, Dai Bingguo, the former state councilor who was primarily in charge of China's foreign affairs and reported directly to President Hu Jintao, previously served as director of the CILD from 1997 to 2003. Dai obtained his position in the Hu-Wen government partly because, as the CILD director, he often accompanied Hu Jintao on foreign visits prior to Hu's ascent to the presidency in 2003, and thereby earned Hu's confidence.

The CILD has also played an important role in issues related to North Korea. Former director Wang Jiarui, a protégé of Jiang Zemin's, was the PRC's principal diplomat on North Korean issues in the past decade. Wang's junior colleague from a few years ago, former CILD deputy director Liu Hongcai, served as the PRC ambassador to North Korea from 2010 to 2015. Liu's successor, current PRC ambassador to North Korea Li Jinjun, also previously served as deputy director in the CILD. Another former deputy director,

Zhang Zhijun, is now director of the State Council's Taiwan Affairs Office. Current PRC ambassador to the United Nations Liu Jiyi also previously served as deputy director of the CILD. Neither Wang Jiarui nor former director of the Central United Front Work Department Ling Jihua obtained a seat in the current Politburo; instead, both concurrently serve as vice-chairs of the CPPCC. Ling was later purged on corruption charges. Wang Jiarui's successor, current director of CILD, Song Tao, advanced his early career in Fujian where he first met Xi Jinping. Song previously served as the PRC Ambassador to Guyana (2002–04) and the Philippines (2007–08) and vice minister of Foreign Affairs (2011–13).

The Central Party School, currently led by Liu Yunshan, is a key player in Chinese politics, partly because of its role as the CCP's principal training ground for cadres and partly because of its function as the "brain" of the top leadership. Over the past two decades, it has become one of the most influential think tanks in Beijing. Like the Central General Office and the Central Propaganda Department, the Central Party School has also had a very impressive list of heavyweight CCP politicians serve as president of the school. These include Liu Shaoqi (1948–53), Hua Guofeng (1977–82), Wang Zhen (1982–87), Qiao Shi (1989–93), Hu Jintao (1993–2002), Zeng Qinghong (2002–07), and Xi Jinping (2007–12). In the reform era, top leaders Deng Xiaoping, Jiang Zemin, and Hu Jintao all tapped the Central Party School for human resources and ideas that would help them consolidate their power and influence. Chapter 4 provides a more detailed discussion of the Central Party School's important role in the professional training and political socialization of China's political elite.

There are other important bodies in the party apparatus that, despite being less important than the six institutions discussed above, still exert great influence in some specific functional areas. The Central Policy Research Center formulates and reviews major policies in domestic and foreign affairs. The Central Party History Research Center, the Central Party Literature Research Center, and the Central Archives mainly compile historical materials, including former senior leaders' memoirs. From time to time, these party organs "use history to make a point for the issue of the day." The Central Translation Bureau not only publishes CCP documents and top leaders' works in foreign languages but also translates a large number of new and important foreign publications for Chinese readers. *People's Daily, Guangming Daily,* and *Qiushi (Seeking Truth)* magazine are the official organs of CCP propaganda. In addition to its other responsibilities, the Central Secrecy Bureau advises the top leadership on what sort of information should be released to the public.

The Central Leading Groups and the National Security Committee: Interagency Mechanisms of Governance

In addition to these formal leadership institutions, the CCP also has a number of informal interagency decisionmaking bodies at the national leadership level. Focused on major functional issue areas, some of these "leading groups" (领导小组, *lingdao xiaozu*) or "coordination groups" (协调小组, *xietiao xiaozu*) are more or less permanent, whereas others are temporary task forces convened to handle an immediate concern. For example, in preparation for the 2008 Beijing Olympic Games, the Chinese authorities established the Central Leading Group on the Olympic Games, which was led by then vice-president of the PRC and PSC member Xi Jinping. This leading group ceased to exist soon after the end of the games. Similar leading groups also exist in the lower levels of leadership. Permanent central leading groups currently cover the following crucial areas: foreign affairs, national security, politics and law, ideology and propaganda, cultural development, party building, finance and the economy, cybersecurity, human resources, rural work, Taiwan, and Hong Kong and Macao.[41]

The main purpose of these central leading groups is to coordinate the implementation of policies across top decisionmaking bodies such as the Politburo, the State Council, and the CMC. While these central leading groups are important, they are primarily ad hoc coordinating institutions, and their members are often formally affiliated with other leadership bodies. Central leading groups report directly to the Politburo and work closely with the PSC. In fact, the most important central leading groups are normally headed by PSC members. For example, Zhang Dejiang heads the Central Hong Kong and Macao Work Coordination Group; Yu Zhengsheng heads both the Central Tibet Work Coordination Group and the Central Xinjiang Work Coordination Group; Liu Yunshan heads both the Central Party Building Leading Group and Central Leading Group for Propaganda and Ideological Work; and Wang Qishan heads the Central Leading Group for Inspections.[42]

Some of the central leading groups are located in the government rather than the party. For example, Premier Li Keqiang heads the National Science and Technology and Education Leading Group. Executive Vice-Premier Zhang Gaoli heads the newly established Leading Group of Joint Regional Development of Beijing, Tianjin, and Hebei. Vice-President Liu Yandong serves as the head of the State Council Leading Group for Health Reform and the head of the newly established Leading Group for the Reform and Development of Soccer in China.[43]

As discussed in chapter 1, Xi Jinping presently heads a number of the most critical central leading groups, including those addressing national security, foreign affairs, Taiwan affairs, finance and the economy, cybersecurity, military and defense reform, and the newly established Central Leading Group for Comprehensively Deepening Reforms (CLGCDR). At the Third Plenum of the 18th Central Committee in the fall of 2013, Xi Jinping announced a remarkably ambitious reform agenda, encompassing fifteen areas, sixty tasks, and over three hundred policies. According to Chinese authorities, most of these policies will be fully implemented within three years, and the entire agenda will be completed by 2020.

To effectively implement these policies, Xi needs to consolidate his power and build strong and efficient institutional mechanisms. The establishment of the CLGCDR reflects this objective. From Xi's perspective, deepening economic reforms is his mandate and, thus, also a crucial part of his legacy. He will not let any other leader—certainly not Premier Li Keqiang, who is from the rival camp—receive credit for future achievements in the economic domain. In contrast to norms set by the previous two administrations, in which Premier Zhu Rongji and Premier Wen Jiabao were in charge of finance and economic affairs, Xi now heads the Central Leading Group for Financial and Economic Work, thus significantly marginalizing Premier Li. In a way, the CLGCDR has become the main organ through which Xi runs the Chinese economy.

According to Chinese authorities, the CLGCDR is supposed to "provide top-level design, coordinate all of the relevant leadership bodies, pursue overall progress based on solid research, and carry out reform initiatives."[44] More specifically, the CLGCDR has divided its leadership responsibilities into six main functional areas: (1) economy and ecology; (2) political and legal reforms; (3) cultural development; (4) social development and social stability; (5) party building; and (6) party discipline.[45]

Table 2-2 shows the composition of the CLGCDR. It is remarkable that fourteen Politburo members, plus an additional four PSC members, make up 57 percent of this particular leading group. In its membership, the CLGCDR also includes the top leaders of the State Council (the premier and all four vice-premiers), one of the two vice-chairs of the CMC, and the heads of both the Supreme People's Court and the Supreme People's Procuratorate. With the exception of the governor of the People's Bank of China and vice-chair of the CPPCC Zhou Xiaochuan, all other members of this twenty-three-person leadership body are full members of the 18th Central Committee.

Director of the CCP Central Policy Research Office Wang Huning, a member of the Politburo, serves as the secretary-general and office director of the CLGCDR. According to Chinese official sources, the Office of the CLGCDR is located in the Central Policy Research Office. Two deputy office directors are vice-minister of the NDRC Mu Hong (Xi's confidant who

TABLE 2-2. Composition of the Central Leading Group for Comprehensively Deepening Reforms, as of May 2016

Name	Position	Age (2016)	Central Committee membership	Concurrently held position	Main functional area of responsibility
Xi Jinping	Head	63	PSC	Party General Secretary and PRC President	Party building
Li Keqiang	Deputy Head	61	PSC	Premier of the State Council	Economy and ecology
Liu Yunshan	Deputy Head	69	PSC	Executive Secretary of Secretariat	Propaganda and cultural development
Zhang Gaoli	Deputy Head	70	PSC	Executive Vice-Premier	Economy and ecology
Wang Huning	Office Director	61	Politburo	Director of the CCP Central Policy Research Office	Party building
Ma Kai	Member	70	Politburo	Vice-Premier of the State Council	Economy and ecology
Liu Yandong	Member	71	Politburo	Vice-Premier of the State Council	Propaganda and cultural development
Liu Qibao	Member	63	Politburo	Director of the Propaganda Department	Propaganda and cultural development
Xu Qiliang	Member	66	Politburo	Vice-Chair of the CMC	National defense and social stability
Li Jianguo	Member	70	Politburo	Vice-Chair of the NPC	Political and legal development
Wang Yang	Member	61	Politburo	Vice-Premier of the State Council	Economy and ecology
Meng Jianzhu	Member	69	Politburo	Secretary of the PLC	Political and legal development
Zhao Leji	Member	59	Politburo	Director of the Organization Department	Party building
Li Zhanshu	Member	66	Politburo	Director of the CCP Central General Office	Party building
Du Qinglin	Member	70	Secretariat	Vice-Chair of the CPPCC	Social development and social stability
Zhao Hongzhu	Member	69	Secretariat	Executive Deputy Secretary of CCDI	Party discipline
Wang Chen	Member	66	Full Member	Vice-Chair and Secretary-General of the NPC	Political and legal development

(continued)

TABLE 2-2. (*continued*)

Name	Position	Age (2016)	Central Committee membership	Concurrently held position	Main functional area of responsibility
Guo Shengkun	Member	62	Full Member	State Councilor and Minister of Public Security	Public security and social stability
Zhou Qiang	Member	56	Full Member	President of Supreme People's Court	Political and legal development
Cao Jianming	Member	61	Full Member	Procurator General of Supreme People's Procuratorate	Party discipline
Zhang Qingli	Member	65	Full Member	Vice-Chair and Secretary-General of the CPPCC	Social development and social stability
Zhou Xiaochuan	Member	68	None	Governor of People's Bank of China and Vice-Chair of CPPCC	Economy and ecology
Wang Zhengwei	Member	59	Full Member	Minister of State Ethnic Affairs Commission and Vice-Chair of CPPCC	Social development and social stability

Note and Source: CC = Central Committee of the CCP; CCDI = Central Commission for Discipline Inspection; CMC = Central Military Commission; CPPCC = Chinese People's Political Consultative Conference; NPC = National People's Congress; PLC = Politics and Law Committee; PRC = People's Republic of China. Author's database.

often accompanied him on domestic and international travel when he was vice-president) and deputy director of the Central Planning Department Pan Shengzhou. Almost immediately following the establishment of the CLGCDR, all of China's thirty-one province-level administrations also founded equivalent leading groups, often headed by the provincial party secretaries. The next few years will reveal whether the CLGCDR will be able to fulfill its pronounced objectives.

In addition to establishing the CLGCDR, the Xi administration also founded the National Security Committee (NSC) at the Third Plenum of the 18th Central Committee. According to Chinese authorities, the NSC functions as an important leadership body that coordinates key areas of national security, including national defense, intelligence, diplomacy, and public security. While China's NSC is similar to the National Security Council in the United States in that it is the principal arm for coordinating security and foreign policies among various government agencies, it is different in at least three important ways. First, in contrast to the U.S. National Security Council, which is a part of the executive branch of the government, China's NSC is a party organization that reports to the Politburo and the PSC. This new leadership body is another sign that the CCP leadership remains committed to the principle of maintaining a party-controlled army, as opposed to a state-controlled army.

Second, although the 9/11 terrorist attack on the United States has led the U.S. National Security Council to pay much greater attention to homeland security, its primary concerns are still national defense and foreign affairs. China's NSC has said explicitly that it holds "dual imperatives" (双重压力, *shuangchong yali*): the need to maintain sovereignty, protect national security, and promote development in foreign affairs and the need to maintain domestic political safety and social stability."[46] At present, China's NSC considers domestic security its top priority.

Finally, as a military and economic superpower with troops stationed worldwide, the United States has engaged in global affairs for the past two centuries. U.S. foreign policy pronouncements continue to emphasize maintaining American leadership in world affairs. In contrast, China can hardly afford to take a leadership role in world affairs at present, despite its growing economic power and political influence. Thus, domestic development has remained the primary concern in the eyes of Chinese leaders.

The Chinese authorities have released only the names of the most senior leaders of the NSC: Xi Jinping as chair and Li Keqiang and Zhang Dejiang as vice-chairs.[47] Organizationally, the NSC consists of several Standing Committee members and regular members, but those names have not been made public. It is widely believed that director of the Central General Office of the CCP Li Zhanshu, also a Politburo member, serves as the secretary-general and office director of the NSC, which is located in the Central General Office. Two other Politburo members, secretary of the PLC Meng Jianzhu and Xinjiang party secretary Zhang Chunxian, serve as standing committee members of the NSC.

The opacity of the NSC, and the growing number and importance of the central leading groups, has engendered criticism from Chinese public intellectuals. Some critics believe that the NSC's function and the way in which it was established represent a major turn away from constitutionalism. The NSC's secrecy allows it to evade common institutional and political procedures and thus grants it unrestricted power. Critics believe that, if left unaltered, the NSC will become a powerful institutional organ—or, more likely, a "tool of special interest groups in power"—to crack down on political dissent, human rights, religious rights, and demands from ethnic and other minorities for equality in the name of national security.[48]

Critics have raised fundamental questions regarding the notion that the leading groups can reduce bureaucratic barriers. Among these critics, some assert that they actually make institutions more bureaucratic. Some even sense that the strongman working through leading small groups is not all that more efficient than the PSC working through the State Council.[49]

Interestingly, Premier Li recently claimed that from March 2013 to June 2014, the State Council abolished a total of 1,441 coordinating bodies, including various forms of leading groups, in thirteen of the country's provinces.[50] But a large number of leading groups remain, and new and more powerful groups such as provincial and municipal leading groups that oversee comprehensively deepening reforms have recently been established.

In a recent article entitled "Leading Group Politics and Institutional Resilience," Yang Xuedong, a scholar at the Institute of Global Governance and Strategic Development of the CCP Central Translation Bureau, observes that the "leading group" mechanism is not uniquely Chinese. Other countries and international institutions also adopt similar mechanisms to focus on daunting challenges, especially new and urgent issues.[51] These ad hoc coordinating groups can break institutional barriers, enhance efficiency, and more directly implement policies. According to Yang, an overemphasis on institutional procedures and departmental responsibilities may undermine effectiveness of both decisionmaking and implementation. Yang argues that, in the case of China, department parochialism (部门本位主义, bumen benweizhuyi) has severely obstructed decisionmaking on major policies over the past decade, and so the establishment of leading groups is essential. However, Yang also suggests that although the leading groups may be able to surpass narrow departmental interests, they should neither serve as substitutes for these departments nor marginalize the existing system of checks and balances.[52]

The Organizational Structure of the Government of the People's Republic of China

The Chinese Constitution declares that "all power in the PRC belongs to the people. The organs through which the people exercise state power are the National People's Congress and the local people's congresses at different levels."[53] People's congresses serve as the legislative branch of the government and operate at every administrative rank in the PRC, from the national to rural township and urban district levels. Like other state organizations, the congresses operate under strict party scrutiny and exercise power only as allowed by the CCP leadership.

Figure 2-4 provides an overall organizational structure of the PRC. The bottom level of the Chinese governance consists of 650,000 villages. These are not considered a formal level of administration and are technically self-governing, as villages carry out direct elections. In rural areas, deputies to county and township people's congresses are directly elected by all eligible citizens in that locale. Similarly, for the lowest level of formal urban administration, which is called the district (街道, *jiedao*), deputies to people's congresses are also selected through direct elections. Elections at all higher levels are indirect, meaning deputies are elected by the people's congress at the next lowest level. For example, deputies to the NPC are elected by the people's congresses at the provincial level.

The National People's Congress: "China's Legislature"

Deputies to the NPC are allocated to each province according to that province's population.[54] Recently, the NPC equalized representation of urban and rural areas. Prior to this change, every 960,000 rural residents and every 240,000 urban residents had one NPC deputy representative, respectively, which gave China's cities much more clout in forming legislative outcomes.[55] In July 2014 the State Council announced that China would abolish the distinction between urban and rural residents, a historical step to end the "Chinese version of apartheid."[56]

Under current regulations, the province with the smallest population is guaranteed at least fifteen deputies. Special administrative regions such as Hong Kong and Macao have a set quota of deputies, as does the PLA. The present NPC, formed in 2013, has 2,987 deputies who were each elected to five-year terms. Deputies do not serve as full-time lawmakers, and when the NPC is not in session, they return home to their regular occupations. Some Chinese scholars have been critical of the fact that China's NPC has the largest number of congressional deputies in the world. In their view the large size of the Congress prevents it from serving as an effective venue for policy

FIGURE 2-4. State Organization of the People's Republic of China

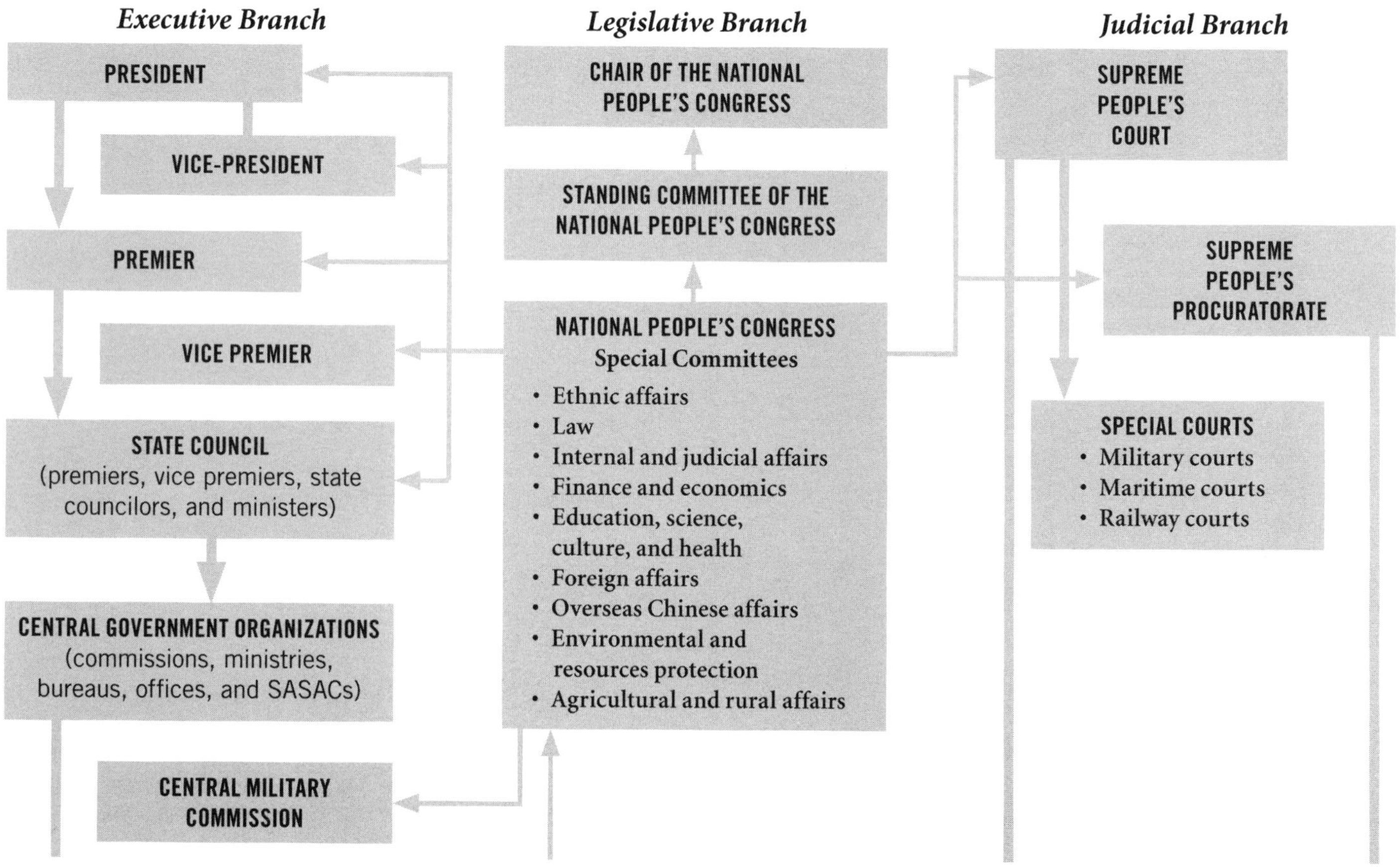

Judicial Branch

SUPREME PEOPLE'S COURT

SUPREME PEOPLE'S PROCURATORATE

SPECIAL COURTS
- Military courts
- Maritime courts
- Railway courts

Legislative Branch

CHAIR OF THE NATIONAL PEOPLE'S CONGRESS

STANDING COMMITTEE OF THE NATIONAL PEOPLE'S CONGRESS

NATIONAL PEOPLE'S CONGRESS
Special Committees
- Ethnic affairs
- Law
- Internal and judicial affairs
- Finance and economics
- Education, science, culture, and health
- Foreign affairs
- Overseas Chinese affairs
- Environmental and resources protection
- Agricultural and rural affairs

Executive Branch

PRESIDENT

VICE-PRESIDENT

PREMIER

VICE PREMIER

STATE COUNCIL
(premiers, vice premiers, state councilors, and ministers)

CENTRAL GOVERNMENT ORGANIZATIONS
(commissions, ministries, bureaus, offices, and SASACs)

CENTRAL MILITARY COMMISSION

LOCAL PEOPLE'S PROCURATORATE
(at the provincial, municipal, county, and other lower levels)

LOCAL PEOPLE'S COURTS

Higher People's Courts (provinces)

Intermediate People's Courts (cities)

Basic People's Courts (counties and townships)

CHINESE PEOPLE'S POLITICAL CONSULTATIVE CONFERENCE
(advisory only)

LOCAL PEOPLE'S CONGRESS
(at the provincial, municipal, county, and other lower levels)

VILLAGES
Village Head
Village Committee, Villager Representative Assembly

LOCAL PEOPLE'S GOVERNMENTS
(at the provincial, municipal, county, and other lower levels)

Notes and Source: Thick arrows = direct supervision; thin arrows = indirect oversight or reporting. Chinese villages are technically self-governing. Cheng Li, "China's Communist Party-State: The Structure and Dynamics of Power," in *Politics in China*, 2d ed., ed. William A. Joseph (Oxford University Press, 2014).

discussion, debate, and decision.[57] At the 5th NPC, held in 1978, there were as many as 3,497 deputies. According to the latest regulations of the NPC, the total number of deputies cannot exceed 3,000.[58] Lower levels of China's people's congresses also have a large number of deputies: 400–1,000 at the provincial level, 200–800 at the municipal level, and 100–500 at the county level.[59]

Currently, the 12th NPC includes 409 ethnic minority deputies (13.7 percent) and 699 female deputies (23.4 percent). A total of 1,027 deputies were reelected (34.4 percent).[60] Of the current NPC deputies, 1,042 are party and government officials (34.9 percent), 610 are professional and technical personnel (20.4 percent), and 401 are workers and peasants (13.4 percent). A large portion of the remaining deputies are entrepreneurs, but Chinese official sources have not released the exact number—perhaps due to recent criticism in China and overseas that business tycoons have begun to dominate the country's legislature. According to a report by Bloomberg News, the combined net worth of the 90 current NPC deputies whose wealth could be traced was 637 billion yuan (US$104 billion).[61]

Just as the National Congress of the CCP elects party leaders every five years at its fall meeting, the NPC elects a new state leadership in the spring of the year following the party congress, and usually those who will be elected are predetermined by party leadership. But unlike the party congress, whose delegates only meet once every five years, the NPC convenes in its entirety every March for a two-week session, during which deputies discuss reports by the premier and other government leaders and approve laws and legislative regulations. This March meeting of the NPC and the March meeting of the CPPCC are held roughly at the same time. They are often called the "two annual meetings" (两会, lianghui) and receive heavy domestic media coverage. In recent years the NPC has increasingly served as a more genuine venue for policy debates, although politically sensitive or controversial topics are off limits. And though the work of the NPC has become more substantive in terms of drafting laws and regulations and providing a venue for policy discourse, it is still basically a rubber stamp for decisions made by the party leadership.

The 12th National People's Congress has one chair and thirteen vice-chairs—nine of whom are CCP members and five who are not. Two are ethnic minorities—one Tibetan and the other Uighur. NPC chair Zhang Dejiang concurrently serves on the PSC as the third-highest-ranking official in the country. The executive vice-chair Li Jianguo concurrently serves on the Politburo. When the NPC is not in session, the Standing Committee of the NPC—not to be confused with the much more powerful CCP Politburo Standing Committee—takes responsibility for any issues that require congressional consideration. The Standing Committee of the NPC has a total of 161 members, not including the aforementioned chair and vice-chairs. The

Standing Committee of the NPC generally convenes every two months, with each meeting lasting about one week. The NPC also appoints nine special committees to draft legislation on various policy issues, including the economy, education, energy, and the environment (see figure 2-4).

In theory, NPC deputies are not only supposed to elect the members of the Standing Committee of the NPC but are also constitutionally entitled to elect the president and vice-president of the PRC. The president and vice-president must meet three basic criteria: (1) they must be PRC citizens; (2) they must have the right to vote and stand for election; and (3) they must be forty-five years or older.[62] The president and vice-president can serve two five-year terms. If the president dies or is unable to fulfill his or her duty due to serious illness or other reasons, the vice-president will succeed the president. If the position of vice-president is vacant, the NPC will elect a new one. If the positions of both president and vice-president are vacant, the NPC will elect both, and during the vacancy period, the chair of the NPC will serve as interim president. The PRC Constitution does not specify the number of vice-presidents allowed to serve at a given time, but there has been only one vice-president over the past three decades.

NPC deputies also elect the chair of the state Central Military Commission (which is also the party CMC—essentially one identical institution with two different names), the president of the Supreme People's Court, and the procurator general of the Supreme People's Procuratorate—the PRC's top law enforcement official, roughly equivalent to the attorney general of the United States. As discussed earlier, the judiciary is not a separate independent branch of government in the PRC. The CCP uses the *nomenklatura* system and other means of control to keep a close watch on all aspects of China's legal system.

According to the PRC Constitution, the NPC is empowered to approve the premier, who is appointed by the president, as well as the other members of the State Council and the CMC. In reality, however, all candidates for the aforementioned positions are chosen by the PSC. This formal process is hardly competitive. When Xi Jinping was elected PRC president in 2013, the vote was 2,952 for, 1 against, with 3 abstentions. Vice-President Li Yuanchao won a slightly more contested election: the tally was 2,839 for, 80 against, with 37 abstentions.[63]

This lack of competitiveness notwithstanding, it is an interesting and fairly recent phenomenon that NPC deputies sometimes vote against nominees for important positions. For example, Zhou Shengxian, the 2013 nominee to the second term for the post of minister of the Environmental Protection Ministry won "only" two-thirds of the vote. This might have been a reflection of widespread public unhappiness with air pollution and other ecological problems.

According to the laws and regulations of the NPC, any bill or proposal to be deliberated at the NPC should be cosigned by thirty deputies and sent to an NPC special committee for review first. Any proposal for constitutional amendment can be initiated only by the Standing Committee of the NPC, with the signatures of at least one-fifth of the deputies. In practice, as some Chinese scholars have observed, the CCP Politburo first proposes the constitutional amendment and then the NPC Standing Committee cosigns it.[64] Occasionally, major proposals made by the CCP leadership face strong criticism and almost fail to pass. One example of broad dissent occurred in April 1992, when NPC deputies voted on the plan for the construction of the Three Gorges Dam, a project championed by then premier Li Peng. The tally was 1,767 in favor, 172 against, and 664 abstentions. Another 25 people did not even touch the voting button.[65]

Chinese People's Political Consultative Conference: An Advisory Body

The CPPCC consists of more than 2,000 members who represent a wide range of constituencies.[66] The PRC Constitution stipulates "a system of cooperation and political consultation led by the CCP."[67] In addition to the CCP, China also has eight smaller political parties, which are officially referred to as the registered minor parties or the "democratic parties" (民主党派, *minzhu dangpai*).[68] Most of these parties have the word "democracy" or "democratic" in their name, for example, the China Democratic National Construction Association and the China Democratic League. They are composed mostly of academics, scientists, writers, artists, professionals, and entrepreneurs and have a total membership of about 700,000.[69] They must swear allegiance to the CCP, and they do not compete with or challenge the CCP in any meaningful way.

The majority of the members in the CPPCC are noncommunists (more than 60 percent), yet the organization is bound by its charter to accept the leadership of the CCP. The current CPPCC leadership, its twelfth iteration, has one chair and twenty-three vice-chairs. Yu Zhengsheng, a PSC member and the fourth-highest-ranking leader in the country, serves as the chair of the CPPCC. Executive Vice-Chair Du Qinglin concurrently serves on the Secretariat of the CCP. Among the twenty-three vice-chairs, eleven are CCP members and the other twelve are not. Unlike the NPC, the CPPCC does not have deputies or delegates. It has only 2,237 members, including 299 Standing Committee members. Among these 2,237 members, 1,100 are first-timers (49.2 percent).[70]

CPPCC members represent thirty-four constituencies (界别, *jiebie*), including the CCP, the aforementioned eight "democratic parties," nonparty independents, China's Communist Youth League, the All China Federation of Trade Unions, the All China Women's Federation, the All China Youth Federation, the All China Federation of Industry and Commerce, the China Association for Science and Technology, the China Federation of Taiwan Compatriots, and the All China Federation of Returned Overseas Chinese. Eleven "walks of life"—culture and art, science and technology, social science, economics, agriculture, education, sports, the press, medicine and public health, foreign exchanges, social welfare and social security—are also represented, along with the ethnic and religious circles, invitees from Hong Kong, invitees from Macao, and other specially invited members.[71]

Like the NPC, the CPPCC also has nine special committees, but the committees are not parallel in scope. The CPPCC's special committees cover the following nine functional areas: (1) bills and proposals; (2) economy; (3) population, resources, and environment; (4) education, science, and sports; (5) social and legal development; (6) minorities and religions; (7) Hong Kong, Macao, Taiwan, and overseas Chinese affairs; (8) foreign affairs; and (9) culture and history. The conference meets each year for about two weeks, concurrent with the annual session of the NPC (as part of the "two annual meetings" described above). The CPPCC has no legislative power of its own; its function is merely to advise the government.

The State Council: China's Cabinet

Although the PSC is the ultimate decisionmaker, the State Council is the source of many important policy initiatives.[72] The State Council reports to the NPC, or to the NPC Standing Committee when the NPC is not in session. The State Council is headed by the premier, and its Executive Committee consists of the premier, four vice-premiers, and five state councilors (senior government leaders with broad responsibilities). One of the state councilors also concurrently serves as the secretary-general of the State Council and manages the day-to-day business of the government. All of these officials hold their positions for no more than two terms.

Among the many political norms that have developed over the last two decades, one of the most significant is that the top two leaders on the State Council—the premier and executive vice-premier—sit concurrently on the PSC. In addition, all vice-premiers (sometimes along with a couple of state councilors) also serve concurrently on the Politburo. The State Council coordinates China's domestic and foreign policies, and the premiership has always been one of the most powerful positions in the country. Several premiers in PRC history—Zhou Enlai, Zhao Ziyang, Zhu Rongji, and Wen Jiabao—have been widely perceived as the "face" of China, in part because of their extensive leadership activities.

The State Council is an enormous bureaucracy with multiple layers of decisionmaking bodies. Its two most important venues are the State Council executive meeting (国务院常务会议, *guowuyuan changwu huiyi*) and the State Council plenary meeting (国务院全体会议, *guowuyuan quanti huiyi*). The former is generally held every week and the latter is held every six months. Those who are entitled to attend the executive meeting informally make up the aforementioned Executive Committee of the State Council.

In addition to Executive Committee members, the State Council full meeting attendance includes twenty-five nonexecutive senior members, including ministers or commissioners who head functional departments such as the Ministry of Foreign Affairs and the National Reform and Development Commission, the central bank governor, and the auditor-general, who oversees the government's budget. At present, all except one of these ministerial-level leaders are members of the CCP, and the vast majority are members of the party's Central Committee. The only non-CCP member is Wan Gang, minister of Science and Technology. Wan received his Ph.D. in physics from Technische Universität Clausthal in 1991 and worked as a senior manager at the Audi Company in Germany for over a decade between 1991 and 2002. Before being appointed minister of Science and Technology, Wan served as the president of Tongji University in Shanghai from 2004 to 2007. In comparison, among the thirty-eight ministers of the State Council, formed in 1959, nine were non-CCP ministers, accounting for almost one-fourth of total membership.[73]

Ministers are the key players in decisionmaking and policy implementation in the functional areas for which their ministries or commissions are responsible. Experience in the central government enhances an official's credentials and often bolsters the official's candidacy for a top leadership position. Ministers of the State Council constitute an important pool of candidates for Politburo membership, perhaps surpassed only by provincial party secretaries and directors of the CCP's central departments.

In addition, the State Council directly manages the following five sets of central government agencies:

— Special Organization under the State Council, which oversees only the State-owned Assets Supervision and Administration Commission (SASAC);
— Organizations under the State Council (sixteen), including the General Administration of Customs and the State Administration of Taxation;
— Offices of the State Council (seven), including the Overseas Chinese Affairs Office of the State Council and the Research Office of the State Council;

— Institutions directly under the State Council (thirteen), including the Xinhua News Agency, the Chinese Academy of Social Sciences, and the China Banking Regulatory Commission; and
— State bureaus under the management of the ministries and commissions of the State Council (nineteen), including the National Energy Administration, and the State Tobacco Monopoly Administration.[74]

Heads of these five sets of central government agencies also usually attend the full meetings of the State Council. With a few exceptions, these fifty-six leaders of the five sets of central government agencies are less prominent than the twenty-five ministerial-level leaders and are therefore generally considered to be the third tier of the State Council, after the members of the Executive Committee and nonexecutive ministers.[75]

It is important to note that some of these third-tier institutions of the State Council carry significant weight in China's economy. This is especially true of the SASAC, which currently controls the 112 so-called SASAC companies (央企, *yangqi*), which are large national flagship firms whose assets are owned in majority by the state. This does not include the SOEs that are run by local (provincial or municipal) governments. As of 2010 China had approximately 114,500 SOEs, which is a significant decrease from its peak of 159,000 in 2003.[76] Another important group of state-owned firms in the banking and financial industries at the national level, central financial firms (金融央企, *jinrong yangqi*), are overseen by the China Banking Regulatory Commission, the China Securities Regulatory Commission and the China Insurance Regulatory Commission, all of which are under the leadership of the State Council. As of January 2012 there were twenty-two such firms.

As China's state-owned flagship companies and financial institutions become increasingly formidable and assertive in domestic and international markets, the CEOs of these firms are also becoming more aggressive in their quest for power in CCP and state government leadership. The proportion of CEOs of large enterprises who are also members of the national leadership is still relatively small, but some heavyweight politicians hold significant leadership positions in China's SOEs. For example, current PSC member Wang Qishan served as president of China Construction Bank from 1994 to 1997; current Politburo member Zhang Chunxian served as general manager of China National Packaging and Food Machinery Corporation in the early 1990s; current state councilor and minister of Public Security Guo Shengkun served as general manager of the Aluminum Corporation of China from 2001 to 2004; and current state councilor Wang Yong served as chair of the SASAC from 2010 to 2013. Two former PSC members, Jia Qinglin and Zhou Yongkang, also advanced their careers via leading SOEs. The former served as general manager of the China National Machinery and

Equipment Import & Export Corporation from 1978 to 1983, and the latter was general manager of China National Petroleum Corporation in the late 1990s.

While top provincial leadership experience, especially the posts of provincial party secretary or of governor, remains the most important stepping-stone to top national officialdom, it is evident that young, entrepreneurial, politically connected, and globally minded Chinese CEOs are increasingly holding positions in national leadership. Several former CEOs now serve as provincial governors. They include Governor Zhang Qingwei of Hebei (former general manager of the China Aerospace Science and Technology Corporation), Governor Lu Hao of Heilongjiang (former deputy general manager of the Beijing Textile Holding Group), Governor Hao Peng of Qinghai (former general manager of the AVIC Lanzhou Flight Control Instrument Factory), Governor Guo Shuqing of Shandong (former chair of the China Construction Bank), Governor Li Xiaopeng of Shanxi (former general manager of the China Huaneng Group), and Mayor Yang Xiong of Shanghai (former chair of Shanghai Airlines). The first three governors were born in the 1960s and are considered rising stars in China's upcoming sixth generation of leadership.

This development may not only broaden the channel of political recruitment in the PRC but also significantly change the rules of the game in Chinese elite politics. Indeed, the overlap between the business elite and the political elite will have immense consequences for Chinese leadership as a whole, and it will profoundly influence the government's policy choices and decisionmaking.

SUMMARY

Crucial to any analysis of Chinese politics is an understanding of where true power lies, how decisions are made, what role top leaders and key institutions play, and what interaction one can expect between them. This is even more important now, given the growing tensions between Xi's consolidation of power and institutional demands for representation and between the need for effective policy implementation and the imperative for checks and balances.

Without a doubt, power in the PRC resides in the ruling party. More precisely, decisions are made by the Politburo, especially the PSC, rather than by the state government (the NPC or the State Council). As all of its members concurrently hold top posts in other important leadership bodies in the party and government, the PSC is ultimately where directives are born, decisions are made, and deals are cut. Some may be surprised to learn that eight registered political parties—and a host of other noncommunist constituencies—are represented in the government apparatus (usually through positions in the CPPCC). However, these roles are merely advisory; they carry no legislative power.

Where non-CCP voices are explicitly separated from the reins of power, the Politburo and PSC achieve supremacy over the CCP as a whole through a more implicit arrangement. Although the PRC Constitution grants the NPC authority to elect the country's president, vice-president, and numerous other top leaders, including the members of the State Council and the CMC, in reality this body enacts the will of the PSC. Likewise, although the Central Committee is responsible for selecting members of the Politburo and the PSC, in practice this is a carefully managed top-down process.

Some political fragmentation and departmental parochialism is inevitable in a system of collective leadership. It is understandable that the new Zhongnanhai boss, Xi Jinping, has attempted to establish new institutions; some of these may be temporary, like the Central Leading Group for Comprehensively Deepening Reforms, and others may be permanent, like the National Security Committee, but they all serve to consolidate power and influence, as evidenced by Xi's holding the top posts in the CLGCDR, the NSC, and ten other groups. However, these two new leadership bodies not only consist of top leaders from the PSC and the Politburo; they are also in both theory and practice overseen by the same two powerful groups.

In similar fashion, China's president is chosen through the CCP's hierarchical structure, rather than elected as a bipartisan or multiparty leader with a clean mandate. Xi's power and authority, therefore, are significantly restrained by Chinese bureaucratic institutions and political norms. Even with the leading groups themselves, there is significant debate over whether these ad hoc leadership bodies can cut through the bureaucracy to achieve their objectives, or if they constitute merely another layer of red tape.

This does not necessarily mean that the new institutional mechanisms and structural changes are insignificant. Experts have noted that when it comes to implementing socioeconomic policies, Zhongnanhai has become less effective in controlling China's provinces, major cities, and even key SOEs. Especially in the final years of his administration, Hu Jintao was widely criticized for his "inaction." His two five-year terms have been regarded by some critics as "the lost decade." A popular barb—"the premier cannot control a general manager" (总理管不了总经理, *zongli guanbuliao zongjingli*)—reflects the serious challenge to the central leadership's administrative capacity.[77] In that regard, the establishment of the CLGCDR and its local branches may be an effective way to break bureaucratic barriers and mitigate local resistance. The limitations of the previously omnipotent PLC's power and the ongoing tough anticorruption campaign led by the more powerful CCDI are two welcome structural changes. The CCDI's recent calls for more supervision over the power of top officials at various levels of administration and its pronounced plan for a gradual transition to a more vigorous legal process in preventing corruption may reinforce the division of responsibility within the collective leadership.

Meanwhile, new paths to important leadership positions are beginning to form. In particular, CEOs of state-owned firms are becoming more aggressive in their pursuit of party and state power, with several former CEOs now holding provincial governorships. The country's future decisionmakers could bring with them a new set of backgrounds, experiences, and priorities, all of which could influence the party's agenda-setting and policy implementation processes.

This structural analysis illuminates both the institutional adjustments the PSC has made to execute collective leadership and the enormous challenges it still faces. The following chapter will link CCP personnel dynamics to issues in the Chinese political structure, illustrating the remarkable transformation of China's elite—the high turnover rate, the growing diversity in recruitment, and the trend toward regional representation—during the reform era.

CHAPTER 3

Elites

Composition and Representation
on the 18th Central Committee

Government offices are solid as iron, but the officials working in them are like flowing water. [铁打的衙门流水的官]
—CHINESE PROVERB

A t a delegation meeting of the 17th National Party Congress in October 2007, then vice-president of the People's Republic of China (PRC) Zeng Qinghong—a Dick Cheney–like figure in Chinese politics—offered the following insight:[1]

> The Chinese Communist Party has a great forward-looking cause. This cause is like a sturdy barrack through which our party cadres at various levels of leadership come and go like one crop of soldiers after another.

Though Zeng's statement glorifies the Chinese Communist Party's (CCP's) cause and overlooks the major flaws in China's political system, he is largely correct in how he characterizes the fluidity of elite circulation in the party. While CCP officials have circulated very rapidly within the organization, the Chinese party-state structure has remained more or less the same over the past sixty-seven years. Certain institutional rules and norms adopted in the 1980s have proven both enduring and effective, including the mandatory retirement age, term limits, regional representation, and multicandidate elections for the Central Committee. Although these institutional mechanisms and personnel management procedures do not eliminate the favoritism and nepotism inherent in China's party-state system, they have nevertheless fostered a new sense of consistency and fairness, and have even changed the competitive political behaviors of elites. There are five primary, interlinked realms from which CCP officials are recruited: the central party's apparatus, ministerial leadership, the military, flagship state-owned enterprises, and provincial administrations. Provincial leadership experience is the most important stepping-stone to top national positions, which highlights the regional foundations of China's collective leadership.

PLACING ELITE TURNOVER AT THE 18TH PARTY CONGRESS IN CCP HISTORICAL CONTEXT

One major reason that the CCP has continued to hold power for over six decades, especially during the development and turmoil of the past quarter century, is the fluidity of elite turnover within the party and state government. An examination of personal backgrounds, demographic distribution, career paths, promotion patterns, and bureaucratic and regional representations of the 376 members of the 18th Central Committee illustrates some of the institutionalized rules and norms that have governed elite circulation and political succession in the CCP.[2]

The turnover rate for Central Committee members has been remarkably high over the past thirty years. Newcomers have constituted an average of 62.3 percent in each of the seven Central Committees held from 1982 to 2012 (see figure 3-1). The leadership change at the 18th National Party Congress, held in 2012, primarily followed the extant rules and norms regarding age limits; members and alternates of the previous Central Committee who were born in or before 1944 could no longer serve on the new Central Committee. By the same token, no one who was born in or before 1939 served on the previous 17th Central Committee. As a result, the turnover rate was remarkably high for the important leadership organs selected at the 18th National Party Congress. Figure 3-2 shows that newcomers make up 64 percent of the current Central Committee, 77 percent of the Central Commission for Discipline Inspection, 86 percent of the Secretariat, 60 percent of the Politburo, 71 percent of the Politburo Standing Committee (PSC), and 64 percent of the Central Military Commission (or 70 percent of all military members).

Among the full members of the 18th Central Committee, 88 (42.9 percent) were reelected, 59 (28.8 percent) were promoted from the previous Central Committee, where they had served as alternates, and 58 (28.3 percent) were first-timers. Among the alternate members, 46 (26.9 percent) were reelected and 125 (73.1 percent) were new. The member turnover rate at the 18th Central Committee, including alternate members in the previous Central Committee who were promoted to full members, was 64.4 percent. Excluding the full members who were promoted from their alternate status on the 17th

FIGURE 3-1. Turnover Rate of the Central Committee, 1982–2012

Percent

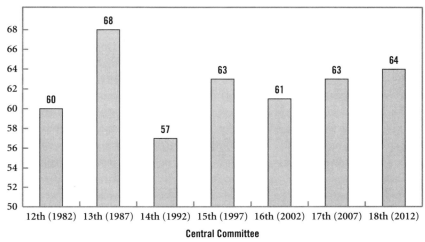

Central Committee

Note and Source: The turnover rate of the Central Committee also includes alternate members in the previous Central Committee who are promoted to full members. Cheng Li and Lynn White, "The Sixteenth Central Committee of the Chinese Communist Party: Hu Gets What?," *Asian Survey*, vol. 43, no. 4 (July/August 2003). The data on the 17th and 18th Central Committees were derived from the author's database, with additional research in 2013.

Central Committee (59), 183 leaders on the 18th Central Committee (comprising 58 new full members and 125 new alternates) are first-timers (48.7 percent of the total). Similarly, at the 16th Central Committee, formed in 2002, 180 leaders (67 new full members and 113 new alternates) were first-timers, accounting for 50.6 percent of the entire 356-member Central Committee.[3] These two cases suggest that although Chinese authorities cannot absolutely control the voting of congressional delegates, their aim is to ensure that roughly half of the Central Committee is completely new to the top leadership.

On the 18th Central Committee, PSC member Liu Yunshan boasts the longest tenure; he served as an alternate member on the 12th Central Committee formed in 1982. He did not serve on the 13th Central Committee but regained his alternate membership on the 14th Central Committee in 1992. No current member of the Central Committee served on the 13th Central Committee, and only six other members in addition to Liu Yunshan served on the 14th Central Committee as alternate members, namely, Zhang Dejiang, Yu Zhengsheng, Li Jianguo, Du Qinglin, Xu Qiliang, and Wu Anying. Li Keqiang began his tenure as a full member of the Central Committee at the 15th National Party Congress in 1997, and Xi Jinping began as an alternate

FIGURE 3-2. Turnover Rate in Top Leadership Bodies at the 18th Party Congress

Percent

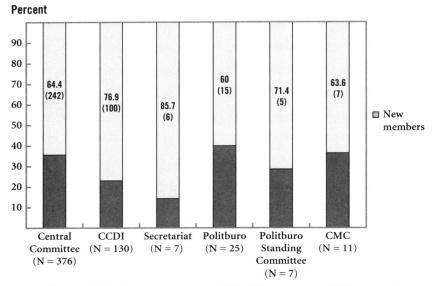

Note and Source: CCDI = Central Commission for Discipline Inspection; CMC = Central Military Commission. Cheng Li, "Opportunity Lost? Inside China's Leadership Transition," *Foreign Policy*, November 16, 2012.

that same year. Among all of the 193 returning members on the 18th Central Committee (including those full members who were promoted from alternate status on the previous Central Committee), 143 (74.1 percent) had previously served only one term on the 17th Central Committee. When the 18th Central Committee convened in 2012, 98 percent of the 376-member committee had entered the Central Committee after 1997. Similarly, 98 percent of the full members on the 15th Central Committee, formed in 1997, had joined the Central Committee after 1982.[4] The numbers outlined above reflect the relatively short-term nature of membership on the Central Committee and show that the committee generates rapid elite turnover in the CCP leadership.

The rapid elite circulation in the CCP leadership evident at the 18th National Party Congress is the norm rather than the exception in the reform era since 1978, especially in the past three decades. Table 3-1 provides a comprehensive overview of the turnover rates for the Central Committees and Politburos formed in each of the eleven National Party Congresses held since the founding of the PRC. The highest turnover rate (81 percent) occurred at the 9th National Party Congress, a result of the large-scale political purge in the early years of the Cultural Revolution of the so-called capitalist roaders (走资派, *zouzipai*)—leaders who were seen as followers of Liu Shaoqi and Deng Xiaoping. At that National Party Congress, a large number of Maoists, or Cultural Revolution radicals, primarily consisting of workers, peasants, and younger military officers, replaced those leaders who were veterans of the Communist Revolution. The extraordinarily long break (thirteen years) between the 8th and 9th National Party Congresses is another possible reason for the unusually high turnover at the latter.

It should be noted that not all Central Committees experienced high elite turnover rates in the history of the PRC and that the high turnover rates in the past three decades do not have much to do with purges. Some political purges before the Deng era—namely, at the 10th National Party Congress in 1973 after the Lin Biao incident and the 11th National Party Congress in 1977 after the downfall of the "Gang of Four" (四人帮, *sirenbang*)— did expel a significant number of Central Committee members who were associated with Lin Biao and the Gang of Four, but the overall turnover rates were relatively low (35 percent and 43 percent, respectively; see table 3-1). Similarly, when Hua Guofeng lost his top leadership post at the 12th National Party Congress in 1982, he and several of his followers remained in the Central Committee. Despite the demotion of Hu Yaobang prior to the 13th National Party Congress in 1987 and the demise of both Zhao Ziyang and the "generals of the Yang family" (杨家将, *yangjiajiang*) prior to the 14th National Party Congress in 1992, most protégés of these senior leaders were reelected. Hu Yaobang and Yang Baibing kept their seats in the Politburo, and only Zhao Ziyang and his political *mishu* Bao Tong lost their seats in the Central Committee.

The 13th National Party Congress adopted Deng Xiaoping's initiative to recruit a large number of younger leaders into the Central Committee, and thus it had the second-largest turnover rate (68 percent) in CCP history. Since that congress, the process of elite circulation has become more institutionalized in regulations and norms. Over the past three decades, every Central Committee has exhibited a fairly high turnover rate (all above 57 percent).

Over the past thirty years, the Politburo and its Standing Committee have also had a high turnover rate on average. The mean of the seven Politburos turnover rates between 1982 and 2012 was 53.3 percent. The relatively high turnover rates of the 14th, 16th, and 18th Politburos follow the rhythm of the once-per-decade generational transition—namely, the leadership handovers from Jiang Zemin's third generation to Hu Jintao's fourth generation, and to Xi Jinping's fifth generation, respectively.[5] For example, among the twenty-five full and alternate members of the 16th Politburo formed in 2002, 60 percent were first-timers. Moreover, except for Hu Jintao, the other eight members (88.9 percent) of the PSC were new. Six of the seven previous PSC members stepped down from this supreme decisionmaking body during

TABLE 3-1. Elite Turnover on Central Committees and Politburos, 1956–2012

| Central Committee | Year held | Central Committee | | | | | | Politburo | | | | | |
| | | Full member | | | Alternate member | | | Total Central Committee | | | | | | | | % of reelected from the previous Politburo |
		No.	New	%	No.	New	%	No.	New	%	No.	New	%	Reelected	%	
8th	1956	97	32	33	73	70	95	170	102	60	23	13	43	10	57	83
9th	1969	170	122	71	109	104	95	279	226	81	25	15	60	10	40	43
10th	1973	195	55	28	124	58	46	319	113	35	25	9	36	16	64	64
11th	1977	201	71	35	132	75	56	333	146	43	26	11	46	15	54	60
12th	1982	210	96	45	138	114	82	348	210	60	28	14	50	14	50	54
13th	1987	175	114	65	110	79	72	285	193	68	18	12	66	6	34	21
14th	1992	189	84	44	130	97	75	319	181	57	22	15	68	7	32	39
15th	1997	193	109	57	151	106	70	344	215	63	24	8	33	16	67	73
16th	2002	198	107	54	158	113	72	356	220	61	25	15	60	10	40	42
17th	2007	204	107	52	167	125	73	371	232	63	25	9	36	16	64	64
18th	2012	205	117	57	171	125	73	376	242	64	25	15	60	10	40	40

Note and Source: The "new" column under full members includes those who have been promoted from alternate to full membership. The "new" column under alternate members excludes those demoted from full to alternate membership. The "new" column under the total Central Committee includes new full plus new alternate members. The increase in the total number of new Central Committee members can be determined using the number promoted from alternate to full membership. On the 16th Central Committee, for example, 40 full members were promoted from alternate status, so the total number of completely new members is 180 (including 67 completely new full members and 113 new alternate members), or 50.6% of the committee. See Li Cheng and Lynn White, "The Thirteenth Central Committee of the Chinese Communist Party: From Mobilizers to Managers," *Asian Survey,* vol. 28, no. 4 (April 1988): 371–99; Li Cheng and Lynn White, "The Army in the Succession to Deng Xiaoping: Familiar Fealties and Technocratic Trends," *Asian Survey,* vol. 33, no. 8 (August 1993): 757–86; and Li Cheng and Lynn White, "The Fifteenth Central Committee of the Chinese Communist Party: Full-Fledged Technocratic Leadership with Partial Control by Jiang Zemin," *Asian Survey,* vol. 38, no. 3 (March 1998): 231–64. Cheng Li and Lynn White, "The Sixteenth Central Committee of the Chinese Communist Party: Hu Gets What?," *Asian Survey,* vol. 43, no. 4 (July/August 2003): 560. The data on the 17th and 18th Central Committees were derived from the author's database.

the 16th National Party Congress. They were Jiang Zemin (CCP general secretary), Li Peng (chair of the National People's Congress [NPC]), Zhu Rongji (premier), Li Ruihuan (CPPCC chair), Wei Jianxing (secretary of the CCDI), and Li Lanqing (executive vice-premier). This was the largest turnover in the history of the PSC.[6] At the 18th National Party Congress, only Xi Jinping and Li Keqiang remained on the PSC, and the seven other previous members had retired, including the four highest-ranking leaders at the time: Hu Jintao (CCP general secretary), Wu Bangguo (NPC chair), Wen Jiabao (premier), and Jia Qinglin (CPPCC chair).

Institutional Norms and Regulations

The rapid elite circulation in the CCP leadership during the past three decades is a result of the effective implementation of institutional norms and regulations. Most of these norms and regulations began to emerge at the 12th National Party Congress in 1982 and have gradually been expanded and reinforced. In August 2006 the General Office of the CCP Central Committee issued three important and comprehensive documents to more systematically guide cadre promotions: *Interim Regulations of the Tenure of Party and Government Officials, Regulations of Exchange of Party and Government Officials*, and *Interim Regulations of Position Avoidance of Party and Government Officials*.[7] In January 2014, the Central Committee of the CCP issued an updated edition of *Regulations and Laws of the Recruitment and Promotion of Party and Government Officials*, which is an amendment of the 2002 edition of the same document.[8] The amendment reinforces the importance of collective leadership in personnel matters.[9] The following formal regulations and informal norms are particularly essential in governing the recruitment and retirement of CCP elites.

Term Limits

In 1982 both the 12th National Party Congress and the Standing Committee of the 5th National People's Congress announced the abolishment of lifetime tenure for party and government positions and the adoption of the cadre tenure system (干部任期制, *ganbu renqizhi*), which is generally known in China as the term limit system (限任制, *xianrenzhi*). With few exceptions, top leadership posts in both the party and the government have a term limit of five years. An individual leader cannot hold the same position for more than two terms, and no leader can remain at the same level of leadership for more than fifteen years.

Table 3-2 provides an overview of all sixty-two party secretaries, mayors, and governors in China's thirty-one provincial-level administrations in

TABLE 3-2. Current Provincial Chiefs (Party Secretaries and Governors), as of May 2016

Province	Party secretary				Governor or mayor			
	Name	Birth year	Since	Birthplace	Name	Birth year	Since	Birthplace
Beijing	Guo Jinlong	1947	2012	Jiangsu	Wang Anshun	1957	2013	Henan
Tianjin	Huang Xingguo	1954	2014	Zhejiang	Huang Xingguo	1954	2008	Zhejiang
Hebei	Zhao Kezhi	1953	2015	Shandong	Zhang Qingwei	1961	2012	Hebei
Shanxi	Wang Rulin	1953	2014	Henan	Li Xiaopeng	1959	2013	Sichuan
Neimenggu	Wang Jun	1952	2012	Shanxi	Buxiaolin (f)	1958	2016	Neimenggu
Liaoning	Li Xi	1956	2015	Gansu	Chen Qiufa	1954	2015	Hunan
Jilin	Bayanqolu	1955	2014	Neimenggu	Jiang Chaoliang	1957	2014	Hunan
Heilongjiang	Wang Xiankui	1952	2013	Hebei	Lu Hao	1967	2013	Shanghai
Shanghai	Han Zheng	1954	2012	Shanghai	Yang Xiong	1953	2013	Zhejiang
Jiangsu	Luo Zhijun	1951	2010	Liaoning	Shi Taifeng	1956	2015	Shanxi
Shandong	Jiang Yikang	1953	2008	Shandong	Guo Shuqing	1956	2013	Neimenggu
Zhejiang	Xia Baolong	1952	2012	Tianjin	Li Qiang	1959	2013	Zhejiang
Anhui	Wang Xuejun	1952	2015	Hebei	Li Jinbin	1958	2015	Sichuan
Fujian	You Quan	1954	2012	Hebei	Yu Weiguo	1955	2015	Shandong

Henan	Xie Fuzhan	1954	2016	Hubei	Chen Run'er	1957	2016	Hunan
Hubei	Li Hongzhong	1956	2010	Shandong	Wang Guosheng	1956	2011	Shandong
Hunan	Xu Shousheng	1953	2013	Jiangsu	Du Jiahao	1955	2013	Zhejiang
Jiangxi	Qiang Wei	1953	2013	Jiangsu	Lu Xinshe	1956	2011	Shandong
Guangdong	Hu Chunhua	1963	2012	Hubei	Zhu Xiaodan	1953	2012	Zhejiang
Guangxi	Peng Qinghua	1957	2012	Hubei	Chen Wu	1954	2013	Guangxi
Hainan	Luo Baoming	1952	2011	Tianjin	Liu Cigui	1955	2015	Fujian
Sichuan	Wang Dongming	1956	2012	Liaoning	Yin Li	1962	2016	Shandong
Chongqing	Sun Zhengcai	1963	2012	Shandong	Huang Qifan	1952	2010	Zhejiang
Guizhou	Chen Min'er	1960	2015	Zhejiang	Sun Zhigang	1954	2015	Henan
Yunnan	Li Jiheng	1957	2014	Guangxi	Chen Hao	1954	2014	Jiangsu
Tibet	Chen Quanguo	1955	2011	Henan	Losang Jamcan	1957	2012	Tibet
Shaanxi	Lou Qinjian	1956	2016	Guizhou	Hu Heping	1962	2016	Shandong
Gansu	Wang Sanyun	1952	2011	Shandong	Lin Duo	1956	2016	Shandong
Qinghai	Luo Huining	1954	2013	Zhejiang	Hao Peng	1960	2013	Shaanxi
Ningxia	Li Jianhua	1954	2013	Hebei	Liu Hui (f)	1959	2013	Tianjin
Xinjiang	Zhang Chunxian	1953	2010	Henan	Shohrat Zakir	1953	2015	Xinjiang

Note and Source: (f) = female. "Difang dangwei lingdao ren ziliao ku" [Database on local level party committee leaders], *People's Daily Online* (http://renshi.people.com.cn/GB/353032/index.html). Tabulated and featured by the author.

TABLE 3-3. Average Length of Tenure of Provincial Party Secretaries and Governors, 1985–2013

Year	Average tenure (years)	
	Provincial party secretaries	Governors
1985	4.5	2.5
1990	4.2	3.9
1995	4.8	3.5
2000	3.3	2.3
2013	2.5	2.2

Source: China Directory (Tokyo: Radio Press, 1985, 1990, 1995, 2000, and 2013). Data accumulated and tabulated by the author.

May 2016. Without exception, they have honored the two-term limit. In fact, an overwhelming majority of these leaders are still in their first term. Fifty-one (82 percent) of the current party secretaries, mayors, and governors were appointed to their present position in or after 2012. A majority of these provincial chiefs were appointed after the 18th Party Congress. The provincial party secretary with the longest tenure is the Shandong party secretary, Jiang Yikang, who has held office since 2008. The longest-tenured mayor, Huang Xingguo of Tianjin, who assumed the post in 2008, will likely hand over the position to his successor in the coming months, because he was promoted to acting party secretary in December 2014. The recent chemical explosion in Tianjin Binhai District, however, may raise concerns about Huang's future career advancement.

Table 3-3 illustrates the average tenure of the sixty-two provincial party secretaries and governors in five different years (1985, 1990, 1995, 2000, and 2013). The figures reveal a significant decrease in the length of the average tenure over the past three decades. This is most noticeable among the provincial party secretaries: their average length of time in power decreased from 4.5 years in 1985 to 2.5 years in 2013. Also, throughout this period, the turnover rate of governors was higher than that of provincial party secretaries. The short tenures in both leadership positions demonstrate the effective implementation of regulations on term limits and highlight the astonishingly fast turnover in top provincial leadership in present-day China.

Table 3-4 shows the tenures of the current cabinet members of the State Council, along with their respective Central Committee membership status. With the exception of the People's Bank governor, Zhou Xiaochuan, all members fall within the two-term limit. Zhou failed to obtain a seat on the 18th Central Committee and was expected to retire at the NPC meeting in March 2013. However, apparently Zhou's patrons in the top leadership found some excuse to grant this exception. Perhaps top decisionmakers believe Zhou to be a critical figure in financial leadership, as his position is equivalent to the chair of the board of governors of the Federal Reserve System in the United States.[10] Zhou was also elected vice-chair of the CPPCC in March 2013. Four other ministers (Minister of Justice Wu Aiying, Minister of Science and Technology Wan Gang, Minister of State Security Geng Huichang, and Minister of Water Resources Chen Lei) assumed their posts before 2008, but the majority of the thirty-three cabinet members (85 percent) are still in their first five years of service. Except for Wan Gang (a non-CCP member), Zhou Xiaochuan, and Chen Jining (the newly appointed minister of Environmental Protection), the remaining ministers all serve on the 18th Central Committee as full members. Five of them also sit on the Politburo, and two of the five (Premier Li Keqiang and Executive Vice-Premier Zhang Gaoli) sit on the PSC.

As discussed in the previous chapter, there is no term limit for Central Committee, Politburo, or PSC membership. But there is a term limit for their other positions. Since all Politburo members and PSC members concurrently hold other senior leadership positions in the party, government, or military, a leader must move to a different leadership post after ten years to maintain his or her membership in any party leadership organ. After fifteen years of service at the same level of leadership, a leader must either move to a higher level or retire.

Age Limits for Retirement

Officials above a certain level of leadership cannot exceed a set age limit. For example, any provincial chief (party secretary or governor) or cabinet minister who is over sixty-five years old must retire, and any deputy provincial leader and vice-minister who is over sixty-three is also encouraged to retire. Among current provincial chiefs and ministers, almost all are under sixty-five, with the exceptions of the sixty-seven-year-old Beijing party secretary, Guo Jinlong, and the sixty-six-year-old People's Bank governor, Zhou Xiaochuan. Guo and Zhou were granted exemptions because both concurrently hold even higher positions in the Politburo and the CPPCC, respectively. Based on CCP regulations and norms, provincial chiefs with Politburo membership have an older retirement age (seventy-two years old), as do cabinet ministers who concurrently serve in national party and state leadership positions, such as the vice-chair of the CPPCC. Guo is the only current provincial chief who was born in the 1940s (see table 3-2), and Zhou is the oldest among the twenty-five ministers of the State Council and one of three in the group born in the 1940s (see table 3-4).

TABLE 3-4. Tenure and Central Committee Membership Status of Current State Council Members, as of May 2016

Position	Name	Year born	Tenure since	Central Committee status
Premier	Li Keqiang*	1955	2013	PSC
Executive Vice Premier	Zhang Gaoli*	1946	2013	PSC
	Liu Yandong (f)*	1945	2013	Politburo
Vice Premier	Wang Yang*	1955	2013	Politburo
	Ma Kai*	1946	2013	Politburo
	Yang Jing*	1953	2013	Full member
	Chang Wanquan*	1949	2013	Full member
State Councilor	Yang Jiechi*	1950	2013	Full member
	Guo Shengkun*	1954	2013	Full member
	Wang Yong*	1955	2013	Full member
Minister/Chair				
Foreign Affairs	Wang Yi	1953	2013	Full member
Defense	Chang Wanquan		see above	
NDRC	Xu Shaoshi	1951	2013	Full member
Education	Yuan Guiren	1950	2009	Full member
Science & Technology	Wan Gang	1952	2007	Non-CCP
Industry & Information Technology	Miao Wei	1955	2010	Full member
State Ethnic Affairs Commission	Bater	1955	2016	Full member
Public Security	Guo Shengkun	1954	2013	Full member
State Security	Geng Huichang	1951	2007	Full member
Supervision	Huang Shuxian	1954	2013	Full member
Civil Affairs	Li Liguo	1953	2010	Full member
Justice	Wu Aiying (f)	1951	2005	Full member
Finance	Lou Jiwei	1950	2013	Full member
HRSS	Yin Weimin	1953	2008	Full member
Land & Natural Resources	Jiang Daming	1953	2013	Full member
Environmental Protection	Chen Jining	1964	2015	None
HURD	Chen Zhenggao	1952	2014	Full member
Transportation	Yang Chuantang	1954	2012	Full member
Water Resources	Chen Lei	1954	2007	Full member
Agriculture	Han Changfu	1954	2009	Full member

TABLE 3-4. (*continued*)

Position	Name	Year born	Tenure since	Central Committee status
Commerce	Gao Hucheng	1951	2013	Full member
Culture	Luo Shugang	1955	2014	Full member
NHFPC	Li Bin (f)	1954	2013	Full member
People's Bank	Zhou Xiaochuan	1948	2002	None
National Audit Office	Liu Jiayi	1956	2008	Full member

Note: * Refers to members of the Executive Committee of the State Council. PSC = Politburo Standing Committee; (f) = female; NDRC = National Development and Reform Commission; CCP = Chinese Communist Party; HRSS = Human Resources and Social Security; HURD = Housing and Urban-Rural Development; NHFPC = National Health and Family Planning Commission.

Although there is no term limit for membership in the top leadership bodies of the CCP, there is a strict age limit. In 2002 the Central Organization Department, when nominating candidates for the 16th Central Committee, followed three guidelines: (1) with few exceptions, the full and alternate members of the preceding Central Committee nominated for reelection should be younger than sixty-four years old; (2) full ministers and provincial chiefs nominated for new Central Committee membership should be younger than sixty-two; and (3) nominated vice-ministers and vice-governors should be younger than fifty-seven.[11] Furthermore, all of the members born before 1944 retired from the 18th Central Committee in 2012. Because a Politburo and PSC member must also be a member of the Central Committee, this age limit for membership on the Central Committee indirectly applies to members of the Politburo and PSC as well.

The age limit also applies to the military elites. Since the late 1990s, the Chinese authorities have effectively implemented a well-defined regulation of age-based retirement for military officers.[12] There is a specific age limit for military officers serving at various levels, from the platoon to the Central Military Commission.[13] In 2000 the Standing Committee of the National People's Congress passed *The Law of Officers in Service*, which stipulates that all officers at the level of army command should be demobilized from military service when they reach the age of fifty-five; at the level of division command, when they reach the age of fifty; and at the level of regiment command, when they reach the age of forty-five.[14] Also according to this regulation, generals who serve as deputy chief at the military region level should retire when they reach sixty-three years old, and generals who serve as full officers at the military region level should retire when they reach sixty-five.

In June 2015 the Politburo passed a new trial-based regulation on the promotion and demotion of cadres in both civilian and military leadership.[15] This new regulation not only requires the strict enforcement of age limits in retirement but also calls for the removal of leaders who are incapable, incompetent, or inactive as a result of health or other reasons. This will likely pave the way for Xi's leadership to remove a large number of leaders (both civilian and military) who would otherwise be qualified based on age to stay in their positions, thus further accelerating the leadership turnover.

Regional Representation of Full Central Committee Members

Since the 15th Central Committee, each provincial-level administration has held two full membership seats (usually occupied by the provincial party secretary and the governor or mayor) on the Central Committee. Just as each American state is allotted two seats in the Senate, each Chinese province gets two full memberships on the Central Committee (although the powers of these two bodies are, of course, very different). Provincial chiefs may later be promoted to the central government or transferred to other provinces or cities, but when the Central Committee is initially selected, seats are allocated according to this norm.

Table 3-5 shows that, with only a few exceptions, regional distribution has been fairly equal for the past four Central Committees.[16] Regions with a high population of ethnic minorities, like Tibet and Xinjiang, are often the outliers since their representation is not constrained by these norms. As part of Chinese "affirmative action," they usually have more than two seats. Additionally, the multicandidate election process to select members of the Central Committee has also affected the representation of some provinces. For example, the governors of Sichuan and Jiangxi failed to attain full membership in the 18th Central Committee, leaving these two provinces with only one representative each. It is also interesting to note that the Politburo elected in 2012 has at least one current member who has worked extensively in each of China's major geographic regions: the northeast, north, northwest, east, south central, and southwest.

The even distribution of full memberships among provincial administrations at the time of the four most recent Central Committee elections is nonetheless an institutional development. Top leaders can still try to manipulate outcomes before or after balloting, but they are now more constrained by formal rules and informal norms in the regional distribution of seats in the Central Committee. Consequently, neither top leaders nor various factions can dominate the Central Committee. Leaders from wealthy coastal provinces may still dominate the Politburo, especially the powerful

TABLE 3-5. Distribution of Provincial Leaders Holding Full Membership Seats on the 15th, 16th, 17th, and 18th Central Committees, 1997–2012

	15th CC (1997)	16th CC (2002)	17th CC (2007)	18th CC (2012)
Beijing	2	2	2	2
Tianjin	2	2	2	2
Hebei	2	2	2	2
Shanxi	2	2	2	2
Neimenggu	2	2	2	2
Liaoning	2	2	2	2
Jilin	2	2	2	3
Heilongjiang	2	2	2	2
Shanghai	2	2	2	2
Jiangsu	2	2	2	2
Shandong	2	2	2	2
Zhejiang	2	2	2	2
Anhui	2	2	2	2
Fujian	2	2	2	2
Henan	2	2	2	2
Hubei	2	2	2	2
Hunan	2	2	2	2
Jiangxi	2	2	2	1
Guangdong	2	2	2	2
Guangxi	2	2	2	2
Hainan	2	2	2	2
Sichuan	2	2	2	1
Chongqing	2	2	2	2
Guizhou	2	2	2	2
Yunnan	1	2	2	2
Xizang	2	3	3	2
Shaanxi	2	2	2	2
Gansu	2	2	2	2
Qinghai	2	2	2	2
Ningxia	2	2	2	2
Xinjiang	2	4	4	3
Total	61	65	65	62

Note and Source: CC = Central Committee. Cheng Li, "The Local Factor in China's Intra-Party Democracy," in *Democratization in China, Korea, and Southeast Asia: Local and National Perspectives*, ed. Kate Zhou, Shelley Rigger, and Lynn White (London: Routledge, 2014), 92.

PSC, but representatives from inland provinces command a majority in the Central Committee when an election is held.

"More Candidates than Seats" Elections

The CCP has incorporated some new election methods to choose the members of the Central Committee and other high-ranking leaders. As discussed in chapter 1, since the 13th National Party Congress in 1987, CCP authorities have adopted a multicandidate election process known as a "more candidates than seats election" (差额选举, *cha'e xuanju*) to select Central Committee members. For example, if the CCP Central Organization Department plans to have a 350-member Central Committee, it may place 370 names on the ballot. The twenty candidates who receive the fewest votes on the ballot are eliminated.

At the election for full members of the 18th Central Committee in 2012, for example, over 2,200 congressional delegates chose 205 full members from the 224 candidates on the ballot (9.3 percent were eliminated). Similarly, they elected 171 alternate members from a candidate pool of 190 (11.1 percent were eliminated).[17] In fact, the percentage of eliminated candidates gradually increased over the last decade from 5.1 percent for full members and 5.7 percent for alternate members at the 16th Central Committee to 8.3 percent for full members and 9.6 percent for alternate members at the 17th Central Committee.[18]

The delegates to the party congresses have often used this limited mechanism of "intraparty democracy" (党内民主, *dangnei minzhu*) to block princelings and other candidates favored by top leaders. For example, since the 1990s, Jiang Zemin has promoted many of his protégés, especially those from Shanghai (the so-called Shanghai Gang), to important leadership positions in Beijing and elsewhere. To counter the growing power of Jiang's Shanghai Gang, delegates elsewhere often voted against his protégés for membership on the Central Committee. The leaders who received the fewest number of votes for alternate membership on the Central Committee in the past four party congresses were, respectively, princeling Xi Jinping on the 15th Central Committee in 1997, You Xigui (Jiang's bodyguard) on the 16th Central Committee in 2002, Jia Ting'an (Jiang's *mishu*) on the 17th Central Committee in 2007, and princeling Li Xiaopeng (former premier Li Peng's son) on the 18th Central Committee in 2012.

Candidates who were eliminated at the 18th National Party Congress election included prominent figures such as the minister of Commerce, Chen Deming (a protégé of Jiang's widely believed to be considered for a seat in the 18th Politburo), Shanghai executive vice-mayor Yang Xiong (another protégé of Jiang's who was later appointed to serve as Shanghai mayor even though he failed to obtain an alternate seat on the 18th Central Committee), and the minister of Supervision (the body that monitors government officials), Ma Wen (a protégé of Wen Jiabao's and one of the most influential female leaders in the country). Notably, the governor of the People's Bank, Zhou Xiaochuan, the minister of Finance, Xie Xuren, the minister of the National Development and Reform Commission, Zhang Ping, and the deputy chief of the General Staff in the PLA, Zhang Qinsheng, were not elected to the 18th Central Committee.

Secret Ballot Voting to Decide Major Personnel Matters

Full party committees, with the attendance of at least two-thirds of the members at higher levels of leadership, "vote on a secret ballot" (票决制, *piaojuezhi*) to determine the party secretaries and deputy party secretaries for the lower-level party committees.[19] In general, major personnel and policy decisions are now often decided by votes in various committees rather than solely by the committee's party secretary. This practice has been used primarily at the provincial and municipal levels of party standing committees, reinforcing the decisionmaking procedures of collective leadership.

"Law of Avoidance" in Selecting Top Local Leaders

The Chinese authorities now require that provincial party secretaries, secretaries of the discipline inspection commissions, heads of the organization department, and police chiefs be nonnative outsiders who have transferred from another province or from the central administration.[20] Among the thirty-one current provincial party secretaries, only two (the Shanghai party secretary, Han Zheng, and the Shandong party secretary, Jiang Yikang) work in the province or city in which they were born. However, Jiang left Shandong in 1985 and subsequently worked in Beijing and Chongqing for twenty-three years before returning to become party secretary of Shandong.

Without exception, all secretaries of the provincial discipline inspection commissions work in provinces other than their birthplaces. Among the governors and mayors, only five were born in the province or city where they now serve (Zhang Qingwei of Hebei, Buxiaolin of Neimenggu, Li Qiang of Zhejiang, Chen Wu of Guangxi, Losang Jamcan of Tibet). CCP regulations generally prohibit natives from serving as full governors, mayors, and county chiefs in their birthplaces. Consequently, over the past decade, fewer top provincial leaders have served in their home provinces and cities. By contrast, in 2006, fourteen governors and mayors (45.2 percent) and eleven secretaries of the provincial discipline inspection commissions (35.5 percent) served in their places of birth.[21] But a large number of deputy party secretaries, deputy governors, deputy mayors, and deputy county chiefs serve in their native birthplaces. This is particularly the case in lower levels of leadership.

A recent case study conducted in Xinye County in Henan Province by a doctoral student in sociology at Peking University shows that the county has a total of 1,013 officials at the deputy section level (副科级, *fukeji*) or above.[22] Yet, there are 161 "political families" in the county, including 21 families that have five or more members working as officials and 140 families that have two to five officials. This case illustrates the prevalence of nepotism in elite formation at the lower levels of leadership in the country. Apparently, the regulations and norms of elite recruitment and promotion can be quite different at various levels of leadership.

All of the institutional regulations and norms outlined above have generated a fluidity of membership in the CCP's most crucial (and high level) leadership bodies. Consequently, no individual, faction, institution, or region can dominate the power structure. These developments have reinforced the norm of checks and balances in the Chinese collective leadership and have influenced elite behaviors. Rather than relying entirely on mentor-protégé ties and political connections, leaders must now pay more attention to the establishment of their legitimacy through institutional channels.

POLITICAL NATURE OF THE CHINESE COMMUNIST PARTY ELITE GENERATIONS

The leadership transition at the 18th National Party Congress was supposed to be a generational change of the top leadership. The fourth generation of leaders, who were mostly born in the 1940s and completed their college education prior to the Cultural Revolution, were to hand the reins of power over to the fifth generation of leaders, who were mostly born in the 1950s and lived their formative years during the Cultural Revolution. In China, as in other countries, the concept and definition of elite generations can be quite imprecise and highly political. As some scholars in generational studies have observed, it is difficult to define "where one generation begins and another ends."[23] Membership of a certain generation is often determined through a combination of birth year, shared major life experience and memories, and collective sociopolitical attitudes within peer groups.

Political generations in the PRC have often been based on the distinct collective political experience of the elite. Several examples of political generations include the Long March generation (the first generation), the Anti-Japanese War generation (the second generation), and the Socialist Transformation generation (the third generation).[24] These categories have largely been driven by political considerations of major players such as Deng Xiaoping and Jiang Zemin. It was Deng who initiated these generational terms during his meeting with other top leaders after the Tiananmen crackdown. As a participant in the Long March, Deng is not a natural member of the Anti-Japanese generation of his protégés, Zhao Ziyang and Hu Yaobang. By identifying himself as the "core" of the second generation and Jiang as the "core" of the third generation, Deng hoped to foster smoother political succession in the wake of the failed ascensions of Hu and Zhao, his previously anointed successors. Jiang was more than ready to use generational identity to consolidate his political legitimacy as heir to Deng. During the mid-1990s, when Deng's health deteriorated, Jiang frequently referred to this categorization to secure his position as the "core" of the third generation.[25]

Both the fourth and fifth generations of Chinese leaders can be regarded as members of the Cultural Revolution generation. Fourth-generation leaders Hu Jintao and Wen Jiabao and fifth-generation leaders Xi Jinping and Li Keqiang had their most important formative experiences during the Cultural Revolution.[26] However, the party's informal subdivision within the Cultural Revolution generation has extended the rule of political leaders who experienced their most formative years in the earlier half of that turbulent decade. This indicates that the boundaries of political elite generations are highly political and often subject to change.

The political nature of the concept of China's elite generations is also evident in the changes of top leadership that occurred at the 18th National Party Congress. Xi Jinping and Li Keqiang were the youngest members of the PSC formed in 2007 and retained that distinction as members of the PSC selected at the 18th Party Congress five years later. Xi and Li are the only two leaders in the new PSC who were born in the 1950s. They are now surrounded by five new members of the 18th PSC who are only three to five years younger than the outgoing leaders of the fourth generation, Hu Jintao and Wen Jiabao. The average age of 18th PSC members is 63.4, which is older than the average age (62.3) of 17th PSC members during their time in office (see table 3-6).

Table 3-6 also shows that the average age of the 18th Politburo (61.2) is slightly younger than that of the previous Politburo (61.8). However, the average age of the 18th Secretariat (61.9) is more than five years older than that of the previous Secretariat (56.8). The average age of members of the Secretariat being higher than that of members of the Politburo (which oversees the Secretariat) represents a shift in the rational "echelon structure" of the top leadership organs, which has generally been consistent over the past three decades, as indicated in table 3-6.

The average age of the entire 18th Central Committee (56.1) is also higher than that of the previous three Central Committees (see table 3-7). Fifty-two full and alternate members of the 18th Central Committee are younger than

TABLE 3-6. Average Age of the Core Leadership Groups of the Chinese Communist Party, 12th–18th Central Committees

Central Committee	Year held	PSC	Politburo	Secretariat
12th	1982	73.8	71.8	63.7
13th	1987	63.6	64	56.2
14th	1992	63.4	61.9	59.3
15th	1997	65.1	62.9	62.9
16th	2002	62	60.4	59.4
17th	2007	62.3	61.8	56.8
18th	2012	63.4	61.2	61.9

Note and Source: PSC = Politburo Standing Committee. Cheng Li and Lynn White, "The Sixteenth Central Committee of the Chinese Communist Party: Hu Gets What?," *Asian Survey*, vol. 43, no. 4 (July/August 2003): 566. The data on the 17th and 18th Central Committees were calculated by the author.

fifty, in contrast to seventy-two under that age on the 16th Central Committee (see figure 3-3).[27] The number of officials younger than forty-five has fallen to only four on the 18th Central Committee, from fifteen on the 16th Central Committee and twenty-one on the 15th Central Committee.[28] Currently, the youngest full member is Lu Hao (governor of Heilongjiang), born in 1967. The youngest alternate member is Liu Jian, who was born in 1970 and currently serves as party secretary of Hami Prefecture in Xinjiang.

Nevertheless, figure 3-3 shows that on the 18th Central Committee, an overwhelming majority of members—272 full and alternate (72.4 percent)—were born in the 1950s and thus belong to the fifth generation. In comparison, thirty-three members (8.8 percent) were born in the late 1940s and seventy members (18.5 percent) were born in the 1960s. One member (the aforementioned Liu Jian) was born in the 1970s, accounting for only 0.3 percent. Despite the prominence of members born in the 1950s, some relatively young leaders, such as Supreme People's Court president Zhou Qiang (born 1960) and Hebei governor Zhang Qingwei (1961), served as full members on the 16th Central Committee in 2002.

The rather sharp narrowing of age cohorts and the incomplete nature of generational transition at top levels of the party reveal the vicious struggle for power at the 18th Party Congress. This intense elite competition reflects the strong desire of many senior leaders to stay in power, even if their victory comes at the expense of the party's ability to bolster its legitimacy by presenting to the country a fresh leadership team for the next decade. As a result of this desire, many younger-generation leaders are not allowed to

TABLE 3-7. Average Age of 8th–18th Central Committee Members

Central Committee	Year held	Average age	DA/DY
8th	1956	56.4	
9th	1969	59	+0.20
10th	1973	62	+0.75
11th	1977	64.6	+0.65
12th	1982	62	−0.52
13th	1987	55.2	−1.36
14th	1992	56.3	+0.22
15th	1997	55.9	−0.08
16th	2002	55.4	−0.10
17th	2007	55.3	−0.02
18th	2012	56.1	+0.16

Notes and Source: DA = difference of age; DY = difference of year. Cheng Li and Lynn White, "The Sixteenth Central Committee of the Chinese Communist Party: Hu Gets What?," *Asian Survey,* vol. 43, no. 4 (July/August 2003): 566. The data on the 17th Central Committee are based on Zhang Shenggeng, *Shiliuda dao shibada de Zhongguo* [China from the 16th Party Congress to the 18th Party Congress] (Beijing: Renmin chubanshe, 2012). The data on the 18th Central Committee are based on Chang Hong and Liu Rong, "Shuzi shibada" [Statistics of the 18th Party Congress], *People's Daily Online,* November 16, 2012.

enter the Central Committee, known as the "first rung on the ladder of top leadership"—a factor that will likely give rise to greater political anxiety and resentment in the upcoming generation of elites.

Because of age limits, five of the seven members of the PSC will retire at the 19th National Party Congress in 2017. In a sense, the leadership change at the 18th National Party Congress is a prelude to a full-fledged generational transition that will occur at the 19th National Party Congress. It seems as though the next round of competition for seats on the PSC will begin much earlier than expected. Arguably, it has already begun, as will be discussed further in the last two chapters of this volume.

Despite the rationality of the mandatory retirement age, such a mechanism may have side effects. Term and age limits have forced many capable leaders in good health to step down in their late fifties. Some of them have made a career change to pursue business activities (下海, *xiahai*) after retirement, and some have seized the opportunity to use political power for corrupt dealings or other malfeasance (known in China as "the age fifty-nine phenomenon"). As a result of the strict implementation of institutional regulations and norms over the past two decades, the number of retired leaders

FIGURE 3-3. Members of the 18th Central Committee, by Year of Birth

Number of members

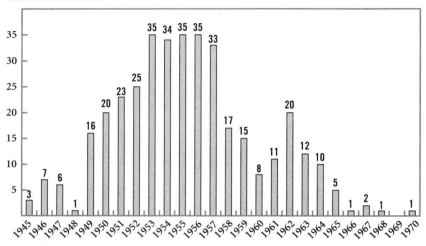

Source: Author's database.

has increased substantially. Many of these former officials have become important political forces in their own right. However, unless CCP authorities adopt more nuanced election mechanisms for the selection of senior leaders, governance issues—such as age discrimination in leadership and the potential for retired officials to challenge top leaders' nepotism and favoritism—will likely become more acute.

DEMOGRAPHIC CHARACTERISTICS

As in many parts of the world, elite distribution in terms of gender, ethnicity, and geography is an important issue. This study of Chinese political elites, especially the 376 members of the 18th Central Committee, provides much empirical data on the subject. This will help assess the composition of Chinese elites—not only from a historical perspective but also through cross-country analysis.

Gender

Since the founding of the PRC in 1949, and especially during the Cultural Revolution, Chinese authorities have often trumpeted the CCP's attention to women's issues. However, women's representation in the party leadership has often been negligible. Except in 1973 and 1977, women have never made up more than 10 percent of the total Central Committee full membership

TABLE 3-8. Female Representation on the Central Committee, 1956–2012

Central Committee	Year	Full members		Alternate members		Total	
		No.	%	No.	%	No.	%
8th	1956	4	4.0	3	4	7	4.0
9th	1969	13	7.6	10	9.1	23	8.0
10th	1973	20	10.2	17	13.7	37	11.5
11th	1977	14	6.9	24	18.1	38	11.4
12th	1982	11	5.2	13	9.4	24	6.9
13th	1987	10	5.7	12	10.9	22	7.7
14th	1992	12	6.3	12	9.2	24	7.5
15th	1997	8	4.1	17	11.3	25	7.3
16th	2002	5	2.5	22	13.9	27	7.6
17th	2007	13	6.4	24	14.4	37	10.0
18th	2012	10	4.9	23	13.5	33	8.8

Source: Cheng Li and Lynn White, "The Sixteenth Central Committee of the Chinese Communist Party: Hu Gets What?," *Asian Survey*, vol. 43, no. 4 (July/August 2003): 570. The data on the 17th and 18th Central Committees were calculated by the author.

(see table 3-8). Only a handful of female leaders have ever been in the Politburo or Secretariat. Most were wives of top leaders, such as Jiang Qing (Mao's wife), Ye Qun (Lin Biao's), and Deng Yingchao (Zhou Enlai's), or symbolic model workers such as Wu Guixian and Hao Jianxiu during the Cultural Revolution. It is therefore encouraging that on the current Central Committee, for the first time since the end of the Cultural Revolution, two women (the vice-premier, Liu Yandong, and the director of the Central United Front Work Department, Sun Chunlan) serve on the Politburo. It should be noted, however, that following the 1997 National Party Congress, no woman has held a seat in the Secretariat, and throughout CCP history, no woman has ever served on the PSC. In recent years much discussion in China has revolved around the need to have a woman serve on the nation's highest decisionmaking body.[29]

Female representation decreased from 10 percent on the 17th Central Committee to 8.8 percent on the 18th Central Committee. The decrease in female full members was even more significant: from thirteen (6.4 percent) on the 17th Central Committee to ten (4.9 percent) on the current Central Committee. Most female leaders usually serve as vice-ministers, deputy provincial party secretaries, or vice-governors. Among the current party secretaries of the fifteen subprovincial cities (副省级市, *fushengjishi*), there is only one woman, Huang Lixin, who serves as party secretary of Nanjing.[30]

Among the current twenty-five ministers, only two are women: the minister of Justice, Wu Aiying, and the minister of the National Health and Family Planning Commission, Li Bin. In 2003, when the 10th NPC selected cabinet members of the State Council, all twenty-nine full ministers were men.[31] Today, the vice-premier, Liu Yandong, is the only woman on the ten-member executive committee of the State Council.

At present, out of China's thirty-one provincial-level administrations, no woman serves as provincial or municipal party secretary. Only two women serve as governor (Buxiaolin, the governor of Neimenggu and Liu Hui, the governor of Ningxia). In addition to the aforementioned four female full Central Committee members (Liu Yandong, Sun Chunlan, Wu Aiying, and Li Bin), the other six women on the current Central Committee are the chair of the China Federation of Supply and Marketing Cooperatives, Wang Xia; the vice-chair of the NPC, Shen Yueyue; the first secretary of the All China Women's Federation, Song Xiuyan; the secretary of the China Federation of Literature, Zhao Shi; the deputy procurator of the Supreme People's Procuratorate, Hu Zejun; and the chair of the All China Writers Association, Tie Ning. Some of these leadership posts are mainly ceremonial.

Before the National Party Congresses, the CCP Central Organization Department often convenes a special meeting to encourage the promotion of women leaders. The department typically proposes that there be at least one or two women on the Politburo and that the number of female ministers on the State Council increase.[32] The Central Organization Department has also required lower levels of leadership to make a greater effort at recruiting female cadres. According to an official report, the percentage of women in the CCP overall increased from 16 percent in 1997 to 18 percent in 2002, while the percentage of female cadres increased from 34 to 38 percent, and the portion of women who served as county, prefecture, or province leaders rose from 7.7 to 9 percent during the same period.[33] On the eve of the 18th National Party Congress, the percentage of women in the CCP was 23.8, and the percentage of female cadres on party committees at the provincial, municipal, and county levels had increased from the previous National Party Congress by 12.1 percent, 3.3 percent, and 12.2 percent, respectively.[34] Female officials made up 23 percent of the total delegates in the 18th National Party Congress, which was 2.9 percent higher than the proportion of female delegates in the 17th National Party Congress.[35]

These generally low percentages may rise in the future, as the number of college-educated women in China continues to increase rapidly. The percentage of female university students grew from 24 percent in 1978 to 34 percent in 1990, and from 38 percent in 1998 to 49.7 percent in 2010.[36] At the postgraduate level, the portion of women increased from 10 percent in 1980 to 23 percent in 1990 and then to 50.4 percent in 2010.[37] In 2010, female students accounted for 35.5 percent of the Ph.D. candidates in the country.[38] As overseas universities tend to admit applicants on a gender-blind basis, a large number of PRC women are now also receiving education abroad (chapter 4 will provide more empirical data on this topic). According to a Chinese official source, females accounted for 58 percent of China's foreign-educated returnees.[39]

Some of these well-educated women have entered the field of public administration and joined the CCP leadership at various levels. According to a survey released by the CCP Central Organization Department, 59 percent of female leaders at all levels of China's party and government are college-educated—3 percent higher than the same figure when assessing all leaders.[40] An "open recruitment examination" (公开招考, *gongkai zhaokao*) in 2001 for deputy bureau chief posts in Beijing resulted in the selection of 30 leaders from 581 candidates. Four-fifths of those selected had postgraduate education, and three-tenths were women.[41] In a country where educational credentials are highly prized in elite recruitment, the growing ranks of female students with an advanced degree may eventually contribute to an increase in female representation in party and government leadership. But for now, the CCP national and provincial leadership posts remain male dominated, and there is no foreseeable strong opposition to this trend.

Ethnicity

As for the ethnic composition of the CCP leadership, recent uprisings across the Tibetan region of China, as well as terrorist attacks in some PRC cities by Uighur separatists seeking independence for Xinjiang, have highlighted the challenges that the CCP faces in governing a Han-dominated but multiethnic China. How China handles the "ethnicity issue" will be a crucial factor in maintaining social stability. Top leaders in China have long recognized the value of ethnic diversity among the party-state elites, both for party propaganda purposes as well as for convincing minorities that the current system offers opportunities for their career advancement. But the party has also maintained a firm grip on power in minority-dominated political units by appointing ethnic Hans to the most important positions in those regions.

Minority leaders, however, are relatively well represented in the government. The party has used legislation to promote ethnic minority officials. In 2002, for example, China's NPC revised the Law of Ethnic Minority Autonomous Areas of the People's Republic of China.[42] The revised law now specifies that the top post of the local government in all ethnic minority autonomous areas should be held by a leader who hails from the same ethnic group as the majority of the citizens in that area. China has 155 ethnic minority autonomous areas, including 5 provincial-level regions, 30 prefectures, and 120 counties. According to one official Chinese source, currently *all* the heads of the local government for these areas are non-Han ethnic minority leaders.[43] A Chinese official source released just before the 18th National Party Congress reported that the percentage of ethnic minorities at the provincial, municipal, and county levels of the party leadership increased in the five years preceding the Congress by 8.7 percent, 11.5 percent, and 7.3 percent, respectively.[44]

Indeed, all of the governors of China's five provincial-level ethnic minority autonomous regions (the Tibetan Autonomous Region, the Xinjiang Uighur Autonomous Region, the Inner Mongolia Autonomous Region, the Ningxia Hui Autonomous Region, and the Guangxi Zhuang Autonomous Region) have ethnic minority backgrounds. Despite this apparent diversity, a Han Chinese cadre occupies the most important leadership position (party secretary) in each of these five provincial-level ethnic minority autonomous regions.

The 18th Central Committee has thirty-nine full and alternate ethnic minority members (10.3 percent), one fewer than the previous 17th Central Committee (see table 3-9). Ethnic minority leaders have occupied more seats on this important decisionmaking body in the reform era than during the Mao era. In the six congresses held since 1987, ethnic minority members usually constitute about 10 to 11 percent of the membership, which is almost double the average from the five previous congresses. The 18th Central Committee includes five Huis, five Tibetans, four Mongolians, and four Zhuangs (see table 3-10). No ethnic minority leader serves in the 18th Politburo. The previous Politburo had one minority member, Vice-Premier Hui Liangyu, a Chinese Muslim (Hui). One ethnic minority leader, State Councilor Yang Jing, a Mongolian, serves in the 18th Secretariat. Ten ethnic minority leaders are full members of the 18th Central Committee (4.9 percent); by contrast fifteen ethnic minority leaders were full members of the 17th (7.4 percent). The decrease in ethnic minority cadres in CCP senior leadership seems to reaffirm the observation that competition for high offices became so intense at the 18th National Party Congress that the rival political camps decided to buttress their own faction rather than push for ethnic diversity.

Birthplace

It has been widely noted that certain geographic regions in China produce a disproportionate amount of the country's leaders.[45] Representatives from eastern provinces, especially Jiangsu and Shandong, have been extremely important in the composition of China's post-Mao elite.[46] On the 15th Central Committee, 45 percent of full members were born in eastern China.[47] During the early 1990s, Shandong natives alone accounted for over one-quarter of

TABLE 3-9. National Minority Representation on the Central Committee, 1956–2012

Central Committee	Year	No. of minorities/total	%
8th	1956	9/170	5.2
9th	1969	13/279	4.6
10th	1973	18/319	5.6
11th	1977	19/333	5.7
12th	1982	31/348	8.0
13th	1987	32/285	11.2
14th	1992	33/319	10.3
15th	1997	38/344	11.0
16th	2002	35/356	9.8
17th	2007	40/371	10.7
18th	2012	39/376	10.3

Source: Cheng Li and Lynn White, "The Sixteenth Central Committee of the Chinese Communist Party: Hu Gets What?," *Asian Survey*, vol. 43, no. 4 (July/August 2003): 570. The data on the 17th and 18th Central Committees were calculated by the author.

China's senior military officers.[48] At the State Council that was formed at the 1998 NPC, sixteen of twenty-nine ministers (55 percent) were natives of eastern provinces, including eight born in Jiangsu.[49] Among the twenty-eight ministers selected at the 2013 NPC, eight were born in Jiangsu (28.6 percent) and five (17.9 percent) were from Shanghai.

Table 3-11 shows the birthplaces of the full members of the 18th Central Committee by province, as compared with the previous two CCs. The eastern provinces, especially Shandong and Jiangsu, continue to be overrepresented in national leadership, despite the significant increase in officials from Hebei and Henan. Individuals from eastern China have constituted on average 40 percent of the full membership in the three most recent CCs.

In the 18th Politburo, the eastern region is also overrepresented. Representatives from the east occupy fifteen of twenty-five seats, or 60 percent of the Politburo membership. This is a significant increase from the 17th Politburo (eleven members, or 44 percent of the total). The current Politburo members from eastern provinces include four natives of Shandong (Wang Huning, Sun Zhengcai, Li Jianguo, and Xu Qiliang), four natives of Jiangsu (Liu Yandong, Li Yuanchao, Meng Jianzhu, and Guo Jinlong), and three natives of Anhui (Li Keqiang, Wang Yang, and Liu Qibao). In contrast, no current Politburo members were born in the southern or southwestern regions, which together make up more than a quarter of China's population.

TABLE 3-10. Distribution of Ethnicities of Members of the 18th Central Committee

Ethnicity	No.	%
Han	337	89.6
Hui	5	1.3
Tibetan	5	1.3
Mongolian	4	1.1
Zhuang	4	1.1
Bai	3	0.8
Korean	2	0.5
Li	2	0.5
Manchu	2	0.5
Miao	2	0.5
Tujia	2	0.5
Uyghur	2	0.5
Buyi	1	0.3
Dai	1	0.3
Kazakh	1	0.3
She	1	0.3
Yao	1	0.3
Yi	1	0.3
Total	376	100.0

Source: Author's database.

A total of only five full members or fewer from the southern region have served on any of the three Central Committees over the past fifteen years, even though that region contributes approximately 12.7 percent of the country's GDP. This is approximately only 2 percent of the average full Central Committee membership during this period (see table 3-11). Most astonishingly, there is not a single Cantonese representative—a native of China's richest and most populous province—among the 205 full members of the 18th Central Committee. Two Cantonese members became alternates at the 18th Central Committee: then Guangzhou party secretary Wan Qingliang and Inner Mongolia executive vice-governor Pan Yiyang. In 2014 Wan and Pan were both purged on corruption charges.

It is also interesting to note that no Sichuan native serves as a full member on the 18th Central Committee (the six in the group for Sichuan/Chongqing in table 3-11 are actually all natives of Chongqing). This is in contrast to the early years of the reform era when the country was largely controlled by

TABLE 3-11. Distribution of Birthplaces by Province of Central Committee Full Members, 1992, 2002, and 2012

Native province	14th CC (1992) (N = 189)		16th CC (2002) (N = 198)		18th CC (2012) (N = 205)		Population, 2010 (%)	GDP, 2012 (%)
	No.	%	No.	%	No.	%		
North	38	20.0	21	10.5	47	22.9	12.30	14.81
Beijing	4	2.1	6	3.0	10	4.9	1.46	3.09
Tianjin	4	2.1	3	1.5	3	1.5	0.97	2.24
Hebei	22	11.6	8	4.0	21	10.2	5.36	4.61
Shanxi	7	3.7	3	1.5	9	4.9	2.67	2.10
Neimenggu	1	0.5	1	0.5	4	2.0	1.84	2.77
Northeast	17	9.0	21	10.6	24	11.7	8.18	8.74
Liaoning	7	3.7	9	4.6	14	6.8	3.27	4.30
Jilin	8	4.2	7	3.5	5	2.4	2.05	2.07
Heilongjiang	2	1.1	5	2.5	5	2.4	2.86	2.37
East	74	39.1	75	37.9	85	42.0	25.99	33.96
Shanghai	3	1.6	6	3.0	5	2.4	1.72	3.49
Jiangsu	25	13.2	29	14.7	19	9.3	5.87	9.38
Shandong	24	12.7	17	8.6	31	15.1	7.15	8.68
Zhejiang	14	7.4	13	6.6	14	6.8	4.06	6.0
Anhui	5	2.6	8	4.0	12	5.9	4.44	2.99
Fujian	2	1.1	2	1.0	5	2.4	2.75	3.42
Taiwan	1	0.5	–	–	–	–	–	–

(continued)

TABLE 3-11. (*continued*)

Native province	14th CC (1992) (N=189)		16th CC (2002) (N=198)		18th CC (2012) (N=205)		Population, 2010 (%)	GDP, 2012 (%)
	No.	%	No.	%	No.	%		
Central	25	13.2	26	13.1	28	13.7	19.52	15.12
Henan	5	2.6	8	4.0	11	5.4	7.02	5.17
Hubei	10	5.3	6	3.0	5	2.4	4.27	3.86
Hunan	8	4.2	10	5.1	7	3.4	4.90	3.84
Jiangxi	2	1.1	2	1.0	5	2.4	3.33	2.25
South	5	2.6	5	2.5	2	1.0	11.88	12.66
Guangdong	4	2.1	4	2.0	0	0	7.79	9.90
Guangxi	1	0.5	1	0.5	2	1.0	3.44	2.26
Hainan	0	0	0	0	0	0	0.65	0.5
Southwest	13	6.9	13	6.5	7	3.4	14.39	9.22
Sichuan (inc. Chongqing)	9	4.8	7	3.5	6	2.9	8.15	6.13
Guizhou	1	0.5	2	1.0	0	0	2.59	1.18
Yunnan	2	1.1	2	1.0	0	0	3.43	1.79
Xizang (Tibet)	1	0.5	2	1.0	1	0.5	0.22	0.12

Northwest	6	3.2	15	7.6	11	5.4	7.22	5.52
Shaanxi	3	1.6	9	4.6	5	2.4	2.79	2.51
Gansu	1	0.5	2	1.0	2	1.0	1.91	0.98
Qinghai	0	0	1	0.5	1	0.5	0.42	0.33
Ningxia	0	0	1	0.5	2	1.0	0.47	0.4
Xinjiang	2	1.1	2	1.0	1	0.5	1.63	1.30
Unknown	8.7		11.1				0.52*	
Total	189	100.0	198	100.0	205	100.0	100.0	100.0

Note and Source: * Refers to those who are registered in the People's Liberation Army and whose area of residence is difficult to determine. For the 14th Central Committee, see *China News Analysis*, nos. 1588–89 (July 1–15, 1997): 15–20; Zang Xiaowei, "The Fourteenth Central Committee of the CCP, Technocracy or Political Technocracy," *Asian Survey*, vol 33, no. 8 (August 1993): 795. Cheng Li and Lynn White, "The Sixteenth Central Committee of the Chinese Communist Party: Hu Gets What?," *Asian Survey*, vol. 43, no. 4 (July/August 2003): 571. The data on the 18th Central Committee are updated by the author. For populations, see National Bureau of Statistics of China, *Diliuci quanguo renkou pucha gongbao* [The Sixth National Census of the Population of the People's Republic of China], 2011. For GDP data, see "2012 Nian gesheng, qu, shi GDP da paiming," *People's Daily Online* (http://finance.people.com.cn/GB/8215/356561/359047) and "Weihe gedi GDP xiang jia dayu quanguo zhi he?" *People's Daily Online* (http://finance.people.com.cn/n/2012/1023/c70846-1935514l.html).

"strongmen" from Guangdong (for example, Ye Jianying) and Sichuan (for example, Deng Xiaoping, Yang Shangkun, and Yang Baibing). They appointed many of their fellow natives, including Xie Fei from Guangdong and Xiao Yang from Sichuan, to important positions.[50] As with other sources of elite divisions, birthplace ties can be instrumental both in factional conflict and political compromise. During the Jiang Zemin era, for example, leaders from Shanghai and its neighboring areas dominated the PSC, which, on the one hand, contributed to elite cohesion but, on the other, caused tremendous factional tensions. This will be further discussed in chapter 7.

CHANNELS OF BUREAUCRATIC ADVANCEMENT AND STRONG PROVINCIAL REPRESENTATION

During the reform era, there have been five primary (and non-mutually exclusive) channels through which CCP officials have obtained Central Committee membership and been recruited to national leadership positions: the central party apparatus, ministerial leadership, the military, flagship state-owned enterprises, and provincial administrations. Table 3-12 shows the bureaucratic affiliations of the full members on the 14th, the 16th, and the 18th CCs within these five groupings. While some bureaucratic channels have largely retained the same level of representation in the Central Committee over the past few decades, the distribution for others has fluctuated.

Central Party Apparatchiks

Party apparatchiks are officials who control some of the most crucial functional domains of the Chinese political system: leadership operation (daily administration), organization (personnel), and ideology (propaganda). As discussed in chapter 2, the general office and the four central departments of the CCP all play very important roles. The representation of party apparatchiks in the Central Committee has increased slightly over the past two decades (see table 3-12). At the time of the 18th National Party Congress, Xi Jinping, Liu Yunshan, and Wang Huning—as officials that ascended to power within the central party channel—all made significant strides in their leadership careers. Also, all of the directors and executive deputy directors of the general office and the four central departments obtained full membership seats on the 18th Central Committee, as did top officials in other important party organizations like the Central Commission for Discipline Inspection, the Politics and Law Committee, the Central Policy Research Office, and the Central Party School.

TABLE 3-12. Principal Bureaucratic Affiliations of Central Committee Full Members, 1992, 2002, and 2012

Principal current position	14th CC (1992) (N=189)		16th CC (2002) (N=198)		18th CC (2012) (N=205)	
	No.	%	No.	%	No.	%
Central party organization	17	9.0	20	10.1	25	12.2
Central government organization	75	39.7	58	29.3	59	28.8
Military	43	22.8	43	21.7	41	20.0
SOEs and financial firms (and also mass/social organizations)	5	2.6	12	6.1	17	8.3
Provincial administration	49	25.9	65	32.8	63	30.7
Total	189	100.0	198	100.0	205	100.0

Note and Source: Percentages do not add up to 100 because of rounding. Author's database.

Central Government Leaders

The group that is recruited through the central government not only consists of leaders from the State Council but also a few CCP officials in the NPC and the CPPCC. Even though all except two of China's cabinet members serve on the 18th Central Committee as full members, the central government's representation in the Central Committee has decreased by more than 10 percent over the past two decades (see tables 3-4 and 3-12). Ministers of the State Council still constitute an important pool of candidates for Politburo membership, because government experience often enhances an official's credentials for a top leadership position in the party. Regarding the CCP elite recruitment, however, the background of serving as a cabinet minister is not nearly as important as the work experience gained by serving as a provincial party secretary.

Some cabinet ministers later served as provincial party secretaries, through which they were finally able to obtain seats in the Politburo. Several officials entered the 18th PSC and the Politburo via that route. They include Yu Zhengsheng (first as minister of Construction and then as party secretary of Hubei and Shanghai), Sun Zhengcai (first as minister of Agriculture and then as party secretary of Jilin and Chongqing), Wang Yang (first as executive deputy secretary-general of the State Council and then as party secretary of Chongqing and Guangdong), Liu Qibao (first as deputy secretary-general of the State Council and then as party secretary of Guangxi and Sichuan), and Zhang Chunxian (first as minister of Transportation and then as party secretary of Hunan and Xinjiang). Several PSC and Politburo members also have served as vice-ministers in the central government and then as provincial party secretaries. Examples include Zhang Dejiang (vice-minister of Civil Affairs and party secretary of Jilin, Zhejiang, Guangdong, and Chongqing) and Li Yuanchao (vice-minister of Culture and party secretary of Jiangsu). Only one Politburo member advanced his career the other way around: Meng Jianzhu served first as party secretary of Jiangxi and then as minister of Public Security.

Military Officers

Military representation in the top party leadership has largely remained constant. Of the full members of the three CCs represented in table 3-12, an average of 21.5 percent are affiliated with the military. Military representation in the Politburo has also been consistently low over the past two decades (about 8 percent). It should be noted, however, that military representation in the Politburo in the early decades of the PRC history was remarkably high (40 percent in 1969 and 31 percent in 1977).[51] At present, no marshal or general (like past strongmen Lin Biao, Xu Shiyou, Ye Jianying, Yang Baibing, or Zhang Zhen) is among the highest-ranking party officials. Of the ten generals who served on the Central Military Commission of the 17th Central Committee, seven retired in 2012, including two vice-chairs. These two Central Military Commission vice-chairs, Xu Caihou and Guo Boxiong, were recently arrested on corruption charges, with Xu dying of cancer shortly thereafter.

SOE Executives

Representatives of state-owned enterprises and financial firms constitute a relatively new group in the Central Committee. This sector's representation in the full membership has gradually increased from five (2.6 percent) on the 14th Central Committee, to twelve (6.1 percent) on the 16th Central Committee, and to seventeen (8.3 percent) on the 18th Central Committee (see table 3-12).[52] The group of business leaders serving on the 18th Central Committee includes the chair of the Aviation Industry Corporation of China, Lin Zuoming, former chair of the Bank of China Xiao Gang, former president of the China Aerospace Science and Technology Corporation Ma Xingrui, and former president of China North Industrial Group Corporation Zhang Guoqing. Some of them later moved to different leadership positions after the 18th National Party Congress. Xiao Gang later served as chair of the China Security Regulatory Commission before being fired in early 2016; Ma Xingrui and Zhang Guoqing serve as deputy party secretaries of

Guangdong and Chongqing, respectively. Like cabinet ministers who strive to bolster their leadership credentials by serving as provincial party secretaries, many promising politicians who started in SOEs are also interested in gaining provincial leadership experience. Several current provincial chiefs advanced their careers primarily by working in SOEs, including Hebei governor Zhang Qingwei, Shandong governor Guo Shuqing, Shanxi governor Li Xiaopeng, and Shanghai mayor Yang Xiong. With the exception of Yang, all of the aforementioned officials serve on the 18th Central Committee.

It may still take some time for business leaders to become central players in Chinese elite politics. Yet, the number of current and former managers of China's large SOEs who have already served on the Central Committee continues to grow; some of these leaders have already been appointed to the Politburo and PSC. Zhang Chunxian served as general manager of China National Packaging and Food Machinery Corporation in the early 1990s, and Wang Qishan worked in the financial sector for many years earlier in his career and served as president of the China Construction Bank in the mid-1990s. The emergence of business elites as political rising stars in the CCP leadership presents the country with both challenges and opportunities in solving many of the emerging SOE-related problems, such as industrial overcapacity, the real estate bubble, shadow banking, local debts, and state monopoly and interest group interference. The interchange between the business and the political elites will have immense consequences for the CCP leadership as a whole (as further discussed in chapter 5). In an increasingly globalized economy, the varied backgrounds and work experience of the business elites will contribute to the development of a more diversified leadership and pluralistic decisionmaking process.

Provincial Leaders

Since the reform era, provincial leadership posts have become the most important stepping-stones to national leadership positions. This should not come as a surprise, as the provinces and municipalities that these leaders have governed are large socioeconomic entities themselves. It is often said that a province is to China what a country is to Europe. In population size Chinese provinces are much bigger than most countries in the European Union. China's three largest provinces—Guangdong, Shandong, and Henan—are more populous than Germany, the most populous country in the European Union. According to the 2010 PRC census, Guangdong Province has a population of 104,300,000.[53] Besides China, only ten other countries in the world have a population over 100 million.[54]

The economic outputs of these provinces are substantial. The total GDP of Guangdong Province has already surpassed that of Singapore and Taiwan.

TABLE 3-13. Type of Membership of Provincial Chiefs on the 18th Central Committee, as of January 2014

Current membership	Number of leaders	%
Politburo member	6	9.7
Full member	46	74.2
Alternate member	8	12.9
None of the above	2	3.2
Total	62	100.0

Source: Author's database.

In 2010 the Guangdong governor claimed that the province's GDP would surpass that of South Korea within a decade.[55] China's provincial chiefs, like top leaders in European nations and East Asian neighbors, are constantly concerned about regional economic development and have coped with daunting challenges such as unemployment, distributive justice, social stability, health care, and the welfare needs of those in their jurisdictions.

Table 3-13 shows that in early 2014, among the sixty-two provincial chiefs, fifty-two (84 percent) served on the 18th Central Committee as full members; among those on the Central Committee, six served as Politburo members. At that time, only two provincial chiefs, Shanghai mayor Yang Xiong and Sichuan governor Wei Hong, were not on the 18th Central Committee.

Former top party leader Jiang Zemin was promoted to general secretary of the CCP in 1989 from the post of party secretary of Shanghai, where he was credited with the "successful" handling of the prodemocracy demonstrations. Hu Jintao had served as party secretary in both Guizhou and Tibet before being promoted to the PSC in 1992. Among the current top leaders, Xi Jinping and Li Keqiang served as party secretaries in two provincial administrations (Xi in Zhejiang and Shanghai; Li in Henan and Liaoning). As discussed earlier, Zhang Dejiang has uncommonly broad provincial leadership experience: he has served as provincial chief in four different provinces. In the 18th PSC, six of the seven members had previously served as provincial chiefs. The sole exception is executive member of the Secretariat Liu Yunshan. He has never been a provincial chief, but he did serve as deputy party secretary of Neimenggu.

As shown in figure 3-4, there has been an increase over the past twenty years in the number of Politburo members with experience in provincial administrations. Beginning at 50 percent in 1992, the portion of Politburo members who were previously provincial chiefs rose to 59 percent in 1997, 67 percent in 2002, and then to 76 percent in both 2007 and 2012. More than

FIGURE 3-4. Politburo Members with Provincial Chief Experience at the 14th–18th Central Committees

Percent with experience

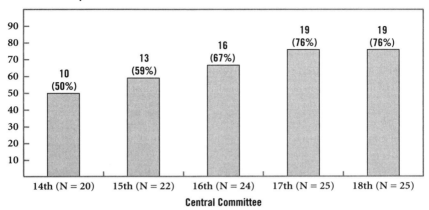

Source: Author's database.

three-quarters of the current Politburo members (nineteen out of twenty-five members) have previously served as provincial chief. Additionally, all seven members of the Secretariat have had substantial experience in provincial leadership. Five of them previously served as provincial party secretaries— Liu Qibao (Guangxi and Sichuan), Zhao Leji (Qinghai and Shaanxi), Li Zhanshu (Guizhou), Du Qinglin (Hainan and Sichuan), and Zhao Hongzhu (Zhejiang)—and one, Yang Jing (Neimenggu), served as a governor. The fact that China's top leaders have substantial experience at the provincial level speaks to the importance of this path to reaching the pinnacle of power. Since two members of both the 17th and 18th Politburos traditionally come from the military, the percentage of civilian top officials with provincial leadership experience is even higher.

In what appears to be a new political norm, the party secretaries of the four major cities under the direct leadership of the central government— Beijing, Tianjin, Shanghai, and Chongqing—are now guaranteed seats in the Politburo. This also seems to be the case for Guangdong Province, where three PSC or Politburo members (Zhang Dejiang, Wang Yang, and Hu Chunhua) have either concurrently or previously served as party bosses. Two other PSC members, Wang Qishan and Zhang Gaoli, also served as vice-governors of Guangdong Province earlier in their careers. Also, since 2002, the party secretary of Xinjiang has also concurrently held a seat in the Politburo, as in the cases of Wang Lequan and now Zhang Chunxian.

A majority (52 percent) of the current Politburo members obtained their seats on the 18th Central Committee in 2012 while serving as party secretaries in provincial administrations, which is a much higher rate than the corresponding 22.7 percent in the 14th Politburo, 20.8 percent in the 15th Politburo, and 40 percent in both the 16th and 17th Politburos (see table 3-14). The current heavy representation of provincial chiefs in the top echelons of the party reflects the growing power and influence of leading politicians in the country's thirty-one provincial administrations, especially those of major cities and large provinces like Guangdong.

One of the most important measures employed by the central leadership to control the localities is the use of promotions as an incentive to ensure that provincial chiefs remain loyal to Beijing rather than develop closer allegiances with the provinces and cities in which they serve. But top national leaders also need to build political capital and tap resources through close ties with some of the most important regions in the country. Deng Xiaoping's strong ties with Sichuan, Jiang Zemin's power base in Shanghai, and Xi Jinping's Shaanxi ties are all good examples. The significance of serving as provincial party secretary, especially in major provinces and cities, in competing for top national leadership positions further enhances the political weight of local power in present-day China.

SUMMARY

The norms underlying Chinese elite politics have gradually become more institutionalized throughout the reform era. The most important and impressive aspect of this political institutionalization has been the fluidity of elite circulation. The seven CCP Central Committees formed between 1982 and 2012 have averaged a turnover rate of 62.3 percent. An overwhelming majority of members during that period—about 98 percent of both the 15th Central Committee in 1997 and the 18th Central Committee in 2012—served on the Central Committee for fifteen years or less. All of the important leadership bodies formed at the 18th National Party Congress consist primarily of newly promoted first-timers, who constitute 71 percent of the PSC, 86 percent of the Secretariat, 77 percent of the Central Commission for Discipline Inspection, and 70 percent of the military members of the Central Military Commission. Similarly emblematic of this trend, the average tenures of provincial party chiefs have decreased substantially over the last three decades.

The large scale and scope of the leadership change and its consistency over time reflect the effective implementation of regulations and norms, including mandatory retirement ages and term limits. Most important, despite political infighting, scandals, and manipulation on the part of some heavyweight party leaders, China has witnessed peaceful, orderly, and institutionalized transitions of power twice in its recent past: from Jiang Zemin's third

TABLE 3-14. Principal Bureaucratic Affiliation of Politburo Members before Politburo Tenure, 14th–18th Party Congresses

Principal current position	14th Politburo		15th Politburo		16th Politburo		17th Politburo		18th Politburo	
	No.	%	No.	%	No.	%	No.	%	No.	%
Central party organization	5	22.7	6	25.0	8	32.0	6	24.0	4	16.0
Central government organization	10	45.5	11	45.8	5	20.0	7	28.0	6	24.0
Military	2	9.1	2	8.3	2	8.0	2	8.0	2	8.0
Provincial administration	5	22.7	5	20.8	10	40.0	10	40.0	13	52.0
Total	22	100.0	24	99.9	25	100.0	25	100.0	25	100.0

Note and Source: Percentages do not add up to 100 because of rounding. Cheng Li and Lynn White, "The Sixteenth Central Committee of the Chinese Communist Party: Hu Gets What?," *Asian Survey*, vol. 43, no. 4 (July/August 2003): 574. The data on the 17th and 18th Central Committees were calculated by the author.

generation of leaders to Hu Jintao's fourth generation at the 16th National Party Congress in 2002, and then to Xi Jinping's fifth generation at the 18th National Party Congress in 2012. China's political succession process—including its newly developed experimental elections—is still deficient in some areas and subject to failure. It remains to be seen whether CCP's elites will continue to adopt more ambitious and wide-ranging reforms to make the succession process more transparent and open for all social classes in the years to come.

The demographics of elite representation, which is a central concern in any political system, has also become a pronounced challenge in China during the reform era. A review of the composition of the Central Committees over the past three decades shows the continued dominance of male, Han Chinese officials. Although two women now serve on the Politburo for the first time since the Cultural Revolution, the overall share of women holding full membership in the Central Committee decreased markedly after the last leadership transition. However, there is reason to expect that the gender ratios of China's top leadership may become more balanced in the future. Women now make up nearly half of all college students, and academic credentials are highly prized in elite recruitment.

Ethnic minorities have increased their representation at lower levels of the leadership, in part thanks to revised laws requiring local governments in ethnic minority regions to fill top posts with candidates from the ethnic group that makes up the majority in that region. Even so, ethnic minorities have experienced a setback in their representation at the higher rung of the Central Committee, probably due to heightened competition between top political factions.

In terms of the birthplaces of leaders, the coastal region, particularly the eastern provinces of Shandong and Jiangsu, are overrepresented, as evidenced by the Central Committee and Politburo formed at the 18th National Party Congress. In sharp contrast, not a single native of Guangdong or Sichuan serves among the 205 full members of the 18th Central Committee, despite these being China's two most-populous provinces, not to mention that in the early years of the reform era the country was largely controlled by Cantonese or Sichuanese "strongmen." This shift seems to suggest that region-based favoritism plays a crucial role in Chinese elite formation and is therefore liable to change drastically depending on which top leader, faction, or coalition holds power.

As with previous leadership transitions, the 18th National Party Congress was supposed to represent a generational change, but instead this already imprecise concept has become murkier still. In particular, the narrowing of the age gap between the previous and current leadership cohorts suggests that many top leaders wish to remain in power, thereby reducing openings in the Central Committee for rising leaders of younger generations. On the flip side, in June 2015 the Politburo passed a new regulation that reinforces age requirements and allows cadres in both the civilian and military leadership to be removed for reasons other than age, perhaps suggesting that turnover will continue at a high rate, or even accelerate.

In addition to bolstering its legitimacy by regularly turning over a fresh crop of leaders, the central leadership has used promotions and other incentives to better control the localities, ensuring that provincial chiefs remain loyal to Beijing rather than to the provinces or cities in which they serve. But due to the growing importance of local interests and the increasing use of formal, transparent election methods, provincial chiefs have often found that maintaining strong ties with their geographical power bases is essential to the advancement of their political careers in Beijing. Consequently, some heavyweight politicians in both the national and provincial leadership have increasingly associated themselves with a particular province, city, or region.

But overall, the fact that the career prospects of provincial leaders depend on their superiors in Beijing also illustrates the enormous power the central party-state wields over local administrations in China's exceedingly hierarchical, authoritarian system. Indeed, promotions at the topmost levels of the party and the government continue to be carefully orchestrated processes. The Central Committee, for instance, has not seen much improvement in the realms of open politicking and overt electoral competition among candidates over the past two decades, except for the notable cases of Bo Xilai and Wang Yang in the lead-up to the 2012 Party Congress. Furthermore, the party has never used a multiple-candidate election to help select the Politburo or the PSC.

Meanwhile, the even distribution of membership seats across provinces and regions in the Central Committee has become increasingly institutionalized. Although provincial and municipal leaders who had experience working in economically advanced coastal provinces occupy more seats in the 18th Politburo, their advantage is far less evident on the Central Committee. Since the 15th Central Committee, a strong political norm in Chinese elite recruitment has been that almost every provincial-level administration holds two full membership seats on the committee, usually occupied by the party secretary and the governor or mayor.

Having a large portion of leaders with experience as provincial chiefs (76 percent in the 18th Politburo and 86 percent in the PSC) reinforces the growing power and influence of the politicians who run the country's thirty-one provincial administrative units. This new emphasis has raised the stocks of regional and local posts, which aspiring national leaders now view as crucial stepping-stones. Cooperation and tension between local leaders, and between the center and provinces, merit further attention, particularly for their impact on elite selection, the rise of new elite groups like business executives, and other trends in elite representation.

These developments have the potential to impart a much-needed sense of legitimacy to China's ruling elite and further change the game of elite competition. Elite transformation in China is an ongoing process. The scale, scope, and speed of changes in leadership are significant. But what has made this transformation most remarkable is that it is not just generational, but also professional. Understandably, the educational attributes of Chinese political elites have also undergone profound changes. This important development will be the focus of the next chapter.

CHAPTER 4

Education

Advanced Degrees, Part-Time Training, and Study Abroad

The philosophy of the schoolroom in one generation will be the philosophy of government in the next.
—ABRAHAM LINCOLN

People are favored by nature, birth, or fortune; they outdo others by talent, effort, and luck.
—THOMAS GRIFFITH

Education has long been perceived as the primary means of preparing political elites to take their place of prominence in Chinese society. Confucius asserted that the principal purpose of education was "to study to become an official" (学而优则士, *xueeryou zeshi*). Various Chinese regimes have made great efforts to legitimize certain types of knowledge they view as essential and have designated certain elites to embody that knowledge. During their rule over China, gentry-scholars, nationalist reformers, bureaucratic compradors, peasants-turned-warlords, and communist ideologues have each claimed that their particular expertise was most valuable.[1]

He Huaihong, a distinguished philosopher and historian at Peking University, summarizes well the age-old emphasis on elite recruitment and the enduring search for effective mechanism and applicable selection criteria in the Middle Kingdom.

> Throughout its history, China has never escaped its concentration on the political or the concentration of values and resources in the state and its officials: not during the hereditary hierarchical society before the Spring and Autumn period or the hierarchical selection society

that came after it; not during the "wandering masters" period of the Warring States period; not during the violent upheavals of the twentieth century. But there have been changes in the criteria by which the ruling classes have been selected: sometimes by birth, sometimes by level of education, sometimes by some special ability or virtue, sometimes by loyalty to an institution or even an individual. Sometimes it was no more than Machiavellian politics.[2]

He Huaihong's study of the circulation of Chinese elites over time, or what he calls the dynamics between "the hereditary society" and "the selection society" (Chinese meritocracy), provides a new perspective on China's 3,000-year history, pointing to the development of a unique sociopolitical structure—a system that holds cultural and intellectual elites in high regard and promotes social mobility and equal opportunity.[3] While the system was certainly not free from the abuse of power, nepotism, factionalism, and corruption, traditional China did establish a "true selection society in which learning was for the purpose of advancement."[4] As He Huaihong has documented, in China's long history, the door to membership in the ruling class was often open to those of humble origins. In the Ming Dynasty, for example, over 50 percent of officials (进士, *jinshi*) were born into three-generation nonofficial families.[5]

This historical fact, as He Huaihong argues, shows that China was a part of the global march toward modernity in Tocqueville's terms, as it reflects a shift toward equality and political institutionalization in elite selection.[6] Other distinguished historians, most notably the late Ho Ping'ti, share a similar view.[7] Arguably, Deng Xiaoping's initiatives to institutionalize the leadership turnover and promote fast elite circulation in the CCP since the 1980s reflect a return to such a long-standing Chinese political tradition.

A review of anti-intellectualism in elite recruitment in the Mao era, followed by an overview of the rapid increase in education levels among members of the Central Committee since the Deng era, highlights the growing number of Chinese leaders who have advanced degrees. The current leadership, in particular, consists of a large number of post–Cultural Revolution graduates from "the famous class of 1982," officials who obtained party school training and the prevalence of part-time academic degrees, especially postgraduate degrees, and leaders who had study abroad experiences, often as visiting scholars. All of these features in the education profiles of the CCP leadership will likely have profound implications for the country's governance in the years to come.

"Red versus Expert": The Contrast between the Mao and Deng Eras

In the Mao era, especially during the Cultural Revolution, the causes of violent social conflict and elite power struggle could be at least partially attributed to differences in the educational and professional backgrounds of the participants.[8] In the first three decades of the PRC, elite recruitment was primarily based on family background (the preferred categories being peasant or worker), ideological loyalty, and political activism, rather than on education credentials and managerial skills. This politicized pattern of recruitment was expressed in the dichotomous notion of "red versus expert" (红与专, *hongyuzhuan*); it was better to be "red" than an "expert." The "reds" were cadres who had advanced their careers on the strength of their revolutionary pedigree and ideological purity, while "experts" were members of the political or intellectual elite who had distinguished themselves by their education credentials and technical skills.

When it came to elite recruitment and promotion, reds almost always prevailed over experts in the Mao era. Thus, from 1949 through the early 1980s, the education levels of party cadres and members were extremely low. In 1955, for example, only 5 percent of national leaders had a junior high school education or above.[9] This poor level of academic attainment is not surprising, given that the CCP rose to power as a military organization, and its leaders were mostly soldiers, peasants, and members of the urban lower class.[10] Beginning in the early decades of the last century, a large number of poor peasants (many who were illiterate) flocked to the Red Army and the CCP. Some of these revolutionaries later made up a large segment of the PRC's ruling elite, holding a majority of leadership posts above the county level following the CCP victory in 1949. In 1963, of the 2,074 county and municipal party secretaries, 98 percent participated in the anti-Japanese and civil wars.[11] In 1985, only 4 percent of CCP members were educated beyond the high school level, and a majority of the CCP members (52.2 percent) had either received only a primary school education or were illiterate.[12] These numbers reflect the low value placed on educational accomplishments and technical know-how within the CCP before the reform era.

When Deng Xiaoping returned to the top leadership in 1978, one of his most significant initiatives was in the area of education. Deng reopened the Chinese higher education system to recruit students based on their academic capabilities, and almost simultaneously, began to send students and scholars to study in the West. Over the decade that followed, Deng and the party establishment recruited college-educated elites—most of them engineers-turned-technocrats—into various levels of leadership in an attempt to promote China's economic development, bolster the CCP's legitimacy and generate greater support for its rule (discussed in detail in chapter 5).

During the past three decades, the education level of CCP members has increased significantly, as technical expertise, instead of ideological purity, has become much more valued in the recruitment process. According to the official data released by the CCP Central Organization Department, the percentage of cadres who were college graduates increased from 5.8 percent in 1951 to 18.8 percent in 1981 and reached 37.6 percent in 1994.[13] In 1998, among the sixty-one million CCP members, eleven million were college graduates (17.8 percent); by mid-2013, about thirty-four million CCP members (40 percent) held at least a two-year college degree.[14]

The elite transformation that has taken place in China during the post-Mao era is part of a wider and more fundamental political change: a shift from revolution to reform in Chinese society. Turning away from the emphasis on class struggle and ideological indoctrination that characterized previous decades, Deng and his technocratic protégés stressed fast-paced economic and technological development at home, along with increased economic integration with the outside world. The educational and professional characteristics of the Chinese ruling elite are therefore important indicators of the political and socioeconomic changes in the country.

As one's academic background has played an increasingly crucial role in determining the social mobility of elites, changes in preference for certain credentials have frequently reflected new trends in social values and the policy orientation of the country.[15] Variations in education (academic fields, length of college programs, part-time versus full-time student status, and domestic versus overseas study) have distinguished some elites, and have sometimes even become new sources of elite contention. An analysis of the educational experience of today's Central Committee members, and ministerial and provincial frontrunners (elites who will become tomorrow's national decisionmakers) offers a better understanding of some of the defining characteristics of the current and future leaders of China.

ADVANCED DEGREES: EDUCATIONAL ATTAINMENT
OF CENTRAL COMMITEE MEMBERS

Not only has the percentage of current college-educated national and provincial leaders reached a zenith in the history of the PRC, but many of them now also hold advanced postgraduate degrees. Growth in the number of national-level party leaders who have pursued higher education has been particularly dramatic. In 1982 not a single member of the Politburo had completed a university education. In contrast, on the 18th Central Committee, formed in 2012, all twenty-five members of the Politburo had college-level

TABLE 4-1. Percentage of College-Educated Members on the 8th–18th Central Committees

	Year held	%
8th	1956	44.3
9th	1969	23.8
10th	1973	NA
11th	1977	25.7
12th	1982	55.4
13th	1987	73.3
14th	1992	83.7
15th	1997	92.4
16th	2002	98.6
17th	2007	98.7
18th	2012	99.2

Note and Source: Cheng Li and Lynn White, "The Sixteenth Central Committee of the Chinese Communist Party: Hu Gets What?," *Asian Survey*, vol. 43, no. 4 (July/August 2003): 578. The data on the 17th and 18th Central Committees were calculated by the author.

degrees: nineteen from civilian universities, one from a military academy, and five from the Central Party School (CPS). Similarly, the percentage of college-educated top provincial leaders increased from 20 percent in 1982 to a full 100 percent in 2010.[16]

Table 4-1 shows that 99.2 percent of the full and alternate members of the 18th Central Committee attended college, including two- to three-year junior colleges (大专, *dazhuan*). The proportion of Central Committee leaders with a college education has now reached an all-time high; only three members of the 18th Central Committee did not graduate from college, including the chair of the China Writers Association, Tie Ning, and deputy political commissar of the People's Armed Police, Zhang Ruiqing. The portion of delegates to the National Party Congress that are college educated has also increased significantly over the past two decades: from 71 percent in 1992 to 84 percent in 1997, followed by 92 percent in 2002, 93 percent in 2007, and 94 percent in 2012.[17]

Figure 4-1 displays the year that leaders were awarded their undergraduate degrees. Among the 306 leaders with such information identified in their biographies, none graduated before 1966—the beginning of the Cultural Revolution. Eleven leaders (3.6 percent) started college before the Cultural Revolution and graduated during the early years, before political turmoil interrupted the education system. They include senior leaders such as the CPPCC chair Yu Zhengsheng, who studied at the Harbin Institute of

FIGURE 4-1. Undergraduate Graduation Years of the Members of the 18th Central Committee, including the Famous "Class of 1982"

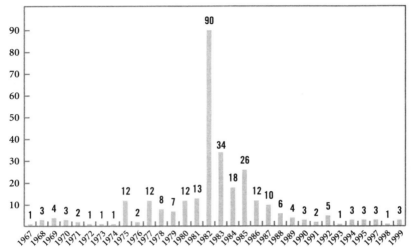

Source: Author's database.

Military Engineering from 1963 to 1968; the executive vice-premier Zhang Gaoli, who studied economic planning and statistics at Xiamen University from 1964 to 1970; the National People's Congress vice-chair Li Jianguo, who majored in Chinese at Shandong University from 1964 to 1969; the vice-premier Liu Yandong, who majored in chemical engineering at Tsinghua University from 1965 to 1970; and the navy commander Wu Shengli, who studied at the PLA Institute of Surveying and Mapping from 1964 to 1967.

In 1970 the Maoists decided to recruit a small number of students (approximately 40,000) for China's colleges, which had not accepted any students since 1966. From 1970 to 1976, a total of 940,000 enrolled, and they were known as members of the worker-peasant-soldier student class (工农兵学员, *gongnongbing xueyuan*).[18] Forty-six leaders of the 18th Central Committee (15 percent) enrolled in college during this time. All of the recruited students were, as their name suggests, young workers, peasants, and soldiers rather than high school graduates. Admission was thus based on class and political background instead of educational credentials.

A significant portion of these worker-peasant-soldier students were sent-down youths (插队知青, *chadui zhiqing*)—urban teenagers who were sent to live and work in the rural areas during the Cultural Revolution. While a large number of teenagers, regardless of class or family background, participated in the movement, sent-down youths from cadre family backgrounds usually returned to the cities earlier than those from other backgrounds. Many youths from cadre families attended college as worker-peasant-soldier students. According to a Chinese documentary film on the sent-down youths in Yunnan, approximately 99 percent of those from cadre family backgrounds returned to their native urban centers within the first few years, while a majority of those from noncadre backgrounds remained in the countryside for approximately a decade.[19]

Three current PSC members were sent-down youths and later went to college as worker-peasant-soldier students: Xi Jinping, who attended Tsinghua University as a chemical engineering major from 1975 to 1979; National People's Congress chair Zhang Dejiang, who studied Korean language at Yanbian University from 1972 to 1975; and CCDI secretary Wang Qishan, who studied history at China's Northwestern University from 1973 to 1976. This group also includes the director of the Taiwan Affairs Office of the State Council Zhang Zhijun, who studied at Peking University from 1971 to 1973; commissar of the PLA National Defense University Liu Yazhou, who studied English at Wuhan University from 1972 to 1975; and former navy commissar Liu Xiaojiang, who majored in Chinese at Heilongjiang University from 1972 to 1975. While they attended college as worker-peasant-soldier students, most of the leaders mentioned above are scions of prominent official families. In general, worker-peasant-soldier students spent most of their college years participating in political campaigns and ideological indoctrination, rather than academic studies.

The Famous Class of 1982 and Li Keqiang's College Years

Almost three-quarters of the members (225 out of 306, or 73.5 percent) of the 18th Central Committee completed their undergraduate education in the 1980s. The graduates of "the famous class of 1982" alone account for 29 percent of total membership (see figure 4-1). This was the first class that entered college through the national examination system for higher education admission, which was established in 1977, after the Cultural Revolution, as a result of Deng Xiaoping's policy initiatives. A total of 11.6 million people, ranging from their late teens to early thirties, registered for the exams in late 1977 and 1978. The admission rate was less than 3 percent for both classes, with only approximately 401,000 students being admitted.[20] The ratio of those who took the exam to those who were admitted in 1977 was 29:1; the ratio was roughly 2:1 in 2007.[21] In March and October of 1978 two classes matriculated in several hundred universities across China. This "famous class of 1982" (both groups graduated in 1982) was extraordinary not only for having passed one of the most competitive college entrance exams in PRC history but also because, as Chinese dissident intellectual Wang Juntao (who himself was a member of the class of 1982) has argued, "this unique group would most likely produce the country's most talented scientists, writers, philosophers, educators, artists as well as statesmen in the future."[22]

Because the college admission process was no longer based on political loyalty, ideological purity, or a revolutionary or proletarian class status, the class of 1982 became known for having diverse family backgrounds and remarkable life experiences from the Cultural Revolution, especially from the sent-down youth movement. At the same time, the years after the Cultural Revolution constituted an exciting period marked by the Chinese youth enthusiastically absorbing Western liberal ideas.[23] Shaped by the extraordinary experiences of the Cultural Revolution, the class of 1982 has prominent representation in the CCP national leadership, including premier Li Keqiang, who majored in law at Peking University; PRC vice-president Li Yuanchao, who first attended the Shanghai Normal University as a worker-peasant-soldier student from 1972 to 1974 and then reenrolled as an undergraduate majoring in mathematics at Fudan University from 1978 to 1982; office director of the Central Leading Group for Financial and Economic Work Liu He, who studied economics at Renmin University; president of the Supreme People's Court Zhou Qiang, who studied law at the Southwestern University of Political Science and Law; minister of Finance Lou Jiwei, who studied computer science at Tsinghua University; Hubei party secretary Li Hongzhong, who studied history at Jilin University; Shandong governor Guo Shuqing, who studied philosophy at Nankai University; and minister of Education Yuan Guiren, who graduated from the Department of Philosophy at Beijing Normal University.

Li Keqiang's college experience and the divergent career paths of some of Li's classmates are particularly revealing. Li enrolled in the Department of Law at Peking University, one of the most prestigious universities in the country, from 1978 to 1982. During his college years, academic and interdisciplinary study groups were very popular at Peking University, which had a long tradition in liberal arts education. Li actively participated in various public lectures and debates organized by these groups and studied under Professor Gong Xiangrui, a well-known British-educated expert on Western political and administrative systems.[24] Li was particularly interested in the subjects of foreign constitutional law and comparative government.[25] Li and his classmates translated important legal works from English to Chinese, including Lord Denning's *The Due Process of Law* and *A History of the British Constitution*.[26] Li also published articles on legal development, scientific management, rural economic reform, poverty alleviation, and other socioeconomic issues of the day.

While Li Keqiang pursued his political career through the leadership of the Chinese Communist Youth League (first at Peking University and then in the national offices), his classmates at the university followed drastically different professional career paths, some becoming leading legal professionals, public intellectuals, independent scholars, political dissidents, religious leaders, and human rights lawyers and activists. Notable examples include He Qinhua, who later served as president of East China University of Political Science and Law; Tao Jingzhou, who later went to France, where he attended the Université Paris 1 Panthéon-Sorbonne and practiced in the law firm Jeantet & Associés, and is now a famous lawyer in the field of international commercial arbitration; Wang Shaoguang, who went to the United States to study politics at Cornell University and then taught at Yale University for many years and is now professor of political science at the Chinese University of Hong Kong; Hu Ping, chief editor of the overseas dissident journal *Beijing Spring*; Zhang Wei, another political dissident who taught economics at the University of Cambridge and now works as executive director of the Hong Kong conglomerate Mingly; Yuan Zhiming, who later became a priest and the founder of the San Francisco–based China Soul for Christ Foundation; and the aforementioned Wang Juntao, who was jailed for many years because of his involvement in the 1989 Tiananmen protest movement before he went to the United States to study politics at Columbia University, and is now chairman of the California-based Chinese Constitutionalist Association.

In the early 1980s Li Keqiang and his classmates at Peking University were all enthusiastically engaged in school and local elections. For example, in 1980 Hu Ping was elected to serve as a delegate to the People's Congress of Haidian District (where Peking University is located) in what was later called the "first free local election" in the PRC. Zhang Wei was the first elected president of the Student Union (学生会, *xueshenghui*) of Peking University after the Cultural Revolution. Li Keqiang was elected head of the Executive Committee of the Student Assembly (常代会, *changdaihui*), which supervised and oversaw the work of the Student Union.[27] The principle of fair and open elections was a central political issue at Peking University in the early 1980s. Although according to Wang Juntao some conservative CCP leaders at the time wanted to crack down on campus elections, Li Keqiang was supportive of open elections.[28]

Li is the only student in his law school class who became a fifth-generation political leader. Understanding his college experience, which was both similar to and different from that of his peers, is important to analyzing Li's background, personality, and worldview. All of these examples not only underscore the liberal academic atmosphere at the time when the class of 1982 was attending college but also the remarkable diversity of the students—both in precollege experiences and in postgraduate careers.

Twenty-four members (7.8 percent) of the 18th Central Committee graduated from college in the 1990s. Most of them studied part-time at the CPS and the National Defense University. They include PSC member Liu Yunshan, who attended the correspondence undergraduate program in party-state management at the CPS from 1989 to 1992; vice-premier Wang Yang, who attended the same correspondence program at the CPS in the same years; Ningxia party secretary Li Jianhua, who majored in political economy at the CPS from 1991 to 1993; and air force commander Ma Xiaotian, who attended a part-time program in the Military Basic Systems Department at the NDU from 1993 to 1994.

Higher Degrees

Table 4-2 shows the highest level of educational attainment of the members of the 18th Central Committee. Two hundred ninety-one (77.4 percent) have obtained advanced degrees, and among them, ninety-nine (26.3 percent) have received doctoral degrees. By comparison, on the 17th Central Committee, the percentages of members with postgraduate degrees and doctoral degrees were 52.3 percent and 13.2 percent, respectively.[29] This also contrasts sharply with the education levels of fourth-generation leaders, most of whom completed only their undergraduate education as a result of the Cultural Revolution.[30] At the end of 2014, among the sixty-two provincial chiefs, fifty-six (90 percent) had received postgraduate education, and nine of them (14.5 percent) held Ph.D.s.[31]

In the Politburo, advanced postgraduate degrees have prevailed; the number of members with such education credentials has increased from one Politburo member (5 percent) in 1992 to two (8 percent) in 1997, four (16 percent) in 2002, ten (40 percent) in 2007, and finally to sixteen (64 percent) in 2012. Five leaders have attained doctoral degrees: Xi Jinping (law and politics from Tsinghua University in 2002), Li Keqiang (economics from Peking University in 1994), Li Yuanchao (law and politics from the CPS in 1995), Liu Yandong (law and politics from Jilin University in 1998), and Sun Zhengcai (agronomy from China Agricultural University in 1997). All of them pursued their doctoral degrees on a part-time basis.

Table 4-3 shows the graduation year of those Central Committee members who received postgraduate degrees (insofar as information is available). A significant number of leaders (21.6 percent of master's degree holders and 48.8 percent of doctoral degree holders) received their advanced education after 2000, reflecting the fact that most of them attended these programs on a part-time basis well into their careers. For example, the director of State Administration of Press, Publication, Radio, Film, and Television Cai Fuchao received his doctoral degree in journalism from Renmin

TABLE 4-2. Distribution of the Highest Level of Educational Attainment of 18th Central Committee Members

Educational attainment	No.	%
Ph.D.	99	26.3
MBA/MPA/MA/MS	192	51.1
BA/BS	73	19.4
Junior college	9	2.4
High school	3	0.8
Total	376	100.0

Source: Author's database.

TABLE 4-3. Distribution of Advanced Degrees Received by 18th Central Committee Members, by Year

Year	Master's degree		Ph.D. degree	
	No.	%	No.	%
Before 1979	2	0.9		
1980–84	25	11.0	1	1.2
1985–89	45	19.8	16	19.5
1990–94	26	11.5	9	11.0
1995–99	80	35.2	16	19.5
2000–04	35	15.4	25	30.5
2005–09			11	13.4
After 2010	14	6.2	4	4.9
Total	227	100.0	82	100.0

Note and Source: For those who received more than one master's degree, this study only counts the first graduation year. Data from author's database.

University in 2010, and the director of the Organization Department of the Jiangxi Provincial Party Committee Zhao Aiming and Gansu deputy party secretary Ouyang Jian both received their doctoral degrees in management from Tsinghua University as recently as 2011.

PARTY SCHOOL TRAINING AND PART-TIME PROGRAMS

During the reform era, Deng Xiaoping and his successors all called for building "a governing party committed to learning." The leadership has placed much emphasis on midcareer education for party officials. For CCP political elites, especially for those who might not have a solid educational background otherwise, training in the CPS and other executive education programs has become requisite in their career development.

The CPS has a long history. Founded as the Marxist Communism School in Ruijin, Jiangxi Province, in 1933, the school received its current name in 1935 when the Red Army arrived in northern Shaanxi after the Long March. Mao Zedong served as president of the school in 1942. The CPS moved to Beijing after the Communist victory in 1949, but closed during the Cultural Revolution up until its reestablishment in 1977. The school has three departments: the Advanced Studies Department runs programs for cadres at the ministerial-provincial and prefecture-department levels and for city and county party secretaries; the Training Department trains young and middle-age reserve cadres and ethnic minority officials in Xinjiang and Tibet; and the Graduate School offers doctoral and master's degree education and trains faculty from the party school system. Every semester, the CPS trains 2,500 high- and middle-level cadres. By July 2012 the CPS had granted 3,074 advanced degrees through its graduate program.[32]

The large numbers of reserve cadres who have potential for further promotion (as discussed in chapter 2) are the main participants in the party school programs. Consequently, numerous institutions facilitating the education of midcareer CCP leaders have merged and developed over the past three decades. In the 1980s, for example, there were altogether 8,800 party schools and similar cadre-training institutions.[33] Due to many mergers in the 1990s, the total number of schools fell to about 3,000, employing 80,000 full-time staff. At present, the country has a total of 5,000 party schools and similar training institutions that party, government, and state-owned enterprise officials at various levels of leadership can attend.[34] Although to a certain extent the party school system can be seen as a set of educational institutions that run in parallel with normal schools and colleges, the academic requirements of the former are usually less vigorous and the disciplinary concentrations are much narrower (mainly focusing on party affairs and economic management) than the latter.

Each of China's provinces has its own party school and institute of socialism. All ministries of the State Council, all central organs of the CCP Central Committee, and many major companies under the State-owned Assets Supervision and Administration Commission (SASAC) also have their own party schools, cadre training centers, or both.[35]

A variety of other training centers have been established over the last two decades to educate leaders in the party and government. The Central Institute of Socialism, which is run by the CCP Central Committee's United Front Work Department, trains officials who are non-CCP members. In 1994 the Chinese Academy of Governance was established, and some provinces and cities also founded local branches for the purpose of training leaders at various levels of government.

In 2005 three important new executive leadership academies were founded, with locations in Pudong, Jinggangshan, and Yan'an; the following year, the China Business Executive Academy was founded in Dalian. These four academies, along with the aforementioned CPS and the Chinese Academy of Governance, are what the Chinese call "one school and five academies" (一校五院, *yixiao wuyuan*), and they form the most important training grounds for civilian elites.[36] In 2008 alone more than 2,000 county-level party secretaries were enrolled in these six schools for further training.[37] China Executive Leadership Academy at Pudong, for example, ran a total of 1,200 programs and trained about 60,000 participants, including about 1,200 ministerial- and provincial-level leaders and PLA generals, as well as almost 20,000 department- and bureau-level leaders as of June 2012.[38]

In addition, thirteen other leading institutions of higher education have been designated by the Central Organization Department as principal training bases for officials, namely, Tsinghua University, Peking University, Renmin University, Beijing Normal University, Fudan University, Xi'an Jiaotong University, Harbin Institute of Technology, Zhejiang University, Nanjing University, Sichuan University, Nankai University, Wuhan University, and Zhongshan University. Provincial, ministerial, and major state-owned enterprises have also established partnerships with twenty-three other universities for leadership training.

According to a recent study by prominent Chinese political scientist Yu Keping, every year the Central Organization Department is responsible for arranging the executive training of 500 provincial and ministerial leaders, 3,000 prefecture and departmental leaders, 500 municipal and county party secretaries, and 4,000 civil service-clerks.[39] The content of the training is quite broad, including Marxist theory, China's structural reforms, economic growth models, urbanization strategies, democracy and law, ecological civilization, public administration, Internet management, world affairs, crisis management, and public relations. Developing the governing capacity of the CCP, as Yu observes, is the central objective of cadre training.[40]

With its degree programs, the CPS has played a leading role in boosting the educational levels of China's senior leaders. Table 4-4 lists the top ten schools at which the 18th Central Committee members pursued their undergraduate and graduate education. With nineteen graduates, Peking University boasts the most alumni among leaders with an undergraduate degree, including prominent figures such as Li Keqiang, Li Yuanchao, Zhao Leji, Hu Chunhua, Lu Hao, Cai Wu, and Zhang Zhijun. Renmin University ranks second in the total combined number of both undergraduate and postgraduate degrees awarded, notably surpassing both Peking University

TABLE 4-4. Schools at Which Members of the 18th Central Committee Pursued Their Undergraduate and Graduate Studies, Top 10 Schools

Rank	Undergraduate level		Graduate level		Both levels	
	School	No. of graduates	School	No. of graduates	School	No. of graduates
1	Peking University	19	Central Party School	81	Central Party School	94
2	Central Party School	18	Renmin University	17	Renmin University	26
3	Renmin University	14	Jilin University	15	Peking University	25
4	Tsinghua University	11	Tsinghua University	12	Tsinghua University	20
5	National Defense University	11	Chinese Academy of Social Sciences	12	Jilin University	19
6	Jilin University	9	Harbin Institute of Technology	10	Harbin Institute of Technology	14
7	Shandong University	9	Peking University	9	Chinese Academy of Social Sciences	11
8	Fudan University	6	Nankai University	9	National Defense University	10
9	Southwest University of Political Science and Law	5	Fudan University	4	Fudan University	10
10	Harbin Institute of Technology	4	Nanjing University	4	Shandong University	8

Note and Source: For those who attended the same school for both undergraduate and graduate degrees, this study only counts the school once. Data from author's database.

and Tsinghua University. Elites who completed their undergraduate education at Renmin University include Fujian party secretary You Quan and the minister of Agriculture, Han Changfu. Those who received their postgraduate education at Renmin University include the vice-premier Liu Yandong, the vice-premier Ma Kai, the former chair of the China Securities Regulatory Commission Xiao Gang, and the Beijing deputy party secretary Ji Lin. The office director of the Central Leading Group for Financial and Economic Work, Liu He, completed both his undergraduate and graduate studies in economics at Renmin University.

Graduates of Tsinghua University dominated the CCP leadership during the first two decades of the reform era. They include former PSC members Zhu Rongji, Hu Jintao, Song Ping, Yao Yilin, Wu Bangguo, Wu Guanzheng, and Huang Ju and Politburo members Hu Qiaomu, Li Ximing, and Zeng Peiyan.[41] Xi Jinping and several prominent leaders of the 18th Central Committee, such as Liu Yandong and the minister of Finance Lou Jiwei, are graduates of Tsinghua University, along with two former party secretaries of the Tsinghua Party Committee, the executive deputy director of the Central Organization Department Chen Xi and Shaanxi governor Hu Heping, who both serve on the 18th Central Committee as well. However, aside from the leaders mentioned above, overall representation of Tsinghua graduates in the Chinese leadership has declined. Tsinghua seems to have lost its standing as "the cradle of the leaders of the People's Republic" and as the dominant force in political networking.[42]

However, one should not underestimate the continuing strong presence of Tsinghua graduates in various sectors, especially finance and public administration. In 2012 Tsinghua University and the People's Bank of China jointly established the People's Bank of China School of Finance. People's Bank governor Zhou Xiaochuan, an alumnus of Tsinghua University, currently serves as honorary dean, and former bank vice-governor Wu Xiaoling serves as dean. The board of directors includes current People's Bank vice-governor Pan Gongsheng, former bank vice-governor and founding chairman of the China Securities Regulatory Commission Liu Hongru, and former bank vice-governor Du Jinfu. Wu Xiaolin and Du Jinfu were graduates of the People's Bank of China School of Finance, as was People's Bank vice-governor and chair of the Import and Export Bank of China Hu Xiaolian.[43] In addition, the Tsinghua School of Economics and Management and the Tsinghua School of Public Policy and Management offer part-time degree programs that have attracted a number of rising stars in the Chinese leadership. For example, Liaoning party secretary Li Xi attended the master's degree program at the School of Economics and Management from 2008 to 2011, and the executive deputy director of the Central Propaganda Department of the CCP Central Committee Huang Kunming attended the doctoral program at the School of Public Policy and Management from 2005 to 2008.

In general, rather than coming from one particular university, the fifth generation of CCP leadership includes graduates from a wide range of schools. Although graduates of the CPS, Renmin University, Peking University, and Tsinghua University are still relatively well represented in the CCP leadership, the fifth generation in general constitutes a more diverse group in terms of the distribution of schools from which leaders graduated. Due to the varying sociopolitical backgrounds and educational experiences of its members (the worker-peasant-soldier student class versus the famous class of 1982, graduate- versus undergraduate-degree holders, part-time versus full-time program attendees, and so on), the fifth generation does not have the strong factional ties that the Tsinghua clique previously held.[44]

The only exception, however, is the CPS, which has had a disproportionally large number of graduates in top leadership positions. Table 4-4 shows the overrepresentation of leaders who attended the CPS both as undergraduates and graduates. According to Chinese official sources, between 1997 and 2002, nearly 3,000 provincial- and ministerial-level leaders attended training programs at the CPS, the State Administration Institute, and the National Defense University.[45] In Guangxi Province, for example, among the top fifteen leaders (including the party secretary, the governor, and deputies) in 2001, fourteen had attended the CPS.[46] On the 18th Central Committee, ninety-four full and alternate members (25 percent) have attended the CPS for degree programs. The number of CPS attendees far surpasses that of Renmin University (the school with the second-largest representation in the party), which has twenty-six graduates on the 18th Central Committee. In addition, sixty-three full and alternate members (16.8 percent) of the 18th Central Committee participated in year- or month-long training programs at the CPS. Altogether, 41.8 percent of the 18th Central Committee members attended the CPS. Similarly, among the sixty-two provincial chiefs, forty-one (66 percent) went to the CPS.

The CPS offers several full-time degree programs, but due to the leadership responsibilities of the attendees, a majority of its programs are on a part-time or correspondence basis. For instance, a majority of 18th Central Committee members who hold postgraduate degrees earned them through part-time or correspondence programs. Experience at the CPS not only enhances these leaders' education credentials but also facilitates political socialization and networking.[47]

As figure 4-2 shows, more than three-quarters of the postgraduate degree holders (75.9 percent) on the 18th Central Committee obtained academic titles through part-time programs. Many 18th Politburo members pursued postgraduate studies on a part-time basis as well. Among the sixteen current

FIGURE 4-2. Educational Background of Members of the 18th Central Committee: Ratio of Part-Time to Full-Time Study

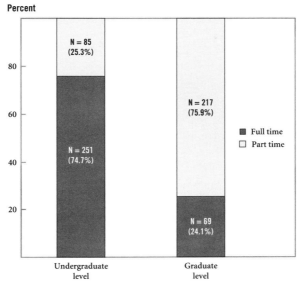

Note and Source: In the 376-member 18th Central Committee, the educational backgrounds of 40 members are not identified. Among the 291 members who received graduate-level education, 5 do not identify whether they did so on a full-time or part-time basis. Xinhua News Agency (www.news.cn/politics/leaders/index.htm). Calculated by author.

Politburo members who have obtained advanced degrees, fourteen (87.5 percent) did so on a part-time basis (see figure 4-3). More astoundingly, a significant number of CCP leaders (25.3 percent of the members of the 18th Central Committee and 32 percent of Politburo members) pursued their undergraduate education on a part-time basis (see figures 4-2 and 4-3). Similarly, forty-eight out of sixty-two (77 percent) provincial chiefs received their highest academic degree through a part-time study program.

It is widely believed in China that many of these part-time degree programs, especially those offered to party officials at the CPS, do not meet high academic standards. These part-time and correspondence programs are criticized for helping political officials "become gilded" (镀金, *dujin*), rather than providing substantive academic training. Some of these part-time academic degrees may turn out to be a political liability. Some critics call this phenomenon of inflated advanced degrees among Chinese officials a sign of "systemic cheating."[48] Wang Yukai, professor in the Chinese Academy of Governance, points out, "When you see these part-time degrees obtained by senior leaders, you cannot rule out the possibility that they are fraudulent."[49]

FIGURE 4-3. Educational Background of Members of the 18th Politburo: Ratio of Part-Time to Full-Time Study

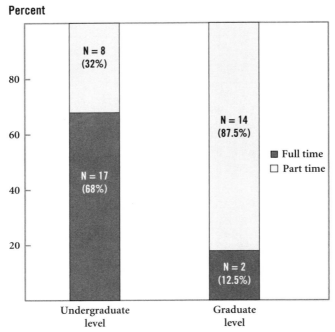

Source: Xinhua News Agency (www.news.cn/politics/leaders/index.htm). Calculated by author.

Zheng Yefu, a professor at Peking University who has studied the inflation of advanced degrees, especially from the CPS, argues that this phenomenon has undermined the political legitimacy of the CCP leadership.[50] His study shows that the number of CCP Central Committee members who have obtained degrees from the CPS has increased drastically—from ten on the 15th Central Committee to nineteen on the 16th Central Committee, sixty on the 17th Central Committee, and ninety-three on the 18th Central Committee.[51] In his view, combating the trend of inflated advanced degrees held by high-ranking officials must involve both academic quality control of these part-time programs and also fundamental changes to the elite selection process. However, all party and government officials at the county level or above are required to attend the cadre training program run by the CPS, executive leadership academies, and other similar institutions, either before their promotion or within a year after their promotion.[52]

Also, it would be inaccurate to conclude that most leaders with college experience have only attended party schools or matriculated on a part-time basis. The discussion earlier in this chapter about the large proportion of the leadership that graduated as part of the famous class of 1982 shows the overall distribution of academic credentials among fifth-generation leaders. Table 4-4 shows that many have also studied at China's elite universities. Among the ninety-nine doctoral degree holders on the 18th Central Committee, one-third attended full-time programs, and most of them completed their education before serving in leadership posts. For example, the president of the Chinese Academy of Sciences, Ba Chunlin, obtained his doctoral degree in chemistry from the Chinese Academy of Sciences in 1985, the executive vice-president of the Chinese Academy of Governance, Ma Jiantang, obtained his doctoral degree from the Chinese Academy of Social Sciences in 1985, former Shenzhen party secretary Wang Rong received his doctoral degree in economic management from the Nanjing Agricultural Institute in 1985, former Liaoning party secretary Wang Min (recently purged) received his doctoral degree in engineering from the Nanjing Aeronautical Institute (now Nanjing University of Aeronautics and Astronautics) in 1986, and Guangdong deputy party secretary Ma Xingrui obtained his doctoral degree in engineering from the Harbin Institute of Technology in 1988.

One factor that has contributed to the strong emphasis on education in the elite selection process of present-day China is the implementation of a civil service-employment and a civil service-exam, both adopted in the reform era. In 1987, at the 13th National Party Congress, the Chinese authorities decided to establish a system of civil service-employment through open competition and national exams. The system was first instituted in 1993 when the Chinese government issued "Provisional Regulations on State Civil Servants."[53] Twelve years later, in 2005, the National People's Congress promulgated the "Civil Service-Law of the People's Republic of China," which stipulated that nonleadership positions of director-level clerks (主任 科员, *zhuren keyuan*) and other equivalent or lower positions should be selected through civil service-exams at the national or provincial level.

At the national level, the civil service-exam is held once a year, usually in the fall, while the provincial-level exam is held once or twice a year. An applicant can apply for both exams but must be a PRC citizen, hold a degree from a two-year college or the equivalent, and be between the ages of eighteen and thirty-five (or forty for an applicant who holds a master's or doctoral degree). Since 2001 the civil service-exam has become institutionalized. The enrollment number has risen dramatically over the years, from about 30,000 in 2001 to 1,410,000 in 2011—a forty-two-fold increase in only a decade.[54] In 2001 the admission rate was 13.7 percent. Eleven years later, in 2011, the rate was 1.2 percent.[55]

This intense competition for employment in public administration reflects the lack of enthusiasm and opportunity in the private sector for young college graduates under the Hu-Wen leadership. For example, in 2010, the State Bureau of Energy Administration received 4,961 applications for a single open position.[56] This situation has led to higher levels of education among office clerks. In recent years, especially after the Xi administration launched the large-scale anticorruption campaign and promoted market reform, enrollment for the civil service-exam began to decline. In 2014, 1,409,000 enrolled for the exam, 115,000 fewer than the previous year. The admission rate in 2014 was 1.6 percent, higher than the 1.3 percent admission rate of 2013.[57] It remains to be seen whether this decline of enrollment for the civil service-exam is a short-term reaction to the ongoing anticorruption campaign or a long-term trend due to more diversified career opportunities. According to Chinese official data released in 2013, about 92 percent of civil service-employees are college graduates, and many of them hold advanced degrees.[58] Civil service-clerks, especially those who work as *mishu* for senior leaders, also provide a pool of future leadership candidates, as will be discussed in chapter 6.

FOREIGN STUDIES

Another important trend in the educational background of Central Committee members is the influx of returnees from overseas study programs during the reform era. The Chinese who studied abroad more than three decades ago, as part of Deng's open-door policy for international educational exchanges, have recently emerged as a distinct elite group. These foreign-educated returnees are known as "sea turtles" in Chinese (海归, *haigui*).[59] The official Chinese definition of a returnee (留学回国人员, *liuxue huiguo renyuan*) is someone who was born in the PRC, studied overseas as a student or visiting scholar for over one year, and then returned to China to work on either a temporary or permanent basis.[60] According to this definition, returnees do not include foreign-born ethnic Chinese or Chinese immigrants to foreign countries who return without having studied abroad. Over the past decade, returnees have increasingly played an important role in virtually all walks of life in China, including in public administration and CCP leadership.

Foreign-educated returnees are a diverse group. They differ in terms of foreign experience, professional expertise, and worldview, as well as in the ways in which they interact with the Chinese party-state system. Most of them work in educational and research institutions or in various industries in the business sector. Some currently serve as advisers to top leaders, and a few hold national leadership positions as ministers in the State Council or as senior officials in the CCP. Some returnees are considered critics or even political dissidents who try to exert their influence on China's domestic and foreign policy discourse primarily through new social media. Several factors have profoundly contributed to this growing influence, namely, the unprecedentedly large foreign study movement and waves of returnees, the collective leadership's need for scholarly input to formulate and justify policies, and the growing importance of think tanks, where returnees often choose to work after their foreign studies.

The Largest Foreign-Study Movement in Chinese History

The first contributing factor is the unprecedented, large-scale study abroad movement initiated by Deng Xiaoping over three decades ago. Between 1978, when Deng first made the landmark decision to send a large number of students and scholars to study abroad, and 2014, approximately 3,518,400 Chinese nationals studied in foreign countries.[61] According to the Chinese official source, by the end of 2014, altogether 1,708,800 Chinese students and scholars remained abroad (among them, 1,088,900 were still attending educational and research programs) and 1,809,600 had returned to work in China.[62] Figure 4-4 provides an overview of the growth of China's study abroad movement from 1978 to 2014, illustrating the exponential increase in recent years. This phenomenon largely reflects the rapid growth of the middle class and the enthusiasm of middle-class families for sending their children to study abroad, especially at a young age.

In the 2005–06 academic year, only 65 Chinese students were enrolled in high schools in the United States. From 2012 to 2013 that number had skyrocketed to 23,795, a 365-fold increase in only seven years.[63] The number of PRC undergraduates enrolled in U.S. colleges increased from 9,309 in 2005–06 to 93,768 in 2012–13.[64] A similar trend can be found among the Chinese students who study in other Western countries. This new wave of younger students studying in the West deserves scholarly attention, as it can have a potentially significant impact in the future on both Chinese sociopolitical life and China's integration with the outside world. Young people in Shanghai, Beijing, and Shenzhen are more similar to their peers in Taipei, Tokyo, Washington, and New York than to their parents. Despite some cultural differences, these young Chinese (who have studied both abroad and at home) and their peers elsewhere share similar lifestyles, cosmopolitan contacts, and sociopolitical aspirations. This will be an important force for change.

Another interesting phenomenon in China's study abroad movement in the reform era is the dramatic change in gender distribution. In the 1980s an overwhelmingly majority of Chinese students studying abroad who were sponsored by the government were male; the ratio of male to female was 9:1.[65] This ratio changed significantly in the 1990s, reaching 7:3, as during that period privately funded students became the majority. By 2014, 51 percent

FIGURE 4-4. People's Republic of China Students and Scholars Studying Abroad, 1978–2014

Number of students

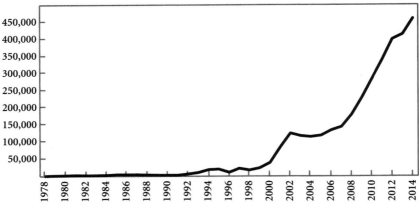

Sources: National Bureau of Statistics and the Ministry of Education, "65 nian liuxue licheng" [Study abroad movement over the past 65 years], September 28, 2014 (http://data.163.com/14 /0928/23/A792D5UR00014MTN.html) and Wang Yucheng and Shi Rui, "2014 Zhongguo chuguo liuxuerenyuan zaizeng" [Continuing increase of Chinese students and scholars studying abroad], Caixin Newsnet, March 6, 2015 (http://china.caixin.com/2015-03-06 /100788923.html).

of Chinese students in the United States were female; in the United Kingdom 63 percent of Chinese students were female. Similarly, there were more Chinese female than male students studying in Canada and Australia.[66] If returnees will be a main source of future leaders in China, this change in gender ratio has profound implications.

According to Chinese official sources, in 2005 and 2009, Chinese students and scholars who studied in the United States accounted for the largest portion (approximately 37 percent) of PRC citizens studying abroad.[67] In 2015 the total number of Chinese students studying in the United States was about 304,000, a significant increase from the number in 2010 (about 100,000).[68] In the 2014–15 academic year, almost 460,000 Chinese students went abroad to study, an increase of 45,900 (11 percent) compared with the previous year. About 92 percent of these Chinese students were self-funded (自费, *zifei*), and about 60 percent of them attended schools in the United States.[69] In 2015 China ranked top in the number of foreign students enrolled in U.S. schools, accounting for 31.2 percent of all foreign students, two times more than India, the country with the second-largest number of students in the United States.[70] At the University of Illinois at Urbana-Champaign, Chinese students accounted for as many as 47 percent of all foreign students.[71]

FIGURE 4-5. Destinations of Chinese Students and Scholars Studying Abroad, 2014

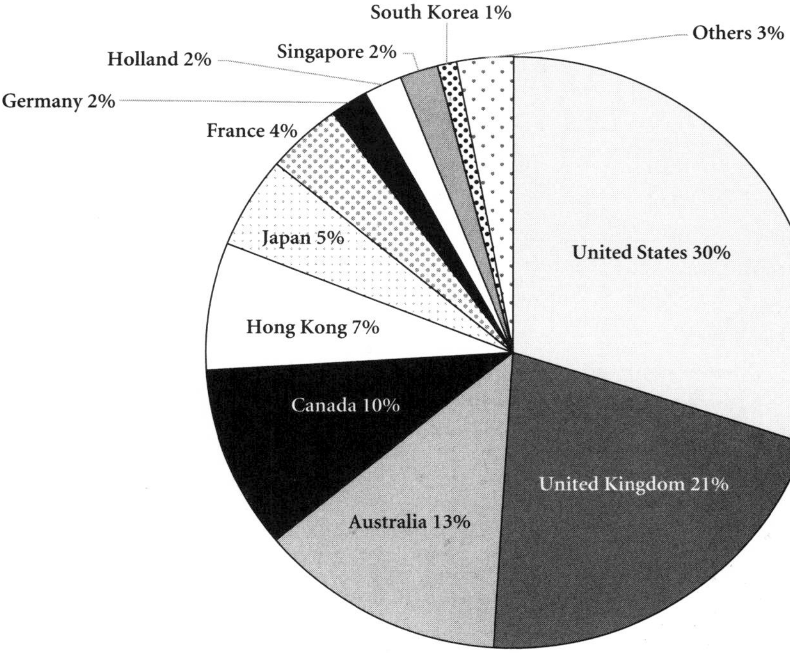

South Korea 1%

Others 3%

Holland 2%

Singapore 2%

Germany 2%

France 4%

Japan 5%

Hong Kong 7%

Canada 10%

Australia 13%

United States 30%

United Kingdom 21%

Source: "2014 nian chuguo liuxue qushi baogao" [Report on the status and trends of study abroad in 2014]. *Zhongguo jiaoyu zaixian* [China Education Online], October 12, 2014 (www .eol.cn/html/lx/2014baogao/content.html).

Figure 4-5 shows the distribution of PRC students and scholars by destination country in 2014. The United States has the largest percentage (30 percent) of PRC citizens studying abroad, followed by the United Kingdom (21 percent), Australia (13 percent), and Canada (10 percent). These four English-speaking Western countries have hosted almost three-quarters of the total number of Chinese students and scholars pursuing foreign studies.

In the past decade, China has also witnessed a tidal wave of returnees, with some 353,500 foreign-educated Chinese citizens returning to the PRC in 2013 alone.[72] By comparison, in that year a total of 413,900 Chinese students went abroad to study.[73] Figure 4-6 shows that the rapid growth in returnees between 1978 and 2013 is similar to the trend for Chinese citizens leaving to study abroad during that same period. As many Chinese nationals are still pursuing their studies abroad, an even greater number are expected to return to China in the years to come.

FIGURE 4-6. Foreign-Educated People's Republic of China Citizen Returnees, 1978–2014

Number of returnees

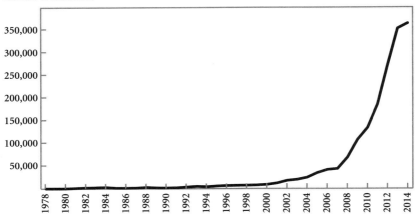

Source: National Bureau of Statistics and the Ministry of Education, "65 nian liuxue licheng" [Study abroad movement in the past 65 years], September 28, 2014 (http://data.163.com/14 /0928/23/A792D5UR00014MTN.html), and Wang Yucheng and Shi Rui, "2014 Zhongguo chuguo liuxuerenyuan zaizeng" [Continuing increase of the Chinese students and scholars studying abroad], Caixin Newsnet, March 6, 2015 (http://china.caixin.com/2015-03-06 /100788923.html).

The current study abroad movement is undoubtedly the largest one in Chinese history. It will likely continue to gain momentum, partly because a rapidly emerging Chinese middle class can afford to send their children abroad, and partly because the state is steadily increasing funding for post-graduate education overseas. According to the PRC's Ministry of Education, 130,000 Chinese students used their own family funds to study abroad in each of the three years from 2007 to 2009.[74] During the same period the China Scholarship Council provided full scholarships each year to at least 5,000 students to pursue advanced degrees abroad. In 2009 the fund offered scholarships to 12,000 students, half of whom enrolled in graduate programs for master's or doctoral degrees overseas.[75] An overwhelming majority of these students opted to study in either Western countries or Japan.

Returnees in the Political Leadership in Contemporary China

Foreign-educated returnees have now played important roles in virtually every field in the country, and some have emerged as political leaders. The presence of returnees in Chinese decisionmaking circles is, of course, not a new phenomenon. In fact, returnees have played an important role in the Chinese government ever since the founding of the Republic of China in

1911. The founders of the Nationalist and Communist parties, Sun Yat-sen, Chiang Kai-shek, Chen Duxiu, and Li Dazhao, all studied overseas before the 1911 Revolution. Tang Shaoyi (the first premier of the Republic of China), Liang Tunyen (minister of Foreign Affairs before the 1911 Revolution), and Hu Shi (minister of Foreign Affairs in the Republic era) were all returnees from the United States, where they had studied with the support of the Boxer Rebellion Indemnity Scholarship. In the short-lived cabinet of Sun Yat-sen after the 1911 Revolution, fifteen of the eighteen ministers and vice-ministers were returnees, a stunning 83 percent.[76]

In the latter half of the twentieth century, several of the most prominent figures in Chinese politics had participated in the study abroad movements of the 1920s and 1930s, including Zhou Enlai, Deng Xiaoping, Liu Shaoqi, and Chiang Ching-kuo. Experience overseas allowed the first three to develop the Communist ideals and political skills they would later use to help the CCP seize power. Chiang, for his part, used his experience abroad to become the second president of Taiwan and later initiated the democratic transformation of the island. Deng and Chiang both rose to preeminent leadership positions and implemented ambitious economic reforms.

Among the 11,000 PRC citizens who studied abroad between 1949 and early 1960, an overwhelming majority went to the Union of Soviet Socialist Republics (USSR).[77] Most leaders from that group are now retired. Among their ranks were Jiang Zemin, Li Peng, Luo Gan, and Li Lanqing, all of whom previously served on the PSC. Fourth-generation leaders generally attended Chinese universities, which is not surprising given that throughout the 1960s and 1970s China hardly sent any students abroad.

Collective Leadership and the Growing Importance of Think Tanks

The decline of strongman politics and the emergence of a collective system of leadership have prompted officials to seek legitimacy for their policies through "scientific decisionmaking" (科学决策, *kexue juece*). Prominent think tanks populated by returnees serve as the primary venues for this kind of research. Just as the current wave of returnees has its antecedents, think tanks (智库, *zhiku* or 思想库, *sixiangku*) are by no means new to China. On the contrary, one could argue that they have played an important role in Chinese society since the time of Confucius. However, during much of the PRC's history, and especially during its first four decades, the role and influence of think tanks largely depended on the preferences and characteristics of the country's paramount leader.

Mao Zedong did not value modern science and technology and, thus, disregarded rationality in affairs of the state and held intellectuals in low esteem. Major decisions during the Mao era were largely made by Mao alone, as discussed in chapter 1. These decisions included the launching of the Cultural Revolution, the movement to shift China's national defense industry to the so-called interior third front, and the initiative to pursue rapprochement with the United States in the early 1970s.

Although Deng Xiaoping greatly improved the economic and sociopolitical status of intellectuals during his reign, he felt no need to consult think tanks when making decisions. Indeed, Deng's most significant decisions—opening China to foreign investment, sending a large number of students to study in the West, normalizing Sino-U.S. relations so as to contain the former Soviet Union, and establishing Special Economic Zones in southern China and then in Shanghai's new Pudong District—have all been attributed to his own visionary thinking and political courage. It has been widely noted in the Chinese public that in his final years Deng preferred to listen to his daughters' gossip rather than read expert reports.

When Hu Yaobang and Zhao Ziyang were in charge of political and economic affairs for both the party and the government in the 1980s, they were the "patron saints" of a group of liberal intellectuals affiliated with government think tanks and, to a certain extent, with the research units connected to the Central Committee of the CCP. Some of these scholars later lent their support to the 1987 liberal movement and the 1989 Tiananmen student movement. As a consequence of these two events, which brought about the fall of both Hu and Zhao, many liberal intellectuals, including Yan Jiaqi, Su Shaozhi, and Wu Guoguang, sought amnesty in the West, and Bao Tong, personal secretary to Zhao, was arrested.

Although certain think tanks were closed as a result of the Tiananmen Square incident, the think tank system survived and even became more institutionalized over the ensuing two decades or so. This has largely been attributed to the fact that China's growing integration with the world economy required more scholars with professional expertise, especially in the areas of international economics and finance. Without a doubt, Jiang Zemin, Zhu Rongji, and their generation of technocratic leaders paid more attention to the role of think tanks than did their predecessors.

Meanwhile, a large number of returnees have chosen to simultaneously teach in the country's top universities and work in think tanks at these schools after their study overseas. The dominant role of foreign-educated returnees in China's think tanks, especially in the areas of economics and international affairs, is truly remarkable. Tsinghua University and Peking University are now home to some of the most influential think tanks in the country. By September 2014, for example, there were altogether 319 research centers and institutes at Tsinghua.[78] This includes 60 research centers and institutes on social sciences, economics and finance, and international affairs. The most notable of these think tanks are the Center for China

Studies, the Center for the Study of Contemporary China, the National Center for Economic Research, the Institute of International Studies, the Institute of International Strategic and Development Studies, and the newly established National Institute of Management. The most important resources for think tanks, of course, are research scholars. For this reason, it is not surprising that research centers and institutes are often "built around a single, strong-minded individual," as Barry Naughton observed in his study of China's economic think tanks.[79] Hu Angang (Center for China Studies), Hu Zuliu (National Center for Economic Research), Li Qiang (Center for the Study of Contemporary China), Yan Xuetong (Institute of International Studies), Chu Shulong (Institute of International Strategic and Development Studies), and Cheng Jianping (National Institute of Management) are good examples. All are returnees who either received their Ph.D.s from foreign universities or spent many years abroad as visiting scholars. To a great extent, these individuals are the public faces, strategic minds, and intellectual souls of their respective think tanks.

The Center for China Studies, headed by Hu Angang, a returnee from the United States, has been particularly active in contributing to policy changes in the Chinese government over the past decade.[80] The center was established jointly by Tsinghua University and the Chinese Academy of Sciences in 1999, with a mission to serve as a think tank for the highest-level decisionmaking circles in the country.[81] The center's broad mission is to forecast China's long-term development and to influence policies. In the last decade the center has issued over 1,000 "reports on the state of China" (国情 报告, *guoqing baogao*), with some of them submitted directly to the State Council and the Secretariat of the CCP Central Committee. Hu was among the first Chinese scholars to advocate the concept of "green GDP growth."[82] According to his proposals, China should not measure development merely by "black GDP numbers" but should also factor in the enormous costs of environmental degradation in order to measure "green GDP growth," a more accurate gauge of real development. Hu attended the 18th National Party Congress as a delegate, and his concept of green GDP growth has recently been accepted by the CCP leadership. As discussed in chapter 1, Hu has also been known for his research in and advocacy of the "collective presidency" in China.

It has been widely recognized that in the early 1990s Jiang Zemin often received advice from returnee scholars at Shanghai-based institutions such as Fudan University, the East China University of Political Science and Law, the Shanghai Academy of Social Sciences, and the Shanghai Institute of International Studies. Indeed, throughout the 1990s several prominent young scholars with experience in the field of foreign studies moved from Shanghai to Beijing, where they worked closely with Jiang in areas such as policy planning, propaganda, Taiwan affairs, and foreign relations. For example, Wang Huning, then dean of the law school at Fudan University (who studied at the University of Michigan, Iowa State University, and the University of California at Berkeley), later served as a personal assistant to Jiang. It is believed that Wang was a principal contributor to the development of Jiang's "theory of the three represents," discussed in the following chapter. Cao Jianming, then professor and president of the East China University of Political Science and Law (who was a visiting professor at the law schools of San Francisco State University and Ghent University in Belgium), assisted Jiang in both China's World Trade Organization negotiations and Taiwan affairs. Wang Huning is now a Politburo member, one of the twenty-five most influential politicians in the country, and Cao Jianming is president of the Supreme People's Procuratorate. In the 1980s and early 1990s former premier Zhu Rongji also relied heavily on the advice of scholars, including several young returnee economists at Tsinghua University's School of Economics and Management, where Zhu served as dean for many years.

Following in Jiang's footsteps, Hu Jintao turned the CPS into a prominent think tank when he served as its president in the late 1990s. For over a decade the CPS has functioned as a leading research center for the study of China's domestic political reform and international relations. Both Zheng Bijian, former vice-president of the CPS, and Wang Jisi, then director of the Institute of International Strategic Studies of the CPS and former dean of the School of International Studies at Peking University, played crucial roles in the development of Hu's theory of "China's peaceful rise."[83] Wang Jisi spent many years studying and working abroad. He was a visiting scholar at St. Antony's College at Oxford University from 1982 to 1983, at the East Asian Institute of the University of California at Berkeley from 1984 to 1985, and in the Department of Politics at the University of Michigan in 1990 to 1991, and he taught at Claremont McKenna College in 2001.

A few other prominent aides to Hu Jintao, for example, Xia Yong (then director of the State Bureau of Secrecy and currently deputy director of the Legislative Affairs Office of the State Council) and Yu Keping (then deputy director of the Central Bureau of Translation of the CCP), were also returnees. Xia had previously spent several years studying in Western countries before working with Hu. Xia studied at Harvard University as a postdoctoral fellow for two years, and Yu taught as a guest professor at Duke University and the Free University in Germany and also served as a visiting scholar at Harvard's Kennedy School of Government. These two aides were instrumental in the formation of Hu's domestic and foreign policies, including the development of the "governing capacity of the CCP" concept.[84]

Xi Jinping is the first leader in the PRC who has publicly endorsed the important role of think tanks in enhancing the country's soft power. Xi made remarks on a number of occasions in the past few years declaring the strategic goal of developing new think tanks with Chinese characteristics.[85] Xi has particularly emphasized the need for innovation, diversity, and global outreach in China's new think tanks. In April 2016, in an important speech delivered at the Internet and Information Security Work Conference, Xi proclaimed that China should adopt a mechanism common in many foreign countries, whereby think tanks serve as a "revolving door" (旋转门, *xuanzhuanmen*) for political and intellectual elites to move between government, enterprises, and think tanks themselves.[86] In fact, some of his most important aides and advisors are from think tanks and universities. Xi Jinping's two confidants, Liu He (director of the Office of the Central Economic Leading Group of the CCP Central Committee) and Chen Xi (executive deputy-director of the CCP Central Organization Department), are U.S.-educated returnees. Liu received an MPA degree from Harvard's Kennedy School of Government and currently serves as the chief economic advisor to Xi Jinping. Known as "China's Larry Summers," Liu played a very important role in drafting the pivotal economic reform agenda announced at the Third Plenum of the 18th Central Committee. Chen, who served as a visiting scholar to Stanford University from 1990 to 1992, is now Xi's appointed man in personnel matters. Chapter 8 will further elaborate the important roles of Liu and Chen in the Xi administration.

Xi also likes to consult the views of returnee experts on global economic and financial development. When he was party secretary of Shanghai, Xi came to know Fang Xinghai, then deputy secretary of the Financial Affairs Committee of the Shanghai Municipal Party Committee and director of the Shanghai Financial Services Office. Fang was born in 1964 and attended Tsinghua University's School of Economic Management from 1981 to 1986, majoring in Information Systems Management.[87] He pursued graduate-level education at Stanford University from 1986 to 1993 under the guidance of Joseph Stiglitz, who was awarded the Nobel Prize in economics in 2001. After receiving his doctoral degree in economics in 1993, Fang worked in the prestigious young professionals program at the World Bank for several years (1993–98). He returned to China in 1998 and served as director of the coordination department of the China Construction Bank (1998–2000), secretary-general of the Galaxy Securities Regulatory Commission (2000–01), and vice-president of the Shanghai Stock Exchange (2001–05) before working in the Shanghai municipal government. Fang has developed a close relationship with Xi and often sends him memos regarding financial development in China and around the world.[88] Soon after Xi became general secretary of the CCP, Fang was transferred to Beijing, where he currently serves as bureau chief of the General Office of the Central Economic and Financial Leading Group. There, he directly supports Liu He in drafting blueprints of China's financial and economic policy. Since November 2015, Fang has concurrently served as vice-chairman of the China Securities Regulatory Commission, therefore playing a very important role in China's financial reform. As China emerges as a global power, the firsthand foreign knowledge that returnees hold is a vital asset in the political establishment, providing valuable advice to the top leadership.[89]

Returnees in the Central Committee

The wave of returnees has not only provided much-needed talent to China's universities and think tanks, particularly in formulating public policy for the leadership, but it has also broadened the recruitment channels of Chinese political elites. In 1999 Zeng Qinghong, then director of the CCP Central Organization Department and who later served as vice-president of the PRC, claimed that "returnees from study overseas"—including both degree holders and yearlong visiting scholars—should be seen as a major source for political recruitment.[90] Zeng also specified that some outstanding returnees be immediately appointed to leading bureau-level posts. These returnees may eventually be promoted to even higher positions after serving as bureau heads for a few years. Zeng's successor, Li Yuanchao, former director of the CCP Central Organization Department and now vice-president of the PRC, not only initiated the Thousand Talents Program to incentivize top-notch foreign-educated Chinese nationals to return to China but also made efforts to promote returnees to various leadership positions.[91] On the eve of the 18th Party Congress, the Central Organization Department issued a long report with 100 cases, praising the achievements made by returnee leaders to the country in various fields, especially public administration.[92]

A few returnees who participated in the Thousand Talents Program also served as delegates to the 18th National Party Congress. According to a Chinese official source, delegates to the 18th National Party Congress included about 120 scholars, most of whom had foreign study backgrounds.[93] These scholars included two additional delegates allocated to Beijing by the Central Organization Department. Zhang Xueji (who participated in the Thousand Talents Program) is professor and director of the Bioengineering and Sensing Technology Research Center of Beijing University of Science and Technology. He completed his postdoctoral research and served as visiting professor at several universities in the United States. The other additional delegate was the aforementioned Hu Angang, who had pursued his postdoctoral research at both Yale University and MIT.

Table 4-5 shows the gradual increase of foreign-educated returnees in the past three Central Committees—from 6.2 percent on the 16th Central Committee, to 10.5 percent on the 17th Central Committee, to 14.6 percent

TABLE 4-5. Foreign-Educated Returnees in the Membership of the 16th, 17th, and 18th Central Committees

Membership	16th Central Committee (2002) No. of returnees/ total	%	17th Central Committee (2007) No. of returnees/ total	%	18th Central Committee (2012) No. of returnees/ total	%
Full members	9/198	4.5	17/204	8.3	20/205	9.8
Alternate members	13/158	8.2	22/167	13.2	35/171	20.5
Total members	22/356	6.2	39/371	10.5	55/376	14.6

Source: Cheng Li, "Shaping China's Foreign Policy: The Paradoxical Role of Foreign-Educated Returnees," *Asia Policy*, no. 10 (July): 73. The data on the 18th Central Committee have been updated by the author.

on the 18th Central Committee. Most of these returnees serve as leaders in education, academic research, finance, or foreign affairs. Only a small number of them have advanced their careers through provincial leadership posts, which are generally the surest launch pads to top-echelon positions, as discussed in chapter 3. But the bottom line is that Western-educated returnees have already made it into the ruling elite. This distinct group of leaders will likely increase their number and convening power in the years to come.

Among the fifty-five leaders on the 18th Central Committee who spent more than one year studying abroad, twenty are full members (9.8 percent of the total). These returnees also include one PSC member, Zhang Dejiang, who studied in North Korea, and two Politburo members, the aforementioned Wang Huning, who studied in the United States, and Sun Zhengcai, who studied agriculture as a visiting scholar at the Rothamsted Experimental Station in England in 1991. Wang has played a crucial role in China's domestic and foreign policies, as he has been at the side of top leaders (Jiang, Hu, and Xi) during their local and international trips over the past two decades. Sun previously served as minister of Agriculture and Jilin party secretary before being appointed Chongqing party secretary in 2012. He is one of the top two rising stars of the sixth generation.[94] Both Wang and Sun are candidates for PSC seats in the next leadership succession in 2017.

Other prominent leaders on the 18th Central Committee who have studied abroad include State Councilor Yang Jiechi, who studied at the University of Bath and the London School of Economics and Political Science from 1973 to 1975; Foreign Minister Wang Yi, who studied at Georgetown University as a visiting scholar from 1997 to 1998; the director of the Hong Kong and Macao Affairs Office of the State Council, Wang Guangya, who

TABLE 4-6. Overseas Educational Experience of Members of the 18th Central Committee

Overseas educational experience	No.	%
Post-doctoral study	3	5.5
Ph.D.	10	18.1
MBA/MPA/MA/MS	7	12.7
BA/BS	3	5.5
Visiting scholar	27	49.1
Administrative/technical work	5	9.1
Total	55	100.0

Source: Author's database.

studied in the United Kingdom twice—first at Welsh Atlantic Union College from 1972 to 1975 and then at the London School of Economics and Political Science from 1981 to 1982; Henan party secretary Xie Fuzhan, who was a visiting scholar first at Princeton University from 1991 to 1992 and then at Harvard University in 2003; political commissar of the National Defense University Liu Yazhou, who studied English literature at Stanford University as a visiting scholar from 1986 to 1987; and the aforementioned Cao Jianming and Chen Xi. All of these returnee leaders are full members of the 18th Central Committee.

Almost half of these returnees (49.1 percent) pursued their foreign studies as visiting scholars (see table 4-6). Among the thirty-three Central Committee members who attended full-time degree programs, ten obtained their doctoral degrees. Table 4-7 provides the background information of these ten members (including one member who received a doctoral degree from Hong Kong) along with that of four master's degree holders. They include prominent leaders such as Minister of Commerce Gao Hucheng and the aforementioned Liu He.

Five of these degree holders attended universities in the United States. Table 4-8 outlines the foreign countries in which these returnee leaders studied. The United States ranks at the top, not only among degree candidates (27.8 percent) but also among visiting scholars (37.9 percent). Table 4-9 shows the duration of study for each high-ranking leader. More than three-quarters of them (76.4 percent) spent less than three years abroad, reflecting the relatively short-term, one-year visiting scholarship programs in which many of these leaders participated. Only eleven leaders (20 percent) have stayed overseas for more than four years. Most of these years were spent in intensive study for an academic degree. Very few have taught at foreign universities or have had long-term research experience after completing formal

TABLE 4-7. Selected Members of the 18th Central Committee Who Received Foreign Advanced Degrees

Name	Born	Current position	Country	Foreign school	Years	Degree	Academic field
Gao Hucheng	1951	Minister of Commerce	France	Paris No. 7 University	1982–85	Ph.D.	Sociology
Zhou Ji	1946	President of the Chinese Academy of Engineering	USA	SUNY, Buffalo	1980–84	Ph.D.	Engineering
Hu Heping	1962	Shaanxi Deputy Party Secretary	Japan	Tokyo University	1992–95	Ph.D.	Engineering
Li Jiayang	1956	Vice Minister of Agriculture	USA	Brandeis University	1985–91	Ph.D.	Genetics
Li Peilin	1955	Vice President of the Chinese Academy of Social Sciences	France	University of Lyon; Paris No. 1 University	1983–87	Master/Ph.D.	Sociology
Wan Lijun	1957	President of China University of Science and Technology	Japan	Tohoku University	1996–99	Ph.D.	Chemistry
Yin Li	1962	Sichuan Governor	Russia (Soviet Union)	Public Health, Economic and Health Service Institute	1988–93	Ph.D.	Medicine
Gong Ke	1955	President of Nankai University	Austria	Technical University of Graz	1983–86	Ph.D.	Engineering
Yang Hui	1964	Chief-of-Staff of Nanjing Military Region	Yugoslavia	University of Belgrade	1985–88	Ph.D.	Literature

(continued)

TABLE 4-7. (*continued*)

Name	Born	Current position	Country	Foreign school	Years	Degree	Academic field
Cao Shumin	1967	President, Telecommunications Research Institute in Ministry of Industry and Information Technology	Hong Kong	The Hong Kong Polytechnic University	2003–07	Ph.D.	Management
Liu He	1952	Office Director of Central Economic Leading Group	USA	Seton Hall Univ; Harvard Kennedy School	1992–95	Master	Business/Public Administration
Lan Tianli	1962	Vice Governor of Guangxi	Singapore	Nanyang Technological University	2006–07	Master	Public Administration
Li Qun	1962	Party Secretary of Qingdao	USA	University of New Haven	2000	Master	Public Administration
Song Liping	1962	President of Shenzhen Stock Exchange	USA	University of Dallas	1986–88	Master	Business Administration

Source: Author's database.

TABLE 4-8. Foreign Countries in Which Members of the 18th Central Committee Studied

Country	Foreign study in general		Foreign study resulting in an advanced degree	
	No.	%	No.	%
USA	25	37.9	5	27.8
England	11	16.7	2	11.1
Japan	6	9.1	3	16.7
Germany	4	6.1	1	5.6
France	3	4.5	2	11.1
Russia	3	4.5	1	5.6
Canada	2	3.0		
Holland	2	3.0		
Italy	2	3.0		
Austria	1	1.5	1	5.6
Yugoslavia	1	1.5	1	5.6
Singapore	1	1.5	1	5.6
Sweden	1	1.5		
Belgium	1	1.5		
New Zealand	1	1.5		
North Korea	1	1.5		
Zaire	1	1.5	1	5.6
Total	66	99.8	18	100.3

Note and Source: If a leader studied in more than one country, each country is counted. Total percentages do not add up to 100 due to rounding. Data from author's database.

schooling. One exception is president of Shanghai Jiaotong University Zhang Jie, who served as a visiting scholar at Oxford University in the United Kingdom, the University of Tokyo in Japan, and the Max Planck Institute of Quantum Optics in Germany for a total of nine years (from the late 1980s to the late 1990s). Zhang's substantial time abroad and solid academic credentials make him the kind of talent China needs most at present, especially in the high-level decisionmaking circle. But as analysis of the educational background of returnees on the 18th Central Committee reveals, Zhang Jie is an exception rather than the norm.

According to Chinese official sources, China dispatched some 9,400 party or government officials and 5,100 managers of large state-owned enterprises to study abroad on a short-term basis in 2003 and 2004.[95] Harvard University's Kennedy School, Syracuse University's Maxwell School, Stanford University, Yale University, and the University of Maryland at College

TABLE 4-9. Duration of Study Abroad among Members of the 18th Central Committee

Duration (years)	No.	%
1	26	47.3
2–3	16	29.1
4–5	7	12.7
6–7	3	5.5
8–9	1	1.8
Unknown	2	3.6
Total	55	100.0

Source: Author's database.

Park, among many others, also offer public administration programs for young Chinese officials at the ministerial, provincial, municipal, and bureau levels of leadership. To date, more than one hundred universities, business firms, and international organizations in thirty countries have been engaged in executive training programs for Chinese officials.[96] Nanyang Technological University in Singapore, nicknamed "China's overseas party school," has trained 130,000 PRC officials over the past two decades, including about 1,200 officials who have been granted master's degrees.[97]

In addition to the fifty-five Central Committee members who had more than a year's experience studying abroad, some other members of the 18th Central Committee have also attended short-term (3–6 months) programs overseas. Table 4-10 lists seventeen members who participated in the short-term training program in public administration at Harvard University's Kennedy School of Government. Since 2001 the CCP Central Organization Department along with the State Council Development Research Center and the School of Public Policy and Management at Tsinghua University have organized an annual advanced research seminar on public policy and management. So far, eleven classes of Chinese leaders have attended this seminar. The participants include prominent leaders such as PRC vice-president and Politburo member Li Yuanchao, Hubei party secretary Li Hongzhong, and the secretary-general of the Central Political and Legal Committee, Wang Yongqing. Other than Li Hongzhong, all of them attended the program in the 2000s. Most of these leaders were born in the 1960s and thus are considered rising stars in the sixth generation. It is interesting to note that three of them, former party secretary of Nanning City Yu Yuanhui, former party secretary of Nanjing Yang Weize, and former deputy party secretary of Yunnan Qiu He, were recently purged on corruption charges. They were all considered protégés of Vice-President Li Yuanchao.

TABLE 4-10. Members of the 18th Central Committee Who Have Attended a Short-Term Program at Harvard University's Kennedy School of Government

Name	Born	Current position	Position when attending the Harvard program	Program year
Li Yuanchao	1950	Vice President of the PRC and Politburo Member	Party Secretary of Nanjing City, Jiangsu Province	2002
Li Hongzhong	1956	Party Secretary of Hubei Province	Mayor of Huizhou City, Guangdong Province	1999
Wang Yongqing	1959	Secretary General, Central Political and Legal Committee	Deputy Director of the Legislative Affairs Office of the State Council	2006
Xie Fuzhan	1954	Governor of Henan	Deputy Director of the State Council Development and Research Center	2003
Zhang Guoqing	1964	Deputy Party Secretary of Chongqing City	Deputy General Manager of China North Industries Group Corporation	2001
Zhao Zhengyong	1951	Party Secretary of Shaanxi Province	Vice Governor of Shaanxi Province	2007
Ma Shunqing	1963	Member of the Qinghai Provincial Party Committee	Director of Department of Land Resources in Qinghai Provincial Government	2006
Yu Yuanhui	1964	Former Party Secretary of Nanning City (purged)	Secretary of Guangxi Committee of the Chinese Communist Youth League	2004
Zhao Jin	1962	Director of the Propaganda Department of Yunnan Province	Deputy Director of Propaganda Dept. of Yunnan Provincial Party Committee	2006

(continued)

TABLE 4-10. (*continued*)

Name	Born	Current position	Position when attending the Harvard program	Program year
Yang Weize	1962	Former Party Secretary of Nanjing City, Jiangsu Province (purged)	Mayor of Suzhou City, Jiangsu Province	2004
Huang Lixin	1962	Party Secretary of Nanjing City	Vice Governor of Jiangsu	2010
Zhao Aiming	1961	Director of the Organization Department of Jiangxi Provincial Party Committee	Party Secretary of Panzhihua City, Sichuan Province	2005
Wu Zhenglong	1964	Party Secretary of Taiyuan City	Head, Wanzhou District, Chongqing City	2005
Yin Li*	1962	Governor of Sichuan Province	Inspector of Social Development Division of Research Office of the State Council	2003
Liu Jian	1970	Party Secretary of Hami Prefecture, Xinjiang	Deputy Secretary of the Chinese Communist Youth League in Beijing City	2004
Qiu He	1957	Former Deputy Party Secretary of Yunnan Province (purged)	Party Secretary of Suqian City, Jiangsu Province	2005
Shang Yong	1957	Party Secretary of China Association for Science	Vice Minister of Science and Technology	2005

Note and Source: * In the School of Public Health at Harvard University. From author's research.

TABLE 4-11. Academic Fields Studied Abroad by Members of the 18th Party Congress

Field	No.	%
Engineering & science	21	38.2
Engineering	7	12.7
Agronomy/forestry	2	3.6
Biology	1	1.8
Chemistry	3	5.5
Geology	1	1.8
Information technology	2	3.6
Medical science	2	3.6
Physics	3	5.5
Economics & management	13	23.6
Management (including MBA)	6	10.9
Economics/statistics	5	9.1
Finance	2	3.6
Social science & law	18	32.7
International affairs	5	9.1
Law	2	3.6
Political science	2	3.6
Public administration	7	12.7
Sociology	2	3.6
Humanities	3	5.5
Education	1	1.8
Foreign language/literature	2	3.6
Total	55	100.0

Source: Author's database.

The members of the 18th Central Committee who studied abroad—including both on long-term and short-term bases—are unlike the Chinese students who went to the USSR and Eastern Europe in the 1950s for engineering or natural sciences. The academic fields of the returnees today are more diverse. In the most recent decade those who went to the West, Japan, Singapore, or other countries usually studied economics, social sciences, law, or public administration, rather than engineering or natural sciences, which were the dominant fields in the 1980s. Table 4-11 shows the academic fields that members of the 18th Central Committee pursued while studying abroad. Although those who studied engineering and natural sciences still constitute the largest group (38.2 percent), the percentage of leaders who studied social sciences and law account for one-third of the total (32.7 percent). The number of leaders who studied public administration is equal to that of those who studied engineering—both were tied for number one in terms of academic fields pursued.

The returnees not only have their own distinct foreign education backgrounds but also differ from PRC-educated leaders in other ways. Returnees generally advance their careers through sectors such as foreign affairs, science and technology, or education and finance, but may not have strong regional constituencies. Even in 2003, in China's universities and research institutes, 51 percent of college-level senior administrators were returnees, and a full 94 percent of the leaders of research departments and teams at the Chinese Academy of Sciences were returnees.[98] Returned students are now well represented in the leadership of the aforementioned areas. This trend in career experience among returnee-turned leaders contrasts with the main career paths of current top leaders, a majority of whom advanced their careers step by step from county, city, and especially provincial levels of administration, as discussed in the previous chapter. Thus, whether returnees are able to serve at the provincial level of leadership is likely to affect their chances of advancing to top leadership positions.

But with the increasing number of Chinese students and scholars returning to China over the past decade, returnee representation in the Chinese political leadership will likely increase significantly in the near future. Table 4-12 illustrates returnee representation in the top three ranks of ministerial leadership, namely, ministers, vice-ministers, and assistant ministers. It is interesting to note that, as one moves lower in the ranks of leadership, the proportion of returnees rises. Since future full ministers will likely be chosen from current vice-ministers and assistant ministers—who, for vice-ministers, are usually five to ten years younger or, for assistant ministers, ten to twenty years younger than full ministers—this matrix suggests that the representation of ministers with returnee backgrounds will likely increase in the years to come.

With the inevitable generational change in the leadership, the new cohort of returnees may differ profoundly from the current generation in level of education and life experiences abroad. This is particularly evident in the different groups of princelings. In the second generation, veteran communist leaders like Deng Xiaoping, Chen Yun, and Li Xiannian all had their children study in the West. So did third-generation leaders like Jiang Zemin, Li Peng, and Zhu Rongji, though their children usually studied abroad as either visiting scholars or postgraduate students when they were already in their thirties. Additionally, they usually studied science or engineering. Examples include Deng Zhifang (Deng Xiaoping's son), who was born in 1952, and studied in the United States when he was in his thirties and received a

TABLE 4-12. Returnee Representation in the Ministerial Leadership, 2010

Positions	Total no.	No. of returnees	%
Full minister	27	4	14.8
Vice-minister	148	30	20.3
Assistant minister	18	7	38.9
Total	193	41	21.2

Source: "China's Midterm Jockeying: Gearing Up for 2012. Part 2: Cabinet Ministers," *China Leadership Monitor,* no. 32 (Spring 2010), 8.

Ph.D. in quantum physics from the University of Rochester in the late 1980s; Chen Weili (Chen Yun's daughter), who was born in 1942 and studied physics at Stanford University as a visiting scholar in 1984; General Liu Yazhou (Li Xiannian's son-in-law), who was born in 1952 and studied English literature at Stanford University as a visiting scholar from 1986 to 1987 when he was in his mid-thirties; Jiang Mianheng (Jiang Zemin's son), who was born in 1951 and went to study at Drexel University in Philadelphia in 1986 and received his Ph.D. in electrical engineering in 1991 when he was already forty years old; Shaanxi governor Li Xiaopeng (Li Peng's son), who was born in 1959 and served as a visiting scholar at both the Ontario Hydro Administration and the University of Manitoba in Canada from 1987 to 1988 when he was in his late twenties; and Zhu Rongji's son, Zhu Yunlai (Levin Zhu), who was born in 1958 and went to the United States when he was already in his early thirties. Zhu received his Ph.D. in atmospheric physics from the University of Wisconsin in 1994 and his master's degree in accounting from DePaul University in Chicago in 1995.

In contrast, the grandchildren of the second and third generations and the children of the current fifth generation usually began their studies in the West at a very early age. Many of them began their foreign studies during high school or even earlier, and almost all obtained their undergraduate education abroad, usually in the social sciences, law, economics, or public administration. These princelings include Deng Zhuodi (David Zhuo, Deng Xiaoping's grandson, J.D. from Duke), Chen Xiaodan (Chen Yun's granddaughter, B.A. in economics from Duke and MBA from Harvard), Jiang Zhicheng (Alvin Jiang, Jiang Zemin's grandson, B.A. in economics from Harvard), Xi Mingze (Xi Jinping's daughter, B.A. in sociology from Harvard), and Liu Chunhang (Bryan Liu, Wen Jiabao's son-in-law, B.A. in economics and English from Williams College, MA in economics from Cambridge, MBA from Harvard, and Ph.D. in political science from Oxford). Deng Zhuodi, Chen Xiaodan, and Liu Chunhang also attended middle school in the United States. Exposure to education and life experiences in the West during the formative years of the younger generation of princelings—and in fact among Chinese middle-class children in general, as discussed earlier in the chapter—is an important sociopolitical development that merits more research.

The presence and growing power of Western-educated elites in the Chinese leadership will arguably contribute to the diversity of the ruling elite and is an important indicator of the openness and political transformation of the country. For example, two spokespersons for the Ministry of Defense appointed in July 2015 are both returnees. Colonel Yang Yujun, director of the Press Bureau of the Ministry of Defense, was born in Beijing in 1970 and joined the PLA after graduating from China's Foreign Affairs University in 1993. Yang later received a master's degree in public policy from the Queen Mary University of London. Yang's deputy, Colonel Wu Qian, deputy director of the Press Bureau, was born in Beijing in 1973. Wu graduated from PLA International Relations College in 1995 and later received an MBA from the University of Birmingham in England. Wu also served as deputy defense attaché at the PRC embassy in the United States. Yang and Wu's educational backgrounds and life experiences differ significantly from their predecessors.[99]

It remains to be seen whether the number of returnees will substantially increase in the CCP top leadership; whether China-educated elites, often called "land turtles" (土鳖, *tubie*), and foreign-trained elites will cooperate well; whether the Western-educated leaders can better communicate China's interests and concerns with the outside world and thus reduce misunderstandings; whether the differences in the speeds and courses of their career promotion will affect the norms of political succession; and whether those returnees in the decisionmaking circle will help propagate international norms and values as a result of their foreign experiences. In a broader perspective, the contrast between foreign-educated returnees and domestically trained elites not only reflects two distinct and increasingly divergent paths in political leadership but may also signify a potential for conflict over power and policy between these two groups.

SUMMARY

This study of the educational backgrounds of the 18th Central Committee of the CCP, based on both qualitative and quantitative analysis, reveals three interesting developments. First, while the current percentage of college-educated CCP leaders is the highest in the history of the PRC—and many of these leaders also hold advanced postgraduate degrees—an astonishingly high number of them obtained their college educations, especially postgraduate training, through part-time and correspondence programs.

The Chinese public generally believes that these part-time training programs lack academic rigor and only help to "gild" political officials.

Second, current Chinese leaders are graduates of a wide range of universities. Tsinghua University alumni no longer dominate the political leadership, as was the case with the third and fourth generations of leaders. However, an overwhelming majority of 18th Central Committee members attended the CPS for yearlong mid-career training and degree programs as a substitute for or in addition to their education in regular academic institutions. The ubiquitous role of the CPS in the education of current Chinese leaders might have satisfied the need for ideological indoctrination and political networking, but it has perhaps undermined rather than enhanced the academic credentials of those attendees who do not have more-conventional educational experiences.

And third, an increasing number of CCP leaders have had academic experiences abroad, either as visiting scholars or degree candidates. However, most have only studied overseas for a year or so and have not accumulated substantial work experience beyond school. Also, most of these returnee leaders have pursued their careers in education, finance, or foreign affairs rather than in provincial leadership, which is the traditional stepping-stone for top positions. Despite all the rhetoric from top Chinese officials claiming that they want to recruit foreign-educated returnees to leadership posts, China's political system is neither open nor bold enough to accommodate a large number of returnees in the most important decision-making bodies.

Yet, some new developments may make returnees more favorable and more competitive in the elite selection process in the future. For example, President Xi's call for promoting new, innovative, and globally oriented think tanks will favor returnees, as they are often well represented in these organizations. In addition, members of the newest generation of returnees generally complete their foreign education at a very young age, and are then able to pursue grassroots political careers after returning home. For instance, the increasing number of foreign-educated returnees at lower ranks of leadership suggests that, over time, the representation of returnees in ministerial and other leadership positions will increase. Either way, the study abroad movement is likely to continue gaining momentum as a middle class with the means to send its children abroad emerges and as the government increases funding for overseas education. This further suggests that the number of foreign-educated returnees in China will continue to increase. These emerging trends will have profound implications for China's leadership politics in the years to come.

The prevalence of undergraduate and postgraduate degrees among China's leadership is a stunning development from the Mao era, when the education levels of China's leaders were extremely low. Political recruitment at that time followed a "red versus expert" approach, favoring revolutionary experience and a pure ideological pedigree over academic expertise. When Deng came to power in 1978, he reestablished a college education system based on academic ability, centered on an entrance examination system. The first year's examination—the most competitive in the PRC's history—precipitated "the famous class of 1982," whose members make up 29 percent of the 18th Central Committee. Later in the reform era Chinese leaders implemented civil service employment, determined by a civil service examination, which has also contributed to an increased emphasis on educational attainment.

More broadly, Deng and his successors called for "a governing party committed to learning." Accordingly, leaders have emphasized and developed opportunities for officials to pursue midcareer education. There are currently about 5,000 different party schools and training institutions that party, government, and state-owned enterprise officials can attend. As academic credentials are a major factor in career advancement, the main participants in these programs are reserve cadres with the potential for promotion. From top leaders' perspectives, the primary purpose of these programs is to enhance the governing capacity of the CCP, so all party and government leaders at the county level or above are required to attend various programs within a year of their promotion.

Overall, the educational backgrounds of Chinese political elites are increasingly divergent in terms of academic majors, degree programs (part-time versus full-time), and setting (domestic versus foreign). Although diversity in the academic, occupational, and administrative backgrounds of leaders is perhaps a positive development that can potentially contribute to political pluralism, the history of contemporary China has shown that differences in educational backgrounds and career experiences among political leaders are often sources of tension and conflict. Yet, precisely because of their differences in expertise, credentials, and experience, contending elite groups need to rely on each other and therefore must share power. The next chapter will further examine how the occupational diversity of Chinese elites is keeping pace with increasing variations in educational backgrounds and what this means for leadership politics and the governance of the country.

CHAPTER 5

Occupations

From Rule by Technocrats to a More Diverse Leadership

There is nothing noble in being superior to your fellow man;
true nobility is being superior to your former self.
—ERNEST HEMINGWAY

Vilfredo Pareto and Gaetano Mosca, Western classic scholars in elite studies, described the "circulation of elites" as the key to the survival of any ruling group. In Mosca's view, governing groups decline in influence when they cease to find an arena for the talents they drew upon as they rose to power—that is, if they can no longer provide the services they once rendered or if their strengths become less relevant in the face of socioeconomic changes.[1] Pareto explains that a revolution—or in his words, a "wholesale circulation of elites"—becomes likely when a "piecemeal circulation of elites" is too slow. In other words, a cohort of old elites can clog channels of political recruitment and prevent "new blood" from entering the power structure.[2] Any enduring regime will try to maintain its internal integrity not only by defining who can rule but also by adapting to its external environment through the recruitment of fresh talent—new ambitious elites who may otherwise become potentially formidable challengers of the system.

The Chinese Communist Party (CCP) leaders have shown an understanding of the importance of opening the door to elites with new professional credentials and occupational backgrounds. Therefore, the makeup of the party leadership has changed significantly over the past three decades. The shift in educational characteristics, including the emphasis on more diverse academic backgrounds, reflects the objective of circulating elites and has certainly contributed to the occupational diversity of CCP political elites.

163

Over the last three decades, the professional composition of the CCP leadership has undergone a sweeping change not just once, but twice. The party has been transformed: first from a revolutionary party, consisting primarily of peasants, soldiers, and urban workers, to a governing party dominated by engineers-turned-technocrats; then to a ruling elite, which increasingly includes members trained in social sciences, especially economic management and law. Entrepreneurs and lawyers have emerged as new players in Chinese socioeconomic and political life, and some of them serve in prominent positions in the party-state structure. Therefore, understanding these new groups of governing elites is crucial to analyzing China's political system and its trajectory. This is even more important now with regard to political trends in China, as political elites with new professional credentials and more diverse occupational backgrounds emerge to run the country in the next decade and beyond.

THE "TECHNOCRATIC TAKEOVER" AND ITS SUBSEQUENT DECLINE

The CCP in its earlier, revolutionary period was primarily led by former peasants and soldiers whose formative experiences for the most part had been in times of war.[3] At the beginning of the reform era in the early 1980s, farmers and workers—the traditional base of the Communist Party—made up 63.4 percent of the CCP membership.[4] Under Deng Xiaoping's leadership, the party began to recruit new members from different social and occupational backgrounds, especially to serve in its elite corps. As figure 5-1 shows, farmers and workers accounted for only 38.3 percent of the CCP members in 2013—a decrease of about 25 percent in three decades. Although farmers continue to constitute the largest single segment of the CCP, the current occupational composition of the party reflects the impact of China's modernization and the ideological reorientation of the party.

In the last two decades or so the CCP has drastically reversed its recruitment policies and actively sought members from groups that only came into existence in the reform era. This includes the new social strata (新社会阶层, xin shehui jieceng) composed of private entrepreneurs, technical personnel and managers in private firms, foreign joint ventures and foreign-funded enterprises, intellectuals, independent professionals, and the self-employed. As a result, the managerial, professional, and technical staff members in enterprises and public institutions became the second-largest occupational group in the CCP, constituting 23.7 percent of the total membership in 2013, which is a 1.7 percent increase from five years earlier.[5]

From a broader perspective, the remarkable changes in the occupational backgrounds of the CCP elites can be best illustrated in terms of the "technocratic turnover" within China's party-state leadership through the 1980s

FIGURE 5-1. Occupations of Chinese Communist Party Members, 2013

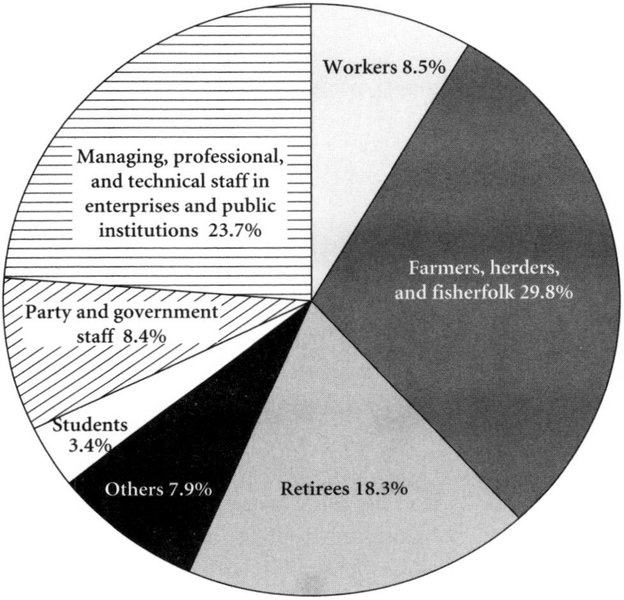

Workers 8.5%

Managing, professional, and technical staff in enterprises and public institutions 23.7%

Farmers, herders, and fisherfolk 29.8%

Party and government staff 8.4%

Students 3.4%

Others 7.9%

Retirees 18.3%

Source: Xinhua, June 30, 2013 (http://news.xinhuanet.com/politics/2013-06/30/c_116344187 .htm).

and 1990s and its subsequent decline. A technocrat is defined as a person who *concurrently* holds specialized training in engineering or natural science, a professional occupation, and a leadership position. Strictly speaking, those leaders who receive specialized training in the fields of economics and finance are not regarded as technocrats. In a broad sense one may call these leaders "economic technocrats," a term that distinguishes them from "technocrats" or "engineers-turned-technocrats."

In 1982 technocrats constituted only 2 percent of the total full members on the Central Committee; but by 1987 they made up 19 percent of the full members, and by 1997 they made up over half (see figure 5-2). More important, the nine members of the Politburo Standing Committee elected in 1997 were all engineers, including the three top leaders: General Secretary Jiang Zemin (electrical engineer), the chair of the National People's Congress, Li Peng (hydroelectric engineer), and Premier Zhu Rongji (electrical engineer). This was also true of the top three leaders elected in 2002: General Secretary Hu Jintao (hydraulic engineer), National People's Congress chair Wu Bangguo (electrical engineer), and Premier Wen Jiabao (geological engineer).

The representation of technocrats also rose dramatically in other high-level leadership positions, such as State Council ministers, provincial party secretaries, and governors. In 1982 only one minister in the State

FIGURE 5-2. Technocrat Representation among Full Members of the Central Committee, 1982–2012

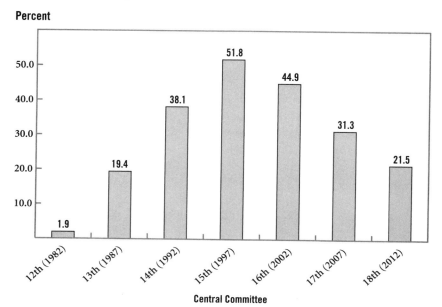

Note and Source: If a leader's undergraduate major differs from his or her postgraduate education focus, this study only counts the latter. Chinese Communist Party Organization Department and Research Office on the History of the Chinese Communist Party, comp., *Zhongguo gongchandang lijie zhongyang weiyuan dacidian, 1921–2003* [Who's who of the members of the Central Committees of the Chinese Communist Party, 1921–2003] (Beijing: *Zhonggong dangshi chubanshe,* 2004). Xinhua News Agency, www.news.cn/politics/leaders/index.htm. Calculated by the author.

Council—the minister of the Electric Power Industry, Li Peng—could be called a technocrat, and no provincial party secretaries or governors had a college-level technical education. In contrast, at the turn of the century, 70 percent of the ministers in the State Council, 74 percent of the provincial party secretaries, and 77 percent of the governors were technocrats (see figure 5-3).

The rise of technocrats and their dominance in the Chinese leadership during the Jiang Zemin and Hu Jintao administrations was particularly striking considering the following three facts. First, in 2010, only 7 percent of China's labor force had received a college education.[6] Second, China was traditionally a meritocratic society in which social status was largely determined by success in imperial examinations. Scientific knowledge and technical competence—which have been esteemed in the West for centuries—were always subordinate to literary and cultural achievements in the Confucian worldview. Third, China's meritocratic tradition underwent an extreme

FIGURE 5-3. Technocrat Representation in Ministerial/Provincial Leadership Posts, 1982–2013

Percent who are technocrats

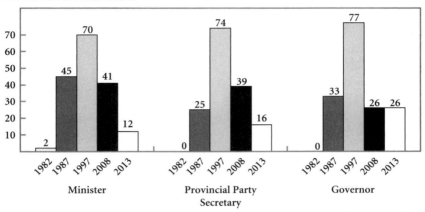

Source: Data for 1982, 1987, and 1997 are based on Hong Yung Lee, *From Revolutionary Cadres to Party Technocrats: The Changing Cadre System in Socialist China* (University of California Press, 1991), 268; Kenneth Lieberthal, *Governing China: From Revolution through Reform* (New York: W. W. Norton, 1995), 236; and Cheng Li and Lynn White, "The Fifteenth Central Committee of the Chinese Communist Party: Full-Fledged Technocratic Leadership with Partial Control by Jiang Zemin," *Asian Survey,* vol. 38, no. 3 (March 1998): 251. Data for 2008 and 2013 were compiled by the author.

reversal during the Mao era, especially during the Cultural Revolution, when professionals or "experts" were repeatedly targeted as enemies of the people (see chapter 4).

The technocratic takeover in the 1980s and 1990s reflects the fluidity of elite composition in post-Mao China and parallels the remarkable economic growth, educational development, and social change in the country. Also, technocratic rule was directly linked to "construction fever" during that period, most noticeably a rapid emergence of skyscrapers—first in Shenzhen, then in Shanghai's Pudong District, and gradually across the country's major cities. The construction of giant engineering projects, including the Three Gorges Dam, was also seen as a crowning achievement of the technocratic leadership.[7]

Beginning with the 17th National Party Congress in 2007, technocratic dominance in the Chinese leadership began to wane, and leaders with non-technical education started to rise rapidly. Ten of the twenty-five members (40 percent) elected to the Politburo that year were technocrats, down from nineteen out of twenty-five (76 percent) in 2002. In the current twenty-five-member Politburo formed in 2012, measured by highest degree obtained, only four (16 percent) are technocrats. In the current seven-member Politburo Standing Committee, only Yu Zhengsheng studied engineering and worked

FIGURE 5-4. Technocrat Representation in the Politburo and the Politburo Standing Committee, 1992–2012

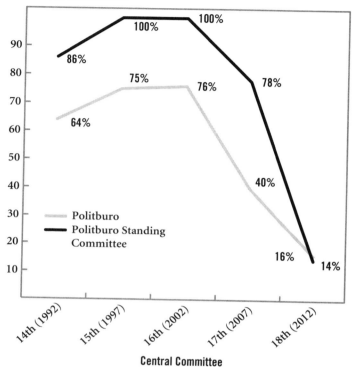

Note and Source: If a leader's undergraduate major differs from his or her postgraduate education focus, this study only counts the latter. Chinese Communist Party Organization Department and Research Office of the History of the Chinese Communist Party, comp., *Zhongguo gongchandang lijie zhongyang weiyuan dacidian, 1921–2003* [Who's who of the members of the Central Committees of the Chinese Communist Party, 1921–2003] (Beijing: *Zhonggong dangshi chubanshe,* 2004). Xinhua News Agency, www.news.cn/politics/leaders/index.htm. Calculated by the author.

as an engineer during his early years. The technocrats' representation in the Central Committee also dropped from its peak of 51.8 percent in 1997 to 44.9 percent in 2002, 31.3 percent in 2007, and 21.5 percent in 2012 (see figure 5-2).

Figure 5-4 illustrates the dominance—and then dramatic decline—of technocrats in China's top leadership (the Politburo and the Politburo Standing Committee) over the past two decades. An overwhelming majority of the current members of the Politburo and the Politburo Standing Committee studied economics, political science, law, or humanities. Although

Xi Jinping's undergraduate education was in chemical engineering, he never worked as an engineer. Xi holds an advanced degree in law and political science. Li Keqiang received his undergraduate degree in law and a doctoral degree in economics. Leaders who are educated in a broad range of fields may well bring more diverse perspectives to policymaking and problem solving.

SIMILAR ELITE TRANSFORMATION IN TAIWAN

It is particularly interesting to note that despite the significant differences between the political systems and socioeconomic developments of mainland China and Taiwan, both sides of the Taiwan Strait experienced similar elite transformations.[8] Under the premiership of Chiang Ching-kuo, the ruling Nationalist Party in Taiwan, the Kuomintang, promoted a large number of technocrats to leadership beginning in the early 1970s. Among the most noticeable were Sun Yun-suan (an engineer who was trained at the Harbin Institute of Technology), Li Kwoh-ting (a physicist who was educated at the University of Cambridge), Chen Li-an (an MIT-trained engineer who also held a Ph.D. in mathematics from New York University), and Lee Teng-hui (who held a Ph.D. in agronomy from Cornell University). Sun later succeeded Chiang as the premier of the Republic of China; Li and Chen both served as ministers of economic affairs and played an instrumental role in Taiwan's economic takeoff; and Lee later succeeded Chiang as the president of the Republic of China.

Like China in the Deng era, Taiwan in the late 1970s and throughout most of the 1980s was ruled by a strongman, Chiang Ching-kuo, who was surrounded by a group of technocrats. Also comparable to China's experience, Taiwan underwent an economic miracle with double-digit GDP growth and broad changes in urban development during those two decades. The era of technocratic dominance is apparently coming to an end in the PRC, as it did in Taiwan about fifteen years ago. CCP leaders trained in the social sciences, economic management, and law have now moved to the center stage of Chinese politics. Meanwhile, PRC business elites have also become increasingly influential, and some have begun to serve in the provincial and national leadership.

In the wake of the most recent political succession, both Chinese official media and social media are filled with discussions about how many CCP leaders have studied social sciences and law and how many private entrepreneurs and SOE executives have served as delegates to the 18th National Party Congress. Similarly, lawyers and entrepreneurs in Taiwan also emerged as important political players both in the government and opposition party during the final years of the Chiang Ching-kuo era. The political role of entrepreneurs and the rise of legal professionals in Taiwanese politics clearly paralleled the consolidation of the legal system and the broad democratic transition on the island. This similarity demands greater scholarly attention be focused on the ongoing elite transformation in mainland China.

THE RISE OF BUSINESS ELITES

The upward social mobility of entrepreneurs—owners and managers of private businesses and executives at SOEs—represents a momentous change in Chinese society. In the West entrepreneurs are defined as businesspeople who assume the "risks of bringing together the means of production, including capital, labor, and materials, and receive reward in the form of profit from the market value of the product."[9] According to Joseph Schumpeter, entrepreneurs are primarily innovators whose dynamic "creative response" to the economic environment makes them central to the promotion of material growth.[10] Entrepreneurs characteristically engage in risk taking in a market economy. In the Chinese context an entrepreneur is defined as a manager or owner of private property—a person who holds property either through capitalization of personal income or through private operation of a collective, public, or joint venture enterprise.[11]

Traditional Chinese society, which was dominated by the scholar-gentry class, tended to devalue merchants because they made a living by profiting off others, rather than through "honest" mental or manual labor.[12] This anti-capitalist bias reached its extreme during the first few decades of the PRC. The four million private firms and stores that had existed in China before 1949 all disappeared by the mid-1950s as part of the transition to socialism.[13] During the Cultural Revolution, anything related to capitalism was branded poisonous; top leaders such as Liu Shaoqi and Deng Xiaoping were purged for allegedly taking China down "the capitalist road."

Several factors contributed to the reemergence of entrepreneurs in the PRC. They include rapid development of rural industries, rural–urban migration, urban private enterprises, foreign joint ventures, adoption of a stock market and land leasing, a real estate boom, and technological revolution—especially the fast growth of the Internet and the dynamic new commercial transactions associated with online banking.

Private Entrepreneurs

Private enterprises that employed a large number of laborers did not emerge in China until 1989. Over the past quarter century, the number of private firms has greatly increased, from some 90,000 in 1989 to 5,210,000 in 2007 and then to 10,598,000 in 2013.[14] The private firms accounted for 60 percent of the total number of enterprises across the country in 2007.[15] According to Wang Jianlin, CEO of Wanda, private firms now account for over 90 percent of the total number of enterprises in China.[16] In addition, roughly forty million people run small, individually owned firms that employ only a handful of people, usually family members and relatives.[17] By the end of 2012 these two types of private enterprises contributed 60 percent of China's gross domestic product and accounted for more than 80 percent of urban employment and over 90 percent of new jobs.[18]

Chinese entrepreneurs have been a diverse and dynamic bunch ever since their emergence in the 1980s. Among the private entrepreneurs, there are three distinct subgroups: first, self-made entrepreneurs—peasants-turned-industrialists in rural areas and owners of business firms of different sizes in cities; second, bureaucratic entrepreneurs—corrupt officials and their relatives who made their fortunes by abusing power in various ways throughout the process of market reform; last, technical entrepreneurs—computer and information technology specialists (including those who pursue commercial activities primarily through online stores and banking) who became wealthy as a result of rapid technological development and economic globalization.[19]

Each of these three groups has a distinctive family and occupational background. Self-made entrepreneurs usually come from humble family environments and receive relatively little education. By contrast, a host of bureaucratic entrepreneurs receive undergraduate degrees in economics and even master's degrees in business administration, usually through part-time, midcareer programs. Furthermore, most of them are already CCP members or officials when they begin to engage in private business. Some come from official family backgrounds or have strong political connections, which helps them earn what the Chinese call the "first pot of gold" (第一桶金, *diyitongjin*)—financial resources with which to launch their private business. Technical entrepreneurs may or may not have powerful family connections and are often seen as China's "yuppies." They are usually well educated, with some having studied or worked abroad. To a large extent, these three subgroups represent different phases in China's economic development during the market reform period, and each reflects the particular socioeconomic environment from which it has emerged. These three subgroups are not mutually exclusive, of course, and each of them has recently experienced a generational change, further contributing to the dynamic development and growing diversity of the Chinese business community.

The rise of the entrepreneurs' political influence can be traced to July 2001, when then CCP general secretary Jiang Zemin gave an important speech on the eightieth anniversary of the party's founding.[20] In his speech Jiang claimed that the party should be representative of three components of society:

FIGURE 5-5. Private Entrepreneurs with Chinese Communist Party Membership

Percent with CCP membership

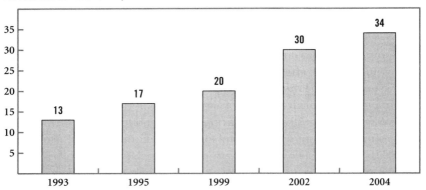

Source: United Front Department of the Chinese Communist Party Central Committee, "2005 nian Zhongguo siying qiye diaocha baogao" [A survey of private enterprises in 2005]. See also www.southcn.com/finance/gdmqgc/gdmqyyrl/200502030218.htm and *Xingdao ribao*, December 13, 2004, 1.

advanced social productive forces, advanced culture, and the interests of the overwhelming majority. Known as the "theory of the three represents" (三个代表, *sange daibiao*), Jiang's statement lifted ideological taboos against privately owned business. This new concept broadened the CCP's base of power to include entrepreneurs, intellectuals, and technical specialists. The theory of the three represents was endorsed by the Sixth Plenum of the 15th Central Committee in September 2001 and was then added as an amendment to the CCP constitution at the 16th National Party Congress, paving the way for the political advancement of new elite groups, especially entrepreneurs, in the years to come.

A 2004 official study by the United Front Work Department of the CCP Central Committee found that 34 percent of private enterprise owners were party members, up from just 13 percent in 1993 (see figure 5-5). Of that group, however, only 9.4 percent had joined the CCP *after* Jiang's 2001 speech, which reflects the fact that during the Jiang era from the 1990s to the beginning of the 2000s, a large number of private entrepreneurs obtained CCP membership.[21] Jiang's ideological embrace was at most a formal acknowledgment that a large number of party members were already engaged in private business activities.

In 2006 a survey revealed that 35 percent of the 500 richest people (multi-millionaires or billionaires) in China are CCP members.[22] Further research conducted in 2012 by the Chinese Academy of Social Sciences showed that the percentage of CCP members classified as private entrepreneurs remained the same as in 1993 (about one-third), but 53 percent of entrepreneurs whose firms possessed at least 100 million yuan in assets were CCP members. This was much higher than in 1993.[23] The study also showed that private firms with CCP committees or branches increased from 27.5 percent in 2002 to 30 percent in 2004, 36.7 percent in 2006, and 38.7 percent in 2008.[24]

Private entrepreneurs have recently begun to acquire positions in the provincial and national political leadership. In 2002, for the first time in PRC history, seven private entrepreneurs attended the National Party Congress as a distinct group, and some served as members of the presidium of the Congress.[25] Although the thirty-four private entrepreneurs who were selected to participate in the 2012 CCP National Party Congress made up only about 1 percent of the total number of delegates, that was more than twice the number of private entrepreneur delegates to the 2007 National Party Congress.[26] The group of private entrepreneurs that attended the 2007 Congress included Wang Jianlin, aforementioned chairman of the Dalian Wanda Group, the world's largest operator of movie theaters after its purchase of AMC Entertainment Holdings for US$2.6 billion in 2013. Wang himself was listed as the wealthiest person in China that year with a net worth of US$14.2 billion (mostly in real estate), according to Bloomberg News.[27]

The private entrepreneur delegates to the 2012 National Party Congress also included some Chinese household names: Wu Xie'en, chairman of the Huaxi Group, one of the most successful township and village enterprises in the country; Liang Wengen, chairman of the SANY Group, a global leading company in the construction machinery industry; and Chen Feng, chairman of Hainan Airlines.[28] The three entrepreneurs are the owners of multibillion-dollar private business firms. Zhang Ruimin, the CEO of China's Haier Group, a multinational consumer electronics and home appliances manufacturer, has served on the Central Committee as an alternate member since 2002.[29]

Wealthy business executives have been more visible in the less powerful state institutions—the National People's Congress and its advisory body, the Chinese People's Political Consultative Conference. According to Rupert Hoogewerf, who has issued annual rankings of the wealthiest individuals in China for *Forbes* magazine since 1999, China's one hundred richest people in 2006 included nineteen delegates of the National People's Congress and another nineteen members of the Chinese People's Political Consultative Conference, a significant increase from the previous year (nine delegates and sixteen members, respectively).[30] At the 2013 meeting of these two bodies, eighty-three deputies were billionaires, according to a report in the *Financial Times*.[31] By contrast, there are no billionaires in the U.S. Senate or House of Representatives.

One important trend in contemporary China is that prominent private entrepreneurs have increasingly formed clubs and associations in their business circles (商业圈子, *shangye quanzi*) and beyond.[32] These clubs usually include the country's most successful business elites. The China Entrepreneur Club, for example, was established in 2006 by thirty-one business leaders (including Lenovo chairman Liu Chuanzhi and Alibaba chairman Jack Ma), economists (such as Wu Jinglian and Qian Yingyi), and diplomats (for example, former WTO trade negotiator Long Yongtu and former PRC ambassador to France Wu Jianmin). In 2011, CEOs of forty-six firms who also serve as directors on the board of the club possessed assets totaling more than 2 trillion yuan. This is equivalent to 4.2 percent of China's GDP that year.[33] The China Entrepreneur Club has established critical convening power in China and abroad. Since 2009 it has organized annual conferences to explore challenges and opportunities for the country, such as environmental degradation and public health crises. In 2013, when the club delegation visited France and Belgium, the heads of those two states and the president of the EU held an audience with the delegation.

Some clubs have a significant number of members. Positive Sum Island (正和岛, *zhenghedao*) was founded in Beijing in 2012 by Liu Donghua, former publisher of *Chinese Entrepreneurs* magazine. It currently has over 2,400 members, including about 2,000 entrepreneurs and 400 public intellectuals, media elites, and other professionals, with annual membership dues of 20,000 yuan.[34] Positive Sum Island provides an active online platform for discussing major issues of the day and organizes many public events, including an annual business leadership summit. Distinguished business leaders such as Liu Chuanzhi, Jack Ma, Wang Jianlin, Zhang Ruimin, Wang Shi (chairman of China Vanke), Lu Guanqiu (chairman of the Wanxiang Group Corporation), Guo Guangchang (chairman of Fosun International Limited), and Li Shufu (chairman of Zhejiang Geely Holding Group Co.) are among the group's founders and major supporters. In the past two years Positive Sum Island has established branches and offices in Jiangsu, Zhejiang, Shanghai, Guangdong, Shandong, and Sichuan.

Some clubs are extremely exclusive. Chang An Club was founded in the heart of Beijing on the famous Chang'an Avenue in 1996 by Chan Laiwa, chairwoman of Fu Wah International Group. The club consists of business tycoons from Hong Kong and mainland China. Prominent government officials, especially financial technocrats such as governor of the People's Bank Zhou Xiaochuan, and former governor of the China Development Bank Chen Yuan, serve as advisers to the club.[35] The annual membership fee for Chang An Club is 200,000 yuan (about US$32,500).

Another exclusive club, the Taishan Industrial Research Institute, also known as Taishan Club (泰山会, *taishanhui*), was founded in 1994 by Duan

Yongji (CEO of Stone Group Holdings). Hu Deping (vice-chairman of the All China General Chamber of Industry and Commerce and former deputy director of the United Front Work Department of the CCP Central Committee) serves as an adviser to the club. Hu Deping is the son of former CCP general secretary Hu Yaobang. Business gurus such as Liu Chuanzhi, Robin Li (CEO of Baidu), and Feng Lun (CEO of the Vantone Group) later became key members of the club. According to the club's bylaws, it recruits only one new member each year. Its discussions are always off the record, and no local leaders are invited to the meetings. As of 2014, the club had only sixteen members. Because of its members' strong desire to maintain the club's low profile, some critics consider the club a "secret society."[36]

Memberships in these elite clubs are not mutually exclusive. Jack Ma, Liu Chuanzhi, Wang Shi, and Feng Lun are associated with several clubs. Many of these top business leaders have attended executive master of business administration (EMBA) programs or CEO programs in the country's two leading business schools—Cheung Kong Graduate School of Business (CKGSB) and China Europe International Business School (CEIBS). CKGSB was founded in Beijing by Hong Kong business tycoon Li Ka-shing in 2002 (it now has campuses in Shanghai and Shenzhen). CEIBS, a joint venture between the Chinese government and the European Commission, was founded in Shanghai in 1994 (it now has campuses in Beijing and Shenzhen). By the end of 2013, the CKGSB had seven thousand alumni and thirty-six alumni associations around the world. Among them, 4,000 had received EMBA degrees, and 76 percent of them served in companies at the vice-president level or higher.[37] Jack Ma, Guo Guangchang, and Niu Gensheng (the founder of the China Mengniu Dairy Company) are graduates of CKGSB's CEO program, and Feng Lun and Li Dongsheng (CEO of TCL) attended the EMBA program at CEIBS.

Many political leaders have also attended CEIBS. Chongqing Mayor Huang Qifan obtained his MBA degree from CEIBS in 1999 when he was the deputy chief-of-staff of the Shanghai Municipal Government. Similarly, Du Jiahao, former director of the Pudong District and current governor of Hunan Province, received his EMBA from CEIBS in 2007. Du also served as chief-of-staff of the Shanghai Municipal Government from 2003 to 2004, assisting then mayor Han Zheng. The newly appointed governor of Yunnan Province, Chen Hao, attended the CEIBS's MBA program from 2001 to 2003 when he was the deputy chief-of-staff of the Shanghai Municipal Party Committee. The social connections facilitated by both entrepreneur clubs and executive education programs at elite business schools promote the economic and political networking of this rapidly emerging group of entrepreneurs.

In March 2014 the China Entrepreneur Club organized what it called an "unprecedented dialogue among leaders" in China on the political participation of Chinese private entrepreneurs, featuring Liu Chuanzhi and Wang

Shi.[38] During the conversation, Liu stated that Chinese businesspeople "should be primarily concerned about business" (在商言商, *zaishang yanshang*) in order to protect themselves in China's current sociopolitical environment and avoid becoming victims of politics. By contrast, Wang used the recent persecution of businesspeople in Chongqing under Bo Xilai to illustrate that Chinese entrepreneurs cannot and should not shy away from politics. Wang argued that Bo would have launched a nationwide campaign to persecute entrepreneurs if he had become a top national leader, as he had done in Chongqing. Not interested in seeking any leadership position, though, Wang believes that businesspeople should exert their political influence on the country's future trajectory through various channels. For example, some influential entrepreneurs could seek political office to ensure their interests are protected.

Regarding Liu's argument that "businesspeople should only talk about business," Wu Xiaobo, a well-known scholar in the study of Chinese business elites, believes it serves as a political strategy and it reflects the maturity and diversity of Chinese business communities. Wu asserts that Liu's approach, which emphasizes the political protection of business elites for the time being, does not entirely contradict Wang's call for enhancing the civil rights and responsibilities of entrepreneurs. According to Wu, in the last decade Chinese entrepreneurs have become increasingly active in political discourse and participation. Wu asserts that "the political challenges to the system by Chinese entrepreneurs arguably will be stronger than those by the masses and intellectuals in the years to come because such challenges are backed by financial capital."[39]

The three major groups of entrepreneurs discussed above—self-made, bureaucratic, and technical—are all very active in China today. They have contributed to the dynamics of social mobility and the diffusion of political power, economic wealth, and social prestige. They will likely coexist and share the country's wealth for many years to come, though the size of each group may vary over time. The occupational and demographic differences between these three groups of entrepreneurs have also added to the diversity of cultural values and political ideologies in Chinese society. Each group of entrepreneurs holds a distinctive worldview.[40] Self-made business leaders usually adhere to a strong sense of entrepreneurship, which is fundamentally incompatible with Confucian meritocracy and technocratic credentialism. The latter view has served as an ideological justification for technocratic rule in postreform China.[41] Although both self-made and technical entrepreneurs might have used political connections (关系, *guanxi*), they resent the unfair business competition they have experienced, which is a result of the "capitalization of power" by bureaucratic entrepreneurs.

These three groups of entrepreneurs not only have contrasting world-views but also represent different political and business behaviors. While bureaucratic entrepreneurs rely heavily on political connections, nepotism, and favoritism, technical entrepreneurs embrace technological innovation and market competition, attracting both consumers and venture capitalists. They believe that in the increasingly competitive global market, an entrepreneur's ability needs be more highly prized than political status, academic credentials, seniority, or *guanxi*.[42] They argue that the most important trait is competency (能力本位, *nengli benwei*), and not meritocracy (as in traditional Confucianism) or bureaucratic connections—in Chinese terms, officialdom (官本位, *guan benwei*).[43] Private entrepreneurs play a much more substantial role in the PRC than they did a few years ago. Nevertheless, they still have a long way to go before their political clout comes anywhere close to matching their economic power.

State-Owned Enterprise Executives

The rise of entrepreneurs-turned-political leaders is a relatively new phenomenon in the PRC. Most of them serve or previously worked as senior executives of major SOEs. The proportion of CEOs of large Chinese enterprises in the national leadership is still relatively small. As discussed in chapter 3, full members of the Central Committees with backgrounds in SOEs and financial firms (and also social organizations) are not that common compared with the number of leaders in the provincial leadership, the central government, the central party organization, and the military. However, an increasing number of businesspeople have entered the top leadership over the past two decades (see table 3-12). More crucially, younger, business-savvy, politically connected, and globally minded Chinese CEOs are now viewed as more suitable candidates for CCP leadership, thus greatly broadening the CCP's recruitment options.

Many of these political leaders with strong business backgrounds have advanced their careers through China's flagship state companies under the State-owned Assets Supervision and Administration Commission, which are known as "SASAC companies." Other financial executives represent China's six state-run commercial banks and the three largest state-controlled insurance companies in the country, which are under the administrative supervision of the China Banking Regulatory Commission and the China Insurance Regulatory Commission, respectively. By definition, SASAC companies are large national firms in which the state, or more specifically the SASAC itself, owns the majority of assets. China's SOEs are divided into two main categories: the first includes enterprises that are under the direct administration of the central government; the second includes state enterprises that are governed by provincial or municipal governments.[44]

The total number of SASAC companies has fallen significantly in the last few years—from 196 in 2003 (when the SASAC was established) to 121 in 2010 and then to 112 in spring of 2015—as a result of mergers and acquisitions to enlarge and strengthen several flagship companies. The total assets of the SASAC companies, however, increased from 3 trillion yuan in 2003 to 20 trillion yuan in 2010 and to 35 trillion yuan in 2013.[45]

The rapid political ascent of a particular elite group in any given country is often linked to concurrent changes in the domestic and international environments. The recent emergence of chief business executives in the CCP leadership is no exception. It can be attributed to the meteoric rise and the ever-increasing power of China's large SOEs on the world stage. If the economic success of a given country is measured by the number of its companies on the Fortune Global 500 list, the PRC undoubtedly represents one of the greatest triumphs in the contemporary world.[46] Chinese companies on the Fortune Global 500 have dramatically increased, from three in 1995 to fifteen in 2005, forty-six in 2010, ninety-five in 2014, and ninety-eight in 2015.[47] In 2015 Sinopec Group, China National Petroleum, and State Grid are ranked second, fourth, and seventh, respectively. China has the second-largest number of companies on the list, behind the United States, which leads with 128.

Table 5-1 includes nineteen members of the 18th Central Committee who currently represent business firms in the country. They are from various industries and sectors. A few of them work primarily in technology areas, but most are chairmen or CEOs of flagship companies and financial institutions. With the exception of full member Lin Zuoming (general manager of the Aviation Industry Corporation of China), all are alternate members of the Central Committee. Chairmen of China's three major commercial banks (the Industrial and Commercial Bank of China, China Construction Bank, and China Development Bank) were all listed on the Fortune Global 500 in 2015 and now serve on the 18th Central Committee. All but Zhang Ruimin were born after 1950 and are thus qualified to remain on this important leadership body after 2017. Eleven of the nineteen members (57.9 percent) were born in the 1960s and are considered promising politicians in the Chinese leadership. Some have worked in their current posts for over a decade and others were recently appointed.

It may take some time for leaders with strong administrative experience in business firms to collectively become a central group in Chinese elite politics. Yet, over the past decade some individual leaders have been appointed to the Politburo and its Standing Committee. Table 5-2 lists the current prominent political leaders with administrative experience at SASAC companies and other large SOEs. They include two Politburo Standing Committee

TABLE 5-1. Prominent Business Leaders Who Serve on the 18th Central Committee, 2016

Name	Year born	Current position	Since	CC status
Lin Zuoming	1957	Chairman, China First Aviation Industry Corporation	2012	Full member
Jiang Jianqing	1953	Chairman, Industrial and Commercial Bank of China	2005	Alternate member
Wang Hongzhang	1954	Chairman, China Construction Bank	2011	Alternate member
Hu Huaibang	1955	Chairman, China Development Bank	2013	Alternate member
Qian Zhimin	1960	President, China Nuclear Industry Group Company	2012	Alternate member
Liu Shiquan	1963	Deputy General Manager of China Aerospace Science and Industry Corporation	2013	Alternate member
Jin Zhuanglong	1964	Chairman, Commercial Aircraft Corporation of China, Ltd.	2012	Alternate member
Ren Hongbin	1963	Chairman, China Machinery Industry Group Co.	2013	Alternate member
Zhang Xiwu	1958	Chairman, Shenhua Group	2008	Alternate member
Zhang Ruimin	1949	CEO, Haier Group	2000	Alternate member
Cao Guangjing	1964	Chairman, China Three Gorges Corporation	2010	Alternate member
Wang Yongchun	1960	Vice-President, China National Petroleum Corporation (purged)	2011	Alternate member
Xu Lejiang	1959	Chairman, Shanghai Baosteel Group Corporation	2007	Alternate member
Wang Xiaochu	1958	Chairman, China Telecom	2008	Alternate member
Li Jincheng	1963	Chief Engineer, China Railway Construction Corporation	2003	Alternate member
Guo Jianbo	1960	President, China Electric Power Research Institute	2010	Alternate member
Wu Manqing	1965	Chief Engineer, China Electronics Technology Group Corporation	2012	Alternate member
Jing Donghan	1961	Director, Research Institute of China Shipbuilding Industry Corporation	2004	Alternate member
Zhu Yanfeng	1961	Chairman, Dongfeng Auto Corporation	2015	Alternate member

Note and Source: CC = Central Committee. Author's database.

members and one Politburo member: Wang Qishan, who previously served as vice-president and then president of China Construction Bank from 1989 to 1997 and has been widely known throughout the international business community as a seasoned expert on economics and finance; Zhang Gaoli, who previously served as general manager of Maoming Oil Company and China Petrochemical Corporation in the early 1980s and oversaw the economic and financial reforms in Shenzhen from 1997 to 2001 and in Tianjin from 2007 to 2013; and Zhang Chunxian, who served as general manager of China National Packaging and Food Machinery Corporation in the early 1990s.

Table 5-2 includes two state councilors, Guo Shengkun, general manager of the Aluminum Corporation of China from 2001 to 2004, and Wang Yong, former vice-president of the China Aerospace Electrical Group from 1999 to 2000 and minister of SASAC from 2010 to 2013. Several cabinet ministers have also served as CEOs of major SOEs and commercial banks. Minister of Finance Lou Jiwei was chairman of the China Investment Corporation from 2007 to 2013; Minister of Industry and Information Technology Miao Wei served as general manager of the Dongfeng Motor Corporation, one of the largest Chinese state-owned automobile manufacturers, from 1999 to 2005. Former chairman of the China Securities Regulatory Commission Xiao Gang served as chairman of the Bank of China from 2003 to 2013; another recently appointed chairman of the China Insurance Regulatory Commission, Xiang Junbo, was chairman of China Agricultural Bank from 2007 to 2011. These leaders, along with the others listed on table 5-2, are all full members of the 18th Central Committee and strong contenders for top economic and financial leadership posts in the following round of political succession in 2017 and 2018.

As discussed in chapter 3, the experience of serving as a provincial chief has been the most important stepping-stone to top Chinese national leadership positions. It is interesting to note that an increasing number of political rising stars with backgrounds in leading SOEs have also extended their political careers to provincial administration. Table 5-3 presents the top provincial and municipal leaders with administrative experience at SASAC and other large SOEs. Hebei Governor Zhang Qingwei previously served as chairman of the Commercial Aircraft Corporation of China, a Chinese aerospace manufacturer that builds mid- to large-size passenger aircraft and aims to challenge the dominance of Boeing and Airbus in the global marketplace. From 2001 to 2007 Zhang served as the general manager of the China Aerospace Science and Technology Corporation. It made him the youngest CEO among China's flagship companies at that time. From 2007 to 2011, former Fujian governor Su Shulin served as chairman of the China Petrochemical Corporation (Sinopec), which was ranked fifth on the Fortune Global 500 in 2012, the year after he left.

When Zhang and Su gained membership on the 356-member Central Committee at the 16th National Party Congress in 2002, Zhang was only forty-one years old (the youngest full member on the Central Committee) and Su was one of the three youngest alternates. But their tenures on the Central Committee have been longer than some of the widely recognized forerunners of the sixth-generation leaders, including Politburo members Hu Chunhua and Sun Zhengcai; neither Hu nor Sun joined the Central Committee until 2007. Top leaders in the fourth and fifth generations of leadership were also noted for their early entry into the Central Committee. Hu Jintao and Wen Jiabao joined the Central Committee in 1982 when they were forty years old; in 1997 Xi Jinping and Li Keqiang became an alternate and a full member of the Central Committee, respectively, when they were both in their early forties. The early Central Committee membership helped them advance their positions as fourth- and fifth-generation forerunners in their ascents to the top Chinese leadership.

Su was purged on a corruption charge in October 2015. Zhang is not the only former CEO of a major Chinese company who is well positioned to jockey for power in the future. There are some other rising stars on the 18th Central Committee who now have built up their credentials through both the SOE and provincial leadership. They include Zhang Guoqing (former CEO of China North Industries Group Corporation and now deputy party secretary of Chongqing), Ma Xingrui (former president of the China Aerospace Science and Technology Corporation and now concurrently deputy party secretary of Guangdong and party secretary of Shenzhen), Chen Qiufa (former director of China Atomic Energy Authority and newly appointed Liaoning governor), and Ren Xuefeng (former chairman of the Hong Kong Alliance Group Limited and newly appointed party secretary of Guangzhou). Guo Shuqing, former chairman of China Construction Bank and current governor of Shandong, is a leading contender to succeed Zhou Xiaochuan as governor of the People's Bank of China.

A new term, "the cosmos club" (宇宙帮, *yuzhoubang*), has recently been coined to refer to national and provincial leaders who have advanced their careers through China's space industry.[48] In addition to aforementioned Ma Xingrui and Chen Qiufa, the "cosmos club" includes State Councilor Wang Yong (former vice-president of China Aerospace Electrical Group), Hebei governor Zhang Qingwei (former chairman of the Commercial Aircraft Corp. of China), the executive vice-minister of Industry and Information Technology Xu Dazhe (former president of China Aerospace Science and Industry Group), and Zhejiang executive vice-governor Yuan Jiajun (former vice-president of China Aerospace Science and Technology Corporation). Ma, Chen, Wang, Zhang, and Xu serve as full members of the 18th Central Committee; Yuan was an alternate member of the 17th Central Committee.

TABLE 5-2. Selected Members of the 18th Central Committee with Administrative Experience in the SASACs and Large SOEs, 2016

Name	Year born	Current position	Central Committee status	SASAC/Major company experience
Wang Qishan	1948	Secretary of CCDI	Politburo Standing Committee member	President, China Construction Bank, 94–97
Zhang Gaoli	1946	Executive Vice-Premier	Politburo Standing Committee member	General Manager, Maoming Oil Company, China Petrochemical Corporation, 84–85
Zhang Chunxian	1953	Party Secretary, Xinjiang	Politburo member	General Manager, China National Packaging and Food Machinery Corp, 93–95
Guo Shengkun	1954	State Councilor and Minister of Public Security	Full member	General Manager, Aluminum Corporation of China, 01–04
Wang Yong	1955	State Councilor	Full member	Vice-President, China Aerospace Electrical Group, 99–00; Minister of SASAC, 10–13
Lou Jiwei	1950	Minister of Finance	Full member	Chairman, China Investment Corporation, 07–13
Miao Wei	1955	Minister of Industry and Information Technology	Full member	General Manager, Dongfeng Auto Corporation, 99–05

Wang Zhigang	1957	Party Secretary and Executive Vice-Minister of Science and Tech.	Full member	General Manager, China Electronics Technology Group Corporation, 03–11
Jiang Jiemin	1955	Former Minister of SASAC (purged)	Full member	Chairman, China National Petroleum Corporation, 06–13
Xiao Gang	1958	Former Chairman of the China Securities Regulatory Commission	Full member	Chairman, Bank of China, 03–13
Xiang Junbo	1957	Chairman of the China Insurance Regulatory Commission	Full member	Chairman, China Agricultural Bank, 07–11
Wang Yupu	1956	First Secretary, All China Federation of Trade Unions	Full member	Chairman, Daqing Oilfield Co., 03–09
Xu Dazhe	1956	Vice-Minister of Industry and Information Technology	Full member	President, China Aerospace Science & Industry Corp, 07–13
Yang Dongliang	1954	Former Director of State Administration of Production Safety Supervision (purged)	Full member	Vice-President, Tianjin United Chemical Co., 94–96

Note and Source: CCDI = Central Commission for Discipline Inspection; SASAC = State-Owned Assets Supervision and Administration Commission; SOE = state-owned enterprises. From the author's database.

TABLE 5-3. Top Provincial/Municipal Leaders with Administrative Experience in the SASACs and Large SOEs, 2016

Name	Year born	Current position	Central Committee status	SASAC/Major company experience
Zhang Chunxian	1953	Party Secretary of Xinjiang	Politburo member	General Manager, China National Packaging and Food Machinery Corporation, 93–95
Zhang Qingwei	1961	Governor of Hebei	Full member	Chairman, Commercial Aircraft Corporation of China, 08–11
Su Shulin	1962	Former Governor of Fujian (purged)	Full member	Chairman, Sinopec Group, 07–11
Guo Shuqing	1956	Governor of Shandong	Full member	Chairman, China Construction Bank Corporation, 05–11
Lu Hao	1967	Governor of Heilongjiang	Full member	Vice-President, Beijing Textile Holding (Group) Corporation, 98–99
Zhang Guoqing	1964	Deputy Party Secretary of Chongqing	Full member	CEO, China North Industries Group Corporation, 08–13
Ma Xingrui	1959	Deputy Party Secretary of Guangdong, and Party Secretary of Shenzhen	Full member	President, China Aerospace Science and Technology Corp., 07–13

Chen Qiufa	1954	Governor of Liaoning	Full member	Head of Technology and Industry Bureau of National Defense, 08–13
Li Xiaopeng	1959	Governor of Shanxi	Alternate member	General Manager, China Huaneng Group, 99–08
Jiang Chaoliang	1957	Governor of Jilin	Alternate member	Chairman, China Agricultural Bank, 12–14; Governor, China Development Bank, 08–12; Chairman, China Communications Bank, 04–08
Hao Peng	1960	Governor of Qinghai	Alternate member	General Manager, AVIC Lanzhou Flight Control Instrument Factory, 95–99
Ren Xuefeng	1965	Party Secretary of Guangzhou	Alternate member	Chairman, the Hong Kong Alliance Group Limited, 04–08
Yang Xiong	1953	Mayor of Shanghai	None	Chairman, Shanghai Airlines, 98–01; President, Shanghai Alliance Investment, 93–98

Note and Source: SASAC = State-Owned Assets Supervision and Administration Commission; SOE = state-owned enterprises. From the author's database.

All of them are qualified based on age to serve on the Central Committee for at least another term beyond 2017. The remarkable presence of CEOs of SOEs among the young cohort on the Central Committee reflects a crucial occupational shift among the current Chinese leadership and suggests that some of the future top national leaders may come from this new pool.

The presence of top CCP national leaders with administrative experience at SOEs is not entirely new. Some top leaders in the third and fourth generations served as general managers or directors in factories and companies earlier in their careers. Former president Jiang Zemin served as director of several large factories in Shanghai and Changchun in the 1950s and 1960s. Former premier Li Peng served first as director of a power plant in northeastern China and then as chief of the Beijing Electricity Authority before being appointed vice-minister of the electric power industry in 1979.

There are, however, at least two main differences between the senior leaders Jiang Zemin and Li Peng and the current political leaders with business executive backgrounds, such as Zhang Qingwei. First, the business entities under the administration of the former group and the large companies led by the latter are fundamentally different, both in size and type. Companies such as the Commercial Aircraft Corporation of China are gigantic competitors in the global market. This gives their CEOs not only tremendous power in making financial and economic decisions but also an overwhelming sense of corporate responsibility given the high stakes of their decisions. Although all of these firms are state-owned monopolies enjoying preferential policies, their CEOs must have sharp business minds and global perspectives.

Second, the business leadership backgrounds of Jiang and Li are not considered the defining experiences of their political careers. Zhang and other business executives' experience in running China's flagship companies, however, is likely to be seen as the most salient evidence of their leadership abilities, both at present and in the future. Though business administrative experience did not serve as a major political stepping-stone for Jiang and Li, it likely did for Zhang and others. A majority of the third, fourth, and fifth generations of Chinese leaders did not have much leadership experience in business, and very few served as CEOs. The business leadership experience of Jiang and Li was an exception rather than a norm for their generation.

It is worth noting that the children and grandchildren of many top Chinese leaders are now pursuing careers in the business sector (as discussed in chapter 4), with most working in foreign joint ventures like investment banks rather than climbing the ladder of the CCP political hierarchy as their parents and grandparents did. If some of them aspire to political careers, as is likely, their paths to power will be very different from the precedent set by previous generations. This has important implications for the future of China's communist party-state.

THE RISE OF LEGAL PROFESSIONALS

Along with the economic and political rise of entrepreneurs, there has also been an increase in the power and influence of legal professionals. The Mao era was known for its hostile stance toward both the legal profession and the legal system. As a result, the legal profession was noticeably underdeveloped. At the start of the reform era in the early 1980s, there were only three thousand lawyers in a country of over one billion people.[49] Since then, the number of registered lawyers and law school students has greatly increased. In early 2014, China had a total of 250,000 lawyers in about 20,000 registered law firms.[50] This is still a small number (especially on a per capita basis) compared with the more than one million lawyers in the United States. But the number of lawyers in China has increased dramatically in recent years and will likely continue to grow.

Some of the PRC's lawyers work outside the political establishment to challenge abuses of power, including rampant official corruption, and seek to promote the rule of law at the grassroots level. While activist lawyers are an emerging group in Chinese politics, they are still subject to regulation and persecution by the party-state. All lawyers must be licensed by the government; the authorities often refuse to renew a license if the lawyer is regarded as a troublemaker. For example, the blind activist Chen Guangcheng, who was self-taught in legal procedures, brought a class action lawsuit against officials in his home province, charging them with abuses in connection with China's one-child policy. Chen was subsequently arrested in 2006 and then imprisoned for four years. After his release from prison in 2010, Chen was placed under strict house arrest. He escaped in April 2012 and took refuge in the U.S. embassy in Beijing.

Critics of China's legal development are cynical about the growing number of legal professionals in the CCP leadership, partially due to the controversies over the educational credentials of some leaders. Their major concern, however, is that the new leadership has neither loosened party control over the legal profession nor fostered genuine judicial independence. Instead, liberal legal scholars and human rights lawyers are often among the primary victims of harsh treatment, including imprisonment, as in the case of Xu Zhiyong, a doctoral graduate of Peking University Law School and well-known human rights lawyer.[51] The recent arrests of human rights lawyers in China further illustrate the cruel reality of legal development in the country.[52]

These troubling incidents remind students of Chinese politics both in China and abroad of the formidable obstacles facing proponents of legal and political reform in China. This situation is not surprising, however, given the country's absence of a legal tradition that constrains the political power of the leadership.

Most Chinese legal professionals work within the political or intellectual establishment. The rapid rise of leaders with legal training is nevertheless an important trend in Chinese politics. It is interesting to note that the current top leaders, President Xi Jinping, Premier Li Keqiang, Vice-President Li Yuanchao, and Vice-Premier Liu Yandong, all state in their official biographies that they hold law degrees. Whether these degrees could be called law degrees is controversial. Xi Jinping, Li Yuanchao, and Liu Yandong concentrated their studies on Marxism, socialism, and politics, respectively.[53] The recent controversy over the academic credentials of some law degree holders in the PRC leadership, however, should not overshadow the significance of the rapid rise of Chinese political leaders who have received their college or postgraduate education in the social sciences, including the study of law. Some PRC leaders have obtained law degrees that are more credible by Western standards. For example, Premier Li Keqiang attended a four-year undergraduate program at the Department of Law at Peking University. As a law student at Peking University, Li showed great interest in foreign constitutional law and comparative government. Li, together with his classmates, translated important Western legal works from English into Chinese.

While Li Keqiang did not pursue a career in the legal field after graduation, some of the rising stars in the current Chinese leadership have practiced extensively in the judicial and law enforcement fields. The newly formed 18th Central Committee of the CCP includes two representatives from the Supreme People's Court (President Zhou Qiang and Executive Vice-President Shen Deyong) and two representatives from the Supreme People's Procuratorate (Procurator-General Cao Jianming and Executive Deputy Procurator-General Hu Zejun). They all serve as full members of this crucial decisionmaking body. This stands in sharp contrast to the previous Central Committees, in which only one representative from each of those two supreme legal institutions held full membership. Each of the four aforementioned leaders attended the country's most prestigious law schools at both the undergraduate and graduate levels. Cao Jianming even taught at law schools in both the United States and Europe as a visiting professor. Leaders with similar legal training and professional experience have also emerged in the ministerial and provincial leadership, serving as ministers, provincial party secretaries, and governors.

The Chinese Communist Party's Changing View of and Ambivalent Stance toward Legal Development

The rise of legal professionals has paralleled the ideological change in the party-state. During the first three decades of the PRC, legal nihilism and legal instrumentalism dominated the public view of law. Lawyers and legal professionals were marginalized and occasionally became political targets. A good example of legal nihilism is Mao's remarks at the important CCP Politburo meeting in August 1958: "Every one of our party resolutions is law, and every meeting itself is law, and we can therefore maintain social order through resolutions and meetings."[54] From Mao's perspective, the party line—or his personal authority—was *the* law. The absence of basic legal consciousness was the reason that from 1949 to 1978 the PRC promulgated only two laws, the Constitution and the marriage law.

This historical background influenced the legal development of the reform era. Since economic reforms began in 1978, many top leaders who had suffered from the lawlessness of the Cultural Revolution—including Deng Xiaoping and then chairman of the Legal Committee of the National People's Congress Peng Zhen—have made systematic efforts to build a strong framework of laws in China. In the early 1990s Xi Zhongxun, Xi Jinping's father and then vice-chairman of the National People's Congress, said that China would always be at risk of disaster if the leadership did not figure out where the supreme power of the country should lie: in the party or in the Constitution.[55]

In the last two decades, top CCP leaders have often spoken of the need to strengthen the country's legal system. Jiang Zemin's work report to the 2002 National Party Congress also specified that the nation should establish a new Chinese-style legal system.[56] More recently, both Hu Jintao and Xi Jinping have made widely publicized speeches stressing the importance of the rule of law. In his first month as general secretary of the CCP, Xi Jinping made a speech marking the thirtieth anniversary of the amendment of the PRC Constitution. He claimed that "no organization or individual has the privilege to overstep the Constitution and the law."[57] He also said that the Chinese leadership "must firmly establish, throughout society, the authority of the Constitution and the law and allow the masses to fully believe in the law."[58]

In a very timely move, the Xi leadership devoted the Fourth Plenum of the 18th Central Committee, held in October 2014, to discussing the rule of law and legal reforms. This was the first time in CCP history that a Central Committee plenum focused on the country's legal development. Yet, critics in China and abroad were disappointed with the resolution of the meeting because it did not stress the supremacy of the Constitution over the CCP. Instead, it reaffirmed the party's leadership in establishing constitutional reforms, implying that the party would remain above the Constitution. Two decades after Xi Zhongxun's warning, this fundamental constitutional issue, as well as its accompanying risk, remains unchanged.

Despite the failure of the recent plenum to enact philosophical and ideological change in the CCP's governance of China, it outlined some important legal reforms.[59] In particular, the establishment of circuit courts, which will operate across administrative regions, is likely to bolster judicial independence. This change, along with the development of a mechanism to keep records of officials who interfere in judicial cases, will ostensibly limit the party's influence in legal affairs. The plenum also highlighted the importance of professional training for lawmakers, judges, and prosecutors and initiates a liability accounting system to hold officials responsible for poor decisions.

Over the years, many laws have been established in China, including the criminal law and the code of criminal procedure in 1979, the general principles of civil law in 1987, the administrative procedure law in 1989, the administrative punishment law in 1996, and the property law in 2007. The main motivation for the Chinese leadership to promulgate these laws has not been liberal legal thinking but self-interest, as the late Cai Dingjian, one of the prominent drafters of some of these laws, stated specifically with regard to the CCP leadership's desire to vindicate property rights in the Deng era.[60] China's transition to a market economy necessitated the development of more laws and regulations, without which the economy would fall into anarchy. In July 1981 the State Council established the Research Center of Economic Laws, which was responsible for drafting large-scale economic legislation. Of the 130 laws passed by the National People's Congress from 1979 to 1993, more than half were in the areas of economic and administrative law.[61]

According to the Chinese authorities, the PRC's legal framework had largely been established by the end of 2010. This legal system includes seven main functional areas: the Constitution, civil and commercial law, administrative law, economic law, social law, criminal law, and litigation and non-litigation procedural law. According to official counts, China has promulgated 239 laws in the reform era. The State Council has issued an additional 690 administrative rules and regulations, and local governments have issued about 8,600 laws and regulations.[62] Taken together, these developments are a substantial improvement over the legal vacuum of Mao's China. Although many of these laws have not been implemented or are insufficiently enforced, they represent an important foundation upon which a more effective system can be built.

The legal profession in China has grown alongside this rapid emergence of a Chinese body of law.[63] In the early years of the PRC the country had only four colleges specializing in politics and law.[64] Only a few universities established law departments, and all of these schools and programs were closed during the Cultural Revolution. In 1977 Peking University, Jilin University, and the Hubei Institute of Finance and Economics admitted law students for the first time after the Cultural Revolution; but out of the entire country, only 200 law students registered that year.[65] At that time, the legal specialization remained only part of a broader academic major called "politics and law" (政法, *zhengfa*). By 1980, fourteen colleges and law departments in the country had admitted an underwhelming total of 2,800 undergraduate law students.[66] By contrast, there were about 90,000 full-time students in more than 630 law schools and law departments in 2012.[67] Moreover, programs in legal studies—jurisprudence, constitutional law, administrative law, criminal law, civil law, procedural law, and environmental law—have become well-established professional subfields over the past two decades. The curricula of these legal studies are heavily influenced by similar courses taught in the West, as observed by He Qinhua, former president of East China University of Political Science and Law and current vice president of the Chinese Research Society of Justice.[68] He was a former classmate of Li Keqiang in Peking University's law department.

During his visit to China in 1998, while meeting with his Chinese hosts, President Bill Clinton was said to have exclaimed, "You have too many engineers and we [the United States] have too many lawyers. . . . Let's trade!" Today, in contrast to President Clinton's assumption in 1998, China seemingly no longer needs to "trade" elites with, nor "import" lawyers from, the United States. In a single generation, legal professionals, including many law degree holders, have played an increasingly important role in various areas of Chinese political life. A few have come to occupy some of the most powerful leadership posts. According to an employment survey conducted in 2014 at three law schools (Southwestern University of Political Science and Law, East China University of Political Science and Law, and the China University of Political Science and Law), 43.5 percent of graduates work in the private sector and 31 percent work at governmental organizations. These figures exclude those who are pursuing further studies in China or abroad.[69]

Under all of these circumstances, the educational and occupational composition of the Chinese political elite has changed profoundly. As table 5-4 shows, full members of the Central Committee who are trained in social sciences, law, and economic management have increased substantially over the past decade, replacing leaders trained in engineering and natural sciences. Leaders on the Central Committee trained in social sciences, including law, have significantly increased in the last fifteen years, as illustrated in figure 5-6. Full members of the Central Committee who were trained in social sciences grew from 5.6 percent in 1997 to 38.2 percent in 2012, while those who held law degrees rose from 1.7 percent to 14.1 percent over the same period.

TABLE 5-4. Educational Background of Full Members of the 16th and 18th Central Committees, 2002 and 2012

Subject	16th Central Committee	18th Central Committee
Engineering and science	45.6	11.1
Economics and management	6.7	28.7
Social science and law	11.8	38.2
Humanities	11.8	10.0
Military education	19.5	8.5
Unknown	4.6	3.5
Total	100.0%	100.0%

Note and Source: If a leader's undergraduate major differs from his or her postgraduate education focus, this study counts only the latter. Chinese Communist Party Organization Department and Research Office of the History of the Chinese Communist Party, comp., *Zhongguo gongchandang lijie zhongyang weiyuan dacidian, 1921–2003* [Who's who of the members of the Central Committees of the Chinese Communist Party, 1921–2003]. (Beijing: *Zhonggong dangshi chubanshe*, 2004). Xinhua News Agency, www.news.cn/politics /leaders/index.htm. Calculated by the author.

Legal professionals, including political elites with law degrees, have become an important group within the leadership, regardless of whether they actually practice law. A law degree has become a valuable credential for party standing. As discussed in the previous chapter, a considerable number of the members of the 18th Central Committee received their advanced degree through part-time programs and often at various party schools. Therefore, they might not have met high academic standards. However, putting aside the weakness of the academic credentials of some law degree holders, certain party members did receive a solid legal education. For those studying Chinese elite politics, it is essential to understand the different subgroups of "law degree" holders in the CCP leadership, based on their educational and professional backgrounds.

Law Degree Holders in the Central Committee: Typology and Characteristics

A review of the biographical backgrounds of the newly formed Central Committee of the CCP shows that fifty-two members (thirty-four full and eighteen alternates) hold "law degrees" or have received formal legal education, accounting for about 14 percent of the committee as a whole. In the twenty-five-member Politburo, there are six law degree holders (24 percent). Peng Chun, a scholar of the Chinese legal system at Oxford University, notes that "law/legal studies" (法学, *faxue*) is actually an umbrella term that encompasses

FIGURE 5-6. Full Members of the Central Committee Trained in Law or the Social Sciences, 1997–2012

Percent

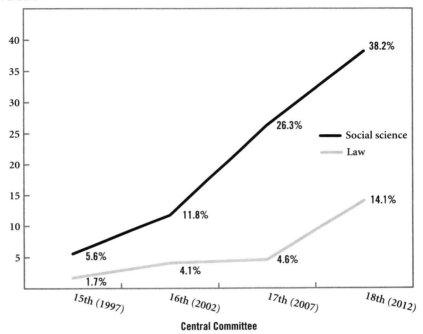

Note and Source: If a leader's undergraduate major differs from his or her postgraduate education focus, this study only counts the latter. Chinese Communist Party Organization Department and Research Office of the History of the Chinese Communist Party, comp., *Zhongguo gongchandang lijie zhongyang weiyuan dacidian, 1921–2003* [Who's who of the members of the Central Committees of the Chinese Communist Party 1921–2003] (Beijing: *Zhonggong dangshi chubanshe*, 2004). Xinhua News Agency, www.news.cn/politics/leaders /index.htm. Calculated by the author.

not only the discipline of law *sensu stricto* but also political science, sociology, ethnography, and Marxism."[70]

This study divides the CCP leaders with law degrees into three categories, based largely on the nature of their academic training and professional experience: (1) leaders who hold a law degree in name only, but actually studied political science or Marxism, (2) leaders who are legally trained but have never practiced law, and (3) leaders who are legal professionals in terms of both educational credentials and professional practice. Table 5-5 shows the distribution of these three types among the fifty-two leaders in this study.

The first category, leaders who hold a law degree in name only, includes four Politburo Standing Committee and Politburo members: President Xi

TABLE 5-5. Subgroups of Law Degree Holders on the 18th Central Committee, 2016

Types	Full member or alternate member		Full-time or part-time education		Total	
	Full	Alternate	Full	Part	No.	%
Law degree in name only	9	3	2	10	12	23.1
Legally trained but nonpracticing	15	12	7	20	27	51.9
Legal professionals	10	3	6	7	13	25.0
Total	34	18	15	37	52	100.0

Source: Xinhua News Agency, http://www.news.cn/politics/leaders/index.htm. From the author's database.

Jinping, Vice-President Li Yuanchao, Vice-Premier Liu Yandong, and Director of the Central Policy Research Office Wang Huning. Xi Jinping attended a part-time doctoral degree program in law (Marxism) at the School of Humanities and Social Sciences of Tsinghua University in Beijing from 1998 to 2002, while he was serving as a top provincial leader in Fujian. Li Yuanchao attended a doctoral degree program in law (scientific socialism) at the Central Party School in Beijing from 1991 to 1995; at the same time, he was working at the CCP Leading Group on Foreign Communication and as a deputy director of the State Council Information Office. Liu Yandong was enrolled in a doctoral degree program in law (politics) at the School of Public Administration of Jilin University in Changchun from 1994 to 1998; during those four years, she was also a deputy director of the CCP United Front Work Department. Wang Huning was enrolled in a master's degree program in law (international politics) at Fudan University in Shanghai from 1978 to 1981 and later served as dean of the Law School at Fudan University in 1994 and 1995. With the exception of Wang, all earned their advanced degrees on a part-time basis.

Some other leaders also obtained a law degree in name only. Former minister of Culture Cai Wu received a doctoral degree in law (international politics) from Peking University. Jiangsu party secretary Luo Zhijun attended a master's program in law (politics) at the Chinese University of Political Science and Law in Beijing from 1994 to 1995, while working in the national leadership of the Chinese Communist Youth League. The chairman of the China Insurance Regulatory Commission, Xiang Junbo, obtained a doctoral degree in law (international politics) from Peking University in 1998, when he was a senior official at the National Audit Office in Beijing. Of the twelve leaders in this category, ten (83 percent) attended their program part-time.

The second category, leaders who are legally trained but have never practiced law, comprises more than half of the law degree holders on the 18th Central Committee. In addition to Premier Li Keqiang, a few other prominent leaders also fall into this category. Politburo member and Chongqing party secretary Sun Zhengcai attended a part-time master's degree program in law at the Central Party School in 2002 and 2003, majoring in legal theory. Du Qinglin, a member of the CCP Secretariat and executive vice-chairman of the Chinese People's Political Consultative Conference, obtained his bachelor's degree in law through a correspondence program from the Law School of Jilin University in 1992 and 1993, during which time he was deputy secretary of Hainan Province. Minister of Agriculture Han Changfu attended a master's degree program in economic law at the Chinese University of Political Science and Law in Beijing from 1990 to 1993, while working at the Chinese Communist Youth League Central Committee. Sichuan party secretary Wang Dongming attended the master's program in law at the Central Party School from 1996 to 1999. The former chairman of the China Securities Regulatory Commission, Xiao Gang, received a master's degree from the Department of Law at Renmin University in 1996. Shandong governor Guo Shuqing received a master's degree in law from the Chinese Academy of Social Sciences in 1988.

Like Premier Li Keqiang, several leaders in this category received solid full-time undergraduate training in law soon after the resumption of the national college entrance examination. The chairman of the Chinese People's Political Consultative Conference of Beijing, Ji Lin, attended the bachelor's degree program in law at Renmin University from 1978 to 1982. The chairman of the Chinese People's Political Consultative Conference of Xinjiang, Nuerlan Abudumanjin, received a bachelor's degree in law from Xinjiang University in 1985. The deputy party secretary of Xinjiang, Han Yong, received undergraduate training in law at Jilin University from 1977 to 1980. Legally trained leaders in this category, however, have neither practiced law as attorneys nor worked in the legal field.

The final category, leaders who are legal professionals in terms of both educational credentials and professional practice, consists of thirteen leaders who not only have received formal training in law but also have practiced as attorneys, judges, prosecutors, and legal scholars or have worked in other fields of law enforcement. Former Executive Vice-Minister of Public Security and current Director of the State Administration of Work Safety Yang Huanning received his bachelor's degree in law and forensic science from the Southwest University of Political Science and Law in 1983 and his master's degree in criminal law from Peking University in 2001. Yang advanced his career almost exclusively in the domain of public security and law enforcement.

Table 5-6 presents biographical information about eight of these leaders. All of them were born in the 1950s or early 1960s and attended the country's best law schools—the Southwest University of Political Science and Law, the Chinese University of Political Science and Law, and Peking University. Most pursued their legal education full-time, especially at the undergraduate level.

Three leaders have studied law overseas. The procurator-general of the Supreme People's Procuratorate, Cao Jianming, served as professor and president of East China University of Political Science and Law for many years before he moved to Beijing and became vice-president of the Supreme People's Court in 1999. In his early years he studied law at Ghent University in Belgium from 1988 to 1989 and then taught at the University of San Francisco in the United States from July to December 1990. The secretary-general of the CCP Central Political and Legal Committee and deputy secretary-general of the State Council, Wang Yongqing, was a visiting scholar at Harvard University's Kennedy School of Government for a short time in 2006. The governor and deputy party secretary of Jiangsu, Shi Taifeng, studied at the Law School of the University of Amsterdam in the Netherlands from 1991 to 1992.

A number of leaders have taught at the top law schools in China. Hu Zejun taught at her alma mater, Southwest University of Political Science and Law, for ten years (1985 to 1995) after she received her master's degree. During the same period she was also serving as secretary of the Chinese Communist Youth League and later as party secretary of the university. Shi Taifeng also taught law at the Central Party School for twenty years (1990 to 2010), during which time he was also chairman of the Department of Law and vice-president of the school in charge of legal studies.

All of those mentioned above have substantial work experience in the legal field. And with the exception of Shi Taifeng, all still work in the legal field. Several of them gained work experience earlier in their careers as *mishu* (personal assistants) to senior lawmakers or justices in the country. In the mid-1990s Zhou Qiang served as a *mishu* to then minister of Justice Xiao Yang, who later became president of the Supreme People's Court, the position that Zhou now holds. The newly appointed director of the PRC central government's Liaison Office in Hong Kong, Zhang Xiaoming, served as a *mishu* to Liao Hui, director of the Hong Kong and Macao Affairs Office of the State Council, between 1986 and 2006. During that time, he witnessed the entire legal and political process (including the diplomatic negotiations) surrounding Hong Kong's handover to the PRC.

Another leader, Wang Yongqing, has worked as a *mishu* in the legal system for almost his entire career. After receiving his bachelor's degree in law from Jilin University and his master's degree in law from Peking University in 1987, Wang began his career as a clerk in the research department of the State Council Legislative Affairs Office. While there, he moved up and became a *mishu* and office director for more than twenty years before assuming the post of deputy chief-of-staff of the State Council in 2008. He now concurrently works as the chief-of-staff of the Central Political and Legal Committee of the CCP Central Committee.

The newly appointed deputy chief-of-staff of the Central Political and Legal Committee, Xu Xianming, is a distinguished legal scholar who played a direct role in 2004 in amending the PRC Constitution with the provision that "the state should respect and protect human rights."[71] Born in Shandong in 1957, Xu attended Jilin University's law school in 1978 as an undergraduate and earned his master's degree in law at the same school in 1985. After graduation, he began to teach law at Shandong University, where he served successively as an instructor, assistant head, and then head of the law department, dean of the law school, and vice-president of the university. He served as president of the Chinese University of Political Science and Law from 2001 to 2007 and as president of Shandong University from 2008 to 2013. He is also a standing committee member of the National People's Congress, vice-president of the China Law Society, and chairman of the Chinese Jurisprudence Research Association.

The president and vice-presidents of China's Supreme People's Court have biographical backgrounds similar to the leaders in this subgroup (see table 5-7). All of them received postgraduate legal education at China's most prestigious law schools. Four of them were also members of the famous undergraduate class of 1982. Five attended the prestigious Southwest University of Political Science and Law and four studied at Peking University's law school. Vice-President He Rong studied in the master's program in civil and commercial law at the University of Technology, Sydney. Vice-President Tao Kaiyuan was a visiting scholar at the University of British Columbia. Both speak excellent English. Wan E'xiang, former vice-president of the Supreme People's Court, was appointed in March 2013 as vice-chairman of the National People's Congress. He received an LL.M degree from Yale Law School in 1987 and also did research at the University of Michigan Law School and the Max Planck Institute for Comparative Public Law and International Law in Heidelberg, Germany, from 1990 to 1991. Former vice-president Xi Xiaoming, who was purged on corruption charges in 2015, also studied law as a visiting scholar at the London School of Economics and Political Science.

All nine of these justices have had substantial legal experience before their current appointment to the Supreme People's Court. In fact, most of

TABLE 5-6. Members of the 18th Central Committee with Formal Training and Professional Experience in the Legal Field

Name	Birth year	Position	Central Committee status	Legal education	Full-time/ part-time	Legal experience
Zhou Qiang	1960	President of the Supreme People's Court	Full member	Bachelor's Degree in Law (Southwest University of Political Science and Law)	Full	Ministry of Justice (1985–95), Supreme People's Court (2013–present)
				Master's Degree in Law (Southwest University of Political Science and Law)	Full	
Shen Deyong	1954	Executive Vice-President of the Supreme People's Court	Full member	Master's Degree in Law (Chinese University of Political Science and Law)	Full	Jiangxi Provincial Higher People's Court (1988–97), Supreme People's Court (1998–06, 2008–present)
Cao Jianming	1955	Procurator-General of the Supreme People's Procuratorate	Full member	Bachelor's Degree in Law (East China University of Political Science and Law)	Full	East China University of Political Science and Law (1986–99), Supreme People's Court (1999–2008)
				Master's Degree in Law (East China University of Political Science and Law)	Full	
Hu Zejun (f)	1955	Executive Deputy Procurator-General of the Supreme People's Procuratorate	Full member	Bachelor's Degree in Law (Southwest University of Political Science and Law)	Full	Southwest University of Political Science and Law (1985–95), Ministry of Justice (1995–2004), Supreme People's Procuratorate (2010–present)
				Master's Degree in Law (Southwest University of Political Science and Law)	Full	

Name	Birth year	Position	Membership	Education	Full/Part	Work experience
Wang Yongqing	1959	Secretary-General of CCP Central Political and Legal Committee and Deputy Secretary-General of the State Council	Full member	Bachelor's Degree in Law (Jilin University); Master's Degree in Law (Peking University); Doctoral Degree in Law (Jilin University)	Full; Full; Part	Legislative Affairs Bureau of the State Council (1987–98); Legislative Affairs Office of the State Council (1998–2008)
Yang Huanning	1957	Director of the State Administration of Work Safety	Full member	Bachelor's Degree in Law (Southwest University of Political Science and Law); Doctoral Degree in Law (Peking University)	Full; Part	Public Security Bureau of Heilongjiang Province (1992–96), Ministry of Public Security (1996–present)
Zhang Xiaoming	1963	Director of the PRC Central Government's Liaison Office in Hong Kong	Alternate member	Bachelor's Degree in Law (Southwest University of Political Science and Law); Master's Degree in Law (Renmin University)	Full; Full	State Council's Hong Kong and Macau Office in charge of Hong Kong basic legal issues (2001–2012)
Shi Taifeng	1956	Governor and Deputy Party Secretary of Jiangsu	Alternate member	Bachelor's Degree in Law (Peking University); Master's Degree in Law (Peking University)	Full; Full	Law Department of the Central Party School (1990–2010)

Note and Source: (f) = female. From the author's database.

TABLE 5-7. Biographical Sketches of President and Vice-Presidents of the Supreme People's Court, 2016

Name	Birth year	Position	Law degree (graduation year)	School	Main legal work experience	Foreign studies
Zhou Qiang	1960	President	Bachelor's (82) Master's (85)	Southwest Univ. of Political Science and Law	Supreme Court (13–present), (Ministry of Justice, 85–95)	
Shen Deyong	1954	Executive Vice-President	Master's (83)	Chinese Univ. of Political Science and Law	Supreme Court (98–06, 08–present), Province Court (Jiangxi, 88–97)	
Jiang Bixin	1956	Vice-President	Bachelor's (82) Master's (85) Doctoral (04)	Southwest Univ. of Political Science and Law, Peking Univ.	Supreme Court (85–04, 07–present), Province Court (Hunan, 04–07)	
Li Shaoping	1956	Vice-President	Bachelor's (82) Master's (87)	Southwest Univ. of Political Science and Law, Peking Univ.	Supreme Court (13–present), Province Court (Sichuan 87–07), Tianjin, 03–13)	

Name	Year	Position	Education	University	Court	Overseas
Nan Ying	1954	Vice-President	Bachelor's (80) Master's (02)	Peking Univ., Southwest Univ. of Political Science and Law	Supreme Court (80–04, 09–present), Province Court (Heilongjiang 04–09)	
Jing Hanchao	1960	Vice-President	Bachelor's (82) Master's (97) Doctoral (03)	Southwest Univ. of Political Science and Law, Peking Univ.	Supreme Court (94–96, 06–present), Province Court (84–94)	
Huang Ermei (f)	1951	Vice-President	Bachelor's (83) Master's (97)	Peking Univ.	Supreme Court (83–present)	
He Rong (f)	1962	Vice-President	Bachelor's (84) Master's (04) Doctoral (06)	Chinese Univ. of Political Science and Law	Supreme Court (11–present), Province Court (Beijing 84–11)	Univ. of Technology, Sydney (02–04)
Tao Kaiyuan (f)	1964	Vice-President	Bachelor's (88) Doctoral (00)	Law School of Wuhan Univ.	Supreme Court (13–present), Province Court (Guangdong, 99–08)	Univ. of British Columbia (02–03)

Note and Source: (f) = female. Supreme People's Court website, http://www.court.gov.cn/jgsz/zgrmfyld. Tabulated and expanded by the author.

them have spent their entire careers after graduation in the court. For example, Vice-President Jiang Bixin began his career as an assistant judge at the research office of the Supreme People's Court in 1985 after receiving his master's degree in law from Southwest University of Political Science and Law. He was an assistant judge at the Administrative Tribunals of the Supreme People's Court from 1988 to 1993 while working in the Xuanwu District Court in Beijing and at the Beijing Higher People's Court. He was promoted to judge in 1993, vice-president in 1995, and president in 1998—all in the Administrative Tribunals of the Supreme People's Court. He was vice-president of the Supreme People's Court from 2002 to 2004. Jiang was transferred to the Hunan Higher People's Court and worked as president for three years. He returned to the Supreme People's Court in 2007 and has since been serving as vice-president.

The law degree holders of the third subgroup, leaders who are legal professionals in terms of both educational credentials and professional practice, do not hold law degrees "in name only." Instead, they are the real legal professionals in the CCP leadership in terms of their educational credentials and work experience. In present-day China they are still first and foremost party officials. It remains to be seen whether this subgroup of law degree holders will expand in number and influence within the party leadership, and even more important, whether their extensive legal training will lead them to promote China's judicial independence.

SUMMARY

During his seven-decade-long academic career, the British historian Joseph Needham tried to explain what Sinologists later called "the Needham paradox."[72] Paradoxically, although imperial China had many talented people and was advanced in science, the country started to decline around the fifteenth and sixteenth centuries. According to Needham, a primary reason for China's decline was that the country "lost its edge" by suppressing technicians and merchants, "whose power posed a threat to the Emperor."[73]

The conditions that Needham identified persisted in China through the twentieth century, but the landscape underwent profound changes beginning in the mid-1990s. This was particularly evident at the 15th National Party Congress in 1997 and the 16th National Party Congress in 2002. Members of the Politburo Standing Committees formed during these two Congresses were *all* engineers by training. Furthermore, the Chinese leadership codified in the CCP Constitution what was already true in practice—the enthusiastic recruitment of merchants, known as "entrepreneurs" by the Chinese, or "capitalists" to Western observers.[74] China's business elites—not only private entrepreneurs in firms of various sizes, but also politically connected and globally minded executives at SOEs—have played an increasingly prominent role in Chinese economic and sociopolitical life.

Do these changes necessarily imply the end of the "Needham paradox"? China has already emerged as an economic powerhouse and as the second-largest economy in the world. It is evident that the PRC's elite transformations and the country's shifts in socioeconomic policy during the reform era were profoundly consequential. China has precipitated its historic rise on the world stage, and this becomes a testimony to the proposition in Western social science literature that the occupational identities of political leaders usually have a bearing on other characteristics of a country's development. If political elites have professional expertise and interest in a certain policy area, they will strive to leave a legacy of strong leadership in that area.[75] Technocrats have been known to devote special attention to economic growth and technological development—subjects they studied early in life or on which they have centered their careers. This tendency is clearly reflected in the legacy of the engineer-dominated third and fourth generations of PRC leadership.

The occupational change in the Chinese political elite during the reform era has been remarkably dynamic, with the so-called rule of the technocrats lasting for only about two decades. In recent years the fifth and sixth generations of Chinese leaders are more known for their educational and professional training in the social sciences, economic administration, and law. Many CCP leaders now seek to earn credentials in the field of law. This may not only indicate an important political and ideological shift in the Chinese political establishment but also reflect societal change and a greater demand for judicial development in the country at large.

It is interesting to note the similar sequences of elite transformation in Taiwan and mainland China during the past half century—from revolutionary military and ideological elites, to technocrats, and then to business elites and lawyers. Does Taiwan's political system today foreshadow a similar political transformation for mainland China tomorrow? Any political predictions about China's future based on comparative studies must seriously consider demographic variations and situational factors. Yet, it is notable that identical elite transformations have occurred in these two culturally similar polities.

However, the study of law by CCP leaders differs profoundly from that of their Taiwanese counterparts. For example, the former president of the Republic of China, Ma Ying-jeou, and the former vice-president Lü Hsiu-lien both received their law degrees from Harvard Law School. The current president of the Republic of China, Tsai Ing-wen, received law degrees from both Cornell University and the London School of Economics and Political Science. While the credibility of some PRC leaders' law degrees is open to dispute, some leaders in the fifth and sixth generations did receive a solid legal education in China or even abroad. This trend is likely to continue.

Chinese liberal scholars have called for legal professionalism, which seems to indicate the desire that lawyers or legally educated leaders will "bring to policymaking not only legal expertise but, more importantly, a deep commitment to justice."[76] It would be naïve and questionable to assume that the legal education of a top leader guarantees a genuine commitment to reinforcing legal frameworks and to strengthening the rule of law in the course of governance. Chen Shui-bian, a lawyer who became president of the Republic of China, was notorious for his disregard of law and his involvement in corruption and other criminal activities. Similarly, Russian president Vladimir Putin is clearly not known for promoting the rule of law or political democracy, despite his possession of a law degree from the prestigious Leningrad State University.

In the early decades of the PRC, law was seen largely as a tool for the ruling class to maintain its power and exercise dictatorship. Not surprisingly, before the late 1990s, while discussing the role of law in the country, Chinese authorities often used the phrase "using law to rule the country" (以法制国, yifa zhiguo) rather than "governing the country according to law" (依法治国, yifa zhiguo).[77] These two phrases have exactly the same pronunciation in Chinese, but fundamentally different connotations. The former emphasizes the utility of law as a means of reinforcing the dominant role of the party, and the latter says that no individual, group, or party should be above the law. Despite the emphasis on constitutional development in the recent Fourth Plenum of the 18th Central Committee, there has been no ideological, philosophical, or legal breakthrough.

The contradicting forces of advanced legal reform and continued CCP interference in the legal system—as evidenced by the growing representation of law degree holders in leadership and the regime's harsh treatment of independent lawyers and NGO activists—are a defining characteristic of contemporary Chinese politics. China's future hinges on whether the continued development of legal professionalism and constitutionalism can resolve this impasse.

It would be a mistake, however, to overlook the importance of the occupational composition of governing elites. In any given country the rise of lawyers often parallels sociopolitical and legal transformation. Strong representation of lawyers is an essential component of a democratic political system. China's legal development—including the authority of lawyers and the influence of the legal community—is, of course, still in its infancy. The potential consequences of this development for the Chinese political system deserve greater scholarly attention.

If one accepts the basic premise of Western elite studies, as discussed in the beginning of this chapter, there must be a relationship or correlation between, on the one hand, greater elite understanding of constitutionalism and the rule of law and, on the other, prospects for subordinating the party to the constitution. The evolution of China's legal system, especially the issuance of an impressively large number of laws and the rapid rise of leaders with law education and training in the last decade, will make it more likely for the country to move toward an independent judiciary. It stands to reason that the current fifth generation and the emerging sixth generation, populated as they are by a higher percentage of leaders educated in social sciences and law, may seek to have an impact on political and legal reforms. This task is particularly crucial for a Chinese political system that has been beset by rampant official corruption and various forms of favoritism and nepotism in elite recruitment.

CHAPTER 6

Mishu

Favoritism and Corruption in Elite Politics

In any country, corruption tends to increase when more respectable
means of social advancement break down.
—KATHERINE BOO

Mentor-protégé ties play an important role in elite formation in virtually
all political systems.[1] But arguably no country gives more prominent
advantage, in terms of promoting those who have previously served as personal assistants to senior leaders, than China. This phenomenon of having a
large set of leaders with such experience has led to the adoption of the Chinese
term *mishu* to refer to this group. At present, more than three-quarters of
cabinet ministers and provincial governors have served as *mishu*.[2] Of the
current twenty-five members of the Politburo, sixteen (64 percent) have served
in such roles, and of the seven-member Politburo Standing Committee (PSC),
five (71 percent) have *mishu* backgrounds.

Equally significant, the recent purges of such senior leaders as Zhou
Yongkang, Xu Caihou, Guo Boxiong, and Ling Jihua all began with the
removal or investigation of their *mishu*. The fall of these very senior leaders of the Chinese Communist Party (CCP) whose scandals were linked to
the operational input of their *mishu* has raised public concern about the
ubiquitous role and tremendous power of *mishu* in the Chinese political
system.

207

THE DEFINITION OF *MISHU*: HISTORICAL ORIGIN AND POLITICAL CONTEXT

By definition, the term *mishu* refers to office clerks who deal with paperwork (respond to mail and file documents), schedule meetings, and assist their bosses in handling their daily routines. *Mishu* are a diverse group, including a wide range of people who differ significantly from one another in terms of nature of work, functional areas, length of experience, level of leadership at which they serve, and responsibilities given to them. Important distinctions should be made between organizational (机关, *jiguan*) and personal (个人, *geren*) *mishu*; between chiefs-of-staff or secretaries-general (秘书长, *mishuzhang*) and office directors (办公室主任, *bangongshi zhuren*); between bodyguards (贴身警卫, *tieshen jingwei*) and civilian secretaries (文职秘书, *wenzhi mishu*); and between aides with high official status (助理, *zhuli*) and office clerks (办事员, *banshiyuan*) whose duties are typically limited to typing correspondence and answering phone calls.[3] During the first few decades of the People's Republic of China (PRC), *mishu* were often referred to as clerks (干事, *ganshi*) in various functional areas such as administration, organization, and propaganda. The differences between these various subgroups of *mishu* are enormous. In general, for example, a *mishu* works for one individual leader, whereas a *mishuzhang* may work on behalf of several people and often also holds institutional responsibilities. The level and scope of influence of *mishu* and *mishuzhang* are therefore quite different.

Secretaries-general or chiefs-of-staff certainly play an important administrative role. The experience of serving as a secretary-general or a director of the general office at the national level of party and government leadership is undoubtedly a stepping-stone to further promotion. Among the eleven leaders who have served (or still serve) as director of the General Office of the CCP Central Committee since the founding of the PRC, all have held the status of "highest-ranking party and state leaders" (党和国家领导人, *dang he guojia lingdaoren*).[4] Seven of them (Yang Shangkun, Wang Dongxing, Yao Yilin, Hu Qili, Qiao Shi, Wen Jiabao, and Zeng Qinghong) later served on the PSC, and three (Wang Zhaoguo, Wang Gang, and Li Zhanshu) served or currently serve in the Politburo. Only Ling Jihua did not make it to the Politburo, and he was recently purged on corruption charges. Ling, however, had served as vice-chair of the Chinese People's Political Consultative Conference before the purge and thus was among the "highest-ranking party and state leaders."

Some of these former or current directors of the General Office of the CCP Central Committee also later served as top state leaders (Yang Shangkun as PRC president, Qiao Shi as chairman of the National People's Congress, Wen Jiabao as premier, and Zeng Qinghong as PRC vice-president). In the

State Council the post of secretary-general was extremely important in its own right. Xi Jinping's father, Xi Zhongxun, for example, had served as secretary-general for six years before being promoted to vice-premier in 1959. In the last three decades, all secretaries-general of the State Council have concurrently served as either vice-premier or state councilor.

Top Chinese Communist Party Leaders and Their Mishu Clusters

In PRC history, top leaders' personal secretaries (贴身秘书, *tieshen mishu*), also known as chief aides (大秘, *dami*), and bodyguards often later became high-ranking senior leaders themselves. For example, Mao's political *mishu* Chen Boda and Hu Qiaomu later served as a PSC member and a Politburo member, respectively. Wang Dongxing, who served as Mao's bodyguard from 1947 to 1958 and worked as director of the Bodyguard Bureau of the General Office of the CCP Central Committee during the Cultural Revolution, later served as vice-chairman of the CCP.

Deng Xiaoping's personal secretary for over three decades, Wang Ruilin, later served as deputy director of the General Political Department of the People's Liberation Army (PLA) with the military rank of full general, and he was in charge of military personnel appointments throughout most of the 1990s. When Deng was purged for the first time in 1967, he was allowed to take an assistant with him to Jiangxi, where he was assigned to do manual labor. Deng chose Wang Ruilin, who had served as his *mishu* since 1952, soon after the founding of the PRC. Both survived the physical hardship and political uncertainty in Jiangxi. When Deng returned to power in the late 1970s and became vice-chairman of the Central Military Commission (CMC), Wang became director of Deng's office.[5] As Deng's most trusted confidant, Wang later also served as secretary of the Discipline Inspection Commission of the PLA (1990–93) and as a member of the CMC (1995–2003). After returning to power in 1978, almost all of Deng Xiaoping's *mishu* were uniformed PLA officers with high military ranking. They included Zhang Baozhong (lieutenant general), Sun Yong (lieutenant general), Nian Fuchun (lieutenant general), Zhao Jiashun (major general), Chen Menghua (major general), and Wang Fuzhong (major general).

Similarly, Jiang Zemin was always keen to promote his *mishu* to key positions in both the civilian and military bureaucracies. In 1989, when Jiang, then party secretary of Shanghai, was promoted to general secretary of the CCP, he took with him two top aides, Zeng Qinghong and Jia Ting'an. Zeng had previously served as Jiang's chief-of-staff (secretary-general of the Shanghai Municipal Party Committee). Zeng continued to serve as Jiang's top aide in Beijing as deputy director (1989–1993) and director (1993–1999) of the General Office of the CCP Central Committee. Zeng played a crucial role in helping Jiang to consolidate power both in Shanghai and Beijing, as elaborated on later in the chapter.

Jia Ting'an began to serve as a *mishu* for Jiang when Jiang was the highest-ranking vice-minister of the Ministry of Electronics Industry in the early 1980s. He followed Jiang to Shanghai in 1985 when Jiang was appointed mayor. Three years later, Jia was promoted to deputy director of the General Office of the Shanghai Municipal Party Committee, assisting then Shanghai party secretary Jiang. In June 1989 Jia served as director of Jiang's office while Jiang held the position of CCP general secretary. Five months later, he also concurrently served as Jiang's *mishu* in the Office of Chairman of the CMC, the position that Jiang held. It is believed that Jia did not join the PLA until this CMC *mishu* appointment. In 1994 Jia was concurrently promoted to deputy director of the General Office of the CMC and director of the Office of the Chairman of the CMC with the military rank of major general. He was promoted to director of the General Office of the CMC in 2003. One year after Jiang stepped down as CMC chairman, Jia was granted the military rank of lieutenant general. Since 2007 Jia has served as deputy director of the General Political Department of the PLA. Like Wang Ruilin, Jia Ting'an was also in charge of discipline affairs in the military for a period of time. Jia was granted the rank of full general in 2011.

Jiang's other *mishu* and bodyguards also were promoted to important leadership positions. For example, Huang Liman, Jiang's *mishu* during his tenure as minister of the Ministry of Electronics Industry in the early 1980s, later served as party secretary of Shenzhen and chairman of the Guangdong People's Congress. Guo Kailang, Jiang's *mishu* in the 1990s when he was the general secretary of the party, now serves as director of the Organization Department of the Hunan Provincial Party Committee. Jiang's most trusted confidant is You Xigui, his former bodyguard (who still works for Jiang). You served as deputy director of the Bodyguard Bureau, in charge of Jiang's security, when Jiang was appointed as party general secretary in 1989. You was promoted to director of the Bodyguard Bureau in 1994 and deputy director of the General Office of the CCP Central Committee in 1997. You was granted the military rank of major general in 1990, lieutenant general in 1997, and general in 2004.

For Hu Jintao, three *mishu*—Ye Kedong, Chen Shiju, and Ling Jihua— provided tremendous support for him in his advancement to the top leadership. Ye Kedong, a native of Guangxi who was born in 1953, studied philosophy at Zhongshan University in Guangzhou. After graduation he worked as a *mishu* for Hu Jintao at the General Office of the Central Committee of the Chinese Communist Youth League (CCYL) from 1983 to 1985, when Hu was in charge of the league. He followed Hu Jintao to work in Guizhou and Tibet in the following years.[6] Ye worked in the field of Taiwan, Hong Kong, and Macao affairs in the last two decades; he served as deputy director of the Office of Taiwan Affairs of the Central Committee of the CCP from 2006 to 2015.

Chen Shiju, who was born in Guizhou in 1963, worked as a *mishu* for Hu Jintao for as many as twenty-seven years. After graduating from Guizhou University in 1985 (and briefly serving as an instructor in the university's philosophy department), Chen Shiju began to work for then Guizhou party secretary Hu Jintao. Chen accompanied Hu to Tibet in 1988 when Hu served as Tibet party secretary, and then Hu brought Chen to Beijing in 1992 when Hu was appointed to membership in the PSC. Chen served as director of General Secretary Hu Jintao's office from 2002 to 2012 and was promoted to deputy director of the General Office of the CCP Central Committee after Hu's retirement in 2013. Chen has continued to serve in that position (with promotion to the full ministerial rank in January 2015).

Ling Jihua had long been regarded as one of President Hu's most important aides. They met in the early 1980s while working together at the CCYL Central Committee. Ling advanced his career largely at the CCYL national leadership. There, Ling served as deputy head of the Theoretical Research Division of the Propaganda Department of the CCYL Central Committee (1985–1988), director of the Office of the CCYL Secretariat (1988–1990), deputy director of the General Office of the CCYL Central Committee and concurrently editor-in-chief of the CCYL magazine (1990–94), and director of the Propaganda Department of the CCYL Central Committee (1994–95). Hu's and Ling's shared identity as CCYL officials (known as *tuanpai*) further consolidated their political bonds. In the middle and late 1990s, when Ling served as an official at the Research Division of the General Office of the CCP Central Committee, he helped draft speeches and memos for Hu, then a PSC member. In 1999 Hu promoted Ling to deputy director of the General Office and director of the vice-president's office (Hu was vice president at the time). In 2007, when Hu began his second term, Ling was promoted to member of the Secretariat and director of the General Office of the CCP Central Committee concurrently. Before the tragic death of his son in a car incident in March 2012 and the subsequent exposure of his corruption scandals, Ling was seen as a strong candidate for PSC membership at the 18th Party Congress.

It is important to know that all of these *mishu* who have served senior leaders have their own administrative ranks (行政级别, *xingzheng jibie*), for example, there are division-level, bureau-level, department-level, and vice-minister-level *mishu*. Both the government and central party systems have their own bureaus of *mishu* (秘书局, *mishuju*) under the leadership of the General Office of the State Council and the General Office of the Central Committee of the CCP, respectively. Table 6-1 presents the career trajectories and the current status of the personal secretaries of all nine PSC members

TABLE 6-1. Career Development and Current Status of Personal Secretaries (*Dami*) of the Politburo Standing Committee Members of the 17th Central Committee, as of August 2015

Name	Boss	Year began as *mishu*	Year born	Birthplace	Education	Last position	Current position (status)
Chen Shiju	Hu Jintao	1985	1963	Guizhou	Bachelor's degree in philosophy, Guizhou University	Director of President Hu Jintao's Office	Deputy Director of the General Office of the Central Committee
Sun Wei	Wu Bangguo	1995	1961	Shandong	Bachelor's degree in geography, Peking University	Director of NPC Chairman Wu Bangguo's Office	Executive Vice-Governor of Shandong
Qiu Xiaoxiong	Wen Jiabao	1985	1955	Guangxi	Bachelor's degree in economics, Peking University; master's degree, Central South University of Technology	Director of Premier Wen Jiabao's Office; Deputy Secretary-General of the State Council	Deputy Director of the State Administration of Taxation
Tong Guangcheng	Jia Qinglin	1997?	1953	Jiangxi	Bachelor's degree	Director of CPPCC Chairman Jia Qinglin's Office	Deputy Secretary-General of the CPPCC
Zhang Jiang	Li Changchun	2002	1956	Liaoning	Bachelor's degree in philosophy, Renmin University	Director of Li Changchun's Office	Vice-President of the Chinese Academy of Social Sciences

Zhong Shaojun	Xi Jinping	2003?	1968	Zhejiang	Master's degree, Zhejiang University; doctoral degree candidate in public policy, Tsinghua University	Head of the Research Team of the Central Military Commission General Office	Deputy Director of President Xi Jinping's Office; Deputy Director of the General Office of the Central Military Commission
Shi Gang	Li Keqiang	2007?	1958	Anhui	Bachelor's degree, China University of Science & Technology; master's degree in management, Shanghai Jiaotong University	Deputy Director of the Research Office of the State Council	Director of Premier Li Keqiang's Office
Ji Wenlin	Zhou Yongkang	1998	1966	Neimenggu	Bachelor's degree in geology, China University of Geosciences	Deputy Director of Central Office of Maintaining Social Stability; Director of Zhou Yongkang's Office	Hainan Vice-Governor (purged)
Liu Mingbo	He Guoqiang	2008	1964	Neimenggu	Bachelor's degree in history	Director of the Office of the Central Commission for Discipline Inspection	Executive Deputy Secretary of the Anhui Provincial Commission for Discipline Inspection

Note and Source: CPPCC=Chinese People's Political Consultative Conference. Wang Xin, "Zhonggong tuixiu qichangwei dami fuchenlu" [The files of personal secretaries of the retired seven Politburo Standing Committee members of the CCP], Duowei Newsnet, July 5, 2013, http://china.dwnews.com/news/2013–07-05/59258258.html; Chen Yifan, *Zhonggong gaoguan de mishumen* [The *mishu* cluster of the high-ranking leaders of the Chinese Communist Party] (New York: Mirror Books, 2010); and the author's database.

of the 17th Central Committee.[7] Eight of them held the rank of vice-minister and vice-governor or higher in 2015 (Zhou Yongkang's *mishu* Ji Wenlin served as vice-governor of Hainan before he was purged in 2014).[8] They were all born after the mid-1950s, and five of them were born in the 1960s. Most of them only received bachelor's degrees (many belonging to the famous 1982 class). Many of them spent most of their professional and political careers as *mishu* even before serving their powerful PSC bosses. Hu Jintao's *mishu* Chen Shiju and Wen Jiabao's *mishu* Qiu Xiaoxiong both began to work for their bosses as early as 1985. Sun Wei (Wu Bangguo's *mishu*), Tong Guangcheng (Jia Qinglin's *mishu*), and Ji Wenlin, for example, all worked as *mishu* soon after their college graduations, and they previously worked as *mishu* for other bosses.

Some longtime personal secretaries of these PSC members were appointed to important leadership positions before the 17th Party Congress. For example, Ling Yueming began to work as He Guoqiang's *mishu* when He was vice-minister of the Ministry of Chemical Industry in 1991. Ling followed He to Fujian and Chongqing when the latter served as provincial top leader in those two places. Ling remained in Chongqing when He was promoted to director of the Central Organization Department in 2002. Ling is currently a Standing Committee member of the Chongqing Municipal Party Committee.

Factors Contributing to the Prominent Role of Mishu

The prominent role of *mishu* in the CCP leadership is certainly not new in Chinese history. In their seminal study of *mishu* in the Chinese leadership, Wei Li and Lucian W. Pye argue that the ubiquitous role of *mishu* reflects Confucian political culture, especially the "intensely personalized element in Chinese politics."[9] This mentor-protégé relationship, as Li and Pye characterize it, is based on the fact that bosses "depend on *mishu* for shelter, comfort and convenience in their lives and work"; and *mishu* depend on bosses "for status, prestige and career advancement" later in their political lives.[10]

Although communist veteran leaders usually had no *mishu* experience themselves, there are two noticeable exceptions. Deng Xiaoping served as secretary-general of the CCP from 1954 to 1956, and former president of the PRC Yang Shangkun served as director of the General Office of the CCP Central Committee from 1958 to 1965. For the first three decades of the PRC, however, *mishu* were largely seen as office clerks rather than powerful figures in their own right. When communist veteran leaders (most of them were considered the first and second generations of CCP leaders) became senile, they tended to rely on their *mishu* to exert their power and influence "behind the scenes." Some of the *mishu* of these gerontocratic leaders later served or still serve in important positions. Examples include Chen Yun's *mishu* Xu Yongyue, who served as minister of State Security for almost ten years; Ye Jianying's bodyguard Cao Qing, who served as deputy commander of the Beijing Military Region with the military rank of lieutenant general; and Yang Shangkun's *mishu* Wang Guanzhong, who currently serves as deputy director of the Joint Staff Department, also with the rank of lieutenant general. Both Cao and Wang currently serve on the 18th Central Committee.

An important contributing factor to the prominent role of *mishu* is that in the early years of the reform era, many children of high-ranking officials, also known as princelings, sought to work as office staff members in important national leadership bodies, particularly as *mishu* to senior leaders who were their fathers' old comrades-in-arms. Examples include Xi Jinping, who served as *mishu* to Minister of Defense Geng Biao, and Zeng Qinghong, who served as *mishu* to Yu Qiuli, then chairman of the State Planning Commission. Bo Xilai and Wang Qishan worked as clerks in the General Office or the Secretariat of the CCP Central Committee, respectively, early in their careers. The son-in-law of Hu Yaobang, former navy political commissar Liu Xiaojiang, served as *mishu* to Liu Huaqing, then deputy chief-of-staff of the PLA and later vice-chairman of the CMC. Their experiences as *mishu* not only provided valuable opportunities for princelings to become familiar with the work and decisionmaking process in the national leadership but also accelerated their political careers owing to these extraordinary credentials.

Ironically, the prominent role of *mishu* is actually attributable in part to the top leadership's concern about preventing the formation of region-based factionalism (both military regions and provincial administrations) in the 1970s and 1980s. To prevent local autonomy and even possible separatist tendencies (山头主义, *shantou zhuyi*), Mao, Deng, and Jiang all continually arranged large-scale reshuffles of top provincial leaders and, more important, top officers in China's greater military regions.[11] This approach aimed to weaken the power bases of military leaders. When top regional leaders—both civilian and military elites—moved to new regions, they could not bring too many of their previous subordinates with them. Yet they were often allowed to bring their personal *mishu* to their new posts.[12] The policy that was supposed to limit factional politics unexpectedly has led to even closer bonds between high-ranking leaders and their aides, contributing to a more powerful role for *mishu* in the Chinese leadership.

Perhaps the most important contributing factor to the *mishu* phenomenon has been the shift in criteria for elite recruitment from revolutionary credentials, such as participation in the communist revolution and mobilization in socialist campaigns, to two new areas of skills. One area is technical, economic, and financial expertise; the other entails administrative skills such as political networking and coalition building—both vertically and horizontally. As an example of the first, current minister of Finance Lou Jiwei served as a *mishu* for Zhu Rongji in late 1980s when Zhu was mayor of Shanghai, and he continued to assist Zhu on tax reform when Zhu was vice-premier and premier. Similarly, Xi Jinping often relies on his aides who received academic degrees at Harvard and Stanford for advice on economic and financial affairs, such as Liu He (office director of the Central Financial Leading Group) and Fang Xinghai (vice-chairman of the China Securities Regulatory Commission). Fang also served as deputy office director and then director of financial affairs in Shanghai when Xi was in charge of the city in 2007.

As for political networking and coalition building, Jiang Zemin's reliance on Zeng Qinghong and Xi Jinping's appointment of Li Zhanshu as his chief-of-staff are both good examples. Zeng is often described as Jiang's "hands, ears, and brain." Zeng began to work in Shanghai in late 1984, a few months before Jiang's arrival. Zeng had strong political connections in the city. His father, Zeng Shan, served as vice-mayor soon after the communist victory in 1949. In the early 1980s three of his father's former junior colleagues—Chen Guodong, Hu Lijiao, and Wang Daohan—held top posts in the city.[13] When Jiang arrived in Shanghai as mayor, Zeng was soon promoted to director of the Organization Department in the city, in charge of personnel affairs. One year later, when Jiang was promoted to party secretary of the city, Zeng became Jiang's chief-of-staff in the Shanghai Municipal Party Committee and they began their "long-term mutually beneficial cooperation."[14]

When Jiang was appointed general secretary of the CCP in June 1989, he brought Zeng with him to Beijing. This was because Zeng was as well connected in the power circles in Beijing as he was in Shanghai, largely due to his extremely influential parents.[15] It has been widely reported that over the past two decades Zeng helped Jiang defeat his political rivals, including the "generals of the Yang family" (Yang Shangkun and Yang Baibing), the Deng children, Chen Xitong (former party chief in Beijing), and Qiao Shi (former head of the National People's Congress).[16] More recently, it was believed that Zeng initiated the move to select Xi as the heir apparent at the 17th Party Congress in 2007.[17]

Similarly, it was a very thoughtful decision on the part of Xi Jinping to choose Li Zhanshu as director of the General Office of the CCP Central Committee on the eve of the 18th Party Congress in 2012. Besides their longtime friendship and similar princeling family backgrounds (elaborated on in chapter 8), Li's previous two sets of work experiences are particularly valuable for Xi. First, Li served as a provincial leader in many parts of the country: in Hebei as secretary-general of the provincial party committee, in Shaanxi as deputy party secretary, in Heilongjiang as governor, and in Guizhou as party secretary. These leadership experiences in the northern, northeastern, northwestern, and southwestern regions of the country could bring much-needed broad regional support for Xi's administration. Second,

Li is often seen as a *tuanpai* leader, as he served as secretary of the Hebei Provincial CCYL Committee from 1986 to 1990. This background of Xi's new chief-of-staff could help Xi potentially reconcile the factional tensions in the leadership and contribute to his coalition-building efforts.[18]

Under the directorship of Li Zhanshu, the General Office has gone through major personnel changes over the past three years. All former deputy directors were transferred to other positions: Zhang Jianping was appointed executive deputy party secretary of the Work Committee of Departments under the Central Committee in April 2013; Zhao Shengxuan became vice-president of the Chinese Academy of Social Sciences in May 2013; and Wang Zhongtian began to serve as deputy director of the Office of the South-to-North Water Diversion Project in January 2015. Several bureau heads of the General Office—for example, Director of *Mishu* Bureau Huo Ke, Director of Bodyguard Bureau Cao Qing, Director of Administration Bureau Chen Ruiping, and Director of Research Bureau Ding Xiaowen—were all transferred to ceremonial or less critical positions. Meanwhile, Li's two chiefs-of-staff from when he was party secretary of Guizhou, Liao Guoxun and Liu Qifan, were promoted to director of the Organization Department of the Zhejiang Provincial Party Committee and chief-of-staff of the Guizhou Provincial Party Committee, respectively. Liao was born in 1963 and Liu was born in 1967. Both will likely be further promoted due to their strong ties with Li Zhanshu.[19] In the fall of 2015 Li also appointed his longtime protégé Meng Xiangfeng (born in 1964) as deputy director of the General Office of the CCP Central Committee.

The Prevalent Role of *Mishu* in Rampant Official Corruption

Xi Jinping's ongoing vigorous anticorruption campaign—and subsequent purges of high-ranking officials—follows an interesting pattern wherein *mishu* are often the first to succumb to investigation and arrest. This phenomenon partly reflects the strategy behind Xi's antigraft investigations, and partly shows the relationship between the prevalent role of *mishu* and rampant official corruption in the Chinese political system. This trend is, of course, not new. Throughout PRC history, purges of senior party leaders have in fact usually involved their *mishu*. For example, the purge of former CCP general secretary Zhao Ziyang in the wake of the Tiananmen crisis in 1989 began with the arrest of his political secretary, Bao Tong, on the charge of "leaking state secrets." Bao Tong, a full member of the 13th Central Committee of the CCP, had previously served as deputy director of the National Commission for Economic Restructuring, director of the Research Office on Political Reform of the CCP Central Committee, and director of the Office of Party

General Secretary Zhao Ziyang. Bao was sentenced to seven years in prison and was placed under house arrest after serving his sentence.

The corruption charges brought against former Politburo member and Beijing party secretary Chen Xitong in the Jiang era began with the arrest of Chen's *mishu* Chen Jian two months before the fall of Chen Xitong himself. Similarly, under the Hu Jintao leadership, former Politburo member and Shanghai party secretary Chen Liangyu's *mishu* Qin Yu, was first transferred to serve as head of the city's Baoshan District and then placed under investigation and arrested in 2006, two months before the arrest of Chen Liangyu on corruption charges.

As a widely circulated report released in the Chinese official media recently noted, "Each 'tiger' (high-ranking official sacked on corruption charges) always had a meticulous *mishu* who helped engage in illegal pursuits."[20] The report stated that personal secretaries were so powerful because of the backing from their bosses that the Chinese public often refers to these *mishu* as "No. 2 chiefs" (二号首长, *erhao shouzhang*).[21]

The case of Zhou Yongkang, arguably the largest corruption case in PRC history, involved six of his personal secretaries who worked for him at different periods during his leadership tenure. Table 6-2 presents background information on these six *mishu*. Most of them worked for Zhou for a very long time, often following him as he moved to new leadership positions. Three of them worked under Zhou in the oil industry beginning more than twenty years ago. They all held senior leadership positions (most at the vice-governor level) before they were purged.

Guo Yongxiang, for example, formed his ties with Zhou when they worked together in the Shengli Oilfield in the late 1980s. At the time, Zhou was director and party secretary of the Shengli Oilfield Administration and party secretary of Dongying, Shandong Province, and Guo was director of the Research Office of the Party Committee of the Shengli Oilfield Administration. When Zhou served as general manager and party secretary of the China National Petroleum Corporation (CNPC) from 1996 to 1998, Guo was deputy director of the Research Office of the CNPC. Guo moved to Beijing along with his boss in 1998 to serve as director of the Office of the Ministry of Land and Resources when Zhou became the minister. Soon after Zhou became Sichuan party secretary in 1999, Guo went to Sichuan to serve first as deputy secretary-general and then as secretary-general of the Sichuan Provincial Party Committee, primarily assisting his longtime patron Zhou. Guo was placed under investigation and then arrested on corruption charges in June 2013, six months before the authorities' formal investigation of Zhou Yongkang.

Ji Wenlin began working as a *mishu* for Zhou Yongkang in 1998 when Zhou was appointed as minister of Land and Resources. He followed Zhou

TABLE 6-2. Zhou Yongkang's *Mishu* Cluster

Name	Birth year	Years serving as Zhou's *mishu*	Zhou's position	*Mishu*'s title	Position before the purge
Li Hualin	1962	1988–92	Director of Shengli Oilfield Administration; Party Secretary of Dongying City; Deputy General Manager of CNPC	*Mishu* to Zhou	Vice-President of CNPC
Shen Dingcheng	1963	1992–97	Deputy General Manager of CNPC, then General Manager	*Mishu* to Zhou	Party Secretary of Petro China International
Ji Wenlin	1966	1998–08	Minister of Land and Resources; Sichuan Party Secretary; Minister of Public Security	*Mishu* and Deputy Director of the Office of the Minister of Public Security	Vice-Governor of Hainan
Guo Yongxiang	1949	1989–07	Director of Shengli Oilfield; Party Secretary of Dongying City; Deputy General Manager of CNPC; Minister of Land and Resources; Sichuan Party Secretary	*Mishu*, Director of the Office of the Minister of Land and Resources, Deputy Secretary-General, Secretary-General of Sichuan Provincial Party Committee	Vice-Governor of Sichuan and Vice-Chairman of the Sichuan People's Congress
Yu Gang	1968	2003–12	Politburo member; Politburo Standing Committee member	Deputy Director of the Office of the CCP Politics and Law Committee	Deputy Director of the Office of the CCP Politics and Law Committee
Tan Hong	1972?	2008–12	Politburo Standing Committee member	Bodyguard and *mishu* to Zhou	Division-level staff of the Ministry of Public Security

Note and Source: CNPC = China National Petroleum Corporation; CCP = Chinese Communist Party. Wang Huan, "Zhou Yongkang wuren mishu de mingyun" [The fate of Zhou Yongkang's five *Mishu*] (周永康五任秘书的命运), Xinhua, July 2, 2014, http://big5/forum.home.news.cn/detail/133324958/1.html and the author's database.

to Sichuan in 2000 and served as a *mishu* to Zhou with the title of deputy director of the Office of the Sichuan Provincial Party Committee. He continued to play a supporting role when his boss became minister of Public Security in 2002, after which Ji became deputy director of the Office of the Ministry of Public Security. Ji also served as deputy director of the Central Office of Maintaining Social Stability and director of the Office of Zhou Yongkang when Zhou was in charge of public security in the PSC after 2008. Ji later returned to the Ministry of Land and Resources, where he served as director of the general office in the ministry for two years (2008–10). He served as mayor of Haikou and vice-governor of Hainan before his purge in February 2014. Zhou's cluster of *mishu* formed a broad web of personal connections across different regions and functional areas. Oil, land, and other resources were very lucrative businesses, and Zhou's control over the security apparatus during the years 2002–12 gave him and his protégés the opportunity to abuse political power and to obtain economic resources for personal gain.

The recent major corruption cases involving top military generals have also revealed the heavy involvement of their uniformed *mishu* with senior military ranks. Four former personal secretaries for Xu Caihou, former vice-chairman of the CMC, are all under investigation. They include Major General Zhang Gongxian (former director of the Political Department of the Jinan Military Region), Rear Admiral Li Bin (deputy director of the Political Department of the PLA Navy), Major General Kang Xiaohui (political commissar of the Joint Logistics Department of the Shenyang Military Region), and Major General Qi Changming (deputy chief-of-staff of the Beijing Military Region).[22]

Zhang Gongxian, for example, was born in 1960 and was considered a rising star in the PLA leadership. He served as *mishu* for Xu Caihou in the mid-1990s when Xu was deputy director of the General Political Department of the PLA. Later, Zhang served as secretary-general of the General Office of the Central Political Department. Zhang was recently fired and placed under investigation. According to the Chinese official media, Xu's main crime was selling military ranks and officer positions and accepting a huge amount of bribes.[23] His aforementioned *mishu* were actively involved in this widely spread practice, and they helped solicit bribes. This does not mean that *mishu* tend to corrupt the leaders, but rather that *mishu* usually handle the dirty work in environments conducive to official corruption.

Broadly speaking, strong mentor-protégé ties, evident in the prominent role of *mishu*, have significantly contributed to rampant official corruption and reflect serious deficiencies of Chinese political norms during the reform era.[24]

TABLE 6-3. Percentage of Leaders in Important Leadership Positions with *Mishu* Experience, 2014

Leadership position	No. of leaders with *mishu* experience	Total no. of leaders	%
Politburo Standing Committee member	5	7	71.4
Politburo member	16	25	64.0
Central Committee member	238	376	63.3
Provincial governor	24	31	77.4
State Council minister	19	25	76.0

Source: Author's database.

THE PERVASIVE PRESENCE OF *MISHU* ON THE 18TH CENTRAL COMMITTEE

Despite the Chinese public's recognition of the pervasive role that *mishu* play in official corruption, individuals with *mishu* background continue to have strong representation among the CCP leadership. Table 6-3 shows the percentage of leaders in several of the most important leadership positions in 2014 who had *mishu* experience. In addition to the aforementioned high percentages of leaders with *mishu* backgrounds in both the Politburo (64 percent) and the PSC (71.4 percent), 238 members (including both full members and alternate members) of the 18th Central Committee have had experience as *mishu* (63.3 percent). An even higher proportion of ministerial and provincial leaders have had experience as *mishu*: 77.4 percent among provincial governors and 76 percent among ministers in the State Council. At the provincial leadership level in March 2015, ten governors of China's thirty-one provincial level administrations (32 percent) had previously served as secretary-general or deputy secretary-general either in the provincial party committee or provincial government.[25]

Some of these prominent leaders have advanced their careers primarily or even exclusively through *mishu* work. Table 6-4 presents sixteen full members of the current central committee of the CCP whose careers have been marked primarily by service as a *mishu*, secretary-general, or both. They include two Politburo members—the vice-chairman of National People's Congress, Li Jianguo, and the director of the Central Policy Research Office, Wang Huning. Li Jianguo has spent most of his adult life (thirty-one years, to be exact) as a *mishu* and secretary-general, mainly in Tianjin. Born in Shandong in 1946, Li attended Shandong University as a Chinese major between 1964 and 1969.

TABLE 6-4. Select Civilian Members of the 18th Central Committee Who Advanced Their Careers Primarily as a *Mishu* and/or Secretary-General, 2016

Name	Current position (status)	Central Committee status	Main *mishu*/secretary-general experience	Total no. of years as *mishu*
Li Jianguo	Executive Vice-Chairman of the National People's Congress	Politburo member	*Mishu* in local administration in Tianjin, 1972–78; *Mishu* in Tianjin Party Committee, 1978–81; *Mishu* to Li Ruihuan (Tianjin Party Secretary), 1981–83; Office Director, Deputy Secretary-General, and Secretary-General, Beijing Party Committee, 1983–92; Secretary-General, National People's Congress, 2002–13	31
Wang Huning	Director of the Central Policy Research Office	Politburo member	Special Assistant to CCP Secretary-General and PRC President, 1995–present	20
Ling Jihua	Former Director of the United Front Work Department (purged)	Full member	*Mishu* and Office Director of the Chinese Communist Youth League Central Committee, 1979–83, 1988–94; *Mishu*, Deputy Director and Director of the General Office of the CCP Central Committee, 1995–2012	27
Xu Shaoshi	Minister, National Development and Reform Commission	Full member	*Mishu* and Office Director of Ministry of Geology and Mineral Resources, 1980–93; *Mishu* in the General Office of the State Council, 1993–2000; Deputy Secretary-General, State Council, 2000–07	27
Wang Zhengwei	Minister of State Ethnic Affairs Commission	Full member	*Mishu* in county-level party organization in Ningxia, 1976–84; *Mishu* in Ningxia Party Committee, 1984–89, Office Director in Ningxia Party Committee, 1989–97	21

Lou Jiwei	Minister of Finance	Full member	*Mishu* to Zhu Rongji (Shanghai Mayor and Vice-Premier), 1984–95; Deputy Secretary-General, State Council, 2007–09	13
Yin Weimin	Minister of Human Resources and Social Security	Full member	*Mishu* in the Office of the CCP Organization Department, 1978–2000	13
You Quan	Fujian Party Secretary	Full member	*Mishu* in State Planning Commission and General Office of State Council, 1987–2001; Deputy Secretary-General (*Mishu* to Huang Ju, Executive Vice-Premier), 2001–06, 2008–13	24
Jiang Yikang	Shandong Party Secretary	Full member	*Mishu* in Office of Jinan Municipal Party Committee 1982–85; *Mishu* and Deputy Director General of the CCP Central Committee, 1985–2002	20
Peng Qinghua	Guangxi Party Secretary	Full member	*Mishu* in a grassroots party committee, 1975–79; *Mishu* in the CCP Organization Department, 1983–2001	22
Baima Chilin	Chairman of the People's Congress in Tibet	Full member	*Mishu* and Secretary-General in the Tibet Autonomous Region Government, 1986–2000, 2003–05	16
Liu Weiping	Executive Vice-President of Chinese Academy of Sciences	Full member	*Mishu* in an aerospace factory, 1976–86; *Mishu* to Wu Guanzheng (Jiangxi Governor and Party Secretary), 1986–95; Secretary-General, Qinghai Party Committee, 2003–04	20
Sun Huaishan	Deputy Secretary-General, CPPCC	Full member	*Mishu* and Director in the General Office of the Chinese Communist Youth League Central Committee, 1978–94; *Mishu* and Secretary-General, CPPCC, 1994–present	37
Li Wei	Director of the Development Research Center of the State Council	Full member	*Mishu* to Zhu Rongji (Shanghai Mayor, Vice-Premier, and Premier), 1988–2003	15

(continued)

TABLE 6-4. (*continued*)

Name	Current position (status)	Central Committee status	Main *mishu*/secretary-general experience	Total no. of years as *mishu*
Wang Yongqing	Deputy Secretary-General, State Council	Full member	*Mishu* and Director in Legal Office of the State Council, 1987–2008; Deputy Secretary-General, State Council, 2008–present	28
Jiao Huancheng	Deputy Secretary-General, State Council	Full member	*Mishu* to Chen Yonggui (Politburo member), 1973–82; Deputy Secretary-General, State Council, 2002–present	22

Note and Source: CCP = Chinese Communist Party; CPPCC = Chinese People's Political Consultative Conference. Data from the author's database.

He began his career as a clerk in both the cultural-educational department and the propaganda department at the county level of leadership in Tianjin in 1972. In 1978 he started to work as a *mishu* for the Office of the Tianjin Party Committee. Three years later, at the age of thirty-five, he met his most important mentor, Li Ruihuan, then a rising political star who had just been appointed Tianjin's top leader.

In the following decade, Li Jianguo primarily served as Li Ruihuan's *mishu*, holding posts such as deputy office director and then office director of the Tianjin Party Committee, followed by deputy secretary-general and then secretary-general of the Tianjin Party Committee. After Li Ruihuan became a member of the PSC in 1989, Li Jianguo was promoted to member of the Standing Committee and deputy secretary of the Tianjin party committee. In 1997 Li Jianguo was transferred to Shaanxi Province, where he served as party secretary for ten years and formed a good relationship with the Xi Jinping family, which has its roots in the province. After working briefly as party secretary of Shandong in 2007–08, Li served concurrently as vice-chairman and secretary-general of the National People's Congress from 2008 to 2013. Currently he serves as executive vice-chairman of the National People's Congress.

Unlike Li Jianguo, who began his career as a *mishu*, Wang Huning started off as an academic, only later serving as a *mishu* and an adviser. Wang was born in 1955 in Shanghai (his ancestral home is usually cited as Laizhou County, Shandong Province). He studied French language in the cadre training class at Shanghai Normal University from 1972 to 1977 and attended the graduate program in international politics at Fudan University from 1978 to 1981, where he also received a master's degree in law in 1981. He was a visiting scholar at the University of Iowa and the University of California at Berkeley in 1988–89. He began his career as a cadre in the Publication Bureau of the Shanghai Municipal Government in 1977–78. After receiving his master's degree, he remained at Fudan University, where he worked as an instructor, associate professor, and professor throughout the following decade. He also served as chairman of the Department of International Politics from 1989 to 1994 and dean of the law school in 1994–95. Wang developed mentor-protégé ties with Jiang Zemin and Zeng Qinghong, two top leaders in Shanghai in the late 1980s.

In 1995, at the request of both Jiang and Zeng, who then served respectively as general secretary and director of the General Office of the CCP Central Committee, Wang moved to Beijing. He served as head of the Political Affairs Division of the Central Policy Research Office (CPRO) of the CCP Central Committee from 1995 to 1998, deputy director of the CPRO from 1998 to 2002, and director from 2002 to the present. CPRO is primarily a government think tank, and Wang acts largely as a personal assistant or chief strategist for the top leaders: first Jiang, then Hu, and now Xi. It is believed that Wang was a principal contributor to the development of Jiang's so-called theory of the three represents at the turn of the century.[26] Wang has played a critical role as *mishu* to the party boss for the past two decades.

Before the recent purge of Ling Jihua on corruption charges, Ling had a total of twenty-seven years of experience working as *mishu*, which included many years of serving as Hu Jintao's chief-of-staff. The minister of the National Development and Reform Commission, Xu Shaoshi, previously served as *mishu* for Wen Jiabao, first at the Ministry of Geology and Mineral Resources from 1980 to 1993 when Wen served as vice-minister (1983–85) and then as deputy secretary-general at the State Council from 2000 to 2007 when Wen was first vice-premier and then premier. Several other *mishu*-turned-senior leaders (see table 6-4) previously served as *mishu* for PSC members. They include the minister of Finance, Lou Jiwei, and the director of the Development Research Center of the State Council, Li Wei, who both were *mishu* to Premier Zhu Rongji for many years; Fujian party secretary You Quan, who served as *mishu* to Huang Ju, former executive vice-premier; and Executive Vice President of the Chinese Academy of Sciences Liu Weiping, who served as *mishu* to Wu Guanzheng, former Jiangxi governor and party secretary and later secretary of the Central Commission for Discipline Inspection.

The longest-serving *mishu* or secretary-general in the current Central Committee is Sun Huaishan, deputy secretary-general of the Chinese People's Political Consultative Conference. Sun began to work at the General Office of the CCYL as a *mishu* in 1978 and subsequently served as deputy division head, division head, deputy office director, and office director over the following sixteen years. In 1994 he continued his *mishu* and secretary-general work at the Chinese People's Political Consultative Conference, where he served as deputy bureau head in the general office and now serves as deputy secretary-general. Up to now, he has worked as a *mishu* or secretary-general for a total of thirty-seven years.

Of the 238 members of the 18th Central Committee with *mishu* experience, 148 (62.2 percent) have worked at the national and provincial levels of leadership (see figure 6-1). This further illustrates how important political networking is for *mishu* to access high office. Table 6-5 presents the *mishu* or secretary-general experiences of sixteen members of the current Politburo or PSC. Among them, two leaders—the director of the Central Propaganda Department, Liu Qibao, and the aforementioned Li Jianguo—have served as both *mishu* and secretary-general; eleven served as secretary-general, deputy secretary-general, or office director (exclusively at the national and provincial levels); and three served only as *mishu*.

FIGURE 6-1. Members of the 18th Central Committee with *Mishu* Experience in Different Levels of Leadership

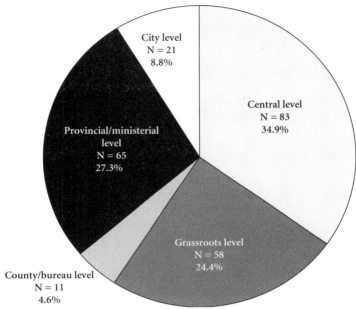

Note and Source: For those who have served as *mishu* in more than two levels of leadership, only the highest level of leadership is counted. Author's database.

Military officers occupy 66 seats in the 376-member 18th Central Committee of the CCP. Among them, twenty-two officers have *mishu* experience, accounting for one-third of this very high-ranking military elite group. It is understandable that military elites usually have less *mishu* work experience than civilian leaders. This is largely because military elites tend to advance step by step in their careers via two distinct tracks: (1) military operations in the posts of commander or chief-of-staff or (2) political affairs in the posts of commissar or political department director.[27] Yet, in fact, a significant number of senior military generals have *mishu* backgrounds. Table 6-6 lists sixteen senior military leaders on the 18th Central Committee with *mishu* experience. They include two members of the powerful CMC—the state councilor and minister of Defense Chang Wanquan, who served as *mishu* to General Han Xianchu (then commander of Lanzhou Military Region) from 1978 to 1980, and the chief of the Joint Staff Department, Fang Fenghui, who served as *mishu* to the party committee of the Twenty-first Group Army in the 1980s. All of these military leaders have the rank of general or lieutenant general. Several of them served as personal assistant or bodyguard to top

TABLE 6-5. Members of the 18th Politburo with *Mishu* and/or Secretary-General Experience

Name	Current position	Central Committee status	*Mishu* experience	Secretary-general experience
Xi Jinping	General Secretary of the Chinese Communist Party; President of the People's Republic of China; Chairman of the Central Military Commission	PSC member	*Mishu* to Geng Biao, Minister of Defense, 1979–82	
Li Keqiang	Premier	PSC member		Secretary-General, All China Students' Federation, 1983
Liu Yunshan	Executive Member of the Secretariat	PSC member		Secretary-General, Neimenggu Party Committee, 1987–91
Wang Qishan	Secretary of the Central Commission for Discipline Inspection	PSC member		Office Director, Rural Reform, State Council Development and Reform Center, 1986–88
Zhang Gaoli	Executive Vice-Premier	PSC member	*Mishu* in grassroots organization, 1971–74	
Ma Kai	Vice-Premier	Politburo member		Deputy Secretary-General and Secretary-General, State Council, 1998–2003, 2008–13
Wang Huning	Director of the Central Policy Research Office	Politburo member	Special Assistant to Chinese Communist Party Secretary-General and People's Republic of China President, 1995–present	

Liu Yandong	Vice-Premier	Politburo member	Deputy Secretary-General, United Front Work Department, 1991–95
Liu Qibao	Director of the Department of Propaganda	Politburo member	*Mishu* in the Office of the Anhui Party Committee, 1977–80
Sun Zhengcai	Chongqing Party Secretary	Politburo member	Secretary-General, Beijing Party Committee, 2002–06
Li Jianguo	Vice-Chairman of National People's Congress	Politburo member	*Mishu* to Li Ruihuan, (Tianjin Party Secretary) 1982–87	Office Director, Deputy Secretary-General, and Secretary-General, Beijing Party Committee, 1983–92; Secretary-General, National People's Congress, 2002–13
Wang Yang	Vice-Premier	Politburo member	Deputy Secretary-General, State Council, 2003–05
Meng Jianzhu	Secretary of the Central Political and Law Commission	Politburo member	Deputy Secretary-General, Shanghai Municipal Government, 1992–93
Hu Chunhua	Guangdong Party Secretary	Politburo member	Secretary-General, Tibet Party Committee, 2001–03
Li Zhanshu	Director of the General Office of the Central Committee	Politburo member	Secretary-General, Hebei Party Committee, 1993–97; Office Director, Party General Office, 2002–present
Han Zheng	Shanghai Party Secretary	Politburo member	Deputy Secretary-General, Shanghai Municipal Government, 1995–98

Note and Source: PSC = Politburo Standing Committee. Data from the author's database.

TABLE 6-6. Select Military Members of the 18th Central Committee Who Began Their Careers as *Mishu*

Name	Current position	Central Committee status	Military rank	Main *mishu* experience
Chang Wanquan	State Councilor and Minister of Defense	CMC, Full member	General	*Mishu* to Han Xianchu (then Commander of Lanzhou Military Region), 1978–80
Fang Fenghui	Chief of the Joint Staff Department	CMC, Full member	General	*Mishu* to the Party Committee of the No. 21 Group Army, 1980s
Liu Xiaojiang	Navy Political Commissar (until Dec. 2014)	Full member	Admiral	*Mishu* to Liu Huaqing (then Deputy Chief-of-Staff of the People's Liberation Army and later Vice-Chairman of CMC), 1980–83
Jia Ting'an	Deputy Director, Political Work Department	Full member	General	*Mishu* to Jiang Zemin (then Minister of Electronics Industry and Mayor of Shanghai) and later Chairman of the CMC, 1982–2004
Cai Yingting	President, Academy of Military Science	Full member	General	*Mishu* to Zhang Wannian (Vice-Chairman of the CMC), 1995–2002
Wang Quanzhong	Deputy Chief of the Joint Staff Department	Full member	Lt. General	*Mishu* to Yang Shangkun; Deputy Director and Director of the General Office of the CMC, 1996–2012
Tian Xiusi	Former Political Commissar, Air Force (until July 2015)	Full member	General	*Head Mishu*, Political Department, No. 13 Artillery Division, 1981–83
Zhu Fuxi	Political Commissar, Western Theater of Operation	Full member	Lt. General	Deputy *Mishuzhang* and *Mishuzhang*, Political Department, 2003–07

Name	Position	Membership	Rank	Secretary experience
Du Hengyan	Deputy Director of Political Work Department	Full member	General	*Mishu*, Commander's Office of the Shenyang Military Region, 1979–88; Deputy *Mishuzhang* and *Mishuzhang*, Political Department of the Beijing Military Region, 1989–96
Zheng Weiping	Political Commissar of Eastern Theater of Operation	Full member	Lt. General	*Mishu* to Li Jinan, General Office of the Political Department, 2001–03
Chu Yimin	Political Commissar, Northern Theater of Operation	Full member	Lt. General	*Mishu*, Commander's Office of the Lanzhou Military Region (time unknown)
Sun Sijing	Political Commissar, People's Armed Police	Full member	General	*Mishu*, Commander's Office of the Jinan Military Region, 1984–91; *Mishu* and *Mishuzhang*, Political Department of the People's Liberation Army General Logistics Department, 1991–99
Wang Hongyao	Political Commissar, Equipment Development Department	Full member	General	*Mishu to* Du Tiehuan, (Political Commissar of Nanjing Military Region)
Cao Qing	Deputy Commander, Beijing Military Region (until Dec. 2015)	Alternate member	General	*Mishu* and bodyguard to Ye Jianying (Vice-Chairman of the CMC), 1972–81
Gao Jianguo	Director, Political Department of Shenyang Military Region (until Dec. 2015)	Alternate member	Lt. General	*Mishu*, Party Committee Office of the Jinan Military Region (time unknown).
Zhang Ruiqing	Deputy Political Commissar, Armed Police	Alternate member	Lt. General	*Mishuzhang*, Political Department of the Armed Police (time unknown)

Notes and Source: CMC = Central Military Commission. Data from the author's database.

leaders for many years. Most of these *mishu*-turned-military officers advanced their career through the political affairs track in the PLA.

Some recently promoted senior military officers who do not serve on the 18th Central Committee also previously served as personal assistants to top military leaders.[28] They include deputy political commissar of the PLA Navy Wang Dengping, who was a *mishu* to former political commissar of the General Logistics Department Zhou Keyu; deputy political commissar of the PLA Navy Ding Haichun, who served as a *mishu* to former deputy commander of the PLA Navy Deng Zhaoxiang; deputy political commissar of the PLA Air Force Fang Jianguo, who was a *mishu* to former vice-chairman of the CMC Chi Haotian; deputy commissar of the Second Artillery Corps Deng Tiansheng, who was a *mishu* to former vice-chairman of the CMC Zhang Zhen; and the vice-president of the Military Academy of Sciences, Ren Haiquan, who was a *mishu* to former director of the PLA General Political Department Li Desheng.[29]

The strong representation of *mishu* in both civilian and military leadership in present-day China is remarkable, particularly in the wake of the public's recognition of the prominent role that *mishu* play in rampant official corruption and the resulting large-scale purges. This observation suggests that mentor-protégé ties based on *mishu* experience will be an enduring phenomenon in Chinese elite politics in the years to come.

XI JINPING'S DILEMMA AND THE DIVERSITY OF HIS *MISHU* CLUSTER

In September 2014 *The Mishu Work*, the official magazine run by the General Office of the CCP Central Committee, published a long article by its director, Li Zhanshu.[30] As a confidant and chief-of-staff for Xi Jinping, Li highlights his boss's recent remarks on the work of the General Office, especially Xi's emphasis on "absolute loyalty" (绝对忠诚, *juedui zhongcheng*) to the party, which is characterized as the key requirement for secretarial staff. In the first webpage of the online version of the same article, the word "loyalty" appears as many as fifty-five times.[31] The author explicitly states that "absolute loyalty has now been raised to unprecedented heights," and the secretarial staff at the General Office "should act and think in a manner highly consistent in accordance with the order from the Central Committee led by General Secretary Xi Jinping."[32] Although the secretarial staff members are supposed to have loyalty to the party, in reality often their first loyalty is to their chief (首长, *shouzhang*) rather than to their office or the abstract notion of the party.

In fact, the General Office of the CCP Central Committee and other important offices in the party, state, and military leadership are now led by

Xi's longtime friends and protégés. Not only does Xi's close friend for over thirty years, the aforementioned Li Zhanshu, serve as director of the General Office, but Xi's protégé from Shanghai, Ding Xuexiang, also serves concurrently as deputy director of the General Office and director of President Xi Jinping's Office. Zhong Shaojun, who has been Xi's personal assistant for the past twelve years, now serves concurrently as deputy director of the General Office of the CMC and director of CMC Chairman Xi's Office with the military rank of senior colonel. Xi's other two aides, Zhu Guofeng and Wang Shaojun, who have had strong personal ties with him for many years, are responsible for logistical details in Xi's diplomatic affairs and security matters, respectively.

As mentioned earlier, Xi Jinping himself served as a *mishu* for the minister of Defense for three years in his late twenties, and this experience helped him tremendously later as he advanced his career, especially by enhancing his credentials in military affairs. Xi's personal assistants, both previous and current, have constituted a major cluster of his inner circle. Because of their very close working relationships with Xi, they are often among his most trusted confidants. As a new boss in Zhongnanhai, Xi needs to appoint his protégés to the most important leadership positions (including the powerful administrative offices that control the agenda) to consolidate his power and push forward his ambitious reform programs.

Apparently, Xi Jinping confronts a serious dilemma: On the one hand he must prevent factional politics from undermining his power, especially by constraining factional politics in the leadership and cracking down on rampant corruption in which *mishu* often are significantly involved. But on the other hand he must avoid backlash from the political establishment for his double standard. Interestingly, Xi Jinping has more friends and protégés with *mishu* backgrounds—and has relied more on support from *mishu*— than most other top Chinese leaders.

This is largely due to two situational factors. First, Xi worked in various leadership posts and in a number of geographical regions throughout his political career before becoming the top leader. Whereas Jiang Zemin worked in only two cities other than Beijing—namely, Changchun and Shanghai— and Hu Jintao worked as a leader in Lanzhou, Guiyang, and Lhasa, Xi held a leadership role in six counties and cities: Zhengding in Hebei; Xiamen, Ningde, and Fuzhou in Fujian; Hangzhou in Zhejiang; and Shanghai. With this case in point, the more rotations in positions and localities that a leader holds, the more *mishu* the leader may have.

Second, since becoming the top leader in November 2012, Xi has established the National Security Committee and several new central leading groups of which he himself serves as the head. This means that Xi has to rely substantially on office directors and secretaries-general of these new leadership bodies. These office directors and secretaries-general are actually responsible for the operation of the central leading groups. Many of them are Xi's trusted confidants and thus influential figures.

Xi's Most Important Mishu to Watch

Table 6-7 presents the twenty-one most important *mishu* for Xi Jinping, both current and former. All of them began serving in their present leadership positions in the last three years; ten of them actually obtained their current posts in the past two years, reflecting Xi's recent aggressiveness in appointing his protégés to high offices. Nine of them serve on the 18th Central Committee, including one Politburo member, four full members, and four alternate members. In addition, Li Shulei currently serves as a member of the Central Commission for Discipline Inspection. The table does not include some of Xi's personal assistants who work very closely with him but do not hold high administrative ranking. Examples include Lü Luhua and Li Yaguang, who always accompany Xi on his travels, both within China and abroad.

All twenty-one of the leaders were born after 1950; therefore, they are qualified to remain in the Central Committee for another term after 2017, and some may have even more-important leadership roles to play. Six of them were born in the 1960s or even the 1970s; and some, especially Ding Xuexiang and Li Shulei, can be viewed as rising stars. Their current membership in the Central Committee or the Central Commission for Discipline Inspection are largely owing to their close personal ties with Xi.

As discussed above, the top five aides presented in table 6-7 work most closely with Xi, constituting the core of his inner circle. Some members of Xi's *mishu* cluster currently serve as office directors or deputy directors in various functional and very important leading groups; for example, director of the Central Foreign Affairs Office and State Councilor (Yang Jiechi), office director of the Central Financial Leading Group (Liu He), deputy director of the Office of the Central Financial Leading Group (Shu Guozeng), office director of the Central Spiritual Civilization Steering Committee (Huang Kunming), office director of the Central Leading Group for Network Security and Information Technology (Lu Wei), executive deputy director of the Office of the National Security Committee (Cai Qi), executive deputy director of the Office of the Central Leading Group for Comprehensive Reforms (Mu Hong), and executive vice-president of the Central Party School (He Yiting). Song Tao, former deputy director of the Office of Central Foreign Affairs, was promoted to director of the International Liaison Department of the CCP Central Committee and executive deputy director of the Office of Central Foreign Affairs in 2015. These *mishu* are in fact chief

TABLE 6-7. Xi Jinping's Current and Former *Mishu*, as of May 2016

Name	Birth year	Birthplace	Current position	Tenure since	Previous position	*Mishu* status	Functional area	Ties to Xi Jinping
Li Zhanshu	1950	Hebei	Director, CCP General Office (Chief-of-Staff for Xi); Politburo member	2012	Guizhou Party Secretary	Current	CCP operation	Colleague in Hebei (both served as party secretaries in two nearby counties)
Ding Xuexiang	1962	Jiangsu	Deputy Director, CCP General Office (Deputy Chief-of-Staff for Xi); Director, President Xi's Office; Alternate CCM	2013	Shanghai CCP Standing Committee member	Current	CCP operation	*Mishu* to Xi in Shanghai
Zhong Shaojun	1968	Zhejiang	Deputy Director, President Xi Jinping's Office; Head of the Research Team of the Central Military Commission General Office	2013	Head of the Political Team of the CCP General Office	Current	Military	*Mishu* to Xi; Deputy Director of the Zhejiang CCP Provincial Committee and Deputy Director of the Shanghai CCP Municipal Committee when Xi was Party Secretary of these two places
Zhu Guofeng	1973	Guangdong	*Mishu* to President Xi	2013	Deputy bureau level *mishu* in the *Mishu* Bureau of the CCP General Office	Current	Foreign affairs	*Mishu* to Xi in diplomatic affairs

(continued)

TABLE 6-7. (*continued*)

Name	Birth year	Birthplace	Current position	Tenure since	Previous position	Mishu status	Functional area	Ties to Xi Jinping
Wang Shaojun	1955	Hebei	Director, Bodyguard Bureau of the General Office of the CCP Central Committee	2015	Executive Deputy Director, Bodyguard Bureau of the General Office of the CCP Central Committee	Current	Military	Chief bodyguard to President Xi
Yang Jiechi	1950	Shanghai	Director of the Central Foreign Affairs Office; Full CCM	2013	Minister of Foreign Affairs	Functional	Foreign Affairs	Chief advisor on foreign affairs
Liu He	1952	Beijing	Office Director, Central Financial Leading Group; Vice-Minister, NDRC; Full CCM	2013	Deputy Office Director, Central Financial Leading Group	Functional	Finance	Childhood friend
Huang Kunming	1956	Fujian	Office Director of the Central Spiritual Civilization Steering Committee; Alternate CCM	2014	Deputy Director of the Central Propaganda Department	Functional	Propaganda	Junior colleague in Fujian and Zhejiang
Lu Wei	1960	Anhui	Office Director of Central Leading Group for Network Security and Information Technology	2013	Vice-Mayor of Beijing	Functional	Cyber issues	Xi's confidant

Name	Birth	Province	Position	Year	Position	Type	Area	Note
Cai Qi	1955	Fujian	Executive Deputy Director, Office of the National Security Committee	2014	Executive Vice-Governor of Zhejiang	Functional	CCP operation	*Mishu* to Xi in Fujian
Shu Guozeng	1956	Zhejiang	Deputy Director, Office of the Central Financial Leading Group	2014	Director of Development Research of the Zhejiang Provincial Government	Functional	Finance	*Mishu* (deputy office director) to Xi in Zhejiang
Mu Hong	1956	Liaoning	Executive Deputy Director, Office of Central Leading Group of Comprehensive Reforms	2014	Deputy Director, NDRC	Functional	Administration	Extensive travels with Xi when Xi was PRC Vice-President
He Yiting	1951	Shaanxi	Executive Vice-President of Central Party School; Full CCM	2013	Executive Vice-Director, Central Policy Research Office	Functional	Propaganda	Assisted Xi in the Central Policy Research Office
Song Tao	1955	Jiangsu	Director of the International Liaison Department of the CCP Central Committee, and Executive Deputy Director of the Central Foreign Affairs Office	2015	Deputy director of the Central Foreign Affairs Office	Functional	Foreign affairs	Vice-President of Fujian International Trust and Investment Corporation when Xi was in charge of this area in Fujian government

(continued)

TABLE 6-7. (*continued*)

Name	Birth year	Birthplace	Current position	Tenure since	Previous position	Mishu status	Functional area	Ties to Xi Jinping
Chen Yixin	1959	Zhejiang	Deputy Director, Office of Central Leading Group of Comprehensive Reforms	2015	Party Secretary of Wenzhou City	Functional	Administration	*Mishu* (deputy secretary-general of the provincial party committee) to Xi in Zhejiang
He Lifeng	1955	Fujian	Deputy Director, NDRC; Alternate CCM	2014	Tianjin CPPCC Chair	Former	Economy	*Mishu* for Xi in Xiamen; junior colleague in Fujian
Li Qiang	1959	Zhejiang	Zhejiang Governor, Alternate CCM	2013	Secretary, Zhejiang CCP Provincial Committee on Politics and Law	Former	Provincial leadership	Chief-of-Staff to Xi; then Zhejiang Party Secretary
Li Shulei	1964	Henan	Discipline Inspection Secretary, Beijing Municipal Party Committee	2015	Vice-President of the Central Party School	Former	Propaganda	Assisted Xi at the Central Party School

Name	Year	Place	Position	Year	Former	Administration	Notes
Chen Baosheng	1956	Gansu	Party Secretary and Executive Vice-President, Chinese Academy of Governance; Full CCM	2013	Former Vice-President of the Central Party School	Administration	Chief-of-Staff to Xi in the Central Party School
Chen Jiayuan	1953	Zhejiang	Executive Vice-Chair, Zhejiang CPPCC	2013	Former Vice-Governor of Zhejiang	Provincial leadership	*Mishu* to Xi in Zhejiang
Fang Xinghai	1964	Shanghai	Vice-Chairman of the China Securities Regulatory Commission	2015	Former Director of the Office of Financial Services in the Shanghai Municipal Government	Finance	Deputy office director and director of financial affairs in Shanghai when Xi was in charge of the city

Note and Source: CCM = Central Committee Member; CCP = Chinese Communist Party; NDRC = National Development and Reform Commission; PRC = People's Republic of China; CPPCC = Chinese People's Political Consultative Conference. Data from the author's database.

advisers and aides to Xi in the crucial areas of finance, economic reforms, foreign affairs, national security, cybersecurity, and propaganda and ideology. All of them also had close ties with Xi earlier in their careers.

Seven leaders listed in table 6-7 were formerly *mishu* to Xi while he served as either a provincial leader or as president of the Central Party School. Although Chen Jiayuan may retire in the next few years, the other five are well positioned for further promotion. He Lifeng, for example, is one of Xi's most trusted confidants, and their mentor-protégé ties can be traced to the mid-1980s when both He and Xi worked in Xiamen. He Lifeng was a *mishu* for Xi during this time—the former served as deputy office director of the Xiamen Municipal Government while the latter was vice-mayor of the city.

He Lifeng was born in Yongding County, Fujian Province (his ancestral home is usually cited as Xingning County, Guangdong Province). He Lifeng completed both undergraduate and graduate programs in finance at Xiamen University. He received his bachelor's degree in 1982, his master's through full-time study in 1984, and his doctoral degree through part-time studies in 1998. Early in his career, He gained substantial leadership experience in the financial sector, serving as deputy director and director of the Bureau of Finance, director of the Municipal Economic and Trade Commission, and director of the Xiangyu Free Trade Zone Management Committee, all of which were in Xiamen. He also served as director of the Tianjin Binghai New Economic Development Zone from 2009 to 2013.[33]

Over the past three decades, He Lifeng's career advancement has often followed Xi's. He assisted Xi on financial affairs in Fujian earlier in his career and was promoted to Fuzhou party secretary and standing member of the provincial party committee when Xi served as provincial deputy party secretary and governor of Fujian. About a year and a half after Xi became vice-president of the PRC and a PSC member, He was appointed deputy party secretary of Tianjin. One year after Xi became president, He Lifeng was appointed vice-minister of the National Development and Reform Commission. Most important, He Lifeng is now in charge of implementing Xi's new regional economic development strategy, known as "One Belt, One Road."[34] This important assignment will give He Lifeng the opportunity to showcase his expertise in financial and economic matters at the national level of leadership.

It is important to note that most of Xi's protégés in economic and financial affairs have been seen as promarket economic technocrats. This is understandable because many of them previously worked (along with their boss Xi Jinping) in the frontier regions of China's economic and financial reforms, such as Fujian, Zhejiang, and Shanghai. As some Chinese analysts have observed, when Xi was party secretary of Zhejiang, his protégés outlined and promoted an economic policy that benefited small- and medium-sized private firms.[35] Fang Xinghai, the aforementioned Stanford-educated financial technocrat who served as deputy office director and director of financial affairs in the Shanghai municipal government under Xi, now plays a crucial role in drafting and implementing the new economic blueprint for the Xi administration. Fang's boss, Liu He, the aforementioned Harvard graduate and an internationally respected liberal economic thinker, is the main drafter of the plan that was adopted at the Third Plenum of the 18th Central Committee to deepen market reforms, as well as the principal designer of the "economic new normal" for China.[36] As will be discussed in detail in chapter 8, Liu He, a childhood friend and trusted confidant of Xi's, has been the chief economic strategist for the current leadership.

The Conservative Team for Propaganda and Ideology

By contrast, Xi's other confidants who are in charge of propaganda and ideological work—namely Huang Kunming, He Yiting, and Li Shulei—are all noticeably very conservative. All three have developed mentor-protégé relations with Xi over many years. Huang Kunming began to work under Xi when the latter was a municipal leader in Fujian in the 1980s. He Yiting and Li Shulei are also members of the so-called "Shaanxi Gang." He Yiting was born in Shaanxi and, like Xi, he was a sent-down youth in the province. Li Shulei served as deputy party secretary of Xi'an in 2004–2006. All three have often been identified by the Chinese media as Xi Jinping's "brain trust" (文胆, wendan).

Huang Kunming is believed to have substantially assisted Xi with preparing the latter's column in Zhejiang Daily called "New Thought in Zhejiang" (之江新语, zhijiang xinyu) in 2003–07 when Xi was Zhejiang party secretary.[37] Xi and Huang frequently exchanged ideas and views during these years and Xi later appointed Huang as director of the Propaganda Department of the Zhejiang Provincial Party Committee in 2007.[38] Similarly, it was reported that He Yiting drafted the eight anticorruption regulations that were enacted in the first year of Xi's leadership and that Li Shulei drafted Xi's speech at the famous cultural and art work forum held in October 2014, in which Xi emphasized the importance of party control of cultural affairs.[39]

All three attended college in the late 1970s after China resumed college entrance examinations. They studied the humanities and social sciences. Huang was enrolled in the political education program at Fujian Normal University (1978–82) and later took a part-time graduate program in politics at the Central Party School (1985–88). Huang also attended the graduate program at Tsinghua University on a part-time basis (2005–08) and received his doctoral degree in management. He Yiting attended Beijing Normal University for both his undergraduate and graduate degrees in history in 1979–85. Throughout his career, he has worked exclusively in the kinds of functional roles best suited for *mishu*, mainly in the area of party building and ideological work. He Yiting worked first as a clerk at the General Office of the CCP Central Committee after graduation, then advanced his career as an official at the Central Policy Research Office and served as executive deputy director of the office from 2009 to 2013, primarily working for then vice-president Xi Jinping. He currently serves as executive vice-president of the Central Party School.

Like Huang and He, Li Shulei received his formal education in China, although he did spend a few months attending a short-term program for senior executives at the Harvard Kennedy School in the spring of 1999.[40] In contrast to Huang and He, who did not begin their college education until their early or late twenties due to the Cultural Revolution, Li Shulei attended the Department of Library Science at Peking University at the age of fourteen, where he earned the nickname "Peking University prodigy" (北大神童, *beida shentong*).[41] Also unlike Huang and He, who attended part-time graduate programs, Li studied Chinese literature on a full-time basis, attending Peking University for his master's (1982–84) and doctorate (1986–89). He took a teaching position in the Department of Literature and History of the Central Party School (1984–86) and then returned to the same department as an assistant professor after receiving his Ph.D. in 1989.

Li served consecutively as associate professor (1991–93), director of the Chinese Literature Division (1993–96, during which he was promoted to full professor in 1995), director of the Socialist Culture Division (1996), deputy director of the Department of Literature and History (1996–99), director of the same department (1999–2002), and dean of the Training Institute of the Central Party School (2002–08). It is unclear when Li first met Xi Jinping, but it is widely believed that Xi played a direct role in promoting Li to provost and vice-president of the Central Party School in 2008 when Xi was president of the school (2007–12). Li was transferred to Fujian Province in 2014, where he served as director of the Propaganda Department of the Provincial Party Committee. This appointment was seen as an effort to broaden Li's leadership experience for further promotion in the future. In December 2015, Li was transferred back to Beijing where he now serves as secretary of the Municipal Commission for Discipline Inspection.

Li Shulei has broad academic interest in history, literature (classic and modern, Chinese and foreign), poetry, literary criticism, psychology, politics, and international relations. For example, he wrote an article discussing the lessons of the Cuban missile crisis based on Robert Kennedy's *Thirteen Days: A Memoir of the Cuban Missile Crisis*.[42] Over the past two decades, he has published nine books (totaling 1.5 million words) and over 200 essays and commentaries. Li's main professional work focuses on reassessing

Confucianism in present-day China, cultural development, and the importance of soft power.[43] These topics and ideas are very much in line with Xi Jinping's notions of "the Chinese dream" and "the great rejuvenation of the Chinese nation."[44] For Xi, China's rise to prominence on the world stage should not lie solely in the economic domain but should also be reflected in the Chinese public's confidence in its cultural values and social ethics.[45]

In his short article "How to Construct an Idol," published in 2011, Li Shulei discusses how Confucius—or, more precisely, Confucianism—was treated and reassessed during the Tang Dynasty and eventually regained its status as the ideological and cultural doctrine of the time.[46] Like Huang Kunming and He Yiting, Li Shulei also has been engaged heavily in advocating Xi's ideas of governance.

In April 2014, soon after Li moved to Fujian and began serving as director of the Propaganda Department in the province, the front page of the official newspaper, *Fujian Daily,* published Li's article on re-reading Xi Jinping's poem in memory of Jiao Yulu. Jiao was a communist hero known for his hard work, devotion, and sacrifice to the party.[47] In the article Li praised Xi's contributions to Fujian in his seventeen years of work there. Li wrote, "Comrade Xi Jinping has not only left Fujian a wealth of ideas and a strategy for development, but also a treasure of work ethics and spirit."[48] Li also initiated a reprint of the book *Out of Poverty,* which Xi wrote during his time as a local leader in Fujian.[49]

The most important individual who has contributed to the promotion of Xi's ideological work is probably He Yiting. In 2014 He compiled the *Study of General Secretary Xi Jinping's Important Speeches,* which included major speeches by Xi following the 2012 National Party Congress. The book has become a must-read for all levels of Chinese officials. As the leader of operations for the Central Party School, He Yiting was instrumental in arranging and hosting seven classes for ministerial and provincial leaders and two classes for senior officials in political and legal affairs to study Xi's speeches from November 2013 to April 2014.[50] He also played a key role in compiling and publishing other books featuring Xi's thoughts on governance, including *Xi Jinping's Nineteen Lectures at the Central Party School.* According to He, a main task for the Central Party School is to "do a good job translating Xi's work" (翻译好, *fanyihao*) for the Chinese public.[51] In another article widely circulated in China, He asserted that "the more frequently one studies General Secretary Xi Jinping's speeches, the more refreshing they become; the more regularly one applies them, the more innovative they turn out."[52]

As some Chinese analysts have observed, in contrast to Wang Huning—another chief aide for top leaders who is known for his expertise in the study of political science—He Yiting is particularly skilled at "party building and official public image making."[53] He Yiting is also famous for his strong views on upholding Marxism as an official ideology, the party leadership, and the socialist road. For example, He stated bluntly that the Chinese Academy of Social Sciences should be the stronghold of Marxism.[54] In his view, all officials "should have absolute respect for the authority of the Central Committee of the CCP led by General Secretary Xi Jinping, respond in an unambiguously positive manner to what the Central Committee expresses, firmly implement the Central Committee's resolutions, and strictly prohibit what the Central Committee bans."[55] Under He Yiting's direct instruction, the official organ of the CCP Central Committee, the journal *Seek the Truth*, published an editorial calling for a firm rejection of five fallacious trends, namely, "universal values, constitutional democracy, historical nihilism, neoliberalism, and the cynicism of reform and opening."[56] The editorial argued that the notion of universal values, with its strong religious component, has always been the "ideological source for Western expansionism and the tool for global domination."[57]

In this sense, Xi Jinping's *mishu* on the ideological and propaganda front (namely, Huang Kunming, He Yiting, and Li Shulei) differ profoundly from his aides for economic and financial matters (namely, Liu He, He Lifeng, and Fang Xinghai). This observation reflects the diversity of Xi's inner circle in terms of background, expertise, and worldview. Perhaps even more revealingly, this may explain why Xi's strategy of governance over the past three years has often been characterized as economically liberal and politically conservative.[58] Under Xi's leadership, market reform has accelerated, especially in terms of financial liberalization, service sector dynamics, and the rapid development of small- and medium-sized private firms. But at the same time, a large number of Chinese public intellectuals have been dismayed by orders instructing them not to speak about seven sensitive issues: universal values, freedom of the press, civil society, civil rights, past mistakes of the CCP, crony capitalism, and judicial independence. Media censorship has tightened, and some participants in human rights activities have encountered political harassment and even arrest.

This contrast is certainly not new in Chinese elite politics. Xi Jinping is not the only Chinese leader in recent decades to have entered office facing high expectations in the realms of political and economic reform. His predecessors Deng Xiaoping, Jiang Zemin, and Hu Jintao all discovered that economic reforms were easier to pursue than political reforms. This is also not unique to China; bureaucratic politics elsewhere encounter the reality that "where policymakers stand largely depends on where they sit," as one phrase neatly captures the phenomenon. To a certain extent, the diversity of Xi's *mishu* cluster broadens his power bases and gives him more options from which to choose—not only an effective and multiskilled team but also a diverse policy agenda—for his second term.

SUMMARY

During the reform era, the post of *mishu* has commonly served as a stepping-stone to leadership positions. Top leaders—Jiang Zemin and Zhu Rongji in the third generation and Hu Jintao and Wen Jiabao in the fourth generation—all served as *mishu* or office directors early in their political careers. Xi Jinping's early experience as a *mishu* to the minister of Defense was a very important credential for him when he became party boss about thirty years later. A large number of the current senior leaders have served as *mishu* or chiefs-of-staff during their political careers. In the three most important leadership bodies, the PSC, the Politburo, and the Central Committee, members with *mishu* experience account for 71 percent, 64 percent, and 63 percent of total members, respectively. Among the military members of the current Central Committee, one-third have *mishu* backgrounds, including the minister of Defense and chief of the joint staff department of the PLA. In 2014, twenty-four of the thirty-one provincial governors (77 percent) and nineteen of the twenty-five State Council ministers (76 percent) had previously served as *mishu* or as chiefs-of-staff or office directors.

The rapid rise of *mishu* and the critical role they play in Chinese politics today are not coincidental. Several situational factors have contributed to the omnipresence of *mishu* in the Chinese leadership: the great need for aides on the part of gerontocratic leaders who returned to power in the early years of the reform era; the desire of princelings to work in high offices and, especially, to serve senior leaders who had been comrades-in-arms of those princelings' fathers; the strong ties and long-term working relationship between *mishu* and their bosses due to frequent job reshuffling that allows only top aides to accompany their bosses; and the necessity to rely on aides who possess technical, administrative, and economic and financial expertise to help guide decisionmaking and governance as China faces increasingly complicated domestic and foreign affairs.

Without a doubt, the prevalence of *mishu* clusters indicates nepotism and favoritism in elite recruitment. The penetration of *mishu* clusters into the Chinese political system not only reflects the importance of mentor-protégé relations in that system but also contributes significantly to rampant official corruption. Not surprisingly, the investigation into Zhou Yongkang's corruption—outrageous in both scale and scope—and his subsequent downfall began with the purge of his six *mishu*. Scandals over Xu Caihou's sale of officer positions and military rankings involved four of his *mishu* (all with the rank of major general) who helped solicit bribes. Ling Jihua, chief-of-staff to Hu Jintao, advanced his career primarily as a *mishu*, through which he gained tremendous power and political influence.

Understandably, Xi Jinping has recently called for the tighter management and party discipline of secretarial staff.[59] His bold anticorruption campaign, especially the purges of heavyweight politicians Zhou Yongkang, Xu Caihou, Guo Boxiong, and Ling Jihua, has enhanced public confidence in his leadership. But paradoxically, Xi Jinping has had to rely on his own *mishu* cluster to consolidate his power and carry out his policy agenda. Xi's emphasis on the "absolute loyalty" of his secretarial staff, as discussed earlier in this chapter, is often interpreted, rightly or wrongly, as demonstrating his obsession with strengthening mentor-protégé ties.

Over the past three years, Xi has appointed many of his former *mishu* to crucial leadership positions, and his current *mishu*, especially those who serve as office directors of the central leading groups, play instrumental roles in assisting Xi in various important functional areas, including finance, economic reforms, national security, cybersecurity, foreign affairs, and ideological affairs. Xi's *mishu* cluster is noticeable for its internal diversity in terms of educational and occupational backgrounds, professional expertise, and the worldviews of its members. While his economic and financial team includes some world-class and liberal-minded financial and economic technocrats, Xi's *mishu* on the ideological front are remarkably old-fashioned hardliners. This may help explain why Xi has adopted an economically liberal and politically conservative governance strategy. It remains to be seen whether this contrast will help Xi balance the interests of different political constituencies in the country or will lead to a deadlock or clash in the implementation of his policy agenda.

Generally speaking, a *mishu* cluster by itself does not form a monolithic organization or an exclusive political faction. Although *mishu* share a political identity, they are loyal to their bosses rather than their peers. Normally, the number of *mishu* that a senior leader has is not enough to form a comprehensive political faction. *Mishu* thus often contribute to the negotiation and interdependence among various factions, foster coalition building, and increase political consultation and compromise in Chinese elite politics.

There are two contrasting views on the implications of the *mishu* phenomenon on the Chinese political system. Some China analysts argue that with the growing importance of *mishu* in the Chinese leadership today, the Chinese political process has become even less institutionalized.[60] Others, such as James Mulvenon and Michael Chase, believe that because *bosses* rarely meet with one another, *mishu* "handle communication and coordination between leaders, and even smooth over personal disputes or policy rifts."[61] If the role of *mishu* is viewed in this light, one can expect that the managerial skills of *mishu*, especially those developed in the process of coalition building and consensus making, become very valuable when they later serve as bosses themselves.

This practical advantage of serving as a *mishu* might explain why elite selection in reform-era China generally favors those who are skilled in coalition building; why the top leaders of the third, fourth, and fifth generations, as well as their chief aides, are often such capable political tacticians; and why political successions over the past two decades, in spite of factional tensions and vicious power struggles, still largely have demonstrated compromise and power sharing in the era of collective leadership.

The top leaders of various factions all engage in coalition-building in their attempts to expand their power and influence. *Mishu* often overlap in their involvement with different political networks and diverse bureaucratic and regional sectors. In that regard they may further contribute to coalition building, political negotiation, and most important, a complex interdependence among competing coalitions—the subject of the next chapter.

CHAPTER 7

Factions

One Party, Two Coalitions?

There's not a liberal America and a conservative America—there's the United States of America.
—BARACK OBAMA

Generally speaking, gentlemen were united as a party by a common principle, while villains were combined into a party by common interests. It was something in the nature of things.
—OUYANG XIU 欧阳修

Regardless of whether they serve in democratic states or authoritarian regimes, politicians tend to emphasize unity and solidarity once they obtain national power. Partisanship and factional struggles based on political, socioeconomic, ideological, and demographic issues, which intensify prior to an election or leadership transition, often give way to an emphasis on shared national identity and common socioeconomic aspirations. Yet, normal political tensions eventually reemerge and spark a new round of intense competition between opposing political forces.

In China's one-party system, the Chinese Communist Party (CCP) holds a monopoly on power. However, this does not necessarily mean that the party leadership today is a monolithic group whose prominent members all share the same ideology, political associations, socioeconomic background, and policy preferences. The preceding chapters have described some of the broad trends of Chinese elite politics in terms of institutional and regional representation, education credentials, occupational identities and career experiences, and mentor-protégé ties through the role of *mishu*. Crucially, the

249

upper echelons of the CCP have also begun to tend toward increasingly dynamic factional politics, resulting in more meaningful alliance building and political grouping in the leadership.

The CCP unambiguously rejects political competition from outside forces. But within the party leadership itself, there is no shortage of checks and balances. The nature of Chinese elite politics has changed over the past two decades, largely as a result of the development of collective leadership in the post-Deng era. Intense elite competition and dynamic political coalitions in the Jiang, Hu, and now Xi administrations, which are often linked to various vested interest groups and geographic regions in the country, have developed a Chinese-style bipartisanship—in a sense, "one party, two coalitions"—similar to systems found in many other countries.[1]

How should one draw a defining line around competing, though still largely informal and implicit, political coalitions in present-day China? On what grounds do factions—large and small, new and old—form major political coalitions in order to be more competitive? What are the new features of the factional lineup in the national leadership after the 18th National Party Congress? What will coalition building and factional dynamics look like on the eve of the 19th National Party Congress? Does Xi Jinping's remarkable consolidation of power—especially the six-to-one split of the Politburo Standing Committee (PSC) in his coalition's favor—mean a shift from factional power sharing to a new "winner takes all" mode of Chinese elite politics? Has Xi's recent anticorruption campaign been largely driven by factional motivations? Is Chinese factional politics becoming more vicious, more arbitrary, and thus more dangerous in the wake of corruption cases like those of Bo Xilai, Zhou Yongkang, Xu Caihou, Guo Boxiong, and Ling Jihua? Will the factional imbalance at the top seriously undermine leadership unity and elite cohesion, thus potentially threatening the sociopolitical stability of the country at large? Will the existing system of collective leadership in China, despite some significant changes, largely continue in the Xi era—or is it headed toward failure?

It is essential for students of Chinese elite politics to address these important questions, especially at a time when rumors and speculation in the public discourse about factional struggles in Zhongnanhai are becoming increasingly sensational, voluminous, confusing, and contradictory. The recent purge of a large number of senior officials on corruption and other criminal charges increases the need for a better understanding of the features of Chinese factional politics. Interestingly enough, the communiqué of the Politburo meeting at the end of 2014 was titled "The party should not tolerate gangs, cliques and nepotism."[2] Seasoned observers of Chinese politics would have no problem understanding the implicit message of this communiqué: factional politics have now become such a serious concern in the leadership that the Politburo needed to hold a meeting focusing on the matter. China's official media, including Xinhua, now also uses the terms "*mishu* clusters," "petroleum faction" (石油帮, *shiyoubang*), and "Shanxi faction" (山西帮, *shanxibang*) to characterize the prevalence of "various factions" (团团伙伙, *tuantuanhuohuo*) that the CCP leadership needs to manage.[3] In the military, the recent purge of senior military officers with Henan native backgrounds led some Chinese analysts to adopt the term "Henan faction" (河南帮, *henanbang*).[4] Factional tensions and dynamics arguably constitute the defining characteristics of present-day Chinese elite politics.

DEFINING CHARACTERISTICS OF CHINESE FACTIONAL POLITICS TODAY

This study argues that two main leadership coalitions—the "elitist coalition" (精英同盟, *jingying tongmeng*, or the Jiang-Xi camp) and the "populist coalition" (民粹同盟, *mincui tongmeng*, or the Hu-Li camp)—have been competing for power, influence, and control over policy initiatives in the post-Deng collective leadership. This bifurcation has created an intraparty mechanism approximating a system of checks and balances in the CCP leadership.

The elitist coalition was born of the Jiang Zemin era and is currently led by Xi Jinping. The elitist coalition is more closely associated with China's east coast—the region that has been known for fast economic growth. The coastal provinces were the country's dominant economic force in the 1990s and have reassumed their role as the pacesetter for China's new phase of economic development under the Xi administration. The region's core political faction used to be the Shanghai Gang—leaders who had advanced their careers in Shanghai under Jiang. The faction's main membership now primarily consists of "princelings"—leaders born into the families of communist revolutionaries or other high-ranking officials, including both Jiang and Xi. They are bound by their shared elite political identity and a sense of entitlement as "red nobility." Due to nepotism, these leaders have usually enjoyed quicker career advancement than leaders who do not come from such backgrounds. More recently, under Xi's leadership, the elitist coalition has expanded to include the so-called "Shaanxi Gang" (which will be discussed in detail in the following chapter) and Xi's other regionally based political networks in Fujian and Zhejiang. This elite group has tended to be economically liberal and supportive of market reform, but politically conservative, especially with regard to control over the media and intraparty elections. Yet, in making anticorruption the centerpiece of their political agenda, Xi Jinping and his principal political ally, Wang Qishan, have shown their commitment to dealing with this particularly corrosive issue.

The populist coalition draws its name from both the well-known political rhetoric of "putting people first" and, consequently, orients its policies toward economic equality, social justice, and more-balanced regional development. The populist coalition consists of factional cliques that support the populist agenda, and its cadres usually come from humble family backgrounds and have worked in poor, inland provinces. The leaders in the populist coalition usually have had more experience at the grassroots level and often have advanced their careers in a step-by-step manner through local leadership. The populist coalition was previously led by former president Hu Jintao and is now headed by Premier Li Keqiang. Its core faction is the so-called *tuanpai* ("league faction"), which includes both Hu and Li and is made up of leaders who have advanced in politics through leadership positions in the Chinese Communist Youth League (CCYL). CCYL leadership experience and the political socialization resulting from such an experience have served as both a distinct identity and an important stepping-stone for *tuanpai* leaders' career advancement. At a time when the Xi-led elitist coalition is rapidly expanding its own power and influence, some other factions, especially the geographically based cliques of inland regions (except Shaanxi Province), tend to lean toward the populist camp of Hu and Li.

Factional politics is, of course, not a new development in the People's Republic of China (PRC). Major events during the Mao and Deng eras, such as the Anti-Rightist campaign, the Cultural Revolution, and the 1989 Tiananmen crisis, were all related to factional infighting within the CCP leadership. At the Eleventh Plenum of the 8th National Party Congress, which was held at the beginning of the Cultural Revolution in August 1966, Mao Zedong made a remarkable statement: "No party outside the party reflects an imperial ideology; no faction within the party is an incredibly bizarre notion."[5] Mao's statement actually echoes the quote used as the second epigraph of this chapter, from Song Dynasty historian Ouyang Xiu's classic essay "On Cliques" (朋党论, *pengdanglun*), on the undeniability of factional politics in a regime.[6]

In the early decades of PRC history, Mao was decisive in purging his factional rivals. The defeated factions—for example, prominent factional leaders such as former minister of Defense Peng Dehuai, former PRC president Liu Shaoqi, and former minister of Defense and CCP vice chair Lin Biao—were all persecuted viciously along with their protégés and associates. All of these factional leaders died tragically and in disgrace.

Factional politics in the era of collective leadership, however, has become less of a winner-take-all game. Neither the elitist nor the populist coalition is capable of defeating the other and monopolizing power. The purges of senior leaders—for example, former Beijing party secretary Chen Xitong in the Jiang era and former Shanghai party secretary Chen Liangyu in the Hu era—did not lead to large-scale replacements or arrests of the protégés of these two leaders. Even after the fall of Bo Xilai, his principal partner in Chongqing, Mayor Huang Qifan, has retained his leadership post and membership in the Central Committee. While the purges of Zhou Yong-kang, Xu Caihou, Guo Boxiong, and Ling Jihua all have led to arrests of some of their associates on corruption charges, it is notable that most of their pa-trons, confidants, and friends have not been targeted. Political deals regard-ing the scale and scope of these purges seemed to be cut between a small number of very senior leaders from both coalitions before the Xi leadership made moves to prosecute Zhou, Xu, Guo, and Ling.

China's current factional dynamics exhibit three main features. First, the two coalitions, which represent the interests of different political elite groups, not only compete for power for their own sake but also compete because they represent different socioeconomic and geographic constituencies and therefore seek to advance contrasting policy agendas. In other words, each coalition has its own strengths and constituencies that the other does not possess. This elite division, which largely hews to socioeconomic backgrounds and geographic constituencies, has been a recurrent phenomenon in con-temporary China. Some critics compare princelings with the offspring of the "Eight Banners" (八旗子弟, *baqi zidi*): households who were known for their "idle, indolent, corrupt and contaminated power abuse" during the late days of the Qing Dynasty in the nineteenth century.[7] But the competing force, the "Han Barrack" (汉军营, *hanjunying*), though weaker overall, provided an alternate source of governance and thus helped sustain the dynasty. Yet, it should be noted that certain politicians tend to push their political en-gagement beyond their usual socioeconomic boundaries, seeking broader public support for their initiatives. This has been most evident in the case of Bo Xilai. Bo, a princeling who came from a privileged family background, belonged to the elitist coalition. But prior to the revelation of his wife's role in the murder of a British businessman and other scandals, Bo had become quite popular among the Chongqing public, if not the entire country. His national bravado earned him the title of "man of the year" in a 2009 online poll conducted by *People's Daily*.[8]

Second, the leaders of the two coalitions have alternated in the driver's seat—the top position in the leadership—as evidenced first in the power transition from Jiang to Hu, and then in the succession from Hu to Xi. These two competing coalitions are almost equally powerful, partly because they are well represented in various national leadership bodies (although each group may not always have equal representation in each leadership body), and partly because their leadership skills, administrative experiences, and political credentials complement each other. The rotation in possession of the driver's seat reflects both the need for collective leadership to make up for the shortcomings of the previous administration led by one coalition and the opportunity to adopt new policy initiatives of the other. The principle of "equal in power distribution" should not be interpreted in a narrow or rigid sense. It instead entails a future-oriented sense of "factional rotation," as described in chapter 1. For example, the dominance of the Jiang-Xi camp in the PSC formed at the 18th Party Congress is balanced by the fact that the Hu-Li camp has remained well represented within the lower tiers of leadership, especially in the 376-member Central Committee. This may explain why the Hu-Li camp quietly accepted its poor showing in the contest for seats in the PSC: future opportunities for their group are still promising.

And third, while the two coalitions compete with each other on certain issues, they are willing to, and sometimes must, cooperate on others. From an individual perspective, cross-coalition personal friendships and other sorts of close connections do exist, as they do in the U.S. political system, wherein politicians from the Republican and Democratic parties can be very good friends. From time to time, political conspiracies and personal deal making across coalitions also occur. The widely perceived political deal between Ling Jihua in the Hu-Li camp and Zhou Yongkang in the Jiang-Xi camp on the eve of the 18th Party Congress is a good example. Ling attempted to make a deal with then PSC member and police tsar Zhou Yongkang, who was involved in the Bo Xilai scandal. The deal was simple: Zhou would help Ling cover up his son's fatal car crash and destroy the evidence of the coverup itself, and in return Ling would refrain from investigating Zhou's involvement in the Bo Xilai case.[9]

From a collective perspective, both camps share fundamental goals: maintaining China's political and social stability, promoting continued economic growth, enhancing China's status as a major international player, and, most important, ensuring the survival of CCP rule. This explains why in recent years both coalitions were willing to accept serious "casualties" as some of their heavyweight leaders were purged—Bo Xilai, Zhou Yongkang, Xu Caihou, and Guo Boxiong for the elitist coalition, and Ling Jihua for the populist coalition. For the CCP establishment, these leaders and their outrageous scandals must be dealt with, but the factions themselves are too strong to be dismantled. The Chinese leaders recognize that they are in the same boat when it comes to dealing with increasingly daunting political, socioeconomic, demographic, and foreign policy challenges. This Chinese style of bipartisanship is, of course, not a fully institutionalized system of checks and balances like the one that operates between the executive, legislative, and judicial branches in the American government. This informal and still largely experimental Chinese mechanism of "one party, two coalitions" provides only limited political choices for the CCP establishment, not to mention the Chinese public.

Nevertheless, the interaction between elitists and populists in the leadership—between the princelings and *tuanpai* factions—reflects a new dynamic of interdependence and power sharing through checks and balances in Chinese politics. Bipartisan collective leadership also entails a more pluralistic decisionmaking process through which political leaders can represent various social and geographic constituencies. It is hard to overemphasize what a dramatic change this marks in the "rules of the game" for CCP leadership politics.

China's "bipartisanship" is, of course, still at risk of failure. Deal cutting, power sharing, and political compromise between coalitions is not always easy. The rivalry between these two camps could get ugly. The fact that there are more ambitious candidates than available seats naturally creates winners and losers, at least for individual leaders. The self-promotion campaigns by ambitious politicians like Bo Xilai and Wang Yang on the eve of the 18th Party Congress, as described in the prologue, will not be the last of such campaigns in the country. Negotiations over personnel appointments, especially when it comes to membership in the PSC, could become contentious and even result in factional infighting that spirals out of control. Increasing diversity among political elites has already spurred concerns about the unity of current leadership. Internal ideological disagreements may become too divisive to reconcile.

Furthermore, Xi's rapid consolidation of personal power could potentially undermine the rules and norms of collective leadership in general and the bipartisan dynamic in particular. Xi's vigorous anticorruption campaigns might be perceived as being driven primarily by his desire to win factional battles. This could create many false friends and real enemies for Xi and lead to an unpredictable and dangerous political situation for the party and the country. Whether Xi and his own coalition can find a more constructive way to deal with the competing group—to share rather than monopolize power in the CCP leadership—is probably the most important issue in Chinese elite politics at present.

Some further clarifications about China's intraparty factionalism are in order. Factional politics and political coalitions in present-day China, although not really opaque to the public, still lack transparency. With a few noticeable exceptions, such as Bo Xilai and Wang Yang, a majority of political leaders in China take a low-profile approach, usually lobbying for promotion in a nonpublic manner. Unlike the decades of Liberal Democratic Party hegemony in Japan (1955–94), for instance, factional politics within the CCP have not yet been legitimized by the party constitution.

Additionally, these camps are not wholly exclusive. Although one can usually identify factional affiliation by political and geographical associations, promotion paths, and patron identities, a few leaders may have dual identities as both princelings and *tuanpai* members. There are *tuanpai* leaders who are of princeling origin; and there are princelings who are not in the Jiang-Xi camp. In these cases, a leader's factional identity and political loyalty is primarily determined by the channel and mentor through which he or she obtained the most crucial appointment in his or her political career. Within each respective camp there are important variations and subgroups, and, as the aforementioned Ling Jihua-Zhou Yongkang deal shows, factional defections and crossfactional conspiracies may occur from time to time.

Why are there only two coalitions? While the possibility of a third division cannot be excluded in theory, in reality no other well-established political force competes in any meaningful way with the two powerful coalitions in present-day China. The intense competition between elitists and populists seems to discourage politicians from allocating precious political resources to a third source of power or a dark-horse leader who does not belong to either of these coalitions. Instead, politicians have tended to assemble around either the current party boss or the heir apparent, one of which has represented each of these two coalitions during the past two decades. Similar observations can also be made about the Democratic Party and the Republican Party in American bipartisan politics. Despite third parties that have from time to time attempted to challenge the political status quo, no one would dispute the fact that bipartisanship in the United States helps illuminate the most-important features of American politics. All the observations above highlight the importance and nature of this emerging bipartisanship in Chinese elite politics.

THE ELITIST COALITION: THE JIANG-XI CAMP OF THE SHANGHAI GANG AND PRINCELINGS

As has been widely noted, Xi Jinping's ascension to China's top leadership—he was made heir apparent at the 2007 Party Congress and attained the top post at the 2012 Party Congress—was attributed to the strong support of Jiang Zemin's elitist camp. His two main patrons were former PRC president Jiang and former vice-president Zeng Qinghong.[10] Xi and these two patrons are all princelings, and all three of them reached the top of China's national leadership by way of Shanghai. This reveals the strong connection—even overlap in these cases—between the princeling group and the Shanghai Gang, the two most prominent factions of the elitist coalition.

Many analysts in both China and abroad interpreted the purges of Zhou Yongkang, Xu Caihou, and Guo Boxiong (all of whom had close ties with Jiang and Zeng) as signifying "the split" between Xi and Jiang, or even "the vicious contention" between Xi's princelings and Jiang's Shanghai Gang.[11] But this assessment is ill grounded, both conceptually and empirically. Xi and Jiang are both princelings and members of the Shanghai Gang, although some prominent Beijing-based princelings consider Jiang's princeling status dubious.[12] There is no evidence that the relationship between Xi and his two patrons is deteriorating in any way. Their political bonds and shared political interests are likely much stronger than most analysts have recognized. On May 24, 2014, CCTV prime-time news featured Xi Jinping's visit to a medical technology company in Shanghai, during which Jiang Zemin's son, Jiang Mianheng, the president of Shanghai University of Science and Technology, served as host to President Xi.[13] Ten days earlier, Zeng Qinghong and Jiang Mianheng, along with Shanghai party secretary Han Zheng, made a highly publicized joint appearance at an art museum in Shanghai.[14]

More important, Xi's strongest political ally, Wang Qishan, is also a longtime confidant of Jiang Zemin's. Of course, this does not necessarily mean that Jiang would have endorsed every important political move or every anticorruption case pursued by his protégé since Xi became the top leader in 2012. Meanwhile, it is in Xi's best interest to quickly dispel the notion that he is under the control of Jiang and Zeng. This explains why Xi fired his bodyguard—the husband of Jiang Zemin's longtime family nanny—shortly after he became the new boss in Zhongnanhai. For the same reason, soon after becoming PRC president in March 2013, Xi quickly reassigned his adviser Shi Zhihong, who had been Zeng Qinghong's longtime confidant, to a ceremonial position as deputy director of the Social and Legal Affairs Committee of the Chinese People's Political Consultative Conference. Shi had served as a *mishu* to Zeng as early as the mid-1980s, when Zeng was a municipal leader in Shanghai. After Zeng's retirement from the post of PRC vice-president, Shi continued working in the office of the vice-president from 2007 to 2012, assisting his new boss, then vice-president Xi, while concurrently holding the position of deputy director of the CCP Central Policy Research Office. Shi routinely accompanied Xi on his domestic and foreign travels and drafted speeches and memos for Xi during these years. Many observers characterized Shi as Zeng's "watchman in Xi's office."[15] Shi's departure from Xi's office was widely seen as part of Xi's effort to assert himself as the real boss of Zhongnanhai.

Like politicians elsewhere, these Chinese leaders understand that in politics there are no eternal allies or enemies. While the relationship between Xi and Jiang—and between Xi and Zeng—is subject to change in China's unpredictable political environment, one should not overlook the fact that, for now, Xi and Jiang very much need each other's support to consolidate the elitist coalition, and the strong bond between the princelings and the Shanghai Gang has been essential to such an effort. In a broader context, Xi and other Chinese leaders should be concerned about the inescapable collateral damage of such a split or the possible fall of a former party boss on

CCP rule as a whole. A review of the formation, background, characteristics, and subgroupings of both the Shanghai Gang and the princelings, including interconnections between these two elite groups and some recent new appointments, can resolve some misperceptions and thus help observers grasp the nature of coalition building in Chinese elite politics throughout the reform era.

The Rise of the Shanghai Gang in Post-Deng China

Membership in the Shanghai Gang is based on political association rather than geographic origin, although a significant number of members were born in Shanghai and two nearby provinces, Zhejiang and Jiangsu. In a stricter sense, "Shanghai Gang" refers to leaders whose careers have advanced primarily as a result of their political association with Jiang Zemin while he was in Shanghai. When Jiang served as mayor and party secretary in the city during the mid-1980s, he began to cultivate a web of mentor-protégé ties with his Shanghai associates. After becoming the party's top leader in 1989, Jiang appointed several of his confidants in Shanghai to important positions in Beijing. In particular, Jiang brought Zeng Qinghong (his chief-of-staff), You Xigui (his bodyguard), and Jia Ting'an (his personal secretary) to Beijing with him. Zeng played a crucial role in helping Jiang consolidate his power in Beijing, as discussed in the previous chapter. You was later appointed director of the Bodyguards Bureau and deputy director of the CCP General Office. Jia served Jiang as director of the office of the PRC president and director of the General Office of the Central Military Commission. These three constituted the most crucial figures in the inner circle of Jiang's administration. A few years after Jiang moved to Beijing, two of Jiang's deputies in Shanghai, Wu Bangguo and Huang Ju, were promoted to Politburo members and later served as members of the PSC.

Over the past quarter century, Jiang has firmly controlled the municipal leadership in Shanghai—arguably his most important power base. A majority of senior leadership positions in the Shanghai municipal government have been filled with candidates from the same city, which violates the norms and regulations of cross-region elite rotation and the law of avoidance (as discussed in chapter 3). For example, current party secretary Han Zheng and Mayor Yang Xiong were both born in Shanghai and have never worked outside of Shanghai. Meanwhile, the leaders who were transferred to top municipal leadership posts in Shanghai over the past three decades usually were confidants of Jiang's or Zeng's. For example, former Shanghai party secretaries Xi Jinping and Yu Zhengsheng are both protégés of Jiang and the princelings. Wang Anshun, who served as director of the Organization Department and later as deputy party secretary of the Shanghai Municipal

Party Committee from 2003 to 2007, came from the petroleum industry, which has been Zeng's power base. Another example is Li Xi, a protégé of Xi Jinping's, who was promoted from 2011 to 2013 to the same positions in Shanghai that Wang Anshun had held earlier. Shen Deyong, who advanced his early legal career in Jiangxi Province, where he served as vice-president of the Jiangxi Provincial Supreme Court and deputy party secretary of the Jiangxi Provincial Party Committee, was transferred to Shanghai in the wake of the Chen Liangyu corruption case. As a trusted political ally of Jiang's, Shen served as secretary of the Shanghai Commission for Discipline Inspection from 2006 to 2008. Shen currently serves as executive vice-president of the Supreme People's Court.

In addition, a significant number of municipal leaders in Shanghai have been promoted to the national leadership or transferred to other provinces and cities where they served as top leaders. For example, former deputy party secretary of Shanghai Meng Jianzhu later served as Jiangxi party secretary and minister of Public Security and is currently a Politburo member and secretary of the Central Political and Law Commission. Other examples include the aforementioned former deputy party secretaries of Shanghai, Wang Anshun and Li Xi, who now serve as mayor of Beijing and party secretary of Liaoning, respectively. Altogether, they have formed a very powerful political network in the country. Therefore, broadly speaking, virtually all senior officials who have served in the municipal leadership of Shanghai over the past three decades can be considered members of the Shanghai Gang.

An important exception is PRC vice-president Li Yuanchao, who was born to a high-ranking official family (his father was vice-mayor of Shanghai in the early 1960s) and advanced his career in Shanghai, where he served as deputy secretary and later secretary of the Shanghai Municipal Youth League Committee in the early 1980s. Li Yuanchao is not usually seen as a member of the Shanghai Gang, but rather as a protégé of two leaders with strong CCYL backgrounds: Chen Pixian (Shanghai party secretary before the Cultural Revolution) and Hu Jintao. For these reasons, the Shanghai Gang has long considered Li as a threat and often blocked his promotion.[16] In 2012 members of the Jiang-Xi camp, especially the Shanghai Gang, successfully prevented Xi's potential rivals, such as Li Yuanchao and Ling Jihua, from obtaining PSC seats.[17]

Political Economy of the "Shanghai Miracle"

Without a doubt, the favorable policies implemented in Shanghai by Jiang Zemin and former premier Zhu Rongji (who also advanced his career by way of Shanghai) explain why and how the city has rapidly risen to economic prominence since the 1990s. Shanghai received a large number of grants and loans from the central government between 1990 and 2002, when Jiang served as CCP general secretary. According to an official Chinese study conducted in 2002, Shanghai received 19.8 billion yuan more than its main domestic competitor, Tianjin, during these twelve years.[18] The high inflow of state grants and loans into Shanghai, in turn, stimulated more foreign direct investment in the city. Between 1978 and 2001, 86 percent of total foreign domestic investment in China went to the coastal region, especially the lower Yangtze River delta; 9 percent went to the central region; and only 5 percent went to the western region, even though the western region accounts for 71 percent of the total area of the country.[19]

According to a Shanghai-based correspondent for the *Far Eastern Economic Review*, in the late 1990s "laborers from the provinces, numbering close to three million, scurried around the city's estimated 21,000 construction sites."[20] A reporter for the *Wall Street Journal* was not entirely exaggerating when he wrote in 1993, "What's going on in Shanghai, and up and down the China coast, might be the biggest construction project the planet has ever seen since the coral polyps built the Great Barrier Reef after the last Ice Age."[21] During his visit to Shanghai in 2004, then French president Jacques Chirac called the development of Pudong, the eastern part of Shanghai, "another project of epic proportion like the Great Wall and the Grand Canal."[22]

History, geography, cultural characteristics, and economic conditions have all contributed to the dynamic development of the city. Shanghai leaders often argue that "the Shanghai miracle" has more to do with the vibrant entrepreneurship of the Shanghainese than with favorable government policies.[23] It is, of course, self-serving for Shanghai leaders to emphasize the distinctiveness of Shanghai's culture—its cosmopolitanism and entrepreneurial work ethic. Yu Tianbai, the author of a best-selling book in the early 1990s, *Shanghai: Her Character Is Her Destiny*, for example, has close connections with the municipal government.[24] Wang Daohan, the former mayor of Shanghai and once Jiang's mentor, wrote the preface for the book. Yu argues that the distinctiveness of Shanghai is both a cause and a consequence of remarkable economic change in the city, because, as the title of the book suggests, "her character is her destiny."

However, the Shanghai Gang and the city's construction fever encountered serious constraints when the populist coalition was in charge of Zhongnanhai after 2002. The macroeconomic control policy adopted by the Hu-Wen administration particularly aimed to cool down the construction boom in Shanghai and surrounding areas. In 2004 overseas media reported that Chen Liangyu, then party secretary of Shanghai and a protégé of Jiang, voiced strong opposition to the Hu-Wen administration's macroeconomic control policy during a Politburo meeting held that summer.[25] Chen, a Politburo member, accused then premier Wen of harming the interests of the

Yangtze River delta—and Shanghai in particular. Citing statistics to illustrate his points, Chen argued that Wen's conservative administrative regulations would not lead to a soft landing and instead would hamper the country's economy in future years, especially its booming real estate industry.[26] Chen stated bluntly that Wen should take "political responsibility" for the damaging consequences of his economic policy. Chen's real target was probably not Wen, but Hu, whose macroeconomic control policy was a key component of his much broader plan to strategically shift China's socioeconomic development toward a more regionally balanced growth. Given the centrality of these policies to his overall vision of China's future development, Hu quickly rejected Chen's criticism, responding that the collective leadership of the Politburo had adopted this macroeconomic policy and that all local governments, including Shanghai, should therefore carry it out.[27]

What followed two years later was the dramatic fall of Chen Liangyu on corruption charges. More specifically, Chen was charged with siphoning 3.45 billion yuan (US$439.5 million) from the Shanghai social security pension fund to make illicit loans and investments.[28] In addition, according to the official Central Commission for Discipline Inspection announcement, Chen was also allegedly involved in other serious discipline violations, such as "helping further the economic interests of illegal business people, protecting staff who severely violated laws and discipline, and furthering the interests of family members by taking advantage of his official posts."[29] The purge of Chen Liangyu was a big victory for the populist camp, and it sent the important message to individual leaders and other political factions, including the formidable Shanghai Gang, that they no longer enjoyed absolute power, even on their own turf.

The pension fund scandal and the fall of Chen Liangyu were major blows to the Shanghai faction. But arguably the most interesting feature of Chen Liangyu's fall was that no other senior official in the Shanghai municipal government lost his or her position. Among the fifteen standing members of the Shanghai Municipal Party Committee, only one, Jiang Sixian (head of the Organization Department and former chief-of-staff for Chen Liangyu), was transferred out of Shanghai.[30] Jiang, a native of Jiangsu, received a master's degree in engineering from Shanghai Jiaotong University, Jiang Zemin's alma mater. Jiang Sixian also served as vice-president of the university before becoming a municipal leader. Soon after the eruption of the Shanghai pension fund scandal, Jiang Sixian was transferred to Hainan Province, where he served as vice-governor, which was at the same level of leadership as his previous post in Shanghai. In early 2014 Jiang Sixian returned to Shanghai to become party secretary of Jiaotong University.

More important, Han Zheng, then mayor of Shanghai and also a rising star in the Shanghai Gang, was selected as acting party secretary of Shanghai after the purge of his former boss in September 2006. It is not yet clear what kind of deal was cut between Hu and Wen on one side and Jiang, Zeng, and other leaders of the Shanghai Gang on the other. But it is reasonable to assume that the nationwide campaign to promote the publication of Jiang's collected works prior to the removal of Chen and the appointment of Han Zheng as the city's acting party secretary (instead of the promotion of a Hu Jintao ally from somewhere else) were parts of the compromise. It is also interesting to note that both the Hong Kong media and the nonofficial mainland media reported that Jiang expressed his anger about Chen Liangyu's "bullying behavior" and "rotten lifestyle."[31] Jiang reportedly told others that "Chen deserves to be punished," despite the fact that Chen's ascent to political prominence, including his membership in the 16th Politburo, was largely attributable to Jiang's patronage.[32]

In March 2007 Xi Jinping was transferred from Zhejiang to take the position of Shanghai party secretary for eight months before moving to Beijing to assume his membership on the PSC. From 2007 to 2012 Yu Zhengsheng served as Shanghai party secretary before moving to Beijing to serve as a member of the PSC and passing this top post to Han Zheng. All of these three top leaders in Shanghai have very strong mentor-protégé ties with both Jiang and Zeng.[33] For Jiang, Shanghai is both the base of his power and a showcase of China's economic progress under his rule. Like any other top leader in China, Jiang is concerned about two things. The first is his legacy, and the second is political security for him and his family. This explains why he would fight so vigorously to maintain control over his turf, even at a huge political cost.

One good example of Jiang's efforts to control his turf was the appointment of Yang Xiong as mayor of Shanghai in 2012. Yang was born in Shanghai in 1953 and is a close friend of Jiang's son, Jiang Mianheng. Yang previously worked as the president of Shanghai Alliance Investment, a large finance, energy, and life sciences company that Jiang Mianheng founded and for which he served as board chairman in the 1990s.[34] With the help of the Jiang family, Yang later served as deputy chief-of-staff of Shanghai's municipal government in 2001, vice-mayor in 2003, and executive vice-mayor in 2008. But Jiang's favoritism, as expressed through the promotion of Yang, sparked a backlash, even in the Shanghai political establishment. In a "more candidates than seats election" for the standing committee members of the Shanghai Municipal Party Committee in May 2012, Yang was eliminated. A few months later, Yang was eliminated again in the election for alternate members of the 18th Central Committee. Despite these embarrassments, Jiang Zemin still insisted that Yang serve as mayor of Shanghai, and he succeeded in making this very unusual appointment. Consequently, for the first time in the past thirty years, the mayor of China's largest economic and financial center was not even an alternate member of the CCP Central Committee.

In a best-selling Chinese book titled *City Monsoon*, author Yang Dongping analyzes the constant changes in the relative economic weight, political power, and cultural influence of China's major cities throughout the nation's development. The author expresses the book's theme with an intriguing question, "In which direction is the city monsoon blowing?"[35] This metaphor may be particularly relevant for China analysts who are interested in the possible correlation between the power status of prominent politicians and the economic prospects of the regions and cities they represent. Just as in 2002, when the populist policy platform of new party boss Hu Jintao drastically changed China's course of development in favor of the inland region, Xi Jinping's ascent to the top leadership quickly led to the establishment of the Shanghai Free Trade Zone in 2013. The city has now reclaimed the status of "head of the dragon"—a pacesetter of China's global outreach in four areas: the economy, finance, trade, and shipping.[36]

Not surprisingly, under the Xi leadership the members of the Shanghai Gang have remained visible on the 18th Central Committee, with six members of the Politburo (24 percent), including two PSC members (28.6 percent). It should be noted that the Shanghai Gang's share of seats on the Central Committee (counting both full and alternate memberships) has always been small (for example, 4.1 percent at the 15th Central Committee and 4.5 percent at the 18th).[37] This reinforces the need for coalition building by the Jiang-Xi camp. Nevertheless, members of the Shanghai Gang tend to occupy some of the most crucial positions in the national leadership, as indicated in table 7-1.

This list does not include some prominent leaders who have strong ties with Shanghai (for example, those who were born in Shanghai), such as the state councilor Yang Jiechi and the director of the Hong Kong and Macau Affairs Office in the State Council, Wang Guangya, both of whom are full members of the 18th Central Committee. Nor does this list include provincial chiefs who are members of the Shanghai Gang but are not on the 18th Central Committee. For example, Chen Hao, new governor of Yunnan, was born in Shanghai in 1954 and served as deputy chief-of-staff of the Shanghai Municipal Party Committee for many years. The following chapter will further discuss Xi Jinping's recent efforts to promote his protégés from Shanghai.

Princelings: Unprecedentedly Strong Presence in the Xi Administration

In China, children of high-ranking officials are usually called princelings, and the princeling faction is also called the "party of princes." Both the original Chinese term and the English translation can be misleading because

TABLE 7-1. Prominent "Shanghai Gang" Members on the 18th Central Committee

Leader	Year born	Current position	Central Committee status	Defining experience in Shanghai
Xi Jinping	1953	Secretary-General of the CCP; President of the PRC	Politburo Standing Committee member	Party Secretary (2007)
Yu Zhengsheng	1945	Chairman of the CPPCC	Politburo Standing Committee member	Party Secretary (2007–12)
Meng Jianzhu	1947	Secretary of the Central Political and Law Commission	Politburo member	Deputy Party Secretary (1996–2001); Vice-Mayor (1993–96); Deputy Chief-of-Staff in Municipal Government (1992–93)
Han Zheng	1954	Party Secretary of Shanghai	Politburo member	Party Secretary (2012–present, 2006–07); Mayor (2003–12); Vice-Mayor (1998–2004)
Wang Huning	1955	Director of the Central Policy Research Office	Politburo member	Dean of the Fudan University Law School (1994–95); Chairman of the Department of International Politics (1989–94)
Xu Qiliang	1950	Vice-Chairman of the CMC	Politburo member	Chief-of-Staff of the Air Force Command in Shanghai (1985–86)
Wang Anshun	1957	Mayor of Beijing	Full member	Deputy Party Secretary (2003–07); Director of the Organization Department (2001–03)
Huang Qifan	1953	Mayor of Chongqing	Full member	Deputy Chief-of-Staff of the Municipal Party Committee (1994–98); Deputy Chief-of-Staff of the Municipal Government (1998–2001)

Name	Year	Position	Membership	Notes
Jia Ting'an	1952	Deputy Director of the CMC Political Work Department	Full member	*Mishu* to Mayor and Party Secretary Jiang Zemin (1985–89)
Lou Jiwei	1950	Minister of Finance	Full member	*Mishu* to Mayor and Party Secretary Zhu Rongji (1988–91)
Li Wei	1953	Director of the State Council Development and Research Center	Full member	*Mishu* to Mayor and Party Secretary Zhu Rongji (1988–91)
Cao Jianming	1955	President of the Supreme People's Procuratorate	Full member	President of the East China University of Political Science and Law (1997–99)
Li Xi	1956	Liaoning Party Secretary	Alternate member	Deputy Party Secretary (2013–present); Director of the Organization Department (2011–13)
Ding Xuexiang	1962	Deputy Director of the General Office of the CCP Central Committee	Alternate member	Secretary of Political and Law Commission (2012–13); Chief-of-Staff of the Municipal Party Committee (2007–12)
Du Jiahao	1955	Hunan Governor	Alternate member	Deputy Chief-of-Staff (2003–04) ; Director of the Pudong District (2004–07)
Jiang Jianqing	1953	Chairman of the Industrial and Commercial Bank of China	Alternate member	President of the Shanghai Branch of the Industrial and Commercial Bank of China (1997–99)
Wang Ning	1955	Commander of the People's Armed Police	Alternate member	Chief-of-Staff of the Shanghai Garrison Command (2003–06)

Note and Source: CCP = Chinese Communist Party; PRC = People's Republic of China; CPPCC = Chinese People's Political Consultative Conference; CMC = Central Military Commission. Author's database.

princelings are not necessarily part of a monolithic organization or a formal network, and they do not necessarily have strong patron-client ties among themselves. Princelings may differ significantly one another in terms of occupational backgrounds, political experiences, and personalities. In addition, the political interests of princelings are not always aligned, and there is often infighting over power and wealth. As an elite group, princelings are far less cohesive than any of the other political networks that were once dominant or are still powerful in the Chinese leadership, such as the "field army association," the "Tsinghua clique," the Shanghai Gang, and the *tuanpai*.[38]

A few prominent leaders with princeling backgrounds—most noticeably, Liu Yandong, Li Yuanchao, and Zhang Qingli—are more closely associated with the *tuanpai* than their fellow princelings. Their career advancement is primarily attributed to the help they received from their *tuanpai* patron Hu Jintao. These leaders are princelings in terms of their family backgrounds, but their career experiences and close political association with Hu Jintao usually make them more loyal to Hu and the populist coalition.

In Chinese elite studies, "princeling" usually refers to a political leader who comes from a veteran communist revolutionary family or has a high-ranking official family background—at least one of the parents or parents-in-law having previously served at the vice-ministerial or vice-governor level of leadership or above. However, a princeling whose father was a vice-minister might differ significantly from a princeling whose father was a vice-premier of the State Council or a Politburo member. That explains why some princelings from the families of vice-premiers and Politburo members usually do not consider leaders who come from less prominent families, including even senior leaders with veteran communist revolutionary family backgrounds like Jiang Zemin, to be princelings.

Despite various differences within this group of "red nobility," the princeling leaders share a strong political identity. All prominent politicians with princeling backgrounds in the fifth generation of leadership greatly benefited early in their careers from their family ties. A large number of them were "born red," arriving in the late 1940s and 1950s as their parents' generation won civil war victories and became the new rulers of the communist regime. They usually received the best education available starting in their adolescent years, as discussed in detail in the following chapter. The formal education of those younger princelings, however, was interrupted during the Cultural Revolution.

A review of the career paths of these most prominent princelings in present-day China also reveals three shared traits. First, many of them served as *mishu* to senior leaders who were their fathers' old comrades-in-arms, as discussed previously. Two well-known red nobles, Kong Dan (former chairman of the China International Trust and Investment Corporation, whose father is Kong Yuan, former director of the CCP Central Investigation Department), and Qin Xiao (former chairman of China Merchants Bank, whose father, Qin Lisheng, was a communist veteran in the Yan'an years) also served as *mishu* for senior leaders in the early 1980s. The former worked for then state councilor and Minister of Finance Zhang Jinfu, and the latter served former Politburo member and director of the CCP Central Organization Department Song Renqiong. Early in their careers, Wang Qishan and Bo Xilai worked as clerks in the General Office and the Secretariat of the CCP Central Committee, respectively. These experiences as *mishu* not only provided valuable opportunities for princelings to become familiar with the work and decisionmaking processes at the national and provincial levels of leadership but also conferred extraordinary credentials that accelerated their political careers.

Second, princelings often received shortcuts for their career advancement. For example, Xi Jinping, Yu Zhengsheng, and Bo Xilai all previously served as mayor or party secretary of Fuzhou, Qingdao, and Dalian, respectively. These three cities are the municipalities whose economic planning is under the direct supervision of the State Council. Such appointments to top municipal leadership positions were catalysts for additional promotions, given that these coastal cities with Special Economic Zone status experienced high economic growth rates and had the potential for even greater growth. Municipal leaders, therefore, could receive credit for economic achievements in these rich coastal cities much more easily than leaders who worked in other cities. Furthermore, the top municipal leaders in these coastal cities automatically receive the administrative rank of vice-provincial governor with no need for approval from the provincial people's congress.

Third, a majority of these princelings, especially those in their fifties, have substantial leadership experience in economic administration, finance, foreign investment, and foreign trade. Wang Qishan, Yu Zhengsheng, Ma Kai, Bo Xilai, Zhou Xiaochuan, Chen Yuan, Lou Jiwei, Liu He, and Xiao Jie have been among the most experienced economic leaders in present-day China. Many of them, such as Xi Jinping and Yu Zhengsheng, had considerable experience leading China's most market-oriented regions. Economic expertise and administrative credentials were among the most important political assets for these princelings when they later competed for top leadership positions with their peer cohort, who typically lacked such experience.

Princelings' privileged life experiences and "helicopter style" career advancements are receiving growing criticism and opposition, not only from Chinese society but also from the deputies of both the National Party Congress and the National People's Congress. The strongest evidence of opposition to nepotism in the selection of Central Committee members is that many candidates on the ballot for the body were not elected despite, or perhaps because of, their high-ranking family backgrounds. Xi Jinping, Bo Xilai, and Chen Yuan, for example, were on the ballot for membership to the 14th Central Committee in 1992, but none of them were elected.[39] In the election of the 15th Central Committee in 1997, Xi Jinping received the lowest number of votes among the 151 alternate members elected. Wang Qishan, Liu Yandong, and Deng Pufang (Deng Xiaoping's son) also ranked among the bottom ten members in the number of votes received in the same election. In 2003 Zhou Xiaochuan received one of the three lowest vote totals among the twenty-nine ministers appointed to the State Council during the confirmation vote of the National People's Congress.[40]

Family ties and nepotism in elite recruitment are certainly not unique to China; they are often instrumental in the advancement of the political careers of leaders in other countries, including democratic states. As Isaac Stone Fish, an editor of *Foreign Policy* magazine, insightfully observed in 2012 regarding heads of states in Asia, "With few exceptions outside the dictatorships in the southeast and central part of the continent, virtually every country in Asia has been ruled by the offspring of a high-ranking politician in the 21st century."[41] In the United States, princelings and spouses of political leaders have been remarkably well represented in presidential and congressional elections in recent decades. However, elections in democracies usually give political legitimacy to an elected top leader, even if he or she comes from a politically powerful family. In an authoritarian regime such as China, where top leaders are *selected* rather than *elected*, privileged family backgrounds of top leaders are usually considered the primary reason for their ascendance to high office, thus diminishing their political legitimacy in some respects.

Some Chinese princelings, however, have recovered their previously poor public image by demonstrating their leadership skills. Wang Qishan, for example, has been seen by the Chinese public as capable and trustworthy during times of emergency or crisis. This was evident in the way he handled the severe acute respiratory syndrome, or SARS, epidemic in the spring of 2003. Beijing was hit hard by the epidemic, and when Wang was appointed as the city's acting mayor, a large number of patients were already dying and medical facilities were far from adequate. Residents had begun panicking, and the government had lost credibility (as a result of its initial attempts to cover up the epidemic), with some foreign observers calling the crisis "China's Chernobyl." Nevertheless, in the following months, Wang proved that he was truly an effective "chief of the fire brigade"—his current moniker in China—as he instituted measures that helped to control the spread of the disease. Unsurprisingly, at the Beijing municipal congress meeting the following year, Wang was confirmed as mayor of Beijing with 742 "yes" votes and only one "no" vote from the delegates.[42]

TABLE 7-2. Princelings on the Politburo Standing Committee

Term	Total members	Princelings	Princelings as % of total members
14th (1992)	7	2	28.6
15th (1997)	7	2	28.6
16th (2002)	9	2	22.2
17th (2007)	9	2	22.2
18th (2012)	7	4	57.1

Source: Cheng Li, "Opportunity Lost? Inside China's Leadership Transition," *Foreign Policy,* November 16, 2012.

TABLE 7-3. Princelings on the Central Military Commission

Term	Total members	Princelings	Princelings as % of total members
14th (1992)	8	1	12.5
15th (1997)	7	1	14.3
16th (2002)	8	2	25
17th (2007)	11	2	18.2
18th (2012)	11	4	36.4

Source: Cheng Li, "Opportunity Lost? Inside China's Leadership Transition," *Foreign Policy,* November 16, 2012.

With the arrival of the Xi administration, Chinese politics seem to be entering a new era characterized by the concentration of princelings at the top. Tables 7-2 and 7-3 show that in both the top civilian and military leadership bodies, the number of princelings is unprecedentedly high, encompassing four of the seven PSC members (57 percent) and four of the eleven Central Military Commission (CMC) members (36 percent). In both leading bodies the percentage of princelings is double that of the previous congress.

Table 7-4 lists some of the most powerful princelings in the civilian leadership of the 18th Central Committee. With the exception of Li Xiaopeng, who is an alternate member, the other twenty princelings are all full members of the Central Committee, including nine members of the Politburo (36 percent). This list does not include all of the princelings on the 18th Central Committee; those who serve in the leadership of universities and state-owned enterprises (SOEs) are not counted. For example, Gong Ke, an alternate member and president of Nankai University, is the son of Gong Yuzhi, who served as deputy director of the Central Propaganda Depart-

TABLE 7-4. China's Most Powerful Princelings in the Civilian Leadership of the 18th Central Committee

Name	Current position	Family background
Xi Jinping*	Secretary-General of the CCP; President of the PRC; Politburo Standing Committee member	Father: Xi Zhongxun, former Vice-Premier; former Politburo member
Zhang Dejiang*	Chairman of the NPC; Politburo Standing Committee member	Father: Zhang Zhiyi, former Major General and Commander of Artillery Force of the Jinan Military Region
Yu Zhengsheng*	Chairman of CPPCC; Politburo Standing Committee member	Father: Yu Qiwei (aka Huang Jing), former Mayor of Tianjin
Wang Qishan*	Secretary of CDIC; Politburo Standing Committee member	Father-in-law: Yao Yilin, former Politburo Standing Committee member; former Vice-Premier
Li Yuanchao**	Vice-President of the PRC; Politburo member	Father: Li Gancheng, former Vice-Mayor of Shanghai
Liu Yandong**	Vice-Premier; Politburo member	Father: Liu Ruilong, former Vice-Minister of Agriculture
Ma Kai**	Vice-Premier; Politburo member	Father: former Vice-Minister-level leader
Li Jianguo**	Vice-Chairman of the NPC; Politburo member	Father: Li Yunchuan, former Vice-Minister of Personnel
Li Zhanshu**	Director of the General Office of the CCP Central Committee; Politburo member	Great-uncle: Li Zaiwen, former Vice-Governor of Shandong Province
Zhang Qingli	Vice-Chairman of the CPPCC; Full CC member	Uncle: General Zhang Wannian, former Vice-Chairman of the Central Military Commission
Lou Jiwei	Minister of Finance; Full CC member	Father: former vice-minister-level leader
Wang Yi	Minister of Foreign Affairs; Full CC member	Father-in-law: Qian Jiadong, former Ambassador to the United Nations in Geneva
Wang Guangya	Director of the Hong Kong and Macao Affairs Office of the State Council; Full CC member	Father-in-law: Chen Yi, former Vice-Premier and Minister of Foreign Affairs
Zhang Zhijun	Director of the Taiwan Affairs Office of the State Council; Full CC member	Father: Vice-President of the PLA General Hospital

TABLE 7-4. (*continued*)

Name	Current position	Family background
Liu He	Office Director of the Central Economic Leading Group; Full CC member	Father: Former vice-governor-level leader in Shaanxi Province
Zhao Kezhi	Party Secretary of Guizhou Province; Full CC member	Uncle: Jiang Chunyun, former Vice-Premier and Politburo member
Luo Zhijun	Party Secretary of Jiangsu Province; Full CC member	Father: Luo Wen, former Deputy Director of the General Armament Department
Xiao Jie	Executive Deputy General Secretary of the State Council; Full CC member	Aunt: Wu Yi, former Vice-Premier and Politburo member
Zhang Mao	Minister of the State Administration for Industry and Commerce; Full CC member	Father-in-law: Gu Mu, former Vice-Premier
Xia Baolong	Party Secretary of Zhejiang; Full CC member	Father: Xia Zhengzhong, former vice-mayor-level leader in Tianjin
Li Xiaopeng	Governor of Shanxi Province; Alternate CC member	Father: Li Peng, former Premier; former Politburo Standing Committee member

Note and Source: * Refers to PSC members; ** refers to Politburo members; CC = Central Committee. Data from the author's database.

ment of the CCP Central Committee and vice-president of the Central Party School. It should be noted that many senior-level Chinese leaders do not identify their family backgrounds in their official biographies. Additionally, not all of these leaders with princeling backgrounds belong to the Jiang-Xi camp; for example, the aforementioned vice-president Li Yuanchao was often viewed as an outsider (异己, *yiji*) by Jiang, Xi, and many other prominent princelings.[43] Within three years after the 18th Party Congress, several of Li Yuanchao's protégés were purged—most noticeably former Liaoning party secretary Wang Min, former Nanjing party secretary Yang Weize, and former Yunnan deputy party secretary Qiu He. A majority of princelings on the list are key political allies of Xi Jinping. Not surprisingly, Xi's administration is first and foremost characterized by the public as the "rule of the princelings" or the "coming of age of the red nobility."[44]

A significant number of senior military officers who hold full membership on the 18th Central Committee come from prominent political families. They include General Zhang Youxia (director of the Equipment Development Department and member of the CMC), the son of Zhang Zongxun, former director of the General Logistics Department; General Liu Yuan (former political commissar of the General Logistics Department), the son of former PRC president Liu Shaoqi; Admiral Liu Xiaojiang (former political commissar of the navy), the son-in-law of former CCP general secretary Hu Yaobang, and General Liu Yazhou (political commissar of the National Defense University), the son-in-law of former PRC president Li Xiannian. Several other senior military officers serve as alternate members on the 18th Central Committee (see table 7-5).

Many military officers with princeling backgrounds do not serve on the Central Committee but instead hold high-ranking positions in the People's Liberation Army (PLA). For example, a recent article published in the overseas Chinese media illustrated the "spectacular rise" of princelings in the PLA leadership.[45] They include the following:

— Vice-Admiral Liu Zhuoming (deputy director of the Science and Technology Commission of the CMC), whose father-in-law is former vice-chairman of the CMC Liu Huaqing;
— Lieutenant General Chen Zaifang (deputy director of the Science and Technology Commission of CMC), whose father is former Politburo member and former commander of the Beijing Military Region Chen Xilian;
— Major General Chi Xingbei (political commissar of the Army Logistics Department), whose father is former vice-chairman of the CMC Chi Haotian;
— Rear Admiral Feng Danyu (director of the Comprehensive Plan Division of the Equipment Development Department of the CMC), whose father is former vice-commander of the North Sea Fleet Feng Hongda;
— Lieutenant General Yin Fanglong (political commissar of the Central Theater Command), whose father-in-law is former director of the General Logistics Department Wang Ke;
— Lieutenant General Zheng Qin (former vice-commander of the Guangzhou Military Region), whose father is former commander of the Beijing Military Region Zheng Weishan;
— Major General Liu Xiaobei (director of the Third Division of the Joint Staff Department), whose father is former vice-commander of the Guangzhou Military Region Liu Changyi;
— Vice-Admiral Ding Yiping (former vice-commander of the navy), whose father is former political commissar of the North Sea Fleet Ding Qiusheng;

TABLE 7-5. China's Most Powerful Princelings in the Military Leadership of the 18th Central Committee

Name	Current position	Family background
Ma Xiaotian	Commander of the Air Force; CMC member; Full CC member	Father: Ma Zaiyao, former Major General and Dean of PLA Political Academy; Father-in-law: Zhang Shaohua, former Deputy Secretary of the Central Military Commission for Discipline Inspection
Wu Shengli	Commander of the Navy; CMC member; Full CC member	Father: Wu Xian, former Vice-Governor of Zhejiang Province
Zhang Youxia	Director of the Equipment Development Department; CMC member; Full CC member	Father: Zhang Zongxun, former Director of the General Logistics Department
Liu Yuan	Political Commissar of the General Logistics Department (until Dec. 2015), Full CC member	Father: Liu Shaoqi, former President of the PRC
Zhang Haiyang	Former Political Commissar, Second Artillery; Full CC member	Father: Zhang Zhen, former Vice-Chairman of the CMC
Liu Yazhou	Political Commissar, National Defense University; Full CC member	Father-in-law: Li Xiannian, former President of the PRC
Liu Xiaojiang	Former Political Commissar, Navy; Full CC member	Father-in-law: Hu Yaobang, former Secretary-General of the CCP; Father: Liu Haibin, former PLA general
Liu Yuejun	Commander of Eastern Theater of Operation; Full CC member	Father: Liu Yide, former Deputy Director of the Political Department of the Hunan Military District
Ai Husheng	Former Deputy Commander of the Chengdu Military Region; Alternate CC member	Father: Ai Fulin, former Deputy Director of the Political Department of the Shenyang Military Region
Liu Sheng	Deputy Director of Equipment Development Department; Alternate CC member	Father: Liu Peishan, former PLA Lt. General

(continued)

TABLE 7-5. (*continued*)

Name	Current position	Family background
Yi Xiaoguang	Deputy Chief of the Joint Staff Department, Alternate CC member	Grandfather: revolutionary veteran and Major General of the PLA; Father-in-law: Meng Guicheng, former Vice-Commander of the Air Force of the Chengdu Military Region
Wang Ning	Commander of the People's Armed Police Force, Alternate member	Father-in-law: Du Ping, Lt. General and former Political Commissar of the Nanjing Military Region
Yin Fanglong	Political Commissar of Central Theater of Operation	Father-in-law: Wang Ke, former Director of the General Logistics Department

Note and Source: CC = Central Committee; CMC = Central Military Commission; PRC = People's Republic of China; PLA = People's Liberation Army. Author's database.

— Lieutenant General Chen Yong (assistant chief-of-staff of the Joint Staff Department), whose father is former commander of the Shandong Province Military District Chen Fangren;

— Lieutenant General Bai Jianjun (former vice-commander of the Beijing Military Region), whose father-in-law is former deputy chief-of-staff of the General Staff Headquarters Xu Huizi;

— Vice-Admiral Xu Lili (vice-president of the PLA Academy of Sciences), whose father-in-law is former vice-commander of the North Sea Fleet Pan Youhong.

Some Red Army veteran leaders from the communist revolution are known as the "family of generals" (将军之家, *jiangjun zhijia*). For example, four sons of General Zhang Zhen, former vice-chairman of the CMC, are all PLA senior officers: Zhang Xiaoyang (former president of the PLA Foreign Language Academy), Zhang Lianyang (former director of the Military Representative Office in the General Staff Headquarters), and Zhang Ningyang (vice-minister of the Bureau of Military Transportation of the General Logistics Department). They all hold the rank of major general. The fourth son, Zhang Haiyang (former political commissar of the Second Artillery) is a full general. In addition, Zhang Zhen's son-in-law Shou Xiaosong is also currently the director of the War Theory and Strategic Studies Department of the Military Academy of Sciences, with the rank of major general.

In recent years, some commentators in China and overseas have adopted the terms "second generation of red communists" or "Red 2G" (红二代,

hong'erdai) and "second generation of officials" or "Official 2G" (官二代, *guan'erdai*) to distinguish between two different subgroups of princelings. The former refers to leaders who come from veteran communist families. This includes leaders whose parents' generation participated in the Long March or were the founders of the PRC in 1949, such as Li Peng, Zeng Qinghong, Yu Zhengsheng, Xi Jinping, Liu Yuan, and Bo Xilai. The latter refers to the offspring of high-ranking officials who were not communist revolutionaries—for example, sons and daughters of Zhu Rongji, Hu Jintao, Wen Jiabao, Zhou Yongkang, and Guo Boxiong.[46] In a way, this distinction makes sense because children of the Hu-Li camp, including children of prominent *tuanpai* leaders such as Hu Jintao, Li Yuanchao, Wang Yang, and Ling Jihua, are also princelings by definition, which seems to blur the factional boundaries between the two camps. Yet, this distinction between the "Red 2G" and the "Official 2G" is problematic in many ways. One can argue that the members of the "third generation of red communists" or the "Red 3G" (红三代, *hongsandai*) are simultaneously the "Official 2G." Examples include Jiang Mianheng and Li Xiaopeng (their fathers or adoptive fathers—Jiang Zemin and Li Peng, respectively—are members of the "Red 2G").

Those military officers with princeling backgrounds are also called the "Red 2G Corps" or "Red II Corps" (红二代军团, *hong'erdai juntuan*).[47] Retired major general Luo Yuan, son of Luo Qingchang (former minister of the CCP Investigation Department and *mishu* to Zhou Enlai), recently gave a widely circulated interview in which he defended the princelings in the PLA. He believed that the term "Red II Corps" is itself an exaggeration.[48] But in the interview, he explicitly reasserted the difference between the "Red 2G" and the "Official 2G." He glorified the former and expressed contempt for the latter, who he believed tended to be corrupt. In his view the "Red 2G" has a strong sense of "collective consciousness and collective loyalty" to continue communist rule. Luo stated that "[o]ur parents established the country, and we are entitled to defend the fruits of our parents' labors."[49] By Luo's calculation, members of the "Red 2G" constitute only 5 to 10 percent of high-ranking party officials or PLA officers.[50]

Along the same lines, Chen Xiaolu, son of Marshal Chen Yi, recently claimed that the "'Red 2G' differs widely from the 'Official 2G' as the former cherishes communist ideals and the latter cares about nothing but greediness for money."[51] Chen's statement drew heavy criticism from the Chinese public. His remarks were widely viewed as political maneuvering by the red nobility to improve its deteriorating reputation in the wake of official corruption scandals. In fact, Chen holds board memberships in some of the country's largest financial and insurance companies, including the Anbang Insurance Group, which was involved in a recent financial and corruption scandal related to Minsheng Bank.[52] Luo Changping, a well-known investigative journalist in Beijing, recently wrote an article criticizing the Chen Xiaolu's hypocrisy and self-congratulatory manner. Luo also employed a new term, "red plutocrat" (赤豪, chihao), to refer to "Red 2G" like Chen Xiaolu who possess enormous power and wealth.[53] Not surprisingly, Luo's provocative article was recently banned in the PRC media.

But it is widely known in China that princelings have dominated the leadership of the country's flagship SOEs or joint venture companies in major industries, especially in leading financial institutions. For example, Wang Jun (son of former PRC vice-president Wang Zhen) serves as chairman of the powerful China International Trust and Investment Corporation (CITIC), Rong Zhijian (Larry Rong, son of former vice-president Rong Yiren) served as chairman of CITIC Pacific, and, until October 2014, Zhu Yunlai (Levin Zhu, son of former premier of Zhu Rongji) served as chairman and CEO of the China International Capital Corporation (CICC). Children of some current high-ranking leaders have also served in important leadership positions in these very wealthy financial firms. For example, until the end of 2012, Liu Lefei (son of current Politburo Standing Committee member Liu Yunshan) served as chairman and CEO of CITIC Private Equity. Fortune magazine ranked Liu Lefei as one of the twenty-five most influential business leaders in Asia in 2011. Liu was then only thirty-eight years old and the youngest person on the Fortune list.

A new trend is that many children of high-ranking officials, mainly the "Red 3G," work in global foreign financial institutions, often located in Hong Kong. Many of these princelings attended elite schools in the United States or other Western countries, as discussed in chapter 4. They are now heavily engaged in international finance, trade, law, and other related fields, capitalizing on the advantages of their excellent educational training and strong political network. The most visible princeling in this regard is Jiang Zhicheng (also known as Alvin Jiang, the grandson of Jiang Zemin). He could be seen as a member of the "Red 4G." Jiang Zhicheng was born in Shanghai in 1986, studied at Jiaotong University, and during his junior year transferred to Harvard, where he received a bachelor's degree in economics in 2010. After working in private equity and focusing on principal investment at Goldman Sachs in Hong Kong for about a year, Jiang Zhicheng established Boyu Capital, a Hong Kong–based private equity fund, where he served as the sole director. Temasek Holdings (a large investment company owned by the government of Singapore) and Li Ka-shing (Asia's richest person) are major investors in Jiang's new financial firm.[54]

In 2013, a year before the student occupations in Hong Kong protesting Beijing's interference in the city's election, a cover story in Taiwan-based magazine The Week used the title "The Princelings Occupy Central" (太子党

占领中环, *taizidang zhanling zhonghuan*) to characterize mainland princelings' omnipresence in Hong Kong's leading financial institutions.[55] The article listed several other prominent princelings in the Hong Kong financial sector. They included former executive chairman of Merrill Lynch China Investment Banking and current chairman of China Nuclear Power and New Energy Industry Investment Fund Feng Shaodong (his English name is Wilson Feng and he is the grandson of former chairman of the National People's Congress Wu Bangguo), managing director of Zeniphs China Capital Chen Xiaoxin (his English name is Charles Chen and he is the grandson of former vice-chairman of the CCP Chen Yun and son of current vice-chairman of the Chinese People's Political Consultative Conference Chen Yuan), and executive chairman of BOC International Holdings Li Dong (daughter of former PSC member Li Changchun).

These princelings who work in the financial sector do not necessarily belong to the Jiang-Xi camp. Children of prominent *tuanpai* leaders also occupy similar positions. One good example is Wang Xisha (daughter of Vice-Premier Wang Yang). She graduated from Tufts University with a master's degree and previously served as a senior manager of the Deutsche Bank branch in Hong Kong. Her husband, Zhang Xinliang (Nicholas Zhang), is also a princeling from a very prominent family. His grandfather is former minister of Defense Zhang Aiping. Zhang Xinliang attended high school in the United States and received his bachelor's degree in international economics from Georgetown University. Zhang has worked in a number of foreign investment banks, including UBS, Goldman Sachs, and Soros Hedge Funds. In 2013 Zhang Xinliang established his own hedge fund called Magnolia Capital Management, registered in Hong Kong. It should be noted that none of the above business activities by princelings have been deemed illegal. Nevertheless, the phenomenon of princelings from various generations dominating China's financial sector will remain a politically controversial and sensitive issue.

Some prominent princelings, such as Ye Xiangzhen (daughter of Marshal Ye Jianying), Xu Xiaoyan (son of Marshal Xu Xiangqian), and Zhou Bingde (niece of Premier Zhou Enlai), have even claimed that none of the officials purged on corruption charges in the past two years were "Red 2G."[56] They have apparently overlooked the fact that the downfall of Bo Xilai, one of the most notorious members of the "Red 2G," led to a legitimacy crisis for CCP rule in the wake of the 18th Party Congress. One does not need to be a political analyst to understand that this distinction between the "Red 2G" and the "Official 2G" is more political than factual.

It is important to note that members of the "Red 2G" have often been strong advocates of the personality cult of Xi Jinping."[57] General Liu Yazhou recently wrote a widely circulated article in the *People's Daily* calling Xi's new book on governance and China's domestic and foreign policy "a thought torch that illuminates the Chinese dream."[58] Liu's entire article is filled with flattery. Liu even stated explicitly that each of the seventy-eight pieces that Xi wrote from November 2012 to June 2014 in the volume reflects the greatness of this visionary leader's "red gene" (红色基因, *hongse jiyin*).[59]

A few prominent officers with princeling backgrounds were recently promoted by Xi to some of the most crucial positions in the military. In December 2014 Xi appointed Wang Ning, deputy director of the General Staff Headquarters, to serve as commander of the People's Armed Police, and in July 2015 Xi granted him the military rank of full general. Wang Ning's father was a major general in the Nanjing Military Region; his father-in-law was Du Ping, a lieutenant general and former political commissar of the Nanjing Military Region; and his uncle was Gu Hui, a general and former commander of the Nanjing Military Region. Wang Ning also served as chief-of-staff of the Shanghai Garrison Command from 2003 to 2006 and as commander of the Thirty-first Group Army from 2007 to 2010. Also, in December 2014 Qin Weijiang, former vice-commander of the Nanjing Military Region and son of former minister of Defense Qin Jiwei, was promoted to deputy chief-of-staff of the General Staff Headquarters.

But the arguments of Luo Yuan, Chen Xiaolu, Liu Yazhou, and like-minded members of the red nobility unintentionally have revealed another important phenomenon that has generated much public concern: of the 160 senior officials purged since the 18th Party Congress, not one was a member of the "Red 2G."[60] Some critics believe that the ongoing anticorruption campaign led by Xi Jinping and Wang Qishan (two princelings) is "selective antigraft" (选择性反腐, *xuanzexing fanfu*). Critics cite the fact that Bo Xilai was purged under the Hu-Wen leadership and that other prominent disgraced leaders, including Zhou Yongkang, Xu Caihong, and Guo Boxiong, are all "common people" (平民, *pingmin*) rather than princelings.[61] Thus, the previous notion of immunity for PSC members on corruption charges has now changed to "immunity for princelings" (刑不上太子党, *xingbushang taizidang*), in the words of critics.[62] However, such a notion is also problematic because a large number of these scandals were linked to very powerful networks such as the petroleum faction (part of the Jiang-Xi camp).

The above observations all reflect the contentious views of and political sensitivities surrounding princelings, especially the "Red 2G," in Chinese politics today. While many analysts in both China and abroad have said the Xi administration is "seizing the full power of the 'Red 2G'" (红二代的全面掌权, *hong'erdai de quanmian zhangquan*), one should not underestimate the enduring power of the competing coalition, especially the strong representation of *tuanpai* officials in the ministerial and provincial leadership.[63]

THE POPULIST COALITION: THE HU-LI CAMP AND ITS CORE *TUANPAI* FACTION

In sharp contrast to the princeling-led elitist coalition, most of the populist coalition's leading figures, such as Hu Jintao and Wen Jiabao in the fourth generation and Li Keqiang and Wang Yang in the fifth generation, usually come from humble or less privileged families.[64] They also tend to have accumulated much of their leadership experience in less developed inland provinces. For example, Hu Jintao spent most of his working life in some of the poorest provinces of China's inland region, including fourteen years in Gansu, three years in Guizhou, and four years in Tibet. Similarly, Wen Jiabao spent fifteen years after graduating from college working in extremely arduous conditions, also mainly in Gansu.

Li Keqiang, Wang Yang, and Liu Qibao—three *tuanpai* leaders who are currently PSC or Politburo members—were all born in Anhui Province and spent their formative years in this less developed inland province. Li Keqiang's longest tenure in the provincial leadership was in Henan, where he served first as governor and then as party secretary for about seven years. Wang Yang spent the first forty-four years of his life in Anhui Province, including four years working in a local food-processing factory when he was a young man. Liu Qibao began his career as a village cadre. After attending Anhui University as a worker-peasant-soldier student during the Cultural Revolution, he worked first as a clerk in the Propaganda Department and then as a *mishu* in the office of the Anhui Provincial Party Committee from 1974 to 1980. Liu advanced his career largely through the CCYL leadership. He served first as deputy chief of the Propaganda Department, then as deputy secretary and secretary of the Anhui CCYL Provincial Committee from 1980 to 1985, and finally as a member of the Secretariat of the CCYL Central Committee from 1985 to 1993—under the direct leadership of Hu Jintao and Li Keqiang. A majority of leaders in the populist coalition advanced their careers from the grassroots level through step-by-step promotion, often through the party, propaganda, and mass (social) organizations rather than in the economic and financial sector.

The populists often voice the concerns of vulnerable social groups such as farmers, migrant workers, and the urban poor. Their populist agenda includes eliminating the agricultural tax on farmers, supporting more lenient policies toward migrant workers, economically prioritizing inland cities to allow them to "catch up," establishing basic health care, and promoting affordable housing projects. One may doubt the effectiveness of the implementation of the Hu-Wen administration's economic policies or Li Keqiang's urbanization plan, but the populist camp has attempted to represent the needs of the common people.

The Definition of Tuanpai *Officials*

Like Li Keqiang, Wang Yang, and Liu Qibao, many other prominent leaders of the populist coalition advanced in politics by way of the CCYL and have therefore gained the *tuanpai* label. Just as princelings function as the core group in the elitist coalition, *tuanpai* form the core group in the populist coalition. Both Hu Jintao and Li Keqiang had distinguished careers in the CCYL. Hu Jintao worked for several years at the provincial and national levels of the CCYL and served as a member of the Secretariat of the CCYL (1982–84) and as first secretary (1984–85). Li Keqiang served as a member of the Secretariat of the CCYL for ten years (1983–93) and as first secretary for another five years (1993–98). Li Keqiang's ties to Hu Jintao have directly helped advance his political career. Li began working on the CCYL Central Committee at the end of 1982, exactly the same time that Hu became a secretary of the CCYL. Li Keqiang worked closely with Hu, assisting him in convening the Sixth National Conference of the All-China Youth Federation in August 1983. Three months later, after being nominated by Hu, Li was promoted to alternate member of the CCYL Secretariat. When Hu was made first secretary of the CCYL in 1985, Li became a full member of the Secretariat. Some foreign analysts have described Li as "a thirteen-year-younger carbon copy of Hu Jintao," reflecting the strong influence Hu has had on the political career and leadership style of Li.[65]

Li is also noted for his keen interest in forming political ties with other prominent leaders who have a CCYL background. When he served as secretary of the CCYL Committee at Beijing University in the early 1980s, he dedicated a great deal of time to playing tennis. Some analysts have suggested that the reason Li became such a tennis aficionado was that a number of political heavyweights who were in charge of the CCYL leadership at the time, such as Hu Qili and Li Ruihuan, were also fond of the game.[66] Both Hu Qili and Li Ruihuan later served as members of the PSC of the CCP.

Another important figure in the formation of the *tuanpai* faction was the late Song Defu. Song served in the CCYL Secretariat between 1983 and 1993, part of which time he also served as first secretary (1988–93). Song had leadership experience in various sectors: the military (as deputy director of the Organization Department under the PLA General Political Department), the party (as deputy director of the CCP Central Organization Department), the State Council (as minister of Personnel), and provincial government (as party secretary in Fujian). In 1982, at the age of thirty-six, Song joined the 12th Central Committee of the CCP. Unfortunately, he had to resign from his leadership work after he was diagnosed with cancer in 2004, and he died three years later. Four current Politburo members (Li Keqiang, Liu Yandong, Liu Qibao, and Li Yuanchao) all worked in the

Secretariat when Song was in charge. Several members of the current Central Committee—for example, Zhang Baoshun, Yuan Chunqing, and Cai Wu—were promoted by Song.

Strictly speaking, *tuanpai* leaders are those officials who worked in the senior levels of CCYL leadership (municipal/prefecture, provincial, and ministerial levels or above) anytime from 1982 to 1998, during which they likely formed close working relationships or even mentor-protégé ties with heavyweight *tuanpai* leaders Hu Jintao, Song Defu, and Li Keqiang. Several *tuanpai* officials served only as CCYL secretaries at the university level or bureau level, but they concurrently served as members of the Central Committee of the CCYL under the leadership of either Hu Jintao or Li Keqiang. Although their actual position within the CCYL might not have been that high, due to their CCYL Central Committee membership and their possible close contact with Hu and Li at the time, they also qualify as *tuanpai* leaders.

Some leaders had work experience in the CCYL central and provincial leadership, but politically they are more closely associated with Jiang and Xi. This study does *not* consider them to be *tuanpai* leaders. They include PSC and Politburo member Liu Yunshan, who is often seen as Jiang's protégé, and Han Zheng, who served as CCYL deputy secretary and secretary in Shanghai but advanced his career primarily through the political networks in Shanghai. This group also includes Li Zhanshu, who was CCYL secretary in Hebei Province and who has been a confidant of Xi Jinping.

This study also does not consider members who had CCYL leadership experience below the municipal level to be *tuanpai* leaders. For example, Sun Chunlan served as CCYL secretary of the Textile Industry Bureau of Anshan City, Liaoning Province, early in her career (1974–77), but she is not counted as a *tuanpai* leader for two reasons. First, her CCYL position was below the municipal/prefecture level of the CCYL leadership, and second, her leadership tenure at CCYL preceded Hu Jintao's. Another example is Zhao Leji. He served as CCYL secretary of the Department of Commerce of the Shaanxi Provincial Government (1983–84), but his position was below the municipal/prefecture level. Instead, he is often viewed as a key member of Xi Jinping's "Shaanxi Gang" (see chapter 8).

Understandably, some *tuanpai* members spent more years in the CCYL leadership than others. Among the aforementioned three *tuanpai* leaders of Anhui origin, for example, Wang Yang spent only three years in a leadership role. In contrast, Li Keqiang and Liu Qibao spent sixteen years and thirteen years, respectively, as CCYL senior officials. But Wang Yang's three-year tenure in the CCYL constituted one of his defining political posts. Wang has been widely considered to be Hu Jintao's confidant, and it is partly for this reason that some observers believe that the Jiang-Xi camp blocked his promotion to the PSC at the 18th Party Congress.[67]

The Role of the CCYL and Its Leaders

Officials of the CCYL have long been a major recruitment source for the party and government leadership in the PRC. The mission of the CCYL states explicitly that this political organization is the "reserve army" (后备军, houbeijun) of the CCP. The precursor of the CCYL, the Chinese Socialist Youth League, was established in 1922, one year after the founding of the CCP, and it changed its name to the CCYL in 1925.[68] The CCYL is an organization for people ages fourteen to twenty-eight. Its purpose is to "add new blood" to the party and to produce successors for all levels of political leadership.[69] In 2013 the CCYL had nearly ninety million members, a staff of over 190,000 full-time cadres (many of whom are older than the age limit for ordinary members), and about 3.6 million local chapters.[70]

In addition to providing ideological and political training, the league runs a variety of social service programs and operates several prominent media outlets, most notably the China Youth Daily newspaper. Membership in the CCYL does not guarantee party membership, nor is participation in the youth organization required to join the CCP. But being active in the CCYL can certainly facilitate full party membership. Several prominent leaders of modern Chinese history—including former PSC members Hu Yaobang, Hu Qili, and Li Ruihuan—advanced their political careers through the channels of the CCYL. In general, for the first five decades of the PRC, the number of officials with CCYL backgrounds in top leadership positions was quite low. Former president of the PRC Liu Shaoqi intended to promote some CCYL leaders, such as Jiang Nanxiang and Rong Gaotang (both were from Tsinghua University), but Mao persecuted them during the Cultural Revolution. Deng did promote Hu Yaobang, Hu Qili, and Wang Zhaoguo, but all of them lost favor in the late 1980s. Jiang Zemin did not value leaders with CCYL backgrounds, although a couple of Jiang's close associates, such as Liu Yunshan and Han Zheng, had previously worked in the CCYL leadership.

During the reform era, most princelings took jobs in major SOEs or local governments in coastal cities, rather than positions within the CCYL. There were a few exceptions in the early 1980s, when a handful of princelings—namely, Li Yuanchao, Liu Yandong, Chen Haosu (son of former foreign minister Chen Yi), and He Guangwei (son of revolutionary veteran He Changgong)—served in the Secretariat of the 11th CCYL Central Committee. Otherwise, most princelings went to work for SOEs or municipal governments on the east coast, as these jobs provided more opportunity for financial gain and political advancement in the 1980s and 1990s. According to Ding Wang's study, since 1983 no princeling at the ministerial or vice-ministerial level of leadership has ever served in the national leadership of the CCYL.[71] In a sense, over the past three decades CCYL leadership has become a channel of promotion primarily for ambitious young politicians from humble and less-privileged family backgrounds.

The Coming of Age of Tuanpai *under Hu Jintao*

It was only with Hu Jintao's rise to the top leadership, however, that the *tuanpai* really came of age in terms of power. Since Hu became general secretary of the party in the fall of 2002, many officials with CCYL backgrounds have been appointed to positions in the ministerial and provincial levels of leadership.[72] According to a study conducted in 2005, about 150 *tuanpai* officials served as ministers, vice-ministers, provincial party secretaries, provincial deputy party secretaries, governors, and vice-governors.[73] In 2005 thirteen provincial party secretaries and governors, seven ministers, and two heads of the CCP central departments were members of *tuanpai*, constituting 21 percent, 25 percent, and 50 percent of total numbers in those three levels of leadership, respectively.[74] They included Li Keqiang, Li Yuanchao, Liu Yandong, and Wang Lequan (all of them later served on the Politburo) but did not include some other rising stars with strong *tuanpai* mentor-protégé ties who then served as deputies at the provincial and ministerial levels of leadership—for example, Wang Yang, Liu Qibao, Ling Jihua, Cai Wu (then deputy head of the CCP International Liaison Department and until recently minister of Culture), Shen Yueyue (deputy head of the CCP Organization Department and now vice-chairman of the National People's Congress), Ji Bingxuan (deputy head of the CCP Propaganda Department and now vice-chairman of the National People's Congress), and Jiang Daming (executive deputy party secretary of Shandong and now minister of Land and Resources). Most of these *tuanpai* rising stars had worked under Hu's leadership in the CCYL during the early 1980s. Therefore, they had close contact with Hu Jintao for more than three decades.

Similarly, among the eleven members in the Secretariat of the 13th CCYL Central Committee (1993–98) when Li Keqiang served as the first secretary, nine are now full members on the 18th Central Committee of the CCP. They include Premier Li Keqiang, Guangdong party secretary Hu Chunhua, president of the Supreme People's Court Zhou Qiang, director of the State General Administration of Sports Liu Peng, deputy director of the Central Leading Group in Rural Work Yuan Chunqing, vice-chairman of the National People's Congress Ji Bingxuan, secretary of the China Federation of Literary and Art Circles Zhao Shi, Jilin party secretary Bayanqolu, and minister of Land and Resources Jiang Daming. One is an alternate member of the 18th Central Committee (Xinjiang deputy party secretary Sun Jinlong). The only one who does not serve on the 18th Central Committee is Huang Danhua, concurrently vice-minister of the State-Owned Assets

Supervision and Administration Commission and vice-chairman of the All-China Federation of Trade Unions. Huang previously served as a member of the 16th Central Commission for Discipline Inspection. For Li Keqiang, these longtime colleagues in the CCYL leadership are now among his most important confidants. Among the members of the Secretariat of the CCYL since the reform era began in 1978, nine later served as Politburo members (and the first four listed also served as PSC members): Hu Qili, Li Ruihuan, Hu Jintao, Li Keqiang, Wang Zhaoguo, Liu Yandong, Liu Qibao, Li Yuanchao, and Hu Chunhua.

In the Politburo elected at the 17th Party Congress in 2007, the *tuanpai* held seven seats (Hu Jintao, Li Keqiang, Li Yuanchao, Liu Yandong, Wang Yang, Wang Lequan, and Wang Zhaoguo), constituting 28 percent of the total; in comparison, the princelings occupied four seats (Xi Jinping, Wang Qishan, Zhang Dejiang, and Yu Zhengsheng). Table 7-6 shows the rapid increase of *tuanpai* representation in the positions of provincial party secretary and governor—the former increased from three spots (9.7 percent) in 2003 to fourteen (45.2 percent) in 2014, and the latter grew from three seats (9.4 percent) in 2003 to thirteen (41.9 percent) in 2010. The positions of provincial chiefs are the most important stepping-stone in the Chinese leadership, and the strong representation of *tuanpai* leaders reflects the enduring power of this important faction.

Continuing Strong Representation of Tuanpai in the Xi Era

Table 7-7 provides an overview of the factional backgrounds of provincial chiefs in May 2016. Among these sixty-two leaders, the Hu-Li camp occupied twenty-one positions (33.9 percent), of which fourteen (22.6 percent) were held by *tuanpai* leaders. In comparison, the Jiang-Xi camp occupied twenty-five positions (40.3 percent), including only three princelings (Shanxi governor Li Peng, newly appointed Neimenggu governor Buxiaolin, whose grandfather is former PRC vice-president Ulanhu, and whose father is former Neimenggu governor Buhe, and Xinjiang governor Shohrat Zakir, whose grandfather is a communist revolutionary martyr and whose father is a former vice-governor of Xinjiang).[75] Within the Jiang-Xi camp in the provincial top leadership, five of the leaders are members of the Shanghai Gang. Since national leaders are usually chosen from among provincial chiefs (as discussed in detail in chapter 3), the political connections and mentor-protégé ties formed at the provincial level are often important foundations of factional politics in China. This observation challenges the recent belief that the *tuanpai* has completely collapsed as a result of Ling Jihua's purge and the princelings' consolidation of power.[76]

TABLE 7-6. Increase in *Tuanpai* Leaders Serving as Provincial Chiefs, 2003–14

Year	Provincial party secretary $(N=31)$		Provincial governor $(N=31)$		Total $(N=62)$	
	No.	%	No.	%	No.	%
2003	3	9.7	3	9.7	6	9.7
2005	6	19.4	7	22.6	13	21.0
2010	8	25.8	13	41.9	21	33.9
2014	14	45.2	8	25.8	22	35.5

Source: Author's database.

As evidenced by elite recruitment norms over the past three decades, a former first secretary of the CCYL Central Committee usually takes his or her next leadership assignment as a provincial chief. This trend is congruent with the promotion patterns of Hu Jintao (Guizhou party secretary), Song Defu (Fujian party secretary), Li Keqiang (Henan governor), Zhou Qiang (Hunan governor), Hu Chunhua (Hebei governor), and Lu Hao (Heilongjiang governor). Other members of the Secretariat were usually transferred to the provincial leadership, where they served as vice-governors.[77] The Hu-Li camp, especially its core faction of *tuanpai* officials, seems to have an advantage over the princelings or the Shanghai Gang in terms of its regional distribution of power and thus it also has an advantage in terms of candidates who are in the pool for potential future membership in the Politburo. In general, *tuanpai* officials usually have the added advantage of their relative youth. As discussed in chapter 3, both the youngest full member, Lu Hao (governor of Heilongjiang), born in 1967, and the youngest alternate member, Liu Jian (party secretary of Hami Prefecture in Xinjiang), born in 1970, are *tuanpai* leaders.

In fact, *tuanpai* leaders enjoy the advantage of relative youth in all echelons of the CCP elite. In 2015, among approximately 400 members of the standing committees of provincial party committees, eighteen leaders belonged to the post-1965 generation. *Tuanpai* leaders are well represented among the youngest of this important leadership group. In addition to Lu Hao and Liu Jian, former CCYL secretary at Tsinghua University and member of the CCYL Secretariat Yang Yue (b. 1968) serves as Fuzhou party secretary; former CCYL secretary of Tsinghua School of Architecture Chen Gang (b. 1966) serves as vice-mayor of Beijing; former CCYL secretary of Hebei Institute of Engineering Ren Xuefeng (b. 1965) serves as party secretary of Guangzhou; former CCYL deputy secretary of Shandong Sun Shougang

TABLE 7-7. Overview of Provincial Chiefs (Party Secretaries and Governors/Mayors), as of May 2016

Province	Party Secretary					Governor/Mayor				
	Name	Birth year	Since	Birthplace	Factional background	Name	Birth year	Tenure since	Birthplace	Factional background
Beijing	Guo Jinlong	1947	2012	Jiangsu	Hu-Li camp	Wang Anshun	1957	2012	Henan	Jiang-Xi camp
Tianjin	Huang Xingguo	1954	2014	Zhejiang	Jiang-Xi camp	Huang Xingguo	1954	2008	Zhejiang	Jiang-Xi camp
Hebei	Zhao Kezhi	1953	2015	Shandong	*Tuanpai*	Zhang Qingwei	1961	2012	Hebei	
Shanxi	Wang Rulin	1953	2014	Henan	*Tuanpai*	Li Xiaopeng	1959	2013	Sichuan	Princeling
Neimenggu	Wang Jun	1952	2012	Shanxi		Buxiaolin (f)	1958	2016	Neimenggu	Princeling
Liaoning	Li Xi	1956	2015	Gansu	Jiang-Xi camp	Chen Qiufa	1954	2015	Hunan	
Jilin	Bayanqolu	1955	2014	Neimenggu	*Tuanpai*	Jiang Chaoliang	1957	2014	Hunan	Jiang-Xi camp
Heilongjiang	Wang Xiankui	1952	2013	Hebei	*Tuanpai*	Lu Hao	1967	2013	Shanghai	
Shanghai	Han Zheng	1954	2012	Zhejiang	Shanghai gang	Yang Xiong	1953	2013	Zhejiang	Shanghai gang
Jiangsu	Luo Zhijun	1951	2010	Liaoning	*Tuanpai*	Li Xueyong	1950	2011	Hebei	Hu-Li camp
Shandong	Jiang Yikang	1953	2008	Shandong		Guo Shuqing	1956	2013	Neimenggu	
Zhejiang	Xia Baolong	1952	2012	Tianjin	Jiang-Xi camp	Li Qiang	1959	2013	Zhejiang	Jiang-Xi camp
Anhui	Wang Xuejun	1952	2015	Hebei		Li Jinbin	1958	2015	Sichuan	Jiang-Xi camp

Fujian	You Quan	1952	2012	Hebei	Jiang-Xi camp	Yu Weiguo	1955	2015	Shandong	Jiang-Xi camp
Henan	Xie Fuzhan	1954	2016	Hubei	Hu-Li camp	Chen Run'er	1957	2016	Hunan	Hu-Li camp
Hubei	Li Hongzhong	1956	2010	Shandong	Jiang-Xi camp	Wang Guosheng	1956	2011	Shandong	
Hunan	Xu Shousheng	1953	2013	Jiangsu		Du Jiahao	1955	2013	Zhejiang	Shanghai gang
Jiangxi	Qiang Wei	1953	2013	Jiangsu	*Tuanpai*	Lu Xinshe	1956	2011	Shandong	
Guangdong	Hu Chunhua	1963	2012	Hubei	*Tuanpai*	Zhu Xiaodan	1953	2012	Zhejiang	*Tuanpai*
Guangxi	Peng Qinghua	1957	2012	Hubei		Chen Wu	1954	2013	Guangxi	
Hainan	Luo Baoming	1952	2011	Tianjin	*Tuanpai*	Liu Cigui	1955	2015	Fujian	Jiang-Xi camp
Sichuan	Wang Dongming	1956	2012	Liaoning	*Tuanpai*	Yin Li	1962	2016	Shandong	
Chongqing	Sun Zhengcai	1963	2012	Shandong	Jiang-Xi camp	Huang Qifan	1952	2010	Zhejiang	Shanghai gang
Guizhou	Chen Min'er	1960	2015	Zhejiang	Jiang-Xi camp	Sun Zhigang	1954	2015	Henan	Shanghai gang
Yunnan	Li Jiheng	1957	2014	Guangxi	Hu-Li camp	Chen Hao	1954	2014	Jiangsu	Shanghai gang
Tibet	Chen Quanguo	1955	2011	Henan	Hu-Li camp	Losang Jamcan	1957	2012	Tibet	*Tuanpai*
Shaanxi	Lou Qinjian	1956	2016	Guizhou	Jiang-Xi camp	Hu Heping	1962	2016	Shandong	Jiang-Xi camp

(continued)

TABLE 7-7. (*continued*)

Province	Party Secretary				Governor/Mayor				
	Name	Birth year	Since	Birthplace	Factional background	Name	Birth year	Tenure since	Birthplace	Factional background
Gansu	Wang Sanyun	1952	2011	Shandong	*Tuanpai*	Lin Duo	1956	2016	Shandong	Jiang-Xi camp
Qinghai	Luo Huining	1954	2013	Anhui		Hao Peng	1960	2013	Shaanxi	Hu-Li camp
Ningxia	Li Jianhua	1954	2013	Hebei		Liu Hui (f)	1959	2013	Tianjin	*Tuanpai*
Xinjiang	Zhang Chunxian	1953	2010	Henan	Jiang-Xi camp	Shohrat Zakir	1953	2015	Xinjiang	Princeling

Note and Source: (f) = female. Xinhua, http://renshi.people.com.cn/GB/353032/index.html and the author's database.

(b. 1965) serves as director of the Propaganda Department of the Shandong Provincial Party Committee; and Mao Chaofeng (b. 1965), who advanced his career in CCYL affairs in Henan Province, serves as executive vice-governor of Hainan. All are alternate members of the 18th Central Committee of the CCP. In addition, Wang Xiao (b. 1968), newly appointed party secretary of Xining; Zhang Xiaolan (b. 1965), secretary of the Discipline Inspection Commission of Gansu; and Zhao Yide (b. 1965), chief-of-staff of the Zhejiang Municipal Party Committee, all previously worked in the central committee of the CCYL.[78]

A study of all the secretaries of the thirty-one provincial CCYL committees in 2013 showed that almost all of them were born in the 1970s.[79] In July 2015 China had 162 department-level leaders who were born after 1975, including 10 at the rank of full department head (正厅级, *zhengtingji*). Among the 10 full department heads, 6 were in the CCYL leadership, including Shanghai CCYL secretary Xu Weiwan (b. 1977), Hubei CCYL secretary Zhang Guihua (b. 1976), Jilin CCYL secretary Cheng Long (b. 1976), Qinghai CCYL secretary Wang Huajie (b. 1976), Sichuan CCYL secretary Liu Huiying (b. 1975), and member of the CCYL Secretariat Fu Zhenbang (b. 1975).[80] Three of the other four young leaders who did not serve in the CCYL leadership in fact previously advanced their careers through the CCYL. They include executive deputy director of the Economic and Information Committee of the Guizhou Provincial Government Ma Ningyu (b. 1976), who was Guizhou CCYL secretary; president of Kunming College He Hua (b. 1976), who served as CCYL secretary of Yunnan University; and Dezhou mayor Chen Fei (b. 1975), who served as deputy secretary and secretary of the Qingdao CCYL Municipal Committee for twelve years.[81]

Among these 162 young and promising leaders in 2015, 123 (75.9 percent) had CCYL leadership experience and 100 (61.7 percent) then served as CCYL officials.[82] The youngest is Zhao Yongsheng (b. 1983), a graduate of Tsinghua Law School, who currently serves as secretary of the Shenyang CCYL Municipal Committee. Several others currently work in student affairs at universities. They include Guo Yong (b. 1977), a member of the standing committee of the Tsinghua Party Committee and party secretary of the School of Public Policy and Management at Tsinghua University; Zhao Bo (b. 1979), CCYL secretary of Tsinghua University; and Ruan Cao (b. 1980), CCYL secretary of Peking University.[83] All of these examples suggest that young leaders with CCYL backgrounds are well positioned for the future generation of CCP leadership.

Furthermore, *tuanpai* officials are well represented among the ministers of the State Council. In January 2016, among the twenty-six ministers, eight were *tuanpai* leaders (see table 7-8), accounting for 30.8 percent of the cabinet ministers. They are all full members of the current Central Committee.

TABLE 7-8. Members of the 18th Central Committee with *Tuanpai* Backgrounds Who Serve as Ministers in the State Council, as of January 2016

Leader	Year born	Current position	Central Committee status	Factional ties and defining experience in CCYL
Wu Aiying (f)	1951	Minister of Justice	Full member	CCYL Shandong Secretary (1982–89)
Han Changfu	1954	Minister of Agriculture	Full member	CCYL Central Committee (1982–91)
Huang Shuxian	1954	Minister of Supervision	Full member	CCYL Jiangsu Secretary (1985–89)
Li Liguo	1953	Minister of Civil Affairs	Full member	CCYL Liaoning Deputy Secretary, (1985–90)
Jiang Daming	1953	Minister of Land and Resources	Full member	CCYL Deputy Director and Director of the Organization Department (1987–93); Secretariat (1993–98)
Yang Chuantang	1954	Minister of Transportation	Full member	CCYL Shandong Deputy Secretary and Secretary (1987–92)
Chen Zhenggao	1952	Minister of Housing and Urban-Rural Development	Full member	CCYL Deputy Secretary of Dalian (1983–85)
Zhang Yi	1950	Minister of the State-Owned Assets Supervision and Administration Commission	Full member	CCYL Secretary of Daxinganling Prefecture, Heilongjiang (1978–82)

Note and Source: (f) = female; CCYL = Chinese Communist Youth League. Author's database.

Although the Jiang-Xi camp achieved a landslide victory at the PSC formed at the 18th Party Congress with a six-to-one advantage, *tuanpai* still occupy a total of six seats (24 percent) in the Politburo (Li Keqiang, Liu Yandong, Liu Qibao, Li Yuanchao, Wang Yang, and Hu Chunhua). An important finding is that *tuanpai* leaders actually occupy 99 seats on the 376-member 18th Central Committee, constituting 26.3 percent of this crucial decisionmaking body, which is a significant increase from 50 members (14 percent) on the 16th Central Committee in 2002 and 86 members (23.2 percent) on the 17th Central Committee in 2007. On the 18th Central Committee, 133 members had leadership experience in the CCYL in their early careers, but 34 of them were not considered to be *tuanpai* leaders, because either they were closer to

FIGURE 7-1. *Tuanpai* and Princelings on the Chinese Communist Party Central Committee, 2002–12

Number of persons

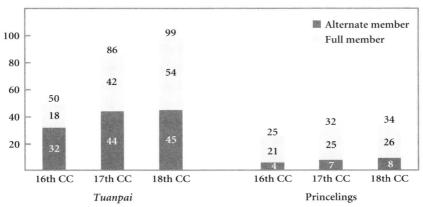

Note and Source: CC = Central Committee. Author's database.

the Jiang-Xi camp or their CCYL leadership experiences were below the municipal/prefecture level. Thus, with the remaining ninety-nine members meeting the definition of *tuanpai*, the faction's representation on the current Central Committee is at its highest percentage in the history of the CCP.

Figure 7-1 compares the representation of *tuanpai* leaders and princelings on the three Central Committees over the past decade (2002–12). Princeling representation has been low in this leadership body over the past decade compared with that of *tuanpai*. Princelings occupied twenty-five seats (7 percent) at the 16th Central Committee, thirty-two seats (8.6 percent) at the 17th Central Committee, and thirty-four seats (9 percent) at the 18th Central Committee. It should be noted that princelings have more commonly served as full members of the Central Committee rather than as alternate members (see figure 7-1). This is consistent with the fact that princelings have often been well represented in the higher levels of the leadership bodies such as the Politburo, and especially the PSC, in recent years.

Table 7-9 shows the representation of *tuanpai* officials in seven very important decisionmaking bodies in the post-18th Congress leadership. In addition to the aforementioned *tuanpai* representation in the Politburo, the Central Committee, the cabinet ministries, and provincial party secretary and governor positions, *tuanpai* officials also occupied three seats (Liu Qibao, Du Qinglin, and Yang Jing) in the seven-member Secretariat and four seats (Li Keqiang, Liu Yandong, Wang Yang, and Yang Jing) on the Executive Committee of the State Council. In contrast, no princeling currently serves on the Secretariat, and only two princelings (Liu Yandong and Ma Kai) served

TABLE 7-9. Representation of Leaders with *Tuanpai* Background in Important Leadership Bodies, as of January 2014

Leadership organ	No. of *Tuanpai*/total	*Tuanpai* as % of total
18th Politburo	6/25*	24
18th Secretariat	3/7*	42.9
Members of the 18th Central Committee	99/376	26.3
State Council Executive Committee	4/10	40
Current Ministers in the State Council	8/26	30.8
Current Provincial Party Secretaries	14/31**	45.2
Current Provincial Governors	8/31	25.8

Note: * Excluding Liu Yunshan, Li Zhanshu, and Han Zheng. ** Excluding Han Zheng.

on the Executive Committee of the State Council. As previously discussed, both Liu and Ma are usually not considered leaders in the Jiang-Xi camp. Of course, both leadership bodies include some prominent members of the Jiang-Xi camp—for example, Liu Yunshan, Zhao Leji, Li Zhanshu, and Zhao Hongzhu are in the Secretariat, and Zhang Gaoli, Yang Jiechi, and Guo Shengkun are on the Executive Committee of the State Council.

It is particularly worth noting that in each and every one of the nine most important leadership organs in the PRC (the PSC, PRC presidency—that is, the president and vice-president—State Council, CMC, CCP Secretariat, National People's Congress, Chinese People's Political Consultative Conference, Supreme People's Court, and Supreme People's Procuratorate), the top leader and the second-highest-ranking leader come from the two competing coalitions, as illustrated in table 1-3 from chapter 1. This suggests that under collective leadership in present-day China, there is a deliberate effort on the part of the top leadership to maintain a factional balance of power in various forms. At least up to now, the rapid consolidation of Xi Jinping's power has not affected the checks and balances in these very important leadership bodies.

Table 7-10 lists the twenty-three most prominent *tuanpai* officials in the post-18th Party Congress leadership. All of them are full members of the current Central Committee and have had substantial leadership experience in the CCYL. With the exception of Liu Yandong and Du Qinglin, who were born in the late 1940s, all others were born after 1950. This means that they are all eligible for at least one more five-year term at the 19th Party Congress. Guangdong party secretary Hu Chunhua and president of the Supreme People's Court Zhou Qiang were both born in the 1960s and are considered front-runners for the sixth generation of leaders.

A couple of leaders on the list may have strong ties to both camps. For example, newly appointed Jilin party secretary Bayanqolu seems to benefit from the support of both Xi Jinping and Li Keqiang. Bayanqolu is the only ethnic minority leader who currently serves as a provincial party secretary in China. A Mongolian, Bayanqolu was born in Etuokeqianqi, Inner Mongolia, in 1955, and early in his life he served in local leadership in his native autonomous region. He accelerated his career largely through the CCYL and served as deputy secretary and secretary of the Inner Mongolia CCYL Committee from 1991 to 1993. He also served as a member (1993–98) and executive secretary (1998–2001) of the CCYL Secretariat. He and Premier Li Keqiang overlapped at the CCYL national leadership, as both served as secretaries of the CCYL from 1993 to 1998. Bayanqolu was transferred to Zhejiang in 2001, one year before Xi Jinping's arrival there. In Zhejiang, Bayanqolu served as vice-governor (2001–03), standing member of the Zhejiang Provincial Party Committee, and secretary of Ningbo City (2003–10). Next, he was transferred to Jilin, where he served as deputy party secretary (2010–14) and concurrently as governor (2013–14). In August 2014 he was promoted to Jilin party secretary. As an ethnic minority leader with broad leadership experience, and aided by his close working relationships with both Xi Jinping and Li Keqiang, he will be a leading candidate for the next Politburo in 2017.

Characteristics of Tuanpai Leaders

Figure 7-2 shows Central Committee members with *tuanpai* backgrounds distributed according to the highest level of leadership they occupied in the CCYL. The largest group (40.4 percent) worked in the ministerial and provincial level of CCYL leadership bodies, usually as deputy secretary, secretary, or both consecutively. The second-largest group (34.3 percent) worked at the central level, including members of the Secretariat or heads of various departments in the CCYL Central Committee.[84] CCYL senior officials at these two levels usually had close working relationships with Hu Jintao and Li Keqiang when they were first secretaries. Members of the Secretariat work together especially closely. In general, full-time officials working in the various levels of the CCYL leadership have tended to form an intimate political network. Consequently, a CCYL career has become a major channel for elite upward mobility in the PRC over the past three decades.

TABLE 7-10. Prominent *Tuanpai* Leaders on the 18th Central Committee

Leader	Year born	Current position	CC status	Defining experience in CCYL	Academic field
Li Keqiang	1955	Premier	PSC member	CCYL Secretariat, 1983–98; First Secretary, 1993–98	Economics
Li Yuanchao	1950	Vice-President	Politburo member	CCYL Secretariat, 1982–90	Law
Liu Yandong (f)	1945	Vice-Premier	Politburo member	CCYL Secretariat, 1982–91	Law
Wang Yang	1955	Vice-Premier	Politburo member	CCYL Anhui Deputy Secretary, Secretary, 1982–84	Economic management
Liu Qibao	1953	Director of the CCP Organization Department	Politburo member	CCYL Anhui Secretary, 1982–83; CCYL Secretariat, 1985–93	Economics
Hu Chunhua	1963	Guangdong Secretary	Politburo member	CCYL Secretariat, 1997–2001; First Secretary, 2006–08	Chinese literature
Du Qinglin	1946	Vice-Chairman of the CPPCC	Secretariat member	CCYL Jilin Deputy Secretary, Secretary, 1979–84	Economics
Yang Jing	1953	State Councilor, and Chief-of-Staff of the State Council	Secretariat member	CCYL Neimenggu Secretary, 1993–96	Politics
Zhou Qiang	1960	President, Supreme People's Court	Full member	CCYL Secretariat, 1995–2006; First Secretary, 1998–2006	Law
Shen Yueyue (f)	1957	Vice-Chairman of NPC	Full member	CCYL Ningbo Secretary, Zhejiang Secretary, 1983–93	Economic management
Ji Bingxuan	1951	Vice-Chairman of NPC	Full member	CCYL Anhui Deputy Secretary, Secretary, 1987–90	Chinese literature

Name	Year	Position	Membership	CCYL Background	Field
Zhang Qingli	1951	Vice-Chairman of CPPCC	Full member	CCYL Central Committee, 1979–86	Politics
Song Xiuyan (f)	1955	ACWF First Secretary	Full member	CCYL Qinghai Deputy Secretary and Secretary, 1983–88	Politics
Wang Xiankui	1952	Heilongjiang Party Secretary	Full member	CCYL Secretary of Mudanjiang Railway Bureau, 1976–85	Economic management
Luo Zhijun	1951	Jiangsu Party Secretary	Full member	CCYL Standing Committee member, 1993–95	Law
Qiang Wei	1955	Jiangxi Party Secretary	Full member	CCYL Beijing Secretary, 1987–90	Law
Wang Rulin	1953	Shanxi Party Secretary	Full member	CCYL Jilin Deputy Secretary, Secretary, 1983–87	Economic management
Wang Dongming	1956	Sichuan Party Secretary	Full member	CCYL Secretary of Jinzhou City, Liaoning, 1983–85	Law
Luo Baoming	1952	Hainan Party Secretary	Full member	CCYL Tianjin Deputy Secretary and Secretary, 1984–92	History
Zhao Kezhi	1953	Hebei Party Secretary	Full member	CCYL Deputy Secretary and Secretary of Laixi City, Shandong, 1980–83	Politics
Zhao Zhengyong	1951	Former Shaanxi Party Secretary	Full member	CCYL Secretary of Maanshan City, Anhui, 1982–85	Politics
Wang Sanyun	1952	Gansu Party Secretary	Full member	CCYL Guizhou Secretary, 1990–92	Politics
Bayanqolu	1955	Jilin Party Secretary	Full member	CCYL Neimenggu Deputy Secretary and Secretary 1991–93; CCYL Secretariat, 1993–98.	Economic management

Note and Source: CCYL = Chinese Communist Youth League; CCP = Chinese Communist Party; CPPCC = Chinese People's Political Consultative Conference; (f) = female; NPC = National People's Congress; ACWF = All China Women's Federation. Data from author's database.

FIGURE 7-2. *Tuanpai* Members on the 18th Central Committee Based on Their Level of Leadership Experience in the Chinese Communist Youth League

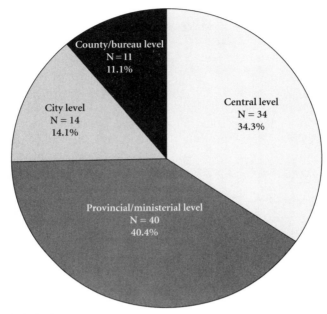

Source: Author's database.

As for the educational backgrounds of Chinese leaders, as discussed in chapter 4, there has been a decline in the number of technocrats and a rise in the proportion of leaders trained in the social sciences, economics, and law in the fifth generation. This trend is particularly evident among *tuanpai* leaders. None of the twenty-three most prominent *tuanpai* leaders listed in table 7-10 received their highest degrees in the fields of engineering or natural sciences. Instead, twelve leaders (52.2 percent) received their highest degrees in law or politics, eight leaders (34.8 percent) specialized in economics or economic management, and the rest studied the humanities (Chinese literature or history). Almost all of them attended either midcareer training programs or degree programs at the Central Party School in the 1990s, when Hu Jintao was the president of the CPS, thus strengthening their ties with him.

This author's study of the twenty-two most prominent *tuanpai* leaders in 2005 found that none had work experience in foreign trade, finance, or banking.[85] Ten years later, among the twenty-three most prominent *tuanpai* leaders listed in table 7-10, hardly any of them (with the possible exception of Vice-Premier Wang Yang) could claim expertise in finance and economic affairs. Among the eight cabinet ministers with a *tuanpai* background, only the minister of Agriculture, Han Changfu, has solid leadership experience in finance and economic affairs, having served as deputy director of the Office of the Central Leading Group from 1998 to 2001 (see table 7-8). Of course, many *tuanpai* leaders have previously served or currently serve as provincial chiefs, and their primary responsibility is to promote economic growth in their cities or provinces. Therefore, these *tuanpai* leaders are not necessarily ignorant or incapable of handling financial and economic issues. Nevertheless, none of the most prominent *tuanpai* leaders has specialized in economic or financial administration, and their experience is especially lacking in the area of international trade and finance. In general, *tuanpai* leaders have worked in rural areas instead of urban industries; they are most experienced in propaganda and party organizational work. The lack of credentials in economics, especially in foreign trade and finance, is an inherent disadvantage for *tuanpai* officials. These officials have to collaborate with other elite groups to handle trade and finance issues and are thus forced to share power.

Since most *tuanpai* leaders have worked in noneconomic areas, as a group they might have less chance (in comparision with some other factional groups) of becoming involved in major corruption scandals. An article written in 2011 by Zhan Guoshu, former editor-in-chief of the overseas edition of the *People's Daily*, observed that since the founding of the PRC, none of the almost one hundred members of the CCYL Secretariat had ever been charged with corruption.[86] Zhan attributed this phenomenon to the positive example set by CCYL top leaders Hu Yaobang, Hu Jintao, Wang Zhaoguo, Song Defu, and Li Keqiang. Zhan's article was controversial, partly because it ignored the prevalence of official corruption in present-day China and partly because it seemed to be motivated by factional politics.

Among the twenty members of the 18th Central Committee who have been purged on corruption charges since 2013, nine were *tuanpai* leaders, including Ling Jihua. For example, former executive vice-governor of Inner Mongolia Pan Yiyang served as a CCYL official from 1989 to 1998, during which time he was deputy secretary and secretary of the Foshan Prefecture CCYL Committee, deputy secretary and secretary of the Guangdong Provincial CCYL Committee, and a member of the standing committee of the CCYL Central Committee, consecutively. Former Guangzhou party secretary Wan Qingliang also served as the secretary of the Guangdong Provincial CCYL Committee and concurrently as a member of the standing committee of the CCYL Central Committee from 2000 to 2003. Former deputy party secretary of Sichuan Li Chuncheng served as deputy secretary and secretary of the Harbin CCYL Municipal Committee and concurrently as a member of the CCYL Central Committee from 1987 to 1992.

The recent fall of Ling Jihua, a prominent and longtime protégé of Hu Jintao's from the CCYL, revealed the pervasive business pursuits and corruption of some *tuanpai* leaders and their political networks.[87] Among the provincial leaders in Shanxi who were purged on corruption charges relating to Ling Jihua, many were Ling's *tuanpai* protégés in his native province. They include former party secretary of the China Association for Science Shen Weichen, who served as deputy secretary of the Shanxi Provincial CCYL Committee from 1984 to 1988; former director of the Organization Department of the Hebei Provincial Committee Liang Bin, who served as deputy secretary and secretary of the Shanxi Provincial CCYL Committee from 1992 to 1996; and former director of the United Front Work Department of the Shanxi Provincial Party Committee Bai Yun, who served as deputy secretary and secretary of the Shanxi Provincial CCYL Committee from 1993 to 2003.[88] Two former party secretaries of Shanxi Province, Zhang Baoshun and Yuan Chunqing, were also Ling's *tuanpai* allies. Though these two *tuanpai* leaders are still in power, their previously bright career prospects have been severely dimmed by the fall of Ling Jihua.

But it is also important to note that except for Ling Jihua, no other prominent power contender with a *tuanpai* background was purged on a corruption charge after the 18th Party Congress. Since Ling Jihua never served as a member of the CCYL Secretariat, the aforementioned observation that none of the almost one hundred members of the CCYL Secretariat have ever been accused on a corruption charge still remains valid. Despite the *tuanpai*'s losing nine seats on the current Central Committee due to the recent anticorruption campaign, a majority of heavyweight *tuanpai* leaders have remained in power.

The most important unanswered question regarding the tension between *tuanpai* leaders and Xi Jinping's protégés concerns the future prospects of Li Yuanchao, current vice-president of the PRC and a Politburo member. As a confidant to Hu Jintao and a *tuanpai* "convenor" who served as director of the Central Organization Department of the CCP before the 18th Party Congress, Li Yuanchao has long been seen as a threat and challenger to the Jiang-Xi camp. For reasons that still remain largely unknown to those studying Chinese elite politics, Li lost his chance for promotion to the PSC at the 18th Party Congress. Arguably, his loss is the biggest in the last political succession. Since October 2013 several of Li's protégés in Jiangsu Province have been purged on corruption charges. They include former mayor of Nanjing Ji Jianye (b. 1957), former standing committee member of the Jiangsu Provincial Party Committee Feng Yajun (b. 1966), former chief-of-staff of the Jiangsu Provincial Party Committee (when Li was party secretary) Zhao Shaolin (b. 1946), former party secretary of Nanjing Yang Weize (b. 1962), and former vice-governor of Jiangsu and deputy party secretary of

Yunnan Qiu He (b. 1957). It remains to be seen whether Xi intends to use these purges to force Vice-President Li into submission and prevent him from fighting back in the next round of leadership turnover, or ultimately purge Li himself. If the latter, the potential political backlash should not be underestimated.

SUMMARY

The greatest challenge to CCP rule probably comes not from external forces but from factors within the party. Over the past three decades, China has been moving away from rule by a single charismatic and all-powerful leader such as Mao or Deng and toward a more collective form of leadership. Collective leadership inherently involves more factional competition and coalition building. In the absence of strongman politics, factional compromise has become more common, as have negotiations and deal making. The CCP's institutional developments in elite recruitment—discussed in previous chapters—do not reduce factional tensions. Rather, they make factional politics all the more dynamic as politicians try to comply with the new rules and norms. Political campaigning or lobbying in various forms has already begun, which was evident in the many dramatic events that occurred before the 18th Party Congress. Political dramas or scandals such as the fall of Chen Liangyu in the Hu era, the Bo Xilai incident on the eve of the 18th Party Congress, and the purge of Ling Jihua in the Xi era are all related to the power ambitions of heavyweight politicians in various factions (namely, the Shanghai Gang, princelings, and *tuanpai*).

Paradoxically, these major political dramas demonstrate that from a collective (not individual) perspective, Chinese factional politics is becoming less a zero-sum game in which the winner takes all and more of a deal-making process. Despite the purges of individual leaders such as Chen Liangyu, Bo Xilai, and Ling Jihua, the powerful factions—the forces propelling political rising stars, such as the Shanghai Gang, princelings, and *tuanpai*— have all survived and continue to be strong and very competitive. Within this emerging system of inner-party bipartisanship between the Jiang-Xi camp and the Hu-Li camp—or between princelings and *tuanpai*—factional winners and losers continually change, and both coalitions occasionally suffer heavy casualties. Such a dynamic balance helps prevent overwhelming power from coming to rest in the hands of one group or individual.

An interesting and important finding in this chapter is that, despite the widely perceived landslide victory of the Jiang-Xi camp at the 18th Party Congress and Xi's six-to-one majority rule in the PSC, *tuanpai* officials in fact hold record-breaking representation (99 seats) in the 376-member Central Committee. With the exception of the PSC and CMC, in which princelings dominate, *tuanpai* leaders generally occupy a significant number of leadership seats in important decisionmaking bodies. *Tuanpai* officials have particularly high representation in top provincial positions—the most important pool from which the top national leadership is drawn. The *tuanpai* faction is also well represented among the younger generations of post-1965 and post-1975 officials.

The "one party, two coalitions" mechanism is more enduring and more sustainable than many analysts in both China and abroad believe. Given the deep legitimacy crisis facing communist rule and the growing public resentment of nepotism associated with the "Red 2G" and the convergence of power and wealth, *tuanpai* leaders may be perceived as a leadership faction that better represents different socioeconomic constituencies. To a certain extent, the CCP's bipartisan factional politics may provide a modicum of checks and balances that helps to keep the party leadership resilient and adaptable to changing circumstances. One can argue that from Xi Jinping's perspective, it will be neither feasible nor desirable to abandon the notion of collective leadership and demolish the *tuanpai* faction or the Hu-Li camp.

Meanwhile, some analysts argue that Xi's rapid consolidation of power since becoming the top party leader in the fall of 2012 reflects Chinese public opinion favoring a stronger and more-effective leadership in contrast to the previous two administrations' reputation for "inaction" or factional deadlock. Others believe that due to the deficiencies of collective leadership, China is now, in line with Xi's personality and political ambition, returning to the era of strongman politics. Regardless of whether Xi aims to replace collective leadership in order to become a Mao-like figure—or alternatively, to transform the current bipartisanship into a more competitive and effective system—one should pay greater attention to key facets of Xi's leadership. These include the kinds of protégés that make up his inner circle, the groups and factions that form his broader political coalition, and how quickly and effectively he places these individuals and groups in the most-important positions—the subject of the next chapter.

CHAPTER 8

Protégés

Xi's Inner Circle

Don't walk behind me; I may not lead. Don't walk in front of me;
I may not follow. Just walk beside me and be my friend.
—ANONYMOUS

Knowing others is wisdom, knowing yourself is enlightenment.
[知人者智, 知己者明]
—LAO TZU 老子

Like successful politicians everywhere, President Xi Jinping assumed China's top leadership role with the support of an inner circle of friends and protégés—individuals who serve as his hands, ears, mouth, and brain.[1] This group has been crucial to Xi's efforts to consolidate power during his first years in office, helping him smoothly manage the Bo Xilai trial, implement a robust anticorruption drive, outline an ambitious market reform agenda at the Third Plenum of the 18th Central Committee in November 2013, and put forward a blueprint for judicial reform at the Fourth Plenum held in October 2014.[2] These bold, wide-ranging economic and political initiatives reflect Xi's growing power and influence.

Xi's inner circle of confidants—leaders whose career advancements are attributable to Xi's support—has played a critical role in the Xi administration. To a certain extent, the 2012 landslide victory by Xi and the Jiang Zemin camp at the 18th National Party Congress was similar to the American presidential election in 2008, when the Democrats won control of the White House. Both President Barack Obama and General Secretary Xi Jinping were aware of their respective political realities; achieving an impressive political victory is one thing, but governing a country effectively is something else entirely. The powerful political allies who helped the two leaders gain power in their respective countries may not be as loyal as the leaders' own longtime protégés.

This explains why, early in his presidency, Obama was also quick to recruit a coterie of people "that had been with him a long time, that worked with him closely and whose judgment he trusted" into his administration.[3] This included individuals from several important political and personal networks. The first group was composed of political advisers from his power base in Chicago: Rahm Emanuel, David Axelrod, and Valerie Jarrett. The second included his "school buds" from Harvard Law School: Michael Froman, Cassandra Butts, and Chris Lu. The third group included the staffers in his Senate office: Pete Rouse, Robert Gibbs, and Alyssa Mastromonaco. And the fourth group included foreign policy strategists from the Brookings Institution and other think tanks: Susan Rice, James Steinberg, and Jeffrey Bader.[4] President Obama frequently turned to these trusted friends to "bounce around ideas and solicit feedback."[5] Some of them became members of Obama's inner circle of advisers. According to American commentators, they served roles as the president's "tacticians," "fixers," "defenders," "messengers," and "whisperers."[6]

Which groups, then, constitute Xi's inner circle? Who serves as Xi's hands, ears, mouth, and brain? How are Xi's political confidants positioned in the national leadership? Just as Obama relies heavily on people he has associated with socially, politically, and professionally throughout his career, Xi also seeks help from the people he has encountered during important phases in his personal and political lives. The dominance of Jiang's political allies in the current Politburo Standing Committee (PSC) has allowed Xi to pursue an ambitious reform agenda during his first term. The effectiveness of Xi's policies and the political legacy of his leadership, however, will ultimately depend on the political positioning of Xi's own protégés both now and during his second term.

This chapter presents the three most important associations or networks that Xi has formed: (1) native-place associations, namely, the so-called "Shaanxi Gang," which includes the "iron triangle" grouping in the PSC; (2) Xi's longtime friends formed through school ties and "big yards" bonds—the political confidants whom Xi met during his childhood and formative years and with whom he has remained close over the past several decades; and (3) Xi's protégés from the provinces and cities in which he served as a top leader and cultivated a web of mentor-protégé ties.

It should be noted that Xi's *mishu* cluster, discussed in detail in chapter 6, also provides an important source of elite advisers for his team. Several individuals work very closely with Xi on a daily basis, and they certainly constitute the core of his inner circle. They include Xi's chief-of-staff, director of the Chinese Communist Party (CCP) General Office Li Zhanshu; Xi's deputy chief-of-staff, deputy director of the CCP General Office and concurrent director of the President's Office Ding Xuexiang; Xi's *mishu* for military affairs, deputy director of the President's Office Zhong Shaojun; Xi's *mishu* for foreign affairs, Zhu Guofeng; and Xi's chief bodyguard, director of the Bodyguard Bureau of the General Office of the CCP Central Committee Wang Shaojun. These individuals mainly established their political ties with Xi early in their careers. The *mishu* cluster and the other political networks under Xi are not mutually exclusively, and this overlap reinforces each network and makes the bonds between them even stronger.

For Xi, these friends and protégés are more trustworthy than political allies with whom he built bonds primarily on shared factional association. Evaluating the individuals who often stand at Xi's side, particularly of some of the advisers who have helped orchestrate major political endeavors and design new policy changes during the first few years of Xi's leadership, can help explain some of the driving forces for change. Likewise, analyzing the political orientation and worldview of the influential figures in Xi's inner circle can provide clues to his political trajectory and the policy options available under his leadership. Xi's ability to promote his own protégés is among the most important indicators of his power and authority at present and moving into the future.

SOURCES AND FOCUSES OF THE STUDY

In an authoritarian political system like that of China, where the inner workings of the leadership are far less transparent than in the United States, it is profoundly difficult to trace out top leaders and their mentor-protégé ties. Despite those inherent limitations, there is a great volume of reliable, publicly available information about Xi's protégés. This is largely because Xi himself has spoken with media both in China and abroad about the relationships he has developed throughout his career. For example, the Chinese official media recently published several articles about Xi's experiences in Zhengding County in Hebei Province, where he served as county leader in the early 1980s. These articles revealed the friendships that he developed with some officials during that period and beyond.[7] Xi has given other clues about the identity of his closest confidants. In the fall of 2013 Xi introduced Liu He, one of his top aides on economic affairs, to the U.S. national security adviser at the time, Tom Donilon, who was visiting Beijing. Xi said, "This is Liu He. He is very important to me."[8]

In recent years the Chinese government has actually made a concerted effort to release more-detailed biographical data about officials at various levels of leadership. Some specialized online websites run by the CCP propaganda apparatus are devoted to biographies of leaders in the party, government, major state-owned enterprises (SOEs), and the military, as explained in chapter 1.[9] Official, semiofficial, and social media in the People's Republic of China (PRC) have all increasingly revealed previously banned information about the mentor-protégé ties of party leaders. Chinese books published in Hong Kong, Taiwan, and abroad feature biographical sketches and information on family background and political networks and provide additional—though often unverified—information about Chinese leaders and their political associations.[10]

This study primarily explores open-source information found in official Chinese publications, both online and in print, with a special focus on the career overlaps and close working relationships between Xi and his protégés. This research also strives to confirm some unverified sources and provides footnotes to indicate any unsubstantiated information. This chapter meticulously tracks familial and personal associations between Xi and his longtime friends through various political networks.

Table 8-1 presents a chronological overview of the main phases of Xi's formative years and career experiences before his designation as the heir apparent in 2007, tracing the political associations and mentor-protégé relationships formed during each of these phases. This analysis includes some of Xi's defining experiences: from his adolescent years in the heyday of the radical Mao era; to toiling as a "sent-down youth" (a rural laborer) in the country's most primitive region, the Loess Plateau; to serving as a "worker-peasant-soldier student" at Tsinghua University toward the end of the Cultural Revolution; to working as a *mishu* for the minister of Defense in the early years of the Deng era; and, finally, to gaining substantial local and provincial leadership experience in Hebei, Fujian, Zhejiang, and Shanghai. During each of these periods, especially his formative years and early career, Xi developed strong personal bonds and lifelong friendships. These key friends and associates are also represented in table 8-1. This study further examines the characteristics of several of Xi's important confidants and links these leaders' current positions with their future political prospects, thus providing a much-needed assessment of the strengths and weaknesses of Xi's inner circle and the implications for China's evolving system of collective leadership in the years to come.

Xi's family members are his core confidants and advisers, especially his wife, Peng Liyuan, his mother, and his daughter, who recently graduated from Harvard University. In addition, Xi's siblings and their spouses are also among his most valued aides. Despite the fact that most or all of them do not play direct leadership roles, their influence on President Xi can be

TABLE 8-1. Xi Jinping's Friends and Protégés before His Tenure in Zhongnanhai

Period	Xi's age	Life and career experiences	Personal and political associations	Main friends and protégés
1953–60	1–7	Family ties	"Shaanxi native place"	Yu Zhengsheng, Wang Qishan, Li Zhanshu, Zhao Leji, He Yiting
1960–68	7–15	Student at Bayi School and Beijing No. 25 School	"Princelings" and grew up in cadre's compound (*ganbu dayuan*)	Zhang Youxia, Liu He, Liu Yuan
1969–74	16–21	Rural laborer in Yanchuan County, Shaanxi	"Sent-down youth" and "Shaanxi connection"	Wang Qishan, Wang Chen
1975–78	22–25	Worker-peasant-soldier student at Tsinghua University	"Tsinghua network"	Chen Xi
1979–82	26–29	*Mishu* for Minister of Defense Geng Biao	Experience with PLA and in affairs regarding Taiwan and Hong Kong	Liu Xiaojiang
1982–85	29–32	County leader in Zhengding County, Hebei	"Hebei connection"	Li Zhanshu, Yang Zhenwu
1985–02	32–49	Leader in Xiamen, Ningde, Fuzhou, Fujian	"Fujian connection"	Zhao Keshi, Cai Yingting, He Lifeng, Cai Qi, Huang Kunming, Song Tao, Wang Ning, Wang Xiaohong
2002–07	49–54	Governor and Party Secretary of Zhejiang	"Zhejiang connection"	Chen Min'er, Li Qiang, Xia Baolong, Zhong Shan, Ying Yong, Lou Yangsheng, Zhong Shaojun, Shu Guo-zeng, Meng Qingfeng, Shen Haixiong
2007	54	Party Secretary of Shanghai	"Shanghai Gang"	Han Zheng, Ding Xuexiang, Yang Xiaodu, Xu Lin, Fang Xinghai

Source: Part of the data is based on Wu Ming, *Zhongguo xinlingxiu: Xi Jinping zhuan* [China's new leader: Biography of Xi Jinping], new enl. ed. (Hong Kong: Wenhua yishu chubanshe, 2010), 572–73. Tabulated and expanded by Cheng Li.

significant. However, to maintain a reasonable scope of research, this study does not account for the influence of family members.

THE "SHAANXI GANG"

It may be pure happenstance that Xi's ascent to the top leadership coincided with the rise of some prominent political leaders with the so-called Shaanxi connection—those who were born in Shaanxi Province (or are natives of Shaanxi by family origin [籍贯, *jiguan*]) and those who spent much of their professional career (or experienced a turning point in their career) in the province.[11] Some analysts have used the term "Shaanxi Gang" to highlight the rapid rise of national leaders (both civilian and military) who have strong ties to Shaanxi.[12]

Native Ties and Chinese Political Networking

It is by no means unusual in contemporary China for national leaders to disproportionately represent certain geographic regions.[13] During the Nationalist era, Guangdong Province produced a significant number of top political and military elites. They included not only those who were Cantonese but also those who studied at the Whampoa Military Academy and those who advanced their professional and political careers in the region.[14]

During the Mao era, a majority of CCP leaders came from central China, especially from Hunan and Hubei Provinces. This was mainly due to the origins of the Chinese Communist movement in the 1920s and 1930s, which attracted many peasants from central China. Two or three decades later, their representatives became national leaders of the newly founded PRC. For example, approximately one-third of the members of the Eighth Politburo of the CCP formed in 1956 were born in Hunan and about one-third of the members of the Ninth Politburo in 1969 were born in Hubei.[15] Most of these Hunan- and Hubei-born leaders had military backgrounds. Altogether, the leaders from provinces in central China occupied half of the seats in the Politburo in these two party congresses.

Deng Xiaoping relied heavily on his fellow Sichuan natives in the leadership of the CCP, most noticeably the Yang brothers (Yang Shangkun, who served as PRC president and vice-chairman of the Central Military Commission [CMC], and Yang Baibing, who served as secretary-general of the CMC). Deng also played a direct role in promoting his Sichuanese protégés, including Sichuan party secretary Yang Rudai and Sichuan governor Xiao Yang, to important leadership posts. As a result of Deng's recommendation, Yang Rudai, provincial party secretary of Sichuan, served as a Politburo member at the 13th Central Committee in 1987. While Deng planned to promote Xiao Yang, then governor of Sichuan, for membership on the 14th Politburo in 1992, Xiao was eliminated in the election for full membership of the Central Committee and thus failed to obtain a seat in the Politburo.

Under the leadership of Jiang Zemin and Hu Jintao, China experienced disproportionate representation of leaders from the east coast, especially from Shandong and Jiangsu Provinces. On the 15th Central Committee in 1997, about 45 percent of full members were born in eastern China.[16] According to a study of military elites in the 1990s, Shandong Province accounted for well over one-quarter of China's senior military officers.[17] A report released in the late 1990s showed that of the forty-two highest ranking PLA generals and admirals whose birthplaces were identified, thirteen were born in Shandong, and six were born in Jiangsu. Twenty-two top military leaders (52 percent) were from eastern China.[18] As discussed in chapter 3, multiple factors could have led to the strong representation of Shandong natives in the military leadership over the last two decades.[19] The high percentage of Jiangsu natives in the civilian leadership is at least partially due to the fact that Jiang Zemin and Hu Jintao, both Jiangsu natives, liked to promote their fellow Jiangsunese.[20]

Like other sources of division among elites, birthplace ties can be instrumental in political consolidation or factional conflict. During the Jiang era, leaders from Shanghai and its neighboring areas dominated the PSC, contributing to elite cohesion on the one hand, while causing tremendous factional tensions on the other.[21] As the new boss in Zhongnanhai, Xi has taken advantage of all available political associations and networks to consolidate his power, especially boosting the careers of those who have strong ties to his birthplace, Shaanxi.

Xi's Family Origin and the "Yellow Earth Attachment"

Xi Jinping's reliance on his fellow natives of Shaanxi reflects a political norm in Chinese elite politics. Xi has been quite outspoken about his strong affection for Shaanxi (陕西情结, *shaanxi qingjie*)—an affinity referred to as his "yellow earth attachment" (黄土地情结, *huangtudi qingjie*), referring to Shaanxi in particular.[22] Shaanxi is not only the native province of his father, Xi Zhongxun, but also where Xi Jinping himself spent his formative years and launched his own political career.

Xi Zhongxun was born in Fuping County in Weinan City, central Shaanxi, in 1913. At the age of fifteen, he was arrested as a result of his participation in the student movement. While in prison, he joined the CCP. When he was released, he took part in peasant guerrilla fighting and helped establish the Shaanxi-Gansu border revolutionary base in 1933. He served as chairman of the Shaanxi-Gansu Border Region of the Soviet government in the mid-1930s. He remained in the region during the Anti-Japanese War and the civil war over the following decade, becoming secretary of the Northwest Bureau of the CCP Central Committee and deputy political commissar of the Northwest Field Army when he was only thirty-two years old.

After the Communist victory in 1949, Xi Zhongxun was based in Xi'an, Shaanxi Province, where he was in charge of the party, government, and military leadership in northwestern China. In 1952 he moved to Beijing, where he served as secretary-general (chief-of-staff) of the State Council, primarily assisting Premier Zhou Enlai. A few years later, he concurrently served as vice-premier of the State Council. Xi Zhongxun spent almost forty years of his early life and career in Shaanxi. Although he was also instrumental in implementing economic reforms in Guangdong Province, such as the establishment of the Shenzhen Special Economic Zone, during the early 1980s his career was primarily defined by his early experience in Shaanxi. The fact that Xi Zhongxun was purged for sixteen years (1962–78) made his political associations in Shaanxi even more important.[23]

Xi Zhongxun had deep familial ties to the region. His first wife was a native of Shaanxi, and he married his second wife, Qi Xin (Xi Jinping's mother), in Suide County, Shaanxi. Five of his seven children from both marriages were born in Shaanxi. When Xi Zhongxun moved to Beijing in the fall of 1952, his wife, who was already pregnant, remained in Yan'an for several months. When she joined Xi Zhongxun in Beijing the following year, Xi Jinping was born. Two years later, their youngest son, Xi Yuanping, was also born in Beijing. Both Xi Jinping and Xi Yuanping have the word "ping" in their names, reflecting their birthplace of Beiping (北平), now called Beijing.[24] Xi Zhongxun's brother, Xi Zhongkai, served consecutively as deputy head of the Commerce Department of the Shaanxi provincial government and as head of the Organization Department of the Shaanxi Provincial Party Committee.

Xi Zhongxun's associations in Shaanxi influenced Xi Jinping's life and career in various ways. Xi Jinping's father-in-law from his first marriage, Ke Hua, who later served as China's ambassador to the United Kingdom, served as deputy head of the Culture Department of the Northwest Military Committee, on which Xi Zhongxun served as vice-chairman during the first few years of the PRC. During the Cultural Revolution, millions of urban middle-school students were rusticated in the countryside, where they worked as farmers and in other manual labor jobs during their adolescent years, becoming known as "sent-down youths." Xi Jinping's strong family ties to Shaanxi and his father's revolutionary legacy in the region explain why, in 1969, at the age of sixteen, young Xi chose Yanchuan County of Shaanxi's Yan'an prefecture as the location to undertake his "sent-down youth" work. Xi spent almost seven years there as a farmer, serving concurrently as the branch party secretary of a local village after 1974.

Through experiencing extraordinary hardships in such a poor and primitive rural region, Xi felt a sense of fulfillment and native attachment. For him, this time in his early career was a relief from Beijing's political turmoil, through which he had suffered as the child of an "enemy of Mao." In Yan'an prefecture, the cradle of his father's revolutionary career, Xi was surrounded by fellow Shaanxi natives and developed deep ties to his native region. Xi recently told the Chinese media that the time he spent in Yan'an as a sent-down youth was a "defining experience" and a "turning point" in his life.[25] Xi identified himself as a "Yan'an native" (延安人, *yan'anren*), claiming Shaanxi as his "root and base" (根, *gen*) and Yan'an as his "soul and spirit" (魂, *hun*).[26] He was particularly grateful for the knowledge, strength, and confidence that his native province instilled in him.[27]

Understandably, Xi Jinping's sentiment toward the "yellow earth" has also led to his favorable view of leaders connected with Shaanxi, which strengthens observers' perceptions of a loosely defined "Shaanxi Gang." According to Jiang Shaofeng, an analyst who has published several articles on this subject in the overseas Chinese media, the members of the Shaanxi Gang now occupy a significant portion of the top leadership in the party, government, and military. Shaanxi Province seems to have become the new power base for the emerging dominant force in the national leadership.[28] Combining the work of Jiang Shaofeng and others, table 8-2 tabulates some of the most prominent members of the Shaanxi Gang in the Chinese civilian and military leaderships at the national level. It is remarkable that the group occupies three out of seven seats (43 percent) on the PSC, seven out of twenty-five members (28 percent) in the Politburo (if Li Jianguo and Ma Kai are included), and four out of eleven members (36 percent) on the CMC.

The "Iron Triangle"

The first three leaders listed in table 8-2, Xi Jinping, Yu Zhengsheng, and Wang Qishan, are all current members of the Politburo Standing Committee. All are princelings, with their fathers or fathers-in-law having served as CCP senior leaders. Yu Zhengsheng's father, Yu Qiwei (also known as Huang Jing), and Wang Qishan's father-in-law, Yao Yilin, were the primary leaders of the December Ninth National Salvation Movement in Beijing in 1935. Yu Zhengsheng was born in Yan'an in 1945, when his father was secretary of the Pingyuan branch of the Northern Bureau of the CCP Central Committee. Yu's mother, Fan Jin, served as the president of *Beijing Daily* and deputy director of the Propaganda Department of the Beijing Municipal Party Committee in 1952, when Xi Zhongxun was director of the Central Propaganda Department of the CCP. It is likely that the Xi and Yu families have known each other for almost seven decades.

TABLE 8-2. Xi Jinping and the "Shaanxi Gang" in the National Leadership

Name	Birth year	Current position	Central Committee status	Shaanxi affiliation	Formative experience in Shaanxi	Leadership experience in Shaanxi
Xi Jinping	1953	CCP Secretary-General, PRC President, CMC Chair	PSC member, CMC member	Shaanxi native	Sent-down youth, 1969–75	
Yu Zhengsheng	1945	Chair, CPPCC	PSC member	Born in Shaanxi		
Wang Qishan	1948	Secretary, CCDI	PSC member		Sent-down youth, 1979–71; Shaanxi Museum, 1971–73, 1976–79	
Li Zhanshu	1950	Director of the CCP General Office	Politburo member			Standing Committee member, Xi'an Party Secretary and Shaanxi Deputy Party Secretary, 1998–2003
Zhao Leji	1957	Director of the Central Organization Department	Politburo member	Shaanxi native		Party Secretary of Shaanxi, 2007–12
Li Jianguo*	1946	Executive Vice-Chair, NPC	Politburo member			Party Secretary of Shaanxi, 1997–2007

Name	Year	Position	Politburo member	Grew up in Shaanxi	
Ma Kai*	1946	Vice-Premier			
Chang Wanquan	1949	State Councilor and Minister of Defense	CMC member		Stationed in Shaanxi as an officer for 28 years, 1974–2002
Fang Fenghui	1951	Chief of the CMC Joint Staff Department	CMC member	Born in Shaanxi	Stationed in Shaanxi for 35 years, 1968–2003
Zhang Youxia	1950	Director of CMC Equipment Development Department	CMC member	Shaanxi native	
Liu Xiaojiang	1949	Former Political Commissar of Navy	Full member	Born in Shaanxi	Sent-down youth, 1968–70
Wang Chen	1950	Vice-Chair and Secretary-General of the NPC	Full member		Sent-down youth, 1969–70; local government, 1970–74
He Yiting	1951	Executive Vice-President of the Central Party School	Full member	Born in Shaanxi	

Note and Source: * It is debatable whether Li Jianguo and Ma Kai should be considered members of the Shaanxi Gang, because their relationship with Xi is not close. CCP = Chinese Communist Party; PRC = People's Republic of China; CMC = Central Military Commission; PSC = Politburo Standing Committee; CPPCC = Chinese People's Political Consultative Conference; CCDI = Central Commission for Discipline Inspection; NPC = National People's Congress. Jiang Shaofeng, "Zhongguo Zhengtan xianchu yige shaanxibang" [The emergence of the Shaanxi Gang in the Chinese leadership], *Waican* [External reference], no. 38, September 2013; and Jiang Shaofeng, "Jiefangjun zhong shaanxibang" [The Shaanxi Gang in the PLA], Mirror Online, October 16, 2013 (http://city.mirrorbooks.com/news/?action -viewnews-itemid-100765), accessed January 16, 2014. Updated, expanded, and tabulated by Cheng Li.

Xi Jinping, Yu Zhengsheng, and Wang Qishan are all very close to former party boss Jiang Zemin, and they are part of the "majority of six" on the 18th PSC. They are often seen as the "center of the core group in the Jiang camp." Even before the 18th National Party Congress in November 2012, some analysts predicted that these three heavyweight politicians would form the "iron triangle" in the top leadership following the Hu-Wen administration.[29]

Both Yu Zhengsheng and Wang Qishan have been extremely supportive of Xi's new policy agenda. Approximately three weeks before the Third Plenum of the 18th Central Committee, Yu Zhengsheng made a widely publicized statement claiming that the reform agenda for the upcoming meeting would be unprecedented in terms of its scale, scope, and depth.[30] At a time when serious pessimism seemed to prevail in the country over what the Xi leadership could do, this forecast by Yu aimed to forcefully mobilize broad support from both the political elite and the public for Xi's new economic reform platform at the Third Plenum. The impressive agenda proposed at the meeting validated Yu's forecast and endorsement.

Wang Qishan: Xi's Longtime Friend and Key Political Ally

Xi Jinping's close relationship with Wang Qishan has arguably been the most important factor in the consolidation of Xi's power and the implementation of his new policy initiatives since the political succession in 2012. It is unclear when Xi and Wang first met, but several Chinese sources reveal that they were already close friends more than forty years ago, when both were sent-down youths in two neighboring counties in Yan'an.[31] According to Zhang Siming, a Yan'an-based writer who interviewed Xi Jinping in 2002, on one trip to Beijing during the early period of his sent-down youth years, Xi stopped by the village where Wang Qishan lived and stayed for a night, during which they shared a single bed and blanket due to the primitive living conditions.[32] From time to time during their years in Yan'an, Xi and Wang visited each other and also exchanged books on economics and the social sciences.[33]

Wang Qishan, whose family originated from Shanxi Province (not to be confused with Shaanxi Province), was born into an intellectual family in Qingdao, Shandong Province, in 1948.[34] His father, a graduate of civil engineering from the prestigious Tsinghua University, worked as a senior engineer at the Ministry of Construction in Beijing beginning in the mid-1950s. In 1969, the same year Xi went to Yan'an, Wang also went there as a sent-down youth. While in Yan'an, Wang fell in love with his future wife, Yao Mingshan, a fellow sent-down youth from Beijing and a daughter of Yao Yilin.[35] Yao Yilin was purged between 1966 and 1973, but later became executive vice-premier and a PSC member. Yao Mingshan's sister, Yao Mingrui, is married to Meng Xuenong, the former mayor of Beijing, whom Wang Qishan replaced during the SARS crisis in 2003.

Wang spent ten years in Shaanxi: first as a farmer, then as an assistant at the Shaanxi Provincial Museum in Xi'an, and later as a student in the Department of History at Northwest University (also in Xi'an). He finally returned to the Shaanxi Provincial Museum as a researcher before moving to Beijing, where he began to work at the Modern History Institute of the Chinese Academy of Social Sciences in 1979. During the three years that Wang worked at the academy, he made many friends in the country's reemerging circle of public intellectuals, and his main research interest switched from history to economics. He and three other young scholars (Weng Yongxi, Huang Jiangnan, and Zhu Jiaming), all in their late twenties and early thirties, wrote a comprehensive report on economic reform in which they explored the periodic shortage crises in socialist economies—a subject that was previously taboo.[36] The report was submitted to senior economic policymakers in the top leadership, such as Premier Zhao Ziyang, Chen Yun, and Yao Yilin, who all offered very positive comments; Zhao even invited them to a roundtable discussion of their report. Because of these extraordinary accomplishments, Wang and the three other scholars earned the nickname "the four gentlemen of the reform proposal" (改革四君子, *gaige sijunzi*).[37] Wang Qishan also spent most of the summer of 1980 in Guangdong as a guest of the provincial government, working on Guangdong's pioneering economic reforms, which would emerge as a model for China's reform and opening up. As part of his work, he briefed provincial senior leaders, including the governor of Guangdong, Xi Zhongxun.[38]

Over the following two decades, Wang Qishan worked primarily in the domain of economic affairs, especially in the areas of agricultural and financial development. He served successively as president of the China Rural Trust and Investment Corporation, vice-governor of the People's Bank of China, and governor of the China Construction Bank. Wang has obtained a reputation in both China and abroad as a statesman with outstanding financial expertise.

Wang's widely recognized nickname in China is "chief of the fire brigade" (救火队长, *jiuhuo duizhang*). Knowing that Wang maintains such a great reputation among the Chinese public, former secretary of the U.S. Treasury Timothy Geithner presented him with an authentic New York City Fire Department hat during Wang's visit to the United States in 2011.[39] The Chinese public has long regarded Wang as a leader who is capable and trustworthy during times of crisis—a "go-to guy" in the Chinese leadership for handling some of the country's most daunting challenges. His experience handling crises includes his appointment as executive vice-governor of Guangdong in 1998 to handle the bankruptcy of a major financial institution in the wake of the 1997 Asian financial crisis; his appointment as party secretary of Hainan Province in 2002 to address the decade-long real estate bubble on the island; his transfer to Beijing at the peak of the SARS epidemic in the spring of 2003; and his role as mayor of Beijing during the 2008 Olympics.

Xi Jinping faced three urgent challenges when he took power from Hu Jintao in November 2012: the trial of Bo Xilai, the prevalence of official corruption, and the slowdown of the Chinese economy. On all three of these fronts, Wang Qishan played an instrumental role in helping to formulate Xi's political and policy objectives and raising public confidence in the new leadership. For example, Wang Qishan was very decisive in pushing for new regulations and reform initiatives for SOEs. According to the new regulations, CEOs and senior executives of the companies under the purview of the State-Owned Assets Supervision and Administration Commission should substantially cut their salaries—from about twelve times the average company employee salary to no more than eight times. The annual bonus for senior executives should not be more than 30 percent of their salary.[40]

Wang Qishan's courage, toughness, popularity, expertise in finance, and his international reputation make him indispensable to Xi. Furthermore, some of Wang's protégés are now well positioned in China's financial and economic leadership, including the minister of Finance, Lou Jiwei, the governor of the People's Bank of China, Zhou Xiaochuan, and the director of the Development Research Center of the State Council, Li Wei. Newly appointed chairman of the Bank of China Tian Guoli (b. 1960) and newly appointed president of China's Merchant Bank Tian Huiyu (b. 1965), a graduate of Columbia University, are both Wang's former *mishu*. Wang Qishan also promoted some of his protégés who worked at the Beijing municipal government when he was mayor to important leadership positions in the Central Commission for Discipline Inspection (CCDI). They include Xiao Pei (b. 1961), former deputy director of the Propaganda Department of the Beijing municipal government, who was first promoted to director of the Propaganda Department of the CCDI in November 2014, and then appointed vice-minister of Supervision in July 2015, and Lin Duo (b. 1956), former director and party secretary of Xicheng District in Beijing, who was appointed secretary of the Discipline Inspection Commission and standing committee member of the Liaoning Provincial Party Committee in August 2014. Lin was promoted to governor of Gansu in April 2016. Other former colleagues from the Beijing municipal government—including former vice-mayor Zhao Fengtong (b. 1954), former chief-of-staff Li Xiaohong (b. 1953), former deputy chief-of-staff Cui Peng (b. 1964), former deputy chief-of-staff Dong Hong (b. 1953), former deputy chief-of-staff of the Beijing Discipline Inspection Commission Wang Rongjun (b. 1959) and Yang Xiaochao (b. 1958) former director of the Audit Bureau of the Beijing Municipal government—

now all work with Wang at the CCDI.[41] Yang currently serves as secretary-general of the CCDI.

These observations reveal that Wang has been the most effective political ally for Xi. Their four-decade-long friendship seems to have had an impact far beyond the personal and social domains.

Other Important Members of the Shaanxi Gang

Of the four Politburo members with a Shaanxi connection, two (Li Zhanshu and Zhao Leji) are often seen as Xi's confidants. Li Zhanshu was born into a Communist revolutionary family in Pingshan County, Hebei Province, in 1950. His great-uncle served as vice-governor of Shandong and secretary of the All-China Federation of Trade Unions, and several of his family members participated in the Anti-Japanese War and the civil war. He gained extensive provincial leadership experience in different parts of China, including Hebei Province (north), Shaanxi Province (northwest), Heilongjiang Province (northeast), and Guizhou Province (southwest). From 1986 to 1990, he also served as secretary of the Hebei Provincial Committee of the Chinese Communist Youth League. As Xi's current chief-of-staff, the broad geographic reach of his leadership experience has proved invaluable. He can help Xi better coordinate provincial-level leadership across the region and make deals with members of the so-called *tuanpai* faction as needed.

It was reported that the friendship between Xi Jinping and Li Zhanshu began about three decades ago, when Xi served as deputy party secretary and then party secretary of Zhengding County in Hebei from 1982 to 1985, and Li Zhanshu served as party secretary of Wuji County in the same province from 1983 to 1985.[42] Both counties belong to Shijiazhuang Prefecture and are geographically in close proximity. Li later spent five years in Shaanxi serving as director of the Organization Department of the provincial party committee, party secretary of Xi'an, and deputy party secretary of Shaanxi. All of these factors help explain why Xi chose Li as his chief-of-staff on the eve of the 18th National Party Congress.

From Xi's perspective, Zhao Leji's role as the man in charge of personnel appointments is perhaps equally as important as Li Zhanshu's role in monitoring the operation of Xi's decisionmaking circle. As discussed in chapter 2, the CCP Central Organization Department (COD) is entitled to make appointments for several thousand senior positions in the party, government, military, SOEs, and other important institutions. Although it is not entirely clear to what extent Zhao owes his own appointment to Xi's support, Zhao had been seen as a rising star in the Chinese provincial leadership for more than a decade. According to some unverified sources, Xi Zhongxun and Zhao Leqi's father were close friends.[43]

Undoubtedly, Zhao has a very strong "Shaanxi connection." As a native of Shaanxi, Zhao speaks with a strong regional accent, and some analysts have identified him as the "spokesperson" of the Shaanxi Gang.[44] Zhao served as Shaanxi party secretary from 2007 to 2012 before he moved to Beijing to head the COD. His brother Zhao Leqin (b. 1960) also served as a local leader in Shaanxi for more than two decades, taking posts such as the party secretary of Shanyang County, deputy director of the Department of Transportation in the Shaanxi provincial government, and mayor of Hanzhong. Zhao Leqin was transferred from Shaanxi to Guangxi a few months after his brother was appointed provincial party secretary of Shaanxi. In January 2013 Zhao Leqin was appointed party secretary of Guilin City, Guangxi.

Over the past two years, as director of the powerful COD, Zhao Leji has aggressively promoted members of the Shaanxi Gang to important leadership posts. They include the newly appointed Liaoning party secretary Li Xi and Anhui governor Li Jinbin. Both leaders advanced their careers from Shaanxi Province under the leadership of Zhao Leji. Deputy party secretary of Tianjin Wang Dongfeng was born in Xi'an, Shaanxi, and spent the first forty-six years of his life in the province. In addition, Yao Yinliang, a native of Shaanxi who has lived and worked exclusively in the province, was promoted from party secretary of Yan'an City to executive vice-governor of Shaanxi Province in June 2015. Jing Junhai, former director of the Propaganda Department of the Shaanxi Provincial Party Committee, left Shaanxi in June 2015 and moved to Beijing where he currently serves as deputy director of the CCP Central Propaganda Department. Jiang Zelin, newly appointed deputy secretary-general of the State Council, also previously served as executive vice-governor of Shaanxi under Zhao Leji. In December 2015, Qi Yu, another Shaanxi native who advanced his early career in Shaanxi, was appointed to deputy director of the COD.

Li Jianguo and Ma Kai are not seen as a protégés of Xi, but both are princelings whose fathers served as leaders at the vice-ministerial level, and both have some sort of Shaanxi connection.[45] Li served as provincial party secretary of Shaanxi for ten years before he passed the post to Zhao Leji in 2007. Over the following five years, Li served concurrently as vice-chairman and secretary-general of the National People's Congress. Li's ascension to the Politburo at the 18th National Party Congress was seen as a surprise, as many analysts believed that Li, like his three predecessors, would retire without obtaining a Politburo seat. Xi Jinping's praise for Li's work in Shaanxi might have played a role in Li's promotion. It is worth noting that Li delivered the keynote address at the forum commemorating the 100th anniversary of the birth of Xi Zhongxun.[46] Ma Kai, on the other hand, appears to have a weaker connection to Shaanxi, although he did grow up in Xi'an and attend an elementary school for the children of officials in the city (the school's previous incarnation was Yan'an Cadre's Children School, founded by Mao Zedong).[47]

Table 8-2 shows that the Shaanxi Gang includes four prominent PLA generals, three of whom serve on the very powerful CMC. Minister of Defense Chang Wanquan was stationed in Shaanxi as an officer for twenty-eight years (1974–2002), both PLA chief-of-staff Fang Fenghui and former political commissar of the navy Liu Xiaojiang were born in Shaanxi, and Fang was actually stationed in the province for thirty-five years (1968–2003). Director of the CMC Equipment Development Department Zhang Youxia is a princeling whose father, Zhang Zongxun, was a close friend of Xi Zhongxun. During the civil war in the late 1940s, the former served as commander of the Shanganning Field Army, and the latter as political commissar of the same army. Later, Zhang Zongxun served as vice-commander of the Northwest Field Army, and Xi Zhongxun served as its deputy political commissar. After the Communist victory in 1949, Xi Zhongxun served as the first vice-chairman of the Northwest Military Committee, on which Zhang served as a member.

Xi Jinping and Zhang Youxia have strong ties with and affection for Shaanxi since their fathers were not only natives of Shaanxi but also "bloody fighting comrades" in the Chinese Communist Revolution in northern China. The friendship between their fathers also extends to Zhang Youxia and Xi Jinping. According to a Reuters source, in 2012 Xi proposed that Zhang be promoted to vice-chairman of the CMC.[48] Both Xi Jinping and Zhang Youxia were born in Beijing and grew up in the nearby "big yards." When Xi was sent to Yan'an to work as a rural laborer, Zhang joined the PLA.

The other three leaders listed in table 8-2 may attribute their recent promotions to Xi. It has been reported in overseas Chinese media that all have close personal ties with him, although it is not always simple to identify their first interactions and determine how important the Shaanxi connection was in the development of their ties.[49] The vice-chairman and secretary-general of the National People's Congress, Wang Chen, traveled to Shaanxi from Beijing as a sent-down youth in 1969, at exactly the same time that Xi Jinping was there. Wang served as a *mishu* in the Yan'an Prefecture party committee from 1973 to 1974, when Xi worked as a grassroots party secretary in the region. When Xi was in charge of the CCP Secretariat between 2007 and 2012, Wang served as the director of the CCP Foreign Publicity Office. Wang took over Li Jianguo's posts in the National People's Congress in 2013 when Li became a Politburo member.

Many of Xi's sent-down youth friends were princelings. For example, Lei Pingsheng and Lei Rongsheng, two brothers who attended the same Bayi School as Xi in Beijing, were Xi's roommates in the village for a few years. The Lei brothers came from an official family, and their father Lei Yingfu served as director of Military Operation Division of the PLA General Staff Department. Lei Yingfu served as a military staffer for Zhou Enlai during the famous 1945 Chongqing negotiation between the CCP and the Nationalist Party. Lei Pingsheng, who pursued post-doctoral studies at University of Virginia in the 1990s, currently works as a professor and medical doctor at the Beijing Union Medical College Hospital, and Lei Rongsheng works as deputy director of the Information Technology Department of the Chinese Academy of Governance.[50] Qiu Yuanping (b. 1953), director of the State Council Overseas Chinese Affairs since 2013, was also a sent-down youth in Yan'an from Beijing. Qiu's father was a senior diplomat and she attended the Beijing Institute of Foreign Languages during the Cultural Revolution, later earning a doctoral degree in international relations from Peking University. She is currently one of a few minister-ranking female leaders in the country.

He Yiting (profiled in chapter 6) served as a close aide to Xi for many years and was often seen as a top speechwriter for Xi. Soon after Xi became party boss, he appointed He Yiting the executive vice-president of the powerful Central Party School. As discussed earlier, He Yiting has played an important role in formulating Xi's ideological stance.

Table 8-2 does not include members of the Shaanxi Gang who currently serve at the provincial level of leadership. Some of them are well positioned for further promotion. Among them, Li Xi probably has the best chance of entering the next Politburo. Li was born in Liangdang County, Gansu Province, in 1956. He worked as a sent-down youth in his native county (1975–76), and served as a clerk in both the Education and Culture Bureau and the office of the county party committee (1976–78). He attended Northwestern Normal University in Lanzhou, Gansu (1978–82), majoring in Chinese language and literature. After graduation, he developed his career largely as a *mishu*, first in the Propaganda Department of the Gansu Provincial Party Committee (1982–85), then in the office of Gansu party secretary Li Ziqi (1985–86), and finally in the Department of Organization of the Gansu Provincial Party Committee (1986–95). Li Ziqi was born in Shaanxi and, as a thirteen-year-old boy in the 1930s, he participated in the communist military uprising in the northwestern region, led by Xi Jinping's father Xi Zhongxun. Li Ziqi was persecuted in the early 1960s—the same period during which Xi Zhongxun was fired. Both were charged for antisocialist activities and later rehabilitated after the Cultural Revolution. In 1983 Xi Zhongxun nominated Li Ziqi to be Gansu provincial party secretary.[51] It was believed that through this important connection, Li Ziqi's *mishu* Li Xi developed a strong personal tie with the Xi family, especially with Xi Jinping.

Over the following decade, Li served as a party official at the prefecture, municipality, and province levels of leadership—all in Gansu Province. In 2004 Li was transferred to Shaanxi Province, where he served as secretary-general of the provincial party committee from 2004 to 2006. He served concurrently as party secretary of Yan'an Prefecture and as a member of the Standing Committee of the Shaanxi Provincial Party Committee from 2006 to 2011, during which time he attended a part-time graduate program in economic management at Tsinghua University and received a master's of business administration degree.

In 2011 Li was transferred to Shanghai, where he served first as director of the Organization Department from 2011 to 2013 and then as deputy party secretary from 2013 to 2014. He was appointed Liaoning governor in 2014. Li served only one year as governor before being promoted to party secretary of the province. According to an overseas Chinese media source, Li Xi's native county was where Xi Jinping's father, Xi Zhongxun, led the revolutionary uprising in 1932—the only military uprising led by the CCP in the northwestern region of the country during the first civil war.[52] As a reporter observed, "Li Xi did an impressive job in highlighting the historical significance of this uprising in the Communist red revolution."[53] Furthermore, when Li Xi was party secretary of Yan'an, he shaped the village where Xi worked as a sent-down youth into a "model village" of the province.[54] Li Xi's recent successive promotions have largely been due to his strong ties with Xi Jinping. The personal contact between Xi Jinping and Li Xi was widely reported in the Chinese media, reinforcing the public perception that Li is a confidant of Xi.[55]

SCHOOL TIES AND "BIG YARDS" BONDS

Just as birthplace has been an important element in Xi's political networking, other kinds of shared early life associations—attending the same school and growing up in the same neighborhood compound—are also significant in the formation of Xi's inner circle. Xi spent most of his childhood years in an elite academic and residential environment. He received his early education at the Bayi School (八一学校, *bayi xuexiao*), which was located in Beijing's Haidian District. Some of the schools in the district, most notably Beijing No. 101 School, were famous for being cradles of "red nobility." Another school with an excellent academic reputation is Beijing No. 4 School, which is located in the city's Xicheng District. Many princelings attended this prestigious school, including Bo Xilai and his two brothers (Bo Xiyong and Bo Xicheng), Ma Kai, Chen Yuan, Kong Dan, and Qin Xiao.[56] Wang Qishan attended the No. 35 High School, which was also located in Xicheng District and is known for producing senior CCP leaders like former PSC member Song Ping and former Politburo member and Beijing party secretary Li Ximin.

The Bayi School did not have the academic reputation of Beijing No. 101 School or of Beijing No. 4 School; it was established primarily for children of senior officers in the PLA. Students who attended the Bayi School in the late 1950s and early 1960s include former deputy director of the National Commission of Defense Science and Technology Nie Li (daughter of Marshal Nie Rongzhen), former vice-commander of the navy He Pengfei (son of Marshal He Long), former member of the CCP Central Committee Deng Pufang (son of Deng Xiaoping), former vice-commander of the Beijing Military Region Su Rongsheng (son of General Su Yu), and PSC member Yu Zhengsheng (son of former Tianjin party secretary Huang Jing).[57] According to one source, Xi Jinping formed a close relationship with Deng Pufang. Deng Pufang and his wife often visited Xi and Peng Liyuan in Fujian when Xi worked there.[58] But both Deng Pufang and Yu Zhengsheng are eight to nine years older than Xi Jinping, so when Xi was enrolled at the Bayi School, Yu Zhengsheng had already been transferred to Beijing No. 4 School. Xi and Yu apparently did not form their friendship through overlapping attendance at the Bayi School, but their family ties and similar upper-crust upbringings likely helped strengthen their personal and political bonds.

A main reason for the high enrollment of princelings in these middle schools and high schools in Beijing is that after the Communist victory in 1949, many high-ranking military officers who had recently moved to the capital (including both those who remained in the military and those who had just been transferred to the civilian leadership) settled in the so-called military residential "big yards" (军队大院, *jundui dayuan*), or "cadre compounds" (干部大院, *ganbu dayuan*). These were sprawling housing areas in the capital for PLA officers and civilian leaders during the early decades of the PRC.[59]

All PLA general departments and service headquarters, as well as all ministries, had their own "big yards," which varied in size. Smaller ones had several dozen families, and larger ones operated very much like self-sufficient communities, with a kindergarten, school, clinics, and so on. The "big yards" became an important venue for socializing among princelings in the late 1950s and early 1960s, including the early period of the Red Guard movement. A half-century later, these "big yards" had become a crucial source of political networking among senior military and civilian leaders.

Of course, not all of Xi's close friends from his formative years have become officials. For example, Nie Weiping, China's most famous professional Go player (who won the inaugural World Amateur Go Championship in 1979) was one of Xi's best childhood friends. Nie's father was an accomplished engineer who served as party secretary of China's Association of Science and as director of the Bureau of Intelligence of the State Science and Technology Commission. Xi Jinping and Nie Weiping have maintained their friendship and close contact since then, even when Xi worked in Fujian,

Zhejiang, and Shanghai.[60] It was reported that when Xi was party secretary of Zhejiang, he asked rich entrepreneurs in the province to fund Nie's Go team.[61] However, Nie has never served in a position in the government and apparently has no political ambitions.

Perhaps because Xi Jinping's father, Xi Zhongxun, had been purged by Mao before the Cultural Revolution, Xi was not an active member of the Red Guard movement. This differentiates him from some radical Red Guards with princeling backgrounds, such as Kong Dan and Bo Xilai, who held strong views about the "theory of bloodline" (血统论, *xuetonglun*), asserting that one's political attitude and moral character are determined by family background or genetic origin.[62] Nevertheless, most of Xi's childhood friends tended to be fellow princelings. In addition to the aforementioned Nie Weiping, another of Xi's close friends at the Bayi School was Liu Weiping.[63] When the Bayi School was dismantled during the Cultural Revolution, both Xi and Liu were transferred to Beijing No. 25 School. Liu Weiping's father, Liu Zhen, was a PLA general and served as vice-commander of the PLA Air Force. Like Xi's father, Liu Zhen was also purged when the Cultural Revolution began. Liu Weiping currently serves as deputy chief-of-staff of the CMC Logistics Support Department with the rank of major general.

Three leaders—Liu He, Liu Yuan, and Chen Xi—with whom Xi established close ties during his formative and school years, are particularly noteworthy. All three have apparently been quite influential in helping Xi devise economic, political, and security policies.

Liu He: A Liberal Financial Technocrat

Like that of many other CCP leaders, the friendship between Xi Jinping and his chief economic adviser, Liu He, began during their childhood years. Liu was born in Beijing in 1952, a year earlier than Xi. According to one source, Liu He's father was a vice-governor-level leader in Shaanxi and may have had family ties with the Xi family.[64] Some foreign and Chinese media have reported that Xi Jinping and Liu He went to the same middle school.[65] In fact, Xi attended the aforementioned Bayi School and Beijing No. 25 School, and Liu went to Beijing No. 101 School in the same district.[66] It is likely that they developed their childhood friendship while growing up together in the same "big yards" or the same neighborhood.

Liu began his career in 1969—the same year that Xi was sent to Yan'an—as a sent-down youth in a primitive rural area in Jilin Province at the age of seventeen. Liu soon joined the PLA, where he served as a soldier for four years (1970–73) in China's elite Thirty-eight Group Army, stationed in Baoding, Hebei Province. He returned to Beijing in 1974 to become a worker, and later a manager, in the Beijing Radio Factory. When China restarted the national examination for college admissions in 1978, Liu passed the exam and enrolled in the Department of Economics at Renmin University, which at that time had the best economics program in the country. He continued his graduate-level studies there and received a master's degree in economic management in 1986.

After briefly teaching at Renmin University, Liu pursued a research career at the Development Research Center of the State Council in 1987 and then continued to work at the State Planning Commission, where he served for a decade, first as deputy director of the Research Office and then as deputy director of the Department of Industrial Policy and Long-term Planning. At the State Planning Commission, Liu worked very closely with Zeng Peiyan, who was then the deputy director of the commission and office director of the Central Financial and Economic Work Leading Group. Zeng later became vice-premier and was appointed to the Politburo. During that early period, Liu spent a few years abroad pursuing advanced degrees. He studied in a master of business administration program at Seton Hall University from 1992 to 1993 and in a master of public administration program (as a Mason fellow) at Harvard University's Kennedy School of Government from 1994 to 1995. Liu He's broad and diverse range of experience in his early career is truly extraordinary, and some Chinese reporters call him the "worker-peasant-soldier plus foreign-educated returnee."[67]

In 1998, along with several other distinguished Chinese economists, including Wu Jinglian (a fellow at the Development Research Center of the State Council and later adviser to Premier Zhu Rongji) and Yi Gang (vice-governor of the People's Bank of China and deputy office director of the Central Financial and Economic Work Leading Group), Liu He founded the Chinese Economists 50 Forum (中国经济 50 人论坛, Zhongguo jingji wushiren luntan).[68] The forum consists of the country's most influential economists and financial technocrats (including the current governor of the People's Bank, Zhou Xiaochuan, and the minister of Finance, Lou Jiwei). The mission of the forum is to provide policy recommendations to the government on major economic issues. Over the past seventeen years, the forum has organized numerous annual conferences, economic policy lecture series, internal roundtable discussions, academic seminars, foreign exchange programs, and policy briefings for the Chinese national leadership.[69] In that regard, Liu has not only helped bridge the divide between academic economists and policymakers but has also contributed to the new function of Chinese think tanks to act as a "revolving door," allowing economists and financial technocrats to play a greater role in the government.

The author of five books and over 200 articles, Liu He covers five broad research areas: the relationship between economic development and the change in industrial structure in China; macroeconomic theories; corporate governance and property rights; the new economy and the information industry; and reforms of Chinese SOEs. In 2013 Liu wrote *A Comparative Study of Two Global Financial Crises*, which later won the prestigious Sun Yefang Book Award in Economics.[70] All of these research areas and academic publications closely relate to Liu's leadership responsibilities. In 1998, for example, he served as director of the National Information Center. Two years later, he was appointed deputy office director of the State Council Information Office, where he introduced innovative and efficient e-government practices and advanced international cooperation.

In 2003 Liu was appointed deputy director of the Office of the CCP Central Financial and Economic Work Leading Group to directly assist top leaders (Jiang Zemin, Hu Jintao, and now Xi Jinping) on economic and financial policies, especially in writing major speeches and resolutions for important party and government gatherings. He has been one of the principal drafters of communiqués for key CCP leadership meetings, including the Third Plenum (2003), the Fifth Plenum (2005), and the Sixth Plenum (2006) of the 16th Central Committee; the full meeting of the 17th National Party Congress (2007); and the Fourth Plenum (2009) and the Fifth Plenum (2010) of the 17th Central Committee.[71] Liu has been deeply involved in drafting five-year plans since the Eighth Five-Year Plan in 1991, when he worked at the State Planning Commission.[72] In addition, Liu has drafted eleven reform initiatives on state industrial policies, five of which were issued by the State Council.[73] During the 2008 global financial crisis, Liu worked closely with Premier Wen Jiabao and became particularly crucial to China's decisionmaking circle by formulating the country's measures to minimize the negative impact of the crisis on the Chinese economy. His proposals led to a quick V-shaped recovery.[74]

Because of the pivotal role that Liu He has played in advising China's top leaders and in designing major economic and financial policies for the country, he has earned the nickname "China's Larry Summers."[75] A soft-spoken and characteristically thoughtful man who keeps a low profile, Liu has earned great respect from academic and political elites in both China and abroad. His economic outlook is remarkably liberal. When he was deputy director and party secretary of the Development Research Center of the State Council from 2011 to 2013, Liu was intimately involved in the collaboration between the World Bank and the Development Research Center to produce the joint report *China 2030: Building a Modern, Harmonious, and Creative Society*. This important report forcefully argues that in order to achieve a structural change in the Chinese economy that would allow for sustainable growth, China must accelerate far-reaching SOE reforms.[76] On many recent occasions, Liu He has also argued that, at a time when many countries in the world have experienced economic slowdowns, responsible governments should particularly avoid pursuing populist (民粹主义, *mincui zhuyi*) or ultranationalist socioeconomic policies.[77]

Not surprisingly, when Xi Jinping became the general secretary of the party, he promoted Liu He to an even more important position. At the 2012 National Party Congress, Liu, for the first time, became a member of the Central Committee; during the following year, at the National People's Congress, he was appointed vice-minister of the National Development and Reform Commission and was promoted to serve as office director of the Central Financial and Economic Work Leading Group.

Liu He now serves as the chief economic adviser to President Xi. It has been widely noted both in China and abroad that Liu served as a chief drafter of the communiqué at the Third Plenum of the 18th National Party Congress, which claimed to be "version 2.0" of China's market development. The Chinese media often compares this meeting to the Third Plenum of the 11th National Party Congress in 1978, during which Deng Xiaoping announced China's decision to "reform and open up." The overall objective of Xi's new economic policy, as evident from the Third Plenum communiqué, is to make the private sector the "decisive driver" of the Chinese economy. Liu He has been a great asset for Xi, as Liu is both an accomplished financial expert and an effective communicator in both Chinese and English. Liu He is also noted for his humble personality. He often tells the media both in China and abroad that it is not appropriate to emphasize any one individual's input into China's economic policy, especially to give him too much credit. Liu said that "China's economic policy in the reform era has been made by a collective leadership, and an individual's role in that process is always limited."[78]

Liu Yuan: A Conservative Military Hawk

Xi's inner circle consists of leaders with different personalities, varied professional expertise, and contrasting ideological stances. It includes liberal economists like Liu He, but also conservative military hawks like Liu Yuan, who served as political commissar of the PLA General Logistics Department before his retirement in the end of 2015. Liu Yuan was born in Beijing in 1951, making him two years older than Xi. Liu attended No. 2 Experimental Elementary School in Beijing and went on to attend the capital's famous No. 4 School. It is unclear when Xi and Liu Yuan first met, but both had very similar experiences in their formative years and early careers. Liu's father, Liu Shaoqi, was the first chairman of the National People's Congress and the second president of the PRC before he was purged during the Cultural Revolution. Xi and Liu were adolescents when their veteran revolutionary fathers were persecuted by Mao, and both families were forced to move out of their prestigious residences in Zhongnanhai. As teenagers, both were sent to destitute rural areas where they worked as farmers for seven years. In Liu's case, he was a sent-down youth in Shanying County, Shanxi Province, from 1968 to 1975. Liu's father was physically and mentally tortured and died after not receiving appropriate medical treatment in 1969. Meanwhile, his mother was held continuously in a maximum-security prison.

Both Xi Zhongxun and Liu Shaoqi were rehabilitated a few years after the end of the Cultural Revolution. In an interview with a Chinese magazine in 2000, Xi Jinping emphasized the close parallels between himself and Liu Yuan, particularly in their early lives and work experiences. According to Xi, at that time only two young leaders with veteran communist family backgrounds decided to leave their office jobs in Beijing to work in grassroots and county-level leadership positions elsewhere: Xi went to Hebei, and Liu worked in Henan.[79] Liu advanced his political career by serving at various levels of leadership in Henan Province: first as deputy head of Qiliying People's Commune (1982–83), then as deputy county head (1983–84) and county head (1984–85) of Xinxiang County, followed by vice-mayor of Zhengzhou City (1985–88) and vice-governor of Henan Province (1988–92).

While Xi shifted from serving in the PLA (as a *mishu* to the minister of Defense) to working in the civilian leadership, Liu Yuan did just the opposite. Liu did not join the People's Armed Police (PAP) until 1992, when he was already forty-one. He first served as second political commissar of the PAP Hydropower Troops. In 1998 Liu was appointed deputy political commissar of the PAP. Five years later, in 2003, at the age of fifty-two, he was transferred to the PLA, where he served as deputy political commissar of the General Logistics Department with the rank of lieutenant general. He then served as political commissar of the PLA Military Academy of Sciences from 2005 to 2010 and was promoted to the rank of general in 2009. In 2010 Liu was appointed political commissar of the PLA General Logistics Department. In a military culture that values seniority, professionalism, and step-by-step promotion, Liu Yuan is understandably unpopular among senior officers, who are skeptical of his "helicopter-like" rise in the military leadership and his "military career" advancement in the PAP (rather than through the more professional PLA). Perhaps more important, Liu Yuan's strong anticorruption initiatives in the PLA leadership have offended many of his peers.

It was Liu Yuan who launched the corruption investigation of Lieutenant General Gu Junshan, which eventually led to the fall of Xu Caihou and Guo Boxiong—the two highest-ranking military officers to be charged with corruption in PRC history.[80] Overseas Chinese media reported that in an enlarged meeting of the CMC held December 25–28, 2011, Liu Yuan not only presented a photo of Gu Junshan's luxurious hometown villa, known as the General's Manor House (将军府, *jiangjunfu*), but also criticized Xu and Guo for "selling" military ranks and officer positions.[81]

Liu Yuan might have gained popularity among the general public and junior officers in the PLA by expressing strong nationalistic sentiments. Liu is known for his politically conservative and chauvinistic views, in addition to his hawkish foreign policy stance. John Garnaut, an Australian journalist who lived in China for many years, observed that from Liu Yuan's perspective, "war is a natural extension of economics and politics" and that Liu "claims . . . 'man cannot survive without killing.'" For Liu Yuan, "history is written by blood and slaughter," and the nation-state is "a power machine made of violence."[82]

In his foreword to the controversial book *Transform Our Cultural Perspective of History,* by Zhang Musheng (a conservative public intellectual who also has a princeling background), Liu Yuan endorses the notion of the zero-sum game in world history and rejects the concept of universal values.[83] Liu states that the term "motherland" should be "fatherland" because the former overlooks the core notion of the Chinese word "forefather" (祖, *zu*), which emphasizes "male worship."[84] He also bluntly argues that the greatness and unity (大一统, *dayitong*) of China lies in the fact that China's neighbors to the east, west, north, and south have all continually exerted pressures on "the fatherland."[85] Liu Yuan took five senior officers to attend Zhang Musheng's book launch event in April 2011, including Major General Luo Yuan (deputy director of the Department of World Military Research of the PLA Academy of Military Sciences), Major General Zhu Chenghu (dean of the National Defense College of the PLA National Defense University), and Major General Qiao Liang (coauthor of the famous book *Unrestricted Warfare* and professor at the Air Force Command College), all of whom are considered to be military hawks.

Liu's vision for domestic development, instead of moving toward liberal democracy, civil society, and rule of law, calls for a "Socialist New Democracy" (新民主主义, *xinminzhu zhuyi*), a concept that was initiated by Liu's father (and Mao) in the early years of Communist China.[86] Zhang Musheng is famous for his outspoken support of Bo Xilai's "Sing the Red Songs and Strike the Black Mafia" campaign in Chongqing, before Bo's dramatic fall. Zhang explicitly expressed hope that Bo's "Chongqing model" would pave the way for a new round of experimentation in Socialist New Democracy. What Liu Yuan and Zhang Musheng considered to be the "Chongqing model" is similar to the Socialist New Democracy movement of the early 1950s in three main characteristics: rural land reforms that aim to please peasants; an urban socialist welfare economy with a strong presence of SOEs that claim to protect the interests of workers; and a moral and authoritarian government that takes a strong stance against corruption.[87]

In the two years leading up to the 18th National Party Congress, Zhang Musheng also launched a remarkably explicit criticism of the Hu-Wen administration. He claimed that "our country is now led by some weak, incompetent, inactive, and antiblood leaders who will drive China into a serious political and social crisis. The incoming team of new leaders will not let this trend continue."[88] Zhang even stated that Liu Yuan would be a highly competent leader with great "ideals and ambition."[89] While Liu's support for Zhang Musheng is unambiguous, it is not clear how Xi Jinping views Zhang's ideological and policy stances on both domestic and international issues. A review of the first few years of Xi's leadership, however, seems to suggest that Xi has learned some important lessons from the preceding Hu-Wen administration. Xi has been bold, ambitious, proactive, and very nationalistic, as evident in his aggressive anticorruption campaign, in his glorification of the Mao era, and in his assertiveness in foreign policy, especially in dealing with ongoing tensions in the East and South China Seas.

It should be noted that Bo Xilai, Liu Yuan, and Zhang Musheng are all prominent princelings who grew up in the "big yards" of Beijing. Despite the suffering of their veteran communist fathers during the Cultural Revolution, their mind-sets, collective memories, ideologies, worldviews, and political behavior were all shaped by the Maoist indoctrination and Red Guard movement during their formative years.[90] In his widely circulated essay on the characteristics of the fifth generation of Chinese leaders, Qian Liqun, a distinguished professor of Chinese literature at Peking University, observes that the fifth generation consists mainly of former Red Guards and sent-down youths.[91] Compared with the preceding cohort, leaders of this new generation, according to Qian, "are more courageous, more active, and have a better understanding of the lives and concerns of grassroots people."[92] But what worries Professor Qian the most is the combination of "imperial arrogance" and "rogue habits" among many new leaders who are princelings and who were also Red Guards in Beijing. Many of those former Red Guards now serve in the national military leadership.

The brutality and violence of the Cultural Revolution, especially the torture and suffering inflicted on their privileged and powerful families, taught Bo Xilai and Liu Yuan realpolitik in a drastic and direct manner: "In order to achieve the goal, you can do anything."[93] This may help explain why these princelings (and Mao's victims during the Cultural Revolution) have ironically embraced Maoism at certain times in their political discourse. Qian presciently warned that the need to prevent both the rise of Chinese militarism in the Asia-Pacific region and military intervention in China's domestic politics would be major challenges for Xi.[94]

The strong bond between Xi Jinping and Liu Yuan was highlighted in overseas Chinese sources and social media in the PRC on three recent occasions.

First, according to Hu Shiying, the son of former Politburo member Hu Qiaomu, as early as 1979, a group of princelings formed a study group in Beijing that met several times a month. Participants included Xi Jinping, Wang Qishan, Liu Yuan, Liu Xiaojiang, Chen Yuan, Fu Yang (son of former National People's Congress chairman Peng Zhen), and the Bo brothers.[95] This study group lasted for more than a year.

Second, in 2006, when Xi Jinping, then the party secretary of Zhejiang Province, visited Beijing, princelings came together for a dinner party reunion at the Zhejiang Mansion in the capital. A photo that has been widely circulated online since the spring of 2012 (released by Hu Shiying) shows that dinner attendees included Xi Jinping, Peng Liyuan (Xi's wife), Wang Qishan, Yao Mingshan (Wang's wife), Liu Yuan, Zhang Musheng, Liu Xiaojiang, Chen Yuan, Fu Yang, Yang Li (daughter of former PRC president Yang Shangkun), Hu Shiying, Hu Muying (Hu Shiying's sister), Song Binbin (daughter of veteran Communist leader Song Renqiong), Qin Xiao, Kong Dan, and Bo Xicheng (Bo Xilai's brother).[96]

Third, in early September 2012, two months before he officially became the president of the PRC, Xi Jinping was reported to have a back injury and was hospitalized in the PLA 301 Hospital. Liu Yuan, as political commissar of the PLA General Logistics Department, was in charge of the medical treatment for China's heir apparent. This reflects the trust and longtime friendship between these two princelings. It was widely believed that Xi had once intended to promote Liu Yuan to the powerful CMC, but some top military leaders at the time, such as Xu Caihou, apparently blocked the proposal.

Many analysts in both China and abroad believed that Liu would win a seat or even a vice-chairmanship on the CMC in recognition of his immense contribution to Xi's antigraft campaign in the military. But instead of obtaining a pivotal position of power, he retired from the PLA in the early stages of military reform and, in February 2016, was appointed vice-chairman of the Financial and Economic Affairs Committee of the National People's Congress, a ceremonial—not high-ranking—post that offers him far less power.

Liu Yuan's early retirement shows that Xi is keenly aware that Liu Yuan could be a liability rather than an asset should Xi continue to rely heavily on such a politically ambitious general. Some liberal intellectuals in China have long considered Liu Yuan a "Bo Xilai-like figure in the military," partly because of Liu's princeling background and his demagogic manipulation of public opinion, but mainly because of his long-standing position as a conservative military hawk with ultranationalistic appeal.[97] The PLA establishment has never had much respect for Liu, primarily because of Liu's thin résumé as a professional soldier. Additionally, Liu has made too many enemies in the PLA leadership. According to an unverified report, in two CMC meetings in the fall of 2015, executive vice-chairman of the CMC Fan

Changlong voted against the proposal to appoint Liu Yuan as secretary of the PLA Discipline Inspection Commission and as a new member of the CMC.[98] It looks as though Xi's effort to promote Liu Yuan failed due to strong opposition in the military establishment. But one could also reasonably argue that, for the reasons discussed above, Xi simply did not have any incentive to promote Liu.

The latter interpretation seems to accord with Liu's own statement that he would "support the resolution of the Central Military Commission, and resolutely obey President Xi's arrangements."[99] According to the overseas Chinese media, Xi Jinping and vice-chairman of the CMC Xu Qiliang hosted a banquet for Liu Yuan at the time of his retirement, calling Liu a man of "noble character and unquestionable integrity" (高风亮节, *gaofeng liangjie*), the same expression that Xi used when Hu Jintao stepped down as chairman of the CMC in the fall of 2012.[100] Beyond the aforementioned political concerns that could explain Liu's premature retirement, other considerations may have factored in to Xi's decision. One may argue that Xi's worldview and policy preferences—especially his economic reform agenda and foreign policy priorities—differ profoundly from Liu's.

Chen Xi: Xi's Roommate at Tsinghua and a Chief Personnel Officer

Xi Jinping has helped advance the careers of many leaders in his inner circle, but perhaps no one has received more direct assistance from Xi than Chen Xi, the current executive deputy director of the CCP's powerful Central Organization Department. Xi Jinping and Chen Xi were classmates and roommates at Tsinghua University from 1975 to 1979, when they were both worker-peasant-soldier students in the Department of Chemical Engineering. It has been reported that Xi greatly values the friendships that he developed during his years at Tsinghua.[101] Throughout his tenure as a top provincial leader in Fujian and Zhejiang, Xi regularly got together with his Tsinghua schoolmates, in Beijing and elsewhere.[102] Even when Xi became China's heir apparent after 2007, he and his wife still attended class reunions in Beijing.[103]

In college both Xi and Chen were sports fans, and they were also both interested in politics and world affairs. They became close friends almost immediately after they met at Tsinghua. Chen not only excelled academically but also won the 100-meter track championship at the Beijing College Athletics Games. On Xi's recommendation, Chen Xi joined the CCP at Tsinghua in November 1978, a few months before graduation.[104]

Soon after Xi became a member of the PSC in 2007, he promoted Chen to vice-minister and deputy party secretary of education. It was believed that this appointment would help Chen eventually obtain the post of minister of

Education, but that did not happen; the promotion went to Yuan Guiren, a protégé of Premier Wen Jiabao, in October 2009.[105] In September 2010 Chen was transferred to Liaoning Province, where he served as deputy party secretary, a role in an important provincial-level administration that could broaden Chen's leadership profile. Seven months later, Chen returned to Beijing and took the post of party secretary of the China Association for Science, a position equivalent to the rank of minister that usually ensures a seat in the Central Committee of the CCP. Indeed, Chen obtained full membership at the 18th National Party Congress. Soon after Xi became the top leader of the CCP, Chen was made executive deputy director of the COD, essentially becoming one of Xi's chief personnel officers.

Chen Xi was born in Putian County, Fujian Province, in September 1953, making him three months younger than Xi. At the age of seventeen, he began his career as a factory worker in a university-run mechanical plant in his hometown of Fuzhou City. After graduating from Tsinghua in 1979, he returned home to teach at Fuzhou University for a few months and then in the fall of 1979 enrolled again in the Department of Chemical Engineering at Tsinghua University for graduate-level studies. After receiving his master's degree, Chen pursued a political career as a Youth League official, serving consecutively as director of the Department of Sports and Military Training, deputy secretary and then secretary of the Youth League Committee of Tsinghua University, and standing committee member of the party committee of Tsinghua University responsible for student affairs (1982–90). In December 1990 Chen went abroad to study chemical engineering at Stanford University as a visiting scholar for fourteen months. After he returned to Tsinghua in 1992, he served as deputy party secretary of the Department of Chemical Engineering; afterward, he held the positions of deputy party secretary, executive deputy party secretary, and then party secretary of the Tsinghua Party Committee in 2008.

Throughout these years, Chen Xi and Xi Jinping maintained close personal ties. When Xi served as a municipal and provincial leader in Chen's hometown of Fuzhou from 1990 to 2002, Chen Xi always spent a great deal of time with Xi Jinping when visiting his parents at home. When Xi studied on a part-time basis for his doctoral degree in Marxism and Law at Tsinghua University from 1998 to 2002, Chen Xi was a top administrator at the university. It was also reported that when Xi was party secretary of Zhejiang Province, he helped Chen Xi establish the Yangtze Delta Region Institute of Tsinghua University in Zhejiang Province.[106]

Just as Chen Xi's immediate boss, Zhao Leji, has recently appointed a number of the members of the Shaanxi Gang to key positions, Chen Xi, as executive deputy director of the COD, has promoted a few of his close associates at Tsinghua to important leadership posts. The most notable examples are Chen Jining, former president of Tsinghua University, who was appointed minister of Environmental Protection in January 2015, and Hu Heping, former party secretary of Tsinghua University, who was first appointed director of the Organization Department of the Zhejiang Provincial Party Committee, then deputy party secretary of Shaanxi Province in April 2015, and then governor of Shaanxi in April 2016.[107] It is expected that the current party secretary of Tsinghua, Chen Xu (b. 1963), will also be appointed to a key post in the national leadership in the next year or so. Chen will likely emerge as one of the most prominent woman leaders in the country.

It is also interesting to note that in 2015 several university presidents (for example, Chen Jining) were appointed ministerial leaders. They include vice-minister of Industry and Information Technology Huai Jinpeng (former president of Beijing University of Aeronautics and Astronautics and a member of the Chinese Academy of Sciences), vice-minister of Science and Technology Hou Jianguo (former president of the University of Science and Technology of China and a member of the Chinese Academy of Sciences), and deputy chief-of-staff of the Beijing Municipal Party Committee Guo Guangsheng (former president of Beijing Industry University). Huai was born in 1962, Hou was born in 1959, and Guo was born in 1963. They all have experience studying overseas and developed strong ties with Chen Xi when they previously worked in universities in Beijing. According to some Chinese journalists, their recent appointments to senior government positions not only reflect the age-old Confucian view that the "person who excels in study can follow an official career" but also herald a new normal of elite recruitment from distinguished scholars and university administrators.[108] But perhaps more important, these new appointments show that, like the previous Jiang Zemin and Hu Jintao administrations, the powerful COD, now led by Xi's confidants Zhao Leji and Chen Xi, has forcefully promoted members of Xi's political networks to important positions.

Xi's Service in the People's Liberation Army

One of Xi Jinping's most important career experiences was his tenure as a *mishu* for the minister of Defense Geng Biao. Xi served in this post from 1979 to 1982, when Xi was in his late twenties and had just finished his studies at Tsinghua University as a worker-peasant-solider student. Geng Biao, who played an important role in both domestic and foreign policies in the early years of the Deng era, was Xi Zhongxun's "comrade-in-arms" during the Anti-Japanese War in the Shaanxi-Gansu-Ningxia border region. According to one source, Xi Jinping actually often stayed in Geng Biao's house from 1979 to 1982.[109] The house was located alongside the Forbidden City, outside of Zhongnanhai, and was close to Deng Xiaoping's personal residence. Living under the same roof, Xi Jinping developed a very close relationship with Geng's family and became a good friend of Geng's son, Geng Zhiyuan (George Geng), who is now a businessman. Even after Xi became a PSC member in 2007, Xi and his wife Peng Liyuan often visited the Geng family during the Spring Festival.[110]

This job as *mishu* established Xi's connection to the military, which is a key leadership credential. It is unclear, however, what types of networks Xi built within the PLA during these years. But Xi has told the Chinese media that serving as a *mishu* for the minister of Defense allowed him to attend many important meetings and expanded his knowledge of military, local, and foreign affairs.[111] Minister Geng had three *mishu* at that time, and Xi was the youngest. Because Minister Geng was also the Politburo member responsible for affairs regarding Taiwan, Hong Kong, and Macao, Xi was heavily involved in work related to those territories.[112]

During these three years, Xi developed a close working relationship with Liu Xiaojiang, the son-in-law of Hu Yaobang and former political commissar of the PLA Navy. From 1980 to 1983 Liu Xiaojiang worked as a *mishu* for Admiral Liu Huaqing, then as deputy chief-of-staff of the PLA, and later as vice-chairman of the CMC. Xi and Liu both worked at the headquarters of China's military leadership. Xi's and Liu's families also have strong ties. Liu Xiaojiang's father and father-in-law both were close friends of Xi Zhongxun. Liu's father, Liu Haibin, a veteran Communist Party leader who participated in the Long March, served as director of the Logistics Department in the Northwest Military Region in 1949 under Xi Zhongxun, who was the political commissar of the region at the time. After Xi Zhongxun moved to Beijing in the early 1950s, Liu Haibing continued to work in Xi'an for many more years.

Liu Xiaojiang was also born in Shaanxi. His father-in-law, Hu Yaobang, former general secretary of the CCP, previously worked as first secretary of Shaanxi Province. When Hu was the director of the CCP's COD in 1977, he made it a top priority to revoke the false charges made against Xi Zhongxun during the Cultural Revolution and then appointed him provincial party secretary in Guangdong Province.[113] A few years later, both men worked together in the Secretariat of the CCP Central Committee. When Hu Yaobang was purged by Deng in 1987 because of his liberal approach to student demonstrations, Xi Zhongxun refused to criticize his longtime friend.[114]

The ties between Liu Xiaojiang and Xi Jinping have not been shaped solely by the friendship between their parents. The two became friends when they were young and were sent-down youth in Shaanxi during the same period.[115] As discussed earlier in the chapter, both participated in a study group in Beijing in their spare time during a later period.

POLITICAL PROTÉGÉS FROM THE PROVINCES

Xi Jinping advanced his career largely through local and provincial administration; he spent twenty-five years (some of the most defining years of his adult life) as an official in county, municipal, and provincial levels of leadership in three important provinces (Hebei, Fujian, and Zhejiang), as well as China's most cosmopolitan city, Shanghai. To top it off, Xi also has solid political ties to Shaanxi Province. Xi's comprehensive work experience in various parts of the country—the northwest, north, southeast, and east—and the close personal contacts he developed in these provinces over the years have evidently helped him build a broad, impressive power base.

Table 8-3 provides biographical information and the current leadership positions of twenty-six leaders—Xi's protégés—who developed their personal and political associations with Xi at the local and provincial levels of leadership. Among them, twelve are members of the 18th Central Committee (two Politburo members, four full members, and six alternate members). One leader, Yang Xiaodu, serves on the CCDI as one of the eight deputy secretaries. They were all appointed to their current positions after 2012, when Xi became party boss. Ten leaders obtained their current leadership posts in 2014 and the other eight were appointed between 2015 and 2016, reflecting the ongoing prevalence of promoting Xi's protégés. It is worthwhile to trace how Xi and these protégés developed personal and political ties through local and provincial leadership.

The Hebei Connection

In March 1982, at the age of twenty-nine, Xi Jinping left the position of *mishu* at the Ministry of Defense and arrived in Zhengding County, Shijiazhuang Prefecture, in Hebei Province, where he served as deputy party secretary of the county. This career move was unusual for princelings like Xi at that time, because most were more interested in working in the offices of the national leadership in Beijing or in major SOEs. Today, however, serving as a county head has become a more popular choice for the new generation of princelings. For example, Deng Xiaoping's grandson Deng Zhuodi, who was born in the United States and is a graduate of Duke University's law school, was made deputy head of Pingguo County in Guangxi's Baise Prefecture in 2013, at the age of twenty-eight.[116] In March 2016, he was promoted to deputy party secretary of Pingguo County. Another example is Hu Jintao's son Hu Haifeng, a Tsinghua University graduate and former general manager of Nuctech (a security scanner supplier), who became deputy mayor of the prefecture-level city Jiaxing in Zhejiang Province in 2013.[117] In March 2016, Hu was promoted to deputy party secretary and mayor of

TABLE 8-3. Xi Jinping's Protégés during His Tenure as a Local/Provincial Leader, as of May 2016

Province/ city	Name	Birth year	Birthplace	Previous position in province under Xi Jinping	Current position	Tenure since	Central Committee status
Hebei	Li Zhanshu	1950	Hebei	Colleague of Xi in Hebei (Wuji County Party Secretary)	Director of the General Office of the Central Committee	2012	Politburo member
	Yang Zhenwu	1955	Hebei	*People's Daily* reporter in Hebei who wrote feature stories about Xi	President, *People's Daily*	2014	None
	Zhao Keshi	1947	Hebei	Stationed in Fujian when Xi was a municipal and provincial leader	CMC member, Director of CMC Equipment Development Department	2012	Full member
Fujian	Cai Yingting	1954	Fujian	Stationed in Fujian when Xi was a municipal and provincial leader	President of Academy of Military Science	2016	Full member
	He Lifeng	1955	Guangdong	Deputy Director of the Office of Xiamen Municipal Government, Fuzhou Party Secretary	Deputy Director of the NDRC	2014	Alternate member
	Cai Qi	1955	Fujian	Deputy Director of the office of the Fujian Provincial Party Committee and Secretary of Shanming City	Deputy Director of the Office of the National Security Committee	2014	None
	Huang Kunming	1956	Fujian	Mayor of Longyan City	Executive Deputy Director of the CCP Propaganda Department	2014	Alternate member

	Name	Year	Origin	Connection	Current Position	Year	Membership
	Song Tao	1955	Jiangsu	Vice-President of Fujian International Trust and Investment Co. when Xi was in charge of this area in Fujian	Director of the International Liaison Department of the CCP Central Committee	2015	None
	Wang Xiaohong	1957	Fujian	Deputy Director of the Public Security Bureau of Fuzhou City when Xi was Party Secretary of the city	Vice-Mayor and Director of Public Security in Beijing	2015	None
	Wang Ning	1955	Jiangsu	Stationed in Zhejiang	Commander of the People's Armed Police	2014	Alternate member
	Lei Chunmei	1959	Fujian	Vice-Mayor of Ningde, Fujian, when Xi was Party Secretary of Ningde	Director of the United Front Work Deartment, Fujian Province	2012	Alternate member
Zhejiang	Chen Min'er	1960	Zhejiang	Director of the Propaganda Department and Vice-Governor	Guizhou Party Secretary	2015	Full member
	Li Qiang	1959	Zhejiang	Secretary-General of the Zhejiang Provincial Party Committee	Zhejiang Governor	2013	Alternate member
	Xia Baolong	1952	Tianjin	Deputy Party Secretary	Zhejiang Party Secretary	2012	Full member
	Zhong Shan	1955	Zhejiang	Zhejiang Vice-Governor	Trade Negotiator, Vice-Minister, Deputy Party Secretary of Commerce	2014	None
	Ying Yong	1957	Zhejiang	Deputy Secretary of Provincial Discipline Inspection Commission	Shanghai Deputy Party Secretary	2014	None

(continued)

TABLE 8-3. (*continued*)

Province/city	Name	Birth year	Birthplace	Previous position in province under Xi Jinping	Current position	Tenure since	Central Committee status
Zhejiang	Lou Yangsheng	1959	Zhejiang	Party Secretary of Lishui City	Shanxi Deputy Party Secretary	2014	None
	Zhong Shaojun	1968	Zhejiang	*Mishu* to Xi; Deputy Director of the Zhejiang CCP Provincial Committee and Deputy Director of the Shanghai CCP Municipal Committee	Deputy Director, President Xi's Office	2013	None
	Shu Guozeng	1956	Zhejiang	*Mishu* (Deputy Office Director) to Xi	Deputy Director, Office of the Central Financial Leading Group	2014	None
	Meng Qingfeng	1957	Shandong	Vice-Director of the Department of Public Security	Vice-Minister of Public Security	2015	None
	Shen Haixiong	1967	Zhejiang	Xinhua reporter based in Zhejiang	Director of Propaganda of the Department of the Guangdong Party Committee	2015	None

Shanghai	Han Zheng	1954	Shanghai	Secretary-General of the Shanghai Municipal Party Committee	Shanghai Party Secretary	2012	Politburo member
	Ding Xuexiang	1962	Jiangsu	Secretary of Discipline Inspection Commission of the Shanghai Municipal Party Committee	Deputy Director of the General Office of the Central Committee	2013	Alternate member
	Yang Xiaodu	1953	Shanghai	Director of the Agriculture Committee of the Shanghai Municipal Government	Deputy Secretary of CCDI	2014	CCDI member
	Xu Lin	1963	Shanghai	Director of the Office of Financial Services in the Shanghai Municipal Government	Executive Deputy Director of the State Internet Information Office	2015	None
	Fang Xinghai	1964	Shanghai		Vice-Chairman of the CSRC	2015	None

Note and Source: CMC = Central Military Commission; NDRC = National Development and Reform Commission; CCP = Chinese Communist Party; CCDI = Central Commission for Discipline Inspection; CSRC = China Securities Regulatory Commission. Data from the author's database.

Jiaxing. Both Deng Zhuodi and Hu Haifeng might have been inspired by Xi's career move three decades earlier.

Xi recently stated that his three years as a county leader were so important to him that he considers Zhengding County his second home (第二故乡, di'er guxiang).[118] He explained that his leadership experience in Zhengding taught him "what politics means."[119] In his words, "Politics is to mobilize all possible positive forces and to unite all people who can be united."[120] While in Zhengding, as a young princeling surrounded by colleagues who joined the CCP in the late 1930s, Xi made great effort to demonstrate respect and humility toward his "older comrades." Xi seemed to benefit greatly from his cultivation of heavyweight veteran leaders. Xi's good working relationship with "old comrades" was reported in the party organ newspapers in Shijiazhuang and Beijing in 1984 and 1985, respectively, and served to accelerate his promotion.[121]

The most important "Hebei connection" for Xi is his friendship with Li Zhanshu, as discussed earlier in the chapter. In 2011, a year before the political succession at the 18th National Party Congress, Xi spent four days traveling in Guizhou, where Li served as provincial party secretary. Li escorted Xi throughout the entire visit, and some analysts speculated that they discussed many important issues regarding Xi's upcoming succession to the top leadership post.[122] It might have been surprising to many that in September 2012, two months before the Congress, Li Zhanshu was appointed director of the very important General Office of the CCP Central Committee, replacing Hu Jintao's confidant Ling Jihua. However, due to their strong personal ties and the trust that Xi and Li cultivated in Zhengding three decades earlier, this appointment was an ideal choice for Xi.

Xi's years in Zhengding also helped him develop his leadership style and tactics—including the aggressive promotion of his friends and the use of the media to enhance his public image—and he has continued this style as a top national leader. In 1982, soon after he arrived in Zhengding, Xi appointed a new friend, a local writer named Jia Dashan, to be chief of the Culture Bureau of Zhengding County, even though Jia was not a member of the CCP.[123] More remarkably, Xi decided that the Culture Bureau would not establish a CCP branch in order to make sure that Jia could effectively run it. Jia later served as vice-chairman of the Zhengding People's Political Consultative Conference and vice-chairman of the Hebei Provincial Writers Association. He died of cancer in 1997, and Xi and his wife visited Jia a few times during his final days. Xi also wrote an article commemorating Jia, and their friendship has been widely reported in the Chinese media.[124]

Yang Zhenwu, the newly appointed president of People's Daily, the official newspaper of the CCP, is another important protégé of Xi from his Zhengding years. Yang was a People's Daily reporter stationed in Hebei Province and first met Xi in Zhengding in the early 1980s. It was reported that Yang wrote some feature stories showing Xi to be a highly effective local leader.[125] Yang's career promotions seemed to parallel Xi's own consolidation of power. After Xi became a PSC member in 2007, Yang was appointed standing committee member and director of the Propaganda Department of the Shanghai Municipal Party Committee. In April 2013 he was promoted to editor-in-chief of the *People's Daily* and, one year later, he was made president of the newspaper, becoming Xi's point man on propaganda and media, especially in domestic affairs.

The Fujian Connection

Due to its proximity to Taiwan, Fujian Province has always played an important role in national security and military affairs. With his previous experience as a *mishu* to the minister of Defense, Xi Jinping was understandably very much interested in military developments in the regions he served. In fact, during his tenure in Fujian, Xi concurrently took a number of military positions (for example, director of the National Defense Mobilization Committee of Fujian Province from 1999 to 2002) while serving primarily as a civilian leader. Through his work in these military outfits, Xi cultivated important relationships with officers who were stationed in the province.

Two prominent military figures with whom Xi built strong personal ties in Fujian were Zhao Keshi and Cai Yingting. General Zhao currently serves as a member of the CMC and director of the CMC Logistics Support Department and General Cai is president of the PLA Academy of Military Sciences. Both of them are now among the highest-ranking officers in the PLA. Zhao and Cai both served in the Thirty-first Group Army for many years, the headquarters of which is located in Tongan County, near Xiamen City, where Xi Jinping held office as vice-mayor from 1985 to 1988. Both primarily advanced their military careers in the Nanjing Military Region, in which each later served as deputy chief-of-staff, chief-of-staff, and then commander. Fujian, Zhejiang, and Shanghai—places where Xi served as a top leader for over twenty-two years—all fall within the Nanjing Military Region. Zhao and Cai kept in close contact with Xi for many years before they moved to Beijing.

Cai Yingting was born in Jinjiang County, Fujian, in 1954 and joined the PLA in 1970 at the age of sixteen. Cai's family background is unclear, but the fact that he served as a *mishu* to CMC vice-chairman Zhang Wannian suggests that he may be a princeling. It was reported in overseas media that Cai formed a close relationship with Xi in Fujian, not only during the time of his service in the province, but also when Cai escorted Zhang Wannian on a visit.[126] According to some overseas analysts, Cai was the first military officer that Xi promoted after he became chairman of the CMC in 2012.[127] What happened to Cai Yingting during the recent military reform is quite surprising. Instead of receiving a promotion or remaining as commander of the Eastern Theater of Operations, Cai was appointed president of the PLA Academy of Military Sciences. Analysts believe that Cai has been marginalized. He may still have a chance for a seat in the CMC if his current position is just transitional. But, at present, Cai is no longer considered a top contender for the next CMC. A rumor circulating in the PLA establishment is that Cai's daughter has married an American and, thus, CCP regulations prohibit him from being considered for a top military post.

Both General Song Puxuan (b. 1954, commander of the Northern Theater of Operations) and General Wang Jiaocheng (b. 1952, commander of the Southern Theater of Operations) served as deputy commanders of the Nanjing Military Region under Commander Cai Yingting. Several other current heavyweight military leaders advanced their careers from the Nanjing Military Region. They include deputy director of the CMC Joint Staff Department Qi Jianguo (b. 1952), deputy director of the CMC Joint Staff Department Yi Xiaoguang (b. 1958), political commissar of the navy Miao Hua (b. 1955), commander of the PAP Wang Ning (b. 1955), deputy director of the CMC Political Work Department Wu Changde (b. 1952), political commissar of the Northern Theater of Operations Chu Yimin (b. 1953), political commissar of the Southern Theater of Operations Wei Liang (b. 1953), political commissar of the Western Theater of Operations Zhu Fuxi (b. 1955), deputy political commissar of Northern Theater of Operations Wang Jian (b.1955), and commander of the Central Theater of Operations Han Weiguo (b. 1956). Among the forty-four highest-ranking officers in China's seven military regions prior to the structural change to the five theaters of operations, fourteen (31.8 percent) advanced their careers primarily from the Nanjing Military Region.[128]

Several of them were from the Thirty-first Group Army, which some Chinese analysts now call Xi's "royal army" (近卫军, jinweijun).[129] This group of Xi's military confidants who served as top officers of the Thirty-first Group Army includes the aforementioned Zhao Keshi, Cai Yingting, Miao Hua, Wang Ning, and Wang Jian. In 2015 alone, several military leaders who had served in the Thirty-first Group Army received major promotions. Former vice-commander of the Thirty-first Group Army Zhang Mingcai was promoted to commander of the Zhejiang Provincial Military District; former director of the Political Department of the Thirty-first Group Army Zhu Shenglin (b. 1957) was promoted to director of the Political Department of the Eastern Theater of Operations; former commander of the Thirty-first Group Army Ma Chengxiao (b. 1964) was promoted to deputy chief-of-staff of the Eastern Theater of Operations; and former political commissar of the Thirty-first Group Army Jiang Yong (b. 1956) was promoted to political commissar of the Beijing Garrison.

Xi Jinping has apparently sped up the promotion process for his protégés. This was particularly noticeable in the promotion of full generals in 2015. According to the regulations governing PLA officer promotion, any lieutenant general will not be considered for further promotion unless and until he or she has held this rank for at least four years and served as a chief in the full military region–level leadership for two years. Wang Ning and Miao Hua did not meet these two criteria, as Wang Ning held the rank of lieutenant general for only three years and Miao Hua held the rank of lieutenant general for only two years. Miao had served as a chief in the full military region–level leadership for only one year.

While in Fujian, Xi also developed friendships with several civilian leaders. He Lifeng, who was recently appointed vice-minister of the National Development and Reform Commission, first met Xi in Xiamen in 1985, when He was the newly appointed deputy director of the General Office of the municipal government and Xi was the newly appointed vice-mayor. Later, He served as deputy director and then director of the Finance Bureau of the Xiamen municipal government, reporting directly to Xi, who was in charge of municipal finance. He also followed Xi through his career moves, serving as Fuzhou party secretary and standing member of the provincial party committee when Xi served as provincial deputy party secretary and governor of Fujian. In 2009, about a year and half after Xi became vice-president of the PRC and a PSC member, He was appointed deputy party secretary of Tianjin. With his important new position as vice-minister of the National Development and Reform Commission, He will likely play greater importance in the economic leadership of the country in the years to come.

Like He Lifeng, Cai Qi also worked in the General Office of the Fujian provincial government when Xi arrived there in 1985. In addition, Cai worked directly under Xi ten years later, in the mid-1990s. At that time, Cai served as deputy director of the General Office of the Fujian provincial party committee, and Xi served as deputy party secretary. Cai Qi also worked with Xi in Zhejiang Province from 2002 to 2007, serving as party secretary and mayor of several counties and cities, including Hangzhou, while Xi was Zhejiang party secretary. Cai later served as standing member and director of the Organization Department of the Zhejiang Provincial Party Committee. It is unusual that Cai served only four months (from November 2013 to March 2014) as executive vice-governor of Zhejiang before being promoted to a higher leadership position. The norm for elite recruitment is that one needs to work in a leadership position for at least two years before being eligible for further promotion, as described in detail in chapter 3. Cai now serves as deputy office director of the newly established National Security Committee.[130]

Another important protégé Xi cultivated during his tenure in Fujian was Huang Kunming, as discussed briefly in chapter 6. Huang was born in Shanghang County, Fujian Province, in 1956. Like Cai Qi, Huang worked with Xi in both Fujian and Zhejiang. After serving as mayor and deputy party secretary in Longyan City in Fujian, Huang was transferred to Wuzhou City in Zhejiang, where he served as mayor from 1998 to 2003, a couple of years before Xi's arrival in Zhejiang as provincial party secretary. Huang later served as party secretary of Jiaxing City, director of the Propaganda Department of the Zhejiang Provincial Party Committee, and party secretary of Hangzhou City. In November 2013, on the eve of the Third Plenum of the 18th Central Committee, Huang was appointed deputy director of the Propaganda Department of the CCP. One year later, Huang was promoted to executive deputy director of the same organization.

Song Tao and Wang Xiaohong are two other leaders who were recently promoted largely due to their strong ties with Xi in his Fujian years. Song Tao was born in Jiangsu and advanced throughout his early career in Fujian after graduating from college in Fuzhou. He served as vice-president of Fujian International Trust and Investment Corporation (1997–2000) when Xi was deputy party secretary and later governor of the province. Song was appointed executive deputy director of the Central Foreign Affairs Office in December 2014 and, less than a year later, he was appointed director of the International Liaison Department of the CCP Central Committee. Wang Xiaohong served as deputy director of the Public Security Bureau of Fuzhou City (1993–98) when Xi was the municipal party secretary and was appointed Henan vice-governor in December 2014. Three months later, in March 2015, Wang was further promoted to vice-mayor of Beijing and director of the Public Security Bureau of Beijing. He Lifeng, Cai Qi, Huang Kunming, Song Tao, and Wang Xiaohong are now well positioned in important functional areas, helping Xi exert influence and more effectively implement his policy initiatives.

In addition, Lei Chunmei (b. 1959), a female leader who served as vice-mayor of Ningde (1988–91) when Xi was in charge of the city, was promoted to member of the Standing Committee of the Fujian Provincial Party Committee in January 2015; Liu Cigui (b. 1955), who advanced his career in Fujian at the time when Xi was a municipal and provincial leader, was appointed Hainan governor in February 2015; and Deng Weiping (b. 1955), who worked under Xi in the early 1990s in Fuzhou, was promoted to discipline secretary of the Ministry of Public Security in March 2015. Lei is currently an alternate member of the 18th Central Committee, and Liu and Deng will likely obtain membership in the Central Committee in 2017.

The Zhejiang Connection

As the top leader in Zhejiang, Xi was far more comfortable promoting his protégés there than in his other regional posts. Xi played a direct role in appointing Chen Min'er, Li Qiang, and others to key positions. Chen Min'er was born in Zhuji County, Zhejiang, in 1960 and advanced his career through positions within the province until 2012, when he was appointed deputy party secretary and governor of Guizhou. In 2015, Chen was promoted to party secretary of Guizhou. During the five years (2002–07) Xi was party boss of the province, Chen served as director of the Propaganda Department and standing member of the Zhejiang Provincial Party Committee. It was widely believed that Chen Min'er provided much support for Xi's weekly columns published in the provincial party newspaper *Zhejiang Daily* during these years.[131] Chen also served as executive vice-governor of Zhejiang. As a full member of the 18th Central Committee and one of three provincial party secretaries born in the 1960s (the other two, Guangdong party secretary Hu Chunhua and Chongqing party secretary Sun Zhengcai, serve in the current Politburo), Chen will likely receive strong support from Xi for future promotions.

Zhejiang governor Li Qiang worked directly under Xi from 2004 to 2007 as chief-of-staff of the Zhejiang Provincial Party Committee. Li was born in Rui'an County, Zhejiang Province, in 1959. He has spent his entire career in his native province, serving consecutively as director of the Industry and Commerce Bureau of Zhejiang Province, party secretary of Wenzhou, and secretary of the Politics and Law Committee of the Zhejiang Provincial Party Committee. It is expected that Li will move to another province to become a provincial party secretary or move to Beijing, where he will work directly for his former boss.

The relationship between Xi and current Zhejiang party secretary Xia Baolong is not entirely clear. Xia, a native of Tianjin who advanced his early career there, was transferred to Zhejiang in 2003, a year after Xi became Zhejiang party secretary. Xia served as deputy provincial party secretary under Xi for three years. For a year, Xia served concurrently as governor of Zhejiang before being promoted to his current position in December 2012. Xia is a conservative leader known for his campaign to demolish a large number of Christian churches in the province.

Xi's six other protégés from his Zhejiang years were also promoted to important positions in 2014. New trade negotiator and vice-minister of Commerce Zhong Shan was vice-governor of Zhejiang from 2003 to 2008. He assisted Xi with foreign trade in Zhejiang. New Shanghai deputy party secretary Ying Yong served as director of the Supervision Department of the Zhejiang Municipal Government (2003–06) and president of the Zhejiang Higher People's Court (2005–07). Ying played a key role in advancing Xi's anticorruption efforts in Zhejiang. New Shanxi deputy party secretary Lou Yangsheng, who was selected for his current position in the wake of major corruption scandals in Shanxi, previously served as party secretary of Lishui City, Zhejiang Province, when Xi was provincial party secretary. Lou has changed leadership positions four times in the past few years—serving consecutively as deputy director of the United Front Work Department of the Zhejiang Provincial Party Committee, director of the Organization Department of the Hainan Provincial Party Committee, director of the Organization Department of the Hubei Provincial Party Committee, and deputy party secretary of Shanxi.

The new deputy director of the Office of the Central Financial Leading Group, Shu Guozeng, was known as Xi's "facile writer" (笔杆子, biganzi) in Zhejiang, where he served first as a mishu to Xi and then as deputy director of the office of the Zhejiang Provincial Party Committee in 2004 when Xi was provincial party secretary.[132] Before his current position, Shu was promoted from director of the Development Research Center of the Zhejiang provincial government. Similarly, the former vice-president of Xinhua News Agency and newly appointed director of the Propaganda Department of the Guangdong Provincial Party Committee, Shen Haixiong, was often called the "imperial reporter" (御用记者, yuyong jizhe) by critics. As a Xinhua reporter based in Zhejiang and Shanghai, Shen wrote extensively to promote Xi's popular image when Xi was in charge of those two places.[133] Wang Ning, former deputy chief-of-staff of the PLA General Staff Department, previously developed strong political ties with Xi in Zhejiang and was appointed commander of the PAP in December 2014.

In addition, Zhong Shaojun (b. 1968), who began to work for Xi in Zhejiang over a decade ago, is now Xi's top aide on military affairs in the CMC General Office. Meng Qingfeng (b. 1957), who worked under Xi Jinping in Zhejiang Province as vice-director of the Department of Public Security of the provincial government, was promoted to vice-minister in the Ministry of Public Security in June 2015. During the Chinese stock market crisis in the summer of 2015, it was Meng Qingfeng who directed law enforcement officials from the Ministry of Public Security to investigate illegal trading in the China Securities Regulatory Commission.[134] This highly publicized event seems to suggest that Meng is one of Xi's confidants in this important bureaucratic organ, which is tasked with maintaining sociopolitical stability in the country. Chen Derong (b. 1961), former party secretary of Wenzhou and vice-governor of Zhejiang under Xi's leadership, was appointed president of the state-owned Baosteel Group in August 2014. In August 2015

Gong Zheng (b. 1960), former vice-governor of Zhejiang under Xi's leadership, was transferred to Shandong to become deputy party secretary there. In December 2015, Chen Yixin (b. 1959), who served as deputy secretary-general of the Zhejiang provincial party committee during Xi's tenure in Zhejiang, was appointed deputy office director of the Central Leading Group for Comprehensive Reforms. These protégés of Xi's all will be candidates for membership on the 19th CCP Central Committee.

The Shanghai Connection

Xi spent only eight months (March to October 2007) in Shanghai as party secretary of the city, which apparently did not give him time to cultivate solid personal ties. While in office, he had to rely on the leadership team that was largely formed by his own mentors, Jiang Zemin and Zeng Qing-hong. However, these eight months gave Xi a chance to identify some capable Shanghai leaders to include on his own team in Shanghai and to consider for high-level positions in the future, when he would become a top national leader. Han Zheng, then mayor of Shanghai, apparently earned Xi's support, as Han earned a Politburo seat after Xi became general secretary of the party. It seems Xi was particularly impressed by Ding Xuexiang, then director of the General Office and deputy chief-of-staff of the Shanghai Municipal Party Committee, for his administrative skills, political counsel, low profile, and humble personality. Within two months, Xi promoted Ding to chief-of-staff and standing member of the Shanghai Municipal Party Committee.

Ding was born in Nantong, Jiangsu Province, in 1962, studied engineering at the Northeast Heavy Machinery Institute (now Yanshan University) in Qiqihar City, Heilongjiang, from 1978 to 1982, and joined the CCP in 1982. After graduation, Ding worked in the Shanghai Research Institute of Materials for seventeen years. He served as deputy director of the Shanghai Municipal Science and Technology Commission from 1999 to 2001 and deputy party secretary and head of Shanghai's Zhabei district from 2001 to 2004. Under the leadership of then Shanghai party secretary Chen Liangyu, Ding took the important position of deputy director of the Organization Department of the Shanghai Municipal Party Committee and concurrently served as director of the Personnel Bureau of the Shanghai Municipal Government (2004–06). He remained in Shanghai to assist Xi's successor, Yu Zhengsheng, from 2007 to 2012. In 2013, soon after Xi became CCP general secretary, Ding moved to Beijing, where he serves concurrently as deputy director of the General Office of the CCP Central Committee and director of the Office of the PRC President—or Xi's principal *mishu*.

New deputy secretary of the CCDI Yang Xiaodu is another Shanghai leader who impressed Xi during his brief tenure there.[135] Yang, a Shanghai native born in 1953, was a sent-down youth in Anhui before he returned to Shanghai as a worker-peasant-soldier student. After twenty-five years advancing his career in Tibet, Yang was transferred back to Shanghai to become vice-major (2001–06), standing member, and director of the United Front Work Department of the Shanghai Municipal Party Committee (2006–12) and secretary of the Shanghai Discipline Inspection Commission (2012–14). In early 2014, at the recommendation of both Xi Jinping and Wang Qishan in a special meeting of the CCDI, the Chinese leadership appointed Yang deputy secretary of this increasingly powerful commission.

Two other Shanghai leaders whom Xi recently promoted are in their sixties. Both Xu Lin and Fang Xinghai, who worked under Xi in Shanghai in 2007, are seen as Xi's protégés. Xu Lin, former director of the Propaganda Department of the Shanghai Municipal Party Committee, worked closely with then Shanghai party secretary Xi in 2007 and was appointed executive vice-director of the State Internet Information Office in June 2015. Because of his broad experience and expertise in global finance, Fang Xinghai plays an important role in China's financial reforms, as discussed in chapter 6.

SUMMARY

What do the dynamics of Xi's inner circle mean for our assessment of his current consolidation of power and his future political trajectory? Four important observations can be made. First, through native-place associations, family connections, school ties, "big yards" bonds, military service, his *mishu* cluster, and broad local and professional leadership experience, Xi has cultivated a large web of political protégés in the civilian and military leaderships, and these protégés are now well positioned at both the national and provincial levels. As most of the friendships can be traced back to Xi's adolescent and formative years—and because these mentor-protégé relationships were often established during Xi's early career—these friends and confidants are more trustworthy than political allies who formed bonds with Xi primarily based on shared factional association. The support and loyalty of Xi's inner circle have been crucial to his rise. Most notably, the four-decade-long friendship between Xi Jinping and Wang Qishan—and their multidimensional bond—constitutes the cornerstone of Xi's power. Due to his remarkable expertise in finance and economics, along with his implementation of the astonishingly strong anticorruption campaign, Wang's contribution to Xi's leadership is unparalleled.

Second, just as he has shown determination in taking over twelve top leadership posts himself, Xi has acted decisively to appoint his confidants to important leadership positions since becoming party boss in 2012. Apparently, Xi is not afraid of being criticized for his emphasis on mentor-protégé ties. His actions seem to echo the Chinese dictum, "Appoint people based on their merits without omitting relatives or friends" (举贤不避亲, *juxian bubiqin*). As table 8-3 shows, Xi's protégés from his days in provincial leadership were all appointed to their current positions after 2012, and most of them were appointed in the past couple of years. Several of them were promoted twice within two years. In addition to the aforementioned cases of Li Xi and Wang Xiaohong, Cai Qi was first promoted to executive vice-governor of Zhejiang Province in November 2013, and then, four months later, promoted again to his current position. Yang Zhenwu was appointed editor-in-chief of the *People's Daily* in April 2013, and one year later he was promoted to president of the publication. All of these cases were out of step with the CCP norm and regulation that leaders should work at one level of leadership for a minimum of two years before being promoted.[136] The quick promotions of Xi's protégés might have not resonated well among the political establishment, but they helped Xi form his team to carry out important policy initiatives in a timely manner.

Third, Xi's team consists of leaders with different expertise and leadership skills. Members of Xi's inner circle have occupied crucial leadership positions in various functional areas, including party discipline, party operation, party organization (personnel management), propaganda, economics, foreign affairs, state security, legislation, and the party's united front work. Due to the growing importance of political power and economic interests in provincial-level administrations, top leaders often find it essential to maintain strong ties with their geographical power bases in order to consolidate their power and influence in Beijing. They often leverage their power bases by appointing protégés as top leaders within provincial administrations and in the national leadership. Among Xi's protégés from his provincial connections, Guizhou party secretary Chen Min'er, Liaoning party secretary Li Xi and Zhejiang governor Li Qiang belong to the former delegation, and National Development and Reform Commission deputy director He Lifeng, executive deputy director of the CCP Propaganda Department Huang Kunming, and deputy secretary of the CCDI Yang Xiaodu are examples of the latter.

Xi's confidants and protégés also differ profoundly in terms of personality, education, occupational background, worldview, and policy preferences. This is most evident in the case of Liu He and Liu Yuan—one is a liberal economic technocrat and the other is a conservative military hawk. Their worldviews could not be more different, but both have constituted the most reliable sources of political support for Xi in his effort to consolidate power during the first few years of his tenure. There is one common bond, however, among Xi's inner circle. Many of Xi's confidants and longtime friends are princelings—most notably Wang Qishan, Yu Zhengsheng, Li Zhanshu, Zhang Youxia, Liu He, Liu Yuan, Liu Xiaojiang, and Liu Weiping. This factor may not simply be a superficial characteristic of Xi's inner circle; these connections may help Xi gain favor with other princelings. However, the majority of Chinese political elites, even those on the 376-member Central Committee, are not princelings. At a time when the Chinese public is resentful of nepotism, favoritism, and the convergence of power and wealth, the reality of having an inner circle consisting largely of princelings may undermine Xi's populist image. Some princelings like Liu Yuan can be political liabilities for Xi for the reasons discussed earlier. The removal of Liu Yuan from his senior military position reflects Xi's recognition of the need for—and his serious efforts to achieve—a delicate balance between these competing political concerns.

And fourth, a central concern for foreign observers of China, especially U.S. policymakers, is the need for well-grounded and insightful assessments of Xi's control of the Chinese military, his worldview, and the possibility that Xi could pursue more-aggressive policy vis-à-vis the United States. In that regard, both General Cai Yingting's dramatic marginalization and the even more surprising end to General Liu Yuan's military career are revealing. These two consequential episodes—largely overlooked in overseas China-watching communities—show the importance of institutional norms and regulations, which apparently continue to constrain Xi's power in this critical domain. Even more important, Xi's decision to remove Liu Yuan, an ultranationalistic, anti-U.S. heavyweight military leader, may reflect the profound difference in worldviews and foreign policy instincts between Xi and Liu.

It is evident that Xi is interested in broadening traditional channels for elite recruitment. During the CCP Central Committee's work conference on united front work held in May 2015, Xi Jinping called for recruiting and promoting three elite groups: (1) foreign-educated returnees (2) representatives of new social media, and (3) businesspeople from the private sector, especially young entrepreneurs.[137] But it is one thing to open up new sources for elite recruitment at various sub-national levels of leadership; it is quite another thing for Xi and the COD to appoint many inexperienced and untested leaders to the national leadership.

If Xi were to drastically overhaul the regulations and norms in a noninstitutional manner, he would face strong resistance from the political establishment and furious criticism from China's liberal intellectuals. The political cost and potential backlash for Xi would be overwhelming, as the concluding chapter will discuss. The second epigraph of this chapter, which quotes the Chinese philosopher Lao Tzu—"Knowing others is wisdom, knowing yourself is enlightenment"—could be particularly instructive to Xi as he navigates this critical period in Chinese elite politics.

CHAPTER 9

Trajectory

The 19th National Party Congress and Changing Dynamics in Chinese Society

The difference between a politician and a statesman is
that a politician thinks about the next election while the
statesman thinks about the next generation.
—JAMES FREEMAN CLARKE

Limited wisdom makes doers; moderate wisdom makes managers;
supreme wisdom makes law-builders. [小智治事，中智用人，大智立法]
—CHINESE SAYING

China's future political transformation is unlikely to follow a linear path. Various possibilities for the nation's political development are in play: a prolonged or even rejuvenated authoritarian system (likely accompanied by a return to a strongman dictatorship), a sudden collapse of Chinese Communist Party (CCP) rule or a military coup, a continual improvement of collective leadership and political institutionalization, or even an incremental transition to Chinese-style democracy.[1] In the process of transformation, these scenarios are not mutually exclusive or collectively exhaustive, and one political scenario may lead to another. While all these scenarios are possible, they are not, however, all equally probable.

The road that China ultimately takes depends on the interplay of many factors, including the prospects for the country's economy, sociopolitical forces (especially the expansion of the middle class), the communication and information revolutions, institutional development, legal reform, intellectual enlightenment, elite unity and diversity, demographic trends, foreign

351

relations, and the international environment. By consulting the reliable information and basic knowledge about these variables that exists, China analysts can make thoughtful assessments and intelligent forecasts.

Walter Laqueur, a scholar of Russian politics, was hesitant to make political predictions about the former Soviet Union in 1990, when the country was undergoing fundamental changes: "Political predictions are easiest to make when they are least needed—when the political barometer points to continuity. They become more difficult at a time of rapid and violent change."[2]

Laqueur's prudent restraint with respect to assessing the Soviet Union is equally applicable to those analyzing China's present and future. Throughout the first twenty-five years of the existence of the People's Republic of China (PRC), the only future that seemed possible was the perpetuation of the status quo. Observers had little doubt that socialist planning of the economy and allegiance to orthodox communist ideology would continue in China. Today, however, a variety of possibilities manifest for the future path of this rapidly changing country. China's economic rise during the last three decades has been a fascinating development—and, for many, quite a surprise. The Middle Kingdom, a country known for its economic backwardness and international isolation over the past couple of centuries, has transformed into the world's frontier of economic globalization. Despite a recent slowdown in GDP growth, the Chinese economy has remained one of the largest and most dynamic in the world.

China's political scene has also experienced many dramatic episodes in recent years. Political conflict and corruption scandals have plagued the leadership, toppling powerful civilian and military leaders like Bo Xilai, Zhou Yongkang, Ling Jihua, Xu Caihou, and Guo Boxiong. The recent crises in Chinese elite politics and the rampancy of official corruption have revealed the vulnerability, fragility, and fundamental flaws of China's political system. Nevertheless, the CCP leadership has withstood these devastating threats to its legitimacy. Despite such a precarious environment, Xi Jinping has risen to the occasion and regained the public's confidence over the first few years of his leadership. Xi launched a bold anticorruption campaign, levying serious charges against heavyweight "tigers" and rallying support for continued CCP rule. How can these seemingly contradictory phenomena be reconciled? Is the Xi leadership's current political maintenance only temporarily effective, and thus unsustainable? Or will China surprise the world again by deepening its political transformation in the years to come?

Two recurring and prevailing mistakes exist in the study of Chinese leadership politics. First, although China analysts consider challenges confronting the Chinese leadership in dynamic terms, they often fail to analyze leaders' policy responses in the same light. They tend to assume that the Chinese leadership is static, single-minded, and stuck in its ways. Analysts often fail to take into account the intriguing personal contradictions of top leaders and the range of options that are available to them, *as well as* the imperative for these leaders to make choices. Various options can have drastically different political implications for the country, and a top leader's ultimate choice of one option over another is by no means predetermined.

In assessing Xi Jinping, many analysts tend to adopt simplistic and one-dimensional characterizations of this complicated leader. They fail to understand Xi's many contradictions—not only his defining characteristics and his power status but also his worldview and policy agenda. To a great extent, Xi's own contradictions increase the degree of uncertainty over China's political trajectory. Xi confronts, however, an unavoidable test at the 19th National Party Congress in the fall of 2017, when the CCP leadership undergoes another substantial turnover. A thoughtful examination of the options for Xi at the upcoming leadership change is urgently needed, particularly as it relates to the formation of the Politburo Standing Committee in his second term. Each of these possibilities will have profound implications for how China is governed in the remaining years of the Xi leadership and beyond.

Second, some analysts pay close attention to individual top leaders and political institutions, overlooking the crucial role of societal forces. Recent political crises like the Bo Xilai scandal have compounded to constitute the most serious threat to the CCP's legitimacy since the 1989 Tiananmen incident. Yet, in the wake of the Bo Xilai incident, China's economy and society have not faced any major upheavals. This reflects the maturation of Chinese society. Before 1989, several key stabilizing forces in today's China either did not exist or were very weak, including the entrepreneurial class, the middle class, the professional legal community, a commercial and increasingly diversified media, and various other interest groups. While many of these actors resent the abuse of power and rampant corruption among officials, they also tend to prefer top-down political and legal reform to bottom-up revolution.

The growing importance of some social forces, especially the emerging middle class and legal community, will serve to constrain the excessive accumulation of power by any individual leader or any single political faction. The intriguing interaction between the political leadership and social forces—the imperative to seek public support versus the incentive to push for leadership that is more representative, accountable, and effective—is, of course, not unique to Chinese politics. Analyzing the interplay between these two trends not only helps demystify China's modern governance by demonstrating how it is subject to the same pressures as many other systems but also highlights the significance and potentially far-reaching impact of ongoing Chinese experiments in political institutionalization.

XI'S CONTRADICTIONS

As discussed in previous chapters, Xi Jinping embodies many paradoxical traits in terms of his defining characteristics, formative experiences, educational background, career trajectory, and leadership style. He is a princeling who comes from a very privileged, high-ranking official family, but his father was purged by Mao in the mid-1960s when Xi was a teenager. At a young age, Xi Jinping not only suffered from political discrimination in Beijing during the years of the Red Guard madness but also endured physical hardship in the primitive rural areas of Yan'an throughout his experience as a sent-down youth. Like many from the age cohort who grew up in the first decades of Communist China, Xi is an idealist. But at the same time, his tough life experiences also nurtured in him strong instincts and inclinations toward realpolitik. Like other politicians in China and elsewhere, Xi blends the qualities of both an idealist and a pragmatist.

Xi attended Tsinghua University, one of China's most prestigious educational institutions. He earned his undergraduate degree from Tsinghua as a worker-peasant-soldier student during the final years of the Cultural Revolution and returned to earn a postgraduate degree through a part-time correspondence program. Both programs are often considered academically substandard, and thus the conditions of Xi's enrollment undermine the prestige of his education credentials. Yet, especially since becoming China's top leader, Xi has exhibited impressive intellect and political wisdom, as well as a broad knowledge of both history and present-day world politics.

Xi advanced his leadership career largely through administrative work in economically developed coastal cities such as Fuzhou, Xiamen, Hangzhou, and Shanghai. But, as discussed in the previous chapter, his strong affection for Shaanxi Province—including his familial roots and his well-known "yellow earth attachment" (stemming from six years spent in Shaanxi as a farmer and village head)—has molded him into a leader who understands the heart of rural China. Additionally, although Xi has experience as a municipal and provincial chief, which is often characterized as the most essential credential for attaining top national leadership positions, the administrative skills he developed through his *mishu* work for the minister of Defense early in his career were instrumental in facilitating his ascent to the pinnacle of power. Not only did he form close ties within the People's Liberation Army (PLA), but he also mastered techniques like political networking and coalition building during this time.

Xi's most important contradictions are not related to his past experiences but instead relate to his paradoxical policy moves and ambiguous ideological stances. A 2014 *Wall Street Journal* article on Xi Jinping begins by asking, "Does Chinese leader Xi Jinping really want to be the next Mao

Zedong? Or is it Deng Xiaoping, the pragmatic architect of China's market reforms, that he's modeling himself after?"[3] The answer should be neither. A simplistic comparison between Xi and Mao or between Xi and Deng that fails to account for the contradictions embodied in Xi's actions and thoughts can be misleading. Indeed, examples of Xi's contradictions abound:

— The overall objective of Xi's economic policy, as demonstrated at the Third Plenum of the 18th Central Committee, held in the fall of 2013, is to make the private sector the decisive driver of the Chinese economy, to promote the development of the service sector, and to build an innovation-driven economy. Xi's initiatives to support private firms and to crack down on monopolized state-owned enterprises (SOEs) and corrupt officials demonstrate his sincere dedication to this development strategy. However, Xi's continued emphasis on promoting China's "national champions" (mainly flagship SOEs), tight control over the Internet, and strong-willed discrimination against foreign IT companies all undermine the vitality of a true innovation-driven market economy.

— Xi's politically conservative approach to governance, which relies on ideological oversight, has alienated the country's liberal intellectuals to a certain extent. But in a contradictory fashion, Xi has prioritized the development and promotion of Chinese think tanks (and, by extension, intellectuals), citing this as a national strategic objective. In addition, Xi's own foreign affairs and economic teams consist of many U.S.-trained financial technocrats and experts on international relations. Publicly, Xi has urged the party leadership to recruit foreign-educated returnees, as discussed in chapter 8.

— The Xi leadership is noted for its strong crackdown on groups and individuals inspired by the "color revolutions" and by what Chinese authorities call the "U.S.-led anti-China conspiracy."[4] This was evident in the draft version of the foreign nongovernmental organization (NGO) law, released by the National People's Congress (NPC) in early 2015. Interestingly, in June 2015 Xi held a widely publicized meeting with Aung San Suu Kyi, who personifies the Burmese democratic movement. Xi's wife and China's first lady, Peng Liyuan, has also become famous for her enthusiastic involvement with foreign NGOs (especially the Bill & Melinda Gates Foundation). She has played an instrumental role in advancing antismoking campaigns, AIDS prevention, and other social causes advocated by China's emerging civil society and foreign NGOs.[5]

— Xi apparently intends to firmly oppose the growing ethnic and religious demands for autonomy. As such, tensions in Xinjiang and Tibet have remained acute under Xi's watch. Yet, followers of Falun Gong, a semireligious group that was viciously suppressed by Xi's predecessors, seem to be far less critical of Xi's leadership. Likewise, many signs suggest that Xi and Pope Francis are considering a historic meeting in China in the near future.[6]

— The most astonishing political achievement of the Xi leadership has been its bold and broad anticorruption campaign. In 2013 alone the Chinese authorities investigated 182,000 officials—the highest annual number of cases in thirty years.[7] By May 2016 the authorities had purged about 160 vice-ministerial- and provincial-level leaders on corruption charges. But Xi has never linked rampant official corruption to fundamental flaws in the Chinese political system. Instead, he asserts that the Chinese should have confidence in China's political system (制度自信, *zhidu zixin*).[8]

— At Xi's direction, the Fourth Plenum of the 18th Central Committee, held in the fall of 2014, was devoted to legal and judicial reform. This was the first plenum in party history that concentrated on law. More than any previous leader, Xi is interested in making the nation's judicial development part of his political legacy. There were many important and concrete measures adopted in the plenum, including establishment of the circuit courts and regulations for transparency of court proceedings. Yet, Chinese authorities recently persecuted several hundred human rights lawyers and legal professionals on charges of "endangering national security."[9]

— In foreign relations, Xi has frequently met with Russian president Vladimir Putin and significantly strengthened Sino-Russian relations. But Xi is chiefly focused on the Sino-U.S. relationship, in which the Chinese hope for a "new type of major power relations" (新型大国关系, *xinxing daguo guanxi*). As for China's position on U.S. military presence in Asia, Xi has contradicted himself by claiming "Asia for Asians" and by stating that "the Pacific Ocean is vast enough to embrace both China and the United States."[10] Also, regarding tensions on the Korean peninsula, Xi has unambiguously sided with his "South Korean sister," Park Geun-hye, over the CCP's "Communist little brother," Kim Jong-un.

These examples by no means suggest that Xi Jinping is a political opportunist. All political leaders have at times been self-contradictory. In the famous words of Oscar Wilde, "The well-bred contradict other people. The wise contradict themselves." As the leader of a rapidly changing country with widely ranging views and values, as well as conflicting interests, Xi Jinping is wise to strike a delicate balance between various constituencies and socioeconomic forces. It is arguably Xi's contradictions that make him a well-rounded and effective leader. The increasingly complex international environment that China faces also leads Xi to be deliberately ambiguous about certain stances and strategies.

Self-contradictions also suggest that Xi Jinping is not a dogmatic leader, but rather is flexible and adaptable. Of course, some of Xi's contradictions may only be temporary phenomena. If Xi hopes to be a great leader in Chinese history, sooner or later he should present a clearly articulated and coherent vision for the country's political trajectory. It is reasonable for Xi, however, to spend the first few years of his leadership determining the best sequence in which to implement his agenda, maximizing public support and accumulating political capital.

A comprehensive understanding of Xi's contradictions is essential for foreign observers. Overstating any one dimension of his leadership while ignoring others can lead to inaccurate conclusions. At least for now, it is premature to make a definitive judgment about Xi's intentions, strategy, capacity, worldview, and historical legacy. As for his consolidation of power, two prevailing—but contrasting—views deserve attention: one sees Xi as the most powerful leader since Mao, while the other believes that Xi simply cannot implement his economic reform policies.

Analysts of Chinese leadership politics must learn to live with complexity, tolerate ambiguity, and expect uncertainty. However, the immense intricacy of the subject, made more difficult by Xi's contradictions, is no excuse for failing to apply good judgment and neglecting to pursue empirically grounded assessments, especially regarding the leadership composition. China analysts should test whether positive expectations of Xi are reasonably foresighted or naïvely misplaced, especially when the next party congress convenes in the fall of 2017.

SELECTION NORMS AND THE CANDIDATE LINEUP FOR THE 2017 NATIONAL PARTY CONGRESS

As a result of retirement-age rules, it is anticipated that five of the PSC's seven current members (everyone except for Xi Jinping and Li Keqiang) will step down at the 2017 National Party Congress. The selection of the new members of this supreme decisionmaking body is consistently regarded as one of the most critical aspects in the study of Chinese elite politics. The composition of the new PSC—especially its generational attributes, individual idiosyncratic characteristics, group dynamics, and factional lineup—will have profound implications for China's economy, social stability, political trajectory, and foreign relations. Arguably, the most intriguing question regarding Xi's power is whether he will be able to position enough of his protégés between now and autumn of 2017 to fashion another landslide victory in the new Politburo and PSC, similar to the one shaped by the Jiang-Xi camp at the 2012 National Party Congress. To better answer this question, it is necessary to understand the regulations and norms associated with the selection process and to be familiar with the candidates.

Two norms in CCP leadership selection are helpful for identifying who will be eligible to become members at the next Politburo and PSC. The first norm is the age requirement for retirement from the Central Committee. At the 2007 National Party Congress, all leaders born before 1940 were barred from continuing to serve on the committee. Similarly, at the 2012 National Party Congress, all leaders who were born before 1945 retired. Extrapolating from this norm, leaders who were born before 1950 will not be eligible for the next committee and are therefore unable to obtain seats on the Politburo or the PSC in 2017. The second norm is that new PSC members are promoted from the previous Politburo, and that all Politburo members are promoted from the full and alternate members of the previous Central Committee.

These norms suggest that five current PSC members (all of them Xi's political allies, including the powerful anticorruption tsar Wang Qishan) will step down. There will be fourteen current Politburo members eligible for the 19th PSC (see table 9-1). Xi Jinping and Li Keqiang will undoubtedly remain. Among the other twelve candidates, seven belong to the Jiang-Xi camp and five belong to the Hu-Li camp. Xi will most likely promote two of his confidants, Li Zhanshu and Zhao Leji, to the PSC at the 2017 National Party Congress.

Han Zheng and Wang Huning, two prominent members of the Shanghai Gang, will also be strong contenders for spots on the PSC. Han Zheng has spent his entire career in Shanghai, and Wang Huning has served almost exclusively as an adviser to top leaders (Jiang, Hu, and Xi). As discussed in chapter 3, over the past three decades virtually all PSC members have served either in provincial or municipal leadership roles or as governmental leaders in the State Council, and most of them have served in more than two provincial-level administrations. These factors put Han and Wang at a slight disadvantage when it comes to winning seats on the PSC. It is speculated that Han and Wang will be assigned to new positions before the 2017 National Party Congress in order to bolster their leadership credentials.

Although he is Xi's political ally, Zhang Chunxian has been noted for his political ambition. His rise to the top leadership is not attributable to Xi. The same can be said about Sun Zhengcai. If Sun, a sixth-generation leader, were to be promoted to the PSC, his ascension would be interpreted as signaling that he is heir apparent to Li Keqiang or even Xi Jinping. Sun is not a member of Xi's inner circle and therefore may not be Xi's choice for these roles. As

TABLE 9-1. Current Politburo Members Who Meet the Age Qualifications for Promotion to the 19th Politburo Standing Committee

Name	Birth year	Age in 2017	Current position	Tenure on Politburo and PSC	Factional background
Xi Jinping	1953	64	CCP Secretary-General, member of PSC, CMC Chair, PRC President	Two terms as Politburo member; one term as PSC member	Jiang-Xi camp
Li Keqiang	1955	62	Member of PSC, Premier	Two terms as Politburo member; one term as PSC member	Hu-Li Camp (*tuanpai*)
Li Zhanshu	1950	67	Politburo member, Director of the CCP General Office	One term as Politburo member	Jiang-Xi Camp (Xi's inner circle)
Zhao Leji	1957	60	Politburo member, Director of the CCP Organization Department	One term as Politburo member	Jiang-Xi camp (Xi's inner circle)
Han Zheng	1954	63	Shanghai Party Secretary	One term as Politburo member	Jiang-Xi camp (Shanghai Gang)
Wang Huning	1955	62	Politburo member, Director of the CCP Policy Research Office	One term as Politburo member	Jiang-Xi camp (Shanghai Gang)
Zhang Chunxian	1953	64	Xinjiang Party Secretary	One term as Politburo member	Jiang-Xi camp
Sun Zhengcai	1963	54	Politburo member, Chongqing Party Secretary	One term as Politburo member	Jiang-Xi camp
Xu Qiliang	1950	67	Politburo member, CMC Vice-Chair	One term as Politburo member	Jiang-Xi camp

(continued)

TABLE 9-1. (*continued*)

Name	Birth year	Age in 2017	Current position	Tenure on Politburo and PSC	Factional background
Li Yuanchao	1950	67	Politburo member, PRC Vice-President	Two terms as Politburo member	Hu-Li camp (*tuanpai*)
Wang Yang	1955	62	Politburo member, Vice-Premier	Two terms as Politburo member	Hu-Li camp (*tuanpai*)
Hu Chunhua	1963	54	Politburo member, Guangdong Party Secretary	One term as Politburo member	Hu-Li camp (*tuanpai*)
Liu Qibao	1953	64	Politburo member, Director of the CCP Propaganda Department	One term as Politburo member	Hu-Li camp (*tuanpai*)
Sun Chunlan (f)	1950	67	Politburo member, Director of the CCP United Front Work Department	One term as Politburo member	Hu-Li camp

Note and Source: PSC = Politburo Standing Committee; CCP = Chinese Communist Party; CMC = Central Military Commission; PRC = People's Republic of China; (f) = female. Data from the author's database.

for General Xu Qiliang, the chances of his gaining a seat on the PSC are slim; no military leader has served on the PSC since the late 1990s.

As for candidates from the Hu-Li camp, Vice-President Li Yuanchao needs a miracle in order to attain a seat on the next PSC. Many of Li's protégés were recently purged, one after the next (the latest being the former Liaoning party secretary in March 2016). Li failed to enter the PSC in 2012, as the Jiang-Xi camp considered him a major threat and thus blocked him at the eleventh hour before the National Party Congress.[11] Given that five of his protégés were recently purged on corruption charges, Li Yuanchao's best hope to avoid charges himself is perhaps to retire gracefully from the Politburo in 2017.[12]

The existing norms and the current lineup of candidates make it highly unlikely that the Jiang-Xi camp will prevent all candidates from the Hu-Li camp from ascending to the next PSC, especially in the case of two-time

Politburo member Wang Yang. Wang has broad leadership experience in Chongqing and Guangdong, having served as party secretary of both, as well as in the State Council, where he served as vice-premier. Given his relatively young age, Wang is the only one of the four current vice-premiers in the State Council who need not retire from his position after the 2018 NPC.

Furthermore, it is reasonable to expect that the new PSC will include one or two representatives from the sixth generation. In addition to the aforementioned Sun Zhengcai (a candidate from the Jiang-Xi camp), Hu Jintao's protégé Hu Chunhua has long been seen as the front-runner of the sixth generation.[13] According to some analysts, Hu Chunhua's selection as a Politburo member in 2012 reflected Deng Xiaoping's political design for "grandpa-designated successor" (隔代指定接班人, *gedai zhiding jiebanren*). This refers to the pattern whereby Deng designated Hu Jintao to be the top leader, Jiang designated Xi Jinping, and Hu Jintao designated Hu Chunhua.[14]

Public expectations for Wang Yang and Hu Chunhua to ascend to the 19th PSC constitute a serious challenge for Xi and his team as they prepare for the next leadership turnover. If Xi intends to prevent Wang Yang and Hu Chunhua from rising to the pinnacle of power, he needs to find some justification to do so. In July 2015 the Politburo passed a new trial-based regulation on the promotion and demotion of cadres in both the civilian and military leadership.[15] This new regulation not only requires the strict enforcement of age limits for retirement but also calls for the removal of leaders who are incapable, incompetent, or inactive as a result of health issues or other concerns. According to official Chinese media, by the end of 2015 a total of 584 leaders at the county level or above lost their leadership positions or were demoted as a result of this new regulation.[16] Some ministerial- and provincial-level leaders were demoted to far lower level positions because of noncriminal wrongdoings. For example, Wei Hong, former governor of Sichuan and Zhang Yun, former president of the Agricultural Bank of China, were recently demoted to positions at the department- and division-level, respectively. A new Chinese term, "falling-off-a-cliff demotion" (悬崖式降职, *xuanyashi jiangzhi*), has been coined to refer to this new phenomenon.[17] This new development will likely make the leadership turnover at the 19th National Party Congress more dynamic and less predictable than in the past.

In particular, this CCP resolution will likely pave the way for Xi and his team to remove a large number of leaders who would otherwise be qualified to stay in their positions or even be promoted. Before the announcement of this new party resolution, overseas Chinese media speculated that Xi's team planned to prevent Liu Qibao (a *tuanpai* leader) from entering the next PSC or even force him to step down on the grounds of incompetence.[18] Some observers believe that Xi's team may use the same reasoning to prevent Hu Chunhua from entering the next PSC. But since the public sees Hu Chunhua as an effective leader, this may not be so easy. Since becoming the party boss of Guangdong in 2012, Hu Chunhua has made some significant achievements in infrastructure development, industrial park growth, and county-level urbanization in the province.[19] As for Sun Chunlan, some conventional obstacles stand in the way of her promotion: no woman has ever served on the PSC in CCP history, and over the past half century, no director of the United Front Work Department, the position that Sun currently holds, has been promoted to the PSC.

Understandably, Xi will consider a large pool of candidates, especially his well-positioned protégés who are qualified in age. Table 9-2 lists twenty-four high-ranking leaders in Xi's inner circle who were born after 1950. Xi's three confidants—Li Zhanshu, Zhao Leji, and Han Zheng—are among the top contenders for the next PSC, and a handful of others may be selected for the first time to serve in the next Politburo or even on the PSC.

Xi's college roommate Chen Xi currently serves as the executive deputy director of the Central Organization Department and will play a key role in the formation of the next Central Committee. Chen Xi, known for his low-profile personality and coalition-building skills, is a strong candidate for Politburo membership. Huang Kunming is also a good candidate. As the current executive deputy director of the Central Propaganda Department, Huang is in line for the directorship and thus a seat in the next Politburo. Another leading candidate for a Politburo seat is He Yiting, who currently plays the same role as Wang Huning (that is, an adviser to senior leaders), especially as it relates to domestic affairs and ideological matters. Wang Chen, who currently serves as vice-chairman and secretary-general of the NPC, is another contender for a seat in the next Politburo. With his predecessor Li Jianguo's promotion to the Politburo as precedent, Wang will likely follow. As discussed in chapter 8, Wang's experience as a sent-down youth alongside Xi Jinping in Yan'an, as well as his leadership experience in propaganda and media, may enhance his opportunities for further promotion.

Liu He has been widely considered an adviser rather than a policymaker. However, Liu's career path, especially over the past two decades, has closely mirrored that of former vice-premier and Politburo member Zeng Peiyan. Thus, Liu could be considered a very strong candidate for a Politburo seat and for vice-premiership in the next round of leadership turnover.[20] He Li-feng, who is currently in charge of the strategic development of the "One Belt, One Road" initiative, is also a candidate for a state councilor position in the State Council and perhaps even a seat in the Politburo.

Provincial leadership has always been the main conduit to Politburo membership. Two of Xi's protégés, newly appointed Guizhou party secretary Chen Min'er and Liaoning party secretary Li Xi, apparently have received strong endorsements from Xi. Both Chen and Li also have a chance for

TABLE 9-2. The Prospects for Xi Jinping's Protégés for the 19th Central Committee in 2017 and the Next State Council in 2018

Name	Birth year	Current position	Tenure since	Ties with Xi Jinping	Functional area	18th Central Committee status	19th Central Committee prospects for promotion
Li Zhanshu	1950	Director of the General Office, Central Committee	2012	Colleague of Xi in Hebei	Party operation	Politburo member	PSC
Zhao Leji	1957	Director of the CCP Org. Department	2012	Shaanxi native	Organization	Politburo member	PSC
Han Zheng	1954	Shanghai Party Secretary	2012	Colleague of Xi in Shanghai	Economy	Politburo member	PSC and Executive Vice-Premier
Chen Xi	1953	Executive Deputy Director of the CCP Organization Department	2013	Roommate at Tsinghua University	Organization	Full member	Politburo (or Secretariat), Director of the Organization Department
Liu He	1952	Director of the Office of the Central Economic Leading Group	2013	Childhood friend	Economy	Full member	Politburo and Vice-Premier
He Yiting	1951	Executive Vice-President of the Central Party School	2013	Shaanxi native and *mishu* to Xi	Propaganda	Full member	Politburo (or Secretariat)
Chen Min'er	1960	Guizhou Party Secretary	2015	Junior colleague of Xi in Zhejiang	Provincial leadership	Full member	Politburo (or Secretariat) and Vice-Premier

(continued)

TABLE 9-2. (*continued*)

Name	Birth year	Current position	Tenure since	Ties with Xi Jinping	Functional area	18th Central Committee status	19th Central Committee prospects for promotion
Wang Chen	1950	Vice-Chair and Chief-of-Staff of the NPC	2013	Fellow sent-down youth in Yan'an, Shaanxi	Legislative	Full member	Politburo and Executive Vice-Chair of the NPC
Zhang Youxia	1950	CMC member, Director of the General Armament Department	2012	Family ties and childhood friend	Military	Full member	Politburo and Vice-Chair of the CMC
Cai Yingting	1954	President of Academy of Military Science	2016	Stationed in Fujian when Xi was a municipal and provincial leader there	Military	Full member	Politburo, Vice-Chair (or member) of the CMC
Zhang Shibo	1952	President, National Defense University	2014	Stationed in Hong Kong and Macao when Xi was in charge there	Military	Full member	Member of the CMC and Minister of Defense
Li Xi	1956	Liaoning Party Secretary	2015	Confidant and member of the Shaanxi Gang	Provincial leadership	Alternate member	Politburo (or Secretariat), Vice-Premier, Full member
He Lifeng	1955	Deputy Director of the NDRC	2014	Junior colleague of Xi in Xiamen and Fujian	Economy	Alternate member	Politburo, Full member, Minister of the NDRC or State Councilor

Huang Kunming	1956	Executive Deputy Director of the CCP Propaganda Department	2014	Junior colleague of Xi in Fujian and Zhejiang	Propaganda	Alternate member	Politburo (or Secretariat), Full member, Director of Propaganda Department
Ding Xuexiang	1962	Deputy Director of the CCP General Office	2013	*Mishu* to Xi in Shanghai	Party operation	Alternate member	Secretariat, Full member
Li Qiang	1959	Zhejiang Governor	2013	Chief of staff to Xi in Zhejiang	Provincial leadership	Alternate member	Secretariat, Full member
Lu Wei	1960	Director of the Cyberspace Affairs Administration	2013	Confidant in media outreach and cyber-space affairs	Propaganda and cyberspace	None	Secretariat, Full member
Yang Xiaodu	1953	Deputy Secretary of the CCDI	2014	Junior colleague of Xi in Shanghai	Party discipline	CCDI member	Secretariat, Full member
Li Shulei	1964	Discipline Inspection Secretary of the Beijing Municipal Party Com.	2015	Colleague at the Central Party School	Propaganda	CCDI member	Secretariat, Full member
Cai Qi	1955	Deputy Director of the Office of the NSC	2014	Deputy Director of the office of the Fujian Provincial Party Committee	State security	None	Secretariat, Full member
Zhong Shan	1955	Trade Negotiator, Vice-Minister of Commerce	2014	Junior colleague of Xi in Zhejiang	Economy	None	Full member and Minister of Commerce

(continued)

TABLE 9-2. (*continued*)

Name	Birth year	Current position	Tenure since	Ties with Xi Jinping	Functional area	18th Central Committee status	19th Central Committee prospects for promotion
Song Tao	1955	Director of the International Liaison Department of the CCP Central Committee	2015	Junior colleague of Xi in Fujian	Foreign Affairs	None	Full member and Director of the International Liaison Department of the CCP
Wang Shaojun	1955	Director of the Bodyguard Bureau of the CCP General Office	2015	Chief bodyguard for Xi	Military	None	Full member and Deputy Director of the General Office of the CCP
Yang Zhenwu	1955	President of *People's Daily*	2014	*People's Daily* reporter in Hebei who wrote feature story about Xi	Propaganda	None	Full member and President of Xinhua News Agency

Note and Source: PSC = Politburo Standing Committee; CCP = Chinese Communist Party; NPC = National People's Congress; CMC = Central Military Commission; NDRC = National Development and Reform Commission; CCDI = Central Commission for Discipline Inspection; NSC = National Security Committee. Data from the author's database.

vice-premiership posts in the next State Council and membership in the next Politburo. Chen, known for his liberal policies promoting market reform and his leadership capacity in running both an economically advanced province (Zhejiang) and an economically underdeveloped province (Guizhou), is a political rising star in the sixth generation. In 2015, Guizhou had the second largest GDP growth (10.7 percent) among China's thirty-one province-level entities, second only to Chongqing (11 percent). The deputy director of the General Office of the Central Committee, Ding Xuexiang, is expected to succeed Li Zhanshu sometime in the near future, when Li takes another top leadership position. Ding will also be a leading candidate for membership in the next Secretariat. If so, Zhejiang governor Li Qiang, an office director for Xi during his Zhejiang years, will likely move to Beijing to take over Ding's current position and thus may also obtain a seat in the Secretariat.

Several other Xi protégés, including Yang Xiaodu, Li Shulei, Lu Wei, and Cai Qi, also have an opportunity to join the next Secretariat. In CCP history, the political weight of the Secretariat has varied. It has the potential to play a crucial role in the top leadership's decisionmaking, as demonstrated at the Fifth Plenum of the 12th Central Committee, which was held in February 1980, two years after Deng took power.[21] The Secretariat formed at that plenum was much younger—in average age—than the corresponding Politburo and the PSC. More important, the Secretariat formed in 1980 was officially designated the "frontline leadership body" (第一线, *diyixian*), rather than an administrative body that only handled paper flow. The main objective of this Hu Yaobang–led Secretariat was to assist Deng Xiaoping in "selecting and nurturing younger successors" (培养接班人, *peiyang jiebanren*).[22]

The Secretariat usually consists of heavyweight figures and rising stars. For example, the Secretariat of the 15th Central Committee (1997–2002) consisted of Hu Jintao, Wei Jianxing, Ding Guangen, Zhang Wannian, Luo Gan, Wen Jiabao, and Zeng Qinghong. Five of them concurrently or later served as members of the PSC, and one later became vice-chairman of the Central Military Commission (CMC). After 2002 Hu became general secretary of the party and PRC president, Zeng Qinghong became PRC vice-president, and Wen Jiabao served as premier of the State Council. In his second term, Xi may entrust the Secretariat with far more power than it now holds.

Among the military leaders, Zhang Youxia, Xi's longtime friend and a fellow princeling from Shaanxi, will likely obtain a Politburo seat. (General Xu Qiliang is also likely to serve his second term in the Politburo.) Cai Yingting, a longtime friend of Xi's from his Fujian years, was a leading candidate for chief of the CMC Joint Staff Department. But in December 2015, Cai was transferred from his position as commander of the Nanjing Military

Region to become president of the PLA Academy of Military Science. Cai may still have a chance for a seat in the CMC if his current position is just transitional. But, at present, Cai is no longer considered a top contender for the next CMC. Rumor is that Cai's daughter has married an American, and thus CCP regulations prohibit him from being considered for a seat in the CMC (as discussed in the previous chapter).

Former commander of the Beijing Military Region and current president of the National Defense University Zhang Shibo developed strong personal ties with Xi while he was stationed in Hong Kong and Macau. During this period of close contact with Zhang—from 2007 to 2012—Xi was in charge of Hong Kong affairs in Zhongnanhai. Zhang is also a candidate for membership in the CMC.

Table 9-2 also lists several Xi protégés who are not in the current Central Committee. They are more likely to obtain full membership in the next Central Committee, rather than Politburo or Secretariat membership. Several are likely to serve in ministerial posts in the State Council, including key positions in various functional areas—Zhong Shan in economic and commercial affairs, Song Tao in foreign affairs, Wang Shaojun in military and security affairs, and Yang Zhenwu in media and public relations.

Although Xi seems to carry more sway over personnel promotion than his predecessor Hu Jintao did, his power still has limits. In fact, Xi does not have a large pool of protégés from which to choose. It is, of course, far too early to know how Xi will manage this challenge to the factional lineup as the next party congress approaches. Even if all of Xi's protégés who are listed in table 9-2 are able to obtain their desired promotions, they can only occupy a total of three seats on the PSC and eleven seats on the Politburo. Therefore, it is debatable whether or not Xi's trusted protégés can truly dominate these two critical leadership bodies in his second term. Even if Xi and his confidants are able to dominate power of these two leadership bodies, what political risks and opposition will Xi and his team face? As some Chinese analysts insightfully point out, the "top leader often realizes that the candidate pool is too small to choose from when one needs to do so" (人到用时方恨少, *rendao yongshi fanghenshao*).[23]

XI'S THREE OPTIONS

Through what process—and according to what criteria—will the members of the next PSC be chosen? Arguably more than anything else, Xi's handling of this crucial question will reveal his stance on the governance and political institutionalization of the country. Barring an entirely unforeseen or aberrant incident, three mutually exclusive options exist for Xi: (1) a firm return to one-person rule similar to the Mao and Deng eras, including a scenario wherein Xi would not only serve more than two terms, but also pick—at his will—members of the PSC who will serve largely as his personal cabinet; (2) a compromise with the competing faction that results in power sharing among a "team of rivals;" and (3) a surprising move to expand election mechanisms, which would allow, for the first time in PRC history, members of the yet-to-be established 19th Central Committee to vote for members of the Politburo and the PSC.

Political circumstances, including both public sentiment and the attitudes of the political establishment, are important factors that will influence Xi's ultimate decision, as will be discussed in the final part of this chapter. Nevertheless, given Xi's noticeable consolidation of power during his first term, China analysts—and the Chinese public—will largely attribute this selection to Xi's personal preferences. Understandably, none of these options is easy to pursue, and each involves serious political risk on the part of the Xi leadership. Analyzing the risks and rewards of each of these vastly different political scenarios is critical to understanding the choices that lie before Xi.

Option One: Forming Xi's Personal Cabinet

Xi can spend any political capital that he accrues during his first term—including through his strong anticorruption campaign, firm control of personnel appointments, bold economic reform initiatives, grand structural reform of the PLA, and important foreign policy accomplishments—to justify a Pyrrhic victory in the selection of the next PSC. Specifically, he can return to the "good old days" under Mao and Deng, during which one paramount leader selected members of the PSC and turned this top leadership body into something resembling a personal cabinet. In a way, this means that Xi would completely abandon both term limits for the party leadership and the collective leadership model of the post-Deng era. To achieve this ambitious objective, however, Xi has to make fundamental changes in three important respects: ideological, conceptual, and institutional.

On the ideological front, the CCP would need to embrace, once again, strongman politics and the personality cult. According to some critics, this has been the trend ever since Xi became the top leader in the fall of 2012. The extensive publication of Xi's thoughts on governance, the establishment of the official "Fan Club of Xi Studies" (学习小组, *xue Xi xiaozu*) on social media, the widely used nickname "Papa Xi" (习大大, *Xi dada*), and the worship of places where Xi worked or visited are often cited as examples of the Xi personality cult.[24] Many China analysts both at home and abroad see the recent political rhetoric to name Xi the "core" (核心, *hexin*) of the CCP leadership as the latest effort to transform Xi from his status as "the first among equals in the PSC" to a Deng-like "paramount leader" above the PSC.[25]

In 2014 Qian Gang, a scholar at the University of Hong Kong, conducted research based on content analysis and found that during the first eighteen months of the Xi leadership, Xi's name appeared 4,725 times in the *People's Daily*, the official mouthpiece of the party. This was a significant increase over mentions of previous leaders. In the eighteen months after the Gang of Four were arrested in 1976, Hua Guofeng (Mao's immediate successor) was mentioned 2,605 times. Likewise, in the first eighteen months after they each became general secretary, Jiang Zemin and Hu Jintao were mentioned 2,001 times and 2,405 times, respectively.[26] The frequency with which Xi's name appeared was second only to that of Mao, who was referenced in the *People's Daily* approximately 7,000 times in the eighteen months after the 1969 National Party Congress.[27]

The military parade in September 2015 commemorating the seventieth anniversary of victory in the Anti-Japanese War was widely perceived as a grand political show, arguably aimed more at enhancing Xi's claim for absolute authority over the PLA than at displaying the capabilities of the Chinese military itself. In a widely circulated article published in *People's Daily*, the deputy chief commander of China's 2015 military parade and vice-political commissar of the Beijing Military Region, Wang Jian, stated firmly that this military parade would first and foremost demonstrate the "immeasurable loyalty" (无比忠诚, *wubi zhongcheng*) and "absolute support" (坚决支持, *jianjue zhichi*) of the PLA to the Central Committee of the CCP and to President Xi Jinping.[28]

According to an old CCP saying, "political power grows out of the barrel of a gun."[29] Although this famous slogan—coined by Mao—emphasizes the communist doctrine that the party commands the army in seizing and retaining state power, it is equally true that a top party leader's personality cult cannot be developed without strong support from the military. And so it is in today's China under the leadership of Xi Jinping, according to some critics. As discussed earlier, when Xi became the top leader at the 2012 National Party Congress, he also assumed chairmanship of the CMC. This move was in remarkable contrast to Xi's predecessor Hu Jintao, who waited two years before taking up the paramount military post in the previous political succession. Even more astounding, Xi made a bold and decisive move to imprison about fifty military generals on corruption charges, including the two highest-ranking military generals from the previous administration.[30] The quick and sweeping military reforms implemented in late 2015 and early 2016 greatly enhanced Xi's power and authority in the PLA.[31]

Some China analysts observe that there has been a strong call for the "return of ideology" (意识形态的回归, *yishi xingtai de huigui*) under the Xi leadership.[32] As discussed in chapter 6, some of Xi's confidants, such as Huang Kunming, He Yiting, and Li Shulei, have been quite aggressive in promoting Xi's conservative ideological stance. Wang Weiguang, a full member of the 18th Central Committee and president of the Chinese Academy of Social Sciences, wrote an article in 2014 claiming that the CCP should continue to embrace the Leninist ideology of class struggle and proletarian dictatorship.[33] Some Chinese critics call Wang's article "a prelude to the new Cultural Revolution."[34]

Of course, the comparison between Mao and Xi ends there; China is *not* preparing to embark on another Cultural Revolution. As has been widely noted, Wang's article received far more criticism than support, because old-fashioned communist ideology has very few adherents. In fact, the CCP leadership has acknowledged a "loss of beliefs" and an "ideological vacuum" in the country.[35] Even the theoreticians and scholars within the CCP establishment openly criticize this new phase of communist ideological indoctrination and personality cult building. Yu Keping, the new dean of the School of Government at Peking University and a well-respected Chinese thinker who until recently served as deputy director of the CCP Central Compilation and Translation Bureau, argued in 2014 that Deng Xiaoping's most important legacy was "the emancipation of the mind, the complete rejection of the Cultural Revolution and personality cults, the reform of the party and state leadership system, and the recognition of peace and development as the overall theme of today's world."[36] Wang Changjiang, director of the Party Building Research Department of the Central Party School and a distinguished party theoretician, recently wrote an essay emphasizing the importance of intraparty democracy and the necessity of preventing the "arbitrary rule of the top-ranked leader" (一把手专断, *yibashou zhuanduan*).[37] In Wang's view, intraparty democracy may undermine the authority of the top leader, but it also enhances leadership legitimacy and thus the viability of the ruling party.[38]

As for the military parade, some Chinese scholars have publicly criticized the Leninist mentality behind this grand event. For example, Zhou Yongkun, a distinguished law professor at Suzhou University, challenged the purpose behind and constitutional justification for the parade by requesting that Chinese authorities disclose the total cost of the military parade.[39] A week after the parade, Zhang Qianfan, a professor of constitutional law at Peking University, told the *Wall Street Journal* that "any country without a sound political system, media freedom and democracy could become the next Fascist nation."[40] Although Zhang's remarks ostensibly referred to Japan, he perhaps had another country in mind.

Zhang's comparison, however, is somewhat sensationalist. Li Weidong, a Chinese dissident intellectual, has offered some basic reasons as to why China will not become the next Nazi Germany: (1) the Nazis had a strong belief system, whereas the CCP no longer has one; (2) elites in Nazi Germany were disciplined and united, but the CCP leadership is beset with factional politics; (3) the Nazis were largely free of economic corruption, but corruption is rampant among CCP elites; and (4) the Nazis had a unified and supportive mass following, but the Chinese public is quite cynical about CCP leadership in general.[41] Also, as discussed in chapter 1, most critics of Xi's personality cult do not believe that Xi will be able to become a Mao-like figure, even if he may so desire.[42]

Some observers believe that Xi and his team's motives are not really about ideology. These ideological indoctrination efforts have nothing to do with the notion of struggle over choosing the right path (路线斗争, *luxian douzheng*), but rather are related to the fact that Xi and the new leadership have had difficulty finding a new legitimacy and mechanism for governance in the wake of the Bo Xilai affair and other recent major scandals.[43] According to Yu Jianrong, a prominent critic in Beijing, Xi Jinping needs to test various waters and determine the best political strategy with which to move forward.[44]

On the conceptual front, in order to return to strongman politics, Xi would have to change the definition of "political elite generations" from the current lineup of five generations (led respectively by Mao, Deng, Jiang, Hu, and Xi) to a lineup of only three generations (Mao, Deng, and Xi). As discussed in chapter 3, the concept and definition of political elite generations can be highly political and manipulated by top leaders. For instance, as a participant in the Long March, Deng probably should not be placed alongside Zhao Ziyang and Hu Yaobang as part of the Anti-Japanese War generation (that is, second generation). Yet, by identifying himself as the "core" of the second generation and Jiang as the "core" of the third generation, Deng was determined to ensure a smooth political succession in the wake of the failures of his two previously appointed successors (Hu and Zhao). Jiang, on the other hand, used generational identity as the "core of the third generation" to consolidate his political legitimacy as heir to Deng. It is interesting to note that the notion of the "core leader" was in fact also used in collective leadership during the Jiang era, so it is not necessarily an indication of a return to strongman politics.

Some observers argue that Xi now intends to change the existing formulation by eliminating Jiang's third generation and Hu's fourth generation. According to Zheng Yongnian, a distinguished Singapore-based expert on Chinese politics, Mao and Deng each ruled China for thirty years, based on their decisionmaking roles and long-term impacts on policy, and Xi may plan to achieve this same length of influence in his own era.[45] In other words, "Mao is the first generation, Deng is the second generation, and Xi is the third generation."[46] With this categorization, there is no need to appoint the previously defined sixth-generation leaders, such as Hu Chunhua and Sun Zhengcai, to the next PSC. Likewise, the question of political succession at the 19th National Party Congress is moot because the 2012–17 period represents only the first five years of Xi's thirty years of control!

On the institutional front, Xi could enhance the role of various central leadership groups and turn the Secretariat into a de facto decisionmaking body, thus substantially undermining the power of the PSC. He could also formally abolish term limits and age requirements for retirement, which would allow him and probably his most important political ally, Wang Qishan, to remain in power beyond their defined tenures. Xi could also change the institutional regulations and norms for the next round of leadership turnover, not unlike the way he has strayed from the practices of collective leadership over the past three years. In the recent military reshuffling, for example, the promotions of Xi's two protégés to the rank of full general (Wang Ning to commander of the People's Armed Police and Miao Hua to political commissar of the navy) did not comply with institutional norms, as explained in chapter 8.

The appointment of Song Puxuan to serve as commander of the Beijing Military Region at the end of 2014 (Song also was commander of the military parade) was a surprise to many analysts because Song is not a member of the 18th Central Committee of the CCP. His predecessors Li Xinliang, Zhu Qi, Fang Fenghui, and Zhang Shibo were all members of the Central Committee when they were appointed to this position. This extraordinary situation reflects Xi's determination to place loyal generals in key positions in the PLA and his heavy reliance on senior officers who advanced their careers from the Nanjing Military Region, especially from the Thirty-first Group Army, to which Xi has strong personal ties.

In the civilian leadership, the rapid promotion of Xi's confidant Li Xi over the past three years is another good example of noncompliance with institutional norms, as discussed in chapter 8. According to a recent report, a number of newly appointed bureau chiefs (at the rank of vice-minister) in the State Council—for example, director of the State Oceanic Administration Wang Hong, director of the State Secrecy Bureau Tian Jing, and director of the National Archives Li Minghua—all jumped ahead of the regular lineup of candidates.[47] As an overseas China watcher observes, Xi likes to appoint leaders who "come from behind" (后来居上, *houlai jushang*).[48]

But the above cases are exceptions, not norms. Conceptual and institutional changes would perhaps be as difficult to achieve as ideological ones. As Henry Kissinger observes, each and every leader of the five elite political generations in the PRC reflects that generation's own historical circumstances and learning experiences, and each generation should be seen as a particular phase of the overall leadership evolution. The achievements of the top leader of one generation often build on the experiences of the preceding generation.[49] Thus, it is not easy to eliminate any generation of leadership from either public perception or historical memory. Some Chinese public intellectuals have bluntly opposed any step backward in institution building. Han Dayuan, dean of the Law School at People's University, argues that China confronts "two core problems." First is lack of public consensus, and the other is power abuse. The Chinese leadership can resolve these two problems by embracing constitutionalism, which would allow for building consensus while constraining power.[50] According to Han, "If there is constitutional authority, China would not have so many central leading groups."[51] Nor would the country's political life be filled with leaders' speeches, official meetings, and party documents. Han further argues that "all other forms of authority—political, party, individual, judicial, institutional—should obey constitutional authority."[52]

Option Two: Sharing Power with Tuanpai

Xi's widely perceived monopolization of power and his personality cult seem to have alienated a large number of public intellectuals, especially liberal-minded intellectuals. Xi's bold anticorruption campaign, though popular among the public, has not only led to new and much broader "inaction" by officials at various levels of leadership but has also created many political enemies among senior leaders. Both of these conditions can seriously undermine Xi's ability to implement his policy agenda. It is not difficult to imagine that Xi's intellectual critics and political rivals will quickly mobilize if a major crisis occurs in his administration's handling of either domestic or international issues. The strongest resistance most likely will come from within the national leadership. The Hu-Li camp, especially the *tuanpai* leaders, will conceivably pose the strongest opposition should a winner-take-all leadership change indeed occur in 2017.

Ironically, while Hu Jintao and Li Keqiang were not seen as aggressive in appointing their protégés to key posts, *tuanpai* officials constitute the largest factional group in the current Central Committee (as fully documented in chapter 7). The recent purges of several prominent *tuanpai* members have not changed the overall high representation of *tuanpai* leaders in the committee and also in the municipal and provincial leadership. Understandably, *tuanpai* leaders will vigorously fight for their political survival—and career prospects—during the next round of leadership turnover.

From Xi's perspective, although the anticorruption campaign and the aggressive promotion of protégés are essential for the consolidation of personal power, they should not be pursued at the expense of creating overwhelming fissures in the leadership. It thus remains an option for Xi to put more emphasis on mitigating tensions between competing factions, broadening his support base, and uniting the CCP leadership as he begins his second term. The idea of turning rivals into allies "for the sake of the greater good," as Abraham Lincoln put it, was widely cited by the mainstream Chinese media during the CCP leadership change in 2007 and 2008.[53] The Chinese discourse surrounding the "team of rivals" concept (政敌团队, *zhengdi tuandui*) emphasizes the need for political compromise that maximizes common interests and political capital in order to ensure the survival of CCP rule.[54]

Some scholars of Chinese elite politics consider it inappropriate—and premature—to conclude that Xi Jinping has abandoned collective leadership. Steve Tsang, head of the School of Contemporary Chinese Studies at the University of Nottingham, observes:

> There is little doubt that Xi is in the driving seat but he has apparently not imposed his will on his colleagues in the Politburo and its Standing Committee in a way that would provoke a backlash, at least not yet. What Xi has so far demonstrated is an attempt to lead from the front and yet he has managed to preserve a collective leadership.[55]

A possible backlash against Xi will not only come from the elite. While the Chinese public generally supports Xi's anticorruption campaign, their stance may change if the campaign looks to be driven by factional politics. According to Tsang, one should not jump to the conclusion that China's collective leadership no longer exists. The fact that Xi's colleagues in the Politburo and the PSC have ceded to him the power needed to implement policies does not necessarily mean that collective leadership has been abandoned at this crucial moment in China's socioeconomic development. This is particularly important if one recognizes that bureaucratic resistance prevented the Hu and Wen administration from accomplishing its policy initiatives. Such an endorsement from the leadership, however, should not be seen as a blank check for Xi—neither now nor in the future. "Much needed economic reforms have been slow to be implemented, again suggesting that Xi is not quite as all-powerful as it may seem," explains Tsang.[56] In a sense, as Tsang further argues, "Xi's outward confidence belies an acute sense of insecurity."[57]

Steve Tsang's observation seems to be substantiated by the fact that Xi has had to compromise and negotiate over personnel appointments despite his reputation of being a very powerful leader. For example, in April 2014 Xi's confidant Li Xi obtained the governor's post in Liaoning by defeating the other strong candidate, Shenyang party secretary Zeng Wei, who is a *tuanpai* leader and former chief-of-staff for Li Keqiang in Liaoning.[58] At the same time, however, Li Xi's predecessor, the former governor of Liaoning Chen Zhenggao, a *tuanpai* leader and a protégé of Li Keqiang, obtained a cabinet post as minister of Housing and Urban-Rural Development in the State Council. Chen is now well positioned to carry out Premier Li's affordable housing program nationwide. A deal seems to have been made on these personnel appointments between Xi Jinping and Li Keqiang, or between their competing political camps.

Term limits, age requirements for retirement, and the once-per-decade generational transfer of power are important political and institutional developments in China during the post-Deng era. These institutional mechanisms may be the contributing factors that allow the CCP to remain in power. As Francis Fukuyama, a distinguished American scholar, writes, "One of the things that I think has made the current Chinese leadership exceptional among authoritarian regimes is the fact that there are term limits. You have these three turnovers of leadership on 10-year intervals. You have retirement, a somewhat mandatory retirement age and so forth. Most dictatorships don't do this."[59] It is interesting to note that first Wang Qishan and then Xi Jinping held private meetings with Francis Fukuyama during his visits to Beijing in 2015.[60]

Some Chinese scholars who are in favor of political institutionalization and power sharing have argued that it is in everyone's interest to avoid vicious power struggles in the leadership. Sun Liping, a distinguished public intellectual and a professor of sociology at Tsinghua University, condemns the brutality in factional politics during the Mao era. He argues that the tragedy of the Cultural Revolution can be traced to the fact that "factional politics failed to be institutionalized," and thus matters often spiraled out of control. Sun calls for the "institutionalization of factional politics" (派系政治制度化, *paixi zhengzhi zhiduhua*) in China's future political development.[61]

Furthermore, some Chinese scholars argue that power sharing in the top leadership could help "reconcile tensions among competing factions and different social groups."[62] The absence of such "an intraparty democratic system," writes Zheng Yongnian, could be a fatal "subversive error" of the party leadership.[63] Zheng asserts that the essence of democracy is compromise. This concept was weak in traditional Chinese culture, which embraced the notion of "the victor becomes a king and the loser a bandit" (胜者为王, 败者为寇, *shengzhe weiwang, baizhe weikou*).[64] In Zheng's view the CCP's internal pluralism (内部多元主义, *neibu duoyuan zhuyi*)—in terms of compromise and power sharing, rather than election (either intraparty election or general election)—should be the most effective way to ensure Chinese political institutionalization.[65]

But the notion of compromise and power sharing is often easier said than done. For Xi this means bringing several ambitious *tuanpai* leaders—notably Wang Yang, Hu Chunhua, and perhaps also Liu Qibao (currently director of the Central Propaganda Department)—into the next PSC. If so, the Hu-Li camp, including returning member Li Keqiang, will take the majority of seats on the PSC. Even if only three *tuanpai* leaders (Li Keqiang, Wang Yang, and Hu Chunhua) make it to the PSC, Xi's current six-to-one overwhelming majority will become a four-to-three marginal majority after the 19th National Party Congress, assuming the new PSC still has seven seats.

Even worse, from Xi's perspective, is that two new PSC members from the rival camp, Hu Chunhua and Wang Yang, will become formidable contenders for power in Xi's second term. Hu will likely be seen as Xi's successor, and Wang will be the top candidate to succeed Li Keqiang as the next premier, and both will significantly undermine the power and influence of Xi himself. Xi may not see any incentive to take this option unless he is absolutely forced to make such a compromise. For Xi's team, it would seem ironic to end up with such a factional lineup in the supreme leadership body after Xi's remarkable effort to consolidate his power throughout his first term.

Option Three: Initiating Elections for Politburo Standing Committee Membership

A third, more unconventional option would be for Xi to adopt some new electoral methods for intraparty competition that enhance political legitimacy and maintain his majority control in the PSC. Through some creative electoral procedures, Xi might be able to maximize his political influence beyond the term limit in the short run and to retain his leadership legacy in the long run. This unprecedented approach would drastically change the existing selection criteria and methods for forming the next Politburo and PSC. Such an approach could take the form of an expansion of electoral mechanisms, or what the Chinese call "intraparty democracy," which could profoundly boost the legitimacy of the CCP leadership.

As discussed in chapter 3, since the 13th National Party Congress in 1987, the Chinese leadership has used multicandidate elections, known as "more-candidates-than-seats elections," for the formation of the Central Committee.[66] At the election for full members of the 17th Central Committee in 2007, for example, over 2,200 congressional delegates elected 204 full members from 221 candidates on the ballot (8.3 percent were eliminated). Similarly, in the election for alternate members of the committee, they elected 167 leaders from a candidate pool of 183 (9.6 percent were eliminated).[67] Xi may increase the percentage of those who will be eliminated in the committee election at the 19th National Party Congress. More important, for the first time in CCP history, Xi may use a "more-candidates-than-seats election" for the formation of the Politburo and even the PSC.

Political circumstances on the eve of the 2017 National Party Congress will be the main determinant of whether Xi chooses this third option. As discussed in chapter 7, in the leadership formed at the 18th National Party Congress, the Jiang-Xi camp achieved a landslide victory in the PSC (winning an overwhelming six-to-one majority) but weaker representation in the Central Committee compared with the Hu-Li camp. But in the lead-up to the 19th National Party Congress, Xi is likely to confront a situation that is just the opposite. Xi may not be able to maintain an overwhelming majority on the next PSC, but on the new Central Committee he will likely be able to replace many members of the Hu-Li camp with his longtime protégés and new loyalists.

As discussed in chapter 3, the CCP leadership has maintained an impressively high turnover rate in the Central Committee. Newcomers constituted on average 62.3 percent of each of the seven committees formed over the past three decades (see Figure 3-1). The membership turnover rate for the 18th Central Committee, for example, was 64.4 percent. Excluding the full members who were promoted from their alternate status on the 17th committee, a total of 183 leaders on the 18th—58 new full members and 125 new alternates—are first-timers (48.7 percent of the total).

One can reasonably expect that the turnover rate on the 19th Central Committee will be even higher than it was for the 18th. Table 9-3 illustrates the prospects for current 18th Central Committee members. A total of 20 members have been purged in Xi's anticorruption campaign over the past three years. Another 142 members (76 full members and 66 alternate members) have already retired or are expected to retire by 2017 given three observations: (1) age limits will require that members born before 1950 retire; (2) some members, despite remaining qualified for the next committee in terms of age, have recently been transferred to ceremonial positions, also known as "being transferred to second-line work" (退居二线, *tuiju erxian*), and are likely to serve on various functional committees of the National People's Congress and the Chinese People's Political Consultative Conference; and (3) some members that were seen as protégés of patrons have recently been purged or are under investigation for corruption.

In addition, a total of 66 members, including 50 full members and 16 alternate members, are likely to retire in the next two years. This observation is based on the fact that these leaders have remained in their current positions for many years—suggesting that they are less promising than those that have frequently been reshuffled or promoted to more-important positions. According to a recent study conducted by PRC scholars, of the 205 current

TABLE 9-3. 18th Central Committee Members' Prospects for the Next Central Committee

18th Central Committee	Purged during the past few years		Already retired		Will likely retire in 2017		Alternate member likely to be promoted to full member		Likely to remain on the 19th Central Committee		Likely to remain on the 19th Central Committee (including those promoted from alternate)	
	No.	%	No.	%	No.	%	No.	%	No.	%	No.	%
Full member N=205	8	3.9	76	37.1	50	24.4	—	—	71	34.6	71	34.6
Alternate member N=171	12	7.0	66	38.6	16	9.4	44	25.7	33	19.3	77	45.0
Total N=376	20	5.3	142	37.8	66	17.6	44	11.7	104	27.7	148	39.4

Source: Author's database.

full Central Committee members, 104 have moved to different positions over the past three years. Eight members were purged and 15 members have "moved to second-line work," but the remaining 81 members have all been promoted or rotated to positions at the same level of leadership to gain more administrative credentials.[68] Most of them will remain on the next committee. By contrast, those who have stayed in their current positions for many years will likely be transferred to "second-line work" before or at the next National Party Congress and thus give up their CCP Central Committee membership.

As for alternate members, this study estimates that 94 will be replaced and 77 will remain on the next Central Committee, including 44 who will likely be promoted to full members. Based on the above analysis, there will be about 230 first-timers on the 19th Central Committee (compared with 183 first-timers on the 18th). The turnover rate will be over 70 percent counting those full members who are promoted from alternate status, or over 60 percent if promoted members are excluded. These estimated turnover rates are higher than the turnover rate of any Central Committee since 1982 (see figure 3-1).

A large number of Xi's protégés will likely enter the 19th Central Committee as first-timers. The top thirty-one candidates are director of the International Liaison Department of the CCP Central Committee Song Tao (b. 1955), commander of the Northern Theater of Operation Song Puxuan (b. 1954), political commissar of the navy Miao Hua (b. 1955), political commissar of the air force Yu Zhongfu (b. 1956), deputy secretary of the Central Commission for Discipline Inspection Yang Xiaodu (b. 1953), party secretary of the Ministry of State Security Chen Wenqing (b. 1960), director of the Office of the Central Leading Group for Network Security and Information Technology Lu Wei (b. 1960), deputy director of the Office of the National Security Council Cai Qi (b. 1955), executive deputy director of the Office of the Central Leading Group for Comprehensively Deepening Reforms Mu Hong (b. 1956), deputy director of the Office of the Central Economic and Financial Leading Group Shu Guozeng (b. 1956), executive vice-director of the State Internet Information Office Xu Lin (b. 1963), minister of Environmental Protection Chen Jining (b. 1964), trade negotiator and vice-minister of Commerce Zhong Shan (b. 1955), Hainan governor Liu Cigui (b. 1955), president of *People's Daily* Yang Zhenwu (b. 1955), Shanghai deputy party secretary Ying Yong (b. 1957), Tianjin deputy party secretary Wang Dongfeng (b. 1958), Shandong deputy party secretary Gong Zheng (b. 1960), Shanxi deputy party secretary Lou Yangsheng (b. 1959), director of the Bodyguard Bureau of the CCP General Office Wang Shaojun (b. 1955), vice-chairman of the China Securities Regulatory Commission Fang Xinghai (b. 1964), deputy director of the General Office of the CMC Zhong Shaojun (b. 1968), deputy director of the General Office of the CMC Wang Anlong (b. 1968?), vice-minister of the Ministry of Public Security Meng Qingfeng (b. 1957), president of the Baosteel Group Chen Derong (b. 1961), discipline secretary of the Ministry of Public Security Deng Weiping (b. 1955), commander of the Central Theater of Operation Han Weiguo (b. 1956), political commissar of the Beijing Garrison Jiang Yong (b. 1956), vice-mayor and director of Public Security in Beijing Wang Xiaohong (b. 1957), secretary of the Discipline Inspection Commission of Beijing Li Shulei (b. 1964), and director of the Propaganda Department of the Guangdong Provincial Party Committee Shen Haixiong (b. 1967).

According to the norms of CCP elite selection, the leaders listed above are likely to secure seats as full or alternate members in the next Central Committee. For example, directors of the CCP central departments, chief PLA officers in various services and theaters of operation (previously greater military regions), ministers of the State Council, and provincial party secretaries and governors usually serve as full committee members, and provincial deputy party secretaries often serve as alternate members. In addition, some leaders in the above list are likely to receive promotions in the months before the 19th National Party Congress as a result of their strong ties to Xi.

The above list includes only Xi's own protégés. Several of Xi's closest confidants—for example, Li Zhanshu, Zhao Leji, and Chen Xi, who currently control personnel matters in the CCP—will surely recruit their own loyalists into the 19th Central Committee. Some of Xi's heavyweight political allies, most notably Wang Qishan, will presumably also bring their followers into the 19th committee. Altogether, they will significantly expand the Xi camp in the next committee. On top of that, approximately thirty returning members to the 19th Central Committee (seventeen full members and thirteen alternate members on the 18th committee) are known as Xi's protégés. While the Hu-Li camp, especially its *tuanpai* faction, will likely remain a considerable force on the 19th committee, it will no longer hold the impressively large number of seats that it does on the 18th, in which ninety-nine members can be identified as *tuanpai* officials (see figure 7-1). Instead, Xi's protégés—including members of the Shaanxi Gang; those who previously worked under Xi in Fujian, Zhejiang, and Shanghai; and Xi's fellow princelings and alumni of Tsinghua University—will likely constitute the largest faction on the 19th Central Committee. Overall, the Xi coalition is expected to hold a majority on the 19th committee.

With this likely new composition of the next Central Committee in mind, Xi Jinping and his team may come to the conclusion that a method for Central Committee members to elect the Politburo or even the PSC will work in their favor. This would change the existing norm by which new PSC members are selected (that is, PSC members are elected only from the previous

Politburo, and new members of the Politburo are chosen exclusively from the previous Central Committee). This would also allow a few Xi protégés who do not serve on the 18th Politburo to occupy seats on the 19th PSC and some first-time Central Committee members to enter the new Politburo. Having launched a bold anticorruption campaign, ambitious market reform, and extensive structural reform in the PLA during his first term, Xi Jinping may be courageous enough to initiate this monumental political change. This would open the door to greater transformation of sociopolitical life in China. In a way, the Bo Xilai and Wang Yang style of political lobbying and campaigning in the lead-up to the 18th National Party Congress, as described in the prologue to this book, would return in a more institutionalized and legitimized fashion. At present, no signs show that Xi and his team are interested in pursuing these bold and consequential intraparty political reforms. Only time will tell if Xi will take this important step in 2017.

Whichever route he decides to take, Xi confronts some tough choices as the 2017 National Party Congress approaches:

— Total dominance by Xi and his camp in the selection of the next Politburo and PSC and the return of strongman politics would inevitably lead to robust resistance from the competing political coalition, provoke sharp criticism from the country's liberal intellectuals, and generate deep anxiety in the international community.

— A compromise and a power-sharing strategy would reinforce the structure of collective leadership that has developed over the previous two decades. This option would help Xi broaden support in the political establishment and unite the party leadership, but this would be at the expense of Xi's personal power and authority. Specifically, this means that Xi would have to step down at the end of his second term.

— A more election-oriented approach would once again profoundly change the game of Chinese elite politics and thus could vastly expand political competition. Through this bold initiative, Xi would likely solidify his historical legacy as the Chinese leader who made a remarkable contribution to Chinese-style democracy. In a sense, Xi's role would be similar to that of Jiang Jingguo (Chiang Ching-kuo), who initiated major political reforms in Taiwan in the late 1980s and thus is widely regarded as "the father of Taiwanese democracy." Xi's influence would extend beyond his decade-long tenure at the top of the CCP leadership. Yet, this option involves tremendous political risks for the party and the country, at least from the perspective of the ruling party. This option also means that Xi would most likely step down as party chief at the 20th National Party Congress in 2022, as CCP rules and regulations would be more vigorously enforced while intraparty democracy deepens.

Any of the three options that Xi adopts could have far-reaching consequences in the structure and governance of the country. However, no one can confidently predict which direction Xi Jinping will pursue. Even in the transparent political system of a country like the United States, where far more information is supposedly available, political analysts would not be able to predict what President George W. Bush or President Barack Obama would do in a given situation.[69] More to the point, even Xi himself might not have his mind made up at this point.

Without offering a prediction as to which of the three possible directions outlined above Xi Jinping is likely to take, analyzing the core meanings of these choices and the likely consequences of each is extremely valuable. This discussion reveals the profound tensions between personal power and institutional constraints in Chinese elite politics today, which is a daunting challenge that Xi Jinping faces. Elite politics, however, is certainly not the only fascinating narrative to emerge from the changing political landscape of the country. Societal changes in present-day China are equally consequential.

DYNAMIC SOCIAL FORCES AND THEIR IMPACT ON ELITE POLITICS

Chinese society has undergone momentous changes throughout the reform era, especially since the beginning of this century. It has been widely believed among China analysts that Chinese society has transformed faster and more substantially over the past few decades than the country's political structure. Just as new elite groups have ascended in the political leadership (for example, well-educated technocrats, rich entrepreneurs, and self-proclaimed or practicing lawyers), new and dynamic social groups have also emerged as important players in the country's political life. They include the country's emerging middle class, foreign-educated (especially Western-educated) returnees, commercialized media outlets, increasingly outspoken and diverse public intellectuals, independent NGO activists, and the legal community. Some large dissatisfied social clusters—including religious groups, unemployed college graduates, and demobilized soldiers—can mobilize quickly in political protest.

Furthermore, as a result of market reforms over the past two decades, every major social class—peasants, workers, intellectuals, and entrepreneurs—has undergone profound changes. Consequentially, substantially different subgroups in each of these classes have come to the fore. For example, within the traditional category of peasants, some have become rural entrepreneurs and others have become migrant workers. Furthermore, these subgroups have experienced generational changes, with younger cohorts differing from their older counterparts.

The dynamic evolution of societal forces, particularly those that are increasingly influential and self-aware, represents a major shift in the landscape of Chinese politics. With the arrival of these new sociopolitical players and an increasingly complicated decisionmaking process, Chinese society has become more and more pluralistic. In a sense, Chinese leaders confront the same question that puzzled former French president Charles de Gaulle in the 1960s: "How can you govern a country that has 246 varieties of cheese?"[70]

Xi Jinping and other Chinese leaders apparently understand the need to pay greater attention to social forces. This explains why Xi has taken seemingly contradictory stances, as discussed earlier in the chapter. Three areas of development in state-society relations deserve particular attention, namely, the strengthening of interest group politics, the growing clout of the middle class, and the evolving dynamics of the legal profession.

New Trends and Tensions in Interest Group Politics

Never in the six-decade history of the PRC have the Chinese leadership and the general public paid as much attention to interest groups as they have in recent years. In contrast to the early years of Communist rule, when the concept of interest groups was politically taboo, China's current leadership has come to recognize the validity of individual and group interests. At the same time, the Chinese people have become more conscious of their own rights and interests.

Like elsewhere in the world, China has many diverse interest groups. They can be based on geographic regions (local governments), industries and sectors, and social classes, to name only a few examples. Local governments in the coastal and inland regions are political interest groups that exert strong influence over Beijing and work to ensure that the central government adopts socioeconomic policies that advance the development of their regions.[71] In 2010 ninety-three of China's one hundred wealthiest counties (including all of the top forty) were located in coastal provinces.[72] One recent study shows that nearly 90 percent of China's exports come from coastal provinces.[73] This remarkable disparity in economic conditions between the coastal and inland regions reveals that localities across China carry contrasting economic interests and policy preferences.

Over the past few years, provincial and local government "liaison offices in Beijing" (驻京办, zhujingban), which are region-based lobbying groups, have rapidly increased in number. Recently, the central government issued new regulations to substantially reduce the permitted number of offices representing local interests and to require financial audits of remaining lobbying groups at the provincial and municipal levels.[74] It is understandable that leaders from various regions in the country would aim to have individuals from their same region in the senior leadership, especially on the Politburo and even the PSC, as a way to better advance or protect their regional and local interests. This is, in and of itself, an important political and institutional mechanism in the formation and representation of the CCP national leadership.

The even distribution of full membership seats in the Central Committee described in chapter 3 is an arrangement that at least ostensibly provides for different regions and constituencies to benefit from collective leadership.[75] Local leaders may differ greatly from one another in diagnosing problems and prioritizing policies. They are naturally inclined to form political coalitions in the national leadership, either to avoid steps that would alter the institutional and personnel apparatus or to adopt new mechanisms and structures to advance their interests. This further explains, from the angle of central-local relations, the source and dynamics of Chinese political change over the past two decades and its enduring impact on the country's political institutionalization.

Chinese interest groups can be categorized into three major groups: corporate and industrial interest groups (known as the "black collar" stratum, 黑领阶层, *heling jieceng*), vulnerable social groups such as migrants ("blue collar" workers), and the emerging middle class ("white collar" professionals). The term "black collar" was created in China during the past decade to refer to the increasing number of rich and powerful players who "dress in black, drive black cars, have hidden incomes, live secret lives with concubines, and have ties to the criminal underground" or "black society" (黑社会, *heishehui*).[76] Most important, they operate their businesses and wield their economic power in an opaque manner. China's most active corporate and industrial interest groups consist mainly of two clusters. The first includes business elites who work in state-monopolized industries such as banking, oil, electricity, coal, aviation, rail, telecommunications, tobacco, and shipping, and the second consists of the lobbying groups who work for state, foreign, or private firms in sectors such as real estate. As has been widely reported in the Chinese media, business interest groups routinely bribe local officials and have formed a "wicked coalition" with local governments.[77]

The various players associated with property development, for example, have become one of the most powerful special interest groups in present-day China. The strong power of this group explains why it took thirteen years for China to pass an antimonopoly law, why the macroeconomic control policy under the Hu-Wen administration was largely ineffective, why the widely acknowledged property bubble has continued to grow, and why low-income affordable housing projects often have met strong resistance and have thus remained noticeably insufficient. In each of these cases, corporate and industrial interest groups have encroached on the governmental decisionmaking process, either by contributing to government policy deadlock or manipulating policies to their favor.[78]

Some Chinese public intellectuals use the term "statist crony-capitalism" (权贵资本主义, *quangui zibenzhuyi*) to refer to the growing trend whereby senior leaders and their families control state-monopolized industries or SOEs for their own profit.[79] The impressive growth of China Mobile, for example, is at least partially attributable to the company's monopoly on domestic telecommunications.[80] This has two troubling consequences. First, no incentive exists for these flagship companies to pursue technological innovation. Over the past two decades, China's large SOEs have dramatically increased their profitability and their standing in the Global Fortune 500, which listed only three Chinese companies in 1995 but ninety-eight by 2015 (an overwhelmingly large majority of which were SOEs). China Mobile's ranking improved significantly among global economic giants, moving from number 336 in 2001 to 230 in 2003, 148 in 2008, 77 in 2010, and 55 in 2015. But interestingly, no single Chinese brand has truly distinguished itself in the global market.[81] Second, the real beneficiaries of China's crony capitalism have been a small number of corrupt officials and their families, many of whom greatly contribute to the outflow of capital. According to a 2011 report released by Washington-based nonprofit Global Financial Integrity, from 2000 to 2009 China's illegal capital outflows were the world's largest, totaling US$2.74 trillion, five times more than the total amount from the next-highest country, Mexico.[82]

Despite—or perhaps because of—their backgrounds as princelings, Xi Jinping and Wang Qishan have made fighting corruption a top priority of the first few years of their leadership. Rampant official corruption has been particularly noticeable among powerful families (including princelings). As discussed earlier in this book, under the Xi-Wang leadership, not only have a large number of high-ranking officials been arrested on corruption charges, but the campaign has also targeted state-monopolized industries such as oil, coal, rail, banking, and telecommunications. With princelings cracking down on princelings, it appears that Xi and Wang have effectively undermined any criticism that the leadership represents the interests of princelings. In addition to greatly enhancing public support for Xi, this sweeping anticorruption campaign might also help sustain CCP rule. From both a personal and systemic perspective, it was wise of Xi and Wang to feature anticorruption as one of the top priorities of their leadership.

Since the 2012 National Party Congress, many new regulations and rules to monitor government officials and SOE executives have been adopted.[83]

They provide specific guidelines on supervision, disclosures, and auditing; regulations on travel, use of vehicles, use of public funds for entertainment, club memberships, gifts, and career development with public funding; and restraints on family members' foreign studies, residence status, and so on. Like elsewhere in the world, vested interests are among the biggest barriers to economic reform and sociopolitical change in China. Both the Chinese authorities and the general public have now persistently demonstrated that dealing with vested interests is a social and political imperative. The tension between the enormous power of the "black collar" stratum and the public resentment of it will likely affect the process and the outcome of the leadership selection.

As for the lower social strata, a manual labor shortage in some coastal cities in recent years reflects the growing political consciousness of these so-called vulnerable social groups (弱势群体, *ruoshi qunti*)—especially the younger generation of migrant workers—in protecting their own rights. They have become increasingly resentful of discriminative policies against migrant workers, farmers, and the urban poor. Migrant workers have moved from one job to the next in order to receive a decent salary, yet China's urbanization policy remains indifferent to their needs. Migrants have become increasingly resentful of middle-class families with multiple homes, not to mention corrupt officials and rich entrepreneurs who buy costly villas for their mistresses. At least partly due to their tireless demands, China has recently witnessed a dramatic increase in wages.

As American political scientist Minxin Pei observes, the Chinese citizenry now routinely challenges the party on a wide range of public policy issues, including economic disparity, social dislocation, environmental degradation, public health care, food safety, social welfare, social justice, rural land reforms, urban construction, religious rights, and ethnic tensions.[84] Official statistics reveal that, in 2012, there were on average more than 500 mass protests each day.[85] Consequently, the financial cost of "maintaining social stability" (维稳, *weiwen*), primarily through the police force, has become astonishingly high. As some Chinese scholars note, in 2007 Guangzhou spent as much as RMB 4.4 billion on its police force, a figure that exceeded total social welfare spending (RMB 3.5 billion) in the city that year.[86] Nationwide, according to a Tsinghua University study, the total amount of money spent on "maintaining social stability" in 2009 was RMB 514 billion, almost identical to China's total national defense budget (RMB 532 billion) for the same year.[87] In 2012 RMB 670 billion was spent on the military and RMB 702 billion on "stability maintenance."[88]

Some Chinese scholars believe that as the Chinese government obtains and dedicates greater financial resources to social welfare, social protests will gradually decline.[89] But it would be naïve to believe that the Chinese government can come up with an easy solution for any of these problems in the foreseeable future. Resources will remain limited as China faces serious demographic challenges in the years to come. These tensions reflect some of the major deficiencies of the Chinese political structure and its system of resource allocation, which are unlikely to be relieved through policy adjustments, but rather will require systematic political changes. Without a more representative and more institutionalized political framework, problems of distributive injustice will become increasingly acute. To a great extent, this, in addition to the local tensions described earlier in the chapter, will create enduring pressure for political institutionalization in elite politics.

From a broad and historical perspective, the growing importance of interest group politics in present-day China should be seen as an encouraging phenomenon. It is interesting to note that corporate and industrial interest groups are probably equally as powerful and influential in some Western countries as they are in China. In the United States, for example, hundreds of lobbying groups have flooded Washington, D.C., and now constitute an essential feature of American politics. From time to time, these business lobbies have been caught manipulating the democratic system for a company's commercial gain. In his classic work on democracy, Robert Dahl argues that the development of Western democracies is a process dominated by many different sets of leaders, each having access to a different combination of political resources and representing the interests of different sectors and groups in society.[90] The democratic pluralist system disperses power, influence, authority, and control away from any single group of power elites sharing the same social background toward a variety of individuals, groups, associations, and organizations.[91] In a sense, democracy is a matter of establishing rules for mediating conflicting interests among social groups in a given society. Yao Yang, a professor at Peking University, argues along the same lines: "An open and inclusive political process has generally checked the power of interest groups in advanced democracies such as the United States. Indeed, this is precisely the mandate of a disinterested government—to balance the demands of different social groups."[92]

The Crucial Role of the Emerging Middle Class

Among the many forces shaping China's course of development, arguably none will prove more significant in the long run than the rapid emergence and explosive growth of the Chinese middle class. China's ongoing economic transition from a relatively poor, developing nation to a middle-class country has been one of the most fascinating human dramas of our time.[93] Just a quarter of a century ago, a distinct socioeconomic middle class was virtually nonexistent in the PRC.[94] Now a large number of Chinese citizens, especially in coastal cities, own private property and personal automobiles, have growing financial assets, and are able to take vacations abroad and send their children overseas for school. After years of scholarly and public debate over its existence, the Chinese middle class has now emerged as the driving force behind Chinese policy development and is becoming the largest body of consumers the world has ever seen.[95]

According to the late distinguished Chinese sociologist Lu Xueyi, based on a definition of the middle class that combines occupation, income, consumption, and innovation, in 2009 the middle class constituted 23 percent (243 million people) of China's total population, up from 15 percent in 2001.[96] In 2015, as Xi Jinping claimed during his state visit to the United States, China had about 300 million "middle income earners" (the official Chinese term for the middle class).[97] The Chinese middle class has already emerged as a core constituency with its own distinct needs and desires. As China's growth shifts from an export-based model to a domestic consumption–based model, the middle class, more than any other group, holds the keys to the governance and prosperity of the country. This transformation is likely to have wide-ranging implications for every aspect of Chinese life, especially the country's long-term economic prospects, energy consumption, and environmental well-being.

The growth of the middle class has brought with it increasing political influence, and the CCP leadership has gradually come to recognize that it must respect the middle class in order to retain its power. During the first three decades of the reform era, the CCP leadership relied on economic development and material incentives to prevent grassroots demand for sociopolitical challenges. New socioeconomic forces, especially entrepreneurs and the middle class, have been widely perceived to be political allies of the CCP regime. But this assumption should be subjected to greater scrutiny. Just as yesterday's political target could be today's political ally, so too could today's political ally become tomorrow's political rabble-rouser. Recent studies conducted in China have found that the Chinese middle class, more than any other social group, tends to be more cynical about the policy promises made by authorities; more concerned about issues such as environmental degradation, public health hazards, and a host of safety problems; more demanding of policy implementation; and more sensitive about official corruption.[98]

Disillusionment with and criticism of the Hu-Wen administration arguably were strongest among the country's middle class. Whether fair or not, the middle class had important reasons to be upset with the Hu-Wen administration, including the aforementioned severity of official corruption, as well as the increasing monopolization of SOEs and the accompanying shrinking of the private sector, a trend the Chinese summarize as "the state advances and private companies retreat" (国进民退, *guojin mintui*). The middle class did not have many investment opportunities beyond real estate, and thus economic problems emerged in the form of shadow banking, local debt, overcapacity, and a property bubble.

Furthermore, members of the middle class often complained that they (rather than the rich class) shouldered most of the burden for Hu Jintao's harmonious society policy, which intended to help vulnerable groups such as farmers, migrant workers, and the urban poor. The high unemployment rate among college graduates (nearly 2 million each year fail to find work), who often come from middle-class families, also angered the middle class. The admission rate for civil service exams was remarkably low under Hu's leadership, reaching just 1.4 percent in 2011, in sharp contrast to the previous decade, when government employees were leaving to "jump into the sea of the private business sector."[99] Not surprisingly, Xi's economic policy, especially his advocacy for the concept of "the Chinese dream," has primarily intended to please the middle class by focusing on promotion of the private sector, the service industry, and loans for small and medium-size enterprises, especially for start-up companies run by college graduates.

Middle-class participation in governance and public policy has been on the rise. Chen Zhiwu, an economist at Yale University, observes that 25.5 percent of fiscal expenditures in China in 2011 were used for social welfare, public health, education, and other public goods, while 38 percent of fiscal expenditures were for administrative expenses. By contrast, in the United States the fiscal expenditures on these two categories were 73 and 10 percent, respectively.[100] In Chen's view, the Chinese middle and lower classes seek a reallocation of resources through democratic reforms in the Chinese political system to correct this disparity.

If the Chinese middle class begins to feel that the voices of its members are being suppressed, that their access to information is unjustly being blocked, or that their space for social action is being unduly confined, increased political dissent may begin to take shape. It is important to note that the commercialized media and social media have increasingly become the main venues to convey middle-class views and values in the country. This has occurred at a time when social media has achieved a level of pervasiveness no one could have imagined only a few years ago. According to an official Chinese source, by May 2014 the number of cell phones in China had reached 1.26 billion.[101] By mid-2015 Internet users in China surpassed 668 million, including 594 million mobile Internet users, and as much as 48.8 percent of the population had Internet access.[102]

In December 2011 thirty-year-old Han Han—China's most popular blogger, whose site has registered well over 580 million hits—published an essay titled "On Revolution."[103] Although Han argued that "revolution is hardly a good option for China," his view of the choice between reform and revolution pointedly reflected—and greatly enhanced—public awareness of the risk of revolution in the country. Talk shows, especially shows that target the urban middle class, have attracted large audiences. Jin Xing, a forty-eight-year-old famous ballerina who had transgender surgery in 1995, is the host of the most popular late-night show in the country, the Jin Xing Show. As a returnee artist known for her sharp criticism of the handling of various social issues, Jin Xing has become a prominent advocate for middle-class values and social justice. Another host of a popular late-night talk show, Zhou Libo, who is nicknamed China's Jay Leno, often imitates top Chinese leaders and comments on important political issues of the day. Han Han, Jin Xing, and Zhou Libo all live and work in Shanghai, the stronghold of the middle class in the country. The role of popular blog discourse and politically influential talk shows reflects a new form of public participation. Chinese leaders may come to realize that in a pluralistic society, such as present-day China, where multiple voices exist even within the middle class, it is most efficient to let legitimate public debate play a role in public policy.[104]

In recent years, however, social media has become so powerful that Chinese authorities have occasionally shut down domestic microblogging services. This is not an effective way to run the country, especially when China is supposed to be moving toward an innovation-driven economy. The reason people rely on social media for news is that the mainstream media does not tell them much. This is particularly the case in the period just before a leadership turnover at the party congress. During this "season of rumors," the more that sensational rumors in social media are suppressed by authorities, the more influential the rumors become. Thus, perhaps the best way to avoid the social media–induced sensationalism is to open up mainstream media. Ten years of Chinese media commercialization have already prepared Chinese journalists to pursue professionalism. The ongoing revolutionary change in social media and telecommunications will only make media censorship more difficult.

As the middle class continues to grow, Chinese politicians should pay increasingly close attention to the concerns of that population. A good example of this can be found in the United States, where the middle class is alluded to in almost all major policy speeches by presidential candidates. It is politically advantageous for politicians to acknowledge middle-class needs and remind members of the class that politicians are focused on them. Similar to their counterparts in the West, the Chinese middle class tends to prefer top-down political and legal reform to bottom-up revolution.

Of course, meaningful political reform may meet strong resistance from conservative leaders and powerful vested interest groups. The threat of revolution from below may push forward-looking political leaders to pursue incremental yet bold political reform. It is interesting to note that one of the most popular books in PRC intellectual circles in recent years has been the Chinese translation of Alexis de Tocqueville's 1856 classic, *The Old Regime and the Revolution*. One frequently quoted passage is Tocqueville's argument that revolutions usually occur not when the old regime resists change, but rather when it begins to attempt reform, only to find expectations outstripping any possible rate of improvement. Notably, senior Chinese leaders are fans of Tocqueville's work. For example, Li Keqiang and Wang Qishan have reportedly recommended this book to their colleagues.[105] It seems inevitable that socioeconomic and political expectations in the country will rise as the Chinese middle class becomes increasingly connected—both digitally and physically—with the outside world. Public demand for a more accountable and more transparent political system can only grow stronger.

Consensus on the Rule of Law and the Growing Demands of the Legal Community

As Chinese society becomes increasing pluralistic, with contrasting views and conflicting interests among political elites and various socioeconomic groups, it will continue to be enormously difficult to reach consensus on governance. Generally speaking, lack of consensus on overall direction and major policy agendas in both domestic and foreign affairs is a distinct feature of present-day China. One noticeable exception, however, is the broad consensus on the necessity and importance of the rule of law.[106] Make no mistake: sharply different views are prevalent about the overall objectives, content, process, timing, and priorities of legal development in the country. To a certain extent, similar disputes and disagreements are observable in some constitutional democracies.[107] An important trend in present-day China is that the general public, various interest groups, public intellectuals (both liberals and conservatives), and political elites all seem to recognize that no one is safe in a country without the rule of law, and therefore the rule of law should be an essential component for China's political reform.

As Francis Fukuyama observes, the feasibility and desirability of political democracy is a contentious issue between elites and the public in China. It is therefore reasonable, Fukuyama argues, that China's search for better governance begins with promoting the rule of law rather than the pursuit of democracy.[108] According to Fukuyama, such a path is by no means unique. Germany and other European democracies have also followed this sequence of political transformation.[109]

Though various interest groups are driven by different motivations, such a consensus is critically important for China's political trajectory. Of all the challenges sparked by China's ongoing economic and sociopolitical transformation, the development of the Chinese legal system is arguably the most consequential. The aforementioned frequent manifestations of social protests, the increasing transparency of factional infighting in the CCP leadership (as evident in the Bo Xilai and Ling Jihua cases), and the ongoing anticorruption campaign and its potentially negative effects all underscore the urgency of developing a credible legal system in China.

While CCP leaders have remained ambiguous about the tension between the supremacy of the PRC Constitution, on the one hand, and the omnipresence of the party in the country's legal system, on the other, they have become increasingly proactive in adopting various laws (albeit some of which have been aimed at protecting their own interests). As discussed in detail in chapter 5, over the past several decades China has transformed remarkably from a lawless state—particularly during the Cultural Revolution—to a country promulgating hundreds of laws (on paper, at least) in virtually all legal domains.

At the Fourth Plenum of the 18th Central Committee, held in the fall of 2014, the party leadership issued a resolution to "systematically promote rule of law in the country" (全面推进依法治国, *quanmian tuijin yifa zhiguo*). The resolution asserts that "any institutions and individuals should respect the authority of the PRC Constitution and act absolutely in accordance with the Constitution."[110] During the first three years of his leadership, Xi made a number of important statements on the rule of law.[111] In December 2012, one month after Xi became the top leader, at the meeting to commemorate the thirtieth anniversary of the 1982 PRC Constitution Amendment, he asserted that the CCP should govern and behave in accordance with the PRC Constitution.[112] He also stated that the "life and authority of the Constitution lies in its implementation."[113] During the Second Plenum of the 18th Central Commission for Discipline Inspection, held in January 2013, Xi emphasized the need for "locking power into the institutional cage" to prevent official corruption.[114] In September 2014, at the meeting to commemorate the sixtieth anniversary of the founding of the NPC, Xi stated that the rule of law should be a fundamental component of governance, and he highlighted the overarching principle of "rule in accordance with the Constitution" (依宪治国, *yixian zhiguo*).[115]

All of these statements, of course, could be seen as lip service—nothing but "paper filled with hollow words" (一纸空文, *yizhi kongwen*)—a term that Xi himself used to describe laws that are not effectively implemented and enforced.[116] Given the recent arrests of a large number of human rights lawyers and the crackdown on demands for real constitutionalism, critics in both China and abroad certainly have reason to be cynical about Xi's rhetoric regarding the rule of law in China. At the same time, it is reasonable to argue that no country could establish a credible legal system from scratch within a few years or even a decade. More important, Xi's statements promoting the rule of law have opened the door for the country's emerging legal community to continue in its painstaking search for justice, and its political implications should not be dismissed too quickly.

As discussed in chapter 5, the legal community has emerged as an important elite group in the CCP leadership over the past decade. In parallel to this important trend in the political establishment, the legal community has played an increasingly dynamic role in society at large. Three subgroups of legal professionals, divided primarily based on their political and institutional affiliations, deserve greater attention.

The first subgroup consists of legal professionals who previously worked in government or have served as advisers to the leadership. Included in this group was Cai Dingjian, a distinguished constitutional scholar whose death in November 2010 led to nationwide yearlong memorial activities honoring his advocacy for the rule of law in China.[117] As a leading scholar of constitutional studies in China, Cai served as a staff member and deputy bureau chief of the Bureau of Staff of the Standing Committee of the NPC from 1986 to 2003. Before his premature death from cancer, he served as a professor of law and the director of the Institute of Constitutional Research at China University of Political Science and Law. Cai's last words—"Constitutional democracy is the mission of our generation"—were widely cited in both the country's official and social media.[118]

The aforementioned Yu Keping, a political scientist with strong interest in legal issues and a former official who ranked at the vice-minister level and who served as deputy director of the CCP Central Compilation and Translation Bureau, also belongs to this subgroup. Yu recently stepped down from his official position and now serves as the dean of the School of Government at Peking University. Yu has been a longtime advocate of democracy, civil society, and rule of law in China.[119] As early as 2007 Yu argued that "the CCP leadership cannot claim it governs the country by law unless the party is subject to the rule of law."[120] In keeping with this conviction, Yu has been instrumental in distinguishing between the notions of "rule by law" and "rule of law" in the Chinese context. The former emphasizes the utility of law as a means of reinforcing the dominant role of the party, while the latter says that no individual, group, or party should be above the law, as discussed in chapter 5. Yu believes that the CCP should embrace the notion of "rule of law" rather than "rule by law."[121] More recently, Yu has been known for voicing his concerns about the possible return of a personality cult and a general turning away from collective leadership and intraparty democracy.[122] In contrast to Francis Fukuyama's view that promoting the development of rule of law before democracy is a reasonable approach, Yu believes that one cannot separate democracy and the rule of law, as they always reinforce each other.[123] Yu's emphatic arguments might explain why he recently resigned from his vice-minister-ranked position.

The second subgroup of legal professionals mainly consists of liberal-minded and independent law professors. In recent years, an increasing number of well-known professors and opinion leaders have demonstrated that they are not afraid to publicly express controversial views, including sharp criticism of CCP authorities. Such remarks would have been considered politically taboo or even "unlawful" just a few years ago. Xu Xin, professor of law and director of the Research Center of the Judicial System at the Beijing Institute of Technology, and He Weifang, a well-known professor of law at Peking University, are among the leading figures in this subgroup. In 2011 Professor Xu bluntly challenged Wu Bangguo, then the second-highest-ranking leader in the PSC and chairman of the NPC. Xu argued that the "strongest resistance to China's legal development comes from the CCP leadership, and this is most evident in senior leader Wu Bangguo's recent statement widely proclaiming the 'five no's' for China."[124] Similarly, in an English book published in 2012, which was based on the Chinese translation of the author's previously published work, He Weifang criticized three leaders who were extremely powerful at the time—Wang Lijun, Bo Xilai, and Zhou Yongkang—for their contempt toward the law.[125] Interestingly enough, He Weifang's writings were published in Chinese in China before Wang Lijun defected to the U.S. consulate in Chengdu and before Bo and Zhou were purged for corruption and other charges of power abuse.

These instances do not necessarily mean that Chinese authorities have loosened control over the legal profession. On the contrary, liberal legal scholars and human rights lawyers are often among the main targets of harsh treatment, including imprisonment. Yet the movement toward rule of law in the country already seems to have reached a moral and political high ground. In addition to expressing their candid criticism of the authorities, these liberal-minded law professors have offered constructive proposals to reform China's legal system.

Xu Xin, for example, proposes prioritizing judicial reforms with a focus on judicial independence. He argues that judicial reforms are in line with the need for social stability and thus should be considered the least disruptive way to ease China's much-needed political transformation.[126] Xu recommends several important systematic changes to China's legal system:

— transferring the leadership of judicial reforms from the Central Commission of Politics and Law of the CCP Central Committee to the NPC in the form of a yet-to-be-established judicial reform committee, one in which legal scholars, lawyers, and representatives of NGOs would constitute more than half of the members;

— adjusting the role of the CCP from appointing presidents of courts and chief prosecutors to only nominating them (an independent selection committee, rather than the party organization department, would make these appointments);

— prohibiting CCP interference in any legal case, especially by prohibiting judges from being CCP members and banning party organizations within law firms;

— reducing the power of both presidents of courts and chief prosecutors in order to enhance procedural justice; and

— establishing a constitutional review system, including a new constitutional committee and constitutional court.

The third subgroup of legal professionals and activists includes individuals like the famous blind human rights lawyer Chen Guangcheng and civil rights activist Xu Zhiyong. Some legal activists are heavily engaged in organized protest movements for social, political, and legal causes. For example, Xu Zhiyong, who received his doctoral degree from the Law School of Peking University, became well known both domestically and internationally through a case relating to the death of a migrant worker. In 2003 a graphic designer from Hubei Province named Sun Zhigang was beaten to death in Guangzhou after being detained for not carrying a registration permit. Xu Zhiyong petitioned the government to repeal the "Regulation for Internment and Deportation of Urban Vagrants," also known as the "custody and repatriation" law, which was adopted by the Chinese government in 1982. News of the petition circulated widely throughout the country. Within a month, Premier Wen Jiabao announced the abolition of the regulation, bringing an end to two decades of legal discrimination against migrants.[127]

Xu Zhiyong was one of the founders of the Gongmeng Law Research Center, an NGO primarily focused on protecting human rights and promoting civil rights issues. This institution has also become a driving force for the so-called New Citizen Movement (新公民运动, *xingongmin yundong*). The Chinese government recently suppressed the movement and sentenced Xu to a four years' imprisonment for "instigating a mob to disturb public order." Yet, in an increasingly pluralistic society, where the right to protection will surely remain one of the public's most important concerns, the CCP leadership apparently faces unprecedented challenges from this new group of legal activists.

Altogether, these three subgroups of legal professionals will likely continue to push for legal and judicial reforms in the years to come. One may reasonably argue that their demand for a constitutional China will be an important factor contributing to an institutionalized and orderly leadership change at the upcoming 19th National Party Congress. Along with the interest group politics and the dynamic role of the emerging Chinese middle class, social forces will likely compel the Chinese decisionmaking process to become more transparent and the composition of the Politburo and the PSC to become more representative.

This concluding chapter highlights two sets of factors that have the potential to contribute to Chinese political institutionalization over the next decade or so. The first set centers on the profoundly important, if often inadequately understood, tensions between, on the one hand, Xi's dominant role and political initiatives and, on the other, the enduring constraints placed on Xi by collective leadership and various institutional requirements. The choice, of course, should not just be between an effective dictator and an ineffective collective leadership. Likewise, one should not mistake a strong and effective leader for a dictator. Despite their limitations, the CCP's institutional norms and regulations, including the "one party, two coalitions" experiment, may gradually overcome the system's deficiencies and improve rather than reverse collective leadership. The incentives for both competition and cooperation among competing elite groups in the leadership—and especially the tough political choices facing President Xi—are likely to make the upcoming leadership change remarkably dynamic and unpredictable. The Chinese search for a safe, sound, and sustainable political system—and the need for new leadership legitimacy—may pave the way for a systemic transition to Chinese-style democracy.

The second set of factors that could promote Chinese political institutionalization in the near future are related to the socioeconomic and political dynamics of Chinese society. Interest group politics, the growing role of the middle class, and constitutional demands from the legal community may contribute further to a fundamental shift in state-society relations. The threat of revolution from below may push Xi and forward-looking political leaders to pursue incremental yet bold political reform from the top. From the perspective of China's economic development, it is difficult to imagine how Xi's agenda for innovation-led economic growth can be achieved without greater political freedom and openness. The complicated interplay between these two sets of factors likely constitutes the most important political puzzle in present-day China. This unfolding drama, wherever it leads, will undoubtedly have profound ramifications far beyond China's borders. Policymakers in the outside world, especially those in the United States, should not dismiss the possibility of Chinese democracy too quickly or, even more problematically, assume that China's domestic political evolution will have no bearing on its foreign relations.

Interestingly, when recently describing his vision of governance, Xi Jinping quoted the Chinese saying that is used as one of this chapter's epigraphs:

"Limited wisdom makes doers; moderate wisdom makes managers; supreme wisdom makes law-builders."[128] The next few years will test Xi's wisdom—especially as he faces the generational change of leadership and political succession, which arguably constitutes his greatest challenge—and reveal whether he can be a truly transformative leader.

ABBREVIATIONS

ACWF	All China's Women Federation
CASS	Chinese Academy of Social Sciences
CCDI	Central Commission for Discipline Inspection
CCP	Chinese Communist Party
CCYL	Chinese Communist Youth League
CEC	China Entrepreneurs Club
CEIBS	China Europe International Business School
CICC	China International Capital Corporation Limited
CILD	Central International Liaison Department
CITIC	China International Trust and Investment Corporation
CKGSB	Cheung Kong Graduate School of Business
CLGCDF	Central Leading Group for Comprehensively Deepening Reforms
CMC	Central Military Commission
CNPC	Chinese National Petroleum Corporation
CNTC	China National Tobacco Corporation
COD	Central Organization Department
CPD	Central Propaganda Department
CPPCC	Chinese People's Political Consultative Conference
CPRO	Central Policy Research Office
CPS	Central Party School
CSRC	China Securities Regulatory Commission

CSCSC	Central Spiritual Civilization Steering Committee
EMBA	Executive Master of Business Administration
HRSS	Human Resources and Social Security
HURD	Housing and Urban-Rural Development
NDRC	National Development and Reform Commission
NGO	Non-Governmental Organizations
NHFPC	National Health and Family Planning Commission
NPC	National People's Congress
NSC	National Security Committee
PLA	People's Liberation Army
PLC	Politics and Law Committee
PRC	People's Republic of China
PSC	Politburo Standing Committee
ROC	Republic of China
SASAC	State-owned Assets Supervision and Administration Commission
SOE	State-Owned Enterprise
USSR	Union of Soviet Socialist Republics

NOTES

PROLOGUE

1. For more on the Chongqing model, see Su Wei, Yang Fan, and Liu Shiwen, *Chongqing moshi* [The Chongqing model] (Beijing: Zhongguo jingji chubanshe, 2011).

2. For a detailed discussion of Bo's campaigns in Chongqing, see Yawei Liu, "Bo Xilai's Campaign for the Standing Committee and the Future of Chinese Politicking," *China Brief* 11, no. 21 (November 11, 2011).

3. For more on these incidents, see Pin Ho and Wenquang Huang, *A Death in the Lucky Holiday Hotel: Murder, Money, and an Epic Power Struggle in China* (New York: Public Affairs, 2013).

4. Anton Wishik, "The Bo Xilai Crisis: A Curse or a Blessing for China? An Interview with Cheng Li," National Bureau of Asian Research, April 18, 2012 (www.nbr.org/research /activity.aspx?id=236).

5. China Newsnet May 6, 2011 (http://r.club.china.com/data/thread/1011/2725/63/41/3 _1.html).

6. For a detailed analysis of the self-promotion campaigns by Bo Xilai and Wang Yang, see Yawei Liu, "Bo Xilai's Campaign for the Standing Committee and the Future of Chinese Politicking," *China Brief* 11, no. 21 (November 11, 2011).

7. Evan Osnos, "Born Red," *New Yorker*, April 6, 2015, 42–55.

8. Cheng Li, "Fighting for a Constitutional China: Public Enlightenment and Legal Professionalism," in He Weifang, *In the Name of Justice: Striving for the Rule of Law in China* (Brookings, 2012), xvii–xlix.

9. "Wang Qishan wu Mei liangdang daibiaotuan" [Wang Qishan met with a bipartisan delegation from the United States], *Beijing qingnianbao* [Beijing Youth Daily], May 8, 2015; also see U.S.-China Perception Monitor (www.uscnpm.com/model_item.html?action=view &table=article&id=3563).

10. Belinda Luscombe, "Ten Questions for Henry Kissinger," *Time* magazine online, June 6, 2011 (http://content.time.com/time/magazine/article/0,9171,2074215,00.html).

CHAPTER 1

1. David M. Lampton, *Following the Leader: Ruling China, from Deng Xiaoping to Xi Jinping* (University of California Press, 2014), 65.

2. Kor Kian Beng, "China Needs a Wise Strongman," *Strait Times*, April 14, 2014 (www .straitstimes.com/news/opinion/eye-the-world/story/china-needs-wise-strongman -20140414); Willy Wo-Lap Lam, *Chinese Politics in the Era of Xi Jinping: Renaissance, Reform, or Retrogression?* (New York: Routledge, 2015); and "Beware of the Cult of Xi" *The Economist*, April 2, 2016 (http://www.economist.com/news/leaders/21695881-xi-jinping -stronger-his-predecessors-his-power-damaging-country-beware-cult).

3. For example, see Alexis Lai, "Was Bo Xilai's Trial in China Truly Transparent?," CNN China, August 27, 2013 (http://edition.cnn.com/2013/08/26/world/asia/china-bo-xilai-trial -transparency).

4. *Shijie ribao* [World Journal], January 10, 2014, A2. Also, according to the data provided by the Supreme People's Procuratorate, during the first eleven months of 2013, 27,236 cases were examined and 36,907 individuals were prosecuted; see *Shijie ribao* [World Journal], January 6, 2014, A5.

5. See "Zhongjiwei bannian dahu ji:16 ming shengbuji huo yishang guanyuan bei chachu" [A diary of the CCDI's six months of hunting tigers: 16 or more provincial or ministerial-level officials under investigation], CCTV Newsnet, July 2, 2014 (http://news .china.com.cn/2014-07/02/content_32830779.htm); and Cheng Li, "Kaiqi yifa zhiguo yiti de yiyi" [The significance of the open discussion of rule of law], *Zhongguo xinwen zhoukan* [China Newsweek], November 24, 2014, 16. For official updates on the purges of the anticorruption campaign, see Xinhua, August 11, 2015 (http://news.xinhuanet.com/legal/2003 -10/30/content_1150976.htm).

6. For an important recent work on foreign analysts' views of Xi's foreign policy, see Robert D. Blackwill and Kurt M. Campbell, *Xi Jinping on the Global Stage: Chinese Foreign Policy under a Powerful but Exposed Leader*, Council on Foreign Relations Special Report, no. 74, February 2016.

7. Xi Jinping, "Rang mingyun gongtongti yishi zai zhoubian guojia luodi shenggen" [Let the community of common destiny concept find its roots in neighboring countries], Xinhua, October 25, 2013 (http://news.xinhuanet.com/politics/2013-10/25/c_117878944.htm).

8. Cao Tongqing, "Zhongemei shangyan sanguo yanyi" [China, Russia and the U.S. stage a new "Three Kingdoms"], *Jiaobao* [China Press], May 21, 2014 (http://news.uschinapress .com/2014/0521/979106.shtml). For a discussion of China's strategic interest in promoting Sino-Russian relations, see Yan Xuetong, "Zhonge guanxi shi zhanlue hezuo" [The core of Sino-Russian relations lies in strategic cooperation], *Zhongguo chanjing xinwen bao* [China Industrial Economy News], May 19, 2014 (http://finance.sina.com.cn/roll/20140519 /014519145696.shtml).

9. For Xi's speech, see "Xi Jinping zai yaxin fenghui zuo zhuzhi fayan" [Xi Jinping's keynote address at the CICA Summit], People Net, May 21, 2014 (http://world.people.com.cn /n/2014/0521/c1002-25046183.html). Also see Zhao Kejin, "Zhongguo waijiao zhu jidiao: fenfa youwei" [The main tone of Chinese diplomacy: Proactive], People Net, May 25, 2014 (http://politics.people.com.cn/n/2014/0525/c1001-25060865.html).

10. Cheng Li, "Promoting 'Young Guards': The Recent High Turnover in the PLA Leadership (Part II: Expansion and Escalation)," *China Leadership Monitor*, no. 49 (February 2016): 1–12.

11. Andrew S. Erickson, "Sweeping Change in China's Military: Xi's PLA Restructuring," *Wall Street Journal*, September 2, 2015.

12. Ibid., quoting Li Nan, an expert on Chinese civilian-military relations who teaches at the U.S. Naval War College.

13. Minnie Chan, "China vows military reform by 2020, with plans for new anticorruption watchdog in PLA," *South China Morning Post*, November 26, 2015 (http://www.scmp.com/news/china/diplomacy-defence/article/1883606/china-vows-breakthrough-long-awaited-military-reform).

14. For the summary of the resolution of the Third Plenum of the 18th Central Committee, see "The Decision on Major Issues Concerning Comprehensively Deepening Reforms in Brief," *China Daily*, November 16, 2013 (www.china.org.cn/china/third_plenary_session/2013-11/16/content_30620736.htm).

15. The financial reforms proposed at the Third Plenum, which encourage the establishment of private banks and joint ventures with foreign financial institutions, are perceived as the driving force for deepening market reforms. This financial liberalization will provide much-needed loans for private firms, especially those in the service sector.

16. For a comprehensive graphic description of the central leading groups in the Chinese leadership, see "Tujie zhongyang ge lingdao xiaozu: Xi Jinping danren sige xiaozu zuzhang" [Graphics of the Central Leading Groups: Xi Jinping assumes leadership of four groups], *Sina News Center*, June 30, 2014 (http://news.sina.com.cn/c/p/2014-06-30/142030444500.shtml).

17. For example, Henri Eyraud, *Chine: La réforme autoritaire, Jiang Zemin et Zhu Rongji* (Paris: Bleu de Chine, 2001) and John Wong and Lai Hongyi, eds., *China into the Hu-Wen Era: Policy Initiatives and Challenges* (Singapore: World Scientific, 2006).

18. Jeremy Page, Bob Davis, and Lingling Wei, "Xi Weakens Role of Beijing's No. 2," *Wall Street Journal*, December 20, 2013; and Zachary Keck, "Is Li Keqiang Being Marginalized?," *Diplomat*, January 7, 2014 (http://thediplomat.com/2014/01/is-li-keqiang-being-marginalized/).

19. Minnie Chan, "Will 'Strongman' Xi Jinping Lead China into Armed Conflicts with Rival Neighbors?," *South China Morning Post*, January 13, 2014 (www.scmp.com/news/china/article/1404451/will-strongman-xi-jinping-lead-china-armed-conflicts-rival-neighbours?page=all).

20. Yang Liuji and Yuan Junhong, "Dang de jitilingdao zhidu de xingcheng yu fazhan" [The formation and development of collective leadership in the Chinese Communist Party], *Zhonggong dangshi yanjiu* [Party History Research Center of the Central Committee of the Chinese Communist Party], no. 4 (1991): 77–88.

21. Wang Chunxi, "Deng Xiaoping dui jianli zhongyang jitilingdao tizhi kuangjia de gongxian." [Deng Xiaoping's contribution to the system of collective leadership of the Central Committee of the Chinese Communist Party], *Dang de wenxian* [Literature of the Chinese Communist Party], no. 5 (2008): 54–58.

22. Hu Angang, *Zhongguo jiti lingdao tizhi* [The system of collective leadership in China] (Beijing: Zhongguo renmin daxue chubanshe, 2013), 21–24.

23. Deng Xiaoping, *Deng Xiaoping wenxuan* [Selected works of Deng Xiaoping], vol. 3 (Beijing: Renmin chubanshe, 1993), 365.

24. Ibid., 310–11.

25. "Hu Jintao: Yi gaige chuangxin jingshen quanmian tuijin dang de jianshe" [Hu Jintao: Promote comprehensive party building in the spirit of reform and innovation], Xinhua, October 15, 2011 (http://news.sina.com.cn/c/2007-10-15/113314089759.shtml).

26. For example, Mirror Books, a leading overseas publishing house on Chinese politics and society, published numerous books and articles on the composition, personnel, factional tensions, and internal operation of the PSC. They include Xie Fanping, *Changwei Zhiguo* [The rule of the Politburo Standing Committee] (New York: Mirror Books, 2014) and Gao Xin, *Lingdao Zhongguo de xin renwu: Zhonggong shiliujie zhengzhiju changwei* [New figures leading China: The Politburo Standing Committee formed at the 16th Party Congress of the Chinese Communist Party], vols. 1 and 2 (New York: Mirror Books, 2003).

27. Jane Perlez, "With Xi, U.S. confronts a one-man show," *International New York Times*, July 10, 2014, 1, 3.

28. Ibid.

29. Tan Xiongwei, "Why Do the Policies of the Central Government Sometimes Fail to Make It Out of Zhongnanhai?" *Zhongguo qingnian bao* [China Youth Daily], November 17, 2005. Quoted from http://www.zonaeuropa.com, February 10, 2006. For more discussion on local resistance to the central government's initiatives, see Cheng Li, "Think National, Blame Local: Central-Provincial Dynamics in the Hu Era," *China Leadership Monitor*, no. 17 (Winter 2006).

30. *Sing Tao Daily*, March 10, 2015; also see its website, http://news.singtao.ca/toronto /2015-03-10/world1425970399d5474726.html.

31. He Pin, "Xi Jinping jiquan di'erji" [The second phase in Xi Jinping's consolidation of power], Mirror Newsnet, February 17, 2015 (http://www.mingjingnews.com/MIB/news /news.aspx?ID=N000077503).

32. Wu Yu, "Xi Jinping ren guoanwei zhuxi, quanli kongqian" [With his appointment as chair of the National Security Committee, Xi Jinping holds unprecedented power], *Deutsche Welle*, January 25, 2014 (www.dw.de/习近平任国安委主席权力空前/a-17386588). Also see Chen Ergao, *Xi Jinping xiongxin: Huangdi haishi zongtong*? [Xi Jinping's ambition: Emperor or president?] (Hong Kong: Insider Publications, 2014).

33. Wu, "Xi Jinping ren guoanwei zhuxi, quanli kongqian" [With his appointment as chair of the National Security Committee, Xi Jinping holds unprecedented power].

34. The quote is from Roderick MacFarquhar. Roderick MacFarquhar, "Xi de chaoji quanli" [Xi's supreme power], Mirror Newsnet, August 4, 2015 (http://www.mingjingnews.com/MIB /news/news.aspx?ID=N000104737); He Qinglian, "Shibajie sanzhong quanhui: jiti lingdao zhi geren zhuanduan de zhuanzhedian" [The Third Plenum of the 18th Central Committee of the CCP: The turning point from collective leadership to personal dictatorship], *Meiguo zhiyin* [Voice of America], November 17, 2013 (http://www.voachinese.com/content/he-qinglian -20131116/1791714.html); and Lam, *Chinese Politics in the Era of Xi Jinping*.

35. He, "Shibajie sanzhong quanhui."

36. For example, Perry Link, "Is Xi Jinping China's New Mao-Like Strongman?," *World Post*, June 3, 2014 (www.huffingtonpost.com/perry-link/xi-jinping-china-mao_b_5439367 .html).

37. Zheng Yongnian, "Jiquan weile gaige, gaige xuyao fenquan" [Centralization of power can carry out reform; and reform requires decentralization], Nanfengchuang [South Reviews], November 19, 2014 (http://www.nfcmag.com/article/5120.html).

38. Steve Tsang, "Why China's Xi Jinping Is Still Far from Chairman Mao Status," *Forbes*, February 16, 2015 (http://www.forbes.com/sites/stevetsang/2015/02/16/why-chinas -xi-jinping-is-still-far-from-chairman-mao-status/).

39. Ibid.

40. See Lampton, *Following the Leader*. For a detailed discussion of strongman politics in the first four decades of the PRC, see Roderick MacFarquhar, *The Politics of China: The Eras of Mao and Deng* (Cambridge University Press, 1997).

41. Hu Angang, *Mao Zedong yu wenge* [Mao Zedong and the Cultural Revolution] (Hong Kong: Strong Wind Press, 2009), 775–80.

42. Frederick C. Teiwes and Warren Sun, *China's Road to Disaster: Mao, Central Politicians, and Provincial Leaders in the Unfolding of the Great Leap Forward 1955–1959* (New York: M. E. Sharpe, 1998), and Hu, *Mao Zedong yu wenge* [Mao Zedong and the Cultural Revolution].

43. Cheng Li and Lynn White, "The Army in the Succession to Deng Xiaoping: Familiar Fealties and Technocratic Trends," *Asian Survey*, vol. 33, no. 8 (August 1993): 771–72.

44. Andrew Jacobs, "General Yang Baibing Dies at 93; Led Tiananmen Crackdown," *New York Times*, January 17, 2013, A24.

45. Ezra F. Vogel, *Deng Xiaoping and the Transformation of China* (Harvard University Press, 2011).

46. He Pin, "Foreword" in Xie, *Changwei Zhiguo* [The rule of the Politburo Standing Committee], 9.

47. Ibid., 12.

48. Link, "Is Xi Jinping China's New Mao-Like Strongman?"

49. Tsang, "Why China's Xi Jinping Is Still Far from Chairman Mao Status."

50. The exception, Zeng Peiyan, also eventually became a Politburo member and vice-premier in the State Council. This discussion is based on Cheng Li, "Xi Jinping's Inner Circle (Part 1: The Shaanxi Gang)," *China Leadership Monitor*, no. 43 (March 14, 2014), 1–2.

51. Cheng Li, "Hu's Policy Shift and the *Tuanpai's* Coming-of-Age," *China Leadership Monitor*, no. 15 (Summer 2005).

52. Jiang's father, Jiang Shijun, was not a CCP official, but rather a Kuomintang propagandist in the 1940s. But Jiang has always claimed that he came from the family of his uncle and foster father, Jiang Shangqing, a communist martyr.

53. For the reason for the landslide victory of the Jiang camp, see Cheng Li, "Rule of the Princelings," *Cairo Review of Global Affairs*, no. 8 (Winter 2013): 34–47.

54. Based on Chinese political norms, at the next party congress in fall 2017, all leaders who were born in or before 1949 will retire from the Central Committee. Among the current seven members of the Politburo Standing Committee, only Xi Jinping and Li Keqiang were born after 1950. For the family ties between Xi and Yu, see Li, "Xi Jinping's Inner Circle (Part 1: The Shaanxi Gang)," 7.

55. Sun Yun, "Xi Jinping jieshang shenyin" [Xi Jinping uses the excuse of a back injury to be 'spirited away'], *Epoch Times*, September 26, 2012 (www.epochtimes.com/gb/12/9/26 /n3691492.htm).

56. Although Liu Yunshan and Li Zhanshu advanced their careers by way of the CCYL, they are closer to Jiang and Xi and thus do not count as *tuanpai* leaders.

57. Research by Cheng Li, Brookings Institution. For a similar observation, also see Willy Lam, "Communist Youth League Clique Maintains Clout Despite Congress Setback," *China Brief*, vol. 12, no. 23 (November 30, 2012).

58. Liu Jingwei and Du Fei, *Zhonggong jieban shuangxiong* [Dual successors of the Chinese Communist Party] (New York: Mirror Books, 2013).

59. Robert Zoellick recently made an insightful observation regarding these three points. See Robert Zoellick, "The Aim of Xi's Reform Is to Preserve Party Control," *Financial Times*, June 12, 2014 (www.ft.com/cms/s/0/ee06f38c-efce-11e3-9b4c-00144feabdc0 .html).

60. For a detailed discussion of the Ferrari crash incident, see Li, "Rule of the Princelings," 38–39.

61. Prior to the 18th Party Congress, some prominent Chinese public intellectuals openly referred to the ten-year period (two five-year terms) of Hu's leadership as "the lost decade." Given China's emergence over these ten years as a global economic giant with astonishing financial, shipping, and trading power—not to mention an average annual growth rate of 9 percent—characterizing this period as a "lost decade" seems entirely unfair, notwithstanding the validity of some criticism relating to rampant official corruption and the monopolization of state-owned enterprises and firms. Beijing's successful hosting of the Olympics, the Shanghai World Expo, the dynamic development of infrastructure in both coastal and inland regions, and the launch of the country's first manned space program were all notable accomplishments that occurred under Hu's watch. But this term began to circulate widely in public discourse in the lead-up to the 2012 leadership transition. See Cheng Li and Eve Cary, "The Last Year of Hu's Leadership: Hu's to Blame?," *China Brief*, vol. 11, no. 23 (December 20, 2011): 7–10.

62. Benjamin Carlson, "7 Things you can't talk about in China," *Global Post*, June 3, 2013 (www.globalpost.com/dispatch/news/regions/asia-pacific/china/130529/censorship-chinese-communist-party).

63. The author is grateful to an anonymous reviewer of an early version of this book for making this observation.

64. These noted exceptions include Lampton, *Following the Leader: Ruling China, from Deng Xiaoping to Xi Jinping;* Joseph Fewsmith, *The Logic and Limits of Political Reform in China* (Cambridge University Press, 2013); Minxin Pei, *China's Trapped Transition: The Limits of Developmental Autocracy* (Harvard University Press, 2008); Tony Saich, *Governance and Politics of China*, 3rd ed. (Hampshire, UK: Palgrave Macmillan, 2011); David Shambaugh, *China's Communist Party: Atrophy and Adaptation* (University of California Press, 2008); Victor C. Shih, *Factions and Finance in China: Elite Conflict and Inflation* (Cambridge University Press, 2009); and Richard McGregor, *The Party: The Secret World of China's Communist Rulers* (New York: Harper, 2010).

65. Both Daniel Bell and Eric Li provide some insights about the inner workings of Chinese leadership politics, but their praise of CCP meritocracy was highly controversial in the light of rampant official corruption, nepotism, and the purchase of official positions. Daniel Bell and Eric Li, "In Defense of How China Picks its Leaders," *Financial Times*, November 11, 2012 (www.ft.com/intl/cms/s/0/903d37ac-2a63-11e2-a137-00144feabdc0.html#axzz38c3msagD). For a more thought-provoking academic discussion, see Daniel Bell, *The China Model: Political Meritocracy and the Limits of Democracy* (Princeton University Press, 2015).

66. Robert Lawrence Kuhn, *How China's Leaders Think* (New York: John Wiley & Sons, 2010).

67. See, for example, Andrew J. Nathan, "Authoritarian resilience," *Journal of Democracy*, vol. 14, no. 1 (2003): 6–17; Alice Miller, "Institutionalization and the changing dynamics of Chinese leadership politics," in *China's Changing Political Landscape: Prospects for Democracy*, edited by Cheng Li (Brookings, 2008), 61–79; Alice Miller, "Leadership Sustains Public Unity Amid Stress," *China Leadership Monitor*, no. 29 (2009); and David Shambaugh, *China's Communist Party: Atrophy and Adaptation* (University of California Press, 2008).

68. Kjeld Erik Brødsgaard, and Zheng Yongnian, "Introduction: Whither the Chinese Communist Party?" in *The Chinese Communist Party in Reform*, edited by Brødsgaard, Kjeld Erikand and Zheng Yongnian (New York: Routledge, 2006), 2.

69. Bruce Dickson, "Populist Authoritarianism: The Future of the Chinese Communist Party," *Occasional Papers* (Carnegie Endowment for International Peace, 2005): 1.

70. Andrew J. Nathan, Larry Diamond, and Marc F. Plattner, "Introduction," in *Will China Democratize?*, edited by Andrew J. Nathan, Larry Diamond, and Marc F. Plattner (Johns Hopkins University Press, 2013), xi.

71. Dickson, "Populist Authoritarianism," 11. Also see Pan Wei, ed. *Zhongguo moshi: Jiedu renmin gongheguo de liushi nian* [China model: A new developmental model from sixty years of the People's Republic] (Beijing: Central Compilation and Translation Press, 2009).

72. Nathan, "Authoritarian Resilience," 6–7.

73. For a detailed critique of the thesis of authoritarian resilience, see Cheng Li, "The End of the CCP's Resilient Authoritarianism? A Tripartite Assessment of Shifting Power in China," *China Quarterly*, no. 211 (September 2012): 595–623.

74. Zhang Lifan, blog entry, February 1, 2012 (http://blog.sina.com.cn/s/blog_4b86a2630100zhuv.html).

75. According to a 2011 report released by Washington-based Global Financial Integrity (GFI), from 2000 to 2009 China's illegal capital outflow totaled US$2.74 trillion, five times more than the total amount from the second-ranked country, Mexico. *Shijie ribao* [World Journal], April 20, 2012, A4.

76. *Shijie ribao* [World Journal], May 3, 2012, A4.

77. Minxin Pei, "The Myth of Chinese Meritocracy," *Project Syndicate*, May 15, 2012 (www.project-syndicate.org/commentary/the-myth-of-chinese-meritocracy).

78. Zhang Lifan, blog entry, February 1, 2012 (http://blog.sina.com.cn/s/blog _4b86a2630100zhuv.html).

79. David Shambaugh, "The Coming Chinese Crackup," *Wall Street Journal*, March 7, 2015, C1–C2.

80. Hu, *Zhongguo jiti lingdao tizhi*, 14, 158–165.

81. Hu Angang, *China's Collective Presidency* (London: Springer, 2014).

82. Ibid., 1.

83. Hu, *Zhongguo jiti lingdao tizhi*, 14.

84. Ibid., 1, 51–142.

85. For some of the criticisms of Hu Angang's thesis, see Dong Fang, "Beijing kandian" [Beijing observation], Voice of America, August 16, 2013 (www.voachinese.com/content /beijing-focus-china-us-20130816/1731039.html).

86. The author is grateful to an anonymous reviewer of an early version of this book for making this observation.

87. For two important recent reports on Xi Jinping's foreign policy, see Jeffrey A. Bader, *How Xi Jinping Sees the World... and Why*, Brookings Foreign Policy Asia Working Group Paper 2, February 2016 (part of Order from Chaos: Foreign Policy in a Troubled World series); and Blackwill and Campbell, *Xi Jinping on the Global Stage*.

88. In the study of Xi Jinping's political associations, Hong Kong-based Mirror Books has published a large number of books, good examples of which include Xiang Jiangyu, *Xi Jinping bandi* [Xi Jinping's confidants] (New York: Mirror Books, 2011); Xiang Jiangyu, *Xi Jinping de tuandui* [Xi Jinping's team] (New York: Mirror Books, 2013); Ke Lizi, *Yingxiang Xi Jinping de ren* [People who influence Xi Jinping] (New York: Mirror Books, 2013); Wen Zixian, *Xi Jinping de xuanze* [Xi Jinping's choice] (New York: Mirror Books, 2012); and Liang Jian, *Xi Jinping xinzhuan* [New biography of Xi Jinping] (New York: Mirror Books, 2012). For some other publishers, see Wu Ming, *Zhongguo xinlingxiu: Xi Jinping zhuan* [China's new leader: Biography of Xi Jinping], new enlarged edition (Hong Kong: Wenhua yishu chubanshe, 2010).

89. For example, the Chinese government's database of party and state leaders in China (http://cpc.people.com.cn/gbzl/index.html).

90. Yang Shangkun, *Yang Shangkun riji* [Yang Shangkun's diary] (Beijing: Zhongyang wenxian chubanshe, 2001); and Yang Shangkun, *Yang Shangkun huiyilu* [Yang Shangkun's memoir] (Beijing: Zhongyang wenxian chubanshe, 2001).

91. For a good summary of this phenomenon, see Feng Shuangqing, Min Jie, Chen Xi, and Gao Mingong, "Xieren lingdaoren zheyang chushu" [The ways in which retired leaders published their books], *Renmin ribao* [People's Daily], overseas edition, January 3, 2014.

92. Ma Ling and Li Ming, *Hu Jintao—Ta cong nali lai, Jiang xiang hechu qu* [Hu Jintao: Where did he come from and where he will go] (Hong Kong: Mingbao chubanshe, 2002); and Ma Ling and Li Ming, *Wen Jiabao* (Taibei: Lianjing chubanshe, 2003).

93. For example, rising stars in provincial leadership with Suzhou origin were profiled in *Nanfang zhoumo* [Southern Weekly], November 18, 2004, A1–2.

94. Zhang Lei, "Nongchaoer" [The man who paddles against the incoming tide], *Nanfang renwu zhoukan* [Southern People Weekly], August 26, 2013; and Wu Rujia and Lin Zijing, "*Wang Qishan lianpu*" [Changing roles of Wang Qishan], *Fenghuang zhoukai* [Phoenix Weekly], December 5, 2013.

95. Xi Jinping, *Zhijiang xinyu* [New thought in Zhejiang] (Hangzhou: Zhejiang renmin chubanshe, 2007).

96. These books are Xi Jinping, ed., *Xiandai nongye lilun yu shijian* [Modern agriculture: theory and practice] (Fuzhou: Fujian jiaoyu chubanshe, 1999); Xi Jinping, (coed.), *Fujian*

shanhai liandong fazhan yanjiu [The study of land and sea joint development in Fujian] (Fuzhou: Fujian renmin chubanshe, 2000); Xi Jinping, *Xinshiji de xuanze: Fujian sheng fada diqu shuaixian shixian nongye xiandaihua yanjiu* [The new century's decision: The study of agricultural modernization led by advanced areas of Fujian Province] (Fuzhou: Fujian jiaoyu chubanshe, 2001); Xi Jinping, *Zhongguo nongcun shichanghua jianshe yanjiu* [Research on market development of rural China] (Beijing: Renmin chubanshe, 2001); Xi Jinping, ed., *Kexue yu aiguo* [Science and patriotism] (Beijing: Tsinghua University Press, 2001).

97. For example, the Chinese official media recently published several articles about Xi Jinping's experiences in Zhengding County in Hebei Province, where he served as deputy party secretary and then party secretary of the county from 1982 to 1985. These articles reveal the friendships that he developed with some officials during that period and beyond. See Cheng Baohuai, Liu Xiaocui, Wu Zhihui, "Xi Jinping tongzhi zai Zhengding" [Comrade Xi Jinping in Zhengding County], *Hebei ribao* [Hebei Daily], January 2, 2014 (http://news.xinhuanet.com/local/2014-01/02/c_125944449.htm) and Xi Jinping, "Yi Dashan" [In commemoration of Jia Dashan], *Guangming Daily*, January 13, 2014, (www.chinanews.com/gn/2014/01-13/5726676.shtml). The piece originally appeared in *Dangdairen* [Contemporary], no. 7 (1998). As for the international audience, Xi introduced Liu He, one of his top aides on economic affairs, to then-U.S. National Security Adviser Tom Donilon in fall 2013. Xi said, "This is Liu He. He is very important to me." Quoted from Bob Davis, "Meeting Liu He, Xi Jinping's Choice to Fix a Faltering Chinese Economy," *Wall Street Journal*, October 6, 2013 (http://online.wsj.com/news/articles/SB10001424052702304906704579111442566524958).

98. The quantitative sources include the Central Organization Department of the CCP and the Research Institute of the CCP History of the Central Committee of the CCP, comp. *Zhongguo gongchandang lijie zhongyang weiyuan dacidian* 1921–2003 [Who's who in the Central Committees of the Chinese Communist Party, 1921–2003] (Beijing: CCP Archive Press, 2004); Liao Gailong and Fan Yuan, comps., *Zhongguo renming da cidian: xiandai dangzhengjun lingdao renwu juan* [Who's who in China: Current party, government, and military leaders], 1994 edition (Beijing: Foreign Languages Press, 1994); Shen Xueming and others, comps., *Zhonggong di shiwujie zhongyang weiyuanhui zhongyang jilü jiancha weiyuanhui weiyuan minglu* [Who's who among the members of the Fifteenth Central Committee of the Chinese Communist Party and the Fifteenth Central Discipline Inspection Commission] (Beijing: *Zhonggong wenxian chubanshe*, 1999); and *China Directory* (Tokyo: Rapiopress, various years from 1985 to 2014). In addition, this study collected biographical information often through search engines and from online websites such as www.xinhuanet.com, www.China.com, www.google.com, www.Chinesenewsnet.com, www.sina.com, www.yahoo.com, www.baidu.com, and www.sohu.com.

CHAPTER 2

1. Part of this discussion on the structure of China's party-state system is based on Cheng Li, "China's Communist Party-State: The Structure and Dynamics of Power," in *Politics in China*, 2d ed., ed. William A. Joseph (Oxford University Press, 2014), 192–223.

2. "Zhonggong dangyuan zongshu 8668.6 wan ming dangyuan duiwu he zuzhi jianshe chengxian xin tedian" [The number of the CPC members has risen to 86.686 Million, the capacity building of party members and party organizations presents new characteristics], Xinhua, June 30, 2014 (http://news.xinhuanet.com/politics/2014-06/30/c_1111379852.htm); and *Shijie ribao* [World Journal], July 1, 2015, A5.

3. "CPC members exceed 82 million," *China Daily*, June 30, 2012 (http://www.chinadaily.com.cn/china/2012-06/30/content_15538974.htm).

4. Shen Lutao, Wang Li, Zou Shengwen, and Zhang Zongtang, "Quanguo renda changweihui bangongting jiu gongwuyuanfa cao'an juxing xinwen fabuhui" [General Office of

the NPC Standing Committee held a press conference on the draft Law on Civil Servants], Renmin Newsnet, April 28, 2005, http://npc.people.com.cn/GB/14957/3354809.html.

5. Ibid.

6. Constitution of the People's Republic of China (1982), chapter 1, article 1.

7. "CPC Issues Document on Ruling Capacity," *China Daily*, September 27, 2004 (www .chinadaily.com.cn/english/doc/2004-09/27/content_378161.htm).

8. For the latest version of the CCP Constitution, amended in November 2012, see "(Shouquan fabu) Zhongguo gongchandang zhangcheng" [Authorized release: Constitution of the Chinese Communist Party], Xinhua, November 28, 2012 (http://news.xinhuanet .com/18cpcnc/2012-11/18/c_113714762.htm).

9. "Zhonggong qu niandi dangyuan renshu 8668.6 wan xin fazhan rudang renshu shouci xiajiang" [By the end of last year, the number of CPC members has risen to 86.686 million, the number of new members fell for the first time], *Guanchazhe* [Observer], June 30, 2014 (www.guancha.cn/politics/2014_06_30_242290.shtml).

10. "Wang Jingqing: Shengchan he gongzuo yixian daibiao bili tigao 2.1 ge baifendian" [Wang Jingqing: the percentage of party representatives who work on the front line has risen by 2.1%], CCP Newsnet, August 14, 2012 (http://cpc.people.com.cn/n/2012/0814 /c164113-18739640.html).

11. There was some variation in official accounts of the number of delegations to the 18th National Party Congress. On the eve of the congress, Xinhua news announced that the total number of delegations was thirty-eight, which differed from the previous official number of forty delegations; see Xinhua, November 7, 2012 (http://cpc.people.com.cn/18/n /2012/1107/c350837-19515872.html). For the earlier account, see "Chuxi dang de shibada daibiao mingdan (huizong)" [Representatives of 18th Party Congress name list (summary)], Chinese Economics Newsnet, May 11, 2012 (http://district.ce.cn/newarea/sddy/201205/11 /t20120511_23315093.shtml).

12. *Dangde shibada wenjian huibian* [Collection of the documents of the 18th Party Congress] (Beijing: Dangjian duwu chubanshe [Party-building Readings Press], 2012).

13. Wang Ya, "Sizhong shibianxia de zhongjiwei and zhengfawei" [Changing roles of the CCDI and PLC on the eve of the Fourth Plenum of the 18th Central Committee], Duowei Net, August 6, 2014 (http://china.dwnews.com/news/2014-08-06/59602172.html).

14. "Zhongjiwei tan quanli jiandu: Shidang fenjie zhuyao lingdao ganbu quanli zeren" [Central Commission for Discipline Inspection of the CPC commented on the supervision of power: reduce the power and responsibility of main political leaders], China Newsnet, December 4, 2013 (www.chinanews.com/gn/2013/12-04/5581480.shtml).

15. *Shijie ribao*, December 31, 2013, A13.

16. "Zhong jiwei tan quanli jiandu: Shidang fenjie zhuyao lingdao ganbu quanli zeren" [Central Commission for Discipline Inspection of the CPC commented on the supervision of power: reduce the power and responsibility of main political leaders], China Newsnet, December 4, 2013 (www.chinanews.com/gn/2013/12-04/5581480.shtml).

17. *Renmin ribao* [People's Daily], July 11, 2014, 1, 6. Also see "Zhongjiwei kaishi jiandu zhongyang jigou bei ping zouxiang duli hua" [Central Commission for Discipline Inspection started to supervise central organs of CPC, commentators say it is becoming independent], Duowei Net, July 20, 2014 (http://china.dwnews.com/news/2014-07-20/59491951.html).

18. Zhonggong zhongyang jilü jiancha weiyuanhui zhonghua renmin gongheguo jianchabu jubao wangzhan [Central Commission for Discipline Inspection of the CPC and Ministry of Supervision reporting of official wrongdoing website], "Zhonggong zhongyang jilü jiancha weiyuanhui zhonghua renmin gongheguo jianchabu" [Central Commission for Discipline Inspection of the CPC and Ministry of Supervision], January 16, 2015 (www.12388.gov.cn/).

19. "Liu Tienan he ta de nengyuan ju" [Liu Tienan and his National Energy Administration], Sohu Net, August 15, 2013 (http://business.sohu.com/s2013/ltn-nyj/).

20. For the straw poll in 2007, see Alice Miller, "The Case of Xi Jinping and the Mysterious Succession," *China Leadership Monitor*, no. 30 (November 19, 2009): 8–9.

21. The secretary of the CCDI in 1992–97 was Wei Jianxing, who served concurrently only as a member of the Secretariat and the Politburo of the CCP.

22. The Jiang-Xi camp has long considered Li Yuanchao a political threat. Some conservatives such as former premier Li Peng were also concerned about Li's liberal stance during the Tiananmen event in 1989.

23. All the provincial, municipal, and county party committees have their own politics and law commissions.

24. Ji Weiren, "Zhou Yongkang ba zhengfawei gaocheng duli wangguo" [Zhou Yongkang turns the Politics and Law Committee into his own independent kingdom], *Diaocha* [Investigation], July 4, 2014 (www.mirrorbooks.com/MIB/magazine/news.aspx?ID=M000001119).

25. Ibid.

26. China Economic History Forum, May 3, 2006. Also see "He Weifang, zai xishan huiyi de fayan" [He Weifang's speech at the Xishan Conference], Baidu Library (http://wenku.baidu.com/view/a2fa0c8da0116c175f0e4825.html).

27. He Weifang, "The Police and the Rule of Law: Commentary on 'Principals and Secret Agents.'" *China Quarterly*, no. 191 (September 2007), 672.

28. For more discussion of He Weifang's criticism, see He Weifang, *In the Name of Justice: Striving for the Rule of Law in China* (Brookings, 2012).

29. The General Office of the CCP Central Committee, *Dangzheng lingdao ganbu zhiwu renqi zanxing* guiding [Interim regulations of the tenure of party and Government Officials], Xinhua, August 6, 2006 (http://news.xinhuanet.com/politics/2006-08/06/content_4926300.htm).

30. Ibid.

31. Xiang Jiangyu, *Xi Jinping de tuandui* [Xi Jinping's team] (New York: Mirror Books, 2013).

32. "Jiemi quanqiu zuida chaoji HR zhongzubu" [Revealing the world's largest human resources department: Central Organization Department], *Zhongguo xinwen zhoukan* [China Newsweek], September 4, 2014 (http://news.sohu.com/20140904/n404074530.shtml).

33. Based on the author's interviews with COD officials in Beijing during the summer of 2009. Also see "Jiemi quanqiu zuida chaoji HR zhongzubu."

34. The CCP Central Organization Department, *Guanyu xiuding Zhonggong Zhongyang guanli de ganbuzhiwu mingchengbiao de tongzhi* [Notice on the revision of the list of official posts managed by the CCP Central Committee], July 14, 1984.

35. For a recent study of the CCP cadre reserve system, see Wen-Hsuan Tsai and Chien-Wen Kou, "The Party's Disciples: CCP Reserve Cadres and the Perpetuation of a Resilient Authoritarian Regime." *China Quarterly* 221 (March 2015): 1–20.

36. The CCP Central Organization Department, *Guanyu xiuding Zhonggong Zhongyang guanli de ganbuzhiwu mingchengbiao de tongzhi* [Notice on the revision of the list of official posts managed by the CCP Central Committee].

37. CCP Central Organization Department, "Guanyu jianli shengbuji houbei ganbu zhidu de yijian" [Plan on the establishment of the reserve system for provincial and ministerial cadres], Duowei Net, December 7, 2011 (http://18.dwnews.com/news/2011-12-07/58382373.html).

38. Ibid.

39. Tsai and Kou, "The Party's Disciples," 1–20.

40. Richard McGregor, "The Party Organizer," *Financial Times*, September 30, 2009 (www.ft.com/cms/s/0/ae18c830-adf8-11de-87e7-00144feabdc0.html#axzz1L7M0fcuH).

41. For more discussion of the leading groups, see Alice L. Miller, "The CCP Central Committee's Leading Small Groups," *China Leadership Monitor*, no. 26 (Fall 2008): 1–21.

42. "Tujie zhongyang ge lingdao xiaozu: Xi Jinping danren sige xiaozu zu zhang" [Illustrations explaining the Central Leading Groups: Xi Jinping chairs four of them], Renmin Net, June 30, 2014 (http://news.sina.com.cn/c/p/2014-06-30/142030444500 .shtml).

43. *Shijie ribao*, June 26, 2015, B4.

44. "Xi Jinping zhuchi zhaokai zhongyang quanmian shenhua gaige lingdao xiaozu diyici huiyi Li Keqiang Liu Yunshan Zhang Gaoli chuxi" [Xi Jinping hosted the first meeting of Central Leading Group for Comprehensively Deepening Reforms, Li Keqiang, Liu Yunshan and Zhang Gaoli attended the meeting], *Renmin ribao* [People's Daily], January 23, 2014 (http://cpc.people.com.cn/n/2014/0123/c64094-24201660.html).

45. Ibid.

46. "Quanfangwei jiedu 'zhongyang guojia anquan weiyuanhui' he 'zongti guojia anquan guan'" [Interpreting the National Security Commission and the Overall National Security Outlook], Xinhua, April 17, 2014 (http://news.xinhuanet.com/politics/2014-04/17 /c_126397122.htm).

47. "Xi Jinping ren zhongyang guojia anquan weiyuanhui zhuxi" [Xi Jinping takes office as the chairman of National Security Commission], Xinhua, January 24, 2014 (http://news .xinhuanet.com/politics/2014-01/24/c_119122483.htm).

48. Wu Yu, "Zhongguo guojia anquan weiyuanhui" [China's National Security Committee]. *Deutsche Welle*, November 13, 2013 (www.dw.de/中国国家安全委员会习近平亲自执掌 /a-17223469).

49. The author is grateful to an anonymous reviewer of an early version of this book for making this observation.

50. "Li Keqiang duixian chengnuo zhonggong jingjian 1441 ge 'lingdao xiaozu'" [Li Keqiang honored his word, the CPC dismissed 1,441 Leading Groups], Duowei News, July 1, 2014 (http://china.dwnews.com/news/2014-07-01/59484381.html).

51. Yang Xuedong, "*Xiaozu zhengzhi yu zhidu tanxing*" [Leading group politics and institutional resilience], *Renmin luntan* [People's Forum], May 7, 2014 (www.21ccom.net/articles /zgyj/ggcx/article_20140627108496.html).

52. Ibid.

53. Constitution of the People's Republic of China (1982), chapter 1, article 2.

54. For a more detailed discussion of the role and the reform of the NPC, see Shi Hexing, "The People's Congress System and China's Constitutional Development" (and Jacques deLisle's comments), in *China's Political Development: Chinese and American Perspectives*, ed. Kenneth Lieberthal, Cheng Li, and Yu Keping (Brookings, 2014), 103–135.

55. For a comprehensive review of the unequal distribution of delegate seats between urban and rural areas during the first six decades of the PRC, see Han Dayuan, "'Chengxiang anxiangtong renkou bilü xuanju renda daibiao' de guifan fenxi jiqi yingxiang" [Electing deputies of the National People's Congress in the same quota of population between urban and rural areas: analysis of regulations and their impact], *Zhongguo xianfaxue* [China's constitutional law], (http://lesson.calaw.cn/article/default.asp?id=240).

56. State Council, *Guowuyuan guanyu jinyibu tuijin huji zhidu gaige de yijian* [State Council's resolution to further promote the reform of the household registration system] (Beijing: Renmin chubanshe, 2014). For the comparison between Chinese urban-rural segregation and South Africa's apartheid, see Madison Park and C. Y. Xu, "Is Migrant System China's Apartheid?" CNN, December 25, 2012 (http://edition.cnn.com/2012/12/25/world /asia/china-migrant-family/).

57. Yang Hongshan, *Dangdai Zhongguo zhengzhi guanxi* [Political relationships in contemporary China] (Beijing: Jingji ribao chubanshe, 2002), 188.

58. Chen Xiao, *Dangdai Zhongguo zhengfu tizhi* [Contemporary Chinese government system] (Shanghai: Shanghai Jiaotong daxue chubanshe, 2005), 70.

59. Yang, *Dangdai Zhongguo zhengzhi guanxi*, 188.

60. "Shi'er jie quanguo renda daibiao mingdan gongbu gongnong daibiao zhan bi mingxian shangsheng" [The name list of the 12th National People's Congress is released, the percentage of workers and farmers rose significantly], *Zhejiang gongren ribao* [Zhejiang Workers' Daily], February 28, 2013 (www.zjgrrb.com/zjzgol/system/2013/02/28/016136133 .shtml).

61. Michael Forsythe, Michael Wei, and Henry Sanderson, "China's Richer-Than-Romney Lawmakers Reveal Reform Challenge." *Bloomberg News*, March 7, 2013 (www .bloomberg.com/news/2013-03-06/china-s-richer-than-romney-lawmakers-show-xi-s -reform-challenge.html).

62. In the 1956 PRC Constitution the eligible age was thirty-five years or older; it increased to forty-five years or older in the 1982 Constitution. Wei Na and Wu Aiming, *Dangdai Zhongguo zhengfu yu xingzheng* [Contemporary Chinese government and administration], 3d ed. (Beijing: Zhongguo renmin daxue chubanshe, 2012), 22.

63. "Dangxuan guojia zhuxi Xi Jinping quanmian zhizheng" [Xi Jinping was elected president and has started to run the government comprehensively], *Shijie ribao*, March 16, 2013 (www.boxun.com/news/gb/china/2013/03/201303160120.shtml).

64. Chen Xiao, *Dangdai Zhongguo zhengfu tizhi*, 75.

65. Wei and Wu, *Dangdai Zhongguo zhengfu yu xingzheng*, 85–86.

66. For a more detailed discussion of the role and the reform of the CPPCC, see Lin Shangli, "Political Consultation and Consultative Politics in China" (and Joseph Fewsmith's comments), in Lieberthal, Li, and Yu, eds., *China's Political Development*, 136–64.

67. Constitution of the People's Republic of China (1993), Amendment 2.

68. These eight parties are (1) Revolutionary Committee of the Kuomintang (中国国民党革命委员会 or 民革, 81,000 members), (2) China Democratic League (中国民主同盟 or 民盟, 181,000 members), (3) China Democratic National Construction Association (中国民主建国会 or 民建, 108,000 members), (4) China Association for Promoting Democracy (中国民主促进会 or 民进, 103,000 members), (5) Chinese Peasants' and Workers' Democratic Party (中国农工民主党 or 农工党, 99,000 members), (6) Zhigongdang of China (中国致公党, 2,800 members), (7) Jiusan Society (九三学社, 105,000 members), and (8) Taiwan Democratic Self-Government League (台湾民主自治同盟 or 台盟, 2,100 members). See Information Office of the State Council, *Zhongguo zhengdang zhidu* [The party system of China] (Beijing: Information Office of the State Council, 2007).

69. Ibid.

70. "Di shi'er jie quanguo zhengxie weiyuan mingdan chulu Yu Zhengsheng ren quanguo zhengxie weiyuan" [The name list of the 12th National Committee of Chinese People's Political Consultative Conference was released, Yu Zhengsheng was elected member], *Nanfang ribao* [Southern Daily], February 3, 2013 (http://theory.people.com.cn/n/2013/0203 /c49150-20414891.html).

71. "Quanguo zhengxie de jiebie" [The Constituencies of the National Committee of Chinese People's Political Consultative Conference], Xinhua, February 21, 2012 (http:// news.xinhuanet.com/ziliao/2002-02/21/content_284912.htm).

72. For a very comprehensive review of the evolution of the State Council in the first five decades of the PRC, see Guojia xingzheng xueyuan [China's National Academy of Administration], ed., "Zhonghua renmin gongheguo zhengfu jigou wushi nian" [Government organs of the PRC in the past fifty years] (Beijing: Dangjian duwu chubanshe, 2000).

73. Yang, *Dangdai Zhongguo zhengzhi guanxi,* 128.

74. For a more comprehensive discussion of the institutions affiliated with the State Council, see "Zhonghua renmin gongheguo guowuyuan," Xinhua, March, 2013 (http://news .xinhuanet.com/ziliao/2013-03/16/c_115043640.htm).

75. The exceptions include SASAC, a very powerful ministerial leadership body that controls China's flagship companies. Also, the heads of agencies who concurrently serve as heads of CCP organizations can be more important than ministers. One such agency head

is Zhang Zhijun, director of the Taiwan Affairs Office of the State Council, who concurrently serves as director of the CCP Central Office for Taiwan Affairs.

76. Li Rongrong, "I consider Zhu Rongji a role model and Putin an idol," Xinhua, September 8, 2010 (http://news.xinhuanet.com/fortune/2010-09/08/c_12530988.htm). Also see Chen Zhiwu, *Shuo Zhongguo jingji* [Assessing the Chinese economy] (Taiyuan: Shanxi jingji chubanshe, 2010), 103.

77. *Shijie ribao*, April 19, 2010, A10.

CHAPTER 3

1. Zeng Qinghong, "Zai jiwang kailaizhong chuangzao women dangde shiye xinhuihuang" [To keep abreast of time in order to create new glories for our party's cause in the future], *Renmin ribao* [People's Daily], November 16, 2007 (http://cpc.people.com.cn/GB/104019/104099/6381699.html). Zeng's metaphor is an adaptation of the title of a famous Chinese song 铁打的营盘流水的兵 (*tiedade yingpan liushuidebing*), which is itself a modification of the Chinese proverb used as the epigraph for this chapter.

2. The data were primarily compiled by the author using biographical information released by the Xinhua News Agency along with Chinese-language search engines provided by Google and Baidu. They are usually cross-checked with additional sources including The Central Organization Department of the CCP and the Party History Research Center of the CPC Central Committee, comp. *Zhongguo gongchandang lijie zhongyang weiyuan dacidian* 1921–2003 [Who's who among China current leaders]; Liao Gailong and Fan Yuan, *Zhongguo renming dacidian: xiandai dangzhengjun lingdao renwu juan*; Shen Xueming and others, *Zhonggong di shiwujie zhongyang weiyuanhui zhongyang jilü jiancha weiyuanhui weiyuan minglu* [Name list of members of 15th Central Committee and Central Commission for Discipline Inspection of the CPC]; and *China Directory* (Tokyo: Radiopress, various years from 1985 to 2014).

3. Cheng Li and Lynn White, "The Sixteenth Central Committee of the Chinese Communist Party: Hu Gets What?," *Asian Survey*, vol. 43, no. 4 (July/August 2003): 560.

4. Cheng Li and Lynn White, "The Fifteenth Central Committee of the Chinese Communist Party: Full-Fledged Technocratic Leadership with Partial Control by Jiang Zemin," *Asian Survey*, vol. 38, no. 3 (March 1998): 253.

5. For a more detailed discussion of the concept and definition of the political elite generations, see Cheng Li, *China's Leaders: The New Generation* (Lanham, MD: Rowman & Littlefield, 2001). For a comprehensive study of the fifth generation, see Cheng Li, "China's Fifth Generation," in *Emerging Leaders in East Asia: The Next Generation of Political Leadership in China, Japan, South Korea and Taiwan*, ed. Kenneth B. Pyle (Seattle: National Bureau of Asian Research Press), 15–53.

6. The second-largest turnover of the PSC occurred at the 1987 Party Congress. Out of the officials of the previous six-man PSC, only Zhao Ziyang remained.

7. The most important document that explains the norms and regulations of CCP elite recruitment is the General Office of the CCP Central Committee's *Dangzheng lingdao ganbu zhiwu renqi zanxing guiding* [Interim regulations of the tenure of party and government officials]. Two additional documents are the General Office of the CCP Central Committee's *Dangzheng lingdao ganbu jiaoliu gongzuo guiding* [Regulations of exchange of party and government officials], Xinhua, August 6, 2006, and *Dangzheng lingdao ganbu renzhi huibi zanxing guiding* [Interim regulations of position avoidance of party and government officials], Xinhua, August 6, 2006.

8. Zhonggong zhongyang [Central Committee of the CCP], "Dangzheng lingdao ganbu xuanba renyong gongzuo tiaoli" [Regulations and laws on the recruitment and promotion of party and government officials], in Zhonggong zhongyang zuzhibu ganbu yiju [No.1 Bureau of Cadre of the Central Organization Department of the CCP Central Committee],

comp., *2014 Dangzheng lingdao ganbu xuanba renyong gongzuo tiaoli xuexi fudao* [Guide on the regulations and laws on the recruitment and promotion of party and government officials, 2014] (Beijing: Dangjian duwu chubanshe, 2014), 4–30.

9. Ibid., 5.

10. China Merchant Bank (blog), "Liwai" [An exception], March 3, 2013 (http://blog.sina .com.cn/s/blog_4fcd03e90102e747.html).

11. *Wenhui bao* [Wenhui Daily], Hong Kong, November 15, 2002.

12. See http://www.qianlong.com, November 18, 2002. Quoted from the section on China in *Shijie junshi nianjian 2001* [World military yearbook, 2001] (Beijing: PLA Press, 2001).

13. Ibid.; see also Cheng Li, "Promoting 'Young Guards': The Recent High Turnover in the PLA Leadership (Part I: Purges and Reshuffles)," *China Leadership Monitor*, no. 48 (Fall 2015).

14. Quoted from *Wenhui bao* [Wenhui Daily], August 15, 2003; see also http://www.sina .com.cn, August 15, 2003, and the Ministry of National Defense of the PRC website, March 10, 2015 (http://www.mod.gov.cn/policy/2015-03/10/content_4574014.htm).

15. General Office of the CCP Central Committee, *Tuijin lingdao ganbu nengshang nengxia ruogan guiding (shixing)* [A number of trial provisions to promote the mobility of cadres], Renmin Newsnet, July 29, 2015 (http://politics.people.com.cn/n/2015/0729/c1001 -27375974.html).

16. One exception was Yunnan Province, which had only one full member on the Central Committee in 1997.

17. Zhang Sutong, Qin Jie, Huo Xiaoguang, and Li Yajie "Shibajie zhongyang weiyuanhui weiyuan cha'e bilü wei 9.3%" [The full membership of the 18th Central Committee has an elected ratio difference of 9.3%], *People's Daily Online*, November 15, 2012 (http:// politics.people.com.cn/n/2012/1115/c1001-19584526.html).

18. Zhang Lixin, "Shiliuda yilai de zhongyang weiyuan, houbu weiyuan cha'e xuanju" [The multicandidate elections of full members of the Central Committee since the 16th National Party Congress], Xinhua, November 13, 2012 (http://news.xinhuanet.com/politics /2012-11/13/c_113680755.htm).

19. Zhang Lizhou, " 'Piaojuezhi': Ganbu renyong juece de zhongyao gaige" [Secret ballot voting is a major reform mechanism to select cadres], *Renmin ribao*, December 26, 2002 (http://news.xinhuanet.com/zonghe/2002-12/26/content_670280.htm), and Zhonggong Zhongyang [Central Committee of the CCP], "Dangzheng lingdao ganbu xuanba renyong gongzuo tiaoli" [Regulations and laws on the recruitment and promotion of party and government officials], 18.

20. Zhonggong zhongyang [Central Committee of the CCP], "Dangzheng lingdao ganbu xuanba renyong gongzuo tiaoli" [Regulations and laws on the recruitment and promotion of party and government officials], 25.

21. Cheng Li, "Local Government: The Big Shake-up," *China Economic Quarterly*, vol. 2, no. 1 (March 2007): 25.

22. Feng Junqi, "Zhongxian 'zhengzhi jiazu' xianxiang diaocha" [Investigation of 'political families' in Zhongxian], *Nanfang zhoumo* [Southern Weekend], September 2, 2011 (http://www.infzm.com/content/62798).

23. Ruth Cherrington, "Generational Issues in China: A Case Study of the 1980s Generation of Young Intellectuals," *British Journal of Sociology*, vol. 48, no. 2 (June 1997): 304.

24. Li, *China's Leaders*, 6–14.

25. Paul Cavey, "Building a Power Base: Jiang Zemin and the Post-Deng Succession," *Issues and Studies*, vol. 33, no. 11 (November 1997): 1–34.

26. The author's previous study defines the Cultural Revolution generation as consisting of leaders born between 1941 and 1956. They were ten to twenty-five years old when the Cultural Revolution began in 1966. See Li, *China's Leaders*, 10–13. The prominent Chinese scholar Hu Angang, however, defines the Cultural Revolution generation as those who were born between 1949 and 1959, *Lianhe Zaobao* [United Morning News], January 15, 2007.

27. Li and White, "The Sixteenth Central Committee of the Chinese Communist Party," 565.

28. Ibid.; see also Li Feng, *Shiwuda zhonggong gaoceng xin dang'an* [New profiles of the leadership of the Fifteenth Central Committee of the CCP] (Hong Kong: Wenhua chuanbo, 1997), 158.

29. Zeng Haisheng, sister of former Vice-President Zeng Qinghong and a major general of the PLA, serves as a member of the CPPCC. At the annual meeting of the CPPCC on the eve of the 18th National Party Congress, she explicitly expressed her desire that a female leader—her family friend Liu Yandong—enter the PSC. "Zeng Shan zhi nü: Xiwang shibada you nüxing jinru lingdaoceng" [Zeng Shan's daughter hopes female leaders will emerge in the leadership of the 18th party congress], Duowei Net, March 7, 2012 (http://18.dwnews.com/news/2012-03-07/58642821.html).

30. Subprovincial cities refer to Harbin, Changchun, Shenyang, Dalian, Nanjing, Jinan, Qingdao, Hangzhou, Ningbo, Xiamen, Wuhan, Guangzhou, Shenzhen, Xi'an, and Chengdu. Party secretaries of these cities are usually considered well-positioned leaders who will be further promoted.

31. Cheng Li, "China's Fifth Generation: Is Diversity a Source of Strength or Weakness?," *Asia Policy*, no. 6 (July 2008): 63.

32. For example, see Duowei Net, August 8, 2001 (www.chinesenewsnet.com).

33. Xinhua, March 7, 2002 (www.xinhuanet.com).

34. "Zhongzubu fuzeren jiu sheng shi xian xiang siji dangwei huanjie da jizhewen" [Central Organization Department answers journalists' questions on the leadership transition of provincial, municipal, county and township level party committees], Xinhua, August 3, 2012 (http://news.xinhuanet.com/politics/2012-08/03/c_112621847_2.htm).

35. "Canjia zhonggong shibada de nüxing daibiao" [Female representatives at the 18th party congress], Caixin Net, November 8, 2012 (http://china.caixin.com/2012-11-08/100457944.html).

36. Xu Meide (Ruth Hayhoe), *Zhongguo daxue 1895–1995: Yi ge wenhua chongtu de shiji* [China's universities 1895–1995: A century of cultural conflict], trans. Xu Jiemei (Beijing: Jiaoyu chubanshe, 2000), 165; National Bureau of Statistics, comp. *China Statistical Yearbook, 1999* (Beijing: China Statistics Press, 1999), 651; and Zhongguo gaoxiao nüsheng bili buduan shangsheng" [The proportion of female students in Chinese colleges and universities keeps increasing], Science Net, October 25, 2012 (http://news.sciencenet.cn/htmlnews/2012/10/270876.shtm).

37. "Zhongguo yanjiusheng nannü bili nüxing nixi" [Gender ratio of Chinese graduate students, female surpassed male], Xinhua, March 26, 2014 (http://edu.sina.com.cn/kaoyan/2014-03-26/1105413290.shtml).

38. "Zhongguo gaoxiao nüsheng bili buduan shangsheng" [The proportion of female students in Chinese colleges and universities keeps increasing], Science Net, October 25, 2012 (http://news.sciencenet.cn/htmlnews/2012/10/270876.shtm).

39. *Shijie ribao* [World Journal], August 3, 2013, A12.

40. Duowei Net, March 7, 2002 (www.chinesenews.net.com).

41. Duowei Net, November 23, 2001 (www.chinesenews.net.com).

42. For the 2004 amendment to this law, see State Ethnic Affairs Commission, "Renda changwei hui guanyu xiugai 'Zhonghua renmin gongheguo minzu quyu zizhi fa' de jueding" [Decision of the Standing Committee of the National People's Congress on Amending the Law of the People's Republic of China on Regional National Autonomy], July 2004 (www.seac.gov.cn/gjmw/zcfg/2004-07-10/1168742761853498.htm).

43. "Zhongguo de shaoshu minzu zhengce ji qi shijian" [China's ethnic minority policy and practice](www.china.com.cn/ch-book/shaoshu/shaoshu1.htm).

44. "Zhongzubu fuzeren jiu sheng shi xian xiang siji dangwei huanjie da jizhewen" [Central Organization Department answers journalists' questions on the leadership

transition of provincial, municipal, county and township level party committees], Xinhua, August 3, 2012 (http://news.xinhuanet.com/politics/2012-08/03/c_112621847_2.htm).

45. For example, see Li Cheng and Lynn White, "The Army in the Succession to Deng Xiaoping: Familiar Fealties and Technocratic Trends," *Asian Survey,* vol. 33, no. 8 (August 1993): 757–86; Li and White, "The Fifteenth Central Committee of the Chinese Communist Party," 231–64; and Zang Xiaowei, "The Fourteenth Central Committee of the CCP: Technocracy or Political Technocracy?" *Asian Survey,* vol. 33, no. 8 (August 1993): 787–803.

46. For more detail, see Li, *China's Leaders,* 59–62.

47. Li and White, "The Fifteenth Central Committee," 246–47. Previously unknown figures are added based on recently released official biographical information.

48. Li and White, "The Army in the Succession to Deng Xiaoping," 766–67.

49. *China News Analysis,* April 1, 1998, 4–6.

50. As Alice Lyman Miller has observed, "The coalition of leaders that governed China in the 1980s consisted mainly of leaders who either were from or had had long career experience in China's Southwestern province of Sichuan . . . or South China." See "Overlapping Transitions in China's Leadership," *SAIS Review,* vol. 16, no. 2 (Summer–Fall 1996): 24.

51. Li and White, "The Fifteenth Central Committee," 256.

52. Like the previous Central Committees, this group at the 18th Central Committee also includes representatives of so-called mass or social organizations such as the Chinese Academy of Social Sciences and the Chinese Academy of Engineering. Thus, the actual number of representatives of SOEs and financial firms is smaller.

53. The National Bureau of Statistics of the People's Republic of China website, "The Report of the 2010 Census in the People's Republic of China," April 28, 2011 (http://www .stats.gov.cn/tjsj/tjgb/rkpcgb/).

54. *Henan ribao* [Henan Daily], January 11, 2010, 1. The foreign countries with a population over 100 million are India, the United States, Indonesia, Brazil, Pakistan, Bangladesh, Nigeria, Russia, Japan, and Mexico.

55. Cheng Li, "China's Midterm Jockeying: Gearing Up for 2012 (Part 1: Provincial Chiefs)," *China Leadership Monitor,* no. 31 (Winter 2010): 3.

CHAPTER 4

1. Ho Ping-ti, *The Ladder of Success in Imperial China: Aspects of Social Mobility, 1368–1911* (Columbia University Press, 1962) and Robert North and Ithiel Pool, *Kuomintang and Chinese Communist Elites* (Stanford University Press, 1952).

2. He Huaihong, *Moral Decay or Ethical Awakening? Social Ethics in a Changing China* (Brookings, 2015), 67.

3. He Huaihong, *Zixuan ji* [Selected works] (Guilin: Guangxi Normal University Press, 2000), 358.

4. He, *Moral Decay or Ethical Awakening?,* 51.

5. He Huaihong, *Xuanju shehui* [The selection society], rev. ed. (Beijing: Peking University Press 2011), 100.

6. He, *Moral Decay or Ethical Awakening?,* 53.

7. Ho Ping-ti, *The Ladder of Success in Imperial China: Aspects of Social Mobility, 1368–1911* (Columbia University Press, 1962).

8. Hong Yung Lee, *The Politics of the Chinese Cultural Revolution: A Case Study* (University of California Press, 1978); Susan L. Shirk, "Educational Reform and Political Backlash: Recent Changes in Chinese Educational Policy," *Comparative Education Review* 23, no. 2 (June 1979): 185; and Anita Chen, "Dispelling Misconceptions about the Red Guard Movement: The Necessity of Re-Examining Cultural Revolution Factionalism and Periodization," *Journal of Contemporary China* 1 (September 1992): 62–85.

9. *Xinhua banyuekan* [Xinhua Bimonthly), January 2, 1957, 89; cited in Franz Schurmann, *Ideology and Organization in Communist China*, 2d ed. (University of California Press, 1968), 283.

10. Robert A. Scalapino, "Introduction," in Robert A. Scalapino, *Elites in the People's Republic of China* (University of Washington Press, 1972) and Li, *China's Leaders*, 33–34.

11. "Jiemi quanqiu zuida chaoji HR zhongzubu." [Revealing the world's largest super human resources department: Central Organization Department], *Zhongguo xinwen zhoukan* [China Newsweek], September 4, 2014, http://news.sohu.com/20140904/n404074530.shtml.

12. Hong Yung Lee, *From Revolutionary Cadres to Party Technocrats in Socialist China* (University of California Press, 1990), 302.

13. Zhongguo zuzhibu [CCP Central Organization Department], *Zhongguo ganbu tongji wushinian* [Statistics on the Chinese Cadres in the Past 50 Years] (Beijing, 1999), 13–14.

14. Xinhua, June 30, 2013 (http://news.xinhuanet.com/politics/2013-06/30/c_116344187.htm).

15. For a detailed discussion of the correlation between educational background and social mobility in the 1980s and 1990s, see Liu Jingming, "A Study of the Relationships of Education and the White-Collar Stratum," *Social Sciences in China* (Spring 2002): 100–108.

16. Cheng Li, "China's Midterm Jockeying: Gearing Up for 2012 (Part 1: Provincial Chiefs)," *China Leadership Monitor*, no. 31 (Winter 2010): 12.

17. See China Net, November 6, 2002 (www.China.com.cn); Renmin Net, August 4, 2007 (http://cpc.people.com.cn/GB/64107/64109/6070469.html); and *Renmin ribao* [People's Daily], August 17, 2012 (http://cpc.people.com.cn/n/2012/0817/c64387-18762767.html).

18. Hai Tian and Xiao Wei, *Wode daxue: 1970–1976 gongnongbing daxuesheng* [My college years as a worker-peasant-solider student in 1970–1976] (Beijing: Zhongguo youyi chubangongsi, 2009).

19. *Gungun hongchen: Zhongguo zhiqing minjian jiyi jishi* [Red Waves: The Grassroots Memory of China's Sent-down Youths], documentary film (Shantou Ocean Audio-Video Publishing House, 2006).

20. *Zhongguo shibao* [China Times], May 15, 2006.

21. *Shijie ribao* [World Journal], January 7, 2008, A3.

22. John Pomfret of the *Washington Post* has described the entrance exams as "the most intense [they] ever had been and ever would be in Communist China's history." John Pomfret, *Chinese Lessons: Five Classmates and the Story of the New China* (New York: Henry Holt, 2006), 10. For Wang's remarks, see Wang Juntao, "Beida fengyun jiuyou dianping" [Comments about a few distinguished alumni of Peking University], December 25, 2005 (www.blogchina.com).

23. For an excellent recollection of the college experiences of students during that period, see Wang Huiyao, Xu Xiaoping, and Xiong Xiaoge, eds., *Nasanjie: qiqi, qiba, qijiu ji daxuesheng de Zhongguo jiyi* [These three classes: The China Memories of the Classes '77, '78 and '79] (Beijing: China Translation and Publishing, 2014).

24. Leng Gun, "Li Keqiang tudiao Liaoning de xuanji" [The meaning of Li Keqiang's transfer to Liaoning] *Qianshao* [Frontier], March 27, 2005 (http://news.boxun.com/news/gb/pubvp/2005/03/200503272355.shtml).

25. Zhao Lei, "Beida falüxi: 'Huangpu yiqi nabanren' " [The "Graduates of the First Class of the Huangpu Academy": The students of the first post–Cultural Revolution class in the law department of Peking University], *Nanfang zhoumo* [Southern Weekend], June 7, 2007.

26. Li Meng, "Li Keqiang suozai de beida falüxi 77 ji" [Li Keqiang and the class of '77 at the Department of Law at Peking University], *Minzhu yu fazhi* [Democracy and Law], October 26, 2009; also see (http://news.ifeng.com/history/zhiqing/ziliao/200910/1026_6858_1404826.shtml) and *Zhengzhou wanbao* [Zhengzhou Evening News], March 16, 2013 (http://www.ce.cn/xwzx/gnsz/gdxw/201303/16/t20130316_24204792.shtml).

27. This is based on Wang, "Beida fengyun jiuyou dianping" [Comments about a few distinguished alumni of Peking University].

28. Ibid.

29. The author's database.

30. Cheng Li, "Jiang Zemin's Successors: The Rise of the Fourth Generation of Leaders in the PRC," *China Quarterly*, no. 161 (March 2000): 1–40.

31. Author's database.

32. Zhonggong zhongyang zuzhibu ganbu jiaoyuju [The Cadre Education Bureau of the Central Organization Department of the Chinese Communist Party], comp., *Zhongguo ganbu jiaoyu peixun jigou yaolan* [An overview of educational and training institutions of Chinese officials] (Beijing: Dangjian duwu chubanshe, 2012), 25.

33. Yu Keping, "Zhonggong de ganbu jiaoyu yu guojia zhili" [CCP cadre education and state governance], *Zhonggong Zhejiang shengwei dangxiao xuebao* [Journal of the Party School of the CCP Zhejiang Provincial Committee], no. 3 (2014).

34. Ibid.

35. For a very comprehensive survey and introduction of these schools and training centers, see Zhonggong zhongyang zuzhibu ganbu jiaoyuju [Cadre Education Bureau of the Central Organization Department of the Chinese Communist Party], *Zhongguo ganbu jiaoyu peixun jigou yaolan* [An overview of educational and training institutions of Chinese officials].

36. Li Song, "Zhongguo ganbu peixun jiemi" [Revealing the secret of the training of China's leaders], *Liaowang zhoukan* [Outlook Weekly], August 11, 2012 (http://renshi .people.com.cn/n/2012/0811/c139617-18721947.html).

37. Ibid.

38. Zhonggong zhongyang zuzhibu ganbu jiaoyuju [Cadre Education Bureau of the Central Organization Department of the Chinese Communist Party], *Zhongguo ganbu jiaoyu peixun jigou yaolan* [An overview of educational and training institutions of Chinese officials], 33.

39. Yu, "Zhonggong de ganbu jiaoyu yu guojia zhili" [CCP cadre education and state governance].

40. Ibid.

41. See Li, *China's Leaders*, 106–13.

42. For the dominance of Tsinghua graduates in the leadership over the last decade, see Cheng Li, "University Networks and the Rise of Qinghua Graduates in China's Leadership," *Australian Journal of Chinese Affairs*, no. 32 (July 1994): 1–32.

43. The PBOC School of Finance, or Wudaokou School of Finance (五道口金融学院), originated from the Graduate School of the PBOC, which was founded in 1981. Between 1981 and 2011, 1,814 master's degree holders and 247 doctoral degree holders of the school worked for PBOC and other major banks and central financial institutions. In 2012, this school became part of Tsinghua University. *Shijie ribao* [World Journal], May 27, 2013, B8.

44. Ibid.

45. Duowei News, September 24, 2002 (www.chinesenewsnet.com).

46. Guangxi government website, December 7, 2001 (http://gxi.gov.cn).

47. David Shambaugh, "Training China's Political Elite: The Party School System," *China Quarterly*, no. 196 (December 2008): 827–44.

48. Pei, "The myth of Chinese meritocracy."

49. Xinhua, July 4, 2012 (http://news.xinhuanet.com/politics/2012-07/04/c_123366738 .htm).

50. Zheng Yefu, "Congzheng hebi gaoxueli" [No need for politicians to have high academic degrees], *Nanfang Zhoumo* [Southern Weekend], October 24, 2013, F31.

51. Ibid.

52. Zhonggong zhongyang [Central Committee of the CCP], *Dangzheng lingdao ganbu xuanba renyong gongzuo tiaoli* [Regulation on the recruitment and promotion of party and government officials], 8.

53. Ministry of Personnel of the People's Republic of China, "Guojia gongwuyuan luyong zanxing guiding" [Provisional Regulations on State Civil Servants], Renmin Web, July 24, 2003 (www.people.com.cn/GB/guandian/28296/1983116.html).

54. *Fazhi wanbao* [Legal Evening News], October 13, 2011 (http://edu.sina.com.cn /official/2011-10-13/1400315263.shtml).

55. Ibid.

56. Han Xu, "Zhongguo gongwuyuan baokao renshu huoda 200 wan" [The number of applicant enrollments for the civil service-exam may reach 2 million], Xinhua, October 22, 2012 (http://gb.cri.cn/27824/2012/10/22/6011s3895551.htm).

57. *Shijie ribao* [World Journal], November 30, 2014, A12.

58. Zhao Chao, "2012 nian Zhongguo gongzhaolu gongwuyuan 18.8 wan ren" [China admits 188,000 civil servant employees in 2012]. Xinhua, January 8, 2013 (http://news .xinhuanet.com/2013-01/08/c_124204712.htm).

59. In Chinese, the words for "returnee" and "sea turtle" have the same pronunciation.

60. *Renmin ribao*, January 7, 2003, 10.

61. Wang Yucheng and Shi Rui, "2014 Zhongguo chuguo liuxuerenyuan zaizeng" [Continuing increase of the Chinese students and scholars studying abroad], Caixin Newsnet, March 6, 2015 (http://china.caixin.com/2015-03-06/100788923.html); and also "2014 nian chuguo liuxue qushi baogao" [Report on the status and trends of study abroad in 2014], *Zhongguo jiaoyu zaixian* [China Education Online], October 12, 2014 (www.eol.cn/html /lx/2014baogao/content.html).

62. Wang and Shi, "2014 Zhongguo chuguo liuxuerenyuan zaizeng" [Continuing increase of the Chinese students and scholars studying abroad].

63. Ibid.; and *Shijie ribao* [World Journal], March 25, 2014, A12.

64. "2014 nian chuguo liuxue qushi baogao" [Report on the status and trends of study abroad in 2014].

65. "Huaren liuxuesheng guaixiang" [A strange phenomenon in Chinese students abroad], China Education Online, May 4, 2015 (http://www.wenxuecity.com/news/2015 /05/04/4241660.html).

66. Ibid.

67. See "2009 nian Zhongguo chuguo liuxuerenyuan zongshu dadao 22.93 wan" [The total number of Chinese students and scholars who studied abroad in 2009 was 229,300], China News, March 29, 2010 (www.chinanews.com.cn/lxsh/news/2010/03-12/2166360.shtml). The total number of Chinese students and scholars who have studied in the United States is based on the speech delivered by China's ambassador to the United States, Zhou Wenzhong, in Seattle on June 1, 2005. See Chinese News Net, June 6, 2005 (www.chinesenews net.com).

68. China News Net, January 28, 2014 (www.chinanews.com/lxsh/2014/01-28/5794212 .shtml); and for the data of 2010, see "2010 nian zhongguo fumei liuxue zongshu jiangda shi wan" [The total number of Chinese students who study in the United States is expected to reach 100,000 in the year 2010 alone] (http://edu.qiaogu.com/info_21391/). The total number of students who came to study in the United States in 2009 was approximately 98,000. See "Jinnian mei liuxue renshu jiang chuang xingao" [This year's total number of Chinese students who study in the United States is expected to break records] (http://news .sina.com.cn/o/2010-03-03/031117154305s.shtml). For the data for 2015, see *Shijie ribao* [World Journal], November 16, 2015, A6.

69. Wang and Shi, "2014 Zhongguo chuguo liuxuerenyuan zaizeng" [Continuing increase of the Chinese students and scholars studying abroad].

70. *Shijie ribao* [World Journal], November 16, 2015, A6.

71. Wang and Shi, "2014 Zhongguo chuguo liuxuerenyuan zaizeng" [Continuing increase of the Chinese students and scholars studying abroad].

72. "2014 nian chuguo liuxue qushi baogao" [Report on the status and trends of study abroad in 2014].

73. Ibid.

74. See "Zhongguo liuxue renshu meinian jin shisan wan ren" [Some 130,000 Chinese citizens left to study abroad every year], February 11, 2009 (http://news.china-b.com/lxdt /20090211/14484_1.html).

75. See "2009 nian guojia liuxue jijin zizhu shenqing" [China Scholarship Council Application, 2009], October 17, 2009 (www.taisha.org/abroad/topic/gongpai).

76. *Nanfang zoumo* [Southern Weekend], April 15, 2005; see also "Zhumu dishidai haigui guanyuan" [Focusing on the tenth generation of returnees who now serve as government officials], Xinhua, April 15, 2005 (http://news.xinhuanet.com/report/2005-04/15/content _2833349.htm).

77. Li, *China's Leaders*, 17–18.

78. Tsinghua University website (www.tsinghua.edu.cn/publish/newthu/newthu_cnt /research/research-2.html); accessed on November 10, 2014.

79. Barry Naughton, "China's Economic Think Tanks: Their Changing Role in the 1990s," *China Quarterly*, no. 171 (September 2002): 629.

80. For a comprehensive discussion of Hu Angang and his work, see Cheng Li, "Introduction: A Champion of Chinese Optimism and Exceptionalism," in Hu Angang, *China in 2020: A New Type of Superpower* (Brookings, 2011), xv–xl.

81. The CCS has recently expanded to become an institute, called the Institute of China Studies, but it has retained its original English name.

82. Joshua Cooper Ramo, *The Beijing Consensus* (London: Foreign Policy Centre, 2004), 22–23.

83. For a detailed discussion of the theory of China's peaceful rise, see Zheng Bijian, *China's Peaceful Rise: Speeches of Zheng Bijian 1997–2004* (Brookings, 2005).

84. Yu Keping, *Democracy Is a Good Thing: Essays on Politics, Society, and Culture in Contemporary China* (Brookings, 2009) and Cheng Li, "The Status and Characteristics of Foreign-Educated Returnees in the Chinese Leadership," *China Leadership Monitor*, no. 16 (Fall 2005), 17.

85. Zhang Guozuo, "Zuoqiang xinxing zhiku tisheng guojia ruanshili" [Building a new type of think tank to enhance China's soft power]. Also see *Renmin ribao* [People's Daily], October 14, 2014 (www.chinanews.com/sh/2014/10-14/6675278.shtml).

86. Xi Jinping, "Zai wangluo anquan he xinxihua gongzuo zuotanhui shang de jianghua" [Speech at the internet and information security work conference]. Xinhua Newsnet, April 25, 2016 (http://news.xinhuanet.com/politics/2016-04/25/c_1118731175.htm).

87. For Fang's early career, see Sun Tao, "Guogan Fang Xinghai" [Bold Fang Xinghai]. Also see *Jingrong shijie* [Financial World], August 2012 (http://blog.sina.com.cn/s/blog _695557320101d583.html).

88. George Chen and Daniel Ren, "Shanghai Booster Fang Xinghai Lands Beijing Financial Advisory Role," *South China Morning Post*, June 18, 2013.

89. Cheng Li, "Shaping China's Foreign Policy: The Paradoxical Role of Foreign-Educated Returnees." *Asia Policy*, no. 10 (July): 65–85.

90. Zeng Qinghong "Chongfen fahui guangda liuxuerencai zai quanmian jianshe xiaokang shehui zhong de dute lishi zuoyong" [Giving full play to the unique role of a large number of returnees in the history of building a moderately prosperous society]. *Shenzhou xueren* [Chinese Scholars], No. 12 (2003): 3–6.

91. David Zweig and Huiyao Wang, "Can China Bring Back the Best? The Communist Party Organizes China's Search for Talent," *China Quarterly*, no. 215 (September 2013):

590–615. For Li Yuanchao's role in promoting returnees, see State Administration of Foreign Experts Affairs website, "Mr. Li Yuanchao attended the High-Level Foreign Experts Seminar of the 14th OCS," January 4, 2012 (www.safea.gov.cn/english/content.php?id=12742915).

92. Zhonggong zhongyang zuzhibu ganbu jiaoyuju, Waijiaobu waishi guanliju, and Guojia waiguo zhuanjiaju chuguo peixun guanliju [The Cadre Education Bureau of the Central Organization Department of the Chinese Communist Party, Foreign Affairs Administrative Bureau of the Ministry of Foreign Affairs and Department of Foreign Studies of the State Administration of Foreign Experts Affairs], comp., *Lingdao ganbu jingwai peixun chengguo yibaili* [100 cases of the overseas training of cadres] (Beijing: Dangjian duwu chubanshe, 2012).

93. *Dongfang zaobao* [Oriental Morning News], October 9, 2012.

94. The other is Hu Chunhua, who is the same age and serves as a Politburo member and party secretary of Guangdong.

95. *Renmin ribao*, March 22, 2005, 9.

96. Yu, "Zhonggong de ganbu jiaoyu yu guojia zhili" [CCP cadre education and state governance].

97. "Jiemi peiyang Zhonggong gaoguan de haiwai dangxiao" [Revealing the secret of the overseas party school that trains CCP senior officials], Duowei Net, November 22, 2012 (http://china.dwnews.com/news/2012-11-22/58976646-all.html).

98. See Sina (http://www.sina.com.cn), June 19, 2003.

99. Zhou Chunxia, "Guofangbu xinwen fayanren 'huanjiang,' shouxian 'shuang haigui' dadang" [Changes of spokespersons of the Ministry of Defense: dual returnees for the first time], *Beijing qingnian bao* [Beijing Youth Daily], July 12, 2015.

CHAPTER 5

1. Gaetano Mosca, *The Ruling Class* (New York: McGraw-Hill, 1936).

2. Vilfredo Pareto, *The Rise and Fall of Elites: An Application of Theoretical Sociology* (Totowa, NJ: Bedminster, 1968).

3. Robert A. Scalapino, *Elites in the People's Republic of China* (University of Washington Press, 1972) and Li, *China's Leaders*, 33–34.

4. Hong Yong Lee, *From Revolutionary Cadres to Party Technocrats in Socialist China* (University of California Press, 1990), 291.

5. Cheng Li, "China's Communist Party-State: The Structure and Dynamics of Power," in William A. Joseph, ed., *Politics in China* (Oxford University Press), 178; also see http://news.xinhuanet.com/newscenter/2008–07/01/content_8471350.htm, July 1, 2008.

6. "China's Labor Force Lags Behind in Higher Education," *People's Daily*, May 21, 2010 (http://english.peopledaily.com.cn/90001/90782/6994379.html).

7. For a detailed discussion of the role of technocrats in the Three Gorges Dam project, see Cheng Li, *Rediscovering China: Dynamics and Dilemmas of Reform* (Lanham, MD: Rowman & Littlefield, 1997), 165–190.

8. For a comparative study of technocrats across the Taiwan Strait in the 1970s and 1980s, see Cheng Li and Lynn White, "Elite Transformation and Modern Change in Mainland China and Taiwan: Empirical Data and the Theory of Technocracy," *China Quarterly* 121 (March 1990): 1–35.

9. *Encyclopedia Americana* (International edition) (Danbury, CT: Grolier, 1992), vol. 10, 477.

10. Joseph A. Schumpeter, *Capitalism, Socialism and Democracy* (New York: Harper Torchbooks, 1975), 132.

11. Zhang Houyi, "The Position of the Private Entrepreneur Stratum in China's Social Structure," *Social Sciences in China* 16, no. 4 (1995): 33.

12. Lucian W. Pye, *China: An Introduction* (New York: HarperCollins, 1991), 32–59 and Lucian W. Pye, *The Mandarin and the Cadre: China's Political Cultures* (Ann Arbor: Center for Chinese Studies, University of Michigan, 1988).

13. *China News Analysis*, no. 1501 (January 1, 1994), 2.

14. For the data on 2007, see *Renmin ribao*, August 16, 2007, 1. For the data on 2013, see "Zhongguo zaice siying qiye shuliang tupo qianwanjia" [The number of registered private enterprises in China has reached ten million], Xinhua, February 1, 2013 (http://news .xinhuanet.com/fortune/2013-02/01/c_114587467.htm).

15. *Renmin ribao*, August 16, 2007, 1.

16. Wang Jianlin, "Minying qiye youyichun jianghui daolai" [Another spring is around the corner for China's private firms], *Zhongguo qiyejia* [China's entrepreneurs], February 8, 2014 (www.iceo.com.cn/mag2013/2014/0208/274804.shtml).

17. "Zhongguo zaice siying qiye shuliang tupo qianwanjia."

18. "China's Individual, Private Businesses Expand Fast," *China Daily*, December 5, 2012 (www.chinadaily.com.cn/business/2012-12/05/content_15986334.htm).

19. For more discussion of this subject, see Bruce J. Dickson, *Wealth into Power: The Communist Party's Embrace of China's Private Sector* (Cambridge University Press, 2008) and Cheng Li, "'Credentialism' versus 'Entrepreneurism:' The Interplay and Tensions between Technocrats and Entrepreneurs in the Reform Era," in Chan Kwok Bun, ed., *Chinese Business Networks: State, Economy and Culture* (New York: Prentice Hall, 1999), 86–111.

20. "Jiang Zemin's Speech at the Meeting Celebrating the 80th Anniversary of the Founding of the Communist Party of China," July 1, 2001; see China Org Webnet (www .china.org.cn/e-speech/a.htm).

21. The United Front Department of the CCP Central Committee, *2005 nian Zhongguo siying qiye diaocha baogao* [A survey of private enterprises in 2005]. See also www.southcn .com/finance/gdmqgc/gdmqyyrl/200502030218.htm.

22. See "Hu Run's List of the 500 Richest People in China in 2006" (http://news.xinhuanet .com); accessed on October 11, 2006. Also see Bruce Dickson, *Wealth into Power: The Communist Party's Embrace of China's Private Sector* (Cambridge University Press, 2008).

23. Chinese Academy of Social Sciences, *2013 Social Blue Book* (Beijing: Shehui kexue wenxian chubanshe, 2013), reported at http://dailynews.sina.com/bg/chn/chnpolitics/sinacn /20121219/13274074905.html.

24. Ibid.

25. *Shijie ribao*, November 12, 2002, A3.

26. "CPC Delegates from Private Sector Doubled," *China Daily*, November 7, 2012 (www .chinadaily.com.cn/china/2012cpc/2012-11/07/content_15888973.htm).

27. Michael Wei, "Property Mogul Wang Emerges as China's Richest Person," *Bloomberg News*, August 19, 2013; also see www.bloomberg.com/news/2013-08-18/property-mogul -emerges-as-china-s-richest-person-person.html.

28. For more detailed information about the private entrepreneur delegates to the 18th National Party Congress, see "Shibada zhong de minying qiyejia" [Private entrepreneur delegates to the 18th National Party Congress] (www.360doc.com/content/12/1112/15 /10987246_247402288.shtml).

29. Some official Chinese sources do not view Zhang Ruimin as a private entrepreneur anymore because his company now includes large investments from the SOEs, as listed on both the Shanghai and New York Stock Exchanges.

30. Ni Yangjun, "Zhongguo fuhao 35% wei Zhonggong dangyuan, shihao shihuai" [Is it good or bad that 35% of China's richest people are CCP members?], Guangming web, October 21, 2006 (www.gmw.cn/content/2006-10/21/content_493408.htm).

31. Jamil Anderlini, "Chinese Parliament Holds 83 Billionaires," *Financial Times*, March 7, 2013 (www.ft.com/intl/cms/s/0/4568598e-8731-11e2-9dd7-00144feabdc0.html# axzz2QCJa8AdR).

32. For an excellent review of these business circles, see Wu Jie, "Zhongguo shida shangye quanzi yilan" [An Overview of China's Top Ten Business Circles], *Qiye guancha bao* [Enterprise Observer], November 19, 2013; also see http://finance.sina.com.cn/china /20131119/104017365471.shtml.

33. For the China Entrepreneur Club's website, see www.daonong.com/html/cec/about /2013/0813/41211.html.

34. For Position Sum Island's website, see www.zhisland.com/introduce/ret_about.

35. For Chang An Club's website, see www.changan-club.com/key-executives.php?l=2.

36. "Zui ju yingxiangli de shige quanzi: Huaxia tongxuehui taishanghui" [The ten most influential circles: Taishan Chinese Alumni Association], *Zhongguo qiyejia wang* [China Entrepreneur Website], June 5, 2013 (www.iceo.com.cn/com2013/2013/0605/267596_2.shtml).

37. Jiu Zhang, "Jiemi Zhongguo zuigui shangxueyuan" [Revealing the secrets of China's most expensive business school], *Wenhui Daily*, December 16, 2013 (http://news.wenweipo .com/2013/12/16/IN1312160034.htm).

38. The China Entrepreneur Club website, March 14, 2014 (www.daonong.com/cec /green/2014nh/dongtai/2014/0314/47208.html).

39. Wu Xiaobo, "Liu Chuanzhi qishi shi zaishang bu yanshang" [Liu Chuanzhi in fact implies that business elites should be concerned more than business], Phoenix Net, November 6, 2013 (http://finance.ifeng.com/a/20131106/11016046_0.shtml).

40. Some analysis of the subject has also appeared in Cheng Li, "Diversification of Chinese Entrepreneurs and Cultural Pluralism in the Reform Era," in Shiping Hua, ed., *Chinese Political Culture* (New York: M. E. Sharpe, 2001), 219–245.

41. For further discussion of credentialism versus entrepreneurism, see Cheng Li, "'Credentialism' Versus 'Entrepreneurism': The Interplay and Tensions between Technocrats and Entrepreneurs in the Reform Era," in Chan Kwok Bun, ed., *Chinese Business Network: State, Economy and Culture* (New York: Prentice Hall, 1999), 86–111.

42. Han Qingxiang, "*Wo weishenme tichang 'nengli benwei'*" [Why do I favor "competency"?], *Zhongguo rencai* [China Talents], no. 6 (2000): 11–15.

43. Ibid.

44. For more discussion of the status and classification of SOEs, see "Zhongyang qiye xianzhuang yu fenlei" [The status and classification of central state-owned enterprises], August 18, 2010 (http://finance.vip168168.com/caijingxueyuan/118140.html).

45. Chen Zhiwu, *Shuo Zhongguo jingji* [Assessing the Chinese economy] (Taiyuan: Shanxi jingji chubanshe, 2010), 103 and *Jinghua Shibao* [Beijing Times], July 27, 2014 (http://news.xinhuanet.com/fortune/2014-07/27/c_126801263.htm).

46. Li Rongrong, former head of SASAC, recently stated that the most important criterion for China's rise to the status of a global economic giant is the number of Chinese companies that make it on the Global 500 list. See Li Rongrong, "Yi Zhu Rongji weibangyang, yi Pujing wei ouxiang" [I consider Zhu Rongji a role model and Putin an idol], Xinhua, September 8, 2010 (http://news.xinhuanet.com/fortune/2010-09/08/c_12530988.htm).

47. See Cheng Li, "China's Midterm Jockeying: Gearing Up for 2012. Part 4: Top Leaders of Major State-Owned Enterprises," *China Leadership Monitor*, no. 34 (Winter 2011): 10; *China Daily*, July 8, 2014 (www.chinadaily.com.cn/business/2014-07/08/content_17673632 .htm); and Scott Cendrowski, "China's Global 500 companies are bigger than ever—and mostly state-owned." *Fortune*, July 22, 2015 (http://fortune.com/2015/07/22/china-global -500-government-owned).

48. Geng Shenzhen, "Zhongguo zhengzhi diliudai lingdaoceng 'yuzhoubang' jueqi" [The rise of "Cosmos Club" members in the sixth generation of Chinese leaders], *Zhongyang ribao* [Central Daily], May 6, 2015; also see http://chinese.joins.com/gb/article.do ?method=detail&art_id=134840.

49. The Center for Chinese Legal Studies, Columbia University (www.law.columbia.edu /focusareas/asianlegal/china); Gu Xin, "Revitalizing Chinese Society: Institutional

Transformation and Social Change," in *China: Two Decades of Reform and Change*, ed. Wang Gungwu and John Wong (Singapore: Singapore University Press and World Scientific Press, 1999), 80.

50. Among these 250,000 lawyers, 225,000 are full-time lawyers, 10,000 are part-time attorneys, over 5,400 are legal aid lawyers, and 9,200 are military and public corporate lawyers. Lawyers with a bachelor's degree or above accounted for 82.1 percent of the total, with more than 40,000 lawyers holding postgraduate degrees. Zhou Bin, "Woguo zhiye lüshi renshu zengzhi 25.09 wan" [The number of China's registered lawyers increased to 250,900], *Fazhi ribao* [Legal Daily], March 10, 2014 (www.legaldaily.com.cn/xwzx/content/2014-03/10/content_5343043.htm).

51. For the recent imprisonment of Xu Zhiyong, see Hua Ze, "Misrule of Law," *New York Times*, August 21, 2013 (http://cn.nytimes.com/opinion/20130821/c21hua/en-us/).

52. Samuel Wade, "New Accounts Detail Rights Lawyer Detentions," *China Digital Times*, August 4, 2015 (http://chinadigitaltimes.net/2015/08/new-accounts-detail-detentions-in-rights-lawyer-crackdown/).

53. "Lingdao ren huodong baodao ji" [Activities of Leaders] Xinhua, February 23, 2015 (http://www.xinhuanet.com/politics/leaders/) and "Xi Jinping," *Xinhua renwuku* [Xinhua Elite Profiles], February 23, 2015 (http://news.xinhuanet.com/rwk/2013-02/01/c_114586554.htm).

54. Quoted from Chen Su, *Dangdai Zhongguo faxue yanjiu, 1949–2009* [Research on law in contemporary China, 1949–2009] (Beijing: Zhongguo shehui kexue wenxian chubanshe, 2009), 27.

55. Qiangguo website [Strong Nation Website], September 22, 2014 (http://bbs1.people.com.cn/post/1/1/2/142079138.html).

56. "Full Text of Jiang Zemin's Report at the 16th Party Congress," *People's Daily* online, December 10, 2002 (http://english.peopledaily.com.cn/200211/18/eng20021118_106983.shtml).

57. Quoted from Zhao Yinan, "Uphold Constitution, Xi Says," *China Daily*, December 5, 2012; also http://usa.chinadaily.com.cn/china/2012-12/05/content_15985894.htm.

58. Ibid.

59. "Xinhua Communiqué about the 4th Plenum," *China Copyright and Media*, October 23, 2014 (https://chinacopyrightandmedia.wordpress.com/2014/10/23/xinhua-communique-about-the-4th-plenum-translation-ongoing).

60. Cai Dingjian, "The Development of Constitutionalism in the Transition of Chinese Society," *Columbia Journal of Asian Law* 19, no. 1 (Spring–Fall 2005): 27.

61. Cai Dingjian, "Yifa zhiguo" [Rule of Law], in *Zhongguo Zhili bianqian sanshinian: 1978–2008* [China's political reform toward good governance: 1978–2008], ed. Yu Keping (Beijing: Shehui kexue wenxian chubanshe, 2008), 142.

62. Ren Miao, "Falü wenben chengxing, fazhi rentong shangyuan" [The texts of laws are all available, but the rule of law is still far off], *Duowei shibao* [Duowei Times], March 18, 2011, 17.

63. For a discussion of a more optimistic view of China's legal development in terms of professional expansion, see Cheng Li and Jordan Lee, "China's Legal System," *China Review* 48 (Autumn 2009): 1–3.

64. Chen, *Research on Law in Contemporary China*, 13.

65. He Weifang, He Qinhua, and Tian Tao, eds., *Falü wenhua sanrentan* [A tripartite discussion of legal culture] (Beijing: Peking University Press, 2010), 87.

66. Chen, *Research on Law in Contemporary China*, 114.

67. Kou Guangping and Liu Dawei, "Legal Education Must Accord with National Construction of the Rule of Law," *Legal Daily*, January 11, 2012; also Ren, "The texts of laws are all available, but the rule of law is still far off," 17.

68. He Qinhua, "Zhongguo faxue yanjiu sanshinian" [30-year development of China's legal studies], Law School of Huazhong University of Science and Technology, March 26, 2012 (http://law.hust.edu.cn/Law2008/ShowArticle.asp?ArticleID=10806).

69. China Law (blog), January 31, 2015 (http://chuansong.me/n/1126657).

70. Chun Peng, "Is the Rule of Law Coming to China?," *The Diplomat*, September 10, 2013 (http://thediplomat.com/2013/09/10/is-the-rule-of-law-coming-to-china/).

71. Luo Luo, "Renquan xuezhe Xu Xianming ren zhengfawei fu mishuzhang" [Human rights scholar Xu Xianming appointed to be deputy chief-of-staff of the Central Political and Legal Committee]. Caixin website, April 26, 2015 (http://china.caixin.com/2015-04 -26/100803911.html).

72. John King Fairbank, the late dean of modern China studies at Harvard University, echoes Joseph Needham's argument; see *The United States and China*, 4th ed. (Harvard University Press, 1983), 74–76.

73. Ibid.

74. Bruce J. Dickson, *Red Capitalists in China: The Party, Private Entrepreneurs, and Prospects for Political Change* (Cambridge University Press, 2003).

75. For example, see Robert D. Putnam, *The Comparative Study of Political Elites* (New York: Prentice Hall, 1976).

76. Chun, "Is the Rule of Law Coming to China?"

77. Yu Keping, *Yifa zhiguo yu yifa zhidang* [Governing the country and the party by law] (Beijing: Zhongyang bianyi chubanshe, 2007), 2.

CHAPTER 6

1. Some of the discussion in this chapter previously appeared in the author's series Xi Jinping's Inner Circle, *China Leadership Monitor*, "Part 4 (The *Mishu* Cluster I)," Winter 2015 and "Part 5 (The *Mishu* Cluster II)," Spring 2015. Data and discussion have been substantially updated.

2. James Miles, "The Gatekeepers: A String of Arrests Sparks Debate about the Role of Leaders' All-Powerful Assistants," *The Economist*, May 10, 2014 (which was based on Cheng Li's database). Also see the online version (http://www.economist.com/news/china /21601870-string-arrests-sparks-debate-about-role-leaders-all-powerful-assistants -gatekeepers).

3. For further discussion of the distinctions between various types of *mishu*, see Wei Li and Lucian W. Pye, "The Ubiquitous Role of the *Mishu* in Chinese Politics," *China Quarterly*, no. 132 (December 1992): 916–25; and Cheng Li, "The *Mishu* Phenomenon: Patron-Client Ties and Coalition-Building Tactics," *China Leadership Monitor*, no. 4 (Fall 2002): 1–13.

4. The "highest-ranking party and state leaders" is a unique Chinese term that refers to leaders who hold any of the following very senior positions in the PRC: PSC members, Politburo members, members of the Secretariat, CMC members, Central Commission for Discipline Inspection secretary, PRC president and vice-president, National People's Congress chair and vice-chairs, premier, vice-premiers, and state councilors in the State Council, president and vice-presidents of the Supreme People's Court, president and vice-presidents of the Supreme People's Procuratorate, and Chinese People's Political Consultative Conference chair and vice-chairs.

5. Cheng Li, *China's Leaders: The New Generation* (Lanham, MD: Rowman & Littlefield, 2001), 149.

6. Chen Yifan, *Zhonggong gaoguan de mishu men* [The *mishu* cluster of the high-ranking leaders of the Chinese Communist Party] (New York: Mirror Books, 2010), 24–31. But according to some official sources in China, Ye actually worked as Hu's *mishu* in Guizhou only for six months and then moved to Beijing, where he returned to work in the CCYL Central Committee, specializing in Taiwan, Hong Kong, and Macao affairs. See the Taiwan Affairs Office of the State Council website, March 8, 2015 (http://www.gwytb.gov.cn/gtb /yekedong/).

7. This list differs from several widely circulated Chinese lists on the personal secretaries of the PSC members of the 17th Central Committee. For example, Wang Xin's report included Guo Yongxiang as Zhou Yongkang's personal secretary and Ling Yueming as He Guoqiang's personal secretary, which was correct in the sense that both served such roles before Zhou and He became PSC members, but neither of them served as *dami* when they were in the PSC. Wang Xin, "Zhonggong tuixiu qichangwei dami fuchenlu" [The files on the personal secretaries of the seven retired CCP Politburo Standing Committee members], Duowei Newsnet, July 5, 2013 (http://china.dwnews.com/news/2013-07-05/59258258.html).

8. Both the party general secretary and the premier can have full-minister-level rank *mishu*.

9. Li and Pye, "The Ubiquitous Role," 915.

10. Ibid., 930.

11. Li Cheng and Lynn White, "The Army in the Succession to Deng Xiaoping: Familiar Fealties and Technocratic Trends," *Asian Survey* 33, no. 8 (August 1993): 757–86, and Cheng Li and Lynn White, "The Fifteenth Central Committee of the Chinese Communist Party: Full-Fledged Technocratic Leadership with Partial Control by Jiang Zemin," *Asian Survey* 38, no. 3 (March 1998): 255–56.

12. For the policy related to reshuffling of military officers along with their *mishu*, see Li and Pye, "The Ubiquitous Role," 925.

13. Chen was the first party secretary of Shanghai, Hu was the chairman of the Shanghai Municipal People's Congress, and Wang was mayor.

14. Xiao Chong, *Zhonggong disidai lingdaoren* [The fourth generation of leaders of the Chinese Communist Party] (Hong Kong: Xiafeier guoji chubangongsi, 1998), 23 and Li, *China's Leaders*, 161–62.

15. For a more detailed discussion of Zeng's political connections in Beijing, see Li, *China's Leaders*, 160–61.

16. For more on the power struggle between Jiang and his rivals, see Li and White, "The Fifteenth Central Committee of the Chinese Communist Party," 236–39.

17. "Zeng Qinghong de dali jingangzhang, ba Xi Jinping tuishang dawei" [Zeng Qinghong pushes for granting important position to Xi Jinping], *Da Shijian* [Major Event], December 2, 2014; also see http://www.peacehall.com/news/gb/china/2014/12/201412021542 .shtml#.VKWYqiiPCfQ.

18. For more discussion of Li's value to the Xi administration, see Xiang Jiangyu, *Xi Jinping de tuandui* [Xi Jinping's team] (New York: Mirror Books, 2013), 197–205.

19. Sun Lan, "Guizhou yimai tuqi" [Rising together from Guizhou]. Duowei Newsnet, May 6, 2015, http://china.dwnews.com/news/2015-05-06/59651779.html.

20. Zhao Julin, "'Erhao shouzhang' de shishifeifei" [The right and wrong of "no. 2 bosses"], East Day Newsnet, March 9, 2015 (http://news.eastday.com/china/jiaodianzt /gaoguanmishu/index.html).

21. Ibid.

22. *South China Morning Post*, July 2, 2014.

23. "Xu Caihou an yisong shencha qisu" [The Xu Caihou case transferred to the prosecution], Xinhua, October 29, 2014 (http://www.js.xinhuanet.com/2014-10/29/c_1113020249 .htm).

24. For more discussion on the political culture of the *mishu* phenomenon, especially the powerful role of secretaries-general, see Luo Changping, "Ling Jihua he mishuzhang de quanlichang" [Ling Jihua and the power circle of chiefs-of-staff], 21st Century Network, December 24, 2014 (http://www.21ccom.net/articles/china/ggzl/20141224118010_all .html).

25. Cheng Li's database.

26. In contrast to the Marxist notion that the Communist Party should be the "vanguard of the working class," Jiang's theory claims that the CCP should represent the

"developmental needs of the advanced forces of production," the "forward direction of advanced culture," and the "fundamental interests of the majority of the Chinese people."

27. Cheng Li and Lynn White, "The Army in the Succession to Deng Xiaoping: Familiar Fealties and Technocratic Trends," *Asian Survey*, vol. 33, no. 8 (August 1993): 757–86 and Cheng Li and Scott Harold, "China's New Military Elite," *China Security*, vol. 3, no. 4 (Autumn 2007): 62–89.

28. "Cong muhou zouxiang taiqian, pandian naxie dangguo dami de jiangjun" [Stepping into the limelight from behind the scenes: meeting the generals who previously served as *mishu*], Duowei Net (http://china.dwnews.com/photo/2014-07-24/59498370.html).

29. Ibid.

30. Li Zhanshu, "Zhongshi jianxing 'wuge jianchi,' zuo dangxing jianqiang de zhongbanren" [Faithfully implement the "five adhere to" and serve as loyal officials with strong principals in the General Office of the CCP Central Committee], *Mishu gongzuo* [*Mishu Work*], no. 9 (2014).

31. See People's Net, September 29, 2015 (http://cpc.people.com.cn/n/2014/0929/c164113 -25759006.html).

32. Ibid.

33. This economic development zone recently experienced a devastating chemical explosion that killed over 100 people and injured several hundred others. It remains to be seen how this incident will affect the career trajectories of several ambitious political leaders who previously worked or currently serve in Tianjin.

34. "Fagaiwei mingque fuzhuren He Lifeng zhuguan 'yidaiyilu' gongzuo" [The National Development and Reform Commission designates its deputy director He Lifeng to be in charge of 'One Belt and One Road' work], Beijing Newsnet, January 4, 2015 (http://www.bj -news.com/finacial/fin/2015/0104/262454.html).

35. Ma Haoliang, "'Zhijiang xinjun' zouxiang Zhonggong zhengzhi wutai zhongxin" [The new elite cohort from Zhejiang moves to the center stage of CCP politics], Dagong Network, December 30, 2014 (http://opinion.dwnews.com/news/2014-12-30/59626834.html).

36. Wang Ya, "Xi Jinping muliao jin hezai" [Where are Xi Jinping's aides now?], Zhongguo Shuzi Shidai Wang [China Digital Times Online], January 28, 2015. (http://chinadigital times.net/chinese/2015/01/多维｜习近平浅邸幕僚今何在/)

37. The articles that appeared in the column were later published as a book; see Xi Jinping, *Zhijiang xinyu* [New thoughts from Zhejiang] (Hangzhou: Zhejiang renmin chubanshe), 2007.

38. Ye Maozhi and Liu Ziwei, "Xi Jinping qiaoqiao daju tiba xinfu" [Xi Jinping promoted confidants, quietly but aggressively], Mirror Newsnet, May 10, 2014 (http://www .wenxuecity.com/news/2014/05/10/3257474_print.html).

39. "Xianggang meiti pu Xizong shenbian de qiwei zhongyao zhinang" [Hong Kong media reveals seven top advisers in Xi's inner circle], Sina Newsnet, February 3, 2015 (http://club.mil.news.sina.com.cn/thread-701804-1-1.html).

40. Shi Bielou, "Cong wenyi dao zhengzhi: Chongdu Li Shulei" [From literature and art to politics: re-reading Li Shulei], Shanghai Observer Newsnet, September 24, 2014 (http:// web.shobserver.com/news/detail?id=346).

41. Ibid.

42. Li Shulei, "Jiedu Robert Kennedy *Guba daodan weiji jiqi jiaoxun*" [On Robert Kennedy's *Thirteen Days: A Memoir of the Cuban Missile Crisis*], *Zhanlue yu guanli* [Strategy and Management], no. 5 (2001).

43. For example, see Li Shulei, "Guoji jingzheng zhong de wenhua jianshe" [Cultural construction in international competition], *Ershiyi shiji jingji baodao* [21st Century Business Herald], October 31, 2007.

44. Xi Jinping, *Guanyu shixian Zhonghuaminzu weida fuxing de Zhongguomeng lunshu zhaibian* [Excerpts on the realization of the great rejuvenation of the Chinese dream] (Beijing: Central Literature Publishing House), 2013.

45. For more discussion of Xi Jinping's effort to promote Confucian values, see Evan Osnos, "Confucius Comes Home," *New Yorker*, January 13, 2014.

46. Li Shulei, "Ouxiang ruhe goujian" [How to construct an idol] *Liaowang dongfang zhoukan* [Oriental Outlook Weekly], June 21, 2011; also see Confucius Studies website, July 18, 2011 (http://www.rujiazg.com/article/id/4160/).

47. Li Shulei, "Gandan chang ruxi: zaidu Xi Jinping tongzhi Nian nujiao, zhuisi Jiao Yulu" [Dedication and courage: re-reading Comrade Xi Jinping's poem in memory of Jiao Yulu], *Fujian ribao* [Fujian Daily], April 15, 2014, 1.

48. Ibid.

49. Xiu Yangfeng, "Li Shulei: chongyin faxing *baituo pinkun* dui Fujian fazhan you zhongda zhidao yiyi" [Li Shulei: Reprinting [Xi Jinping's book] *Out of Poverty* is of great significance to the development of Fujian], Renmin website, August 19, 2014 (http://fj .people.com.cn/n/2014/0819/c181466-22028755.html).

50. He Yiting, "Qunzhong luxian yiyong jiuling" [The effectiveness of the mass line], Hunan Normal University website, January 22, 2015 (http://qzlx.hunnu.edu.cn/info/1008 /1707.htm).

51. Ibid.

52. 常学常新常用常新, *changxue changxin, changyong, changxin*. He Yiting, "Xi Jinping zongshuji jianghua changxue changxin changyong changxin" [The more frequently one studies General Secretary Xi Jinping's speeches, the more refreshing they become; the more regularly one applies them, the more innovative they turn out], *Xuexi shibao* [Study Times], January 20, 2014; also see http://theory.people.com.cn/n/2014/0120/c40531-24167530 .html.

53. Yu Feng, "He Yiting: Xi Jinping 'wendan' " [He Yiting: Xi Jinping's "brain trust"]. China Focus Newsnet, January 8, 2014 (http://www.cbfau.com/news_detail.aspx?strnew =14102).

54. He Yiting, "Jiang zai dangxiao ge zhuti banci kaishe Xi Jinping jianghua zhuantike" [The Central Party School will offer thematic seminars on the study of Xi's speeches], Chinese Social Sciences Net, November 1, 2013 (http://news.takungpao.com.hk/mainland /focus/2013-11/2007973.html).

55. He Yiting, "Zuo Xi Jinping zongshuji yaoqiu de 'siyou' ganbu" [Being the "officials with four possessions" required by General Secretary Xi Jinping], *Xuexi shibao* [Study Times], January 19, 2015; also see http://theory.people.com.cn/n/2015/0119/c40531-26410993 .html.

56. Qiu Shi, "Gonggu dang he renmin tuanjie fendou de gongtong sixiang jichu" [Consolidate the common ideological basis of the party and the people], *Qiu shi* [Seek the Truth], October 16, 2013; also see http://www.qstheory.cn/zxdk/2013/201320/201310/t20131012 _278250.htm.

57. Ibid.

58. Cheng Li and Ryan McElveen, "Can Xi's Governing Strategy Succeed?" *Current History*, vol. 112, no. 755 (September 2013): 203–209.

59. Wang Ya, "Xi Jinping hanhua 'mishubang' " [Xi Jinping addresses the issue of the *mishu* cluster], Duowei Newsnet, October 12, 2014 (http://china.dwnews.com/news/2014 -10-12/59612796.html).

60. Li and Pye, "The Ubiquitous Role," 930.

61. James C. Mulvenon and Michael S. Chase, "The Role of Mishus in the Chinese Political System: Change and Continuity," in *Chinese Leadership in the Twenty-first Century: The Rise of the Fourth Generation*, ed. David M. Finkelstein and Maryanne Kivlehan (Armonk, NY: M. E. Sharpe, 2002), 141.

CHAPTER 7

1. For a more detailed discussion of the origin of the "one party, two factions" system, see Cheng Li, "Emerging Partisanship within the Chinese Communist Party" *Orbis* (Summer 2005): 387–400 and Cheng Li, "China's Inner-Party Democracy: Toward a System of 'One Party, Two Factions'?" *China Brief*, vol. 6, no. 24 (December 2006): 8–11.

2. Zhonggong zhongyang zhengzhiju [The Politburo], "Dangnei juebu rongren gao tuantuanhuohuo, jiedangyingsi, labangjiepai" [The Party should not tolerate gangs, cliques, and nepotism], Xinhua, December 29, 2014 (www.xinhuanet.com).

3. Wu Mengda and Chen Hongyi, "Fanfu dadiao de naxie 'tuantuanhuohuo'" [Anticorruption campaign knocked out "various factions and gangs"], Xinhua, January 3, 2015 (http://news.xinhuanet.com/politics/2015-01/03/c_1113856708.htm).

4. They include former deputy director of the General Logistic Department Gu Junshan, former deputy director of the General Political Department Zhang Shutian, and former deputy director of the Department of the Informationalization of the General Staff Dong Youxin. The current deputy director of the General Political Department, Jia Ting'an, is also a heavyweight figure in the "Henan Gang." *Shijie ribao*, June 26, 2015, A5.

5. 党外无党，帝王思想；党内无派，千奇百怪 (*dangwai wudang, diwang sixiang; dangnei wupai, qianqibaiguai*). Mao's remarks are actually a direct quote from Chen Duxiu, "Guomindang sizijing" [Four character classic for the Nationalist Party], Douban, November 5, 2011 (www.douban.com/note/182330698). Also see Liu Dezhong, "Mao Zedong sixiang yanjiu zhong lishizhuyi sanyao" [Three main aspects in the study of Mao Zedong thought and historicism], *Mao Zedong sixiang* [Mao Zedong Thought], December 12, 2014 (www.mzdthought.com/html/lypl/2014/1212/18050.html).

6. Ouyang Xiu, *Ouyang wenzhong gongwenji* [Collections of Ouyang Xiu], the Yuan Dyansty edition). Also see Baike website (http://baike.baidu.com/view/541618.htm).

7. Niu Lei, "Xi Jinping moding Hu Chunhua" [Xi Jinping and Hu Chunhua], ComeFromChina, March 7, 2014 (www.comefromchina.com/news/59555).

8. *Shijie ribao*, January 3, 2010, A2.

9. For more discussion on this subject, see Wang Ya, "Pengdang: Jinri Zhongguo de zhengzhi mima" [Cronies: present-day China's political password], Duowei Net, December 30, 2014 (http://china.dwnews.com/news/2014-12-30/59626915.html).

10. Wu Ming, *Zhongguo xin lingxiu: Xi Jinping zhuan* [China's new leader: biography of Xi Jinping], new enlarged edition (Hong Kong: Wenhua yishu chubanshe, 2010) and Xia Fei, Yang Yun, and Bai Xiaoyun, *Taizidang he Gongqingtuan: Xi Jinping PK Li Keqiang* [Xi Jinping versus Li Keqiang: princelings and the Chinese Communist Youth League faction] (New York: Mirror Books, 2007).

11. For example, Michael Sheridan, "Chairman Xi crushes rivals to seal lifetime in power," *Sunday Times*, December 28, 2014.

12. The author's interviews in both Beijing and Shanghai in 2013–2015.

13. Ying Zhi, "Xi Jinping kaocha Shanghai Jiang Mianheng peitong" [Accompanied by Jiang Mianheng, Xi Jinping visits Shanghai], Duowei Net, May 26, 2014 (http://china.dwnews.com/news/2014-05-26/59474012.html).

14. *Shijie ribao*, May 15, 2014, A11.

15. Aozhou xinwenwang [Australian Newsnet], April 1, 2014 (www.huaglad.com/zh-tw/lovecn/20140401/92962.html).

16. Cheng Li, "China's Two Li's: Frontrunners in the Race to Succeed Hu Jintao," *China Leadership Monitor*, no. 22 (Fall 2007); also see Shi Guangjian, "Dixi Yang Weize luoma, Li Yuanchao kaishi mafan [The fall of protégé Yang Weize begins to cause trouble for Li Yuanchao], *Mingjing News* [Mirror News], January 4, 2015 (www.mirrorbooks.com/MIB/magazine/news.aspx?ID=M000002407).

17. Yi He, "Tuanpai laojiang Li Yuanchao de chulu" [The future of tuanpai veteran leader Li Yuanchao], Kaifang Net [Open Net], March 9, 2013, (www.open.com.hk/content .php?id=1199).

18. See www.chinesenewsnet.com, July 22, 2004.

19. This is based on the official data released from the conference of the 21st Century Forum held in Beijing in December 2003. See www.xinhuanet.com, December 18, 2003.

20. Yatsko, *New Shanghai*, 26.

21. James P. Sterba, "A Great Leap Where?," *Wall Street Journal*, December 10, 1993, R9.

22. Quoted from www.justholiday.com/china/shanghai/pudong.html, August 25, 2004; also see www.xinhuanet.com, August 16, 2004.

23. Cheng Li, "The 'Shanghai Gang': Force for Stability or Cause for Conflict?" *China Leadership Monitor*, no. 2 (Winter 2002).

24. Yu Tianbai, *Shanghai: xingge ji mingyun* [Shanghai: Her character is her destiny] (Shanghai: Wenyi Press, 1992).

25. *Straits Times* (Singapore), July 10, 2004.

26. *Shijie ribao*, July 11, 2004, A1.

27. See www.chinesenewsnet.com, July 28, 2004; also see Cheng Li, "Cooling Shanghai Fever: Macroeconomic Control and Its Geopolitical Implications," *China Leadership Monitor*, no. 12 (Fall 2004).

28. Cheng Li, "Was the Shanghai Gang Shanghaied? The Fall of Chen Liangyu and the Survival of Jiang Zemin's Faction," *China Leadership Monitor*, no. 20 (Winter 2007).

29. See www.chinaview.cn, September 25, 2006.

30. Li, "Was the Shanghai Gang Shanghaied?," 13.

31. *Duowei yuekan* [Duowei Monthly], no. 19 (October 2006). Also see www.chinese newsnet.com, October 23, 2006.

32. *Pingguo ribao* [Apple Daily], December 7, 2006, 1.

33. Li, "The 'Shanghai Gang.'"

34. Liu Dong, "Xi Jiang zhenying 'zuoyou fenming'" [The Xi-Jiang camp: the division between "the left and the right"], *Mingjing yuekan* [Mirror Monthly], October 2014.

35. Yang Dongping, *Chengshi jifeng: Beijing he Shanghai de wenhua jingshen* [City monsoon: the cultural spirit of Beijing and Shanghai] (Beijing: Dongfang Press, 1994), 1.

36. "Han Zheng tan Shanghai zimaoqu shiyan" [Han Zheng's comments on the Shanghai Free Trade Zone], *Jiefang wang* [Liberation Daily Online], September 24, 2014 (www .jfdaily.com/zt/news/ss2014/2040_781/12/201409/t20140924_803743.html).

37. Li, "The 'Shanghai Gang,'" 6.

38. For further discussion of the factional networks in the CCP, see Jing Huang, *Factionalism in Chinese Communist Politics* (Cambridge University Press, 2000) and Li, *China's Leaders*.

39. Xiao Chong, *Zhonggong disidai mengren* [The fourth generation of leaders of the Chinese Communist Party] (Hong Kong: Xiafeier guoji chubangongsi, 1998), 337.

40. The other two were then minister of Education Zhou Ji and then minister of Railways Liu Zhijun; see Tianya Web, March 19, 2003 (http://bbs.tianya.cn/post-free-1162809 -1.shtml).

41. Isaac Stone Fish, "Dynasty: Why Are So Many Asian Countries Run by Families?," *Foreign Policy*, December 20, 2012 (http://foreignpolicy.com/2012/12/20/dynasty).

42. *Xinjingbao* [New Beijing Daily], February 23, 2004, 1.

43. Jin Zhong, "Jiang Zemin san dian jianyi daozhi Li Yuanchao Wang Yang chuju" [Jiang Zemin's three comments prevented Li Yuanchao and Wang Yang from entering the Politburo Standing Committee], *Kaifang* [Opening], February 2013.

44. Cheng Li, "Rule of the Princelings." *The Cairo Review of Global Affairs*, no. 8 (Winter, 2013): 34–47.

45. Mai Duo, "Jie jundui hong'erdai fenbu xuanji, hongse jiyin shengjing yu moluo" [Exploring the distribution of the Red 2G in the military: the spectacular rise and inevitable decline of the Red Gene], Duowei Net, February 20, 2015 (http://china.dwnews.com /news/2015-02-20/59636875.html).

46. Lin Baohua, "'Hong'erdai' yu 'guan'erdai'" ["The second generation of red communists" and "the second generation of officials"], *Free Asia Radio*, September 4, 2013 (www .rfa.org/mandarin/pinglun/linbaohua/lbh-09042013112942.html).

47. Mai Duo, "Jiangshan weibianse: yinmide hong'erdai juntuan" [The regime has not changed its color: the hidden "Red II Corps"], Duowei Net, January 12, 2015 (http://china .dwnews.com/news/2015-01-12/59629457.html).

48. Guo Yuandan, "Luo Yuan tan 'hong'erdai'" [Luo Yuan comments on "Red 2G"], *Huanqiu ribao* [Global Times], January 8, 2015; also see People's Net (http://military.people .com.cn/n/2015/0108/c1011-26349254-2.html).

49. Ibid.

50. Ibid.

51. Du Qiang and Lin Shanshan, "Chen Xiaolu: Hong'erdai guangpu" [Chen Xiaolu: Second-generation red communists along the political spectrum], *Nanfang renwu zhoukan* [Southern People Weekly], November 10, 2013 (www.nfpeople.com/story_view.php?id =4959).

52. "Anbang luxian" [The path of Anbang Insurance Group, Inc.], *Nanfang zhoumo* [Southern Weekly], January 29, 2015; also see www.360doc.com/content/15/0202/11/13358165 _445655855.shtml.

53. Luo Changping, "Chihao yu tamende shidai" [Red plutocrats and their era], *Changshi*, February 4, 2015 (www.525789.com/hot/4037.html).

54. Alex Stevens, "Meet Alvin Jiang: Jiang Zemin's Grandson, and Also Quite Possibly China's Hottest Name in Private Equity," *Shanghaiist*, April 11, 2014 (http://shanghaiist .com/2014/04/11/alvin-jiang-chinas-hottest-name-in-private-equity-reuters-extensive -report.php).

55. *Yizhoukan* (The Week), no. 1224, August 22, 2013.

56. Li Ping, "Luoma gaoguan quanshi pingmin chushen?" [Do all of the purged officials come from humble family backgrounds?], *Pingguo ribao* [Apple Daily], September 9, 2014.

57. For a more detailed discussion of the recent personality cult of Xi Jinping, see Tom Phillips, "Xi Jinping: The Growing Cult of China's 'Big Daddy Xi,'" *The Telegraph*, December 8, 2014 (www.telegraph.co.uk/news/worldnews/asia/china/11279204/Xi-Jinping-the -growing-cult-of-Chinas-Big-Daddy-Xi.html).

58. Liu Yazhou, "Zhaoyao Zhongguomeng de sixiang huoju" [A torch of ideas to illuminate the Chinese dream], *Renmin ribao*, February 4, 2015; also see People Net, February 4, 2015 (http://politics.people.com.cn/n/2015/0204/c1001-26502540.html).

59. Ibid.

60. Ibid.

61. Li Ping, "Luoma gaoguan quanshi pingmin chushen?"

62. "Daode doushi hanmen tanguan, taizidang gengjia jinshen didiao" [Purged officials are all from humble families, and princelings have become more cautious and low-profile], *Mingbao* [Ming Daily], August 8, 2014; see also Boxun Web (www.boxun.com/news/gb /china/2014/08/201408080645.shtml).

63. For an argument of the prevalence of the "Red 2G," see Lü Jiayi, *Hong'erdai: Zhonggong quangui jiazu* [The second generation of red communists: China's privileged power families] (New York: Mirror Books, 2014).

64. There is some controversy over Li Keqiang's "humble family background." Some observers have argued that Li can be regarded as a princeling as well. Li Keqiang's father, Li Fengsan, served as head of Fengyang County, president of the Intermediate People's Court of Bengbu City, and deputy director of the Office of Local History, all in Anhui Province.

His father's official rank is not high enough to meet the criteria of princeling, but Li Keqiang's father-in-law, Cheng Jinrui, who was deputy secretary of the CCYL provincial committee of Henan, might have had the rank of vice-minister.

65. Peter Harmsen, "Mining Disaster Bad Luck for Rising Political Star," *The Standard*, February 21, 2005.

66. Chen Xiaoming, "Li Keqiang zheng chengwei diwudai lingpaozhe" [Li Keqiang: The frontrunner of the fifth generation], December 11, 2006 (www.chubun.com/modules/article/view.article.php/c95/28925).

67. "Zhonggong laochangwei queding shibada xinchangwei" [Retired Politburo Standing Committee members decide the new PSC members for the 18th Party Congress], *Back-China*, October 17, 2012 (www.backchina.com/news/2012/10/17/216915.html).

68. It was briefly renamed as the Chinese New Democracy Youth League (中国新民主主义青年团, *zhongguo xinminzhu zhuyi qingniantuan*) between 1949 and 1957.

69. For more discussion of the origin and growth of the CCYL, see Ding Wang, *Hu Jintao yu gongqingtuan jiebanqun* [Hu Jintao and the Successors of Chinese Communist Youth League] (Hong Kong Celebrities Press, 2005) and Cheng Li, "Hu's Followers: Provincial Leaders with Backgrounds in the Communist Youth League," *China Leadership Monitor*, no. 3 (Summer 2002).

70. "Gongqingtuan zuzhibu: Quanguo gongyou tuanyuan 8990.6 wanming" [Organization Department of the CCYL: China has a total of 89,906,000 CCYL members], Xinhua, May 3, 2013 (http://news.sina.com.cn/c/2013-05-03/160827018253.shtml).

71. Ding, *Hu Jintao yu gongqingtuan jiebanqun*.

72. Ibid.

73. *Zhongguo shibao* [China Times], July 13, 2005, 1.

74. Cheng Li, "Hu's Policy Shift and the *Tuanpai*'s Coming-of-Age," *China Leadership Monitor*, no. 15 (Summer 2005): 9–10.

75. Xia Baolong concurrently served as Tianjin party secretary and mayor and thus was double counted. Newly appointed Hainan governor Liu Cigui is regarded as a *tuanpai* leader, as he served as executive deputy secretary of the Fujian Province CCYL Committee, but some other sources cite him as a protégé of Xi Jinping's, as he and Xi worked together in Fujian.

76. Xiao Man, "'Gongqingtuanpai' kuibai" [The collapse of *tuanpai*]. Radio France Internationale Chinese website, May 3, 2015 (http://cn.rfi.fr/中国/20150503-"共青团派"溃败-是否还能东山再起).

77. Mai Duo, "Gongqingtuan shengweishuji zhongshengxiang" [Identities of the CCYL provincial secretaries], Duowei Net, May 22, 2013 (http://china.dwnews.com/news/2013-05-22/59186296-all.html).

78. Zhao Yide is often considered Xi's protégé rather than a *tuanpai* leader because he advanced his career in Zhejiang Province when Xi was in charge. Ji Beiqun, "'65 hou' jieban tidui" [The "post–1965 generation leaders" in the lineup for succession], Duowei Net, May 11, 2015 (http://china.dwnews.com/news/2015-05-11/59652922.html).

79. Mai, "Gongqingtuan shengweishuji zhongshengxiang."

80. Luo Luo, "Tuanpai houlang tui qianlang" [The new wave of promotion of *tuanpai* leaders]. Duowei Net, July 13, 2015 (http://china.dwnews.com/news/2015-07-13/59666941.html).

81. The only post-1975 official who has the rank of full department head is Qie Yingcai (b. 1975), mayor of Suizhou, Hubei Province, who advanced his career through *mishu* work at the General Office of the CCP Central Committee.

82. Luo Luo, "Zhonggong zhengtan 75 hou zhengrong chulu" [The emergence of the post-1975 generation in the CCP leadership], Duowei Net, May 4, 2015 (http://china.dwnews.com/news/2015-05-04/59651360.html).

83. Ibid.

84. In contrast to the CCP Central Committee, which has four operational departments, the CCYL Central Committee consists of nine operational departments: the departments of organization, propaganda, united front work, international affairs, urban youth work, rural youth work, school work, juvenile affairs, and safeguarding the interests of young people.

85. Li, "Hu's Policy Shift and the *Tuanpai*'s Coming-of-Age," 12.

86. Zhan Guoshu, "Tuanzhongyang shuji weihe bu fubai" [Why members of the CCYL Secretariat are not corrupt], *Zhongguo jingji zhoukan* [China Economic Weekly], February 14, 2011. Also see http://china.dwnews.com/news/2011-02-14/57391014.html.

87. For a more detailed discussion, see Zhou Wei and others, "Lingshi xiongdi" [The Ling Brothers], *Caixin*, no. 50, December 29, 2014; also see Caixin Net (http://weekly.caixin.com/2014-12-26/100768395.html).

88. Mai Duo, "Tuanpai 'judian' bengjie" [The Disintegration of the *tuanpai* "stronghold"], Duowei Net, December 30, 2014 (http://china.dwnews.com/news/2014-12-30/59626897.html).

CHAPTER 8

1. Some of the discussion in this chapter previously appeared in the author's series Xi Jinping's Inner Circle, *China Leadership Monitor*, "Part 1 (The Shaanxi Gang)," Spring 2014; "Part 2 (Friends from Xi's Formative Years)," Summer 2014; and "Part 3 (Political Protégés from the Provinces)," Fall 2014. Data and discussion are substantially updated.

2. Evan A. Feigenbaum and Damien Ma, "After the Plenum: Why China Must Reshape the State," *Foreign Affairs*, December 16, 2013 (www.foreignaffairs.com/articles/140557/evan-a-feigenbaum-and-damien-ma/after-the-plenum).

3. Anne E. Kornblut and Scott Wilson, "Obama's Inner Circle about to Break Open," *Washington Post*, September 23, 2010 (www.washingtonpost.com/wp-dyn/content/article/2010/09/22/AR2010092206151.html).

4. For President Obama's heavy reliance on classmates from his Harvard years, see Carrie Budoff Brown, "School Buds: 20 Harvard Classmates Advising Obama," *Politico*, December 5, 2008 (www.politico.com/news/stories/1208/16224.html). Some of the individuals from these political networks overlap. For example, Chris Lu, who was Obama's Harvard classmate, also served as his staffer in the Senate before joining the White House as secretary of the cabinet.

5. Kornblut and Wilson, "Obama's Inner Circle about to Break Open."

6. For example, Ken Thomas, "A Look at President Barack Obama's Inner Circle," Associated Press, July 19, 2012 (http://bigstory.ap.org/article/look-president-barack-obamas-inner-circle).

7. See Cheng Baohuai, Liu Xiaocui, and Wu Zhihui, "Xi Jinping tongzhi zai Zhengding" [Comrade Xi Jinping in Zhengding County], *Hebei ribao* [Hebei Daily], January 2, 2014, 1 (http://news.xinhuanet.com/local/2014-01/02/c_125944449.htm), and also Xi, "Yi Dashan."

8. Quoted from Bob Davis, "Meeting Liu He, Xi Jinping's Choice to Fix a Faltering Chinese Economy," *Wall Street Journal*, October 6, 2013.

9. For example, the database of party and state leaders in China serves this purpose (http://cpc.people.com.cn/gbzl/index.html).

10. In the study of Xi Jinping's political associations, Hong Kong–based Mirror Books has published many books, good examples of which include Xiang Jiangyu, *Xi Jinping bandi* [Xi Jinping's confidants] (New York, 2011); Xiang Jiangyu, *Xi Jinping de tuandui* [Xi Jinping's team] (New York, 2013); Ke Lizi, *Yingxiang Xi Jinping de ren* [People who influence Xi Jinping] (New York, 2013); Wen Zixian, *Xi Jinping de xuanze* [Xi Jinping's choice] (New York, 2012); and Liang Jian, *Xi Jinping xinzhuan* [New biography of Xi Jinping] (New

York, 2012). For some other publishers, see Wu Ming, *Zhongguo xinlingxiu* [China's new leader: biography of Xi Jinping], new enlarged edition (Hong Kong: Wenhua yishu chubanshe, 2010).

11. According to Chinese custom, people often identify themselves as natives of a place based on where their parents (and grandparents) came from (祖籍, *zuji*), not necessarily where they themselves were born (出生地, *chushengdi*). This explains why families' geographic origins play a very important role in the heritage and habits of Chinese people, helping to form various subcultural identities.

12. Jiang Shaofeng, "Zhongguo zhengtan xianchu yige shaanxibang" [The emergence of the Shaanxi Gang in the Chinese leadership], *Waican* [External Reference], no. 38 (September 2013).

13. Other countries have areas that function similarly, as in the United States, where Virginia is considered to be the "mother of presidents."

14. Chen Jianhua, ed., *Huangpu junxiao yanjiu* [Whampoa Military Academy Study], series (Canton: Zhongshan University Press, 2008).

15. For an earlier discussion of the origins of the CCP leaders, see Franklin W. Houn, "The Eighth Central Committee of the Chinese Communist Party: A Study of Elites," *American Political Science Review*, 51 (June 1957); Robert Scalapino, ed., *Elites in the People's Republic of China* (University of Washington Press, 1972); Paul Wong, *China's Higher Leadership in the Socialist Transition* (New York: Free Press, 1976), 190–203.

16. Li and White, "The Fifteenth Central Committee of the Chinese Communist Party," 246–47. Some previously unknown figures are updated based on recently released official biographical information.

17. Li and White, "The Army in the Succession to Deng Xiaoping," 766–67.

18. *China News Analysis*, nos. 1615–16 (August 1–15, 1998), 15–19.

19. It was unclear whether the strong representation of Shandong natives in China's senior military leadership in the 1990s was due to the fact that many Shandong guerrillas joined the CCP and the PLA in the late 1940s (and then became top officers some forty years later) or due to regionally based favoritism in elite promotion or other reasons.

20. For further discussion on this subject, see Cheng Li, "Political Localism Versus Institutional Restraints: Elite Recruitment in the Jiang Era," in Barry Naughton and Dali L. Yang, eds., *Holding China Together: Diversity and National Integration in the Post-Deng Era* (Cambridge University Press, 2004), 29–69.

21. See Li, "The 'Shanghai Gang'" and Li, "Was the Shanghai Gang Shanghaied?"

22. For example, the Chinese official media reported that Xi is particularly fond of the cuisines of two regions: his native Shaanxi and his wife's birthplace, Shandong. See Zhang Xinzhu, "Xi Jinping de 'Zhongguo zuqiumeng'" [Xi's "Chinese Soccer Dream"], *Zhongguo xinwen zhoukan* [China Newsweek], March 29, 2013 (http://insight.inewsweek.cn/report-8713-page-all.html). For the "yellow earth attachment," see Liang, *New Biography of Xi Jinping*, 105.

23. Xi Zhongxun spent these sixteen years between Beijing (in the Central Party School) and Henan Province's Luoyang City, where he served as a deputy factory director. Liang, *New Biography of Xi Jinping*, 54.

24. Liang, *New Biography of Xi Jinping*, 34.

25. *Yan'an ribao* [Yan'an Daily], August 20, 2007, 1; also see Liang, *New Biography of Xi Jinping*, 104.

26. Jiang, "The Emergence of the Shaanxi Gang in the Chinese Leadership."

27. Wang Jun, "Xi Jinping qinshu dangnian zai Shaanxi Liangjiahecun chadui jingli" [Xi Jinping tells his sent-down youth experience in Shaanxi], *Dagong*, May 6, 2013 (http://news.takungpao.com/mainland/zgzq/2013-05/1590913.html) and Liang, *New Biography of Xi Jinping*, 104.

28. "Zhengtan shaanxibang jueqi" [The Emergence of the Shaanxi Gang in Politics], *Shijie ribao*, September 5, 2013, A12.

29. Sun Yun, "Xi Jinping jieshang 'shenyin'" [Xi Jinping uses the excuse of a hurt back to be "spirited away"], *China News Online*, September 26, 2013.

30. Yu Zhengsheng, "Sanzhong quanhui gaige fanwei lidu jiang kongqian" [The reforms proposed at the Third Plenum will be unprecedented in scope and effort], Xinhua, October 27, 2013 (http://news.xinhuanet.com/fortune/2013-10/27/c_125604227.htm).

31. Zhang, "Nongchaoer" and Wu and Lin, "*Wang Qishan lianpu.*"

32. Zheng Furen, "Wang Qishan he Xi Jinping you 'tongchuang zhiyi'" [Wang Qishan and Xi Jinping have a close friendship], *Mingjing yuekan* [Mirror Monthly], November 29, 2013 (http://city.mirrorbooks.com/news/?action-viewnews-itemid-101628). Zhang Siming was then the chairman of the writers' association of Yanchuan County.

33. Zhang, "The man who paddles against the incoming tide."

34. Guo Qing, *Cong Yao Yilin dao Wang Qishan* [From Yao Yilin to Wang Qishan] (Hong Kong: Caida chubanshe, 2009), 111–12.

35. According to a recent report published in China, Wang Qishan and Yao Mingshan knew each other in Beijing before their sent-down years in Yan'an. See Zhang, "The man who paddles against the incoming tide."

36. Wu and Lin, "The Changing Roles of Wang Qishan."

37. Ibid. Weng Yongxi, former deputy director of the Agricultural Policy Research Office of the CCP Central Committee, is now an entrepreneur, deputy director of the Management Committee of the Agricultural Development Fund, and a guest fellow at the Institute of International Relations at Peking University. Huang Jiangnan, former deputy director of the Foreign Trade Committee of the Henan provincial government, is now vice-chairman of the U.S. Chardan China Acquisition Corp. Zhu Jiaming, former deputy director of CITIC International Studies, now teaches at the University of Vienna.

38. Wu and Lin, "The Changing Roles of Wang Qishan."

39. See http://publicintelligence.net/everybody-loves-chinese-vice-premier-wang-qishan, accessed January 20, 2014.

40. *Shijie ribao*, November 21, 2014, A13.

41. For a more detailed discussion of Wang's protégés in Beijing who now work at the CCDI, see Bi Wei, "Wang Qishan renshiquan kuaisu jueqi" [The rapid rise of Wang Qishan's protégés]. *Zhongguo mibao* (Chinese cryptogram), May 9, 2015; also see Mirror Newsnet, http://www.mingjingtimes.com/2015/05/blog-post_29.html.

42. Xiang, *Xi Jinping's Team*, 204.

43. Unverified sources have stated that Zhao Leji's father was Zhao Shoushan, who served as Shaanxi governor in the 1950s, but Zhao Shoushan, who was born in 1894, seems too old to have been Zhao Leji's father. Zhao Shoushan's close relationship with Xi Zhongxun, however, is well-documented. Li Jingning, "Xi Zhongxun he Zhao Shoushan" [Xi Zhongxun and Zhao Shoushan], *Yanhuang shijie* [Glory World], no. 3, 2012; also see http://news.ifeng.com/history/zhongguoxiandaishi/detail_2013_01/23/21513395_0.shtml. According to another unverified source, Zhao's father used to be president of the Shaanxi Education Publishing House. See Xiang, *Xi Jinping's Team*, 235.

44. Ibid., 230, also Yang Qingxi and Xia Fei, *Shibada zhuhou jinjing* [Provincial chiefs go to Beijing for the 18th Party Congress], (New York: Mirror Books, 2010).

45. Li Jianguo is a protégé and *mishu* of Li Ruihuan, former chairman of the Chinese People's Political Consultative Conference and PSC member. Li Ruihuan has long been a critic and political rival of Jiang Zemin, and thus he and his protégé Li Jianguo are usually considered members of the Hu-Wen coalition. Ma Kai has been seen as a protégé of Wen Jiabao.

46. See *People's Daily*, October 16, 2013 (www.chinanews.com/gn/2013/10-16/5384270.shtml).

47. "Fuzongli Ma Kai gen shaanxibang" [Vice-Premier Ma Kai and the Shaanxi Gang], *Waican* [External reference], October 13, 2013 (http://info.51.ca/news/china/2013/10/13 /313834.shtml).

48. Benjamin Kang Lim and Ben Blanchard, "Failure to End China's Labor Camps Shows Limits of Xi's Power," *Reuters*, November 6, 2013 (www.reuters.com/article/2013/11 /06/us-china-politics-xi-insight-idUSBRE9A514U20131106).

49. Jiang, "The Emergence of the Shaanxi Gang in the Chinese Leadership."

50. This was based on the author's interview in Washington, D.C., on March 7, 2015, with a Chinese scholar who is a friend of the Lei family.

51. For the strong ties between Li Ziqi and Xi Zhongxun, see Li Ziqi, "Shenqie mianhuai Xi Zhongxun tongzhi" [Deeply cherish the memory of Comrade Xi Zhongxun], *Meiri Gansu* [Gansu Daily], October 10, 2013 (http://gansu.gansudaily.com.cn/system/2013/10 /10/014708123.shtml).

52. Chu Wen, "Zhengtan 'Shaanjun' jueqi, sida hanjiang buru Zhonggong hexinquan" [The political rise of the 'Shaanxi Gang': Four heavyweight leaders have entered the core power circle of the Chinese Communist Party] Duowei Net, July 3, 2015 (http://china .dwnews.com/news/2015-07-03/59664886.html).

53. Ibid.

54. Ibid.

55. Shi Qing, "Xi Jinping huanying Li Xi shuai Yan'an shi dangzheng daibiaotuan laihu fangwen" [Xi Jinping welcomes Li Xi–led party and government delegation from Yan'an to visit Shanghai], *Oriental*, August 18, 2007 (http://sh.eastday.com/qtmt /20070818/u1a343068.html) and Fang Ledi, "Li Xi lüxin Liaoning" [Li Xi takes new office in Liaoning], *Dagong*, April 28, 2014 (http://news.takungpao.com/mainland/focus /2014-04/2446110.html).

56. For an excellent discussion of the role of princelings in the Red Guard Movement at the No. 4 School in Beijing, see Liu Huixuan, "Zuoye xingchen zuoyefeng: Beijing sizhong de hongweibing wangshi" [Last night's stars and last night's wind: stories of the Red Guard movement in Beijing No. 4 School], *Minjian lishi* [Folk History], the Universities Service Centre of the Chinese University of Hong Kong (http://mjlsh.usc.cuhk.edu.hk/book.aspx ?cid=6&tid=157&pid=3239).

57. Wu Nan and Gao Xiao, *Xi Jinping yu Peng Liyuan* [Xi Jinping and Peng Liyuan], (Taipei: Hayek Publishing House, 2013).

58. Zhou Yahui, "Xi Jinping yu Deng Pufang guanxi miqie" [Xi Jinping and Deng Pufang have a close relationship], *Boxun*, October 22, 2010 (http://blog.boxun.com/hero /201010/zhouyahui/42_1.shtml).

59. Ian Johnson, "Dynasty of Different Order Is Reshaping China," *New York Times*, November 13, 2012, A1.

60. Gao Jun, "Faxiao Nie Weiping bao Xi Jinping ersanshi" [A few episodes about Xi Jinping by his childhood friend Nie Weiping], Duowei Net, October 24, 2010 (http:// politics.dwnews.com/news/2010-10-24/56584020-2.html). Nie Weiping was also a regular guest in Deng Xiaoping's home for two decades before Deng's death in 1997, as both were famous for playing bridge. See http://book.sina.com.cn/jiyizhongdeyingxiang/excerpt/sz /2008-06-23/1859239080.shtml.

61. Gao Jun, "A few episodes about Xi Jinping by his childhood friend Nie Weiping."

62. For a discussion of the roles of these radical Red Guards with princeling backgrounds, see Jiang Yanbei, *Cong Bo Yibo dao Bo Xilai* [From Bo Yibo to Bo Xilai] (Hong Kong: Caida chubanshe, 2009), 102–107.

63. Gao Xiao, "'Sanping': Xi Jinping, Nie Weiping he Liu Weiping" [Three close friends: Xi Jinping, Nie Weiping, and Liu Weiping], *Mirror*, October 22, 2010 (http://city.mirrorbooks .com/news/?action-viewnews-itemid-17652).

64. This is based on the author's interview in Washington, D.C., in February 2014 with a Chinese scholar who went to the same high school as Liu He. Some other sources indicate that his father was a bureau-level leader rather than a vice-minister-level official.

65. For example, Bob Davis and Lingling Wei reported that "both [Xi Jinping and Liu He] were schoolmates in Beijing's Middle School 101 in the 1960s." See "Meet Liu He, Xi Jinping's Choice to Fix a Faltering Chinese Economy," *Wall Street Journal*, October 6, 2013 (http://online.wsj.com/news/articles/SB1000142405270230490670457911 1442566524958). Chinese Wikipedia also states that Xi Jinping attended Beijing No. 101 Middle School (see http://zh.wikipedia.org/wiki/习近平), but Chinese official sources reported Xi went to the Bayi School for his elementary and middle school education and later transferred to Beijing No. 25 School. Also see Wu, *China's New Leader: Biography of Xi Jinping*, 572.

66. Several prominent leaders attended Beijing No. 101 School, such as former vice-president Zeng Qinghong, former Politburo member Li Tieying, former Beijing party secretary Liu Qi, and former director of the State Council's Hong Kong and Macao Office Liao Hui.

67. "*Gongnongbing jia haigui* (工农兵加海归)." Wang Ziyue, "Pandian Zhongnanhai caijing gaoji zhinang" [Analyzing senior financial advisers in Zhongnanhai], *Diyi caijing ribao* (China Business News), August 29, 2014; also see http://www.yicai.com/news/2014/08/4013279.html.

68. For the website of the forum, see www.50forum.org.cn/index_home2.asp.

69. For a more detailed discussion of the Chinese Economists 50 Forum and its "revolving door" function, see Cheng Li, "China's New Think Tanks: Where Officials, Entrepreneurs, and Scholars Interact," *China Leadership Monitor*, no. 29 (Summer 2009): 10–13.

70. Liu He, *Liangci quanqiu weiji de bijiao yanjiu* [A Comparative Study of the Two Global Crises] (Beijing: Zhongguo jingji chubanshe, 2013).

71. Lian Zhong, "Jiemi Xi Jinping zhinang Liu He" [The inside story about Xi Jinping's adviser Liu He], *Lianzheng liaowang* [Governance Outlook], November 1, 2013. Also see http://news.sina.com.cn/c/sd/2013-11-01/115228593457.shtml.

72. Ibid.

73. *Diyi caijing ribao* [First Financial Daily], December 12, 2013.

74. Ibid.

75. Michael Forsythe and Dune Lawrence, "Liu He as China's Larry Summers Makes Politburo Appreciate U.S." *Bloomberg News*, September 24, 2009 (www.bloomberg.com/apps/news?pid=newsarchive&sid=aKp9wybwC4HM

76. The World Bank and Development Research Center of the State Council, the People's Republic of China, *China 2030: Building a Modern, Harmonious, and Creative Society* (Washington, D.C.: World Bank, 2013).

77. Liu Xiaoguang, "Liu He neibu baogao: jingti mincuizhuyi xingqi" [Liu He's internal report: Alert on the rise of populism], *Juece cankao* [Decisionmaking Reference], November 6, 2013; also see http://finance.ifeng.com/business/special/fhsd9/.

78. Tian Liang, "Liu He: Zongshuji de jingji zhinang" [Liu He: The General Secretary's Brain Trust in Economic Development], *Huanqiu renwu* [Global Figures], July 12, 2015.

79. Xi Jinping, "Wo shi ruhe kuaru zhengjiede" [How I entered politics], *Zhonghua ernü* [China's Offspring], no. 7, 2000; also see http://china.dwnews.com/news/2012-02-21/58609785- all.html.

80. This view has been widely circulated on Chinese social media, including Baidu and Tencent, since January 2012. See http://zhidao.baidu.com/question/1859848115454599427.html and www.sydneytoday.com/n/bencandy.php?fid=11&id=99950.

81. "Liu Shaoqi zhi zi Liu Yuan bandao jundui jutan Gu Junshan de diandi xijie" [Details of how Liu Shaoqi's son Liu Yuan revealed the huge corruption scandal of military officer Gu Junshan] (www.fnmhw.com/html/Special/cw/Index.html). Also see Meng Mei,

"Zonghou Gu Junshan bei shui naxiade?" [Who caught Deputy Director of the General Logistics Department Gu Junshan?] (www.pifamm.com/news/201401/21/news_info _9895.html).

82. John Garnaut, "Chinese General Rattles Sabre," *The Age*, May 23, 2011.

83. Liu Yuan, "Foreword," in Zhang Musheng, *Gaizao women de wenhua lishiguan* [Transforming our cultural perspective on history] (Beijing: PLA Military Academy of Sciences Press, 2011).

84. Ibid.

85. Ibid.

86. Garnaut, "Chinese General Rattles Sabre."

87. Wei Pu, "Liu Yuan zhinang Zhang Musheng de mafan" [Liu Yuan's adviser Zhang Musheng faces some trouble], *Da shijian* [Major Events], no. 11, July 9, 2012. Also see http://city.mirrorbooks.com/news/html/79/n-54879.html.

88. Ibid.

89. Ibid.

90. Zhang Musheng's father, Li Yingji, was a *mishu* to such top veteran Communist leaders as Zhou Enlai and Dong Biwu. Li also served as deputy director of the Foreign Economic and Trade Commission before he committed suicide during the Cultural Revolution. See Zhang Huan, "Zhang Musheng: Zaiju xin minzhuzhuyi daqi" [Zhang Musheng: raise anew the banner of new socialist democracy], *Nanfang renwu zhoukan* [Southern People Weekly], November 28, 2011.

91. Qian Liqun, "Lao hongweibing dangzheng de danyou" [Fears about former Red Guards in power], *Wenzhai* [Digest] February 19, 2012.

92. Ibid.

93. Ibid.

94. Ibid.

95. Lu Jiayi, *Hong erdai: Zhonggong quangui jiazu* [Red Generation II: Powerful Chinese Communist families], (New York: Mirror Books, 2014).

96. See *Kan Zhongguo* [China Watch Web] (http://m.secretchina.com/node /494566).

97. For a more detailed discussion of the controversies about Liu Yuan, see Cheng Li, "Xi Jinping's Inner Circle (Part 2: Friends from Xi's Formative Years)," *China Leadership Monitor*, no. 44 (Summer 2014): 10–15.

98. Sun Lan, "Liu Yuan tuiyi neimu baoguang: Fan Changlong toule fanduipiao" [Insider exposes Liu Yuan's retirement: Fan Changlong voted against Liu's CMC membership], Duowei Net, January 3, 2016 (http://china.dwnews.com/news/2016-01-03/59707933 .html).

99. Ibid.

100. Song Ruxin, "Huoyu Hu Jintao xiangtong zanyu: Xi Jinping gaoguige huansong Liu Yuan" [Liu Yuan receives high praise from Xi Jinjing, who did the same to Hu Jintao in farewell], Duowei Net, January 5, 2016 (http://china.dwnews.com/news/2016-01-05/59708411 .html).

101. Gao Xiao, "Qinghua tongchuang yanzhong de gongnongbing xueyuan Xi Jinping" [Xi Jinping's years as a worker-peasant-solider student at Tsinghua: in the eyes of Xi's fellow students], *BackChina* (www.backchina.com/news/2011/02/06/126017.html).

102. Zhang Li, "Xi Jinping, Chen Xi shi tongchuang haishi tongdang" [Xi Jinping and Chen Xi are not only classmates but also party cohorts], *Mirror*, May 31, 2013 (http://city .mirrorbooks.com/news/?action-viewnews-itemid-87605).

103. Ibid.

104. Gao Xin, comments on Radio Free Asia website, April 17, 2014 (www.rfa.org /mandarin/zhuanlan/yehuazhongnanhai/gx-04172014100823.html), and April 30, 2013 (www.rfa.org/mandarin/zhuanlan/yehuazhongnanhai/gx-04302013112626.html).

105. *Lianhe zaobao* [United Morning Post], October 31, 2009. Also see www.aboluowang .com/2009/1031/148038.html#sthash.99VSAQqC.rjOfuYaV.dpuf and www.hoover.org/sites /default/files/research/docs/clm44cl.pdf.

106. Gao, comments on Radio Free Asia website, April 17, 2014.

107. According to overseas observers, due to Chen Xi's strong support, Chen Jining was promoted from a department-level (*tingji* 厅级) official to a full minister—a three-step promotion—within three years. Ji Beiqun, "Sannian sanliantiao guansheng zhengbu" [A three-step promotion in three years], Duowei Net, January 28, 2015 (http://china.dwnews .com/news/2015-01-28/59632710.html).

108. He Jingjun, "'Xue'er youzeshi' de 'xinchangtai' hua" [The "new normal" of good scholars becoming officials], *Xinmin zhoukan* (Xinmin Weekly), no. 11 (2015), 65–67.

109. This was based on the author's correspondence with Michael R. A. Wade, a former U.S. government official.

110. Ibid.

111. Geng Ying and Geng Yan, "Xi Jinping ruhe pingjia ziji wei Geng Biao zuo mishu de nasannian" [How does Xi Jinping evaluate his three years of experience working as a *mishu* for Defense Minister Geng Biao?], *Phoenix News*, December 23, 2013. Also see http://news .ifeng.com/history/zhongguoxiandaishi/detail_2013_12/23/32380395_0.shtml.

112. Ibid.

113. Xu Qingquan, "Xi Zhongxun he Hu Yaobang" [Xi Zhongxun and Hu Yaobang], *Zhongguo xinwen zhoukan* [China Newsweek], October 19, 2013 (http://news.ifeng.com /shendu/zgxwzk/detail_2013_10/19/30476138_0.shtml).

114. Ibid.

115. Xiang, *Xi Jinping's Team*, 568–80.

116. China News Net, June 24, 2014 (www.chinanews.com/gn/2014/06-24/6312987 .shtml).

117. *Jiaxing ribao* [Jiaxing Daily], May 24, 2013, 1.

118. Yong Huaqi, "Xi Jinping yi Zhengding suiyue" [Xi Jinping's recollections of his years in Zhengding], in Wu, *China's New Leader*, 605.

119. Ibid., 602.

120. Yong, "Xi Jinping yi Zhengding suiyue."

121. Wu, *China's New Leader,* 137.

122. Xiang, *Xi Jinping's Team*, 204

123. Wu, *China's New Leader,* 135–36.

124. Xi, "Yi Dashan."

125. Kan Zhongguo Web, September 10, 2014 (http://m.secretchina.com/node/496409).

126. *Xingdao Daily*, November 2, 2012 (http://news.singtao.ca/calgary/2012-11-02 /china1351843867d4175398.html).

127. Ibid.

128. Xiang Dan, "Gaoji jiangling Sulu'zhadui'" [Senior Officers Cluster in Jiangsu and Shandong], Duowei Newsnet, May 10, 2015 (http://china.dwnews.com/news/2015-05-10 /59652510.html).

129. Sun Lan, "'Wansuijun' lingxian" [The "Royal Army" Leads], Duowei Net, July 15, 2015, (http://china.dwnews.com/news/2015-07-15/59667471.html) and Shi Yu, "Jiemi 'jinweijun' Xiamen 31 jituan yijun tuqi" [Unmasking the "Guards": the rapid rise of the Thirty-first Group Army based in Xiamen], Duowei Net, December 12, 2015 (http://china.dwnews .com/news/2015-01-12/59629345.html).

130. Wu Yu, "Xi Jinping qinxin Cai Qi jiang diaoren guo'anwei?" [Will Xi's confidant Cai Qi be transferred to the National Security Committee?], *Deutsche Welle*, March 28, 2014 (www.dw.de/习近平亲信蔡奇将调任国安委/a-17527436).

131. Apollo News Network, December 19, 2012 (http://tw.aboluowang.com/2012/1219 /274159.html).

132. Wang Ya, "'Tianzi' yong jiubu, zhengtan Zhejiangbang jiti shangwei muhou" ["Princeling" promotes his protégés: the rise of the Zhejiang Gang], Duowei Net, December 22, 2014 (http://china.dwnews.com/news/2014-12-22/59625495.html).

133. "Xi Jinping yuyong jizhe Shen Haixiong lüxin, shengren Xinhuashe zui nianqing fushezhang" [Xi Jinping's 'imperial reporter' Shen Haixiong appointed the youngest vice-president of Xinhua], Literature City Network, July 14, 2014 (http://www.wenxuecity.com /news/2014/07/14/3430045.html).

134. Wang Shu, Zhang Yuan, and Guo Yongfang, "Gong'anbu daidui fu Zhengjianhui de Meng Qingfeng shi shui?" [Who is Meng Qingfeng, the man who led a delegation from the Ministry of Public Security on a visit to the China Securities Regulatory Commission?]. China Newsnet, July 10, 2015 (http://www.chinanews.com/gn/2015/07-10/7396558 .shtml).

135. Xi praised Yang for his broad leadership experience and his good work on ethnic affairs in the press conference on the Shanghai Municipal Party Committee in 2012. *Xingdao ribao*, November 20, 2013.

136. General Office of the CCP Central Committee, *Dangzheng lingdao ganbu zhiwu renqi zanxing guiding*.

137. "Xi Urges Strengthening of United Front," *China Daily*, May 21, 2015; also see the online version, http://www.chinadaily.com.cn/china/2015-05/21/content_20785494.htm.

CHAPTER 9

1. For an earlier discussion of competing political scenarios, see Cheng Li, "China in the Year 2020: Three Political Scenarios," *Asia Policy*, no. 4 (July 2007): 17–29.

2. Walter Laqueur, "The Moscow News, Tomorrow: Forecasting the Soviet-Russian Future," *Encounter* (May 1990): 3.

3. Russell Leigh Moses, "Deng Redux? Parsing the Grand Ambitions of China's President," *Wall Street Journal*, China Real Time blog, August 22, 2014 (http://blogs.wsj.com/chinarealtime /2014/08/22/deng-redux-parsing-the-grand-ambitions-of-chinas-president/).

4. John W. Garver, "China's Misperception of a US Anti-China Conspiracy," *U.S.-China Perception Monitor*, July 29, 2015 (http://www.uscnpm.org/blog/2015/07/29/chinas -misperception-of-a-us-anti-china-conspiracy/).

5. For Peng Liyuan's important contribution to China's tobacco control and antismoking campaign, see Cheng Li, *Zhongguo yancao de zhengzhi bantu: Yancao hangye yu kongyan yundong boyi* [China's tobacco industry and antismoking campaign: politics and policies] (New York: Mirror Books, 2013), 126–129.

6. Rosie Scammell, "Pope Francis praises China in latest effort to thaw chilly relations," *National Catholic Reporter*, February 3, 2016; also see http://ncronline.org/news/vatican /pope-francis-praises-china-latest-effort-thaw-chilly-relations.

7. "China Punishes More Than 182,000 Corrupt Officials," Voice of America, January 10, 2014 (http://www.voanews.com/content/china-punishes-thousands-of-corrupt -officials/1827251.html).

8. Xi Jinping, "Jianding zhidu zixin bushi yao gubuzifeng" [Confidence in China's political system does not necessarily mean that we should resist any change], Xinhua, February 17, 2014 (http://cpc.people.com.cn/n/2014/0217/c64094-24384920.html).

9. "Zhongguo zhenya weiquan lüshi renshu yida 249" [The number of rights lawyers being persecuted in China reaches 249], Voice of America, September 7, 2015 (http://www .voachinese.com/content/china-crackdown-human-rights-laywyers-20150714/2860931 .html).

10. Curtis Chin, "Xi Jinping's 'Asia for Asians' mantra evokes imperial Japan," *South China Morning Post*, July 14, 2014 (http://www.scmp.com/comment/insight-opinion/article

/1553414/xi-jinpings-asia-asians-mantra-evokes-imperial-japan); "Xi tells Kerry: Pacific Ocean big enough for China and U.S," AFP website, May 17, 2015 (http://news.yahoo.com /xi-tells-kerry-pacific-ocean-big-enough-china-164047724.html).

11. Cheng Li, "Cuoshi liangji de shibada?" [Opportunity lost at the 18th National Party Congress?], Waican [External Reference], no. 32 (January 2013): 18–21.

12. These recently purged confidants of Li Yuanchao include former Yunnan deputy party secretary Qiu He, former Nanjing party secretary Yang Weize, former Nanjing mayor Ji Jianye, and former chief-of-staff of Jiangsu provincial party committee Zhao Shaolin, in addition to former Liaoning party secretary Wang Min; also see Minnie Chan, Stuart Lau and Li Jing, "Chinese Vice-President Li Yuanchao Hits Back at Rumours He Is Target of Looming Graft Probe," *South China Morning Post*, January 24, 2015 (http://www .scmp.com/news/china/article/1690087/chinas-vice-president-li-yuanchao-apparent -move-deny-online-founder-group?page=all).

13. Zhang Ping, "Zhonggong diliudai lingdaoren zai chuanyanzhong dansheng" [The sixth generation of leaders in the Chinese Communist Party was born out of speculations], Deutsche Welle website, November 21, 2012 (http://www.dw.com/zh/中共第六代领导人在传言中诞生/a-16396812).

14. Ibid.

15. General Office of the CCP Central Committee, "Tuijin lingdao ganbu nengshang nengxia ruogan guiding (shixing)" [A number of trial provisions to promote the mobility of cadres], Renmin Newsnet, July 29, 2015 (http://politics.people.com.cn/n/2015/0729/c1001 -27375974.html).

16. Hua Chunyu, "Tuijin lingdao ganbu nengshangnengxia" [Promoting the mobility of cadres]. Xinhua Newsnet, January 28, 2016. (http://news.xinhuanet.com/politics/2016-01 /28/c_1117927335.htm).

17. *Shijie ribao* [World Journal], January 30, 2016, B5.

18. Suo Fei, "Xi Jinping qiangduo biganzi, Liu Qibao beibi 'rangxian,'" [Xi Jinping forces propaganda chief Liu Qibao to step down], Radio France International, April 10, 2015 (http://cn.rfi.fr/中国/20151004-习近平抢夺笔杆子-刘奇葆被逼"让贤").

19. Hu Chunhua has received much praise for his effective leadership in Guangdong. See Ji Beiqun, "Hu Chunhua nanyue zaifali, 'sanda zhuashou' bu duanban" [Hu Chunhua's great effort to implement three policies to overcome disadvantages in Guangdong's development], Duowei Net, August 20, 2015 (http://china.dwnews.com/news/2015-08-20/59675866.html).

20. Zeng Peiyan, a longtime friend and confidant of Jiang Zemin, also served as a top leader in the State Council Information Office, the National Development and Reform Commission, and the Office of the CCP Central Financial and Economic Work Leading Group, as did Liu He.

21. Luan Xuefei and Zhang Dongwang, "Zhonggong zhongyan shujichu de yange" [The history of the Secretariat of the CCP Central Committee], *Dongbei shida xuebao* [Journal of Northwestern Normal University], no. 5 (1997): 71.

22. Ibid.

23. Ji Beiqun, "Nianmo xipai weituo chaojiu, Xi Jinping yongren zhuojinjianzhou" [Year-end reshuffling did not go beyond the norms, and Xi seems to be stretched in personnel appointments], Duowei Net, January 1, 2015 (http://china.dwnews.com/news/2015 -01- 01/59627340.html).

24. Xi Jinping, *The Governance of China* (Beijing: Foreign Language Press, 2014). For the official Webchat account "Xue Xi Xiaozu" [Learn from Xi], see http://chuansong.me /account/xuexixiaozu. For the nickname of "Papa Xi" and the worship of places where Xi has visited, see Andrew Jacobs and Chris Buckley, "Move Over Mao: Beloved 'Papa Xi' Awes China," *New York Times*, March 7, 2015 (http://www.nytimes.com/2015/03/08/world /move-over-mao-beloved-papa-xi-awes-china.html?_r=0).

25. Chris Buckley, "Xi Jinping Assuming New Status as China's 'Core' Leader," *New York Times*, February 4, 2016 (http://www.nytimes.com/2016/02/05/world/asia/china-president -xi-jinping-core.html?_r=0).

26. Qian Gang, "Yuxiang baogao: Lingdaoren xingming chuanbo qiangdu guancha" [Content analysis: leaders' name transmission intensity observed], China Digital Times website (http://chinadigitaltimes.net/chinese/2014/07/钱钢-语象报告：领导人姓名传播强度观察/).

27. Ibid.

28. Wang Jian, "Liande shi duilie, zhude shi junhun" [Practice queue and cast the soul], *Renmin ribao* [People's Daily], August 30, 2015; also see Renmin Web, August 30, 2015 (http://military.people.com.cn/n/2015/0830/c1011-27531473.html).

29. Mao Zedong, *Selected Works of Mao Zedong*, vol. 2, 2nd ed. (Beijing: Renmin chubanshe, 1991), 224.

30. For details of the military purge under the Xi leadership, see Cheng Li, "Promoting 'Young Guards': The Recent High Turnover in the PLA Leadership (Part I: Purges and Reshuffles)," *China Leadership Monitor*, no. 48 (Fall 2015): 1–14.

31. Li, "Promoting 'Young Guards': The Recent High Turnover in the PLA Leadership (Part I: Purges and Reshuffles)."

32. Zheng Yongnian, "Zhongguo yishixingtai de huigui jiqi yingxiang" [The return of ideology in China and its impact], China Election and Governance Net, February 17, 2015 (http://www.chinaelections.org/article/105/236299.html).

33. Wang Weiguang, "Jianchi renmin minzhu zhuanzheng bingbu shuli" [One should proudly insist on the people's democratic dictatorship], *Hongqi wengao* [Red Flag Presentation], September 23, 2014.

34. Li Wen, "Zhongguo shekeyuan yuanzhang zhuanwen datan jiejidouzheng yin reyi" [The article on class struggle written by the president of CASS causes many controversies], BBC Chinese, September 24, 2014 (http://www.bbc.com/zhongwen/simp/china/2014/09 /140924_cn_struggle).

35. Li Weidong, "Zoubutong de 'hongse diguo zhi lu'" [The dead end of the "Red Empire Road"], *Taipingyang yuekan* [Pacific Monthly], October 17, 2013 (http://article.wn.com /view/WNAT3b018b02893a5024b9d562142b26e6c6/).

36. Yu Keping, "Deng Xiaoping yu Zhongguo de zhengzhi jinbu" [Deng Xiaoping and China's political development], *Wenhui bao* [Wenhui Daily], August 26, 2015 (http://news .wenweipo.com/2014/08/26/IN1408260067.htm).

37. Wang Changjiang, "Minzhu shi lianghao zhengzhi shengtai de yaojian" [Democracy is an important condition for healthy political ecology], Consensus Media Net, July 14, 2015 (http://www.21ccom.net/articles/china/ggzl/20150710126642_all.html).

38. Ibid.

39. Hai Yan, "Zhou Yongkun jiaoshou shenqing gongkai dayuebing feiyong" [Professor Zhou Yongkun calls for publication of military parade expenses] (http://www.mingjingnews .com/MIB/news/news.aspx?ID=N000110793).

40. Quan Ye, "Shui zai paozhi Faxisi Zhongguo?" [Who is concocting a Fascist China?], Duowei Net, September 8, 2015 (http://china.dwnews.com/news/2015-09-08/59680158 .html).

41. Li, "Zoubutong de 'hongse diguo zhi lu.'"

42. See, for example, Yu Yingshi, "Zouxiang ducai de Xi Jinping" [Xi Jinping intends to become a dictator], Free Radio of Asia, March 18, 2015 (https://translate.google.com/#zh -CN/en/走向独裁的习近平) and Perry Link, "Is Xi Jinping China's New Mao-Like Strongman?," *World Post*, June 3, 2014 (www.huffingtonpost.com/perry-link/xi-jinping-china -mao_b_5439367.html).

43. Yu Jianrong, "Hefaxing yu Zhongguo weilai de zhengzhi fazhan: dangqian yishixingtai zhenglun zhi pingjia" [Legitimacy and China's future political development: assessing

the current ideological debate], *Tianzhe shuangzhou luntan* [Unirule Biweekly Forum] (http://www.unirule.org.cn/index.php?c=article&id=3651).

44. Ibid.

45. Zheng Yongnian, "Xi Jinping de zhengzhi luxiantu" [Xi Jinping's political road map], Chao Global Net, October 20, 2014 (https://chaoglobal.wordpress.com/2014/10/20 /cheng-yung-nien/).

46. Ibid.

47. Su Mi, "Xi Jinping yongren 'houlai jushang?'" [Does Xi Jinping like to appoint leaders who "come from behind?"], Duowei Net, September 1, 2015 (http://china.dwnews.com /news/2015-09-01/59678753.html).

48. Ibid.

49. Su Mi, "Jixin'ge: Xi Jinping zui jiechu" [Kissinger: Xi Jinping is truly outstanding], Duowei Net, September 13, 2015 (http://china.dwnews.com/big5/news/2015-09-13/59681217 .html).

50. Wang Demin, "Zhongguo renmin daxue faxueyuan yuanzhang Han Dayuan; xianfa mei quanwei caihui you nameduo lingdaoxiaozu" [Chinese People's University Law School Dean Han Dayuan: if there were constitutional authority, China would not have so many central leading groups], Fenghuang wang [Phoenix Net], July 5, 2015 (http://mp.weixin.qq .com/s?__biz=MjM5Mjc5OTQ0MA==&mid=208982347&idx=1&sn=ec38f5b5db5aa6f7e 83179952d30a82c&scene=1&from=groupmessage&isappinstalled=0#rd).

51. Ibid.

52. Ibid.

53. President Lincoln's approach for the formation of his leadership team was the main theme of Doris Kearns Goodwin, *Team of Rivals: The Political Genius of Abraham Lincoln* (New York: Simon & Schuster, 2006). For Chinese discussion, see Cai Ziqiang, "Yudi tongmian haishi zhengdi tuandui?" [Sleeping with the enemy or forming a team of rivals?], *Nanfang renwu zhoukai* [Southern People Weekly], December 17, 2008 (www.infzm.com /content/21274).

54. Cheng Li, "China's Team of Rivals," *Foreign Policy* (March/April 2009): 88–93.

55. Steve Tsang, "Why China's Xi Jinping Is Still Far from Chairman Mao Status," *Forbes*, February 16, 2015 (http://www.forbes.com/sites/stevetsang/2015/02/16/why-chinas -xi-jinping-is-still-far-from-chairman-mao-status/).

56. Ibid.

57. Ibid.

58. *Pingguo ribao* [Apple Daily], May 1, 2014 (www.backchina.com/news/2014/05/01 /295409.html).

59. Francis Fukuyama, *Political Order and Political Decay: From the Industrial Revolution to the Globalization of Democracy* (New York: Farrar, Straus and Giroux, 2014); also see Qidong Cao, "Q. and A.: Francis Fukuyama on China's Political Development," Sinosphere blog, May 1, 2015 (http://sinosphere.blogs.nytimes.com/2015/05/01/q-and-a-francis -fukuyama-on-chinas-political-development).

60. Zhang Yuanshuai, "Xi Jinping 'poge' jiejian Fushan shencang xuanji" [Xi Jinping's exceptional meeting with Fukuyama shrouded in deep mystery], *Gang'au ribao* [Hong Kong and Macau Daily], November 6, 2015 (http://www.hkmnews.com/site/root/重磅 /2015/11/06/习近平「破格」接見福山深藏玄機.html).

61. Sun Liping, "Wenge de genyuan: Paixi zhengzhi wufa zhiduhua" [The root cause of the Cultural Revolution: factional politics failed to be institutionalized], Soho blog, April 30, 2012.

62. Zheng Yongnian, "Zhongguo shida keneng de 'dianfuxing cuowu'" [China's top ten possible "subversive errors"], Consensus Media Net, February 24, 2015 (http://www.21ccom .net/articles/thought/bianyan/20150224121329_all.html).

63. Ibid.

64. Zheng Yongnian, "Zhongguo minzhu yingshi 'kaifang de yidangzhi'" [Chinese democracy should be an open one-party system], Fenghuang wang [Phoenix Net], May 19, 2015 (http://news.ifeng.com/opinion/gaojian/special/zfzyn).

65. Ibid.

66. For a detailed discussion of intraparty elections, also see Cheng Li, "Leadership Transition in the CPC: Promising Progress and Potential Problems," *China: An International Journal*, vol. 10, no. 2 (August 2012): 23–33.

67. Zhang Lixin, "Shiliuda yilai de zhongyang weiyuan, houbu weiyuan cha'e xuanju" [The multicandidate elections of full members of the Central Committee since the 16th National Party Congress], *Caixin Net*, November 14, 2012 (http://china.caixin.com/2012 -11-14/100460073.html).

68. "Wuzhongquanhui qian 205 ming zhongyangweiyuan banshu yizhi" [Among 205 Central Committee members, more than half have moved to different positions in three years], Tengxun News, October 24, 2015 (http://news.qq.com/a/20151024/034693.htm).

69. The author is grateful to Michael O'Hanlon for reviewing an early version of this book and for making this insightful observation.

70. Kerry Saretsky, "Follow the Fromage," *Princeton Alumni Weekly*, vol. 115, no. 1 (September 17, 2014).

71. For the local factors in sociopolitical changes in China and other East and Southeast Asian countries, see Lynn White, Kate Zhou, and Shelley Rigger, eds., *Democratization in China, Korea, and Southeast Asia? Local and National Perspectives* (New York: Routledge, 2013).

72. See http://bbs.nhzj.com/viewthread.php?tid=377464.

73. Yao Yang, "The End of the Beijing Consensus: Can China's Model of Authoritarian Growth Survive?," *Foreign Affairs*, February 2, 2010. Also available at http://www.foreign affairs.com/articles/65947/the-end-of-the-beijing-consensus.

74. *Liaowang xinwen zhoukan* [Outlook Weekly], January 23, 2010.

75. The author is grateful to an anonymous reviewer of an early version of this book for making this observation.

76. It is unclear who first coined the term "black-collar stratum." Most online postings in China attribute the label to U.S.-educated economist Lang Xianping (Larry Lang), but Lang has publicly denied that he wrote the widely circulated article popularizing the term. See "The Black-Collar Class" (www.chinatranslated.com/?p=407); translated: "Commentary and Analysis on China's Economic and Political Situation," June 12, 2009.

77. *Zhongguo xinwen zhoukan* [China Newsweek], January 13, 2006, *Liaowang* [Outlook], December 9, 2005; also see http://www.chinesenewsnet.com, December 12, 2005.

78. For more discussion of how the vested special interest groups influence policies, see Sun Liping, "Zhongguo shehui zhengzai zouxiang kuibai" [Chinese society is heading toward collapse], Renmin Net, February 10, 2013 (http://bbs.tianya.cn/post-worldlook -679491-1.shtml).

79. For example, Zhang Ming launched a strong critique of the rampancy of official corruption by dozens of CCP top leaders in March, a few months before the foreign media began to trace "family trees" of crony capitalism among the Chinese leadership. Zhang Ming, "Zhongguo xiang hechuqu?" [Whither China?], *Ershiyi shiji* [21st Century], March 3, 2012. Also see Xu Xiaoning and Xing Shaowen, "Zhongguo zhengzai zouxiang quangui shichang jingji" [China is moving toward an economy of crony capitalism], *Nanfangchuang* [South Window], August 31, 2010.

80. As Kan Kaili, a professor at Beijing University of Posts and Telecommunications, recently observed, China Mobile is notorious for charging fees for services that are usually free in other countries. For example, in 2005, China Mobile charged 49 billion yuan (US$5.9

billion) for roaming fees on cellular phone service, which accounted for half of the company's entire profits. Quoted in Wu Xiaobo, *Jidang sanshi nian: Zhongguo qiye 1978–2008* [Thirty Years of Chinese Business, 1978–2008], vol. 2. (Beijing: Zhongxin chubanshe, 2008), 309.

81. See Fortune Global 500 official website, http://fortune.com/global500/.

82. *Shijie ribao* [World Journal], April 20, 2012, A4.

83. For a comprehensive collection of those official documents, see *Shibada yilai lianzheng xin guiding* [Regulations on governance since the 18th National Congress of the CCP] (Beijing: Renmin chubanshe, 2015).

84. Minxin Pei, "China's Leaders Must Embrace Democracy," *Financial Times*, November 15, 2012 (http://www.ft.com/intl/cms/s/0/5d992eea-2e6f-11e2-8f7a-00144feabdc0 .html).

85. Ibid.

86. Jing Yuejin, "China's Interest Coordination Mechanism," in Kenneth Lieberthal, Cheng Li, and Yu Keping, eds., *China's Political Development: Chinese and American Perspectives* (Brookings, 2014), 308–28.

87. *Shijie ribao*, October 15, 2010, A3.

88. *Shijie ribao*, May 3 2012, A4.

89. Jing, "China's Interest Coordination Mechanism."

90. Robert Dahl, *Who Governs? Democracy and Power in an American City* (New Haven, Conn.: Yale University Press, 1961), 68.

91. Ibid., 252, 270.

92. Yao Yang, "The End of the Beijing Consensus: Can China's Model of Authoritarian Growth Survive?," *Foreign Affairs*, February 2, 2010.

93. For a comprehensive discussion of the Chinese middle class, see Cheng Li, ed., *China's Emerging Middle Class: Beyond Economic Transformation* (Brookings, 2010).

94. For the birth and the prototype stage of the emerging middle class in coastal China in the early 1990s, see Cheng Li, *Rediscovering China: Dynamics and Dilemmas of Reform* (Lanham, Md.: Rowman & Littlefield, 1997).

95. For the scholarly debate about the existence of the Chinese middle class, especially reservations about the concept of the middle class in the PRC, see David S. G. Goodman, ed., *The New Rich in China: Future Rulers, Present Lives* (New York: Routledge, 2008).

96. Lu Xueyi, *Dangdai Zhongguo shehui jiegou* [Social structure of contemporary China] (Beijing: Shehui kexuewenxian chubanshe, 2010), 402–06.

97. Xi Jinping, "Zhongguo you 3 yi zhongdeng shouruzhe" [China has 300 million middle-income earners], Xinhua Finance News Net, September 23, 2015 (http://www.xhcj .net/zgsy/65602.html).

98. "China's New Leadership Confronts Many Challenges: Voices of the Middle Class," *Global Times*, March 13, 2013 (http://news.qq.com/a/20130313/000254.htm).

99. Fenghuang wang [Phoenix Net], November 27, 2011 (http://edu.ifeng.com/official /news/detail_2011_11/27/10932051_0.shtml).

100. Chen Zhiwu, "Zhongguo daole fei minzhu buke de shihou" [It is the time for China to make the transition to democracy], Duowei Net, January 2, 2012 (http://china.dwnews .com/news/2012-01-02/58470187.html).

101. Shen Changchang, "Zhongguo shouji yonghu shuliang jiejin 13 yi ren" [The total number of cell phones in China is reaching 1.3 billion], Renmin Net, June 25, 2014 (http:// mobile.people.com.cn/n/2014/0625/c183175-25195976.html).

102. Gao Kang, "Zhongguo wangmin shuliang yida 6.68 yi ren" [China's netizens reach 668 million], Xinhua, July 23, 2015 (http://news.xinhuanet.com/fortune/2015-07/23 /c_1116022351.htm).

103. "On Revolution" was one of the three articles in Han Han's series, which he wrote on the eve of 2012; the other two were "On Democracy" and "On Freedom" (http://blog .sina.com.cn/s/article_archive_1191258123_201112_1.html). For more discussion, see Eric Abrahamsen, "Han Han's U-Turn?," *International Herald Tribune*, January 26, 2012 (http://latitude.blogs.nytimes.com/2012/01/26/blogger-han-han-controversy-on-democracy -in-china).

104. Lynn White, *Unstately Power*, vol. 1 (Armonk, N.Y.: M. E. Sharpe, 1999), chapter 1.

105. Nailene Chou Wiest, "Tocqueville in China," Caixin Online, September 14, 2012 (http://english.caixin.com/2012-09-14/100438129.html).

106. Cong Riyun, "Xiandai fazhishehui de lixiangmoshi jiqi shixiancixu" [The ideal model and its implementation sequences in modern law-governing society], Consensus Net, August 15, 2015 (http://www.21ccom.net/articles/thought/zhongxi/20150812127839_all .html).

107. Ibid.

108. Francis Fukuyama and Yu Ying, "Zhongguoshi minzhu yaocong fazhi kaishi" [Chinese-style democracy should begin with the rule of law], Fenghuang wang [Phoenix Net], November 24, 2015 (http://news.ifeng.com/opinion/gaojian/special/fszgsmzycfzks/).

109. Ibid.

110. *Zhonggong zhongyang guanyu quanmian tuijin yifazhiguo ruogan zhongda wenti de jueding* [Resolution of the Central Committee of the CCP to fully promote the rule of law] (Beijing: Renmin chubanshe, 2014), 6–7.

111. Ding Feng, "Xi Jinping yanzhong de 'fazhi Zhongguo'" [Xi Jinping's vision of a "legal China"], Xinhua, October 22, 2014 (http://news.xinhuanet.com/politics/2014-10/22 /c_1112936158.htm).

112. Ibid.

113. Chen Feng, "Xi Jinping shen xianfa quanwei weixianbijiu zhidu dai luoshi," [Xi Jinping asserts the authority of the PRC Constitution], Duowei Net, December 6, 2012 (http://china.dwnews.com/big5/news/2012-12-06/59005870-all.html).

114. Ding, "Xi Jinping yanzhong de 'fazhi Zhongguo'" [Xi Jinping's vision of a "legal China"].

115. Ibid.

116. Ibid.

117. Cai Dingjian's main publications include *Xianzheng jiangtan* [Constitutional forum] (Beijing: Law Press, 2010).

118. For example, see Guo Guangdong, "Weishenme zheme duo ren jinian Cai Dingjian?" [Why do so many people commemorate Cai Dingjian?], Nanfang zhoumo [Southern Weekend], November 26, 2010. Also see www.infzm.com/content/52858.

119. For Yu Keping's work, see, for example, *Democracy Is a Good Thing: Essays on Politics, Society, and Culture in Contemporary China* (Brookings, 2009).

120. Yu Keping, *Yifa zhiguo yu yifa zhidang* [Governing the country and the party by law] (Beijing: Zhongyang bianyi chubanshe, 2007), 6.

121. Ibid.

122. Yu Keping, "Guojia dixian: Gongpingzhengyi yu yifazhiguo" [China's bottom line: justice and the rule of law]. *Xuexi shibao* [Study Times], October 20, 2014 (http://www.cctb .net/zjxz/expertarticle1/201410/t20141021_313624.htm).

123. Ibid.

124. Wu Bangguo's famous "five 'no's" refers to no multiple party system, no pluralism in ideology, no checks and balances nor a bicameral parliament, no federal system, and no privatization. He made this statement at the Fourth Plenary Session of the Eleventh NPC, held in Beijing on March 11, 2011. See Zhongguo xinwenwang [China Newsnet], March 11, 2011 (www.china.com.cn/ 2011/2011-03/11/content_22114099.htm).

125. He Weifang, *In the Name of Justice: Striving for the Rule of Law in China* (Brookings, 2012).

126. Li, "Introduction: Fighting for a Constitutional China," in He, *In the Name of Justice*, xviii–xix. Also see Xu Xin, "Zhongguo sifa gaige de dingcengsheji jiqi tuijin celüe" [Top-level design and judicial reform strategy in judicial reforms], Consensus Net, December 26, 2014 (http://www.21ccom.net/articles/china/ggcx/20141226118136_all.html).

127. For a more detailed discussion of the Sun Zhigang case, see Yu Xiang, "Sun Zhigang's Death and Reform of the Detention System," *China Society for Human Rights Studies*, June 27, 2012 (www.humanrights.cn/zt/magazine/20040200482694708.htm).

128. *Shichang daobao* [Market Herald], October 21, 2014 (http://www.zjscdb.com/detail .php?newsid=130077).

GLOSSARY

PROLOGUE

"black box manipulation" (暗箱操作, *anxiang caozuo*)
collective leadership (集体领导, *jiti lingdao*).
"singing red songs and striking at the black triads" (唱红打黑, *changhong dahei*).
"remnants of the Cultural Revolution" (文革余孽, *wenge yunie*)

CHAPTER 1

vice-ministerial- and provincial-level leaders (副省部级, *fushengbuji*)
"proactive" foreign policy approach (奋发有为, *fenfa youwei*)
"inaction" (无为, *wuwei*)
the military reform (军改, *jungai*)
dominance of the army (大陆军, *dalujun*)
rule by the PSC (常委制, *changweizhi*)
head-of-state system (元首制, *yuanshouzhi*)
the interior third front (三线建设, *sanxian jianshe*)
political strongman (政治强人, *zhengzhi qiangren*)
monopolized powerful positions (集权, *jiquan*)
authority and power (威权, *weiquan*).
"ruling from behind a screen" (垂帘听政, *chuilian tingzheng*)
CCYL factional leaders (团派, *tuanpai*)
the Jiang-Xi camp (江习阵营, *jiangxi zhenying*).
the Shanghai Gang (上海帮, *shanghaibang*)
princelings (太子党, *taizidang*)
the Hu-Li camp (胡李阵营, *huli zhenying*)
the "one party, two coalitions" mechanism (一党两派, *yidang liangpai*)

the "iron triangle" (铁三角, *tiesanjiao*)
top-ranked leader (第一把手, *diyibashou*)
second-ranked leader (第二把手, *di'erbashou*)
factional rotation (派系轮换, *paixi lunhuan*)
Southern Tour (南巡, *nanxun*)
the "Three Represents" (三个代表, *sange daibiao*)
"purchase office" (买官, *maiguan*)
presidential system (总统制, *zongtongzhi*)
personal assistant (秘书, *mishu*)
the "Shaanxi Gang" (陕西帮, *shaanxibang*)

CHAPTER 2

civil servants (公务员, *gongwuyuan*)
grassroots units (基层组织, *jiceng zuzhi*)
plenums (全会, *quanhui*)
inspection tour teams (巡视组, *xunshizu*)
discipline inspection teams (纪检组, *jijianzu*)
shared offices and operations (合署办公, *heshu bangong*)
to file a report of official wrongdoing (举报, *jubao*)
"list of official posts" (干部职务名称表, *ganbu zhiwu mingchengbiao*)
official posts at the department level and bureau level (厅局级, *tingjuji*)
official posts at prefecture level (地级, *diji*)
a list of names be put on record (备案, *bei'an*)
reserve cadres (后备干部 *houbei ganbu*)
official posts at the county and division level (县处级, *xianchuji*)
the united front (统一战线, *tongyi zhanxian*)
"leading groups" (领导小组, *lingdao xiaozu*)
"coordination groups" (协调小组, *xietiao xiaozu*)
"dual imperatives" (双重压力, *shuangchong yali*)
department parochialism (部门本位主义, *bumen benweizhuyi*)
lowest level of formal urban administration, the "district" (街道, *jiedao*)
"two annual meetings" (两会, *lianghui*)
the "democratic parties" (民主党派, *minzhu dangpai*)
constituencies (界别, *jiebie*)
the State Council executive meeting (国务院常务会议, *guowuyuan changwu huiyi*)
the State Council plenary meeting (国务院全体会议, *guowuyuan quanti huiyi*)
SASAC companies (央企, *yangqi*)
central financial firms (金融央企, *jinrong yangqi*)
"the premier cannot control a general manager" (总理管不了总经理, *zongli guanbuliao zongjingli*)

CHAPTER 3

capitalist roaders (走资派, *zouzipai*)
the Gang of Four (四人帮, *sirenbang*)
the "generals of the Yang family" (杨家将, *yangjiajiang*)
the cadre tenure system (干部任期制, *ganbu renqizhi*)
the term limit system (限任制, *xianrenzhi*)
"more candidates than seats" election (差额选举, *cha'e xuanju*)
intraparty democracy (党内民主, *dangnei minzhu*)

secret ballot system (票决制, *piaojuezhi*)
officials at the rank of deputy section level (副科级, *fukeji*)
to pursue business activities (下海, *xiahai*)
subprovincial cities (*fushengjishi*, 副省级市)
open recruitment examination (公开招考, *gongkai zhaokao*)

CHAPTER 4

"to study to become an official" (学而优则士, *xueeryou zeshi*).
"red versus expert" (红与专, *hongyuzhuan*)
junior college (大专, *dazhuan*)
the worker-peasant-soldier student (工农兵学员, *gongnongbing xueyuan*)
sent-down youth (插队知青, *chadui zhiqing*)
student union (学生会, *xueshenghui*)
the Executive Committee of the Student Assembly (常代会, *changdaihui*)
"one school and five academies" (一校五院, *yixiao wuyuan*)
"become gilded" (镀金, *dujin*)
the level of director-rank clerks (主任科员, *zhuren keyuan*)
foreign-educated returnees, "sea turtles" (海归, *haigui*)
foreign-educated returnee (留学回国人员, *liuxue huiguo renyuan*)
self-funded (自费, *zifei*)
scientific decisionmaking (科学决策, *kexue juece*)
think tanks (智库, *zhiku* or 思想库, *sixiangku*)
reports on the state of China (国情报告, *guoqing baogao*)
the "revolving door" (旋转门, *xuanzhuanmen*)
China-educated elites, "land turtles" (土鳖, *tubie*)

CHAPTER 5

the new social strata (新社会阶层, *xin shehui jieceng*)
business circles (商业圈子, *shangye quanzi*)
Positive Sum Island (正和岛, *zhenghedao*)
Taishan Club (泰山会, *taishanhui*)
"businesspeople should be primarily concerned about business" (在商言商, *zaishang yanshang*)
political connections (关系, *guanxi*)
competency (能力本位, *nengli benwei*)
officialdom (官本位, *guan benwei*)
"the cosmos club" (宇宙帮, *yuzhoubang*)
politics and law (政法, *zhengfa*)
law/legal studies (法学, *faxue*)
"using law to rule the country" (以法制国, *yifa zhiguo*)
"governing the country according to the law" (依法治国, *yifa zhiguo*)

CHAPTER 6

organizational (机关, *jiguan*)
personal (个人, *geren*)
chief of staff or secretary-general (秘书长, *mishuzhang*)
office director (办公室主任, *bangongshi zhuren*)
bodyguard (贴身警卫, *tieshen jingwei*)

civilian secretaries (文职秘书, *wenzhi mishu*)
aides with high official status (助理, *zhuli*)
office clerk (办事员, *banshiyuan*)
clerk (干事, *ganshi*)
highest-ranking party and state leaders (党和国家领导人, *dang he guojia lingdaoren*)
personal secretaries (贴身秘书, *tieshen mishu*)
chief aide (大秘, *dami*)
administrative ranks (行政级别, *xingzheng jibie*)
mishu bureau (秘书局, *mishuju*)
separatist tendencies (山头主义, *shantou zhuyi*)
"No. 2 chief" (二号首长, *erhao shouzhang*).
absolute loyalty (绝对忠诚, *juedui zhongcheng*)
chief (首长, *shouzhang*)
"brain trust" (文胆, *wendan*)
"New Thoughts in Zhejiang" (之江新语, *zhijiang xinyu*)
Peking University prodigy (北大神童, *beida shentong*)

CHAPTER 7

petroleum faction (石油帮, *shiyoubang*)
Shanxi faction (山西帮, *shanxibang*)
the prevalence of "various factions" (团团伙伙, *tuantuanhuohuo*)
Henan faction (河南帮, *henanbang*)
"elitist coalition" (精英同盟, *jingying tongmeng*)
"populist coalition" (民粹同盟, *mincui tongmeng*)
"On Cliques" (朋党论, *pengdanglun*)
offspring of the "Eight Banners" (八旗子弟, *baqi zidi*)
"Han Barrack" (汉军营, *hanjunying*)
"four big families" (四大家族, *sidajiazu*)
outsider (异己, *yiji*)
"family of generals" (将军之家, *jiangjun zhijia*)
the "Red 2G" (红二代, *hong'erdai*)
the "Official 2G" (官二代, *guan'erdai*)
the "Red 3G" (红三代, *hongsandai*)
"Red 2G Corps" or "Red II Corps" (红二代军团, *hong'erdai juntuan*)
"red plutocrat" (赤豪, *chihao*)
"red gene" (红色基因, *hongse jiyin*)
selective antigraft (选择性反腐, *xuanzexing fanfu*)
"common people" (平民, *pingmin*)
immunity for princelings (刑不上太子党, *xingbushang taizidang*)
"seizing the full power of the 'Red 2G'" (红二代的全面掌权, *hong'erdai de quanmian zhangquan*)
reserve army (后备军, *houbeijun*)
full department head (正厅级, *zhengtingji*)

CHAPTER 8

family origin (籍贯, *jiguan*)
affection for Shaanxi (陕西情结, *shaanxi qingjie*)
the "yellow earth attachment" (黄土地情结, *huangtudi qingjie*)
Yan'an native (延安人, *yan'anren*)

"root and base" (根, *gen*)

"soul and spirit" (魂, *hun*)

"the four gentlemen of the reform proposal" (改革四君子, *gaige sijunzi*)

"chief of the fire brigade" (救火队长, *jiuhuo duizhang*)

the Bayi School (八一学校, *bayi xuexiao*)

military residential "big yards" (军队大院, *jundui dayuan*)

"cadre compounds" (干部大院, *ganbu dayuan*)

the "theory of bloodline" (血统论, *xuetonglun*)

the Chinese Economists 50 Forum (中国经济 50 人论坛, *Zhongguo jingji wushiren luntan*)

populist (民粹主义, *mincui zhuyi*)

the General's Manor House (将军府, *jiangjunfu*)

forefathers (祖, *zu*)

greatness and unity (大一统, *dayitong*)

"Socialist New Democracy" (新民主主义, *xinminzhu zhuyi*)

"noble character and unquestionable integrity" (高风亮节, *gaofeng liangjie*)

second home (第二故乡, *di'er guxiang*)

"royal army" (近卫军, *jinweijun*)

"facile writer" (笔杆子, *biganzi*)

"imperial reporter" (御用记者, *yuyong jizhe*)

"appoint people based on their merits without omitting relatives or friends" (举贤不避亲, *juxian bubiqin*)

CHAPTER 9

confidence in China's political system (制度自信, *zhidu zixin*)

"new type of major power relations" (新型大国关系, *xinxing daguo guanxi*)

the "grandpa-designated successor" (隔代指定接班人, *gedai zhiding jiebanren*)

the "falling-off-a-cliff demotion" (悬崖式降职, *xuanyashi jiangzhi*),

the "front-line leadership body" (第一线, *diyixian*)

"selecting and nurturing younger successors" (培养接班人, *peiyang jiebanren*)

the "top leader often realizes that the candidate pool is too small to choose from when one needs to do so" (人到用时方恨少, *rendao yongshi fanghenshao*).

the "Fan Club of Xi Studies" (学习小组, *xue Xi xiaozu*)

"Papa Xi" (习大大, *Xi dada*)

the "core" (核心, *hexin*)

immeasurable loyalty (无比忠诚, *wubi zhongcheng*)

absolute support (坚决支持, *jianjue zhichi*)

the "return of ideology" (意识形态的回归, *yishi xingtai de huigui*)

"arbitrary rule of the top-ranked leader" (一把手专断, *yibashou zhuanduan*)

struggle over choosing the right path (路线斗争, *luxian douzheng*)

"come from behind" (后来居上, *houlai jushang*)

"team of rivals" concept (政敌团队, *zhengdi tuandui*)

institutionalization of factional politics (派系政治制度化, *paixi zhengzhi zhiduhua*)

"the victor becomes a king and the loser a bandit" (胜者为王, 败者为寇, *shengzhe weiwang, baizhe weikou*)

internal pluralism (内部多元主义, *neibu duoyuan zhuyi*)

"being transferred to the second-line work" (退居二线, *tuiju erxian*)

local governments' liaison offices in Beijing (驻京办, *zhujingban*)

the "black collar" stratum (黑领阶层, *heling jieceng*)

the "black society" (黑社会, *heishehui*)

"statist crony-capitalism" (权贵资本主义, *quangui zibenzhuyi*)

vulnerable social groups (弱势群体, *ruoshi qunti*)

to maintain social stability (维稳, *weiwen*)

"the state advances and private companies retreat" (国进民退, *guojin mintui*)

systematically promote rule of law in the country (全面推进依法治国, *quanmian tuijin yifa zhiguo*)

"rule in accordance with the Constitution" (依宪治国, *yixian zhiguo*)

"paper filled with hollow words" (一纸空文, *yizhi kongwen*)

New Citizen Movement (新公民运动, *xin gongmin yundong*)

BIBLIOGRAPHY

ENGLISH

Abuza, Zachary. "The Lessons of Le Kha Phieu: Changing Rules in Vietnamese Politics." *Contemporary Southeast Asia*, vol. 24, no. 1 (April 2002): 121–45.

Alford, William P., Kenneth Winston, and William C. Kirby, eds. *Prospects for the Professions in China*. New York: Routledge, 2011.

Antholis, William. *Inside Out India and China: Local Politics Go Global*. Brookings, 2014.

Bachrach, Peter. *The Theory of Democratic Elitism: A Critique*. Washington: University Press of America, 1980.

Bader, Jeffery A. *How Xi Jinping Sees the World . . . and Why*. [A Series in Order from Chaos: Foreign Policy in a Troubled World. Brookings Foreign Policy Asia Working Group Paper 2]. February 2016.

Baerwald, Hans. *Party Politics in Japan*. Boston: Allen and Unwin, 1986.

Baum, Richard. *Burying Mao: Chinese Politics in the Age of Deng Xiaoping*. Princeton University Press, 1994.

Baylis, Thomas A. *Governing by Committee: Collegial Leadership in Advanced Societies*. State University of New York Press, 1989.

Bell, Daniel A. *The China Model: Political Meritocracy and the Limits of Democracy*. Princeton University Press, 2015.

Belloni, Frank P. and Dennis C. Beller, eds. *Faction Politics: Political Parties and Factionalism in Comparative Perspective*. Santa Barbara, Calif.: ABC-Clio, 1978.

Bialer, Seweryn. *Stalin's Successors: Leadership, Stability, and Change in the Soviet Union*. Cambridge University Press, 1980.

Blackwill, Robert D. and Kurt M. Campbell. *Xi Jinping on the Global Stage: Chinese Foreign Policy under a Powerful but Exposed Leader*. [Council on Foreign Relations Special Report, No. 74, February 2016].

Bo, Zhiyue. "The 16th Central Committee of the Chinese Communist Party: Formal Institutions and Factional Groups." *Journal of Contemporary China* 13 (May 2004): 223–56.

———. *Chinese Provincial Leaders: Economic Performance and Political Mobility, 1949–1998.* Armonk, N.Y.: M. E. Sharpe, 2002.

Bosco, Joseph. "Taiwan Factions: Guanxi, Patronage, and the State in Local Politics." In *The Other Taiwan, 1945 to the Present,* edited by Murray A. Rubinstein, pp. 114–44. Armonk, N.Y.: M. E. Sharpe, 1994.

Boucek, Francoise. "Rethinking Factionalism: Typologies, Intra-Party Dynamics, and Three Faces of Factionalism." *Party Politics* 15, no. 4 (July 2009): 455–85.

Brodsgaard, Kjeld Erik and Yongnian Zheng, eds. *The Chinese Communist Party in Reform.* New York: Routledge, 2006.

Brown, Kerry. *Friends and Enemies: The Past, Present, and Future of the Communist Party of China.* New York: Anthem Press, 2009.

Bullard, Monte Ray. "People's Republic of China Elite Studies: A Review of the Literature." *Asian Survey* 19, no. 8 (August 1979): 789–800.

Burns, John P. "China's Nomenklatura System." *Problems of Communism* 36, no. 5 (September/October 1987): 36–51.

———. "Strengthening Central CCP Control of Leadership Selection: The 1990 Nomenklatura." *China Quarterly* 138 (June 1994): 458–91.

Carlson, Allen, Mary E. Gallagher, Kenneth Lieberthal, and Melanie Manion, eds. *Contemporary Chinese Politics: New Sources, Methods, and Field Strategies.* Cambridge University Press, 2010.

Chang, Parris. "From Mao to Hua to Hu to Zhao: Changes in the CCP Leadership and its Rules of the Games." *Issues and Studies* 25, no. 1 (January 1989): 56–72.

Chen, Jie and Bruce J. Dickson. *Allies of the State: China's Private Entrepreneurs and Democratic Change.* Harvard University Press, 2010.

Chen, Jie and Chunlong Lu. "Does China's Middle Class Think and Act Democratically? Attitudinal and Behavioral Orientations toward Urban Self-Government." *Journal of Chinese Political Science* 11, no. 2 (2006): 1–20.

Chen, Jie and Yang Zhong. "Valuation of Individual Liberty versus Social Order among Democratic Supporters: A Cross-Validation." *Political Research Quarterly* 53 (2000): 427–39.

Cho, Young Nam. "Elite Politics and the 17th Party Congress in China: Changing Norms amid Continuing Questions." *Korean Journal of Defense Analysis,* vol. 20, no. 2 (June 2008): 155–68.

Chu, Yun-han. "A Born-Again Dominant Party? The Transformation of the Kuomintang and Taiwan's Regime Transition." In *The Awkward Embrace: One-Party Domination and Democracy,* edited by Hermann Giliomee and Charles Simkins, pp. 61–95. Amsterdam: Harwood Academic Publishers, 1999.

———. "The Legacy of One-Party Hegemony in Taiwan." In *Political Parties and Democracy,* edited by Larry Diamond and Richard Gunther, pp. 266–98. Johns Hopkins University Press, 2001.

Curtis, Gerald L. *The Logic of Japanese Politics: Leaders, Institutions, and the Limits of Change.* Columbia University Press, 1999.

Dahl, Robert. *Democracy and its Critics.* Yale University Press, 1989.

———. *Who Governs? Democracy and Power in an American City.* Yale University Press, 1961.

Dickson, Bruce J. *Red Capitalists in China: The Party, Private Entrepreneurs, and Prospects for Political Change.* Cambridge University Press, 2003.

———. *Wealth into Power: The Communist Party's Embrace of China's Private Sector.* Cambridge University Press, 2008.

Diamond, Larry and Richard Gunther, eds. *Political Parties and Democracy.* Johns Hopkins University Press, 2001.

Dittmer, Lowell. "Patterns of Elite Strife and Succession in Chinese Politics." *China Quarterly* 123 (September 1990): 405–30.

Dittmer, Lowell, and Yu-Shan Wu. "The Modernization of Factionalism in Chinese Politics." *World Politics* 47, no. 4 (July 1995): 467–94.

Djilas, Milovan. *The Unperfect Society: Beyond the New Class.* London: Unwin Books, 1957.

———. *The New Class: An Analysis of the Communist System.* New York: Frederick A. Praeger, 1972.

Dreyer, June Teufel. *China's Political System: Modernization and Tradition,* 5th ed. New York: Pearson Longman, 2006.

———. "The New Officer Corps: Implications for the Future." *China Quarterly* 146 (June 1996): 315–35.

Englehart, Neil A. "Democracy and the Thai Middle Class." *Asian Survey* 43 (2003): 253–79.

Falkenheim, Victor. "Bureaucracy, Factions, and Political Change in China." *Pacific Affairs* 57, no. 3 (Fall 1984): 471–79.

Fewsmith, Joseph. *Elite Politics in Contemporary China.* Armonk, N.Y.: M. E. Sharpe, 2000.

———. *The Logic and Limits of Political Reform in China.* Cambridge University Press, 2013.

Friedman, Edward and Joseph Wong, eds. *Political Transitions in Dominant Party Systems: Learning to Lose.* London: Routledge, 2008.

Fukuyama, Francis. *Political Order and Political Decay: From the Industrial Revolution to the Globalization of Democracy.* New York: Farrar, Straus and Giroux, 2014.

Gillespie, Richard, Michael Waller, and Lourdes Lopez Nieto, eds. *Factional Politics and Democratization.* London: Frank Cass and Co., 1995.

Gilley, Bruce and Larry Diamond, eds. *Political Change in China with Comparisons with Taiwan.* Boulder, Colo.: Lynne Rienner, 2008.

Goldstein, Avery. "Trends in the Study of Political Elites and Institutions in the PRC." *China Quarterly* 139 (September 1994): 714–30.

Gonzalez, Francisco E. "The Demise of Mexico's One-Party Dominance in Comparative Perspective." *International Studies Review* 9, no. 2 (2007): 357–67.

Greene, Kenneth F. *Why Dominant Parties Lose: Mexico's Democratization in Comparative Perspective.* Cambridge University Press, 2007.

Gunther, Richard, José Ramón Montéro, and Juan J. Linz, eds. *Political Parties: Old Concepts and New Challenges.* Oxford University Press, 2002.

Harding, Harry. *China's Second Revolution: Reform After Mao.* Brookings, 1987.

He, Huaihong. *Moral Decay or Ethical Awakening? Social Ethics in a Changing China.* Brookings, 2015.

He, Weifang. *In the Name of Justice: Striving for the Rule of Law in China.* Brookings, 2012.

Hsiao, Hsin-Huang Michael, ed. *Exploration of the Middle Classes in Southeast Asia.* Taipei: Academia Sinica, 2001.

———, ed. *The Changing Faces of the Middle Classes in Asia-Pacific.* Taipei: Academia Sinica, 2006.

Hsiung, James C., Liu Hong, Chen Ying, Zhou Xingwang, and Tan Huoshen. *The Xi Jinping Era: His Comprehensive Strategy Toward the China Dream.* New York: Beijng Media Time Books, 2015.

Ho, Pin and Wenquang Huang. *A Death in the Lucky Holiday Hotel: Murder, Money, and an Epic Power Struggle in China.* New York: Public Affairs, 2013.

Ho, Ping-ti. *The Ladder of Success in Imperial China: Aspects of Social Mobility, 1368–1911.* Columbia University Press, 1962.

———. "Aspects of Social Mobility in China, 1368–1911." *Comparative Studies in Society and History* 1, no. 4 (June 1959): 330–59.

Howell, Jude, ed. *Governance in China.* Lanham, Md.: Rowman and Littlefield, 2004.

Hu, Angang. *China in 2020: A New Type of Superpower.* Brookings, 2011.

——. *China's Collective Presidency.* London: Springer, 2014.

——. *The Modernization of China's State Governance.* Beijing: Institute of Contemporay China Studies, Tsinghua University, 2014.

Hu, Shaohua. *Explaining Chinese Democratization.* London: Praeger, 2000.

Huang, Jing. *Factionalism in Chinese Communist Politics.* Cambridge University Press, 2000.

Huang, Yasheng. *Capitalism with Chinese Characteristics: Entrepreneurship and the State.* Cambridge University Press, 2008.

Huntington, Samuel. *Political Order in Changing Societies.* Yale University Press, 1968.

——. *The Third Wave: Democratization in the Late Twentieth Century.* University of Oklahoma Press, 1993.

Joignant, Alfredo. "The Politics of Technopols: Resources, Political Competence and Collective Leadership in Chile, 1990–2010." *Journal of Latin American Studies,* vol. 42, no. 3 (August 2011): 517–46.

Joseph, William A, ed. *Politics in China,* 2d ed. Oxford University Press, 2014.

Kennedy, Scott. *The Business of Lobbying in China.* Harvard University Press, 2005.

Kuhn, Robert Lawrence. *How China's Leaders Think.* New York: John Wiley and Sons, 2010.

Lam, Willy Wo-Lap. *Chinese Politics in the Era of Xi Jinping: Renaissance, Reform, or Retrogression?* New York: Routledge, 2015.

Lampton, David M. *Following the Leader: Ruling China, from Deng Xiaoping to Xi Jinping.* University of California Press, 2014.

——. *Paths to Power: Elite Mobility in Contemporary China.* Ann Arbor, Mich.: Center for Chinese Studies, University of Michigan, 1986.

Lee, Hong Yung. *From Revolutionary Cadres to Party Technocrats: The Changing Cadre System in Socialist China.* University of California Press, 1991.

Lee, Khoon Choy. *Japan between Myth and Reality.* Singapore: World Scientific Publishing, 1995.

Lewis, John Wilson. *Leadership in Communist China.* Cornell University Press, 1963.

Li, Cheng, ed. *China's Changing Political Landscape: Prospects for Democracy.* Brookings, 2008.

——. "China's Communist Party-State: The Structure and Dynamics of Power." In *Politics in China,* edited by William A. Joseph, 165–91. Oxford University Press, 2010.

——, ed. *China's Emerging Middle Class: Beyond Economic Transformation.* Brookings, 2010.

——. "China's Fifth Generation: Is Diversity a Source of Strength or Weakness?"*Asia Policy,* no. 6 (July 2008): 53–93.

——. *China's Leaders: The New Generation.* Lanham, Md.: Rowman and Littlefield, 2001.

——. "The End of the CCP's Resilient Authoritarianism? A Tripartite Assessment of Shifting Power in China." *China Quarterly,* no. 211 (September 2012): 595–623.

——. "Introduction: Fighting for a Constitutional China: Public Enlightenment and Legal Professionalism." In *In the Name of Justice: Striving for the Rule of Law in China,* edited by He Weifang, xvii–xlix. Brookings, 2012.

——. "Introduction: Making Democracy Safe for China." In *Democracy Is a Good Thing: Essays on Politics, Society, and Culture in Contemporary China,* edited by Yu Keping, xvii–xxxi. Brookings, 2009.

——. "Leadership Transition in the CCP: Promising Progress and Potential Problems." *China: An International Journal* 10, no. 2 (August 2012): 23–33.

——. "The New Bipartisanship within the Chinese Communist Party." *Orbis* 49, no. 3 (Summer 2005): 387–400.

——. "The 'New Deal:' Politics and Policies of the Hu Administration." *Journal of Asian-and African Studies* 38, nos. 4–5 (December 2003): 329–46.

———. *The Political Mapping of China's Tobacco Industry and Anti-Smoking Campaign.* John L. Thornton China Center Monograph Series. Brookings, 2012.

Li, Nan. "Organizational Changes of the PLA, 1985–1997." *China Quarterly* 158 (June 1999): 314–49.

Li, Wei. "The Role of the Mishu (Staff) Institution in Chinese Politics." Ph.D. diss., Massachusetts Institute of Technology, 1994.

Li, Wei, and Lucian Pye. "The Ubiquitous Role of the *Mishu* in Chinese Politics." *China Quarterly* 132 (December 1992): 913–36.

Lieberthal, Kenneth. *Governing China: From Revolution to Reform*, 2d ed. New York: W. W. Norton & Company, 2003.

Lieberthal, Kenneth, and David M. Lampton, eds. *Bureaucracy, Politics, and Decision Making in Post-Mao China.* University of California Press, 1992.

Lieberthal, Kenneth, Cheng Li, and Yu Keping, eds. *China's Political Development: Chinese and American Perspectives.* Brookings, 2014.

Lieberthal, Kenneth, and Michel Oksenberg. *Policy Making in China: Leaders, Structures, and Process.* Princeton University Press, 1988.

Lijphart, Arend. *Patterns of Democracy: Government Forms and Performance in Thirty-Six Countries.* Yale University Press, 1999.

Lipset, Seymour Martin. *Political Man: The Social Bases of Politics.* Garden City, N.J.: Anchor Books, 1963.

Lu, Ning. *The Dynamics of Foreign-Policy Decision Making in China*, 2d ed. Boulder, Colo.: Westview Press, 2000.

Lü, Xiaobo. *Cadres and Corruption: The Organizational Involution of the Chinese Communist Party.* Stanford University Press, 2000.

MacFarquhar, Roderick. *The Politics of China: The Eras of Mao and Deng.* Cambridge University Press, 1997.

———, ed. *The Politics of China: Sixty Years of The People's Republic of China*, 3d ed. Cambridge University Press, 2011.

MacFarquhar, Roderick, and Michael Schoenhals. *Mao's Last Revolution.* Harvard University Press, 2008.

Manion, Melanie. *Retirement of Revolutionaries in China: Public Policies, Social Norms, Private Interests.* Princeton University Press, 1993.

McGregor, Richard. *The Party: The Secret World of China's Communist Rulers.* New York: Harper, 2010.

Meisner, Maurice. *Mao's China and After: A History of the People's Republic*, 3d ed. New York: Free Press, 1999.

Michels, Robert. *Political Parties: A Sociological Study of the Oligarchical Tendencies of Modern Democracies.* New York: Free Press, 1962.

Miller, Alice. "China's New Party Leadership." *China Leadership Monitor,* no. 23 (January 2008).

———. "Institutionalization and the Changing Dynamics of Chinese Leadership Politics." In *China's Changing Political Landscape: Prospects for Democracy*, edited by Cheng Li, 61–79. Brookings, 2008.

———. "Leadership Sustains Public Unity amid Stress." *China Leadership Monitor,* no. 29 (August 2009).

Moody, Peter R., Jr. "Political Culture and the Study of Chinese Politics." *Journal of Chinese Political Science* 14 (2009): 253–74.

Moore, Barrington, Jr. *The Social Origins of Dictatorship and Democracy: Lord and Peasant in the Making of the Modern World.* Boston: Beacon Press, 1966.

Mosca, Gaetano. *The Ruling Class.* New York: McGraw-Hill, 1936.

Nathan, Andrew J. "Authoritarian Resilience." *Journal of Democracy* 14, no. 1 (2003): 6–17.

———. "A Factionalism Model for CCP Politics." *China Quarterly* 53 (January/March 1973): 34–66.

———. "The Puzzle of the Chinese Middle Class." *Journal of Democracy* 27, no. 2 (April 2016): 5–19.

Nathan, Andrew J., Larry Diamond, and Marc F. Plattner, eds. *Will China Democratize?* Johns Hopkins University Press, 2013.

Nathan, Andrew J., and Kellee S. Tsai. "Factionalism: A New Institutionalist Restatement." *China Journal*, no. 34 (July 1995): 157–92.

Nicholas, Ralph W. "Segmentary Factional Political Systems." In *Political Anthropology*, edited by Swartz, Marc J., Victor W. Turner, and Arthur Tuden, pp. 49–59. Chicago: Aldine Publishing, 1966.

North, Robert and Ithiel Pool. *Kuomintang and Chinese Communist Elites*. Stanford University Press, 1952.

O'Donnell, Guillermo A. *Bureaucratic-Authoritarianism*. University of California Press, 1988.

———. *Modernization and Bureaucratic-Authoritarianism: Studies in South American Politics*. University of California Press, 1973.

Osnos, Evan. *Age of Ambition: Chasing Fortune, Truth, and Faith in the New China*. New York: Farrar, Straus and Giroux, 2014.

———. "Born Red." *New Yorker*, April 6, 2015, pp. 42–55.

Panebianco, Angelo. *Political Parties: Organization and Power*. Cambridge University Press, 1988.

Pareto, Vilgredo. *The Rise and Fall of the Elites: An Application of Theoretical Sociology*. Totowa, N.J.: Bedminster, 1968.

Pearson, Margaret M. *China's New Business Elite: The Political Consequences of Economic Reform*. University of California Press, 1997.

Peerenboom, Randall. *China's Long March toward the Rule of Law*. Cambridge University Press, 2002.

Pei, Minxin. *China's Trapped Transition: The Limits of Developmental Autocracy*. Harvard University Press, 2008.

Pempel, T. J. *Uncommon Democracies: The One-Party Dominant Regimes*. Cornell University Press, 1990.

Pye, Lucian W. *China: An Introduction*. New York: HarperCollins Publishers, 1991.

———. *The Mandarin and the Cadre: China's Political Cultures*. Ann Arbor, Mich.: Center for Chinese Studies, University of Michigan, 1988.

Randall, Vicky and Lars Svasand. "Party Institutionalization and the New Democracies." In *Democracy and Political Change in the "Third World,"* edited by Jeff Haynes, pp. 75–96. New York: Routledge, 2001.

———. "Party Institutionalization in New Democracies." *Party Politics* 8, no. 1 (2002): 5–29.

Rigger, Shelley. *From Opposition to Power: Taiwan's Democratic Progressive Party*. Boulder, Colo.: Lynne Rienner Publishers, 2001.

Saich, Tony. *Governance and Politics of China*, 3d ed. Hampshire, U.K.: Palgrave Macmillan, 2011.

Saich, Tony, and Benjamin Yang, eds. *The Rise to Power of the Chinese Communist Party: Documents and Analysis*. Armonk, N.Y.: M. E. Sharpe, 1996.

Scalapino, Robert A. *Elites in the People's Republic of China*. University of Washington Press, 1972.

Schattschneider, E. E. *The Semisovereign People: A Realist's View of Democracy in America*. Hinsdale, Ill.: Dryden Press, 1960.

Schurmann, Franz. *Ideology and Organization in Communist China*, 2d ed. University of California Press, 1968.

Schumpeter, Joseph A. *Capitalism, Socialism, and Democracy*, 3d ed. New York: Harper, 1950.

Sferza, Serenella. "Party Organization and Party Performance: The Case of the French Socialist Party." In *Political Parties: Old Concepts and New Challenges*, edited by Richard Gunther, José Ramón Montéro, and Juan J. Linz, pp. 166–190. Oxford University Press, 2002.

Shambaugh, David. *China's Communist Party: Atrophy and Adaptation*. University of California Press, 2008.

———. *China's Future*. New York: Polity, 2016.

———. "Training China's Political Elite: The Party School System." *China Quarterly*, no. 196 (December 2008): 827–44.

Shaw, Victor N. "Mainland China's Political Development: Is the CCP's Version of Democracy Relevant?" *Issues and Studies*, vol. 32, no. 7 (July 1996): 59–82.

Shih, Victor C. *Factions and Finance in China: Elite Conflict and Inflation*. Cambridge University Press, 2009.

Shirk, Susan L. *China: Fragile Superpower: How China's Internal Politics Could Derail Its Peaceful Rise*. Oxford University Press, 2007.

Solinger, Dorothy. "Ending One-Party Dominance: Korea, Taiwan, Mexico." *Journal of Democracy* 12, no. 1 (2001): 30–42.

Taras, Roy. *Leadership Change in Communist States*. London: Routledge, 1989.

Teiwes, Frederick C. *Leadership, Legitimacy, and Conflict in China*. New York: Palgrave Macmillan, 1984.

Tsou, Tang. "Chinese Politics at the Top: Factionalism or Informal Politics? Balance-of-Power Politics or a Game to Win All?" *China Journal* 34 (July 1995): 95–156.

Tsai, Kellee. *Capitalism without Democracy: The Private Sector in Contemporary China*. Cornell University Press, 2007.

Tsai, Wen-Hsuan and Chien-Wen Kou, "The Party's Disciples: CCP Reserve Cadres and the Perpetuation of a Resilient Authoritarian Regime." *China Quarterly* 221 (March 2015): 1–20.

Tsang, Steve. "Why China's Xi Jinping Is Still Far From Chairman Mao Status." *Forbes*, February 16, 2015.

Vogel, Ezra F. *Deng Xiaoping and the Transformation of China*. Harvard University Press, 2011.

White, Lynn, Kate Zhou, and Shelley Rigger. *Democratization in China, Korea, and Southeast Asia? Local and National Perspectives*. New York: Routledge, 2014.

Wong, John and Hongyi Lai, eds. *China into the Hu-Wen Era: Policy Initiatives and Challenges*. Singapore: World Scientific, 2006.

Wuhs, Steven T. "The Legacies of Transition from One-Party Rule: Mexico in Comparative Perspective." *International Studies Review* 9, no. 2 (2007): 348–56.

Xi, Jinping. *The Chinese Dream of the Great Rejuvenation of the Chinese Nation*. Beijing: Foreign Language Press, 2014.

———, *The Governance of China*. Beijing: Foreign Language Press, 2014.

———, *How to Deepen Reform Comprehensively*. Beijing: Foreign Language Press, 2014.

Yang, Dali L. *Remaking the Chinese Leviathan: Market Transition and the Politics of Governance in China*. Stanford University Press, 2004.

Yu, Keping. *Democracy Is a Good Thing: Essays on Politics, Society, and Culture in Contemporary China*. Brookings, 2009.

———. *Globalization and Changes in China's Governance*. Leiden, Netherlands: Brill, 2008.

Zakaria, Fareed. *The Future of Freedom: Illiberal Democracy at Home and Abroad*. New York: W. W. Norton, 2003.

Zhang, Wenxian, Huiyao Wang, and Ilan Alon, eds. *Entrepreneurial and Business Elites of China: The Chinese Returnees Who Have Shaped Modern China*. Bingley, U.K.: Emerald Group Publishing, 2011.

Zhao, Suisheng, ed. *Debating Political Reform in China: Rule of Law vs. Democratization*. Armonk, N.Y.: M. E. Sharpe, 2006.

Zweig, David and Huiyao Wang. "Can China Bring Back the Best? The Communist Party Organizes China's Search for Talent." *China Quarterly*, no. 215 (September 2013): 590–615.

Chinese

2014 dao 2018 nian quanguo dangyuan jiaoyu peixun gongzuo guihua [Plan for the education and training of the CCP members for 2014–2018]. Beijing: Dangjian duwu chubanshen, 2014.

Ai Jiabing. *Guan erdai* [Official 2G]. New York: Mirror Books, 2011.

Ai Yanghua and Cheng Xiaoming. *Tuanhui zhaoyao Zhongguo: Zhonggong zhengtan de mingxing he heima* [China under the shining emblem of the Chinese Communist Youth League: Rising stars and dark horses of Chinese politics]. New York: Mirror Books, 2007.

Ao Daiya. *Siying qiyezhu jieceng de zhengzhi canyu* [Political participation of private entrepreneurs]. Guangzhou: Zhongshan University Press, 2005.

Bai Zhigang. *Liyi gongping yu shehui hexie* [Fairness of interests and social harmony]. Beijing: China Society Press, 2008.

Cai Dingjian. *Minzhu shi yizhong xiandai shenghuo* [Democracy is a modern lifestyle]. Beijing: Shehuikexue wenxian chubanshe, 2010.

Cai Dingjian, and Wang Guyang, comp. *Zouxiang xianzheng* [Toward constitutionalism]. Beijing: Law Press China, 2010.

Cai Tuo. *Quanqiuhua yu Zhongguo zhengzhi fazhan* [Globalization and China's political development]. Beijing: Zhongguo zhengfa daxue chubanshe, 2008.

Central Commission for Discipline Inspection of the CCP, the Central Organization Department of the CCP, the Research Institute of the CCP History of the Central Committee of the CCP, and General Political Department of the People's Liberation Army, comps. *Zhongguo gongchandang zhongyang jiwei weiyuan da cidian 1927–2008* [Who's who in the Central Commission for Discipline Inspection of the Chinese Communist Party 1927–2008]. Beijing: Zhongguo fangzheng chubanshe, 2009.

Central Committee of the Chinese Communist Party. *Zhongguo gongchandang zhangcheng* [Constitution of the Chinese Communist Party], 2007 ed. Beijing: Renmin chubanshe, 2007.

———. *Zhongguo gongchandang zhangcheng* [Constitution of the Chinese Communist Party], 2012 ed. Beijing: Renmin chubanshe, 2012.

Central Organization Department of the CCP and the Research Institute of the CCP History of the Central Committee of the CCP, comps. *Zhongguo gongchandang lijie zhongyang weiyuan dacidian* 1921–2003 [Who's who in the Central Committees of the Chinese Communist Party, 1921–2003]. Beijing: CCP Archive Press, 2004.

Chang Xiaoshi. *Gonggong qingfu Li Wei mishi* [The secret life of Li Wei: The shared mistress]. Hong Kong: Beiyunhe chubanshe, 2011.

Chen Desheng, ed. *Zhonggong shiqida zhengzhi jingying zhenbu yu difang zhili* [Political recruitment and local governance in the 17th National Congress of the Chinese Communist Party]. Taipei: INK yinke chuban, 2008.

Chen Ergao, *Xi Jinping xiongxin: Huangdi haishi zongtong?* [Xi Jinping's ambition: Emperor or president?]. New York: Insider Publication, 2014.

Chen Liansheng and Hao Hongguang, comps. *Chen Liangyu chenfu zhilu* [The fall of Chen Liangyu]. Hong Kong: Zhongtian chubanshe, 2008.

Chen Xiao. *Dangdai Zhongguo zhengfu tizhi* [Contemporary Chinese government system]. Shanghai: Jiaotong daxue chubanshe, 2005.

Chen Xiaoming, Yang Yun, Fang Yanhong, and Xie Guanping. *Zhonggong shiqida buju* [The 17th National Congress of the CCP], 2d ed. New York: Mirror Books, 2007.

Chen Xiaoming, Yang Yun, and Xie Guanping. *Zhonggong shiqida muqianxi* [Power play prior to the 17th Party Congress]. New York: Mirror Books, 2006.

Chen Yao. *Xin quanweizhuyi zhengquan de minzhu zhuanxing* [The democratic transition of authoritarian regimes]. Shanghai: Renmin chubanshe, 2006.

———. *Xinxing minzhu guojia de minzhu gonggu* [Democratic consolidation in new democracies]. Shanghai renmin chubanshe, 2010.

Chen Yifan, *Zhonggong gaoguan de mishumen* [The mishu cluster of the high-ranking leaders of the Chinese Communist Party]. New York: Mirror Books, 2010.

Cheng Gongyi and Xia Fei. *Zhonggong shibada zhengzhiju* [Politburo formed at the 18th Party Congress]. New York: Mirror Books, 2012.

Dang de shibada wenjian huibian [Collected works of the 18th National Congress of the Chinese Communist Party]. Beijing: Dangjian duwu chubanshe, 2012.

Dangzheng lingdao ganbu xuanba renyong gongzuo tiaoli xuexi duben bianxiezu [The draft team of the regulations and laws on the recruitment and promotion of party and government officials], comp. *Dangzheng lingdao ganbu xuanba renyong gongzuo tiaoli xuexi duben* [The regulations and laws on the recruitment and promotion of party and government officials]. Beijing: Hongqi chubanshe, 2014.

Deng Xiaoping. *Deng Xiaoping Wenxuan* [Work of Deng Xiaoping], 1st ed. Vol. 3. Beijing: Renmin chubanshe, 1993.

Ding Xueliang. *Bianlun Zhongguo moshi* [Debating the China model]. Beijing: Shehuikexue wenxian chubanshe, 2011.

Dou Zijia. *Zhonggong zhengtan napi "lang": Wang Yang zhuan* [A "wolf" in Chinese politics: Biography of Wang Yang]. New York: Mirror Books, 2009.

Du Fei. *Zhongguo buwei gaoguan: Cong Wen Jiabao neige dao Li Keqiang neige* [China's ministerial top leaders: From Wen Jiabao's cabinet to Li Keqiang's cabinet]. New York: Mirror Books, 2012.

Du Nianfeng, comp. *Dang de shibada wenjian huibian* [Collections of the documents of the 18th National Party Congress of the Chinese Communist Party]. Beijing: Dangjian duwu chubanshe, 2012.

Du Zhigen and Shen Juan. *Zhongguo xin quangui zhi guanshang qieguo lu* [Convergence of power and money: How the new elite steals state assets]. New York: Mirror Books, 2008.

Fang Ning, comp. *Caogen jingji yu minzhu zhengzhi* [Grassroots economy and democratic politics]. Beijing: Shehuikexue wenxian chubanshe, 2008.

———. *Minzhu de Zhongguo jingyan* [China's experience on democracy]. Beijing: Zhongguo shehuikexue chubanshe and Renmin chubanshe, 2013.

———. *Minzhu zhengzhi shilun: Zhongguo tese shehuizhuyi minzhu lilun yu shijian de ruogan zhongda wenti* [Ten lectures on democratic politics: Major issues in the theory and practice of the Chinese-style socialist democracy]. Beijing: Zhongguo shehuikexue chubanshe, 2007.

———. *Shehuizhuyi shi yizhong hexie* [Socialism is a harmonious system]. Beijing: Zhongguo shehuikexue chubanshe, 2007.

———, ed. *Ziyou quanwei duoyuan: Dongya zhengzhi fazhan yanjiu baogao* [Liberty, authority, diversity: A study of East Asian political development]. Beijing: Shehuikexue wenxian chubanshe, 2011.

———, et al. *Zhongguo zhengzhi canyu baogao 2012* [Annual report on political participation in China in 2012]. Beijing: Shehuikexue wenxian chubanshe, 2012.

———. *Zhongguo zhengzhi canyu baogao 2013* [Annual report on political participation in China in 2013]. Beijing: Shehuikexue wenxian chubanshe, 2013.

Feng Chongyi. *Zhongguo xianzheng zhuanxing* [Constitutional transition in China]. New York: Mirror Books, 2014.

Feng Ping. *Zhonggong jutou zibai* [Confessions of the top leaders of the Chinese Communist Party]. Hong Kong: Wenhua yishu chubanshe, 2011.

Fenghuang zhoukan [Phoenix weekly], comp. *Zhongguo tanguan lu* [Corrupt officials of China]. Beijing: Zhongguo fazhan chubanshe, 2011.

Gao Jian and Tong Dezhi, comps. *Zhongguoshi minzhu* [Chinese democracy]. Tianjin: Tianjin renmin chubanshe, 2010.

Gao Xin. *Jiang Zemin de muliao* [Jiang Zemin's counselors], 4th ed. Hong Kong: Mingjing chubanshe, 1997.

———. *Lingdao Zhongguo de xin renwu: Zhonggong shiliujie zhengzhiju changwei* [New figures leading China: The Politburo Standing Committee formed at the 16th Party Congress of the Chinese Communist Party]. Vols. 1 and 2. New York: Mirror Books, 2003.

Gao Xin, and He Pin (Ho Pin). *Zhu Rongji zhuan: Cong fandang youpai dao Deng Xiaoping jichengren* [Biography of Zhu Rongji: From anti-party rightist to Deng's successor]. Taipei: Xinxinwen wenhua chubanshe, 1992.

Gao Xinmin and Zou Qingguo. *Dangnei minzhu yanjiu: Jian tan minzhu zhizheng* [Studies of inner-party democracy: Democratic governance]. Qingdao chubanshe, 2007.

Gao Zhiyuan. *Shibada yu Xi Jinping shidai* [The 18th Party Congress and the Xi Jinping era]. Hong Kong: Wenhua yishu chubanshe, 2011.

Guo Qing. *Cong Yao Yilin dao Wang Qishan* [From Yao Yilin to Wang Qishan]. Hong Kong: Caida chubanshe, 2009.

Guo Qiushui. *Dangdai sanda minzhu lilun* [Three contemporary theories on democracy]. Beijing: New Star Press, 2006.

Guo Yong. *Jingji zhuangui, zhidu yu fubai* [Economic transition, institution, and corruption]. Beijing: Shehuikexue wenxian chubanshe, 2007.

Guo Zhongjun, *Taiwan diqu minzhu zhuanxing zhong de mincui zhuyi* [Populism in the democratic transition of Taiwan]. Shanghai: Xuelin chubanshe, 2014.

———. *Zhongguo de xuanju minzhu* [China's electoral democracy]. Shanghai: Xuelin chubanshe, 2014.

Guojia xingzheng xueyuan [China's National Academy of Administration], ed. *Zhonghua renmin gongheguo zhengfu jigou wushi nian* [Government organs of the PRC in the past fifty years]. Beijing: Dangjian duwu chubanshe, 2000.

Guowuyuan bangongting mishuju [Secretariat of General Office of the State Council] and Zhongyang jigou bianzhi weiyuanhui bangongshi zonghesi [General Division of the State Commission Office for Public Sector Reform], comps. *Zhongyang zhengfu zuzhi jigou* [Central government organizations]. Beijing: Dangjian duwu chubanshe, 2009.

He Gaoxin. *Zhongguo zui gaoceng* [China's top leadership]. Beijing: Renmin wenxue chubanshe, 2003.

He Huaihong. *Xuanju shehui* [The selection society], rev. ed. Beijing: Peking University Press, 2011.

He Pin (Ho Pin). *Keyi queding de Zhongguo weilai* [China's future can be determined]. New York: Mirror Books, 2012.

———. *Zhongguo xin zhuhou* [The new lords of the PRC]. New York: Mirror Books, 1996.

———. *Zhongguo zhengfu lingdaozhe* [The government leaders of the PRC]. New York: Mirror Books, 1996.

He Pin (Ho Pin), and Gao Xin. *Zhonggong "Taizidang"* [China's Communist "princelings"]. Taipei: Shibao Ch'u-pan Kung-ssu, 1992.

———. *Zhonggong "Taizidang"* [China's Communist "princelings"], rev. ed. Taipei: Shibao chubanshe, 1999.

He Zengke. *Gongmin shehui yu minzhu zhili* [Civil society and democratic governance]. Beijing: Central Compilation and Translation Press, 2007.

Ho Szu-yin, comp. *Zhonggong renming lu* [Who's who in communist China]. Taipei: Institute of International Relations, National Chengchi University, 1999.

Hong Qing. *Ta jiangshi Zhongguo daguanjia: Li Keqiang zhuan* [The man who will be the chief manager of China: Biography of Li Keqiang]. New York: Mirror Books, 2010.

Hong Yuanpeng, Li Huizhong, Tao Youzhi, Kong Aiguo, and Chen Bo. *Liyi guanxi zonglun: Xinshiqi woguo shehui liyi guanxi fazhan bianhua yanjiu de zongbaogao* [An overview of interest group politics in the new era of China's social development]. Shanghai: Fudan daxue chubanshe, 2011.

Hu Angang. *Zhongguo jiti lingdao tizhi* [The system of collective leadership in China]. Beijing: Zhongguo renmin daxue chubanshe, 2013.

Hu Min. *Hu Jintao de wuduo jinhua* [Hu Jintao's five golden flowers]. Hong Kong: Bei yunhe chubanshe, 2010.

Hu Shuli and Wang Shuo, comps. *Zhongguo 2013: Guanjian wenti* [China 2013: What matters most]. Beijing: Xianzhuang shuju, 2012.

Hua Sheng. *Zhongguo gaige zuoduide he meizuode* [What has been accomplished and what has been yet to be done in China's reform]. Beijing: Dongfang chubanshe, 2012.

Huang Ping and Cui Zhiyuan, eds. *Zhongguo yu quanqiuhua: Huashengdun gongshi haishi Beijing gongshi* [China and globalization: The Washington consensus or the Beijing consensus?]. Beijing: Shehuikexue wenxian chubanshe, 2005.

Huang Shudong. *Daguo xingshuai: Quanqiuhua beijingxia de luxian zhi zheng* [The rise and fall of great powers: Contention over direction in the era of globalization]. Beijing: Zhongguo renmin daxue chubanshe, 2012.

Huanqiuyuqing diaocha zhongxin [The Global Public Opinion Research Center], comp. *Zhongguo minyi diaocha* [Chinese public opinion survey]. Beijing: Renmin ribao chubanshe, 2012.

Ji Weiren. *Zhongguo shi zhengbian: Cong Chongqing yinmou dao Beijing yinmou* [The Chinese-style coup d'état: From the Chongqing conspiracy to the Beijing plot]. Taipei: Lingxiu chubanshe, 2012.

Jiang Yanbei. *Cong Bo Yibo dao Bo Xilai* [From Bo Yibo to Bo Xilai]. Hong Kong: Caida chubanshe, 2009.

Jin Chengwei. *Dangnei minzhu* [Inner-party democracy]. Beijing: Central Compilation and Translation Press, 2013.

Jin Qianli. *Diwudai jiangxing: Zhonggong duitai zuozhan zhongjian renwu* [The fifth generation of military generals: The core figures in the CCP's battle against Taiwan]. Hong Kong: Xiafei'er chuban youxian gongsi, 2006.

Jing Yuejing, Zhang Xiaojin, and Yu Xunda, eds. *Lijie Zhongguo zhengzhi: Guanjianci de fangfa* [Understanding Chinese politics: Key terminologies and methodologies]. Beijing: Zhongguo shehuikexue chubanshe, 2012.

Ke Lizi. *Yingxiang Xi Jinping de ren* [People who influence Xi Jinping]. New York: Mirror Books, 2013.

Ke Wei. *Zhonggong diliudai mingxing zhuan* [Biographies of the rising stars of the sixth-generation leaders of the Chinese Communist Party]. Hong Kong: Xin wenhuatushu youxian gongsi, 2010.

Ke Yuqian. *Zhonggong huandai: Cong disidai dao diwudai* [The generational change of the Chinese Communist Party: From the 4th generation to the 5th generation]. New York: Mirror Books, 2012.

Li Cheng. *Tongwang Zhongnanhai zhilu: Zhonggong shibada zhiqian gaoceng lingdao qunti* [The road to Zhongnanhai: High-level leadership groups on the eve of the 18th Party Congress]. New York: Mirror Books, 2012.

———. *Zhongguo yancao de zhengzhi bantu: Yancao hangye yu kongyan yundong boyi* [China's tobacco industry and anti-smoking campaign: politics and policies]. New York: Mirror Books, 2013.

Li Chunling. *Duanlie yu suipian: Dangdai Zhongguo shehuijieceng fenhua shizheng fenxi* [Cleavage and fragment: An empirical analysis of social stratification in contemporary China]. Beijing: Shehuikexue wenxian chubanshe, 2005.

Li Feng. *Shiwuda Zhonggong gaoceng xin dang'an* [New dossiers of the top leaders selected at the 15th Party Congress]. Hong Kong: Wenhua chuanbo shiwusuo, 1997.

Li Gucheng. *Zhonggong zheng tianxia: Lingdaoqun poxi* [Analysis of CCP elite groups competing for power]. Hong Kong: Mingbao chubanshe, 1996.

Li Huibin, ed. *Quanqiuhua: Zhongguo daolu* [Globalization: The China road]. Beijing: Shehuikexue wenxian chubanshe, 2003.

Li Junru, *Xieshang minzhu zai Zhongguo* [Deliberative democracy in China]. Beijing: Renmin chubanshe, 2014.

Li Kaifu. *Weibo gaibian yiqie* [Weibo changes everything]. Shanghai caijing daxue chubanshe, 2011.

———. *Yiwang qingshen* [To student with love: Online dialogue between Kaifu and Chinese students]. Beijing: Renmin chubanshe, 2007.

Li Lulu and Wang Yu. "Dangdai Zhongguo zhongjian jieceng de shehui cunzai: Jieceng renzhi yu zhengzhi yishi" [The social existence of the middle stratum in contemporary China: Strata recognition and political consciousness]. *Shehuikexue zhanxian* [Social Sciences Frontline], no. 10 (2008): 202–15.

Li Peilin, Li Qiang, and Sun Liping. *Zhongguo shehui fenceng* [Social stratification in China today]. Beijing: Shehuikexue wenxian chubanshe, 2004.

———, et al. *Dangdai Zhongguo minsheng* [People's livelihoods in contemporary China]. Beijing: Shehuikexue wenxian chubanshe, 2013.

Li Peilin, and Zhang Yi. "Zhongguo zhongchan jieji de guimo, rentong, he shehui taidu" [The scope, identities, and attitudes of China's middle class]. In *Daguoce tongxiang Zhongguo zhilu de Zhongguo minzhu: Zengliangshi minzhu* [The strategy of a great power: Incremental democracy and Chinese-style democracy], edited by Tang Jin, 188–99. Beijing: Renmin chubanshe, 2009.

Li Sen. *Dangzheng lingdao ganbu suzhi yu nengli peiyang yanjiu* [Studies of the quality and capacity development of cadres]. Beijing: Dangjian duwu chubanshe, 2008.

Li Shitou. *Douzheng de yishu* [The art of struggle]. Beijing: Guojia xingzheng xueyuan chubanshe, 2012.

Li Xiaozhuang. *Zhu Rongji renma* [Zhu Rongji's men]. Taipei: Dujia chubanshe, 1998.

Liang Jian. *Xi Jinping xinzhuan* [New biography of Xi Jinping]. New York: Mirror Books, 2012.

Liao Baoping. *Dalao Zhongguo fenqing* [China's angry youth]. Harbin: Beifang wenyi chubanshe, 2010.

Liao Gailong and Fan Yuan, comps. *Zhongguo renming da cidian* [Who's who in China]. Vol. 3. Shanghai Dictionary Publishing House, 1989.

———. comp. *Zhongguo renming da cidian: xiandai dangzhengjun lingdao renwu juan* [Who's who in China: Current party, government, and military leaders], 1994 ed. Beijing: Foreign Languages Press, 1994.

Lin Hong. *Mincui zhuyi: Gainian, lilun yu shizheng* [Populism: Concept, theory, and empirical practice]. Beijing: Central Compilation and Translation Press, 2007.

Lin Qingpu and Zhao Jinghua. *Li Keqiang zhuan* [Biography of Li Keqiang]. New York: Mirror Books, 2012.

Lin Shangli. *Dangdai Zhongguo zhengzhi xingtai yanjiu* [The study of contemporary Chinese political formation]. Tianjin: Tianjin renmin chubanshe, 2000.

———. *Jiangou minzhu: Zhongguo de lilun, zhanlue yu yicheng* [Constructing democracy: Theories, strategy, and agenda in China]. Shanghai: Fudan daxue chubanshe, 2012.

Lin Yifu. *Jiedu Zhongguo jingji* [Demystifying the Chinese economy]. Beijing: Beijing daxue chubanshe, 2012.

Ling Haijian. *Zhonggong jundui xin jiangxing* [The profiles of prominent military chiefs in China]. Hong Kong: Pacific Century Press, 1999.

Liu Fangyuan. *Li Yuanchao zhuan* [Biography of Li Yuanchao]. New York: Mirror Books, 2010.

Liu Hainan. *Xi Jinping de weiji* [Xi Jinping's crisis]. Hong Kong: External Reference Press, 2014.

Liu Jianfei. *Minzhu Zhongguo yu shijie* [A democratic China and world]. Beijing: New World Press, 2011.

Liu Jie, comp. *Zhongguoshi minzhu: yizhong xinxing minzhu xingtai de xingqi he chengzhang* [Chinese-style democracy: The emergence and growth of a new democratic entity]. Beijing: Shishi chubanshe, 2014.

———. *Zhongguo zhengzhi fazhan jincheng 2007 nian* [The process of China's political development, 2007]. Beijing: Shishi chubanshe, 2007.

Liu Jingwei and Du Fei. *Zhonggong jieban shuangxiong* [Dual successors of the Chinese Communist Party]. New York: Mirror Books, 2013.

Liu Shaojie. *Dangdai Zhongguo yishi xingtai bianqian* [Ideological transition in contemporary China]. Beijing: Central Compilation and Translation Press, 2012.

Liu Tao. *Zhongguo shiji* [Chinese century]. Beijing: Xinhua chubanshe, 2010.

Liu Yanchang. *Jujiao Zhongguo jide liyijituan* [Focus on vested interestsgroups in China]. Beijing: Zhonggong zhongyang dangxiao chubanshe, 2007.

Liu Ying and Qi Xingyuan, eds. *Dangdai Zhongguo zhengzhi zhidu* [The political system in Contemporary China]. Jinan: Shandong renmin chubanshe, 2011.

Liu Zhenggang and Zhang Shuai, comps. *Dang de difang he jiceng zuzhi huanjie xuanju gongzuo* [General election work of the local and grassroots CCP leadership elections], 2nd ed. Beijing: Guojia xingzheng xueyuan chubanshe, 2011.

Liu Zhexin. *Jingying yu pingmin: Zhongguo ren de minzhu shenghuo* [Elite and the masses: Chinese people's democratic life]. Beijing: Falü chubanshen, 2013.

Long Hua. *Hu Wen mianlin de dileizhen* [The minefield confronting Hu and Wen]. Hong Kong: Xinhua Publishing, 2004.

Lü Jiayi. *Hong'erdai: Zhonggong quangui jiazu* [The second generation of red communists: China privileged power families]. New York: Mirror Books, 2014.

Lu Xueyi. *Dangdai Zhongguo shehuijieceng yanjiu baogao: Zhongguo shehui jieceng congshu* [Research report on social strata in contemporary China]. Beijing: Shehuikexue wenxian chubanshe, 2002.

———. *Dangdai Zhongguo shehui liudong* [Social mobility in contemporary China]. Beijing: Shehuikexue wenxian chubanshe, 2004.

———. *Dandai Zhongguo shehui jiegou* [Social structure of contemporary China]. Beijing: Shehuikexue wenxian chubanshe, 2010.

Ma Hui and Wang Huning, et al., comps. *Shiqida dangzhang xiuzheng'an xuexi wenda* [Questions and answers on the studies of the amendment to the Constitution of the Chinese Communist Party]. Beijing: Dangjian duwu chubanshe, 2007.

Ma Licheng. *Jiaofeng sanshi nian: Gaige kaifang sici dazhenglun qinliji* [Clash in 30 years: Four major debates during the period of reform and opening]. Nanjing: Jiangsu renmin chubanshe, 2008.

Ma Ling and Li Ming. *Hu Jintao: Ta cong nalilai, jiangxiang hechuqu* [Hu Jintao: Where he comes from and where he will go]. Hong Kong: Mingbao chubanshe, 2002.

———. *Hu Jintao xin zhuan* [New biography of Hu Jintao]. Taipei: Taidian dianye gufen youxian gongsi, 2006.

———. *Wen Jiabao yu Zhu Rongji youhe butong he Hu Jintao zenyang peihe* [Wen Jiabao: How he cooperates with Hu Jintao and how he differs from Zhu Rongji]. Taipei: Lianjing chubanshe, 2003.

Ma Shengmin. *Chen Liangyu mimi dang'an* [The secret dossier on Chen Liangyu]. Xining: Jishi chubanshe, 2006.

Ma Yingjuan. *Zhengfu jianguan jigou yanjiu* [On government regulatory agencies]. Beijing daxue chubanshe, 2007.

Meng Jun. *Jinquan taizidang* [Princelings holding both money and power]. Hong Kong: Xiafei'er chuban youxian gongsi, 2009.

———. *Zhonggong mishu bang* [The gang of personal assistants of CCP leaders]. Hong Kong: Xiafei'er chuban youxian gongsi, 2009.

Meng Ping. *Jun zhong taizidang* [Princelings in the PLA]. Hong Kong: Xiafei'er chuban youxian gongsi, 2010.

Nan Fanglong. *Shanghaibang de nürenmen* [The Shanghai Gang and their women]. Hong Kong: Lianhe zuojia chubanshe, 2008.

———. *Zhonggong gaoguan furen miwen* [Secret stories of the women of top CCP leaders]. Hong Kong: Lianhe zuojia chubanshe, 2008.

Nan Lei. *Taizidang jinquan diguo* [The money empire of the Princelings]. Hong Kong: Wenhua yishu chubanshe, 2011.

———. *Zhulu shibada* [Political jockeying at the 18th Party Congress]. Hong Kong: Wenhua yishu chubanshe, 2010.

Nandu baoxi wangluo wenzheng tuandui [The Southern Media Group's politics team], comp. *Wangluo wenzheng* [Internet politics]. Guangzhou: Nanfang ribao chubanshe, 2010.

Pan Wei, ed. *Zhongguo moshi: Jiedu renmin gongheguo de liushi nian* [China model: A new developmental model from the sixty years of the People's Republic]. Beijing: Central Compilation and Translation Press, 2009.

Peng Huai'en. *Zhonghuaminguo zhengzhi tixi de fenxi* [Analysis of the political system of the Republic of China]. Taipei: Shibao wenhua chuban, 1983.

Qian Mu. *Zhongguo lidai zhengzhi deshi* [Political gains and losses in Chinese history]. Beijing: Sanlian shudian, 2012.

Qin Hui. *Gongtong de dixian* [Shared baseline]. Nanjing: Jiangsu wenyi chubanshe, 2012.

Qin Lu. *Hulianwang shidai ruhe zhizheng yu weiguan* [How to govern and serve as an official in the internet era]. Beijing: Dangjian duwu chubanshe, 2012.

Qiu Jun. *Diwudai caijing gaoguan* [High-ranking financial and economic leaders in the 5th generation]. Hong Kong: Xiafei'er chuban youxian gongsi, 2013.

Qiu Ping. *Disidai quanzheng neimu* [Insightful stories of political jockeying in the fourth-generation leadership]. Hong Kong: Xiafei'er chuban youxian gongsi, 2003.

———. *Zhonggong diwudai* [The fifth generation of leaders of the Chinese Communist Party]. Hong Kong: Xiafei'er chuban youxian gongsi, 2005.

Ramo, Joshua Cooper, ed. *Zhongguo xingxiang: Waiguo xuezhe yanli de Zhongguo* [China's image: The country in the eyes of foreign scholars]. Beijing: Shehuikexue wenxian chubanshe, 2006.

Ren Huayi. *Diliudai: Zhonggong modai jieban qun* [The sixth generation: The last leadership generation of the Chinese Communist Party]. New York: Mirror Books, 2010.

Ren Zhichu. *Hu Jintao: Zhongguo kuashiji jiebanren* [Hu Jintao: China's first man in the 21st century]. Hong Kong: Mirror Books, 1997.

Shen Xueming, et al., comp. *Zhonggong di shiwujie zhongyang weiyuanhui zhongyang jilü jiancha weiyuanhui weiyuan minglu* [Who's who among the members of the Fifteenth Central Committee of the Chinese Communist Party and the Fifteenth Central Discipline Inspection Commission]. Beijing: Zhonggong wenxian chubanshe, 1999.

Shi Bi. *Hu Jiang fengyun* [Tensions between Hu Jintao and Jiang Zemin]. Hong Kong: Wenhua yishu chubanshe, 2005.

———. *Hu Wen weiji* [The crisis of the Hu-Wen leadership]. Hong Kong: Wenhua yishu chubanshe, 2004.

———. *Shanghaibang de huanghun* [The dusk of the Shanghai gang]. Hong Kong: Wenhua yishu chubanshe, 2003.

Shi Linjie. *Zhongxifang zhengfu tizhi bijiao yanjiu* [A comparative study of Chinese and Western systems of government]. Beijing: Renmin chubanshe, 2011.

Shi Weimin and Zhang Xiaobing. *Zhongguo zhengzhi fazhan moshi de xuanze* [Choices of the models of China's political development]. Beijing: Zhongguo shehuikexue chubanshe, 2013.

Shibada yilai lianzheng xin guiding [Regulations on clean governance since the 18th National Congress of the CCP], 2015 ed. Beijing: Renmin chubanshe, 2015.

Sima Du. *Xin Shanghaibang: Jiang Mianheng shuai "xin Shanghaibang" hengkong chushi* [The new Shanghai Gang]. Hong Kong: Xinshijie chuanmei, 2013.

Sima Nan. *Minzhu hutong sishitiao* [Forty alleys towards democracy]. Beijing: Economic Science Press, 2011.

Song Defu and Zhang Zhijian, comps. *Zhongguo zhengfu guanli yu gaige* [The administration and reform of the Chinese government]. Beijing: Zhongguo fazhi chubanshe, 2001.

The State Council of the PRC. *Zhonghua renmin gongheguo wuquanfa* [The property law of the People's Republic of China]. Beijing: Zhongguo fazhi chubanshe, 2007.

Su Ha. *Zhonggong danei zongguan* [Chiefs-of-staff of the CCP]. Hong Kong: Xiafei'er chuban youxian gongsi, 2003.

Su Wei, Yang Fan, and Liu Shiwen. *Chongqing moshi* [The Chongqing model]. Beijing: Zhongguo jingji chubanshe, 2011.

Sun Liping. *Duanlie: ershi shiji jiushi niandai yilai de Zhongguo shehui* [Cleavage: Chinese society since the 1990s]. Beijing: Shehuikexue wenxian chubanshe, 2003.

——. *Shouwei de dixian: Zhuanxing shehui shenghuo de jichu zhixu* [Minimal responsibility: Basic order of social life in a transformational Chinese society]. Beijing: Shehuikexue wenxian chubanshe, 2007.

——. *Zhuanxing yu duanlie* [Transition and cleavage]. Tsinghua UniversityPress, 2004.

Tang Jin, Tan Huosheng, and Yuan He, eds. *Tongxiang daguo zhilu de Zhongguo minzhu: Zengliangshi minzhu* [Chinese democracy and China on the road to becoming a major power: Incremental democracy]. Beijing: Renmin ribao chubanshe, 2009.

Ting Wang. *Hu Jintao yu gongqingtuan jieban qun* [Hu Jintao and the successors of the Communist Youth League of China]. Hong Kong: Celebrities Press, 2005.

——. *Hu Jintao: Beijing ershiyi shiji lingxiu* [Hu Jintao: Beijing's 21st-century leader]. 3rd ed. Hong Kong: Celebrities Press, 2002.

——. *Wen Jiabao yu jiebanqun: Beijing xin shiji lingxiu* [Wen Jiabao and the successors: Beijing's leaders in the new century]. Hong Kong: Celebrities Press, 1999.

——. *Zeng Qinghong yu xiyang zu qiangren* [Zeng Qinghong and the strongman of the sunset race], 2nd ed. Hong Kong: Celebrities Press, 2001.

Tocqueville, Alexis de. *Jiuzhidu yu dageming* [The old regime and the revolution]. Translated by Henry Livre. Beijing: Zhongguo youyi chuban gongsi, 2013.

——. *Lun Meiguo de minzhu* [Democracy in America]. Translated by Cao Dongxue. Nanjing: Yilin chubanshe, 2012.

Waican bianjibu [External reference department]. *Caozong shibada* [Manipulating the 18th Party Congress]. Hong Kong: Waican chubanshe, 2011.

——. *Xi Jinping jieban* [Xi Jinping's succession]. Hong Kong: Waican chubanshe, 2010.

——. *Zhongguo teshu liyi jituan: Zhonggong taizidang he tanguan* [Special interest group in China: Chinese Communist princelings and corrupt officials]. Hong Kong: Waican chubanshe, 2008.

Wang Changjiang and Jiang Yue, eds. *Shijie zhizhengdang de xingshuai* [Historical lessons of the rise and fall of the world's ruling parties]. Beijing: Zhonggong zhongyang dangxiao chubanshe, 2005.

Wang Changjiang, Zhou Hongyun, and Wang Yongbing, comps. *Dangnei minzhu zhidu chuangxin: Yige jiceng dangwei banzi "gongtui xuanju" de anli yanjiu* [Innovation of inner-party democracy: A case study of a local party committee]. Beijing: Central Compilation and Translation Press, 2007.

Wang Chunxi. "Deng Xiaoping dui jianli zhongyang jitilingdao tizhi kuangjia de gongxian." [Deng Xiaoping's contribution to the system of collective leadership of the Central Committee of the Chinese Communist Party]. *Dang de wenxian* [Literature of the Chinese Communist Party], no. 5 (2008): 54–58.

Wang Dongqi. *Zhiduwai zhengce canyu: Zhuanxing Zhongguo yanjiu* [External participation in policy formation: Studies of transitional China]. Beijing: Zhonggong zhongyang dangxiao chubanshe, 2012.

Wang Huiyao, Xu Xiaoping, and Xiong Xiaoge, eds. *Nasanjie: qiqi, qiba, qijiu ji daxuesheng de Zhongguo jiyi* [These three classes: The China Memories of the Classes '77, '78, and '79]. Beijing: China Translation and Publishing, 2014.

Wang Jian, ed. *Zhongguo zhengfu guizhi lilun yu zhengce* [Chinese government regulation: Theory and policy]. Beijing: Economic Science Press, 2008.

———, ed. *Zhengfu jingji guanli* [Government economic management]. Beijing: Economic Science Press, 2009.

Wang Keli. *Zhonggong sandai da jiaoyi: Shibada muhou de jiuda jiaoyi neimu* [A big leadership deal made by three generations of top leaders: Inside stories of the nine major deals cut behind the curtain of the 18th Party Congress]. Hong Kong: Sanjiaode chuban gongsi, 2012.

Wang Peiying, ed. *Zhongguo bainian xianzheng licheng* [A century-long journey toward constitutionalism in China]. Nanjing: Fenghuang chubanshe, 2012.

Wang Puqu. *Zhongguo zhengzhixue xueshu fazhan huigu yu guihua (2006–2015)* [Review and prospects of the academic development in the Chinese study of political science (2006–2015)]. Tianjin: Tianjin renmin chubanshe, 2011.

Wang Shaoguang. *Zhonggong zhidao* [China's governance]. Beijing: Zhongguo renmin daxue chubanshe, 2014.

Wang Shaoguang, and Fan Peng. *Zhongguo shi gongshi xing juece: "kaimen" yu "mohe"* [The Chinese model of consensus decisionmaking: A case study of healthcare reform]. Beijing: Zhongguo renmin daxue chubanshe, 2013.

Wang Yongbing. *Dangnei minzhu de zhidu chuangxin yu lujing xuanze* [Institutional innovation and path selection of inner-party democracy]. Beijing: Central Compilation and Translation Press, 2010.

Wang Zhi. *Dangdai Zhongguo zhengzhi jiegou bianqian: Yi zhizhengdang wei zhongxin de zhengdang, zhengfu, shehui* [Change of political structure in contemporary China: Parties, government, and society centered around the ruling party]. Beijing: Zhongguo shehuikexue chubanshe, 2010.

Wei Na and Wu Aiming. *Dangdai Zhongguo zhengfu yu xingzheng* [Contemporary Chinese government and administration], 3rd ed. Beijing: Zhongguo renmin daxue chubanshe, 2012.

Wen Jiabao. *Zhengfu gongzuo baogao: 2008* [Government work report: 2008]. Beijing: Renmin chubanshe, 2008.

Wen Siyong and Ren Zhichu. *Hu Jintao zhuan* [Biography of Hu Jintao], 7th ed. New York: Mirror Books, 2004.

———. *Hu Jintao zhuan* [Biography of Hu Jintao], 3rd ed. New York: Mirror Books, 2002.

Wen Tiejun. *Baci weiji: Zhongguo de zhenshi jingyan, 1949–2009* [Eight crises: Lessons from China, 1949–2009]. Beijing: Dongfang chubanshe, 2012.

———. *Wen Tiejun yanjiang lu* [A collection of speeches from Wen Tiejun]. Guangzhou: Guangdong renmin chubanshe, 2004.

Wen Zi and Wu Ji. *Zhonggong xin quangui zhi sunzi shidai* [New bigwigs of the grandchildren generation of Chinese communist veterans]. New York: Mirror Books, 2008.

Wen Zixian. *Xi Jinping de xuanze* [Xi Jinping's choice]. New York: Mirror Books, 2012.

Wu Aiming, comp. *Dangdai Zhongguo zhengfu* [Contemporary Chinese government], 2nd ed. Beijing: Zhongguo renmin daxue chubanshe, 2010.

Wu Aiming, Zhu Guobin, and Lin Zhen. *Dangdai Zhongguo zhengfu yu zhengzhi* [Government and politics in contemporary China]. Beijing: Zhongguo renmin daxue chubanshe, 2010.

Wu Jinglian. *Dangdai Zhongguo jingji gaige jiaocheng* [Tutorials of economic reforms in contemporary China]. Shanghai: Shanghai yuandong chubanshe, 2010.

Wu Jinglian, Fan Gang, Liu He, Lin Yifu, Yi Gang, Xu Shanda, and Wu Xiaoling, comp. *Zhongguo xiajieduan jingji gaige de qianyan wenti* [Cutting-edge issues in the next phase of China's economic reforms]. Beijing: Zhongguo jingji chubanshe, 2012.

Wu Jinglian and Yu Keping, eds. *Zhongguo weilai sanshinian* [China in the next thirty years]. Beijing: Central Compilation and Translation Press, 2010.

Wu Jiaxiang. *Jiaoli shiliuda: Weilai Zhongguo kongzhiquan* [Wrestling for Power: The 16th CCP Congress and the future political map of China]. New York: Mirror Books, 2002.

Wu Kangmin. *Wu Kangmin lun shizheng* [On politics]. Beijing: Central Compilation and Translation Press, 2012.

Wu Ming. *Nantianwang Zhang Dejiang* [China's southern lord Zhang Dejiang]. Hong Kong: Wenhua yishu chubanshe, 2006.

———. *Xi Jinping zhuan* [Biography of Xi Jinping]. Hong Kong: Wenhua yishu chubanshe, 2008.

———. *Zhongguo xin lingxiu: Xi Jinping zhuan* [China's new leader: Biography of Xi Jinping], enl. ed. Hong Kong: Wenhua yishu chubanshe, 2010.

Wu Ming, and Lin Zheng. *Wen Jiaobao jiebanren: Li Keqiang zhuan* [Wen Jiabao's successor: Biography of Li Keqiang]. Hong Kong: Wenhua yishu chubanshe, 2008.

Wu Si. *Qianguize: Zhongguo lishi zhong de zhenshi youxi* [The hidden rules: Real games of Chinese history]. Shanghai: Fudan daxue chubanshe, 2009.

Xi Jinping, coed. *Fujian shanhai liandong fazhan yanjiu* [The study of land and sea joint development in Fujian]. Fuzhou: Fujian renmin chubanshe, 2000.

———, ed. *Kexue yu aiguo* [Science and patriotism]. Tsinghua University Press, 2001.

———, ed. *Xiandai nongye lilun yu shijian* [Modern agriculture: Theory and practice]. Fuzhou: Fujian jiaoyu chubanshe, 1999.

———. *Xinshiji de xuanze: Fujiansheng fada diqu shuaixian shixian nongye xiandaihua yanjiu* [The decision of the new century: The study of agricultural modernization led by the advanced areas of Fujian Province]. Fuzhou: Fujian jiaoyu chubanshe, 2001.

———. *Zhijiang xinyu* [New thoughts in Zhijiang]. Hangzhou: Zhejiang renmin chubanshe, 2007.

———. *Zhongguo nongcun shichanghua jianshe yanjiu* [Research on market development of rural China]. Beijing: Renmin chubanshe, 2001.

———. Li Keqiang, and Liu Yunshan, comps. *Shibada baogao fudao duben* [Guide to the reports of the 18th Party Congress of the Chinese Communist Party]. Beijing: Renmin chubanshe, 2012.

Xia Fei, Yang Yun, and Bai Xiaoyun. *Taizidang he Gongqingtuan: Xi Jinping PK Li Keqiang* [Princelings and the Chinese Communist Youth League faction: Xi Jinping versus Li Keqiang]. New York: Mirror Books, 2007.

Xia Handong. *Shui kongzhi Zhongguo jundui* [Who controls China's military]. New York: Mirror Books, 2013.

Xiang Jiangyu. *Li Keqiang bandi* [Li Keqiang's confidants]. New York: Mirror Books, 2011.

———. *Xi Jinping bandi* [Xi Jinping's confidants]. New York: Mirror Books, 2011.

———. *Xi Jinping tuandui* [Xi Jinping's team]. New York: Mirror Books, 2013.

Xiang Jiangyu, and Ye Maozhi. *Li Keqiang neige* [Li Keqiang's cabinet]. New York: Mirror Books, 2013.

Xiao Chong. *Shangchang taizidang* [Princelings in the business world]. Hong Kong: Xiafei'er chuban youxian gongsi, 2000.

———. *Zhonggong disidai mengren* [The fourth-generation heavyweights of the Chinese Communist Party]. Hong Kong: Xiafei'er chuban youxian gongsi, 1998.

Xiao Gongqin. *Chaoyue zuoyou jijinzhuyi* [Beyond left and right radicalism]. Hangzhou: Zhejiang daxue chubanshe, 2012.

Xie Chuntao, ed. *Zhongguo gongchandang ruhe zhili guojia* [Governing China: How the CCP works]. Beijing: New World Press, 2012.

Xie Fanping. *Changwei zhiguo* [The rule of the Politburo Standing Committee]. New York: Mirror Books, 2014.

Xie Qingkui and Tong Fuling, eds. *Fuwuxing zhengfu yu hexie shehui* [Service-oriented government and harmonious society]. Beijing: Beijing daxue chubanshe, 2006.

Xinxi ziyou guancha gongzuoshi [Observation office of information freedom]. *Bo Xilai Zhou Yongkang miju yu shibada* [The myths about Bo Xilai and Zhou Yongkang and the 18th Party Congress]. Hong Kong: Suyuan shushe, 2012.

Xu Haoran. *Jiedu Zhongguo minzhu: xifang Zhongguoxuejia de shijiao* [Interpreting Chinese democracy: Perspectives of Western sinologists]. Beijing: Zhongguo shehuikexue chubanshe, 2013.

Xu Jiugang, Feng Jincheng, and Liu Runmin. *Zhongguo minzhu zhengzhi yanjiu* [Studies of the Chinese democratic politics]. Beijing: Renmin chubanshe, 2006.

Xu Santong. *Jun zhong shaozhuangpai zhangwo Zhongguo bingquan* [Young Turks in the PLA controlling China's military power]. Hong Kong: Haya chubanshe, 2009.

Xu Youyu. *1966: Women zheyidai de huiyi* [1966: The reminiscences of our generation]. Beijing: Zhongguo wenlian chuban gongsi, 1998.

Xu Zhiyong. *Tangtang zhengzheng zuo gongmin: Wode ziyou Zhongguo* [To be a citizen: A free China]. Hong Kong: New Century Media, 2014.

Yan Jian, ed. *Minzhu xuanju* [Democratic election]. Beijing: Central Compilation and Translation Press, 2013.

Yan Jirong. *Zhengzhixue shiwujiang* [Fifteen lectures on political science]. Beijing: Beijing daxue chubanshe, 2004.

Yang Dongping. *Chengshi jifeng: Beijing he Shanghai de wenhua jingshen.* [City monsoon: The cultural spirit of Beijing and Shanghai]. Beijing: Dongfang Press, 1994.

Yang Hongshan. *Dangdai Zhongguo zhengzhi guanxi* [Political relationships in contemporary China]. Beijing: Jingji ribao chubanshe, 2002.

Yang Liuji and Yuan Junhong, "Dang de jitilingdao zhidu de xingcheng yu fazhan" [The formation and development of collective leadership of the Chinese Communist Party]. *Zhonggong dangshi yanjiu* [Study of History of the Chinese Communist Party], no. 4 (1991): 77–88.

Yang Qingxi and Xia Fei. *Shibada zhuhou jinjing: zhengji, renmai, houtai he paixi* [Provincial chiefs move to Beijing: Achievements, connections, patrons, and factions]. New York: Mirror Books, 2010.

Yang Xuedong. *"Xiaozu zhengzhi yu zhidu tanxing"* [Leading Small Groups Politics and Institutional Resilience]. *Renmin luntan* [People Forum], May 7, 2014.

Yang Yun and Fang Yanhong. *Neige xin sanjiao: Wen Jiabao, Li Keqiang, Wang Qishan yingzhan weiji* [The new triangle in the Cabinet: Wen Jiabao, Li Keqiang, Wang Qishan fight against crises]. New York: Mirror Books, 2008.

Yang Zhongmei. *Xin hongtaiyang: Zhonggong diwudai lingxiu* [New red sun: The fifth generation leaders in the Chinese Communist Party]. Taipei: Shibao wenhua, 2008.

———. *Zhonggong kuashiji jiebanren: Hu Jintao* [Hu Jintao: The cross-century successor of China]. Taipei: Shibao chubanshe, 1999.

———. *Zhonggong xin lingxiu: Hu Jintao* [He Jintao: China's new leader]. Taipei: Shibao wenhua, 2002.

Yi Ming. *Zhonggong disidai quanli bushu* [Succession and power redistribution in the fourth generation of the CCP]. New York: Mirror Books, 2002.

Yin Yungong, Wu Xinxun, and Liu Runsheng, eds. *Zhongguo xinmeiti fazhan baogao, 2010* [Annual report on development of China's new media, 2010]. Beijing: Shehuikexue wenxian chubanshe, 2010.

Yin Zhongqing. *Zhongguo zhengzhi zhidu* [China's political system] 2nd ed. Beijing: Wuzhou chuanbo chubanshe, 2010.

Yu Jianrong. *Diceng lichang* [Standpoint of the lower class]. Shanghai: Shanghai sanlian shudian, 2012.

———. *Kangzhengxing zhengzhi: Zhongguo zhengzhi shehuixue jiben wenti* [Contentious politics: Fundamental issues in Chinese political sociology]. Beijing: Renmin chubanshe, 2010.

Yu Keping. *Dalu ruhe zhili* [How mainland China governs]. Taipei: Qiushuitang wenhua shiye gufen youxian gongsi, 2013.

———, ed. *Hexie shehui yu zhengfu chuangxin* [Harmonious society and government innovations]. Beijing: Shehuikexue wenxian chubanshe, 2008.

———. *Lun guojia zhili xiandaihua* [Essays on the modernization of state governance]. Beijing: Social sciences academic press, 2015.

———. *Zengliang minzhu yu shanzhi* [Incremental democracy and good governance]. Beijing: Shehuikexue wenxian chubanshe, 2003.

———. "Zhonggong de ganbu jiaoyu yu guojia zhili" [The cadre education of the CCP and the state governance]. *Zhonggong Zhejiang shengwei dangxiao xuebao* [Journal of the Party School of the CCP Zhejiang Provincial Committee], no. 3 (2014).

———. *Zhongguo de minzhu zhili yu zhengzhi gaige* [Democratic governance and political reform in China]. Beijing: Central Compilation and Translation Press, 2012.

———. *Zhongguo gongmin shehui de xingqi yu zhili de bianqian* [The emergence of civil society and its significance for governance in reform China]. Beijing: Shehuikexue wenxian chubanshe, 2002.

———, ed. *Zhongguo zhili bianqian sanshinian* [China's political reform toward good governance, 1978–2008]. Beijing: Shehuikexue wenxian chubanshe, 2008.

Yu Keping and Li Kanru (Kenneth Lieberthal), eds. *Zhongguo de zhengzhi fazhan: Zhongmei xuezhe de shijiao* [Chinese political development: Perspectives of Chinese and American scholars]. Beijing: Social Sciences Academic Press, 2013.

Yu Shiping. *Xin taizijun* [New princelings in the military]. New York: Mirror Books, 2010.

Yu Youjun, *Qiusuo minzhu zhengzhi* [Seeking democratic politics]. Beijing: SDX Joint Publishing Company, 2013.

Yuan Shiwei. *Wenhua yu Zhongguo zhuanxing* [Culture and China's transition]. Hangzhou: Zhejiang daxue chubanshe, 2012.

Yuan Tiao. *Shiqida qianhou de Zhongguo* [China before and after the 17th Party Congress]. Hong Kong: Youxian chubanshe, 2005.

Yuan Yue. *Chen nianqing, zheteng ba: Yuan Yue xiegei zai qingchun de shiziluokou paihuai de ni* [We could afford to do different things because we were young]. Shanghai caijing daxue chubanshe, 2012.

Yuan Yue, and Zhang Jun, comps. *Rizi li de Zhongguo: Zan laobaixing zhe ershi nian* [The daily life of Chinese ordinary citizens over the past 20 years]. Beijing: Zhongguo jingji chubanshe, 2012.

Zhang Lei and Liu Lirui. *Wangmin de liliang: Wangluo shehui zhengzhi dongyuan lunxi* [Netizen power: An analysis of the internet's social and political mobilizing power]. Shenyang: Dongbei daxue chubanshe, 2012.

Zhang Mingshu. *Zhongguoren xiangyao shenmeyang minzhu* [What kind of democracy do Chinese people want?]. Beijing: Shehuikexue wenxian chubanshe, 2013.

Zhang Wei. *Chongtu yu bianshu: Zhongguo shehui zhongjian jieceng zhengzhi fenxi* [Conflict and uncertainty: Political analysis of the middle-income stratum in Chinese society]. Beijing: Shehuikexue wenxian chubanshe, 2005.

Zhang Weiwei. *Zhongguo chudong: Baiguo shiye xia de guancha yu sikao* [China's move: Observations and thoughts from an international perspective]. Shanghai renmin chubanshe, 2012.

———. *Zhongguo zhenhan: Yige "wenmingxing guojia" de jueqi* [China shocks: The rise of a "new civilized country"]. Shanghai renmin chubanshe, 2010.

Zhang Wen. *Minzhu bushi shuozhe wande* [Democracy is not a joke]. Beijing: Falü chubanshe, 2011.

Zhao Dingxin. *Minzhu de xianzhi* [Constraints of democracy]. Beijing: China CITIC Press, 2012.

Zhao Qizheng, John Naisbitt, and Doris Naisbitt. *Duihua Zhongguo moshi* [Dialogue on the China model]. Beijing: New World Press, 2010.

Zheng Keyang and Li Zhongjie, comps. *Zhongguo gongchandang dangnei minzhu yanjiu* [Studies of the inner-party democracy of the Chinese Communist Party]. Beijing: Dangjian duwu chubanshe, 2009.

Zheng Xian, Wang Guiling, and Sun Ruihua. *Zhongguo canzhengdang yunxing jizhi* [Operational mechanism of participating parties in China]. Beijing: Xueyuan chubanshe, 2000.

Zheng Yongnian. *Gaige jiqi diren* [Reform and its enemies]. Hangzhou: Zhejiang renmin chubanshe, 2011.

———. *Zhongguo de "xingwei lianbangzhi": Zhongyang difang guanxi de biange yu dongli* [De facto federalism in China: Reforms and dynamics of central-local relations]. Translated by Qiu Daolong. Beijing: Dongfang chubanshe, 2013.

———. *Zhongguo moshi jingyan yu kunju* [The China model: Experience and dilemmas]. Hangzhou: Zhejiang renmin chubanshe, 2010.

Zhonggong zhongyang dangshi yanjiushi [Party History Research Center of the Central Committee of the Chinese Communist Party]. *Zhongguo gongchandang xinshiqi lishi dashiji (1978.12–1998.10)* [Major events of the new era of the Chinese Communist Party, December 1978–October 1998]. Beijing: Zhonggong dangshi chubanshe, 1998.

Zhonggong zhongyang ganbu jianduju [Cadre Supervision Bureau of the Central Committee of the Chinese Communist Party], comp. *Ganbu xuanba renyong gongzuo fagui xuanbian* [Collection of the regulations for cadre recruitment and appointment]. Beijing: Dangjian chubanshe, 2008.

Zhonggong zhongyang guanyu quanmian tuijin yifazhiguo ruogan zhongda wenti de jueding [Resolution of the Central Committee of the CCP to fully promote rule of law]. Beijing: Renmin chubanshe, 2014.

Zhonggong zhongyang xuanchuanbu [Publicity Department of the CCP Central Committee]. *Xin Jinping zongshuji xilie zhongyao jianghua duben* [Reader of General Secretary Xi Jinping's important speeches]. Beijing: Xuexi chubanshe 2014.

Zhonggong zhongyang zuzhibu bangongting [General Office of the Organization Department of the Central Committee of the CCP], comp. *Gaige kaifang sanshinian zuzhi gongzuo dashi ziliao zhaibian* [Collection of the major developments of organizational affairs during the thirty-year reform and opening up]. Beijing: Dangjian duwu chubanshe, 2009.

Zhonggong zhongyang zuzhibu ganbu jianduju [Bureau of Cadre Supervision of the Central Organization Department of the CCP Central Committee], comp. *Ganbu xuanba renyong gongzuo fagui xuanbian* [Collected works on the regulations and laws on the cadre recruitment and promotion]. Beijing: Dangjian duwu chubanshe, 2008.

Zhonggong zhongyang zuzhibu ganbu jiaoyuju [Cadre Education Bureau of the Central Organization Department of the Chinese Communist Party], comp. *Zhongguo ganbu jiaoyu peixun jigou yaolan* [An overview of educational and training institutions of Chinese officials]. Beijing: Dangjian duwu chubanshe, 2012.

Zhonggong zhongyang zuzhibu ganbu jiaoyuju, Waijiaobu waishi guanliju, and Guojia waiguo zhuanjiaju chuguo peixun guanliju [Cadre Education Bureau of the Central Organization Department of the Chinese Communist Party, Foreign Affairs Administrative Bureau of the Ministry of Foreign Affairs and Department of Foreign Studies of the State Administration of Foreign Experts Affairs], comp. *Lingdao ganbu jingwai peixun chengguo yibaili* [One hundred cases of the overseas training of cadres]. Beijing: Dangjian duwu chubanshe, 2012.

Zhonggong zhongyang zuzhibu ganbu yiju [No.1 Bureau of Cadre of the Central Organization Department of the CCP Central Committee], comp. *2014 Dangzheng lingdao ganbu xuanba renyong gongzuo tiaoli xuexi fudao* [Guide on the regulations and laws on the recruitment and promotion of party and government officials, 2014]. Beijing: Dangjian duwu chubanshe 2014.

Zhonggong zhongyang zuzhibu laoganbuju [Bureau of Veteran Leaders of the Central Organization Department of the CCP Central Committee], comp. *Laoganbu gongzuo wenjian xuanbian* [Selected collections of the works of veteran leaders]. Beijing: Dangjian duwu chubanshe, 2009.

Zhonggong zhongyang zuzhibu laoganbuju [Bureau of Veteran Leaders of the Central Organization Department of the CCP Central Committee], comp. *Laoganbu gongzuo wenjian xuanbian* [Collected documents on the work of veteran leaders]. Beijing: Dangjian duwu chubanshe, 2008.

Zhonggong zhongyang zuzhibu yanjiushi [Research Office of the Organization Department of the Central Committee of the CCP], comp. *Zuzhi gongzuo kexuehua duben* [Reading of the scientific management of organizational affairs]. Beijing: Dangjian duwu chubanshe, 2012.

Zhonggong zhongyang zuzhibu yanjiushi (zhengce faguisi) [Research Office (Policy and Legal Regulation Bureau) of the Organization Department of the Central Committee of the CCP], comp. *Ganbu renshi zhidu gaige: Zhengce fagui wenjian xuanbian* [Reform of the cadre personnel system: Collected works on the regulations and laws]. Beijing: Dangjian duwu chubanshe, 2007.

Zhongguo gongchandang di shiqici quanguo daibiao dahui wenjian huibian [Collection of the documents of the 17th National Party Congress of the Chinese Communist Party]. Beijing: Renmin chubanshe, 2007.

Zhongguo gongchandang zhangcheng [The Constitution of the Chinese Communist Party]. Beijing: Renmin chubanshe, 2007, 2012.

Zhongguo jushi fenxi zhongxin [The analysis center of China's current situation]. *Zhonggong zuigao jicececeng: Shiwuda hou de quanli buju* [The supreme decisionmaking body of the Chinese Communist Party: Power distribution in the post–15th Party Congress period]. New York: Mirror Books, 1997.

Zhongguo renmin daxue guojiguanxi xueyuan zhengzhixue xi [Political Science Division of the School of International Studies at Renmin University of China] and Zhongshan daxue zhengzhi he gonggong shiwu guanlixueyuan zhengzhikexue xi [Political Science Department of the School of Public Affairs and International Relations at Sun Yat-Sen University], comps. *Zhuanxing zhong de Zhongguo zhengzhi yu zhengzhixue fazhan* [Political science and Chinese politics in transition]. Vols. 1, 2, and 3. Beijing: Zhongguo renmin daxue chubanshe, 2002.

Zhou Bin, ed. *"Weibo wenzheng" yu yuqing yingdui* [Micro-blog politics and public opinion response measures]. Beijing: Renmin chubanshe, 2012.

Zhou Tianyong, Wang Changjiang, and Wang Anling, eds. *Gongjian: Shiqida hou Zhongguo zhengzhi tizhi gaige yanjiu baogao* [Breakthrough: Report on research about China's political structure reforms after the 17th Party Congress]. Wujiaqu: Xinjiang shengchan jianshe bingtuan chubanshe, 2008.

Zhou Yezhong and Li Binghui. *Xianfa zhengzhi: Zhongguo zhengzhi fazhan de biyouzhilu* [Constitutional governance: The necessary path for China's political development]. Beijing: China Legal Publishing House, 2012.

Zhu Wei. *Minyi zhishi yu quanli: Zhengce zhiding guocheng zhong gongzhong, zhuanjia yu zhengfu de hudong moshi yanjiu* [Public opinion, knowledge, and power: An interactive model of the public, experts, and government in the policy making process]. Nanjing: Nanjing daxue chubanshe, 2014.

Zhu Yunhan (Chu Yun-han), ed. *Taiwan minzhu zhuanxing de jingyan yu qishi* [Taiwan's democratic transition: Experience and inspiration]. Beijing: Shehuikexue wenxian chubanshe, 2012.

Zhuang Yi. *Shibada huanwei: Quandang shangxia jishengguan* [Power transition at the 18th Party Congress: Political succession at various levels of the CCP leadership]. Hong Kong: Haya chubanshe, 2011.

Zhuang Yuecheng and Gan Wudong, comps. *Fei gongyouzhi qiye dangjian yanjiu niandu baogao, 2011 nian* [Annual research report of party building by non-state-owned enterprises for 2011]. Beijing: Dangjian duwu chubanshe, 2011.

Zi Ping. *Zhonggong zhengyao furen* [The wives of China's top political leaders]. Hong Kong: Huanqiu shiye youxian gongsi, 1999.

Zi Zhongyun, ed. *Qimeng yu Zhongguo shehui zhuanxing* [The enlightenment and transformation of Chinese society]. Beijing: Shehuikexue wenxian chubanshe, 2011.

INDEX

"circulation of elites," 163
civil service, 137–38
CKGSB. *See* Cheung Kong Graduate School of Business
Clarke, James Freeman, 351
class of 1982, 125–28
CLGCDR. *See* Central Leading Group for Comprehensively Deepening Reforms
Clinton, Bill, 191
CMC. *See* Central Military Commission
COD. *See* Central Organization Department
collective leadership: Hu Angang's view of, 30–32; origins of, 13; and think tanks, 143–48; Xi's preservation of, 375; Xi's reversal of, 8, 12–14
collective presidency, 31
college-educated women, 100–01
Confucianism, 214, 243
Confucius, 119
corporate/industrial interest groups, 385–87
corruption: among powerful families, 386; *mishu*'s role in, 217–20; *tuanpai* and, 297–99. *See also* anticorruption campaign
CPPCC. *See* Chinese People's Political Consultative Conference
CPRO. *See* Central Policy Research Office
CPS. *See* Central Party School
crony capitalism, 386–87
CSCSC. *See* Central Spiritual Civilization Steering Committee
Cui Peng 崔鹏, 314
Cultural Revolution: 9th National Party Congress purges, 80–81; capitalist purges, 170; and class of 1982, 126; and education, 121, 123–24, 130; and factional politics, 376; legal reform as reaction to, 189; Liu Yuan and, 327; Mao's power, 16; and political generations, 94, 95; and princelings' education, 266; professionals targeted during, 167; PSC's marginalization, 13; Xi's experiences during, 308–09, 354

Dahl, Robert, 388
Dai Bingguo 戴秉国, 57
de Tocqueville, Alexis, 392
Deng Pufang 邓朴方, 268, 320
Deng Tiansheng 邓天生, 232
Deng Weiping 邓卫平, 342, 381

Deng Xiaoping 邓小平: Central Party School, 58; children's education abroad, 158–59; and collective leadership, 13; Cultural Revolution purge of, 170; economic vs. political reform, 25, 244; educational initiatives, 120–22, 125, 129; exercise of power, 17; Hu Chunhua and, 361; Jiang Zemin and, 18; legacy of, 371; and legal reform, 189; limits of nepotism, 268; and *mishu*, 209, 214; and 13th National Party Congress, 81; and political generations, 94–95; promotion of leaders with CCYL backgrounds, 282; provincial connections, 114; and PSC, 49; and reform, 33; reshuffling of leadership under, 215; rise to power, 16–17; Sichuan connection, 108, 306–07; study abroad movement, 138, 139, 143; successor selection, 16–17; and technocrats, 164; and think tanks, 144; and Third Plenum of 11th Central Committee, 47; war/revolution experience, 15
Deng Yingchao 邓颖超, 99
Deng Zhaoxiang 邓兆祥, 232
Deng Zhifang 邓质方, 158–59
Deng Zhuodi 邓卓棣, 159, 333, 338. See also Zhuo, David.
developers, 385–86
Ding Guangen 丁关根, 367
Ding Haichun 丁海春, 232
Ding Qiusheng 丁秋生, 272
Ding Wang 丁望, 282
Ding Xiaowen 丁孝文, 217
Ding Xuexiang 丁薛祥, 233, 234, 303, 345, 367
Ding Yiping 丁一平, 272
doctoral degrees, 128–29
domestic security, 63
Dong Hong 董宏, 314
Donilon, Tom, 303
Du Jiahao 杜家毫, 175
Du Jincai 杜金才, 48
Du Jinfu 杜金富, 133
Du Ping 杜平, 278
Du Qinglin 杜青林: Central Committee tenure, 79; and CPPCC, 70; and Hu-Li camp, 20; legal background, 195; provincial leadership experience, 113; and *tuanpai*, 18, 291, 292
Duan Yongji 段永基, 174–75